Twelve Readers Reading
Responding to College Student Writing

Written Language

Marcia Farr, senior editor
Robert L. Gundlach, consulting editor

Twelve Readers Reading
Responding to College Student Writing

Richard Straub
Florida State University

Ronald F. Lunsford
University of North Carolina-Charlotte

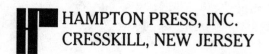
HAMPTON PRESS, INC.
CRESSKILL, NEW JERSEY

Printed in the United States of America

Library of Congress Cataloging-in-Publication Data

Straub, Richard
    Twelve readers reading : responding to college student writing /
Ronald F. Lunsford, Richard Straub.
        p.   cm. – (Written language)
    Includes bibliographical references and index.
    ISBN 1-881303-40-3
    1. English language–Rhetoric–Study and teaching–Evaluation.
2. Written communication–Evaluation. 3. English language–Ability
testing. 4. Grading and marking (Students) 5. Report writing-
-Evaluation. 6. College prose–Evaluation. I. Straub, Richard.
II. Title. III. Series: Written language series
PE1404.L86   1995
808'.042'07–dc20   95-8716
                                                                    CIP

Hampton Press, Inc.
23 Broadway
Cresskill, NJ 07626

For our parents—Joe and Eileen Straub and Chester and Reba Lunsford—who through their example, generosity, and love have shown us what it means to work and love and give and believe in what we do

For Mell, whose generous support, wise counsel, and patience helped make this book possible

For Tamara and Christopher, the continual joys of Ron's life

And for Noni, who has always been there, giving

Contents

Acknowledgments

First and above all, we would like to thank the 12 people—teachers, scholars, and, in the full sense of the term, colleagues—who so graciously agreed to participate in this study: Chris Anson, Peter Elbow, Anne Gere, Glynda Hull, Richard Larson, Ben McClelland, Frank O'Hare, Jane Peterson, Donald Stewart, Patricia Stock, Tillie Warnock, and Edward White. We asked a lot of them and, as will be readily apparent to anyone who looks inside the book, they have given us more than we ever could have expected: more time, more careful work, more risk, more of themselves. We salute their work and professionalism, and we are grateful to them.

We would like to express our appreciation to Kim Haimes-Korn and Tom Thompson, who, as colleagues at Florida State University, helped test and refine the method of analysis developed for this project and helped label the 113 sets of teacher comments that form the basis of the study. We would also like to express our appreciation to Brian Jones, who helped us at various points to turn our text and graphics into a manuscript, and to Bob Stakenas, who assisted us with our statistical analysis.

We would like to thank, formally and lavishly, the friends and colleagues who read and commented thoughtfully and generously on drafts of the manuscript and encouraged us—truly encouraged us—along the way. We are grateful to Bill Smith and Barry Maid, who reviewed an early version of the manuscript and gave us helpful comments. We would also like to thank the graduate-student teachers from LAE 5946, a course for new teachers at FSU, for their helpful feedback on the various drafts of the manuscript, and offer a special note of thanks to Gay Lynn Crossley, whose responses throughout our drafting of the manuscript have been as thoughtful, demanding, and caring as the 12 readers' responses in this study.

We would like to thank Professor James McCrimmon, who has contributed to this book in many ways, first by being a teacher and mentor for Ron when he was a PhD student, second by being a generous senior colleague and mentor to Rick at FSU, then by reading early drafts of the manuscript and providing genuine support for us as we revised, and finally by writing a preface for the book. Our gratitude to, and respect for, Professor McCrimmon span a broad length of time and run deep.

We would also like to thank Richard Larson for turning his thoughts about the assignments in this book into an epilogue essay about the relationship between teacher response and assignment making.

We are exceedingly grateful to Barbara Bernstein for taking on the project late in the process and for holding to—and enabling us to realize—our conception for the book. We know it has taken a lot of work and patience. Thank you. We would also like to thank Marcia Farr for the sharp editorial commentary she gave the manuscript (no small task), and to Diana Dulaney for all the work she has done in getting the book from manuscript to final proofs (again, no small task).

We commemorate the career and life's work of Donald Stewart. His devotion to writing, to teaching, to students, and to the profession resonates in the words he writes in here.

Finally, we would like to thank those who, from the time we started presenting our findings in workshops and conference presentations, have expressed interest in the project, who have encouraged us about its value, and who have waited patiently for its publication. For these teachers—and for the 12 readers whose work we present and study here—we hope it has been worth the wait.

Series Preface

This new series examines the characteristics of *writing* in the human world. Volumes in the series present scholarly work on written language in its various contexts. Across time and space, human beings use various forms of written language—or writing systems—to fulfill a range of social, cultural, and personal functions, and this diversity can be studied from a variety of perspectives within both the social sciences and the humanities, including those of linguistics, anthropology, psychology, education, rhetoric, literary criticism, philosophy, and history. Although writing is not often used apart from oral language, or without aspects of reading, and thus many volumes in this series include other facets of language and communication, writing itself receives primary emphasis.

The study reported here addresses an important issue in writing instruction: How do effective writing instructors respond to their students' writing? Following a tradition they characterize "clinical research," the authors of this volume assembled a set of materials representative of the kinds of writing produced in first-year college writing courses. These materials were then sent to 15 well-known composition teacher-scholars, who were asked to write extensive responses and reflect on the aims and assumed contexts of their comments. The authors' analysis of this unique data offers a fresh perspective on the verbal performances embedded in the familiar exchanges between writing teacher and student. This study thus asks us to consider anew how teachers enact their ideas about writing, about learning, and about the role of the teacher in their responses to students' written work.

While the study of writing is absorbing in its own right, it is an increasingly important social issue as well, as demographic movements occur around the world and as language and ethnicity accrue more intensely political meanings. Writing, and literacy more generally, is central to education, and education in turn is central to occupational and social mobility. Manuscripts that present either the results of empirical research, both qualitative and quantitative, or theoretical treatments of relevant issues are encouraged for submission.

Preface

The real subject of *Twelve Readers Reading* is the nature of teacher comments on student writings and the influence these comments may have on subsequent revisions and on the student's growth as a writer. This subject is developed by inventing a situation in which a dozen distinguished teachers read and comment on some 15 papers representative of the kinds of writing produced in freshman composition courses. Then Straub and Lunsford analyze those comments as models for the teaching of composition.

Such models will be valuable to both beginning and experienced teachers, who, as the Introduction points out, are the principal audience that the authors have in mind. Speaking as one who met his first freshman section in 1937 with no guide except a textbook organized around 101 errors that freshmen were likely to make and a department memo that papers should be failed for any of the following errors—three misspelled words, a period fault, a comma splice, or an obvious disagreement of subject and verb—I would have welcomed *Twelve Readers Reading* as a guide to professional maturity.

The notion that the freshman course in composition is chiefly concerned with correction of errors in usage has been discredited. Thanks to the writings of such teachers as Moffett, Murray, Britton, Sommers, Brannon and Knoblauch, as well as the 12 teachers whose work is featured here, the emphases are now on situation, audience analysis, purpose, organization, and development. In short, composition is the study of written communication, of which the correction of usage is a relatively small part. The main purpose of teacher response, *Twelve Readers Reading* clearly indicates, is admittedly not to correct writing, but to generate it.

The 12 readers seek to achieve this purpose by two major means. First, they emphasize that writing is a process, not an act, and that revision is a normal part of that process. They assume that students are constantly shaping and reshaping their work and that their writing can (and will) get better as they continue to work on it. They illustrate how teachers may examine these drafts as they are done and, through their comments, lead students to see how their writing may be revised.

Even more important than the focus on drafts is the cooperative attitude or mode the teachers display during the revision sessions. In general, they carry on conversations with the students, asking questions, the answers to which lead to a fuller or more satisfactory treatment of the subject, or adding supporting comments to show that they understand and agree with what the students are saying. Throughout these conversations student and teacher move toward a mutual view of the form the paper may take. To the extent that they share such a view, they are approximating Burke's ideal of identification between writer and reader.

In order to be effective writers, students must learn to be effective critics of their own writing. The 12 teachers whose work is presented and analyzed here do a good deal to encourage that learning. If the book did nothing more than display the relationships these teachers establish with students in their comments, it would make a valuable contribution to one's development as a teacher. But the authors go on to do much more, showing in great deal *how* these readers, in their individual ways, lead students back into the possibilities for their writing.

There may be some practical difficulties with implementing these readers' rigorous methods of response in the classroom, especially given the substantial workload of many writing teachers and the kinds of comments students have come to expect from teachers. But the 12 readers' practices provide an ideal toward which teachers and students would do well to strive.

James McCrimmon

Twelve Readers Biographies

Chris Anson

Chris M. Anson is Professor of English and Director of Composition at the University of Minnesota, where he teaches graduate and undergraduate courses in English language and literacy. Among his books are *Writing in Context* (1988), *Writing and Response: Theory, Practice and Research* (1989), *A field Guide to Writing* (1991), *Writing Across the Curriculum* (1993), *Scenarios for Teaching Writing: Contexts for Discussion and Reflective Practice* (1993), *Using Journals in the Classroom: Writing to Learn* (1995), and *The HarperCollins Handbook for Writers and Readers* (forthcoming). His articles have appeared in numerous journals and edited collections. His research interests include writing to learn, response to writing, reflective teaching, and the nature of literacy in and out of schools.

Peter Elbow

Peter Elbow is Professor of English at the University of Massachusetts at Amherst. He has taught at M.I.T., Franconia College, Evergreen State College, and SUNY Stony Brook—where for five years he directed the Writing Program. He is author of *Oppositions in Chaucer, Writing Without Teachers, Writing with Power, Embracing Contraries, What is English,* and (with Pat Belanoff) a textbook, *A Community of Writers* and a peer pamphlet, *Sharing and Responding.* He edited *Voice and Writing* and *Nothing Begins with N: Explorations of Freewriting.* He won the Braddock award for "The Shifting Relationships Between Speech and Writing" (*College Composition and Communication,* October 1985); and the James Berlin award for "The War Between Reading and Writing and How to End It" (*Rhetoric Review,* fall 1993).

Anne Ruggles Gere

Anne Ruggles Gere is Professor of English and Professor of Education at the University of Michigan, where she is Chair of the joint PhD Program in English and Education. Formerly, she served as a member of the English Department at the University of Washington. Her research interests include collaborative writing, literacy, particularly in extracurricular forms, gender and literacy, and service learning. She has published numerous books and journal articles on these topics, including "Common Properties of Pleasure: Texts in Nineteenth Century Women's Clubs" (in *The Construction of Authorship: Textual Appropriation in Law and Literature,* 1994), *Into the Field: Sites of Composition Studies* (1993), and *Writing Groups: History, Theory, and Implications* (1987). She is a former Chair of the College Conference on Composition and Communication and serves as a member of the Executive Committee of CCCC.

Glynda Hull

Glynda Hull is Associate Professor in the School of Education at the University of California, Berkeley, where she teaches in the Division of Language and Literacy. She has published numerous articles in journals in the areas of remediation, technology, and workplace literacy.

Richard L. Larson

Richard L. Larson, Professor of English at Lehman College of The City University of New York, has served as Chair of the Conference on College Composition and Communication and (from 1980 through 1986) as Editor of CCC. Among his many research interests are evaluation of writing programs in public schools and colleges. For many years he compiled the annual Bibliography of Scholarship on Composition and Rhetoric for CCC.

Ben W. McClelland

Ben McClelland is Professor of English and Holder of the Ottillie Schillig Chair of English Composition at the University of Mississippi where he directs the university's comprehensive writing program. Among his book publications are a freshman English textbook, *The New American Rhetoric* (1993), a chapter in *Writing Theory and Critical Theory* (John Clifford and John Schilb, eds., 1994), a chapter in *Theorizing and Enacting Difference: Resituating Writing Programs Within the Academy* (Joe Janangelo and Kristine Hansen, eds., forthcoming), a chapter in *Perspectives in Research and Scholarship in Composition* (With Timothy R. Donovan, 1985), *Writing Practice: A Rhetoric of the Writing Process* (1984), and *Eight Approaches to Teaching Composition* (with Timothy R. Donovan, 1980). Among McClelland's current teaching and research interests are composition, writing theory, and writing program administration. McClelland directs the Writing Program Consultant-Evaluator Board for the Council of Writing Program Administrators.

Frank O'Hare

Frank O'Hare is Professor of English at the Ohio State University, where he served for many years as the Director of Writing. Among his books are a textbook, *The Writer's Work,* and *Sentence Combining: Improving Student Writing Without Formal Grammar Instruction.* His most recent research interest is evaluation of writing across the curriculum programs.

Jane Peterson

Jane Peterson is English Program Coordinator and Assistant Dean of Communications at Richland College, where she also regularly teaches basic writing and freshman composition. A past chair of the Conference on College Composition and Communication and one of five community college participants on the editorial board of Coalition Conference, she has served on the editorial boards of several journals and published articles in *College Composition and Communication* and *College English.* In recent years she has focused on teaching as a mode of learning and on alternative models for faculty development and for teaching and learning within classrooms.

Donald C. Stewart

Donald C. Stewart, a long-time member of the Kansas State University English Department, was the 1983 Chair of the Conference on College Composition and Communication. His many publications include such textbooks as *The Authentic Voice* (1972) and *The Versatile Writer* (1986); a memoir, *My Yellowstone Years* (1989); the journal *Kansas English*, which he edited for nearly a decade; and many articles and book chapters dealing with nineteenth-century American rhetoric and Fred Newton Scott.

Patricia Lambert Stock

Before joining the faculty of Michigan State University, where she is founding Director of the Writing Center and Associate Professor of English, Patricia Lambert Stock taught English literature and composition in schools in New York and Michigan and in The University of Michigan and Syracuse University. In the University of Michigan, she helped to establish the Center for Educational Improvement through Collaboration in which she conducted *praxis*-oriented literacy research with university faculty and school teachers. In Syracuse University, she helped establish a writing program that has earned national acclaim for shaping a culture and a scholarship of teaching. The author of numerous articles about the relationships among talk, writing, and learning; the politics of literacy instruction; the assessment of literacy; and the scholarship of teaching, Professor Stock edits NCTE's journal *English Education* and serves her profession on a number of committees and boards. Her forthcoming book, *The Dialogic Curriculum* argues for the educational and social benefits of community-based literacy instruction.

Edward M. White

Edward M. White is a professor of English at California State University, San Bernardino. He has conducted research in the field of assessing writing for many years. Among his recent books are *Developing Successful College Writing Programs* (1989), *Assigning, Responding, Evaluating* (1992), *Inquiry: A Cross-Curricular Reader* (with Lynn Z. Bloom, 1993), and a revised and expanded edition of *Teaching and Assessing Writing* (1994).

Tilly Warnock

Tilly Warnock currently teaches at the University of Arizona where she directed composition from 1991-1994. She has published articles on composition, writing centers, rhetorical theory, and Kenneth Burke. With Joseph Trimmer, she edited *Understanding Others: Cultural and Cross-Cultural Studies and the Teaching of Literature* for NCTE.

Twelve Readers Reading:
An Introduction

How do well-informed teachers of writing, people whose scholarship we respect and whose classrooms we would like to sit in on, make written responses to their students' writing? How would these teachers, through their example, encourage other writing teachers to respond? What could we learn by looking at their ways of responding?

This study began with these kinds of practical questions about responding to college student writing. The questions were curiosities more than inquiries, meant as much to satisfy our interest as to test the claims of current scholarship or gain new insights into response theory. We saw our principal task as nothing more than to ask a group of established teacher-scholars to respond to a common sampling of essays and share what we had collected, wondered about, and found useful. Although we thought this work would be of interest to the growing community of scholars and researchers working in composition, we envisioned our primary audience as classroom teachers—new teachers with little or no experience in the classroom and experienced teachers who were interested in reexamining their own responding practices. We thought that providing good models and well-thought-out rationales for responding would be powerful ways of helping other teachers develop their own responses.

We decided to focus on one form of response: teachers' written responses. We think that such a focus is appropriate and useful at this time, when different approaches to teaching writing are competing for dominance in composition theory; when poststructuralist theory is helping to redefine our images of writing, reading, and the nature of response; when teachers are decentering the authority of the classroom and distributing it among students; when classwork is increasingly being devoted to peer response; when computer technology is providing innovative ways of putting theory into classroom practice; and when traditional methods of commentary are being transformed by process pedagogies and collaborative approaches to teaching writing. As teachers experiment more and more with different forms of response— written and spoken, in one-to-one settings and in peer groups—it seems a good time to stop and take a close look at what distinguished teachers see as good models of teacher response. We concentrate on written commentary because it is the most widely practiced and the most traditional form of response. It is also the most deliberate form of responding and lends itself to closer scrutiny than other methods of commentary.

We decided to study the responses of well-known, well-informed teachers and scholars in part for the obvious allure they would have for our audience, but mainly for the perspective their work would provide. We believe that there is much to learn about the state of the art of response from teachers who have a range of experience in teaching writing, who have studied evaluation and response, and who have been involved in the training of teachers.[1] Their comments, we believe, will offer models for other teachers who want to develop their own ways of responding to student writing.[2]

As we designed the study and began to see better its potential richness and its complexity, our initial curiosities developed into a series of questions:

How extensively would these teachers respond to a piece of writing?
Would they make more comments on rough drafts or on final drafts?
Would they make as many comments on good pieces of writing as poor ones?
How specific and detailed would they make their comments?

Would the readers address similar issues in the essays?
Would they focus their comments on one or two areas of response?
Or would they try to cover a range of concerns on each paper?
Would they focus on different areas of writing at different stages of drafting?
How would they treat the issue of error?

How much would the readers make use of praise and criticism?
How much would they use comments to help students make revisions?
How much would these teachers make decisions for students?
How much would they leave decisions of writing up to the students themselves?

In what ways would their responses be influenced by a concern for audience?
By a concern for the parameters of the assignment?
By the background and needs of the individual student?

To what extent would they try to help students produce finished written products?
To what extent would they provide instruction in various composing activities?

Which principles and strategies would all 12 readers commonly put into practice?
Which strategies would help distinguish one reader from another?

When over the next year-and-a-half we collected materials from contributors, we were struck by the depth and intricacy of their responses—especially by the different concerns they brought to their readings and the different ways they shaped their comments. We came to see the need for developing a detailed system for analyzing teacher commentary, one that would allow us to capture the nuances in these teachers' responses and help us achieve a better understanding of our central questions. The further we proceeded in our analysis, the more complex the study became. Our initial interest in presenting 12 readers' responses to a common set of student essays turned into an effort to understand the array of strategies these teachers used and to find ways to describe their different responding styles. More and more, we envisioned our audience to be scholars and researchers as much as teachers. Our two-year study turned into a five-year project.

THE 12 READERS

We were fortunate to get an exceptional group of readers—teacher-scholars who have made significant contributions to recent scholarship in composition and who employ various approaches to teaching writing. The group was made up of five women and seven men, some of them recently established in the profession, but most of them veterans. Two are from the South, three from the East, three from the West, and four from the Midwest. The readers and their institutional affiliations are as follows:

Chris Anson, University of Minnesota
Peter Elbow, University of Massachusetts at Amherst
Anne Gere, University of Michigan

Glynda Hull, University of California—Berkeley

Richard Larson, City University of New York—Lehman College

Ben McClelland, University of Mississippi

Frank O'Hare, Ohio State University

Jane Peterson, Richland College

Donald Stewart, Kansas State University

Patricia Stock, Michigan State University

Tilly Warnock, University of Arizona

Edward White, California State University—San Bernardino

THE DESIGN OF THE STUDY

We sent these readers a set of 15 essays—a sampling that we thought to be representative of the kinds of writing produced in first-year college writing courses.[3] In order to allow them a measure of choice, we asked them to respond to 12. In addition, we asked them to:

1. write a brief statement outlining their philosophy of teaching composition;
2. answer a series of questions about their ways of structuring a writing course and their ways of responding to student writing;
3. respond to the essays in our sampling and, if they wanted, explain their choices to us in separate notes; and
4. assign a letter-grade to each of the final drafts.

The sampling was made up of five rough drafts, one invention exercise, and nine final drafts. (Four of these final drafts were presented with earlier drafts or previous writing by the same student.) Five of the writings were expressive essays, six were explanatory, and four persuasive. Half of the writings were written from an impersonal point of view on subjects outside the student's immediate experience, half from the student's personal experiences and perspectives. As a group, the 12 readers made some 3,500 comments on 156 sets of responses.[4]

We knew from the start that our study would be necessarily limited because the teachers would have neither the context of a classroom nor the personal contact with students to inform their reading of the texts. Nevertheless, we set ourselves the task of giving the readers enough information about the writing situation to allow them at least a starting point in building a context within which to work and to direct them as a group, as best we could, to look at each of the student texts in a common light. Typically we included an assignment for the writing as well as information about the stage of drafting, the point in the course at which the paper was written, the focus of instruction, and the previous writing assignments. For half of the writings, we presented, in addition, a brief profile of the student writer. (See Chapter 2 for examples.)

When we first approached teachers about the possibility of taking part in our study, a number of them, although attracted to the project, were hesitant to take it on, feeling that far too much of what goes on in the responding process is geared to the overall context of the writing classroom for such an exercise to be meaningful. Clearly, one of the most difficult—and one of the most interesting—tasks the readers faced was to construct their own hypothetical contexts from the limited information we provided and find a way to employ their typical responding strategies on writings that were not produced by their own students, in their own classrooms.

We would have liked to ask these teachers to respond to the essays "routinely," as they would if they actually received them in their own classes, in order to get as close as we could to their authentic responses. That was simply not possible. Instead, we asked them to feel free to take more time than perhaps they normally would in an actual setting and look at their responses not as samples of real-life exchanges but as models of their ways of responding, perhaps as examples they would use in training teachers.[5]

A NOTE ON RESPONDING "OUT OF CONTEXT"

We realized that our use of hypothetical contexts—and, generally, the study of responses made on student writing outside of actual classroom contexts—would be troubling for many readers. We decided to work with a common sampling of essays that were "out of context" (instead of, for instance, essays from each of the 12 teachers' own classrooms) mainly because it would allow us to control some major variables of response and provide a solid footing for comparisons of the readers' responding styles. We decided to add hypothetical contexts in order to give the readers a better sense of the circumstances behind the writings, to cut down on some of their open-endedness, and to make them more realistic. Aware of the admonishings of contemporary critical theory, we knew full well that readers could not respond to the "texts themselves" without making reference to some context that would define or constrain them. We understood that a teacher's response to student writing is shaped by the text, the individual student, the stage of drafting, the assignment, the rhetorical (and pedagogical) context, the student's prior performance, and the work of other students in the class, as well as by the teacher's course goals, her own values and vacillating expectations, and (let's not forget) the time she can devote to making responses. We realized, further, the rich and complicating influence of other variables: the teacher's personality, her approach to teaching writing, her institutional setting, and her views about what it means to help a student get a college education.[6]

So, we decided to work with the hypothetical nature of the study rather than against it. Instead of asking the teachers to respond to these essays as they would if they were to receive them in their own classes, leaving it completely up to them to create contexts for the writings, we provided background information for each of the essays—some of it based on real circumstances, some of it made up. We asked the readers to make the kinds of comments they would make if they were to receive these essays under the circumstances we defined. We also invited them to modify the specified context as they wished and to note for us any changes they made (see Appendix A for the directions we gave them).

We did not intend to solve the problem of contextuality by simply giving teachers a ready-made context. Our context sheets were not even meant to simulate actual settings because we are convinced that no artificially defined context could adequately reflect the complexities of actual classroom situations. Instead, they were intended to give readers some information by which to begin constructing a sense of context. This information would provide necessary constraints that, we believed, would help readers situate the writings and look at each of them not as the same text—a single static phenomenon—but at least within some common boundaries. Because the meaning that a text comes to have for a reader is a function of her own prior experiences and expectations as well as the words on the page, we realized that the 12 readers, when they sat down to respond to a given student essay, would in each case be reading a different text—a "text" that they would have to create, in a context of their making.[7] But we hoped that such information would help them create texts and contexts that would not be entirely different from those created by their colleagues.

In a sense, we saw ourselves presenting a script and stage directions that would help these readers create, in their own way, through their own background and propensities, texts and contexts that were realistic and would bring the writing to life. By providing these directions, we tried to give readers an opportunity to work from a common script and create texts that would allow us to study their responding styles. We hoped that, as plays may lead us to better understand ourselves, these "put-on" performances by the readers would help us better understand responding theory and practice. As it turned out, a number of the readers had a difficult time with, and sometimes vigorously resisted, some information we provided in these contexts. But the group as a whole generally accepted and worked within these constraints, at times freely elaborating this information, at other times choosing to make slight modifications, yet typically using the information to construct the texts and guide their responses.[8]

Although we recognize that the artificial circumstances must have influenced the readers' readings, we imagine that their responses on these essays are probably not substantially different from the *kinds* of responses they routinely make on writing in their own classrooms—or from the kinds of responses they *would* make on these essays if they were to receive them from students in their own classes.[9] We believe that their responses were influenced most of all by the texts themselves and the teachers' typical ways of looking at student writing. In short, we suspect the readers shaped their responses to the sampling in their own images as classroom teachers.[10]

THE POWERS AND LIMITS OF THE STUDY

Of course, the only way to get a definitive view of teachers' actual ways of responding is to study responses from their own actual classroom settings, optimally, as they unfold. A fuller and more accurate account of these teachers' actual responding styles would require an ethnographic study. Our project adopts the methodology of what North (1987, ch. 7) calls clinical research. It offers quantitative and qualitative descriptions of 12 case-study readers working in an experimental setting.[11] We do not see our research as preferable to an ethnographic study of responding in actual contexts; we see it as preliminary to such a study.

We view this project, then, as a foundational study. It is intended, in part, to contribute to the scholarship on teacher response by presenting 12 accomplished teachers' responses to a common set of student essays, offering a method for analyzing teacher responses, and describing the responding strategies these teachers put into practice. We hope that the study will define richer questions and prompt other work on the subject—with different groups of readers and different student texts, in different settings (experimental and actual), and at different levels of instruction. Above all, the volume is intended to offer good models of teacher commentary, stimulate discussion about various methods of response, and encourage teachers to develop responding styles that allow them to speak as meaningfully as they can with students about their writing.

1 | Issues in Responding to Student Writing

Twelve years ago, in her seminal article "Responding to student writing," Sommers (1982) asserted that although "commenting on student writing is the most widely used method for responding to student writing, it is the least understood" (p. 170). In an article published the year before, "Teacher commentary on student writing: The state of the art" (1981), Sommers's colleagues, Knoblauch and Brannon, had made a similar assertion: "we have scarcely a shred of empirical evidence to show that students typically even comprehend our responses to their writing, let alone use them purposefully to modify their practice" (p. 1).

We need not recount the history of research on response that supported the claims of Sommers and Knoblauch and Brannon because others have rendered broad and thorough reviews (Anson, 1989; Griffin, 1982; Horvath, 1984; Knoblauch & Brannon, 1981; Lawson, Ryan, & Winterowd, 1989), but it may be useful to chart some of the major issues that surfaced in this research. For the most part, researchers have not concerned themselves with whether response to student writing works, or with what "works" might mean in such a sentence. Rather, its general efficacy has been assumed; the researchers' goal has been to determine what kinds of response are most effective. The issues they have studied will sound familiar to anyone who has taken pen or pencil in hand to place marks on a student essay.

One of the most obvious questions researchers have asked concerns the relative effectiveness of long and short teacher comments. No conclusive relation has been found between the length of teachers' responses and the effectiveness of those responses (Arnold, 1962; Clark, 1968). A second question has to do with the placement of responses—marginal comments versus end comments. Again, no obvious connection between the placement of comments and their effectiveness has been found (Bata, 1972; Stiff, 1967). Still another issue is the question of how much praise and criticism should be given in teacher responses. Although some studies have seemed to suggest that responses that praised student work were to be preferred, others have found no correlation between the ratio of praise and criticism and effectiveness of responses.[1]

Many other studies dealing with various issues could be mentioned, but none of them establishes correlations between any of the factors being investigated and improvement in student writing. When the studies are examined carefully from the perspective we now enjoy, it becomes obvious that all were destined to prove little for at least two reasons: (a) they were performed in settings that failed to treat writing as process, and (b) they failed to define what was meant by "improvements in writing." The work of Sommers and Brannon and Knoblauch has done much to move us beyond response research that assumes a product approach to teaching writing. As we shall see below, there is less agreement among writing theorists as to how writing improvement should be defined and, thus, what types of response will result in improvement.

PROCESS TEACHING

Knoblauch and Brannon were among the first to call attention to the product-centered teaching assumed by most early studies of teacher response. In the following passage, they describe what they saw in the typical interactions between teachers and students:

> students write essays and teachers describe their strengths and weaknesses, grading them accordingly. The essays are then retired and new ones are composed, presumably under the influence of recollected judgments of the previous ones. Our assumption has been that evaluating the product of composing is equivalent to intervening in the process. (1981, p. 2)

According to Knoblauch and Brannon, responses that amount to nothing more than post mordems are of limited value. They merely evaluate the work that has been done rather than help writers improve the texts they are working on or develop their writing processes in ways that are likely to result in improved writing over the long term.

Such practices as those described by Knoblauch and Brannon (i.e., responses that tell the student what is wrong with her paper but assume no revisions) seem at odds with writing process theory as it had developed over the 10 or 15 years preceding their study. In *Teaching the Universe of Discourse* (1968/1983, ch. 6), Moffett discussed the feedback students should be given on their writing *while* they are in the process of composing. Moffett compared the writing teacher to a coach: Just as a good coach helps a player improve at his sport by providing "feedback" during the learning process, the writing teacher should provide feedback to the novice writer during the writing process.

Murray, another early influential figure in composition studies, encouraged teachers of writing to question students *while* they are drafting their texts rather than waiting to criticize finished products (1972, p. 29). Garrison (1974) spoke to the same issue. According to Garrison, teachers should not wait to point out problems until the end of the writing process; rather, they should be experts at helping students find and develop strengths in early drafts of their essays (p. 310).

The work of these teachers and that of others led to many converts among teachers of writing across the nation. If one sampled the papers at the annual meeting of the Conference on College Composition and Communication and scores of regional and local conferences on writing during the 1970s, one might assume that the message had been received, that teachers were assisting students in real revisions of their work by responding to student writing throughout their drafting processes.

However, in the seminal article with which we began this review, Sommers suggested otherwise. She found that even though many teachers were responding to drafts of student writing—rather than waiting to respond until the essays were completed—they were treating these intermediate drafts as if they were final products. For example, in responding to a rough draft, a teacher might ask a student to develop her thoughts, but, at the same time, point out mechanical flaws or other infelicities in sentences that very likely would not remain in a revised version of the essay. In such a situation, the student is receiving contradictory messages. On the one hand, she is advised to reconceptualize her essay entirely, in ways that will surely entail completely new sentence and paragraph structures. On the other hand, she is given specific instructions for fixing sentence-level errors in the current draft.[2] In such quasi-process teaching, the student writer is likely to be confused; she may not know whether she should be editing and "fixing" her draft or "rethinking" it. Sommers's work suggested that a genuine process approach to teaching would be one in which teachers adjust their responses to meet the needs of students at various stages of drafting. Specifically, teachers' responses to early drafts must offer students the latitude for real revisions.

Allowing students this latitude, however, is no simple matter. Regardless of what teachers focus on in a draft, they are likely to get in the way of students' revising processes, simply by playing the traditional role of teacher. In that role, teachers approach drafts, not as real "processes," that is, as fluid and unformed gropings toward meaning, but as failed attempts to communicate. In doing so, they fall into the trap of what Sommers called "appropriating" the students' work. As Sommers put it, teachers' comments often "take students' attention away from their own purposes in writing a particular text and focus that attention on the teachers' purpose in commenting" (p. 171).

When the teacher makes his agenda for a piece of writing known, the student is likely to attempt to give the teacher what he wants. Why should she do otherwise? After all, the teacher is the one who holds the power of the grade. The irony here is that what a good teacher of writing wants most is for the student to take charge of her own writing, to set her own goals, and find ways to achieve them. Neither students nor teachers will be able to achieve their goals as long as teachers read students' work as authority figures intent only on judging its ultimate worth. Escape from this apparent Catch-22 is the ultimate challenge for all students and teachers in writing courses.

TEACHER ROLES AND RESPONSE

One way the teacher can combat the artificial situation inherent in the composition classroom is to expand the roles he plays in responding to student texts. Sommers suggests that the composition instructor should read early drafts of student writing, not as a teacher, but "as any reader would, registering questions, reflecting befuddlement, and noting places where . . . [he is] puzzled about the meaning of the text" (p. 176). Such a role helps the teacher avoid identifying problems and pointing out specific changes that the student must make. Rather than trying only to provide what the teacher wants, the student can reflect on the ways in which a reader has responded to what she has written, revising in those instances in which the writing does not seem to say what she intends or have the effect she wishes.

Sommers's comments on teacher roles take us back to Moffett's advice that teachers should assume the role of coaches for their writing students. Moffett reasoned that real learning takes place by trial and error: The learner tries, fails, sees where he has gone wrong, and then makes adjustments before trying again. In the following passage, he uses an analogy between writing and music to explain how a coach can help the learner spot areas in his writing that need attention:

> [S]uppose the learner cannot perceive what he is doing—does not, for example, hear that the notes are rushed—or perceives that he has fallen short of his goal but does not know what adjustment to make in his action. This is where the coach comes in. He is someone who observes the learner's actions and the results, and points out what the learner cannot see for himself. (1968, 1983, p. 189)

Not everyone was content to change the teacher's role to that of coach, however. Even though a "coach" responds differently than a traditional writing teacher, there is a sense in which the teacher as coach would still be an authority figure, the one charged with finding where the student has "fallen short" and suggesting the "adjustment." Murray argued that in assuming these authoritative roles, teachers limit students' growth as writers. Murray (1969) encouraged the writing teacher to lead the way in "constructing an educational system which removes students' responsibilities from the teacher and places them firmly on the student" (p. 140). In a subsequent article, Murray (1973) offered three categories into which teachers may be grouped, depending on the roles they assume in composition instruction. A teacher who evaluates and penalizes "any student who breaks the law" is a judge; a teacher who applies "form when there is not yet content" is a Moses. But a teacher who hears and respects what students want to say plays the role of a listener. Murray would have the teacher spend more time in this role.

Britton, Burgess, Martin, McLeod, and Rosen (1975) offered another view of teacher roles. Britton and his co-authors identified four common relationships between student and teacher: pupil to teacher as trusted adult, pupil to teacher as general audience, pupil to teacher in their particular relationship, and pupil to teacher as examiner. Britton pointed out the fact that teachers will focus on different aspects of the writing process, depending on which role they assume. The "examiner" views the writing as a finished product that must be marked in such a way as to instruct the student writer for her next attempt at writing. The "particular teacher" negotiates meanings with the writer, reading the developing text as one interested in the writer's meaning, as well as in her progress as a writer. The "generalized reader" focuses on the information in the text and shows little interest in the writing situation that generated the information. And finally, the "trusted adult" views the writing as an act of communication and responds to that writing as one being spoken to in earnest.[3] According to Britton, teachers often limit themselves by assuming only the role of examiner.

Building on the work of such theorists as Moffett, Murray, and Britton, Sommers (1982) calls for teachers to move away from the narrow confines of the teacherly role they have become accustomed to assuming. According to Sommers, that role can limit teachers' abilities to read student texts. It leads them to "read with [their] preconceptions and preoccupations, expecting to find errors, and the result is that [they] find errors and misread students' texts" (p. 176). In speaking of the part that readers play in creating meaning, Sommers says that teachers "read student texts with biases about what the writer should have said or about what he or she should have written, and . . . [their] biases determine how . . . [they] will comprehend the text" (p. 176).[4]

As an example of the tendency of teachers to find what they are looking for in a piece of writing, Sommers cites a well-known study by Williams. In an article intended for teachers of writing, Williams (1981) "planted" numerous usage errors in a text dealing with the issue of how readers perceive errors. He expected that teachers would notice relatively few of these errors in the writing of one of their peers because they would be reading his article differently from the way they read student essays. The response Williams received from those reading the essay indicated that, in many cases, his prediction proved correct.

Two studies that followed Sommers's article offer further insight into how the roles teachers assume affect their abilities to read texts. Freedman (1984) reported a study in which she asked teachers to evaluate samples of "student" writing. She did not tell the teachers that the sampling actually contained several pieces by professional writers. Freedman found that although the writing of professionals received high scores on analytical scales measuring voice, syntactic fluency, word choice, and usage, the professionals were consistently rated lower on development and organization. She examined the readers' comments and found complaints about certain "students'" inappropriate informality, their disrespectful expression of distaste for the topic, and their pretentious use of allusions. Freedman concluded that because the teachers could not "take off" for these factors in analytical ratings, they resorted to criticizing more subjective parts of the writing. Would these readers have responded in the same manner, Freedman wondered, had they known they were reading the work of professionals?

The second study, conducted by Brannon and Knoblauch (1982), examined teachers' responses to work students did when asked to compose a summary for the prosecution in the famous Lindberg trial. The teachers were nearly unanimous in criticizing student summaries that were built on emotional appeals against the defendant, insisting that a "good" summarizing statement must deal with the facts of the case. Brannon and Knoblauch noted, however, that these students were being criticized for using the tactic that was actually employed by the prosecutor in the trial. Their study raises the question, then, of whether these teachers would have evaluated the students' summaries in the same fashion had they known they employed the basic strategy used in the trial. Obviously, the prosecution's methods are not necessarily the "correct" methods. Had the teachers actually been asked to respond to an illustrious attorney in such a situation, they might well have raised questions as to why the case was based on emotional appeal. There is little doubt, however, that had the teachers assumed the role appropriate to responding to an attorney, they would have avoided the simple "right" and "wrong" approach that many of them took in responding to student writing.

Such studies led Brannon and Knoblauch to conclude that teachers should avoid responses that place them in the roles of examiner or judge. When teachers take on such roles, they assume they know what the student wants to (or should) say, and they offer responses that "direct" students to make changes that will lead to the "proper" revision—in Brannon and Knoblauch's (1982) terms, the teacher's "ideal" text. Knoblauch and Brannon (1984) prefer "facilitative" responses, comments "designed to preserve the writer's control of the discourse, while also registering uncertainty about what the writer wishes to communicate" (p. 128). Such comments show the teacher responding to the student as a writer who has her own purposes that should be respected. The following are examples of each type of comment:[5]

> This is obvious. (directive)
>
> Run on sentence. Break it up. (directive)
>
> What criteria lead you to decide this? (facilitative)
>
> How important are these factors? Do you imply that they are relative or that they don't always matter? Is your essay going to be about these factors? (facilitative)

It has now been over 12 years since Sommers and Brannon and Knoblauch outlined the various ways in which teachers have tended to "appropriate" student texts in favor of the ideal texts they have in mind. Because it is intuitively clear that teachers who wish to help students take control of their writing need to be sensitive to the meanings intended by those students, one might hope for significant changes in the ways in which teachers now read and respond to student writing. Anson's recent study (1989) would seem to suggest such change has not occurred.

Anson used Perry's scheme for typing thinking styles to categorize writing teachers' various response styles. He found three very different "types" of responders. The first group he labeled (using Perry's terminology) *dualistic*. These teachers' responses, which are directed chiefly at surface features of texts, imply that there are clearly right and wrong ways to complete the assignments in question and that students should make prescribed changes in revising their texts. These changes tend to be spelled out rather specifically by notes in the margins and by comments in the summary statements. A second group of teachers were *relativistic* in their approach. They made almost no marginal comments, preferring to render some type of "casual reaction" in an informal note at the end of the paper. These teachers saw the texts as belonging to the students, and they were unwilling to "trespass" on someone else's property. The final group of teachers, the *reflective* readers, were willing to make suggestions for changes (in the margins and in endnotes), but they were careful in the language of their comments to act as representative readers of the texts, not authority figures. They offered suggestions that the students were free to take, or not, depending on the students' concepts of their own developing texts.

Most significantly for us, Anson found that three-fourths of the teachers in his sampling were dualistic responders. Although most contemporary composition theorists advise teachers to move away from narrowly prescriptive responses that suggest students should be working toward the "right" meaning for their essays, Anson's study suggests many (indeed most) teachers have failed to do so.[6]

GOALS FOR WRITING INSTRUCTION AND RESPONSE

What constitutes improvement in writing? On the surface, of course, this may seem a question hardly worth asking: Writing improves as it communicates more effectively with the writer's intended audience. Freshman writing programs have historically accepted this communication-based definition of writing. But a number of modern writing theorists have explained that there are other purposes that can serve as central to writing courses (Berlin, 1982; Faigley, 1986; Fulkerson, 1979, 1990; Lynn, 1987; Woods, 1981).

In one of the more recent articles dealing with the goals of writing instruction, Fulkerson (1990) offers an illustrative scene from *Alice in Wonderland*:

When Alice asks the Cheshire Cat, 'Would you tell me, please, which way I ought to go from here?' the sage Cat replies, 'That depends a good deal on where you want to get to.' The episode may be read as a parable for teachers, for it enunciates a fundamental principle about ends and means: without the end clearly in mind, it is pointless to ask how to get there. (p. 409)

Fulkerson follows this passage with a brief summary of his earlier article on the subject (1979) in order to outline the four "places" that various composition teachers may be attempting to take their writing students. In that article, Fulkerson used M.H. Abrams's *The Mirror and the Lamp* to label four types of writing teachers. Those who focus on the text itself, and concern themselves with form and correctness in that text, Fulkerson calls *formalists*. If the focus is on the writer of the text, and the teacher emphasizes the ways in which writers may develop and express themselves in their writing, then the method is seen as *expressive*. Teachers who see the primary goal as capturing and presenting the world as it is are labeled *mimeticists*. And finally, those who privilege communication with an intended audience are said to take a *rhetorical* stance. After reviewing the categories in his earlier article, Fulkerson declares the debate over, saying that the rhetoricians have won the day with their focus on communication.[7] He arrives at this conclusion by examining theoretical articles, textbooks on composition, and pedagogical books intended for future teachers of writing. His survey convinces him that "Our disciplinary concern with audience and audience analysis . . . has . . . grown dramatically" (p. 415).

As we reflect on Fulkerson's pronouncements concerning the goals of composition theory, we are inclined to question his assumption that these goals are mutually exclusive. Berkenkotter (1991) compares the way theorists like Fulkerson look at competing composition goals to the way one sees the "figures of the goblet and the profiles . . . in psychology textbooks" (p. 151). When looking at one of these pictures, the viewer is limited to one perspective: "To bring one image into the foreground is to cast the other into the background. One cannot hold in dynamic tension the images of figure and ground simultaneously" (p. 151). Berkenkotter suggests, however, that goals in composition instruction do not operate under the same limitations as these pictures. She believes, in fact, that it is not only possible, but also necessary, that writers give attention to more than one goal as they compose—and by extension, that teachers of writing work toward more than one goal in their instruction.

We agree with Berkenkotter. Thus, one of the basic questions we brought to this study is what purposes, in addition to communication, the 12 readers would pursue in their responses to student texts.

BASIC ASSUMPTIONS AND QUESTIONS INFORMING THIS STUDY

The readers in this study are a select group. These 12 teacher-scholars have helped develop our discipline's theoretical statements on writing instruction. Our study, then, should help us see, not how writing teachers in general respond to student texts, but rather how these teachers would implement their carefully crafted theories of writing in their responses to student writing.

The scholarship allowed us to predict answers to several of the questions we raised in the Introduction. We predicted that:

The readers would make a good many comments that refer to specific items in student texts, rather than the vague "rubber-stamped" comments Sommers talks about.

The readers would adjust their responses according to the drafting stage or maturity of the writing in question; they would tend to deal with matters of error in later stages of drafting.

The readers would assume roles other than the traditional teacherly roles, and would thus be careful not to appropriate or take over students' writing.

Other questions remained very much open for us, among them:

How extensively would readers mark student essays?

Would readers tend to treat similar issues in a given essay?

To what extent would readers use praise and criticism in their responses?

How much would readers use their comments to evaluate the writing?

How much would they use comments to direct or guide the student's revision?

To what extent would readers try to help students produce finished written products?

In what ways would our readers' responses be influenced by the writing assignments students had been given?

To what extent would these readers' responses guide students in the use of various composing activities?

Would readers address their comments to the writer behind the text as well as to the implied writer in the text?

We assumed that the readers in this study would bring a process approach to their reading of student writing. That approach would entail sensitivity to drafts—different amounts and different kinds of advice at different stages. However, we made no assumptions about how they would define improvements in writing and, thus, how their responses would be geared to help students effect those improvements. In a sense we stacked the deck by giving them essays that are attempts at various kinds of writing—expressive pieces, expository pieces, and argumentative pieces. We also included essays written by students who are working their way through sensitive personal issues. We assumed that the readers would, in general, offer advice designed to help students move toward more finished drafts. But we were not sure how readers would define that improvement in a situation in which a student has written a personal narrative (essentially expressive) when he was given an expository assignment. Neither could we guess how much these teachers would address the student behind the text, or how much they would respond to students who have met the requirements of an assignment, but who may have falsified an experience too close for them to deal with truthfully.

At this stage in the development of our discipline, we have no consensus as to what constitutes good writing. But that is not the only complication. As theorists such as Brannon and Knoblauch and North remind us, we must distinguish, in a given situation, whether we are attempting to foster good writing or to help students become good writers.[8] There are times when a teacher may call a halt to continued work on a paper, or at least direct it in ways that do not seem to be leading the student any closer to a product, in order to give the student direct practice in her composing processes or emphasize her long-term development.

We did not expect these 12 readers' responses to provide definitive answers to the questions we have posed. We did hope their responses (and their other statements to us) would help make clear the areas in which they agree and the nature of their disagreements.

2 | The Twelve Readers' Responses

In this chapter, we present the 12 readers' responses to a representative sampling of the essays in our study. The chapter is divided into nine sections, each of them focusing on a single essay. Each section contains the textual information given to the readers, four sets of responses to the sample essay, and a brief commentary in which we note major trends in the four sets of responses presented and in the other readers' responses. We have attempted to display responses that reflect the range of responses given to a particular essay and are, at the same time, typical of an individual reader's overall responding style. In the process of making these selections, we sometimes felt tension between these two aims, but overall we found it possible to achieve both goals.

Before presenting these responses, it is worth noting one important characteristic of several of our readers' responses. We were surprised to find that 6 of the 12 teachers make few, or no, comments in the margins of student papers. Chris Anson and Ben McClelland, for instance, never mark on student papers. Anson responds to each paper with a tape-recorded message in which he discusses various parts of the essay as he reads it and afterward makes general comments about its overall effectiveness. McClelland writes rather formal letters to students in which he often refers to specific passages in texts by way of supporting his evaluations of the essays and offering students ways of revising.

Peter Elbow and Frank O'Hare do make some marks on the students' texts, but they save their written comments for a separate page. Elbow underlines particularly strong passages of a text and draws wiggly lines under passages that "bother" him. He then responds to the essay in an informal letter written as an endnote. Donald Stewart makes many marks on papers, but they are almost exclusively editorial notations; his comments about the substance, organization, and style of the writing are reserved for a lengthy endnote. Patricia Stock always composes a long endnote for the student; at times she marks the student's text heavily to make a point or to offer editing suggestions; at other times, she makes no marks at all on a text.

Though their styles certainly differ and their practices from essay to essay vary, the remaining readers—Anne Gere, Glynda Hull, Richard Larson, Jane Peterson, Tilly Warnock, and Edward White—use some mix of marginal and end comments.

```
WRITING 1
ROUGH DRAFT: [AGAINST THE SEAT BELT LAW]
Featured Responders: Stewart, Peterson, Warnock, Stock
```

BACKGROUND

This is the first rough draft of the third paper of the course. It is the second paper that students will have taken through multiple drafts. The first two papers were personal experience essays.

THE ASSIGNMENT

You have lived for 18, 20, 25 years—or more. There is a list of subjects you know a great deal about. Choose one of these subjects and write an essay in which you discuss this topic in a way that will help your readers see why it is important to you.

Writing 1
Louise P.
First Rough Draft

[Against the Seat Belt Law]

I do not beleve in the seat belt law because I think that it is a   *sp.*

a person's violation of your freedom. It is your right to decide if a selt belt   *sp.*

can save your life or endanger it. It is not only the driver who has

the right to decide, it's the passengers as well. The driver nor the   *Neither*

government has the right to tell a passengers they must wear a seat

belt.

The government forced this law into the states, saying they would   *on*

cut off highway funds if the law wasn't passed. This was a very

communistic way of getting a law passed. If they wanted they law

passed, they should have presented both sides of the issue; not passed

it with threats.

Wearing a seat belt may save some lives, but there are many

accidents *which* that not wearing a seat belt saved lives. Some friends of

mine were in a car accident right before graduation, and the policeman

said if they would have *had* had their seat belts on, they would have never

made it to graduation, that year or any others. Therefore, it should

be up to the individuals in the car to decide if wearing a seat belt

is for them or not.

Louise P., First draft of paper

Good choice of subject, but you have a lot of work to do in
preparing your second draft of this paper. There are two
significant problems with the content of your paper. First,
you were supposed to tell readers why this subject was
important to you. You don't do that. Second, the arguments
you offer to support your position just will not hold up.
Now, let's talk in more detail about these problems.

Explaining your interest in a subject means telling a reader
why this particular problem concerns you. You say the seat
belt law violates your freedom, is communistic, and is even
dangerous to the safety of people who have to obey it, but
these are arguments that we'll talk about in a minute. We
want to know if there is any personal reason this law annoys
you. Were you ever hurt in an accident because you were
wearing a seat belt? Was someone you love hurt because he
or she was wearing a seat belt? Do you get angry when the
government seems to be bullying you around? Why? Have you
had other experiences of this kind? Let me give you an
example from my own experience. Everytime I read about the
government granting oil drilling rights to companies who are
active along the borders of Yellowstone Park, I really get
steamed. I worked in Yellowstone for thirteen summers. I
love the Park and its natural wonders and despise people who
consider it a nuisance because it is an impediment to their
money-making projects. If I argued that Forest Service
policies should be rigorously examined and the organization
given six kinds of hell for so carelessly giving out these
oil drilling leases, readers would first know of my long and
deep attachment to Yellowstone and desire to protect the
wonderful natural features of the Park. So, are there any
personal reasons why this seat belt law aggravates you? If
so, let's hear about them.

Now, let's take a look at your arguments. First, you say
that the law is a violation of a person's freedom. In what
way? You say every person should have the right to decide
whether or not seat belts save or endanger lives. Why? I
have seen a great deal of evidence that clearly demonstrates
the fact that seat belts do save lives. You argue, in your
third paragraph, that this is not so, but in support of your
argument you offer but one rather flimsy example. You will
have to show me a lot of statistical evidence to prove that
wearing seat belts is dangerous. I simply don't believe
you. For that reason, I'm not sure your argument about the
law violating a person's freedom is so strong. If people
aren't smart enough to protect themselves, shouldn't the
government step in and make them save themselves?

That issue leads to a more sophisticated point. I suppose
you can argue that if people want to take risks and kill

themselves, the government shouldn't stop them. That
argument is valid only to a point. If you refuse to wear a
seat belt, get in an accident, and get badly injured, <u>my</u>
medical and car insurance premiums are likely to go up
because somebody has to pay the bills. If there are a lot
of people like you, you could cost the insurance companies
so much money that they would have to raise premiums
significantly. The point I am making is that in a free
society you can do what you want, so long as you do not
infringe upon the rights of others. But if doing what you
want costs me and a lot of other a lot of money--because you
are irresponsible and we're not--you are infringing upon our
rights. Furthermore, who pays the police and ambulance
people who have to clean up after accidents? In your next
draft, then, you will have to deal with these points.
Convince me that wearing seat belts is unsafe and that by
not wearing them you will not infringe upon my rights.

There is another argument that you will have to look over.
You say the government's way of getting states to pass the
bill was communistic. No. You don't understand communism.
I think you mean it was the kind of thing <u>totalitarian</u>
governments (which may be communist or fascist) do. That's
a different point. You also say the government did not
debate both sides of the issue. I was under the impression
that they did. Convince me that I am wrong.

Okay. You have a lot of work to do in developing the
arguments to support your position. The organization of the
paper is satisfactory, and the style is all right. Editing
is quite poor, however. I've indicated changes that should
be made. See me if you don't understand the points I'm
making about your arguments.

PETERSON

Writing 1
Louise P.
First Rough Draft

[Against the Seat Belt Law]

Don't all laws + regulations limit freedom—speed limits, state inspections for cars, life jacket requirements for small boats, etc.?

I do not beleve in the seat belt law because I think that it is a violation of your freedom. It is your right to decide if a selt belt can save your life or endanger it. It is not only the driver who has the right to decide, it's the passengers as well. The driver nor the government has the right to tell a passenger they must wear a seat belt.

are you sure?

The government forced this law into the states saying they would cut off highway funds if the law wasn't passed. This was a very communistic way of getting a law passed. If they wanted they law passed they should have presented both sides of the issue; not passed it with threats.

How important is this to you? If there had been funding riders, would you favor the seat belt law?

What happened? was it day or night? what was the weather like? was it a one car accident or a collision? did the car roll over? etc.

Wearing a seat belt may save some lives but there are many accidents that not wearing a seat belt saved lives. Some friends of mine were in a car accident right before graduation and the policeman said if they would have had their seat belts on they would have never made it to graduation, that year or any others. Therefore, it should be up to the individuals in the car to decide if wearing a seat belt is for them or not.

How many? how close?

Louise, you've chosen a good topic for yourself—one you clearly have strong feelings about. The last ¶ is what really helped me see why it's important to you and that's the point that needs much more detail. Do you know of other instances when seat belts were (or would have been) dangerous? Before you tackle another draft, you might want to do some freewriting or talking to friends to explore the questions I've raised about your first two points (9/5)

Writing 1
Louise P.
First Rough Draft

[Against the Seat Belt Law]

I do not beleve in the seat belt law because I think that it is a violation of your freedom. It is your right to decide if a selt belt can save your life or endanger it. It is not only the driver who has the right to decide, it's the passengers as well. The driver nor the government has the right to tell a passenger they must wear a seat belt.

The government forced this law into the states saying they would cut off highway funds if the law wasn't passed. This was a very communistic way of getting a law passed. If they wanted they law passed they should have presented both sides of the issue; not passed it with threats.

Wearing a seat belt may save some lives but there are many accidents that not wearing a seat belt saved lives. Some friends of mine were in a car accident right before graduation and the policeman said if they would have had their seat belts on they would have never made it to graduation, that year or any others. Therefore, it should be up to the individuals in the car to decide if wearing a seat belt is for them or not.

Louise -
You have selected a topic that clearly matters to you. What more do you want to know about the use of seat belts? What more do you know about your friends' accident? Have you talked to them recently or to the police? What other information do you have for and against the use of seat belts? Who exactly are your readers? Can they change the law? What arguments might convince them? What arguments would people for seat belts have?

Writing 1:   Response

Dear Louise,

     I smiled as I read your essay arguing against the law that requires us to wear seat belts. One of your arguments sounded like one my mother used to offer me. My mother didn't like to wear a seat belt when she was in a car so she always found putting one on an occasion to mention that some people were actually killed in car accidents because they were wearing seat belts. And she could always remember a story that Ethel had told her or Mildred had told her about some individuals who had died because they were wearing seat belts. She often had a few terrible details of those accidents to share with me. I would usually answer my mother's complaints by expressing my horror at the details she mentioned and my sympathy for the injured individuals whom someone she knew knew about. Following her account of a terrible accident, I would customarily ask my mother how Ethel or Mildred learned about the accident, where it had taken place, and so on. Probably it wasn't very nice of me to put my mother on the spot that way. I knew the stories she was sharing with me were her way of resisting the seat belt. Somehow I thought that resistence was more characteristic of older people, who formed their car-riding habits before seat belts were commonplace into cars, than of younger people. That is why I was surprised at your stand on seat belts. And I was really surprised that you offered as support for the position you are taking about seat belts, the same kind of heard or over-heard story my mother used to tell. Nameless people, an authority whose qualifications are questionable, insufficient details. I would not have reached the same conclusion you seem to have accepted because someone told you that a person you do not know, whose judgment you cannot evaluate, had reached such a conclusion.

     Let me ask you to think about it this way: You have a child, a two-year-old. You and she are getting into the car to drive on 1-75. Are you going to put a seat belt on yourself, on her? Why? What kind of facts do you want to know before you make that decision? Will you accept hearsay as fact when it comes to protecting your life and your child's life?

     Maybe the essay you are drafting is not about seat belts; maybe they are just a case in point; maybe your essay is about the government's legislating what is good for its citizens. That is really a different issue. If that is what you are writing about then I have another set of questions I want to ask you: Who or what is the government? How did it force the law into the states? Who are the "they" who will cut off highway funds? The "they" who should have presented both sides of the issue? How do laws get passed? Where? Under what circumstances? What is the difference between a threat and an incentive? Do governments exist to protect the rights of individuals or to secure the safety of the bulk of the population? Or both? Or neither?

     Let's talk in a conference this week as you are working on your second draft of this essay; let's talk about seat belts and the law requiring that we wear them   I'd like to talk with you about these issues not only because you sound like my mother did on the topic of seat belts--and I love to talk with anyone who sounds like my mother--but also because I think you and I might have fun debating the seat belt issue. I warn you, though, I'm off to the motor vehicle bureau and the library to get such facts as I can about seat belt use so that I can give you a tough time when you come in. Be prepared.

P. L. Stock

> **Discussion of Responses to [Against the Seat Belt Law]**
> *Featured Responders: Stewart, Peterson, Warnock, Stock*
> *Featured Issues:*
> • **Readers' views of the writer**
> • **Lack of development**
> • **Student investment in the subject**

Our readers agree that this text is underdeveloped and lacking in specifics. They differ rather significantly, however, in their views of the writer and in the way they respond to this text.

As he indicates in his note to us about his response, Stewart sees Louise as a student who "has paid very little attention to the assignment and has done no serious thinking on the subject." He tells her that "her arguments are as full of holes as a Swiss cheese." Stock, on the other hand, feels that Louise lacks "experience in the variety of ways she may use writing to discover ideas . . . [and a] sense of the work it takes to probe ideas and opinions." Peterson has yet another view of Louise: She sees her as a "somewhat belligerent" student who speaks out frequently and strongly without being aware that others might not understand her or might disagree with her. Finally, Warnock tells us that she does not have a clear sense of who Louise is. She would like to learn more about her (in a conference) and help her "move beyond personal experience to make her views convincing."

These differing views of the student lead to quite different ways of responding to her essay. Stewart tells Louise very directly that her arguments "just will not hold up" and gives her a point-by-point explanation of its flaws. Stock tells Louise the story of how her mother argues against seat belts in an attempt to help her see the logical flaws in her argument. Peterson compliments Louise on her topic selection and suggests that she develop the information in the last paragraph of the essay. Warnock simply asks Louise to consider what more she wants to know about seat belts and what she knows about this specific incident.

Six of the eight respondents not featured for this essay focus on Louise's failure to support her argument with evidence, with five asserting or implying that the paper is underdeveloped because Louise does not really care about her subject. Larson is typical of this approach. He questions whether Louise cares about the topic, but suggests that if she does, she must show the reader why this topic is important to her. McClelland, Anson, Hull, and Elbow also question whether Louise knows or cares enough about the subject to write about it effectively.

White does not speak about Louise's lack of enthusiasm for, or knowledge about, the topic; he simply reports to Louise that her task in revising should be to find evidence for her assertions. Gere and O'Hare, on the other hand, seem to agree with Peterson that the last paragraph in Louise's essay is evidence that she does care about this topic. Like Peterson, Gere sees the graduation day accident as a potential "center of gravity to future drafts," but she hopes Louise "can find ways to draw on this to get out of her cotton wool generalizations." O'Hare also believes that she does "feel strongly about this issue," but he wants to know what reasons have led her to this opinion.

Clearly, then, all the readers of this text agree that it is in need of development. They differ, however, in their views of the student: Some think she lacks motivation to write about this subject; others feel she simply has failed to develop her essay. This crucial difference gives rise to quite different manners and tones of response.

WRITING 2
ROUGH DRAFT: "WHAT IF DRUGS WERE LEGAL?"
Featured Responders: Peterson, Gere, White, Warnock

BACKGROUND

This is the first rough draft of an argumentative response essay. Through the first several weeks of the course, the class has focused on various kinds of expressive writing, and students have been writing essays mostly from their personal experience. Now the class is moving into transactional writing on topics which may include, but which must extend beyond, their first-hand experience. As a bridge into the second half of the course, students are to write a response essay in which they express their views on what another writer has to say about an issue. In anticipation of this assignment, students have been given practice in summarizing and paraphrasing the ideas of others. Although they have written several essays up to this point, this is the first paper that they will take through several drafts and receive another's comments on before they hand in the final draft.

This particular student, Nancy, sees herself as a "good writer." As she has told you a few times already (both verbally and in her course journal), she "has always gotten A's in English." Evidently, she is confused, or even put off, by your view of writing and, particularly, your assessment of her work thus far in the course. She has been somewhat resistant to changing her style and process of writing and has not been very responsive to your comments on the four previous course papers.

THE ASSIGNMENT

Select from a journal, magazine, or newspaper, a recent article on an issue you are interested in, one that presents a view you disagree with or that you find some problem with. In an essay intended for the same publication, write a response to the article. You may respond to the article as a whole or to parts of it. Your task is not to review the article for its own sake but to express your views on what this writer has to say. Your final draft should identify the author, title, and issue you are responding to and summarize what the author says about it, and then present your response.

We'll take this essay through two rough drafts before the final draft is due, two weeks from today. I will respond to both the first rough draft and the second rough draft.

[For additional responses to this essay, see Chapter 4.]

Legalize Drugs

By John LeMoult

STAMFORD, Conn.—As a trial lawyer with some 20 years' experience, I have followed the battle against drugs with a keen interest. Month after month, we have read stories of how the Government has made a major seizure of drugs and cracked an important drug ring. It is reassuring to know that for more than 20 years our Federal, state and local governments have been making such headway against drugs. It reminds me of the body counts during the Vietnam War, when every week we heard of large numbers of North Vietnamese and Vietcong soldiers killed in battle. Somehow, they kept coming, and they finally forced us out and overwhelmed their enemies.

Every elected official from President Reagan on down goes through the ritual of calling for stiffer enforcement of drug and trafficking laws. The laws get stricter, and more and more billions of dollars are spent on the police, courts, judges, jails, customs inspectors and informants. But the drugs keep coming, keep growing, leaking into this country through thousands of little holes. Traffic is funded by huge financial combines and small entrepreneurs. Drugs are carried by organized crime figures and ordinary people. The truth is, the stricter the enforcement, the more money there is in smuggling.

Legalization is not a new idea. But perhaps it is time to recognize that vigorous drug enforcement will not plug the holes. Perhaps it is time to think the unthinkable. What would happen if we legalized heroin, cocaine, marijuana and other drugs? What if they were regulated like liquor and with the protections provided for over-the-counter drugs? Would we turn into a nation of spaced-out drug addicts?

Drugs have been a part of our society for some time. The first antidrug laws in the United States were passed in 1914. They were really anti-Chinese laws, because people on the West Coast were alarmed at the rise of opium dens among Chinese immigrants. Before that, there were plenty of opium addicts in the United States, but they were mostly white middle-class women who took laudanum (then available over the counter) because it was considered unacceptable for women to drink alcohol.

After the first laws were passed, and more drugs added to the forbidden list, the sale of heroin and other drugs shifted to the ghettos, where men desperate for money were willing to risk prison to make a sale. Middle-class addicts switched to alcohol. Today, one in 10 Americans is an alcohol addict. It is accepted. The number of addicts of heroin and other drugs is tiny compared with the number of alcoholics. But these drugs cause 10 times the amount of crime caused by alcohol.

What would happen if the other drugs were legal? Many experts believe there would be no increase in the number of drug addicts. They speak of an addictive personality and say that if such a person cannot easily obtain one drug he will become addicted to another. Many feel that the legalization of heroin and other drugs would mean that such addictive types would change from alcohol to other drugs. A 1972 Ford Foundation study showed that addiction to these other drugs is no more harmful than addiction to alcohol.

But what about crime? Overnight it would be dealt a shattering blow. Legal heroin and cocaine sold in drugstores, only to people over 21, and protected by our pure food and drug laws, would sell at a very small fraction of its current street value. The adulterated and dangerous heroin concoctions available today for $20 from your friendly pusher would, in clean form with proper dosage on the package, sell for about 50 cents in a drugstore. There would be no need for crime.

With addicts no longer desperate for money to buy drugs, mugging and robbery in our major cities would be more than cut in half. The streets would be safer. There would be no more importers, sellers and buyers on the black market. It would become uneconomical. Huge crime rings would go out of business.

More than half the crime in America is drug related. But drugs themselves do not cause crime. Crime is caused by the laws against drugs and the need of addicts to steal money for their purchase. Overnight the cost of law enforcement, courts, judges, jails and convict rehabilitation would be cut in half. The savings in taxes would be more than $50 billion a year.

We may not be ready for a radical step of this kind. Perhaps we are willing to spend $50 billion a year and suffer the unsafe streets to express our moral opposition to drugs. But we should at least examine the benefits of legalization. We should try to find out whether drug use would dramatically increase, what the tax savings would be. I do not suggest that we legalize drugs immediately. I ask only that we give it some thought.

From The New York Times circa 1984

Writing 2
Nancy S.
First Rough Draft

What If Drugs Were Legal?

What if drugs were legal? Could you imagine what it would do to our society? Well according to John E. LeMoult, a lawyer with twenty years of experience on the subject, feels we should at least consider it. I would like to comment on his article "Legalize Drugs" in the June 15, 1984, issue of the New York Times. I disagree with LeMoult's idea of legalizing drugs to cut the cost of crime.

LeMoult's article was short and sweet. He gives the background of the legalization of drugs. For example, the first antidrug laws of the United States were passed in 1914. The laws were put in effect because of the threat of the Chinese imagrants. In addition, he explains how women were the first to use laudanun, an over the counter drug, as a substitute for drinking; it was unacceptable for women to drink. By explaining this he made the reader feel that society was the cause of women using the substitute, laudanun, for drinking. LeMoult proceeded from there to explain how the money to buy drugs comes from us as society. Since drug addicts turn to crime to get money we become a corrupt society. Due to this we spend unnecessary money protecting inocent citizens by means of law enforcment, jails, and ect. LeMoult says that if we legalize drugs that "Overnight the cost of law enforcement, courts, judges, jails and convict rehabilitation would be cut in half. The savings in tax would be more than $50 billion a year."

[handwritten marginalia: this is in his 4th ¶ - what's he doing in the first 3 ¶s?]

[handwritten marginalia: I think you've fallen into the interesting detail trap here.]

[handwritten marginalia: ? crime-filled?]

[handwritten marginalia: good use of quote]

1

LeMoult might be correct by saying that our cost of living in society would be cut in half if drugs were legalized, however, he is justifying a wrong to save money. In my opinion legalizing drugs is the easy man's way out. Just because crime is high due to the fact that the cost of drugs is unbeleivable it doesn't make legalizing them right. We all know drugs are dangerous to the body and society without any explanation, therefore, you shouldn't legalize something that is dangerous.

do we?
All drugs?
cigarettes?
alcohol?
car racing?
those bodies!
how? legal or illegal?

My only and most important argument to LeMoult is the physical harm it would bring by legalizing drugs. People abuse their right to use alcoholic beverages because they are legal. For example, LeMoult himself says the amount of drug addicts is small compared to alcoholics. Why?--of course it is because of the legalization of alcohol. When you make something legal it can and will be done with little hassel. Why allow something to be done with ease when it is wrong? LeMoult's points are good and true but I believe he is approaching the subject in the wrong manner. Drugs are wrong, therefore, should not be legal!

to whom?
all people!
this would mean everyone is an alcoholic because alcohol is legal
do you mean morally wrong or dangerous?

NANCY, your first draft is a good starting point — you clearly understood the structure expected (opening with source info., summarizing the article, responding with your view). Before beginning a second draft, I suggest you do a bare bones outline in the article (you're missing a couple of LeMoult's points) and then do me or your response (you seem to have at least 2 objections instead of one)

2

Writing 2
Nancy S.
First Rough Draft

What If Drugs Were Legal?

What if drugs were legal? Could you imagine what it would do to our society? Well according to John E. LeMoult, a lawyer with twenty years of experience on the subject, feels we should at least consider it. I would like to comment on his article "Legalize Drugs" in the June 15, 1984, issue of the New York Times. I disagree with LeMoult's idea of legalizing drugs to cut the cost of crime.

What about starting with this point?

LeMoult's article was short and sweet. He gives the background of the legalization of drugs. For example, the first antidrug laws of the United States were passed in 1914. The laws were put in effect because of the threat of the Chinese imagrants. In addition, he explains how women were the first to use laudanun, an over the counter drug, as a substitute for drinking; it was unacceptable for women to drink. By explaining this he made the reader feel that society was the cause of women using the substitute, laudanun, for drinking.

How does this advance Le Hoult's argument for legalizing drugs.

LeMoult proceeded from there to explain how the money to buy drugs comes from us as society. Since drug addicts turn to crime to get money we become a corrupt society. Due to this we spend unnecessary money protecting inocent citizens by means of law enforcment, jails, and ect. LeMoult says that if we legalize drugs that "Overnight the cost of law enforcement, courts, judges, jails and convict rehabilitation would be cut in half. The savings in tax would be more than $50 billion a year."

1

LeMoult might be correct by saying that our cost of living in society would be cut in half if drugs were legalized, however, he is justifying a wrong to save money. In my opinion legalizing drugs is the easy man's way out. Just because crime is high due to the fact that the cost of drugs is unbeleivable it doesn't make legalizing them right. We all know drugs are dangerous to the body and society without any explanation, therefore, you shouldn't legalize something that is dangerous.

How can you be sure we all know "without any explanation"?

My only and most important argument to LeMoult is the physical harm it would bring by legalizing drugs. People abuse their right to use alcoholic beverages because they are legal. For example, LeMoult himself says the amount of drug addicts is small compared to alcoholics. Why?—of course it is because of the legalization of alcohol. When you make something legal it can and will be done with little hassel. Why allow something to be done with ease when it is wrong? LeMoult's points are good and true but I believe he is approaching the subject in the wrong manner. Drugs are wrong, therefore, should not be legal!

Can you develop this argument?

Nancy--

You have done a good job of summarizing much of LeMoult's article. I think
you have overlooked a couple of important points, however. Reread the section
where he traces the history of drugs in this country, and look again at his
distinction between drugs and alcohol.

I find your argument against legalizing drugs the most convincing when you
compare the number of alcoholics with the number of drug addicts. Perhaps you
can develop this idea further. In contrast, I find the statements that we all know
drugs are wrong less than convincing. Just exactly why is legalizing drugs the
easy way out? If danger is the issue, how do you respond to the idea that cars
are dangerous? (Think about how many people are killed and maimed in automobile
accidents every year.) In your next draft try to focus on developing more
convincing arguments against legalized drugs.

When you have completed your next draft, try reading it aloud before you
turn it in. I think you will find a number of places where your ears will help you
express your ideas more effectively.

Writing 2
Nancy S.
First Rough Draft

What If Drugs Were Legal?

What if drugs were legal? Could you imagine what it would do to
our society? Well according to John E. LeMoult, a lawyer with twenty
years of experience on the subject, feels we should at least consider
it. I would like to comment on his article "Legalize Drugs" in the
June 15, 1984, issue of the New York Times. I disagree with LeMoult's
idea of legalizing drugs to cut the cost of crime.

LeMoult's article was short and sweet. He gives the background
of the legalization of drugs. For example, the first antidrug laws of
the United States were passed in 1914. The laws were put in effect
because of the threat of the Chinese imagrants. In addition, he
explains how women were the first to use laudanun, an over the counter
drug, as a substitute for drinking; it was unacceptable for women to
drink. By explaining this he made the reader feel that society was
the cause of women using the substitute, laudanun, for drinking.
LeMoult proceeded from there to explain how the money to buy drugs
comes from us as society. Since drug addicts turn to crime to get
money we become a corrupt society. Due to this we spend unnecessary
money protecting inocent citizens by means of law enforcment, jails,
and ect. LeMoult says that if we legalize drugs that "Overnight the
cost of law enforcement, courts, judges, jails and convict
rehabilitation would be cut in half. The savings in tax would be more
than $50 billion a year."

[handwritten margin note:] Now that you are clear on what you have to say (see your last ¶) revise the opening to begin your argument.

[handwritten margin note:] Select the parts of LeMoult's article that are appropriate for your paper and omit the rest. Be sure to quote accurately.

1

Your first argument here: the financial reasons are not good enough for legalization. Focus this ¶ on this argument and develop your case.

LeMoult might be correct by saying that our cost of living in society would be cut in half if drugs were legalized, however, he is justifying a wrong to save money. In my opinion legalizing drugs is the easy man's way out. Just because crime is high due to the fact that the cost of drugs is unbelievable it doesn't make legalizing them right. We all know drugs are dangerous to the body and society without any explanation, therefore, you shouldn't legalize something that is dangerous.

Not so. Look at the previous ¶

My only and most important argument to LeMoult is the physical harm it would bring by legalizing drugs. People abuse their right to use alcoholic beverages because they are legal. For example, LeMoult himself says the amount of drug addicts is small compared to alcoholics. Why?—of course it is because of the legalization of alcohol. When you make something legal it can and will be done with little hassel. Why allow something to be done with ease when it is wrong? LeMoult's points are good and true but I believe he is approaching the subject in the wrong manner. Drugs are wrong, therefore, should not be legal!

Second argument. Now develop this one.

Make this into a full closing ¶.

The paper is a good discovery draft that could become a good paper. As you revise, be sure you focus each ¶ on its central idea. I enjoy the energy of your style.

2

Writing 2
Nancy S.
First Rough Draft

What If Drugs Were Legal?

What if drugs were legal? Could you imagine what it would do to
our society? Well according to John E. LeMoult, a lawyer with twenty
years of experience on the subject, feels we should at least consider
it. I would like to comment on his article "Legalize Drugs" in the
June 15, 1984, issue of the New York Times. I disagree with LeMoult's
idea of legalizing drugs to cut the cost of crime.

LeMoult's article was short and sweet. He gives the background
of the legalization of drugs. For example, the first antidrug laws of
the United States were passed in 1914. The laws were put in effect
because of the threat of the Chinese imagrants. In addition, he
explains how women were the first to use laudanun, an over the counter
drug, as a substitute for drinking; it was unacceptable for women to
drink. By explaining this he made the reader feel that society was
the cause of women using the substitute, laudanun, for drinking.
LeMoult proceeded from there to explain how the money to buy drugs
comes from us as society. Since drug addicts turn to crime to get
money we become a corrupt society. Due to this we spend unnecessary
money protecting inocent citizens by means of law enforcment, jails,
and ect. LeMoult says that if we legalize drugs that "Overnight the
cost of law enforcement, courts, judges, jails and convict
rehabilitation would be cut in half. The savings in tax would be more
than $50 billion a year."

1

Handwritten margin notes:

whats your main point here? If its that you disagree, put that idea up front and explain.

Why do you disagree? Would letting your reader know here clear up a lot of reader expectations?

How do these ideas relate to your purpose as stated in the last sentance of ¶ 1.

You summary the article here but how does what you say here relate to your view stated in the last sentence of ¶ 1?

You've given us a summary of the article — why? You can give your view.

LeMoult might be correct by saying that our cost of living in society would be cut in half if drugs were legalized, however, he is justifying a wrong to save money. In my opinion legalizing drugs is the easy man's way out. Just because crime is high due to the fact that the cost of drugs is unbeleivable it doesn't make legalizing them right. We all know drugs are dangerous to the body and society without any explanation, therefore, you shouldn't legalize something that is dangerous.

My only and most important argument to LeMoult is the physical harm it would bring by legalizing drugs. People abuse their right to use alcoholic beverages because they are legal. For example, LeMoult himself says the amount of drug addicts is small compared to alcoholics. Why?—of course it is because of the legalization of alcohol. When you make something legal it can and will be done with little hassel. Why allow something to be done with ease when it is wrong? LeMoult's points are good and true but I believe he is approaching the subject in the wrong manner. Drugs are wrong, therefore, should not be legal!

Here you're giving your views

here you begin to give your views.

Is this your most original + most important argument? How can you explain + support these views so they will be more convincing to readers of the publication: What specific points that LeMoult makes can you argue with? How?

Nancy—
As you write, you seem to discover what you think. How can you explain + support your views to make them convincing for readers of the publication? What specific points does LeMoult make that you can argue for or against. How?

2

Discussion of Responses to "WHAT IF DRUGS WERE LEGAL?"
Featured Responders: Peterson, Gere, White, Warnock
Featured Issues:
- **Use of outside sources**
- **Logic and support of arguments**
- **Readers' views of the writer**

Our analysis of readers' responses to this essay focuses on three issues. The first two concern textual matters: the incorporation of source materials into a text and the logic and support of arguments. The third takes us beyond the text to the issue of how readers' concepts of the writer affect their responses to that writer's work.

Peterson responds to Nancy's use of her source, suggesting that she has "fallen into the interesting detail trap here." In her endnote, Peterson recommends that Nancy do a "barebones outline" of LeMoult's article in order to get a firmer grasp on just what he is saying. Gere also draws Nancy's attention to problems in her use of the source. Like Peterson, she advises Nancy to reread parts of LeMoult's article to be sure she understands what he is saying. Similarly, White and Warnock ask the student to reconsider what parts of LeMoult's article are appropriate for her paper. Warnock feels that Nancy is summarizing LeMoult when she should be citing specific points in his article that relate to what she wants to say. She follows up on this line of thought in her endnote to Nancy, asking what specific points LeMoult makes that she can argue for or against.

Six of the eight other respondents to this essay suggest that Nancy needs to read her source more carefully and use that improved reading as a springboard to a revised draft of her essay. Stock goes so far as to give Nancy the following protocol of her reading of a section of LeMoult's essay (Stock's reading is italicized and bracketed):

Drugs have been part of our society for some time. [*Okay, so why do you mention that?*] The first antidrug laws in the United States were passed in 1914. [*I didn't know that. I wonder what the significance of the date is.*] They were really anti-Chinese laws, because people on the West Coast were alarmed at the rise of opium dens among Chinese immigrants. [*Oh, so he's arguing that they were racist laws. Laws were passed because Chinese people were smoking opium. The Chinese people were different; therefore, insecure west coast Americans decided their habits were bad. I think I see where he is going with this. I guess that before the Chinese smoked opium in the United States there were no drug laws. Maybe they were racist laws, but isn't smoking opium something to stop before the custom spread in this country? I see in my mind's eye a vision of the emperor's wife in the film "The Last Emperor." Opium smoking is hideous.*] Before that, there were plenty of opium addicts in the United States, [*I didn't know that. What makes him say that? What are his facts?*] but they were mostly white middle-class women who took laudanum (then available over the counter) [*Ah, I didn't know laudanum was opium*] because it was unacceptable for women to drink alcohol. [*That is amazing. It was unacceptable for them to drink alcohol, but it was okay for them to take opium. So, opium was acceptable when mostly-white middle-class women took it, but not when Chinese immigrants took it . . .*]

Although Stock does not say so explicitly, she would seem to be suggesting that Nancy needs to understand how our biases as readers influence what we make a text mean.

Stewart, on the other hand, seems to feel that Nancy has used her source in an appropriate manner. As he tells her, you have "defined the particular issues with which you do not agree and summarized the author's arguments. No problem of note there." Hull is not so satisfied with the use of sourcing here, but she tends to feel that the problem lies in the assignment rather than in the student's failure to carry it out. According to Hull, it is a "false exercise to think that we are somehow abstracting the objective essence of a text, when what we are actually doing is selecting, responding, evaluating as individual readers." Hull is "troubled, too, that we aren't going to allow this student to have her opinion. We're going to make her shape her tirade into a boring little academic paper that uses quotation marks correctly and constructs what westerners think is an appropriate rational 'response.'" Hull would argue, furthermore, that Nancy does not really have a problem with summarizing. She has included in her essay most of the major propositions in LeMoult's article, but rather than attributing to LeMoult his rational, measured tone, Nancy paints him as "this crazy radical type." Hull would "want to examine what it means to write a summary and what's fake about it and why certain topics are harder to deal with in summaries than others."

A second important issue for many readers of this text is Nancy's logic and reasoning. For the most part, their comments focus on questionable assertions and/or her failure to support those assertions. Peterson asks several questions in the margins of the second page of Nancy's draft, all designed to make her think more carefully about the logic of her argument and what kinds of support her readers will need in order to see her assertions as credible. Gere asks one such question in the margin and follows up with a paragraph (the second one) in her endnote dealing in some detail with ways in which the argument can be improved.

White feels that Nancy's lack of support for her arguments is caused, at least in part, by her failure to know what her major arguments are. Thus, he points out what he sees as her two main arguments and suggests that she develop them. Warnock's critique is also designed to help Nancy discover the main points of her argument.

Six of the eight responses not featured also deal, in varying degrees, with Nancy's failure to argue convincingly. Only Stock and Elbow do not concern themselves with this matter. As noted above, Stock spends her time helping Nancy see how she (Stock) reads LeMoult's article, in the hope, apparently, that Nancy will read the article carefully and with more understanding. Elbow focuses on his resistance, as a reader, to Nancy's essay.

With this point, we come to another issue that we do not delve very far into here: the readers' concept of who the writer is. Although Elbow agrees with Nancy's principal argument (in his words: "I don't disagree"), he notes that he finds himself resisting her argument. He explains to her that his resistance may come, in part, from the fact that her arguments "somehow . . . make it seem as though you are having a closed mind and saying 'Let's not even think about it.'" In his note to us, Elbow says that he "is put off" by the essay, but he will not tell Nancy that because he feels they are "drifting into an adversarial relationship—wrestling." He goes on to tell us that "[t]he important principle I've come to realize holds here is this: whenever there is a contest as to whether or not the course will 'reach' someone, the student can *always* win—always has the trump card." Thus, his comments will act as "a kind of holding action" until he can have a conference with Nancy. (For a fuller discussion of how the readers tailored their responses to their concept of who Nancy is, see Chapter 5.)

The readers are, for the most part, in agreement that Nancy needs to work on using her source more effectively and in shoring up her argument. They disagree quite markedly, however, as to "who" Nancy is; this disagreement helps account for important differences in their responses to her essay.

WRITING 5
ROUGH DRAFT: "ATTENTION: BASS FISHERMEN"
Featured Responders: Gere, O'Hare, McClelland, Elbow

BACKGROUND

This is the second rough draft of the third essay of the course, but it is the first time you have looked at the drafting toward this assignment. The strengths and problems you see in this paper are virtually the same ones you have seen in his earlier writing.

THE ASSIGNMENT

In your first two papers you tried to recreate a personal experience that was significant in your life. You concentrated on a single incident and tried to show what happened. In this paper, your first expository essay, your objective is to explain a subject to a reader. You will be concentrating, then, on presenting your understanding about an idea, process, or activity to someone who does not have this knowledge. Rather than talking about a single incident, say, a time when you vacationed in New England, you would be talking about the subject "vacationing." For instance, you might explain the pleasures of touring the New England states by car or describe New England's most enjoyable attractions.

Your assignment, then, is to select an idea, process, or activity that you know about but that many people are unfamiliar with. Assuming the stance of an expert writing a feature column for the school newspaper, write a 600-1000 word essay in which you explain this subject to readers.

Be careful to restrict your topic to a size that will be manageable in the assigned space. And try to develop your ideas with concrete examples and details so that your readers will be able to understand what you have to say about the subject.

You will take this paper through several drafts and receive comments from either me or other students at the various stages.

Writing 5
Steve L.
Second Rough Draft

ATTENTION BASS FISHERMEN

If the feeling of a monster large-mouth bass on the end of your
line sends the same feeling of excitement through your body as it
does mine, the lakes of central Orlando are for you. Orlando is
blessed with an extraordinary number of lakes to fish in. Almost all
of these were formed by sink holes thousands of years ago. The sink
holes were eventually filled with run-off from rain storms and formed
some of the greatest natural fishing holes ever. During my early
childhood the first really fun thing I was taught to do by my
grandfather was to fish for blue-gill. It wasn't until later that I
acquired the skills to fish for large-mouth bass, but after I hooked
my first bass I understood how exciting fishing really is. After
spending the first ten years of my life on the bass infested lakes of
Orlando, I took for granted the great fishing. Only after moving to
Texas did I learn to appreciate the lakes of Orlando. I remember
looking forward to summer vacation because we would always go to
Orlando to visit my grandmother and grandfather for a couple of days
before we would go to New Smyrna Beach. The drive from Texas was
torture, because Florida's I-75 is lined with thousands of potential
fishing holes. The temptation to stop and try my luck was almost
unbearable. Every time I saw a lake I would tell myself it would be
better to hold out until I got to Orlando, where I knew the monster
bass would be lurking.

[handwritten marginal note:] In what way does the paper change here?

[handwritten marginal note:] What would happen if you left yourself out of the description of Orlando's lakes?

1

There is a certain lake in Orlando called Lake Ivenho that is my
favorite place to fish. Lake Ivenho is actually a chain of four lakes
connected by links of water. I have an advantage over most people in
fishing these lakes. I grew up on them and know most of the hidden
underwater structures, like fallen trees and sand-bars that extend out
into the lake. One of the things I love the most about this lake is
that almost all the lake is fishable from the shoreline. This is a
rare occurrence because on most lakes you can only fish in certain
places unless you have a boat or waders. Lake Ivenho is unique
because the only thing between you and the fish are the occasional
patches of lillypads. The best solution to this problem is to work a
top-water buzz bait in the early morning or late afternoon. I have
hooked some big bass using this technique, but if the bass is big
enough to give a good long fight it can be very difficult to get it
through the lillypads. After fishing the lillypads that morning my
next move was to work a plastic worm under the giant oak trees that
hang out over much of Lake Ivenho. Bass like to hang out in these
shady areas during the heat of the day so they can better spot
unsuspecting prey swimming by. This didn't produce the monster bass I
was looking for so my next move was to work a spinner-bait along the
southeast bank of the lake where there is a three foot drop off at the
shore line. This is a especially good place to fish during a change
in barometric pressure. The reason bass do this is because they loose
their sense of equilibrium and must move in close to static underwater
structures to help maintain their sense of balance. This forces you
to place the lure directly in front of the fish or it won't strike.

What differences do you notice between the bracketed portions and the rest?

2

After fishing for about another hour and a half, hot, hungry and tired
from a long day of fishing I decided to call it a day even though I
had failed to catch the "Monster Bass" I was looking for. After
dinner, still wanting to catch a monster I decided to try night
fishing, which has been known to produce some big fish. After putting
on a big black worm I started to fish under a small bridge that went
over the water that conncted two of the lakes. After fishing for
about thirty minutes, I suddenly felt a tug at my line and because it
was dark I couldn't tell if it had the worm in its mouth or not so I
decided to wait for one more sign that it was still at the end of my
line. A split second later I felt it and set the hook hard. It felt
like I set the hook in a tree but the tree was fighting back. After
fighting it in to the shoreline I reached down and pulled out my seven
and a half pound monster.

How would you describe this last portion?

3

Steve--

Your choice of topic is excellent because you clearly know a great deal about bass fishing. Your description of Orlando's lakes and of Lake Ivanho in particular gives me a real feeling for the place and for fishing there because you include so many concrete examples and details. Your accounts of your own fishing experiences provides further detail, but these accounts also raise some problems.

When you begin to recount specific experiences they tend to take over. Instead of explaining fishing you move into a narrative of one event. This is particularly true beginning in the middle of page 2 with the section that begins "After fishing the lillypads that morning..." This account leads into the narrative that closes the paper. By concentrating on this event you abandon your role as expert explaining bass fishing.

As you revise this draft try to concentrate on explaining bass fishing rather than telling the story of one fishing trip. You can certainly draw on your own experiences to illustrate points you make, but try to prevent the narrative from taking over.

Writing 5
Steve L.
Second Rough Draft

ATTENTION BASS FISHERMEN

If the feeling of a monster large-mouth bass on the end of your
line sends the same feeling of excitement through your body as it
does mine, the lakes of central Orlando are for you. Orlando is
blessed with an extraordinary number of lakes to fish in. Almost all
of these were formed by sink holes thousands of years ago. The sink
holes were eventually filled with run-off from rain storms and formed
some of the greatest natural fishing holes ever. During my early
childhood the first really fun thing I was taught to do by my
grandfather was to fish for blue-gill. It wasn't until later that I
acquired the skills to fish for large-mouth bass, but after I hooked
my first bass I understood how exciting fishing really is. After
spending the first ten years of my life on the bass infested lakes of
Orlando, I took for granted the great fishing. Only after moving to
Texas did I learn to appreciate the lakes of Orlando. I remember
looking forward to summer vacation because we would always go to
Orlando to visit my grandmother and grandfather for a couple of days
before we would go to New Smyrna Beach. The drive from Texas was
torture, because Florida's I-75 is lined with thousands of potential
fishing holes. The temptation to stop and try my luck was almost
unbearable. Every time I saw a lake I would tell myself it would be
better to hold out until I got to Orlando, where I knew the monster
bass would be lurking.

There is a certain lake in Orlando called Lake Ivenho that is my favorite place to fish. Lake Ivenho is actually a chain of four lakes connected by links of water. I have an advantage over most people in fishing these lakes. I grew up on them and know most of the hidden underwater structures, like fallen trees and sand-bars that extend out into the lake. One of the things I love the most about this lake is that almost all the lake is fishable from the shoreline. This is a rare occurrence because on most lakes you can only fish in certain places unless you have a boat or waders. Lake Ivenho is unique because the only thing between you and the fish are the occasional patches of lillypads. The best solution to this problem is to work a top-water buzz bait in the early morning or late afternoon. I have hooked some big bass using this technique, but if the bass is big enough to give a good long fight it can be very difficult to get it through the lillypads. After fishing the lillypads that morning my next move was to work a plastic worm under the giant oak trees that hang out over much of Lake Ivenho. Bass like to hang out in these shady areas during the heat of the day so they can better spot unsuspecting prey swimming by. This didn't produce the monster bass I was looking for so my next move was to work a spinner-bait along the southeast bank of the lake where there is a three foot drop off at the shore line. This is a especially good place to fish during a change in barometric pressure. The reason bass do this is because they loose their sense of equilibrium and must move in close to static underwater structures to help maintain their sense of balance. This forces you to place the lure directly in front of the fish or it won't strike.

After fishing for about another hour and a half, hot, hungry and tired from a long day of fishing I decided to call it a day even though I had failed to catch the "Monster Bass" I was looking for. After dinner, still wanting to catch a monster I decided to try night fishing, which has been known to produce some big fish. After putting on a big black worm I started to fish under a small bridge that went over the water that conncted two of the lakes. After fishing for about thirty minutes, I suddenly felt a tug at my line and because it was dark I couldn't tell if it had the worm in its mouth or not so I decided to wait for one more sign that it was still at the end of my line. A split second later I felt it and set the hook hard. It felt like I set the hook in a tree but the tree was fighting back. After fighting it in to the shoreline I reached down and pulled out my seven and a half pound monster.

Writing 5
Steve L.

Steve, this paper has real potential--you seem to know your
subject well and you are a real fan of fishing. You obviously enjoy
fishing and know enough to make it attractive for people who haven't
experienced the Orlando bass-fishing experience.

The strengths of this paper are numbered in the left-hand margins.

1. Everything marked #1 is excellent introductory material connecting
    you to your forthcoming explanation of bass fishing.

2. The #2 sentences are interesting and informative and should prove
    useful in your final draft.

3. Again, useful information, especially about shore-line fishing.

In other words you have selected some first class informative
material for explaining about Orlando bass fishing.

The problem areas in this paper relate directly to the PACES
conceptual frame, especially with regard to purpose and audience. The
last full page of your draft "After fishing" to the end is a narrative
of one day you spent fishing. Your merely mention the fishing you did
at the lilypads, the shady areas beneath the oaks, the southeast bank
for 1 1/2 hours, and then, too briefly, hooking the monster bass.

What is your overall purpose and who is your audience?

I think the two previous personal experience narratives you wrote
have influenced you here. You need to step back from your bass
fishing experiences and decide what makes the different aspects of
bass fishing so exciting. Think of explaining rather than, as in the
second half of your paper, simply narrating.

Is bass fishing more than just "exciting" to you?

You seem interested in the different kinds of techniques demanded
by different locations in that one lake. Should you focus on that
lake exclusively or talk about Central Florida in general?

In other words, what is your overall purpose?

Is your audience people who have never fished before or people who
have never fished for bass, especially in the Orlando area?

Just what aspects of bass fishing led you to the term "exciting"?
Could this term be put into sub-categories?

Steve L.'s Second Rough Draft: "Attention Bass Fishermen"

This text shows you moving away from recreating the personal experience of participating in an activity in and of itself (as you did in the first two assignments) and moving towards "presenting an understanding about" the activity. For you, Steve, this movement is from something like "My Bass Fishing Experience with My Grandfather" to "How to Bass Fish in the Lakes of Orlando."

In a shift of this nature you must guage how much "showing" and how much "telling" to do in the text. As a reader, I want to experience vicariously the primary sensations of the activity, while also needing your commentary to explain how to catch that wondrous large-mouth. What I find most effective in you draft, Steve, is the technical information: where to look for the fish during particular conditions of time and weather, what equipment (rods, lures etc.) to use. I need to know more about specific techniques: HOW to do it. For example, what techniques do you use to work a "top-water buzz bait," a "plastic worm," and a "spinner-bait"? The more scientific information (like that about barometric pressure change) and the more lore (your particular tricks of the trade) you present, the better for us readers who are novices to this sport.

Of course, with such requirements for "telling" us such things you have to make some trade-offs, some reduction in the amount of "showing" us the scene. After all, you are shooting for a 600-1000 word essay and a rough estimate of your draft puts it already at approximately a 750-word length. So you need to examine carefully what to include and what to let drop on the editor's floor. As far as relevance to my needs as a reader, I give a low priority to the reverie about your early childhood days (beginning with the 4th sentence and running to the end of p. 1). There are more than two hundred words tied up it.

Get to work as my mentor, Steve, and show me how to pull a seven-pounder from the waters of Lake Ivenho.

WRITING 5, "ATTENTION BASS FISHERMAN"

Dear Steve,

   I'm a total nonfisherman but (and?) I enjoyed reading your piece. Perhaps that makes me the wrong audience (particularly given your title). (What about that? Do you really want to restrict your audience? You might catch a few nonfisherman on your line with a different title.) I even enjoyed the metaphor of "setting a fish" on the hook--and then realized it's merely the conventional term.

   What I like is your voice and presence and the sense of immediacy through lots of detail. I marked places I especially liked. (I marked your opening sentence-- your "lead"--but I have second thoughts: it's vivid and lively, but I'm bothered because it's used so much--feels like something borrowed from FIELD AND STREAM--I guess the title adds to this feeling--making me fear this will be a stale and "bor- rowed"-feeling piece of writing--which it didn't seem to me to be. But it'll proba- bly work--especially on the school newspaper. Not on teachers, however.)

   I felt something interesting going on here. Seemed as though you had the assignment in mind (don't talk just tell a story of your experiences but explain a subject)--for a while--but then gradually forgot about it as you got sucked into telling about your particular day of fishing. (You'll see my wiggly lines of slight bafflement as this story begins to creep in.)

   The trouble is I like your stories/moments. My preference would be not to drop them ("Shame on you--telling stories for an expository essay") but to search around for some way to save it/them--but make it/them part of a piece that does what the assignment calls for. Not sure how to do it. Break it up into bits to be scattered here and there? Or leave it a longer story but have material before and after to make it a means of explaining your subject? Not sure; tricky problem. But worth trying to pull off. Good writers often get lots of narrative and descriptive bits into expository writing.

Best,

Peter

[On the student's text itself, Elbow notes that the penultimate sentence on page 2 is "interesting." He underlines several passages, including "occasional patches of lillypads" and "during a change in barometric pressure" on page 2, indicating passages that (as he puts it in a note to us) "seem strong or memorable or interesting." He puts a squiggly line underneath several other passages, including "that morning" in the middle of page 2 and "The reason bass do this" at the bottom of the same page, indicating passages that "bother" him.]

Discussion of Responses to "ATTENTION: BASS FISHERMEN"
Featured Responders: Gere, O'Hare, McClelland, Elbow
Featured Issues:
• **Attention to the assignment**
• **Organization/modes of discourse**

Most of the readers see Steve as a very capable writer who, with a bit of direction, can revise this essay quite satisfactorily. However, there is some disagreement as to just what type of advice would be most helpful to Steve and how much that advice should be aimed at moving him in the direction of the essay called for by the assignment. Gere is not satisfied with the narrative structure here, but she feels that "a short conversation would help him see the difference between telling the story of a single incident and explaining fishing." O'Hare thinks this is a paper with "real potential," but he sees it as a "classic example of the narrative/expressive eventually overwhelming the explanatory/expository." He wants Steve to determine his overall purpose and revise to achieve an expository purpose. McClelland agrees with O'Hare. He advises Steve to "gauge how much 'showing' and how much 'telling' to do in the text" and then trade off some of the "showing" in order to "tell" more.

Elbow is also concerned with the issue of how to shape this essay, but, as his comments to Steve make clear, he does not see revision as a simple matter of focusing on an expository purpose. He likes Steve's stories and advises him to "search around for some way to save it/them—but make it/them part of a piece that does what the assignment calls for." He adds that he is "Not sure how to do it."

Anson, whose response is not represented above, also wrestles with this issue of how to help Steve revise his narrative work for an expository purpose. In his note to us, he says that he "wouldn't make such a strong distinction between 'personal' and 'expository' writing." He goes on to add that this "student's essay is a good example of how the two 'types,' if they exist, can often merge in a single text." He tells Steve that although he likes the narrative elements, he feels ultimately that the paper "leans too heavily toward the narrative in places."

With the exception of Hull, the other teachers who responded to this essay—Larson, McClelland, Peterson, Stock, Warnock, and White—all focus on the disjointed nature of the paper. They suggest ways in which the writer can move to an explanatory essay that teaches readers something about bass fishing. Like the other readers in our study, Hull sees Steve as a capable student; in fact, she suspects that Steve understood the assignment in the first place but elected to write this essay instead of what was called for. She objects to the implication in our background statement that, because the student is not making the proper progress, "the teacher ought to do something to shake him up with her comments on this draft." She believes "the motivation for writing has got to come from somewhere else besides fear of teacher reprisal," and, thus, rather than coercing Steve, she would "try to appeal to his talent . . . challenge him with a problem of craft." The first part of her response is designed to show how much she likes this draft:

> I like the feel of this draft. You've captured something of the pleasure and skill involved in bass fishing. Details like using top-water buzz bait in patches of lillypads will make your readers want to buy some waders and head on out to Ivenho.

After this praise, however, she brings Steve back to the assignment at hand:

> In your next draft, keep those wonderful details, but pay attention as well to how you can make this more an expository essay than a personal experience piece.

Although they differ somewhat in the degree of praise they offer Steve for his story and in the directness of their advice for revision, all of those responding to this essay give Steve instruction aimed at helping him fulfill the requirements of this assignment.

WRITING 6
FINAL DRAFT: "THE FOUR SEASONS"
Featured Responders: White, Stewart, Anson, Gere

BACKGROUND

This is the final draft of the fourth essay of the course. You have not responded to previous draftings of this paper.

Students have already written a personal narrative, a thesis-support essay, and a comparison-contrast essay. The class has emphasized writing as a process and has worked on those composing strategies and features of discourse that you would typically emphasize in the first half of Freshman Composition.

You may assume that students have the option of rewriting, for a change in grade, one of their course papers by the end of the term.

David, is a confident, perhaps even a cocky, student who comes across as someone who thinks he is better than (in your view) he is. However, his confidence is by no means groundless. You have been both taken with and disappointed by aspects of his previous writings, and now you receive this paper.

THE ASSIGNMENT

Most of you are off at school and in a new place, away from the people and settings you have become accustomed to and attached to. Similarly, those of you who are from Tallahassee have likely not had the time or the opportunity to visit some of the old places that are special to you.

Choose some place, atmosphere, or situation that you miss from home—or, if you *are* at home, that you have not had the chance to experience for some time, and miss. Depict this scene, mood, or setting in a way that will allow your reader—someone who does not know about it—to see the significance it has for you.

Remember that because your aim is to give your reader a sense of place, you will do well to use specific details.

[For additional responses to this essay, see the introduction to Chapter 3.]

Writing 6
David B.
Final Draft

The Four Seasons

I like Tallahassee very much. The heat and sunshine almost everyday makes each day very pleasant. I intend to spend my next four and one half years here, but I miss my other home, Syracuse, New York. One thing that I truly miss about Syracuse is the four seasons. Each season is distinct and clear in its own way. I will do my best to describe each season to you, but remember that my description cannot compare to experiencing each season for itself.

In the Spring the ground is soft from the melting snow. You can feel the moist ground wanting to seep into your shoes. As the ground begins to dry, the trees begin to blossom and the faint smell of pollen lingers in the air. The flowers work their way out of the ground and bloom for another year. The familiar sound of geese is heard overhead as you look into the sky and see a "V" formation travelling north for the summer. A long winter's nap has ended for the bears, squirrels, rabbits and other hibernating animals. After they awake, their chattering conversations ramble through the forest.

Good detail well observed

which flower is the first to appear?

Not only do the animals come out of their shelter in the springtime, but also people. Many people have a tendency to "hole up" in the wintertime. All your neighbors, that you thought had died, open up their houses to allow the spring breeze to come along and carry away that musty air that built up during winter. You can hear voices and lawnmowers everywhere as people are outside doing their springtime yard work. Wives are planting new flowers while husbands

Tone suddenly becomes flip.

1   *Detail needed. Names?*

This ¶ needs detail + clarity, as well as a distinction (or connection) between nature + people

are raking and mowing the lawn. Spring is the season of awakening where everything becomes (refreshing.) *Notice you use the same term for snow on the next page.*

Following Spring is the season that most people look forward to, that is Summer. Summer is the time of the year when kids are everywhere, because school has been let out. You can hear their voices and giggles <u>fill the atmosphere.</u> *in the parks, playgrounds, beaches, and ball parks.* People are always outside in

People

<u>the summertime</u> because the sun beats down onto the earth and warms *Detail needed* everything up. (There are enormous amounts of) families going to the beach for the weekend or going on vacation for a week. As you look

Nature down the road, you can see heat waves resting on the pavement. The *scrub oaks and pines are*
(foliage) is green and spirits are high. There is a feeling of warmth

People amongst neighbors, friends, and family.

Fall is my favorite season. I do not care for the way Fall *Good detail here* strolls into Tallahassee, the way the leaves and flowers just shrivel away. In Syracuse you can tell when Fall has arrived, because the leaves turn rustic, auburn, garnet, and gold. They fall from the trees onto your lawn, where you spend hours raking the leaves into a pile. After the leaves are sitting neatly in a <u>humongous</u> pile, you *oral tone* may get this crazed feeling. This feeling might just cause you to run and dive into that neat pile. As you are sitting in a natural mattress an aroma of the dried leaves <u>stimulates your olfactories.</u> *artificial tone* This aroma gives you a feeling that you are secure.

When you wake up on a typical fall morning you can look out the window and see the ground lightly dusted with frost. So when you get dressed you may put on a sweater. The fall weather is sometimes referred to as "<u>sweater-weather</u>", because you are able to wear a sweater and be

2

perfectly comfortable. The sweater is just enough to keep the chill
off of you. This is a sign that winter is just around the corner.

Winter is the last season of the year. It ranks a close second
to Fall in my opinion. Many people complain about snow, but I love
it. There is nothing that can compare to the feeling of taking a walk
in the winter at night, when the sky is clear and everything is
placid. The moon glistens off the snow. While you stroll along, you
can hear the soft scrunching of that magical white carpet underneath
your feet. You can "feel Jack Frost nipping at your nose" and the
rosiness in your cheeks. Yet you stay warm, nestled underneath your
winter garb. The atmosphere that surrounds you is serene. It is as *I don't get your meaning here.*
though you could disrobe yourself and still stay warm.

After your walk, in the "winter wonderland", you return to the
homestead. After hanging up your coat, hat, gloves, and scarf, you
shake off the cold and sit by the fire. That burning wood, that has
been seasoned since the summer, smells so wonderful and the heat it
radiates could lull a person to sleep. Winter nights are great to
cuddle up with that special person, by the fire, and listen to the *Detail?*
wind blowing outside or watch the snow fall to the ground. That snow
gives you a refreshing feeling. *You mean something here about watching snow from indoors. What do you mean, precisely?*

These were my brief descriptions of the four seasons in Syracuse.
¶ Of course I have only told of the good things about each season. I enjoy *Are there "not good" things to put in here, as you suggest?*
the changing seasons and when school is through, I intend to move back
up north. The weather down here may be fine for some people, but it
was not meant for me. The only real way to understand what I was
trying to describe is to experience the four seasons for yourself.

3

Comment ⟶

Parts of this paper are very fine, rich with detail and emotion. But sometimes your language gets very general, as if from a greeting card: "feel Frost nipping at your nose,"   "that special person,"   "long winter's nap," and so on. Look closely at the top ¶ on p. 2 for an example of ways to revise, to make your language more clear + detailed.

   Your revision should keep the good organization and concept, but show careful attention to making the ~~new~~ memories yours, by detail, rather than just anyone's.

Writing 6
David B.
Final Draft

The Four Seasons

I like Tallahassee very much. The heat and sunshine almost everyday makes each day very pleasant. I intend to spend my next four and one half years here, but I miss my other home, Syracuse, New York. One thing that I truly miss about Syracuse is the four seasons. Each season is distinct and clear in its own way. I will do my best to describe each season to you, but remember that my description cannot compare to experiencing each season for itself.

In the Spring the ground is soft from the melting snow. You can feel the moist ground wanting to seep into your shoes. As the ground begins to dry, the trees begin to blossom and the faint smell of pollen lingers in the air. The flowers work their way out of the ground and bloom for another year. The familiar sound of geese is heard overhead as you look into the sky and see a "V" formation travelling north for the summer. A long winter's nap has ended for the bears, squirrels, rabbits and other hibernating animals. After they awake, their chattering conversations ramble through the forest.

Not only do the animals come out of their shelter in the springtime, but also people. Many people have a tendency to "hole up" in the wintertime. All your neighbors, that you thought had died, open up their houses to allow the spring breeze to come along and carry away that musty air that built up during winter. You can hear voices and lawnmowers everywhere as people are outside doing their springtime yard work. Wives are planting new flowers while husbands

are raking and mowing the lawn. Spring is the season of awakening
where everything becomes refreshing.

Following Spring is the season that most people look forward to, _—_ _;_
that is Summer. Summer is the time of the year when kids are
everywhere, because school has been let out. You can hear their
voices and giggles fill the atmosphere. People are always outside in
the summertime because the sun beats down onto the earth and warms
everything up. There are enormous _numbers?_ amounts of families going to the
beach for the weekend or going on vacation for a week. As you look
down the road, you can see heat waves resting on the pavement. The _rising from?_
foliage is green and spirits are high. There is a feeling of warmth
amongst neighbors, friends, and family.

Fall is my favorite season. I do not care for the way Fall
strolls into Tallahassee, the way the leaves and flowers just shrivel
away. In Syracuse you can tell when Fall has arrived, because the
sure This
is The leaves turn rustic, auburn, garnet, and gold. They fall from the
right _Them_
word.   trees onto your lawn, where you spend hours raking the leaves into a
pile. After the leaves are sitting neatly in a humongous pile, you
may get this crazed feeling. This feeling might just cause you to run
and dive into that neat pile. As you are sitting in a natural
mattress͵an aroma of the dried leaves stimulates your olfactories. _pretentious_
This aroma gives you a feeling that you are secure.   _language,_

When you wake up on a typical fall morning you can look out the   _cap._
window and see the ground lightly dusted with frost. So when you get
dressed you may put on a sweater. The fall weather is sometimes referred
Commas and
periods always go   to as "sweater-weather", because you are able to wear a sweater and be
inside quotes.

perfectly comfortable. The sweater is just enough to keep the chill off of you. This is a sign that winter is just around the corner.

Winter is the last season of the year. It ranks a close second to Fall in my opinion. Many people complain about snow, but I love it. There is nothing that can compare to the feeling of taking a walk in the winter at night, when the sky is clear and everything is placid. The moon glistens off the snow. While you stroll along, you can hear the soft scrunching of that magical white carpet underneath your feet. You can "feel Jack Frost nipping at your nose" and the rosiness in your cheeks. Yet you stay warm, nestled underneath your winter garb. The atmosphere that surrounds you is serene. It is as though you could disrobe yourself and still stay warm.

After your walk, in the "winter wonderland", you return to the homestead. After hanging up your coat, hat, gloves, and scarf, you shake off the cold and sit by the fire. That burning wood, that has been seasoned since the summer, smells so wonderful and the heat it radiates could lull a person to sleep. Winter nights are great to cuddle up with that special person, by the fire, and listen to the wind blowing outside or watch the snow fall to the ground. That snow gives you a refreshing feeling.

These were my brief descriptions of the four seasons in Syracuse. Of course, I only told of the good things about each season. I enjoy the changing seasons and when school is through, I intend to move back up north. The weather down here may be fine for some people, but it was not meant for me. The only real way to understand what I was trying to describe is to experience the four seasons for yourself.

David B., "The Four Seasons"

This is a good topic for a student who's from Syracuse, New York, but going to school in Talahassee, Florida. Since I'm from a part of the country that has four equally balanced seasons, I don't think I'd like the Sun Belt at all. Like you, I want some change, and I especially like nippy Fall and Winter days. I dislike intense heat and intense cold, but there is no Shangri-La. If I have to choose between summer-like weather most of the time, and the four seasons, I'll take the latter.

Okay. I think you chose a good subject for two reasons: you're in a place where you will not experience the four seasons, and you convince me that you do like that variety.

But now we run into some problems. Have you described the four seasons in Syracuse, or have you described four idealized seasons? I think the latter, and I'll tell you why. In describing Spring, you mention the trees blossoming, flowers working their way out of the ground, geese flying north overhead, and a long winter's nap ending for bears, squirrels, rabbits and other hibernating animals. These are all clichés about Spring. If you must use them, particularize them. Instead of telling us about blossoming trees, tell us how you look forward to the blooming of the redbud tree in your front yard, and of the flowering crab which follows right behind it. Tell us about the particular flowers which blossom in your yard in Syracuse. We'll skip the geese, but let's take a hard look at your list of hibernating animals. How many bears roam the streets of Syracuse? Or do you make frequent trips to the zoo to see them come out of hibernation? If you lived in Yellowstone Park in the winter, mention of hibernating bears would be quite natural. Here, a reader does a double take. What bears are there in Syracuse, or anywhere nearby? Even more to the point, tree squirrels do not hibernate. In winter they are busy digging in places where they buried seeds during the summer. Are you talking about ground squirrels? Do they live in Syracuse? Rabbits don't hibernate, either. The fact that you used these examples suggests to me that you were just tossing off clichéd descriptions of Spring rather than giving us some honest description of Spring in Syracuse. There were, however, a couple of places where you provided some very fine detail. For example, the line, "the faint smell of pollen lingers in the air" is terrific. That's a superb detail. Even the moist ground wanting to seep into one's shoes is pretty good. But the "chattering conversations" of awakening animals "rambling" through the forest is no good at all.

I won't go into excessive detail, but the same kinds of problems show up in your descriptions of the other seasons.

In Summer, for example, you talk about families going to the beach. In Syracuse? Isn't the nearest beach Lake Ontario, and is it fit to swim in? Perhaps it is. I know Erie was a mess and still may be. At any rate, we need to know what beaches you're talking about. The "going-to-the-beach" detail is a Summer cliché for many parts of the country.

In Fall we get "raking Autumn leaves." Can't you tell us something special about Fall in Syracuse? So, the leaves turn. Fine. Aren't there some particularly spectacular maples in the city? Or other hardwoods whose leaves turn a brilliant red? How about shrubs? In my backyard we have a burning bush which I enjoy tremendously every Fall. It turns a brilliant red and stays that way for some time.

Winter turns out to be a popular song. Why don't you tell us what Syracuse winters are really like? Are they as bad as those in Buffalo, with all that snow? How cold does it get? Any ice skating available?

My larger point is that your descriptions of the seasons are conventional and largely clichéd. Why not give us a detailed picture of the seasons as you experience them in Syracuse?

There's not much to say about the organization of the paper. You go from season to season. I've already commented on aspects of the style of this paper. The good details tell us that you are capable of fresh insights, but, for the most part you do not provide them or clothe them in language which is distinctive. I wish you would consistently work up to your potential.

The editing is not much of a problem. I've marked a few things which ought to be corrected.

C

Additional Context

David's composing is erratic, the sign of a writer definitely in the process of transition. Compared to his previous writing, this paper seems to be more carefully structured, but it's hard to tell whether it represents a leap in his abilities because the topic so naturally organizes the paper. In my responses, I've been trying to show David the value of the sorts of studied reflection and careful planning and revising we've been practicing, but his overconfidence has unfortunately limited his potential for improving his work. This is the final draft, and I choose to comment strongly on the limitations of the piece to suggest that he might take more seriously some of the activities in the course. At the same time, I don't want to make it seem that I had something definite in mind in the assignment; I still want David to realize that my course is empowering him, indeed, requiring him, to make good decisions about his writing, and I want to leave the door open to some alternatives. My commentary, then, will be a mixture of expectations/standards and open-ended questions about alternative (and possibly more fruitful) directions.

David's paper (and several others in the class) were a bit disappointing because they didn't seem to fully incorporate some of the ideas we discussed in small-group conference. But my disappointment has caused me to rethink the assignment. As I see it, the problem lies in the strange combination of personal narrative and expository belles-lettre, and it's a mixed genre I don't think either I or my students understand well. In David's case, it's led, I think, to a kind of search for voice, a tension between objective description and authorial involvement. The draft also, however, seems hurried, and I think David could have done more with it in spite of the assignment's limitations. I decide to encourage David to think about some questions of narrative voice. But I am reminded that much of what we get from students is a reflection of our own assignments' excellence--or ineptitude.

Transcription of taped comments on David's final draft

Hi, Dave. Well, having grown up in New England, I share a lot of your feelings about the beauty of the different seasons in the northern part of the country. (In fact, I spoke to my mother yesterday and she said they'd gotten nine inches of snow over the weekend!)

First let me talk about structure. A paper with the topic of the four seasons has a real natural structure; it's hard to see an alternative to, uh, to one section on each of the seasons. It's interesting that you chose to start with spring. That's obviously one way to do it because it's the, traditionally the first season of the year when everything comes to life again, and that forces you to end with winter, which has a kind of serenity, not quite the sense of ending and death that fall conveys but certainly not a feeling of life. Now essentially, if you're sticking to one chunk on each season, you've got four alternatives. One possibity would be to begin with summer, then work your way through to spring, which has, um, gives you the advantage of ending on a note of rebirth and rejuvenation. The one you chose is fine, but you didn't say anything about it in your revision plans following the conference group, and we'd really spent some time talking about these various possibilities.

Uh, I guess my strongest reaction has to do with the question of credibility. Because what you're trying to do here is presumably describe something so that people who haven't experienced it can do so through your words. And in this case, if you romanticize too much, and if it's clear that you're romanticizing, um, your reader may question the credi- . . . well, let me put it this way, your reader may be less prone to accepting the case you make for the beauty of the seasons, especially if you're separating yourself from your readers by implying, you know, "you haven't experienced this, so let me tell you how wonderful it is." Part of the problem, for me anyway, stems from two things--a tendency to exaggerate without providing specific, realistic details, and a tendency to interpret the, uh, the phenomenon you're describing very subjectively, so that **your** impressions, **your** sensations and feelings are at the center of the piece.

The exaggeration problem is pretty quickly remedied. Bruce talked about how he was bothered by the image of bears and squirrels and rabbits all carrying on a kind of woodland conversation, and I think I agree, but you really didn't rethink that much. Along those lines, some specific expressions we questioned in the conference group were things like, um, "enormous amounts of families" (by the way, if you're going to say that, it should be "numbers," and we've talked already about that mass vs. count noun business), and "humongous pile," and "stimulating your olfactories," and the cliche about Jack Frost. And Jody also objected to the sex-role stereotyping of wives planting flowers while husbands rake leaves and mow the lawn. Anyway, all this is a matter of a few stylistic revisions which are easily done.

The other problem is harder to describe, but it concerns, um, how much we as readers depend on your feelings to capture the essense of the seasons. Giving impressions and personal responses is perfectly fine to do, but I think it needs to be balanced with some very descriptive details. And, um, what gives me the sense that you haven't really pushed this piece much from the rough draft we talked about comes in your last line, when you say [flipping through paper], when you say here, um, "The only real way to understand what I was trying to describe is to experience the four seasons for yourself." I think we **all** said to scrap the entire last paragraph because it doesn't do anything, and I even recall that you put a line through it, so what happened? The point of the essay is essentially to give the reader an experience through words, but here it's as if you've told us, "well, you've wasted your time reading this, because I can't capture it in language." And then the whole essay sort of collapses in on itself.

Anyway, I think you get the point here, and I don't want to repeat what we talked about last week. So, what I'd encourage you to do here, Dave, is to spend a lot more time thinking through your drafts before turning them in. Remember that that's where most of the learning comes in; if you, um, if you shortchange yourself at this stage, you'll be giving up that chance to think of alternative strategies, tones, styles, words, and so on.

All in all, this project is about a solid C. Ok, Dave, see you in class.

Writing 6
David B.
Final Draft

The Four Seasons

I like Tallahassee very much. The heat and sunshine almost everyday makes each day very pleasant. I intend to spend my next four and one half years here, but I miss my other home, Syracuse, New York. One thing that I truly miss about Syracuse is the four seasons. Each season is distinct and clear in its own way. I will do my best to describe each season to you, but remember that my description cannot compare to experiencing each season for itself.

In the Spring the ground is soft from the melting snow. You can feel the moist ground wanting to seep into your shoes. As the ground begins to dry, the trees begin to blossom and the faint smell of pollen lingers in the air. The flowers work their way out of the ground and bloom for another year. The familiar sound of geese is heard overhead as you look into the sky and see a "V" formation travelling north for the summer. A long winter's nap has ended for the bears, squirrels, rabbits and other hibernating animals. After they awake, their chattering conversations ramble through the forest.

good description

Do conversations ramble?

Not only do the animals come out of their shelter in the springtime, but also people. Many people have a tendency to "hole up" in the wintertime. All your neighbors, that you thought had died, open up their houses to allow the spring breeze to come along and carry away that musty air that built up during winter. You can hear voices and lawnmowers everywhere as people are outside doing their springtime yard work. Wives are planting new flowers while husbands

1

are raking and mowing the lawn. Spring is the season of awakening *Can women rake and mow lawn?* where everything becomes refreshing.

Following Spring is the season that most people look forward to, that is Summer. Summer is the time of the year when kids are everywhere, because school has been let out. You can hear their voices and giggles fill the atmosphere. People are always outside in the summertime because the sun beats down onto the earth and warms everything up. There are enormous amounts of families going to the beach for the weekend or going on vacation for a week. As you look down the road, you can see heat waves resting on the pavement. The foliage.is green and spirits are high. There is a feeling of warmth *How does this warmth show itself?* amongst neighbors, friends, and family.

Fall is my favorite season. I do not care for the way Fall strolls into Tallahassee, the way the leaves and flowers just shrivel away. In Syracuse you can tell when Fall has arrived, because the leaves turn rustic, auburn, garnet, and gold. They fall from the trees onto your lawn, where you spend hours raking the leaves into a pile. After the leaves are sitting neatly in a humongous pile, you may get this crazed feeling. This feeling might just cause you to run *How could you combine these sentences?* and dive into that neat pile. As you are sitting in a natural mattress an aroma of the dried leaves stimulates your olfactories. This aroma gives you a feeling that you are secure.

When you wake up on a typical fall morning you can look out the window and see the ground lightly dusted with frost. So when you get dressed you may put on a sweater. The fall weather is sometimes referred to as "sweater-weather", because you are able to wear a sweater and be perfectly comfortable. The sweater is just enough to keep the chill off of you. This is a sign that winter is just around the corner.

Winter is the last season of the year. It ranks a close second to Fall in my opinion. Many people complain about snow, but I love it. There is nothing that can compare to the feeling of taking a walk in the winter at night, when the sky is clear and everything is placid. The moon glistens off the snow. While you stroll along, you can hear the soft scrunching of that magical white carpet underneath your feet. You can "feel Jack Frost nipping at your nose" and the rosiness in your cheeks. Yet you stay warm, nestled underneath your winter garb. The atmosphere that surrounds you is serene. It is as though you could disrobe yourself and still stay warm.

After your walk, in the "winter wonderland", you return to the homestead. After hanging up your coat, hat, gloves, and scarf, you shake off the cold and sit by the fire. That burning wood, that has been seasoned since the summer, smells so wonderful and the heat it radiates could lull a person to sleep. Winter nights are great to cuddle up with that special person, by the fire, and listen to the wind blowing outside or watch the snow fall to the ground. That snow gives you a refreshing feeling.

These were my brief descriptions of the four seasons in Syracuse. Of course I only told of the good things about each season. I enjoy the changing seasons and when school is through, I intend to move back *why is this* up north. The weather down here may be fine for some people, but it *weather not* *meant for you?* was not meant for me. The only real way to understand what I was trying to describe is to experience the four seasons for yourself.

3

David--

    This paper is filled with excellent descriptions. You have done a very good job of conveying to your audience the "feel" of the seasons. Phrases like "V formation," "heat waves resting on the pavement," "auburn, garnet and gold," and "soft scrunching" make your descriptions particularly vivid. I come away from this paper with a clear sense of place. Your use of the second person (you) is also effective because it draws the reader into your account. The significance of the four seasons for you remains somewhat vague. Although I understand that you take pleasure in each of the four seasons, I'm still not sure if they have any other meaning for you.

    As noted in the margins, there are several usage problems in this paper. Please check each one and see me if you have questions about any of them.

Discussion of Responses to "THE FOUR SEASONS"
Featured Responders: White, Stewart, Anson, Gere
Featured Issues:
- **Superficially competent writing**
- **Writers with an inflated view of their abilities**

This essay raises two important issues. First, how will readers respond to writing that is competent—but only superficially? David, and writers like him, have the ability to organize paragraphs around a central idea and even to turn a phrase, albeit the phrase smacks very much of Madison Avenue. Nevertheless, that ability is enough to satisfy in many writing situations, and that leads to the second issue, namely, how to deal with a writer who has an inflated opinion of his work.

With the exception of Gere, all readers responding to this text made it clear that they found David's language cliched and uninteresting. (Even Gere says in her note to us that some of his description seems "overdone.") Most of the readers (all but Gere, Hull, Larson, and Warnock) ask David to work on his trite and cliched language. White marks specific passages in the text that need more detail and, in the end comment, asks David to move away from this "greeting card" language. Anson decides to push David by referring to questions about cliched language that were raised by members of his writing group, but not adequately addressed in this revision. Stewart plays back some of David's descriptions and refers to them as "cliches about Spring."

McClelland, whose response is not represented above, rewrites a section of the paper to show David how he might have provided the kind of details the paper needs. Stock compliments David's descriptions of Fall, but then suggests that the descriptions of the other seasons are weak. O'Hare tells the student that "a native of Tallahassee who had never been north could have written" the essay, and then asks, "What details would help make the Syracuse experience unique?"

Larson is also unhappy with the trite language of the essay, but he blames the assignment that seems "to invite the student to fill in some sort of standard pattern." Rather than criticizing the language of this text, he would want to meet with David to see how much he cares about this topic and whether it is worth spending time on revision. Although Warnock seems to agree that this writing is unsatisfactory, her comments are for the most part nonevaluative, asking the writer to assess his own language in light of his purposes for writing.

Hull's initial reaction is to be unhappy with David's glib and cliched writing. But as she continues to read the paper, she comes to feel that many people outside of academia may well like it very much: "It sort of conjures up the American Dream and 2-car garages and 2.5 children and a happy life—an illusion, but a happy one." Her comments are intended to help David examine the differences between audiences who would love this writing and those who would "feel just as strongly in the opposite direction"—and to consider the values and conventions that inform those readings.

Our description of David invited readers to see him as a competent writer (grammatically and mechanically) who has not been asked to examine the lack of substance in his writing and, thus, has a higher opinion of his work than it deserves. The readers' notes to us provide quite a bit of insight into how they deal with overconfident students such as David. White describes David as "a hard nut to crack—the fluent writer who accepts, or even thinks in, cliches." He tells us that he tends "to come down hard on these good writers, who usually slide by without being challenged." Anson feels that David's "overconfidence has unfortunately limited his potential for improving his work." In this final draft, he chooses to "comment strongly on the limitations of the piece" to suggest that he might take more seriously some of the activities in the course.

Stewart also feels that David needs to be encouraged to push himself harder. However, he believes it necessary "to deal sensitively and tactfully with [students like David] so that they will be encouraged to try to improve." If criticisms can be made acceptable to David, he "might develop into a very good writer." Otherwise, he may become "defensive and take refuge in the customary student rationalization that 'his teacher just doesn't like his style.'" Hull is also concerned that she not alienate David. She feels "it will be hard to find a way to convince him of the paper's flaws without offending him." Unlike some of her colleagues, who question David's effort here, Hull believes that David has worked at this piece; however, she sees in his work a "naivete and an unexamined quality that is anathema in the academic world."

Finally, both Stock and Larson share Hull and Stewart's concern that David not be turned off by their responses. Stock tells David that his language is cliched and his organization is formulaic, but she does so only after she has spent considerable time praising him for the parts of the paper that work well. As noted earlier, Larson would elect not to write an end comment, but rather to invite David in for a conference so that he can determine whether he cares enough about this topic to receive criticisms that might help him revise.

The readers, then, view David's writing as competent but uninspiring. They use various techniques designed to help him "push" himself as a writer, with varying degrees of concern for his ego.

WRITING 8
FINAL DRAFT: "TRIBUTE"
Featured Responders: O'Hare, Peterson, Stock, McClelland

BACKGROUND

This essay is written in response to the second assignment in the course. It is handed in as a final draft with no previously required drafts. Up to this point, the class has focused on invention and on substantive content in writing.

You may assume that students have the option of rewriting any of their course papers for a change in grade.

In these first two weeks of the course, you have come to sense that Jennifer, the writer of this paper, is a quiet, sensitive person and a student writer who values both her writing and her teachers' responses to her writing.

THE ASSIGNMENT

Think of a person who has made a strong impression on who you are or on what you think or believe. Describe the impression and explain how he or she made this imprint on you.

Writing 8
Jennifer S.
Final Draft

Tribute

It's a shame how it takes a tragic slap in the face to wake us from our sheltered dreams of life.// We travel through life with an umbrella and while life falls in torrents, we hide until like a bolt of lightning something shatters to make us understand. I know now not to judge a person by the obvious but to look deep into the heart, where the true person lies.// For him I learned too late, for it was with the permanent closing of his eyes that mine were opened for the first time to see him, the real him, as well as everyone, everything else, as if the sun had risen for the first time.//

// Daddy was a smart man, smarter than I'll ever be. I can't remember asking him a question that went unanswered long.// If he didn't know the answer (which seemed rare), he knew how to find it. And if a math problem could be solved, he could solve it.

// He had a love and a talent for music. He used to say that he had missed his calling, that he should have been a musician.// He played the guitar to relax. I find myself humming those familiar tunes that I grew up hearing day after day, though never tiring of.

Daddy was the one I came to with the splinters and loose teeth because they were a little more than mom and a little Bactine could handle. I used to wonder why he didn't become a surgeon. Other times, when he had me laughing so hard that I was crying, I wondered why he didn't become a comedian. At times like that, no one could have asked for a better father.

But alcoholism is a disease that captures and imprisons its victim and offers no escape. It toys with the personality and eventually physically destroys its victim. Daddy was no exception. He was too weak to overcome his opponent, so as time unfolded Daddy became weaker and more addicted. His personality was so different from day to day that we never knew whether it would be "Daddy" or "not." The horrors I experienced through these years turned me almost completely against that wonderful, helpless person who, at that point, needed support probably more than he ever needed it before. How could I have been so blind? Deep down, I knew he didn't mean to act so cruel, but I was too young and too weak myself to cope, to put up with the horrible atmosphere and relentless fear I was trapped in. So I quietly turned against him, left him out in the cold, and slammed the door right in his face.

Then, on a warm summer night, July 20, 1976, we were downstairs when we hard him collapse upstairs, a noise that could have been most anything, but we knew instantly the sound of death. The remainder of the night is rather vague. The siren, the neighbors, the tears, the fear, all centered around a man lying in the floor, his lungs weak and begging for air. Seeing him suffering is still a recurring nightmare. The ambulance came and rushed him to the hospital. But it was too late. He died of a massive heart attack before he ever reached the hospital. The doctor said his heart literally exploded into a million lifeless fragments in his body.

I walked outside the emergency room away from the commotion, the

aroma of medicine the presence of death. The night was warm, but the
chill of death was more dominant. I wanted to cry, but the tears
would not come. Perhaps they just wouldn't have done my feeling
justice. I thought back to when I was a little girl sitting on my
Daddy's knee. What happened to those times? Where did it all go
wrong? I remember looking up at the sky and wondering if he was
looking down at me. "Did you know I loved you, Daddy?", I whispered
to the vast, star-lit night, "Did you know that?"

Then came the tears. I couldn't stop them. They rolled down my
face onto my chin, then into the night, gone forever. I had to get it
out, cry away my sorrow, my regret, but not that a man had died, but
that I had let him slip away without giving him the love and respect
he needed and deserved.

At that moment, on that muggy summer night in July, I learned
something. Like a bolt of lightning it struck, and the truth, like
rain, flooded. I learned not to judge people on the outside, but to
look deep, beyond the surface, to the heart, where the true person
really lives. I can't bring my Daddy back, but I can treat his memory
with enough respect not to let it happen again. Daddy is gone now,
but not completely. A part of him will live on forever within the
hearts and minds of those who believe in him. I am one of those.

Writing 8
Jennifer S.

Jennifer, this is a stunning accomplishment, a real tribute to the memory of your father, whose qualities shine through--musician, tender healer for his little daughter, problem solver, comedian. I am sure that your father knew that you loved him, that you believe in him.

But it is difficult to treat an affliction like alcoholism as a disease. The horrors you experienced over those many years, the horrible atmosphere, the fear can become intolerable. I wish you could see that you probably didn't "let him slip away," that you are being too harsh when you say that you "slammed the door right in his face." Alcoholism corrodes the personality and brutalizes the alcoholic's relatives too. You are both victims of this dread disease.

This paper is an impressive blending of all five elements of PACES. Your overall purpose was clear, and you crafted this essay for your audience with great skill. You have skillfully selected specific incidents from your life with your father to give your readers a sense of his qualities. You also showed respect for your audience (and for your father's memory) by avoiding specific details about the years of suffering.

Paragraphs six through eight are dramatic, effective, convincing. You showed admirable skill in shaping and organizing the story of his death and your reaction to it after you left the emergency room. The self you have projected convinces us of your sincerity and love.

There are, of course, one or two spots where I'd like to see you tighten up your sentence structure, but, quite frankly, I don't want to deal with them now. I want to enjoy this essay--its skillful organization, its powerful details, its maturity, its love.

When I began to bracket in the left-hand margin passages that were especially effective, I thought I might be bracketing too many! As you know, a double bracket (and I rarely double bracket!) means you have produced a real gem.

This paper vibrates with honesty. Well done! Thanks for sharing this memory.

Writing 8
Jennifer S.
Final Draft

Tribute

It's a shame how it takes a tragic slap in the face to wake us
from our sheltered dreams of life. We travel through life with an
umbrella and while life falls in torrents, we hide until like a bolt
of lightning something shatters to make us understand. I know now not
to judge a person by the obvious but to look deep into the heart,
where the true person lies. For him I learned too late, for it was
with the permanent closing of his eyes that mine were opened for the
first time to see him, the real him, as well as everyone, everything
else, as if the sun had risen for the first time.

Daddy was a smart man, smarter than I'll ever be. I can't
remember asking him a question that went unanswered long. If he
didn't know the answer (which seemed rare), he knew how to find it.
And if a math problem could be solved, he could solve it.

He had a love and a talent for music. He used to say that he had
missed his calling, that he should have been a musician. He played
the guitar to relax. I find myself humming those familiar tunes that
I grew up hearing day after day, though never tiring of.

Daddy was the one I came to with the splinters and loose teeth
because they were a little more than mom and a little Bactine could
handle. I used to wonder why he didn't become a surgeon. Other
times, when he had me laughing so hard that I was crying, I wondered
why he didn't become a comedian. At times like that, no one could

Good

1

have asked for a better father.

But alcoholism is a disease that captures and imprisons its victim and offers no escape. It toys with the personality and eventually physically destroys its victim. Daddy was no exception. He was too weak to overcome his opponent, so as time unfolded Daddy became weaker and more addicted. His personality was so different from day to day that we never knew whether it would be "Daddy" or "not." The horrors I experienced through these years turned me almost completely against that wonderful, helpless person who, at that point, needed support probably more than he ever needed it before. How could I have been so blind? Deep down, I knew he didn't mean to act so cruelly, but I was too young and too weak myself to cope, to put up with the horrible atmosphere and relentless fear I was trapped in. So I quietly turned against him, left him out in the cold, and slammed the door right in his face.

a quick example of what the "most" was like (physical abuse? verbal abuse? both?) would help readers understand those comments

Then, on a warm summer night, July 20, 1976, we were downstairs when we hard him collapse upstairs, a noise that could have been almost most anything, but we knew instantly the sound of death. The remainder of the night is rather vague. The siren, the neighbors, the tears, the fear, all centered around a man lying in the floor, his lungs weak and begging for air. Seeing him suffering is still a recurring nightmare. The ambulance came and rushed him to the hospital. But it was too late. He died of a massive heart attack before he ever reached the hospital. The doctor said his heart literally exploded into a million lifeless fragments in his body.

who? doing what?

excellent precision

I walked outside the emergency room away from the commotion, the

2

For me, this part is very powerful because I had a similar experience of when my dad died

aroma of medicine the presence of death. The night was warm, but the chill of death was more dominant. I wanted to cry, but the tears would not come. Perhaps they just wouldn't have done my feeling justice. I thought back to when I was a little girl sitting on my Daddy's knee. What happened to those times? Where did it all go wrong? I remember looking up at the sky and wondering if he was looking down at me. "Did you know I loved you, Daddy?", I whispered to the vast, star-lit night, "Did you know that?"

Then came the tears. I couldn't stop them. They rolled down my face onto my chin, then into the night, gone forever. I had to get it out, cry away my sorrow, my regret, but not that a man had died, but that I had let him slip away without giving him the love and respect he needed and deserved.

At that moment, on that muggy summer night in July, I learned something. Like a bolt of lightning it struck, and the truth, like rain, flooded. I learned not to judge people on the outside, but to look deep, beyond the surface, to the heart, where the true person really lives. I can't bring my Daddy back, but I can treat his memory with enough respect not to let it happen again. Daddy is gone now, but not completely. A part of him will live on forever within the hearts and minds of those who believe in him. I am one of those.

Good idea to return to opening metaphor to give a sense of closure

could just have stopped here

Excellent work Jennifer — you have really enabled me to understand clearly both what you learned and how you learned it. My notes in the middle of page 2 are suggestions for polishing — what could make a strong paper even better. The other area to consider is your introduction where you relied too heavily on 3 cliches ("slap in the face" etc.) and the weather metaphors were a bit confusing. But that too is polishing — your paper overall is well organized with powerful detail and excellent pacing.

Writing 8:   Response

Dear Jennifer,

I was moved by your essay. I found myself liking the father you described. I could hear him patiently explain the answers to the math questions that perplexed you as a child. I could see him strumming a guitar, singing the familiar tunes you find yourself humming now. I could feel him holding your hand reassuringly as he removed the splinters that had pricked their way into your young skin. I could see you pull your face tight with anticipation as he prepared to pull out one of your baby teeth. I did not dislike the man into whom alcoholism transformed your loving father. You did not describe for me a father I might have disliked as you described one I could like. As you write about him, your father is "Daddy"; the man whom alcohol captured and imprisoned is not to be found in your essay. He is not personified or characterized, not even named. He is "not," which I read to mean your way of suggesting your father's absence, his replacement with a stranger whom you did not know, could not know, did not want to know.

I can understand why you avoided the task of presenting a name or a description or specific incidents that might characterize your father when he was suffering from alcoholism. My father was an alcoholic, and I know how painful it is to recall him when he was drinking. Just as your father seemed to be two people to you and your family, my father was two people to my family and me. When he was sober, he was charming, even delightful, clever, bright, and kind. When he was drinking, he was ugly and cruel, abusive. I would find it hard to show that side of him to anyone. It was a side our family protected, hid from view. As I have grown older and reflected on my relationship with my father, I have found that dividing him into two people, one whom I loved, the other whom I loathed, has not been a satisfactory way for me to understand him or myself as his daughter.

It was difficult for my mother, my brother, and I to relate first to the one person my father was and then to the other. But we tried as so many people do who live with alcoholic family members. Like you, we were not able to understand everything; we were not able to forgive everything. My father is still alive so I have not had to face the guilt that you describe you felt when your father died. I know, however, from much reading I have done on the subject that the guilt you felt when your father died is a common feeling in children of alcoholic parents who often conclude, as you have, that they were insufficiently sensitive, insufficiently giving to parents from whom they had no choice but to grow estranged. If you are interested in reading any of the emerging literature on children of alcoholic parents, I would be happy to share any of my books on the subject with you or to give you some titles and authors of such books. I know that it was not easy for you to share these experiences and thoughts with someone you have known for so short a period of time. I want to thank you for the trust you placed in me when you did share them.

Perhaps I am reading too much into your words--perhaps I am reading too much of my own lived life into yours, but I wonder if the experiences about which you are writing are more complicated and conflicted than the first and last paragraph of your essay suggest. The reason why I wonder this is because you have introduced and concluded your discussion, a discussion that suggests the dilemma in which you found yourself relating to a father whose illness altered his personality, with what reads like too neat a formula: As others have, I lived not only insensitive to a loved one but also unable to recognize who he really was until his traumatic death startled me into sensitivity and the commitment to seek and relate to the real selves of individuals.

The difficulty for me with this formulation in your essay is two-fold: It does not capture the complexity of the experiences and emotions about which you have written, and it does not pre-figure or draw together the dilemmas and disorientations you establish in the first two pages of your essay. Rather it suggests how a sensitive--not an insensitive-- young woman worked to make meaning of the death of a father whose debilitating illness had cheated them both of the love and affection they might have shared.   (I also have difficulty with the formulation in general: I don't know how any of us can know what is deep in the heart of an individual but by how they act toward us. But that concern which reading your essay has caused me to think about is not exactly the issue here.)

Instead of framing the complicated and conflicted situations and emotions which you have experienced, in the first and last paragraphs of "Tribute," you rely on formulaic terms: for example, in the first paragraph, "travel through life with an umbrella while life falls in torrents," "bolt of lightning," "look deep into the heart"; in the last paragraph, "Like a bolt of lightning it struck, and the truth, like rain, flooded," "I learned not to judge people on the outside, but to look deep, beyond the surface, to the heart, where the true person really lives." These terms mask, even deny, the pushes and pulls of the affection and the anger you had to grapple with as you were faced with your father's untimely death.

I understand that you are working with the *storm* metaphor to pre-figure one of the primary themes of your essay--when a person puts a barrier between herself and some one who is hurting her, she precludes that person from knowing her; and I understand that you are working with the *surface/depth* metaphor to introduce and summarize the second primary theme of your essay--the side of himself a person shows in the world is not necessarily the real him. What I am questioning is whether these metaphors, these themes, actually introduce and conclude what you are writing about in the body of your essay. In the body of your essay you showed your loving father, suggested your father when he was ill, accounted for your feelings of affection and anger toward him, and demonstrated the emotional anguish you experienced when you were faced with his sudden death. In the introduction and the conclusion of your essay, you indicated not only how your father's death affected you in light of his love, his illness, and your responses to his illness but also how such tramaus as you experienced affect others similarly. In so doing, I think you sacrificed some of the complexity you were working to capture in the body of your paper.

After you re-read "Tribute" now, having had several days away from it, I would be interested in what you think about my reading of the essay. Do the first and last paragraphs do what you want them to do? Are they sufficiently complex to pre-figure and draw together the complex ideas and experiences about which you are writing? Do the *storm* and *depth* metaphors capture all you want them to capture? Do the metaphors compete with one another? Would using just one of them work more effectively? (While I am on the subject of metaphors, let me ask you if *toys* (alcoholism *"toys with the personality,"* ll. 2 and 3 of p. 2) invokes all you want it to bring to your reader's mind. I think you are asking the metaphor to do a lot of work for you because you do not wish to compose the specific details that would allow your reader to see your father when he was ill as you allowed the reader to see you father when he was well. If so, does *toys* serve you suffciently?) As you re-read your essay now, let me invite you to reflect on your use of specific and metaphoric language, on the work you ask each to do, on the balance you establish between them.

Forgive me if with my suggestions and questions, I am asking you to think about issues that, in fact, you have resolved or that you do not wish to think about right now. Please know that I respect the courage it took for you to write this moving "Tribute" to your father. If I may say so, it is also a tribute to his daughter. If you'd like to, I'd like to talk about this essay with you in conference.

P.L. Stock

Jennifer S.' s Final Draft: "Tribute"

Reading "Tribute" is a moving experience; I sense your loving devotion to your father, your conscientious determination to remain loyal to him in the face of his succumbing to alcoholism, and your inward-turning guilt over his death. This latter reaction so troubles me. Your sincerity in this writing is beyond question, Jennifer, but I call on you to reflect further on the nature of revelations that you have experienced. You say that you have gained self-knowledge through this painful relationship that culminated in your father's death. Let me ask you to re-examine some of your text because, while I understand what you are saying, I reject the logic (or psychology) that delivers it.

When you talk at first about your seemingly-omniscient, talented, nurturing, and humorous father, you establish for us his importance to you; we can envision what a loss to you when his personality changed and finally when he died.

In your 5thparagraph, when you introduce the subject of alcoholism, unwittingly you misstate the facts: "But alcoholism is a disease that captures and imprisons its victim and <u>offers</u> <u>no</u> <u>escape</u>" (my emphasis). While alcohol is addictive and the disease is virulent, Jennifer, people can and do recover from it. Moreover, alcoholism is a disease; it is not literally a jailer or some sort of merciless terrorist or superhuman kidnapper. In your text, however, you personify the disease: "it toys with the personality and eventually physically destroys its victim. Daddy was no exception." To characterize alcoholism not as a disease but as a powerful, evil person elevates your father's struggle with it to some imagined heroic level. So when you concede that your father was too weak to work for recovery, it sounds to me as if he were engaged in battle with a omnipotent superhero: "He was too weak to overcome his opponent..."

Then comes the difficult part for me to read. And no doubt it was for you therapeutic but painful to write it: that in the face of horrible years with a cruel man, you turned away from him to protect yourself. This is a sane and healthful; it is normal and typical for a child of an alcoholic, Jennifer. It is also a desperate act for any child. Yes, it must also seem to that child an act of betrayal. And, so when your father has died and you weep in the contradictory emotional release from that horrible life as well as the grief of having lost the father who once meant everything to you, Jennifer, grief and guilt create in you a powerful reaction. For you, as for so many (especially female) children of alcoholics, the complex of grief and guilt turns inward: "I had to get it out, cry away my sorrow, my regret, but not that a man had died, but <u>that</u> I <u>had let him slip away without giving him the love and respect he needed and deserved</u>" (my emphasis). You blame yourself for your father's life and death. Of course, since you do not discuss the family dynamics and whether there were any attempts to help him recover from the disease, we readers cannot speculate on yours and your family's role in his situation. Perhaps, if you choose to revise this essay, you can consider including some such information.

I do not pretend to be a psychoanalyst, Jennifer; however, as you can see, I have some first-hand knowledge of the disease and the difficulties it creates for family members of the alcoholic. For you to become more informed about your psychological response will require some study on your part. By the way, if you would like to read some enlightening books on the subject, there are a number of new titles that deal specifically with these issues. There are also organizations whose role is to assist relatives of alcoholics and to help adult children of alcoholics understand the disease and its human consequences. Please see me if you would like details on these.

The essay you have written is really a tribute to you, Jennifer, for wanting to apotheosize your father's memory. It's a kind and loving thing to desire. But the impulse also comes from an undervaluing of yourself--a psychologically unhealthy dynamic for you to continue. As a reader of your essay, I cannot ignore it. And as someone who cares deeply about your educational success, I must speak up. If you would like some professional assistance in exploring the psychological aspects which gave birth to this essay, I would be pleased to introduce you to one of our counselors with whom you could begin confidential discussions.

Writing is a process of self-discovery and meaning-making, Jennifer. However, the longer I write and read other's writing, the more convinced I become that our original discoveries are not so near the truth as the subsequent making of meaning we do on the basis of those first discoveries. What I am suggesting is that should you pursue this paper further, you may well make more sense for yourself of this painful learning experience than you have thus far.

Discussion of Responses to "TRIBUTE"

Featured Responders: O'Hare, Peterson, Stock, McClelland

Featured Issues:

- **Sensitive personal matters**
- **Depth of insight into subject**
- **Readers' views of the writer**

Nearly all the readers find a good deal to like in this essay. Jennifer's essay reveals a sense of structure and climax, and she writes fluid sentences. Seen from this perspective, Jennifer's writing would elicit nothing but praise for its obvious technical expertise. From another perspective, though, "Tribute" invites teachers to comment on the sensitive issue with which Jennifer is dealing, namely, the degree to which she has understood her father's problems and her relationship with him. The readers differed significantly in their willingness to move beyond the text to talk with Jennifer about this personal matter.

O'Hare, Peterson, and Gere (not represented above) praise the essay and make a few comments intended to show how (or in O'Hare's case to indicate that) the paper might be improved. They do not deal with the issue of how to give constructive criticism to such a personal essay as this.

Larson (not represented above) does not see the writing in such a positive light. He says in his note to us that "the student has followed an urgent private agenda instead of doing what the assignment (as I read it—I could be wrong) asked." His comments to Jennifer are pretty forthright in saying that she has focused on her feelings and that she needs, in a revision, to show how this event affected her. White (not represented above) is also very direct in his advice to Jennifer:

> Stay aware of your reader's need for details and examples. As it now stands, this paper gives us conclusions and responses you feel—and they come off as genuine and deeply felt—but readers will be more convinced by detail than by generalization.

Warnock (not represented above) is not so sure as Larson or White that Jennifer has "missed" the assignment. She notes that "If Jennifer is writing to explain to herself, as the assignment suggests, she has completed the task well." She goes on to say, "One of the most critical decisions I think writers have to make is when to write to discover for oneself and when to revise for specific purposes and audiences." Warnock elects to accept the essay, but to ask the following question in her endnote: "Can you imagine writing this for strangers who might benefit from your experience and understanding?"

Stock and McClelland struggle with the question of how to speak to Jennifer about her feelings. Although McClelland does not offer any note to us on his response, it seems clear that he has decided that Jennifer is confused as to what was happening to her father, and to her. His discussion of her essay, especially the language of the essay, is intended to help her learn something about her experience. One has the feeling that although McClelland would like to see Jennifer write a more successful essay, he is more interested in having her learn something about herself, by means of a close analysis of how she is representing her experience, than in the revised essay she might produce. Stock tells us that at first she "was uncertain whether or not to confine [her] response to the essay's substance or to include in it comments about its effectiveness as a piece of writing." She goes on to explain the strategy she chose:

[B]y commenting on Jennifer's melodramatic use of metaphoric language . . . , I'll ask her to question whether or not she has wrapped her complicated and conflicted feelings into too neat a package.

Hull (not represented above) would apparently like to ask Jennifer some of the same questions. However, she does not feel that she knows Jennifer sufficiently well at this point in the semester to decide whether she is "emotionally stable enough to treat this paper as a paper and not an unrevisable tribute to her father." Thus, she decides to "praise the paper first," and then to ask Jennifer which parts of the paper she thinks need work. "If she is able to do this, to look with a cool eye on her sentences and discourse, then I'll know that I too can suggest changes."

In a similar way, Anson (not represented above) sees this as a "classic dilemma" in which the teacher must "walk the fine line between responding to texts and responding to the lives that those texts embody and inscribe." Deciding that his response "must deal with the paper, to some extent," he tells Jennifer that although he was moved by the paper he was also confused by it; he is not sure whether that confusion is a device Jennifer is using to convey the confused state she was in or whether it is indicative of the fact that she has not yet explained this experience to herself. Thus, he asks her to revise the essay.

What is clear from these responses is that the readers approach a text such as Jennifer's with great care. Some of them focus their attention on the text exclusively, but most of them are inclined to look beyond the text to the troubled relationship it reveals, and most want to help Jennifer use writing as a way of sorting things out for herself. However, their strategies for helping her do so differ significantly.

WRITING 9
FINAL DRAFT: "A BROKEN MAN"
Featured Responders: O'Hare, Anson, Warnock, McClelland

BACKGROUND

This is the final draft of the last essay of the semester, the fifth of five essays written as personal responses to literature in a second-semester freshman writing course. It is in many ways this writer's best paper of the term.

THE ASSIGNMENT

In the last few days we have read several poems and two short stories dealing with good and evil. Using one or more of these literary pieces as a point of departure, write an essay in which you examine what you have learned about good and evil from your own experiences and/or those of others whose lives are connected with yours.

Writing 9
Elizabeth T.
Final Draft

                          A Broken Man

    My father has never read Nathaniel Hawthorne's story, "Young

Goodman Brown." I know he would not have enjoyed the story if he had

read it. My father would have been deeply troubled by the thought

that he typified the fictional character than Nathaniel Hawthorne

ironically calls Goodman Brown. However, my father is a man who is

sad and distrustful, who has lost faith in his family, his friends,

and his church, and who is now wrestling with his own sin and guilt.

    Goodman Brown's change in perception of the nature of man, makes

Hawthorne's "Young Goodman Brown" an initiation story. Hawthorne's

good man is converted from an innocent and virtuous race into a

"congregation, with whom he felt a loathful brotherhood, by sympathy

of all that was wicked in his heart." Originally, Goodman Brown

perceived himself and others as "a race of honest men and good

Christians." However, through his reasoning with the Devil, who bears

"a considerable resemblance to him," Goodman Brown is convinced, but

not without "heavy sickness of heart" and amazement, that "Evil is the

nature of mankind." From this confrontation with evil and

imperfection in man, Goodman Brown becomes "a stern, a sad, a darkly

meditative, a distrustful, if not desperate man."

    My father is presently going through a similar if not identical

initiation. He has begun to see evil in all men. He has begun to

view mankind as a communion of self-righteous, immoral and wicked

hypocrites. In this communion, he first placed his mother, whom he
had reverenced from youth, had deemed holier than himself. Next,
father placed my mother, my brothers, my sister, myself, and the rest
of society. No one was spared, for no one was virtuous. He would not
be deceived again. //

That "Evil is the nature of mankind," arose out of the death of
his mother six years ago. When my father returned home from Ireland,
he was a broken man. His temperament had changed towards all of us.
He was now cold and distant as well as quick to criticize. At first,
I just thought it was because he was depressed over his loss, that he
would return back to the loving and trusting father I remembered." He
never did! //

The first sign that something was definitely wrong was that my
father no longer sang my grandmother's praises, spoke of her with
reverence, or described her as a strong but loving righteous woman
whom had raised him and his seven brothers and sisters alone after the
death of her husband. I don't understand his reasoning, but my father
now believes that my grandmother is responsible for the death of his
father and his sister. As a child, my father told me that my
grandfather had died from cancer, which is true, but now he insists
that the main reason for his early death was a broken spirit caused by
my grandmother forcing him to work jobs that he considered
humiliating, so that she could have the material things she desired.
My father also told me that my aunt had died of natural causes, but
later I discovered that she had committed suicide two days after her
mother's death. Again, my father claimed her death was the result of

the cruelty and hatred my grandmother had always shown my aunt, even
up to the moment of her death. "That pious teacher of the catechism"
is now a "rampant hag," who affected virtues or qualities she did not
have. Now he was undeceived! — "Evil is the nature of mankind."
Therefore, evil must be his only happiness.

My mother is supposedly pushing my father to his death, as my
grandmother had done, by forcing him to become the man she wanted – a
family man. He is tired of doing what other people want him to do.
He doesn't want to end up like his father — dead. My father thinks
that we don't need him anymore because we have our own interests and
that all we want anyway is his money, because we are all takers and
not givers. This is so untrue; all we want to take from him is his
love, but he won't believe us.

Now, to hear my father verbally abuse my mother seems so out of
character. He used to be compassionate and tender towards my mom,
always cuddling and kissing her, even in front of us. My sister,
Kathy, told her husband, Jack, when they were dating, that she hoped
their marriage would be as good as my parents', that they would watch
television on the couch together, side-by-side, with their children on
the floor beside them, just as we had done as children.

It doesn't seem that long ago when he told my sister how
important it was for her to keep her virtue until she was married.
However, when my sister got married last year, my dad told her before
the ceremony, that she should seriously consider living with Jack
because marriage is nothing more than an institution. Kathy was
deeply hurt that my father thought so little of her relationship with

Jack and that she would live in sin as if she had no morals.

In the Summer, after my freshman year of college, I had gotten into an argument with my father. It marked a turning point in our relationship. The dispute was over something one of the women golf professionals, whom my father had been having an affair with, had said about my mother. I was nervous and afraid of how my father would react to the confrontation, but no longer could I stand back and watch him destroy himself and his family. He was furious with my allegations. He said that I had no right to judge him, that I was a little self-righteous hypocrite with my curly hair and makeup and that I could pass off myself as a twenty dollar hooker. He proceeded to tell me that if I did not like the way things were, that I could move out of the house and live with all the other self-righteous hypocrites. The image of my loving and trusting father was shattered. How could this man, who had once held me in his arms to love and console me, be so cruel? I hated my father that day because of what he had called me. It was weeks before I would speak to him. However, like Goodman Brown, he started to see evil in all men even if he had to create it.

// I am still trying to understand my father's actions. I cannot believe that he can find happiness by casting aside his family and by pursuing his goals without the support of his family, or by having an affair. He has lost his faith in those who love him most — his family. //He can no longer look at us or talk to us because of his own guilt and sins. If only he could open his eyes, his arms, and his heart to us, he could see now how great our love is for him. I cry

almost everyday now over losing my father. However, reading "Young
Goodman Brown" has helped me better understand how he came to such a
realization. It depresses me though, to think of my father as Goodman
Brown, "a stern, a sad, a darkly meditative, a distrustful, if not,
desperate man."

Writing 9
Elizabeth T.

I thoroughly enjoyed reading this paper, which is a fine example of the effective blending of audience and code, a skillful mixture of careful organization, effective language, and a clear sense of purpose. Elizabeth, you have a keen sense of what your readers need in order to understand this difficult and complex problem facing you and your family. You assume sensitivity and intelligence in your audience and convince your readers not just by the logic of your evidence and argument, but by the effectiveness of your style. I have marked with ∝ the many instances where your style is particularly effective.

You appear to be fair minded and objective, and, most important, to want to heal and forgive.

A minor note: I'd talk a little more about the theme of initiation or (and I prefer this) delete any mention of it from your essay. It doesn't help.

This paper's organization is very effective. You give your readers enough background information, then you move to effective anecdotes, and then to that excellent opening of the conclusion: "I am still trying to understand my father's actions." You have presented your readers with an effective paradox: How could such a man change, and so abruptly?

An excellent achievement-- a wonderful blending of the different aspects of PACES. Well done, Elizabeth.

Writing 9: "A Broken Man"

Additional Context

Elizabeth has been a model student in the course. Her writing has improved greatly over the term, she's participated fully in conferences and class sessions, and, in spite of the fact that students need simply to achieve a "Pass" grade (roughly equivalent to a "C"), she's put in enough work to merit a high B or perhaps even a low A on a regular grade base.

Transcription of my Taped Commentary on Elizabeth's Final Draft

Hi, Liz. [pause] God, this was a sad paper to read. I really felt the tension in your family life, but you know, there was something about the fact that you foregrounded this with the Goodman Brown story that made it, um, well sort of a peaceful . . . maybe that's not the right word, a *quiet* sort of sadness. I mean, there's more of a questioning tone here than rage or anger, though I feel some bitterness coming through, of course. But it's an interesting feeling; I don't think I've read anything quite like it in the course.

One thing that confused me a little, um, was, is when you talk about how your father had this affair with, um, was it, with a golf professional. By the way, you talk about them in the plural; does he work in golfing or around these golf pros? Anyway, what confuses me is why, how can he be so self-righteous and then lash out against everyone for being evil? Maybe you could explore that a little, I mean, do you suppose that the presence of evil in his own life, you know, his own sense that he's fallen from grace has made him see evil everywhere? Because that's common, for people to protest too much about what they're really feeling in themselves; sometimes it's called "projection," when someone projects their own psychological fears, conflicts, whatever on other people. And that whole business might be worth connecting more explicitly to the story.

Um, this is a strange kind of assignment because it essentially asks you to write a personal reaction as a way of coming to terms with the story, of analyzing it in some way. I like the way you've avoided too much of the traditional literary analysis we've talked about; I mean, could you imagine if you'd gone on a kind of quote binge here, you know, keep stringing pieces from "Young Goodman Brown" in here to support your ideas. I think that would have made it a rather bizarre literary analysis, whereas this is really a personal experience essay punctuated by allusions or quiet references to the story that helped you think about your dad.

I think this is one of the strongest pieces of writing you've done in the course, Liz. Um, you still need to work--and I keep saying this for so many folks, but it's really true--on particularizing your writing. Look for specifics, for detail, for showing instead of telling. I mean, instead of telling us that his temperament changed, how about showing that? There must be specific moments you can call up when he acted with cold indifference, just shrugging off your affections. And, boy, what I'm suggesting might make it even more anguished and hard to read, because this almost makes me want to cry as it is, I mean, that image of your happy family and now so much bitterness and hurt. But I think readers love emotion, and when they read something painful, in a sense it's a kind of catharsis, you know. You finish and you feel almost like a better person for it. I got one of these solicitations in the mail recently, um, from this place outside Las Vegas, I think it's called St. Jude's School for Children or something like that. And it was a letter from father somebody or other there at the school, and essentially it was two pages of paragraphs describing some of the kids' histories. God, it was one of the most moving things I'd ever read. I mean, there was this one little girl, eight years old, and she had been thrown out of her house, and somehow ended up at St. Jude's. So she started saving all her money there until she had enough to buy some construction things and then she made Christmas presents for all her brothers and sisters and mother, and send them off to her home. So a few weeks later, she, um, a big box arrives at St. Judes all wrapped with elegant red paper, and on Christmas morning she's just beaming because it's from her family, and she tears into the box and all of a sudden starts sobbing, and it turns out that all her little presents are inside the box, sent back by her mother. Uffff! I was in tears. And it's funny, because my wife came back from shopping with my little boy, and I was just, I don't know, so happy all of a sudden, and just showering them with affection.

Well, I've rambled on here, but I guess what all that boils down to is that I like your paper a lot, hard though it was to read, and it had an effect on me and I'm sure on Sam and Ellen and Hernando. And I'm glad that the story worked for you; I think it turned out to be a good choice of reading after all.

Ok, Liz. Remember that we have our final one-on-one conference on Friday, and I'll try to put all your work in perspective then. Um, I know you've worried a lot about your performance, so if it helps to relieve any tension, remember that I've been saying all along that you're doing very solid passing work, and that hasn't changed.

Ok, Liz, see you later.

Writing 9
Elizabeth T.
Final Draft

A Broken Man

My father has never read Nathaniel Hawthorne's story, "Young
Goodman Brown." I know he would not have enjoyed the story if he had
read it. My father would have been deeply troubled by the thought
that he typified the fictional character than Nathaniel Hawthorne
ironically calls Goodman Brown. However, my father is a man who is
sad and distrustful, who has lost faith in his family, his friends,
and his church, and who is now wrestling with his own sin and guilt.

Goodman Brown's change in perception of the nature of man, makes
Hawthorne's "Young Goodman Brown" an initiation story. Hawthorne's
good man is converted from an innocent and virtuous race into a
"congregation, with whom he felt a loathful brotherhood, by sympathy
of all that was wicked in his heart." Originally, Goodman Brown
perceived himself and others as "a race of honest men and good
Christians." However, through his reasoning with the Devil, who bears
"a considerable resemblance to him," Goodman Brown is convinced, but
not without "heavy sickness of heart" and amazement, that "Evil is the
nature of mankind." From this confrontation with evil and
imperfection in man, Goodman Brown becomes "a stern, a sad, a darkly
meditative, a distrustful, if not desperate man."

My father is presently going through a similar if not identical
initiation. He has begun to see evil in all men. He has begun to
view mankind as a communion of self-righteous, immoral and wicked

1

Your directness here draws me in

read aloud

hypocrites. In this communion, he first placed his mother, whom he

[handwritten marginal note: Read aloud. I'm not sure here what you're saying.]

had reverenced from youth, had deemed holier than himself. Next,

father placed my mother, my brothers, my sister, myself, and the rest

of society. No one was spared, for no one was virtuous. He would not

be deceived again.

That "Evil is the nature of mankind," arose out of the death of

his mother six years ago. When my father returned home from Ireland,

he was a broken man. His temperament had changed towards all of us.

He was now cold and distant as well as quick to criticize. At first,

I just thought it was because he was depressed over his loss, that he

would return back to the loving and trusting father I remembered. He

never did!

The first sign that something was definitely wrong was that my

father no longer sang my grandmother's praises, spoke of her with

reverence, or described her as a strong but loving righteous woman

whom had raised him and his seven brothers and sisters alone after the

death of her husband. I don't understand his reasoning, but my father

now believes that my grandmother is responsible for the death of his

father and his sister. As a child, my father told me that my

grandfather had died from cancer, which is true, but now he insists

that the main reason for his early death was a broken spirit caused by

my grandmother forcing him to work jobs that he considered

humiliating, so that she could have the material things she desired.

My father also told me that my aunt had died of natural causes, but

later I discovered that she had committed suicide two days after her

mother's death. Again, my father claimed her death was the result of

2

[Warnock makes no more marginal comments on the student's text.]

End Comment:

Elizabeth-

You have been direct in presenting your understanding of your father and how Goodman Brown helps you see him. Would you prefer writing this paper about your father without bringing in the Brown connection, or would you prefer writing about good and evil in the story only? Here you give details about your father's change and suggest that his mother's death and his guilt and sins were the causes, but you say that you still cannot understand. Does Hawthorne explain the causes of Goodman Brown's change? Do you understand that change? How exactly does reading the story help you understand how your father came to his realizaton? Is that your overall purpose here or is it to explore the similarities between your father and Brown? Is your father's story also an initiation story? Try reading your paper aloud to figure out what you want to do next.

[We are presenting Warnock's typewritten version of her endnotes instead of her handwritten comments.]

Elizabeth T.' s Final Draft: "A Broken Man"

This is a poignant essay, Elizabeth, emotionally resonant and intellectually challenging. Your personal response to "Young Goodman Brown" gives us an inside look at a family headed by such a character, even if your essay brings more light to the plight, in yours and your sister's cases, of Faith's innocent children than to the counterpart of <u>Good</u>man who now ironically sees himself and all others as bad men and women.

The intellectual challenge of writing about a matter in which you are deeply implicated emotionally is that it is difficult to analyze human relations when you lack the distance (in emotion and time) from which to view them. In your text the difficulty appears in your seeming inability to comprehend your father's psychological state and consequent behavior: "I am still trying to understand my father's actions." I say "your seeming inability" because, while you present enough information to characterize his problem, you never state it explicitly. For example, you present these bits of information: his drastic change after attending his mother's funeral from loving and trusting to seeing everyone as evil, his having an affair with another woman, his remarks to your sister to avoid the marriage trap and to you that you are a deceptive, hypocritical, sexual temptress. You need not be a psychoanalyst nor to have read <u>Passages</u> to recognize a peculiarly male mid-life crisis. A severe one in your father's case, to be sure. And some mysteries remain. Who knows what strange, strong attachment he had to his mother that caused him in some way to feel betrayed by her dying? Whatever the cause, it was powerful enough to cause him to rewrite family history, casting women as evildoers and men as their victims.

What I'm saying here, Elizabeth, is that you have presented more substantial evidence for defining your father's middle-aged version of a not-so-young Young Goodman Brown than you appear to know. Because of this significant omission, I judge this work slightly above average, a grade of "B-." Overall, the work is a noteworthy accomplishment for you, a fitting way to end your coursework. Thanks for giving a contemporary reading of Hawthorne's tale that causes me both to admire him for his prescient understanding of human psychology and you for your courageous, exploratory view of your father through Hawthorne's text.

Discussion of Responses to "A BROKEN MAN"
Featured Responders: O'Hare, Anson, Warnock, McClelland
Featured Issues:
• **Good (but not flawless) writing**
• **Sensitive personal matters**
• **Literary writing assignments**

The four featured responses represent the rather wide range of readings given to this essay. O'Hare views Elizabeth's paper as "a fine example of the effective blending of audience and code, a skillful mixture of careful organization, effective language, and a clear sense of purpose." Anson and McClelland praise the essay, but they qualify their praise in comments to Elizabeth and in their notes to us. Anson, for instance, tells Elizabeth that he "likes the paper a lot." However, he suggests she examine more closely some of the actions of her father, especially as they relate to "Young Goodman Brown." In contrast to this praise, Warnock characterizes Elizabeth's writing simply as "direct." She then goes on to intimate that Elizabeth should not be satisfied with this paper, by asking questions such as for what audience Elizabeth intended to write the paper and how the experiences of her father connect to the Goodman Brown story.

Clearly, opinions differ as to just how good Elizabeth's essay is. Most of the readers, however, find much to like in the essay. White's response (not represented) may be the most positive overall; his comments to Elizabeth are entirely complimentary, and in his notes to us he mentions no problems.

Other responders noted flaws in the essay, but in responding to Elizabeth they either elected to ignore them or decided to place comments about the flaws within the context of high praise. For example, Patricia Stock (not represented above) elected to praise the essay generously, without naming its "infelicities" (as she called them—it is not clear from her commentary what these infelicities are). Stewart calls the essay moving, but he does question the chronology around the incident involving the father's affair. Similarly, Peterson, Gere, and Elbow, although praising the paper, call attention to some problems in chronology and hint at connections between these problems and the failure to make clear the relationship between the story about Elizabeth's father and Goodman Brown.

Some of the readers felt it important to go beyond the text to talk with Elizabeth about the experience she is relating. Stock tells her that she has done a good job of analyzing the situation, without withdrawing into self pity or self-righteously rewriting history to suit her own purposes. Stewart, however, would like to ask Elizabeth about ways in which she may be failing to fully understand this situation. Even though he tells us that teachers "must never play the amateur psychiatrist," Stewart says that in his comments he has "occasionally nudged [students] into considering help." In his comments to Elizabeth, he calls her story quite troubling and asks if her father has sought counseling. He goes on to tell her that "People who cannot accept the realization that we are all imperfect and in constant need of forgiveness can make life very hard for themselves and their loved ones."

McClelland tells Elizabeth that she "has told herself more about her father's crisis than she knows." He feels that she presents "enough information to characterize his problem," but she never seems to come to terms with (i.e., find the words for) what that problem is. As was the case for "Tribute," McClelland seems more interested in what Elizabeth learns in writing this essay than in offering insights as to how the paper might be improved.

As is obvious, most of our readers are impressed by, or at least satisfied with, "A Broken Man." Several readers, however, see significant problems in the essay that they attribute, at least in part, to the writing assignment. Larson views the assignment as problematic, not because he dislikes literary assignments, but because he would "want the student to grapple with the text, and not just with her/his personal history as it may connect to the text." Elbow agrees. He tells Elizabeth that "'Bouncing off the story' is in a way the main rhetorical problem here—and it's inherent in the assignment itself: how to talk about your own experience using literature as a point of departure."

A major theme of those who criticize the essay is Elizabeth's failure to make meaningful connections between her father's fall from grace and Young Goodman Brown's fall, particularly in regard to how Brown's fall might help explain that of Elizabeth's father. Larson and Elbow would seem to be asking that Elizabeth spell out this connection more clearly, not just write about her personal experiences as a kind of reaction to the story. Warnock, on the other hand, feels that the assignment tried to force a type of connecting that is inherently wrong. She comments that this assignment lends itself to Elizabeth's attempt to "connect literature and life in a way I find disturbing." She goes on to say that it produces a "kind of writing that's limited to school exercises." Anson voices something of the same objection in saying that this assignment "results in . . . a purely academic type of writing, a mixture of personal narrative and literary analysis, which simply doesn't exist in this form beyond the classroom."

Most of our readers see this as a well-written essay—that is clear. They differ rather markedly, however, in their evaluation of the writing assignment given to the student. They also differ significantly in their willingness to address the sensitive father/daughter relationship that gave rise to this essay.

```
WRITING 12
ROUGH DRAFT: "STREET GANGS: ONE POINT OF VIEW"
Featured Responders: Larson, Anson, Hull, Elbow
```

BACKGROUND

This informative paper is the third paper of the course, the third time students have taken an assignment through several drafts with in-draft commentary. The class has been studying the principles of informative writing and paying special attention to the use of examples. Students have already completed invention activities and a first rough draft toward this paper, neither of which you have made written responses to. They will take the assignment through two more drafts.

Rusty is the kind of student who comes into writing classes apprehensive and expecting not to do well, largely because, as he wrote in his journal at the beginning of the course, his "grammar and structure are not too good." He keeps to himself in class, and he has not talked with you after class or in conference about his writing or his performance in the class, even though your written responses on his first two papers indicated that you expected more from him—in substance and correctness—in his future papers. Now he hands in this paper.

THE ASSIGNMENT

For your third paper, I'd like you to write about a hobby or activity in which you regularly engage and in which you have some level of authority or proficiency. In an informative essay of 600-900 words, inform or advise a general audience (say, the members of this class) about an aspect of this hobby or activity. As you write, try to say as best you can what precisely you mean, in a way that perhaps will spark your readers' interest in the subject.

In our work on this paper, we will pay special attention to the use, as distinct from the mere *citation*, of examples to examine and illustrate a point. As you write, keep this objective in mind.

We will take this paper through four drafts. The first is an exploratory draft, a place where you should try to get some words and ideas produced and begin to get them into some general shape. It may well be sketchy and rough. Do what you can to make it a place where you think through and discover what you want to say. You need not concern yourself with being neat and orderly—this is not a draft for readers, but for you as a writer at work. The second and third drafts are working drafts, places where you begin to do more careful shaping and crafting, and perhaps some more discovering and producing, some more experimenting. The fourth is a "final draft"—not in the sense that it is complete and forever done with, but in the sense that you can "finally" let it go now that your writing is ready for readers.

[For additional responses to this essay, see Chapter 4.]

Writing 12
Rusty S.
Second Rough Draft

             Street Gangs: One Point of View

     I'm writing this paper on street gangs because I was once part

of one, and I feel that this gives me some authority to write a

legitimate opinion.

I'M NOT SURE I SEE YOUR "OPINION" IN THE PAPER.

     I never asked or set out to join a gang, it just happened by

association. I knew some guys who were members of the Cripps and by

hanging around them I was sort of "taken in" by the gang and generally

thought to be a part of them by everyone else.

     Unlike some members I tried to maintain a low profile. I didn't

provoke fights or do destructive things on purpose, but we had a

strong bond. If one person was in trouble, no matter who or what kind

it was, everyone was there regardless. *WHERE? AT A POLICE STATION? A HOSPITAL?*

     This sticking together almost always occured in a physical sense.

If one of our guys were to be beaten up, the rest of us would take a

revenge of some sort, whether it be by beating someone up or

vandalizing someones property, we always got even. That was a basic

rule, nobody could "be one up on us", we always had to get even.

     Except for this one occasion, I can't really remember us actually

going out and starting trouble for no "reason". We were at the pool,

and what we did was single out one person at a time. Once we had a

target, one of us would go up to that certain someone and "sucker

punch" him and before he could retaliate the rest of the gang would

break it up.

THE ATTACK?

                          1

Being a member had its ups and downs. The worst part was being
paranoid about something happening to you. It wasn't a frightening
feeling, but more like a burden. You knew something, somehow,
somewhere would eventually happen, either to you or the gang. Many
times I paid the price for being part of the Cripps with black eyes or
broken noses. I even had my windshield busted once.

MIGHT BE USEFUL TO SAY MORE ON THESE EXPERIENCES.

The good side was the family type atmosphere between us, we were
more than friends, almost like cousins or even brothers. That sense
of support that I got from being part of that gang was unmeasurable.
Walking down the halls of school and having everyone know that your in
this gang was great, almost like an "ego-trip". For it did make some
of the guys cocky. This overall feeling is hard to explain, it deals
a lot with acceptance and friendship. I guess these two things were
what kept me in the gang so long. I liked the feeling of being part
of something that (where I come from) is almost like a status symbol.
My parents called this insecurity, this may be, but more importantly
it gave me a purpose and an identity.

During the time I spent in the gang, we were more a "party" gang.
We got into trouble and fights, but not with other gangs. Gangs at
the time were more friendly and were only gangs by name. I mean
everyone knew each other and it was only the name of the gang and
their symbols that separated us.

WORD NEEDED)

Our symbols were one, a blue and red hankerchief worn around the
right ankle, a diamond stud earring in the left ear and most important
the thin white cane each member had. This was in relation with our
name: "THE CRIPPS".

2

I left the gang last year because it started getting to violent,

especially the growing conflicts between gangs. Many gang fights

started to break out in the streets, schools and school related

events. I just couldn't handle this, somebody could get really hurt

or killed. I also felt I didn't need the ego boost anymore. I felt I

could be my own person, with my own traits and characteristics. To

sum it up, I grew up.

SAY MORE ABOUT THE INCIDENTS THAT LED YOU TO GET OUT.

In many respects this is an interesting draft--its story told
with apparent honesty. There is useful detail here, though, as I
hope the notes will suggest, the details could be extended
some, and a few of the experiences you have in mind could have
been rendered more vividly.

But as this piece stands it is essentially an account of a
period in your life: how you got into a gang, what you did, why
you stopped.   The assignment asked, on the other hand,
to discuss an activity in which you "regularly engage"
and on which you can speak from some authority. Clearly you
can speak with authority on street gangs, but your focus,
for this paper, might be on letting readers know how street
gangs operate, what they do, why they do it, rather than on
the chronology of your experiences as a gang member. Your
goal here is to enlarge the reader's knowledge of a subject
that the reader might find important and might genuinely
want to know more about. I think you've got such a subject
(I surely would be glad to learn more about gangs, which I
hear a great deal about). But I'd like to know a bit more
about gangs in general than you tell me. Maybe you could
use your experiences to illustrate more general observations
(observations that might cover many gangs, of different sorts).
In using your experiences so, you might give a few more
details about some of the experiences. On the next draft,
try to accomplish some of the steps I've suggested. The
result probably will be a longer paper, but that should
cause no difficulty; the present draft is a trifle short.

I've underlined some places where I think you should reconsider the punctuation of sentences.

If you need to discuss my suggestions, please come in
and do so.

3

Additional Context

Rusty participated in a special, federally-funded summer program for "at-risk," mostly inner-city minorities who would probably not go to college without being involved in the program. That program involved an intensive, college-preparatory, eight-week basic writing course. On the first day, Rusty showed up in class with a boom-box playing at full blast. Instead of asking him to turn it off, I asked him to turn it down. Then I asked the rest of the class if they wanted him to leave it on during our sessions. Everyone said no. The boom box never returned.

At first Rusty was rather indignant about the course, but eventually he began working hard and improving his writing abilities. About halfway through the course, he went home for the weekend. When he returned, we had a conference about one of his papers. He talked about how his friends thought he was different when he got together with them, how he seemed like an uppety college kid. He also felt an undercurrent of resentment from his family; even though they weren't paying for his participation in the program, he said he felt guilty to think that his parents and two brothers and older sister all had to work while he read his books or lounged around in the dorm or ate free cafeteria food.

 At that time I sensed that Rusty was making a difficult transition from his home culture to the culture of the academy. I worried--as I did about many students in the program--that Rusty might decide the world of college was too rarified, too little like his own world, for him to stay. When, by a stroke of luck, he showed up on the first day of my fall semester basic writing course, I was delighted.

In this paper, however, the third in my course, I sense a little of Rusty's conflict between cultures coming through. Compared with his earlier work, the language of this piece is starting to reflect the influence of the academic setting. There are very few dialect features, for one thing, and, ironically, **some of the life has gone out of his writing, perhaps because he is trying to "play it safe," portray himself as someone not fundamentally "bad" or disenfranchised. I decide, therefore, to take a risk by encouraging Rusty to tell about his experiences in all their color and detail, even if it means painting an ugly picture. The image, I tell him, that he portrays of himself can be just the opposite of the experiences he described, by virtue of showing them for what they are.**

Transcription of my Taped Response to Rusty's Draft

Hi, Rusty. Well, I just got through reading your draft of this paper on, um, your gang paper here. Have the Cripps gotten worse since you were involved with them? For some reason, when I think of the Cripps I keep remembering the murder of that girl over at MLK park and some of the drug busts and all that. Are they a pretty bad gang now, generally, or does it vary from place to place? Or can you be in a piece of the gang that's not up to much harm?

Well, let me give you a couple of brief comments, um, just some reactions and ideas. Remember that the name of the game here is possibility--try things out, experiment a little. You've got nothing to lose, um, because you can just, just toss stuff out that you don't like. But when you open up and really play around with your writing, I think you'll surprise yourself.

Um, for me, the one most important direction I think you might consider here is with the level of detail and also, um, how you, how concerned you are about the way **you** come off in here. I mean, imagine that I asked you to describe as honestly as you could, um, the most outrageous, or awful, or even *interesting* things that happened, as vividly as possible, um, while you were in this gang. Because I think that lots of people have these stereotypes of gangs, you know, they hear a few things on the news, like I have, and see a few results of gangs, but they never really get anything from the inside. And maybe, like you say, it's not as horrendous as we all think, just a bunch of guys trying to be different, hanging together. But from what you've got here, I can't tell, um, it feels to me just as stereotyped, and maybe it's just that you're using a very general language.

Well, here's an example of what I'm saying here, um [flips pages], first page, ok, when you talk about if one of you is beaten up, everyone's there to take revenge. I mean, beaten up by whom? What sort of setting are we seeing here? Can you maybe, um, give us an actual case here, of a time--were you ever beaten up like that? By other gangs, I assume, so with . . . how did they do this? Did they sneak up on you, did they carry knives and all that? What you might try here is listing each episode or idea about the gang itself, and then just list every detail, especially visual, that you can come up with. Um, the same thing happens here at the pool. I can't really see this whole picture; did you, why did you just sucker punch these people? Were they other gang members? What did regular folks do when they saw this? And what sort of weird pleasure, can you analyze what turns people on when they try to harm innocent people for no reason? Is that linked to, um, the point later on here, about your parents telling you it's all about solidarity and feeling like you belong?

So I think you've got a good start here, Rusty. At this point you've got to push it some more, really work on each little chunk here, and see what you can do to embellish it. Don't rely too much on stock language, but, um, it really helps to close your eyes and **see** the experiences, and then try to find the words for what you see. Do that from the very first line, so instead of saying that you're writing a paper, what can you do to throw us right into the scene? "It was a hot Saturday night," you know, that sort of "in the middle of things" beginning we've talked about. Maybe you can take four or five pieces of paper and just list each episode you tell about here and then write as much as you can about it in more specific detail. Because what you've got started here is potentially really interesting, an inside account, something you really know that most of us don't.

Oh, one other thing, I'm attaching an interview from a collection by Studs Terkel on people's jobs. Now whatever you do, don't assume that this is some sort of model for your writing, because it's not, it's a carefully edited transcript of an actual interview the author did with this guy. But what I want you to look at is, um, he asks questions that, if you read carefully, you'll see that the guy he's interviewing is forced to get really specific and detailed, and notice there how, um, how much more interesting his job starts to seem. Well, what you've got to do there is ask yourself . . . better still, talk to someone, maybe in the conference group, about this, and **make them ask you questions** about the gang, and write down what they ask and how you respond. I'm willing to bet you'll really elaborate some of these vague and kind of generalized or, um, almost cliched descriptions of the gang.

Ok, Rusty, see you in the conference group. Again, good start, but push, push, push, make this one move forward. See you later.

Writing 12
Rusty S.
Second Rough Draft

Street Gangs: One Point of View

I'm writing this paper on street gangs because I was once part
of one, and I feel that this gives me some authority to write a
legitimate opinion.

I never asked or set out to join a gang, it just happened by
association. I knew some guys who were members of the Cripps and by
hanging around them I was sort of "taken in" by the gang and generally
thought to be a part of them by everyone else.

Unlike some members I tried to maintain a low profile. I didn't
provoke fights or do destructive things on purpose, but we had a
strong bond. If one person was in trouble, no matter who or what kind
it was, everyone was there regardless. ✳ (see my comments
at the end)

This sticking together almost always occured in a physical sense.
If one of our guys were to be beaten up, the rest of us would take a
revenge of some sort, whether it be by beating someone up or
vandalizing someones property, we always got even. That was a basic
rule, nobody could "be one up on us", we always had to get even. ✳

Except for this one occasion, I can't really remember us actually
going out and starting trouble for no "reason". We were at the pool,
and what we did was single out one person at a time. ✳ Once we had a
target, one of us would go up to that certain someone and "sucker
punch" him and before he could retaliate the rest of the gang would
break it up.

[handwritten margin note:] This is interesting. Somehow I always thought joining a gang involved initiation and so forth.

[handwritten margin note:] Oh, my - were you ever the one to do the punching?

1

Being a member had its ups and downs. The worst part was being
paranoid about something happening to you. It wasn't a frightening
feeling, but more like a burden. You knew something, somehow,
somewhere would eventually happen, either to you or the gang. Many
times I paid the price for being part of the Cripps with black eyes or
broken noses. I even had my windshield busted once. ✳

This is a great way to describe the paranoid feeling.

The good side was the family type atmosphere between us, we were
more than friends, almost like cousins or even brothers. That sense
of support that I got from being part of that gang was unmeasurable.
Walking down the halls of school and having everyone know that your in
this gang was great, almost like an "ego-trip". For it did make some
of the guys cocky. This overall feeling is hard to explain, it deals
a lot with acceptance and friendship. I guess these two things were
what kept me in the gang so long. I liked the feeling of being part
of something that (where I come from) is almost like a status symbol.
My parents called this insecurity, this may be, but more importantly
it gave me a purpose and an identity.

This is interesting, too. I don't think most people recognize the family-like attraction of being in a gang

I admire the way you're able to acknowledge your parents view but go on to give your own.

During the time I spent in the gang, we were more a "party" gang.
We got into trouble and fights, but not with other gangs. Gangs at
the time were more friendly and were only gangs by name. I mean
everyone knew each other and it was only the name of the gang and
their symbols that separated us.

Our symbols were one, a blue and red hankerchief worn around the
right ankle, a diamond stud earring in the left ear and most important
the thin white cane each member had. This was in relation with our
name: "THE CRIPPS".

This is interesting — is it common for gangs to choose names and symbols that could be associated with disability or weakness?

I left the gang last year because it started getting to violent,
especially the growing conflicts between gangs. Many gang fights
started to break out in the streets, schools and school related
events.* I just couldn't handle this, somebody could get really hurt
or killed. I also felt I didn't need the ego boost anymore. I felt I
could be my own person, with my own traits and characteristics. To
sum it up, I grew up.

Rusty— you have the makings of a very interesting paper here. Here are two suggestions for your next draft:

(1) I want you to add some extended examples-- not just one sentence or two, but whole paragraphs. I've marked several places you could make some additions with an asterisk (*). On the first page, for example, you might tell specifically about a time when someone got in trouble and everyone was there. Give details: what time, when, what situation, where. These long examples should be used to illustrate and provide evidence for points you're making.

(2) After you've added the examples, get some scissors and tape, and cut your paper up-- one paragraph per strip of paper. Experiment with putting these paragraphs in different orders. Which ones seem like beginning material? Which ones come next? And 3 so on! If there isn't any order that seems better than another, then try to imagine what you would need to do to your paper to connect up the paragraphs. Then tape your draft together again.

WRITING 12, "STREET GANGS: ONE POINT OF VIEW"

Dear Rusty,

This is interesting to read and sometimes has a strong impact on me.

What I noticed first are the places where you talk about your feelings while being in the gang: the oddly, interestingly, low-key "burden" as you put it. I would feel flat out _fear_. Also the feeling of comfort and support and family-quality. Seems important. I would enjoy getting a bit more exploration here: but not just finding more words for it but more _examples_: what does all that look like in events or scenes?

At the bottom of 1 you give the example of picking on people at the pool. You tell it in a kind of deadpan way, but it's kind of horrifying for me. I think _I_ was the kind of person who was picked on--or always felt I was about to be. There's something intriguing or even moving about your low key tone here, but I'm also curious to know a bit more how you actually felt--and feel. Something mysterious here: perhaps it's more interesting this way, despite my unsatisfied curiosity. But I do know I'd like you to flesh it out more as an example: it's a specific scene or incident, but you don't let us see _any_ particulars.

The symbols of the gang are nice and concrete. I had the thought of somehow starting with them--or at least finding some way to start that has some zip to it; it's a little bit of a soggy opening as you have it. And the ending sentence is very sudden--though now I see you were building to it. I need some kind of help here; not sure what; don't want some abstract discussion of "growing up"--but some-how this important point (I really like it) needs something.

The heart and strength is your investment and relation; the weakness is need for more concretes and specifics.

best,

Peter

Discussion of Responses to "STREET GANGS"
Featured Responders: Larson, Anson, Hull, Elbow
Featured Issues:
- **Development of ideas**
- **Focus and organization**
- **Mechanical issues in a rough draft**
- **Readers' views of the writer**

There is much agreement among the readers as to the relative strengths and weaknesses in this essay. Nearly all of them remark favorably on Rusty's "investment" in this topic; they feel it is a subject he knows and cares about. All of the readers suggest that Rusty needs to include more detail in his next draft. Anson encourages Rusty to learn to question himself (and/or to get a member of his writing group to ask him questions) in order to move away from the overly general and stereotypical language he is now using. Elbow asks questions that should help Rusty see places where he might develop the paper more fully. Similarly, Hull asks Rusty (in her end comment) a series of questions designed to help him develop his thoughts. She keys these questions (via asterisks) to places in the essay that need to be developed. Larson marks in the margin two places where he feels the need for more development and notes (in the end comment) that the experiences "could have been rendered more vividly."

Readers whose responses are not displayed above also called for more detail. O'Hare gives a paragraph-by-paragraph analysis, showing those places where he would like to see development. Stewart suggests that Rusty might think of various "types" of gang members and develop those types in his paper. McClelland gives Rusty a list of questions the essay raised for him. Peterson asks questions in the margins indicating the need for development. She refers to these questions in her end comment in which she tells Rusty that his paper needs more detail.

Other readers, although they call for development, focus their comments on Rusty's need for organization. Gere, whose response is not represented above, calls Rusty's "an almost ideal second rough draft." She does feel, however, that he needs to organize and develop his writing. She suggests that Rusty find a summary sentence for the beginning of the paper, and she raises questions about the connections between parts of the essay. Similarly, White feels the need for more order in a revised draft. He discovers in the writer's last paragraph a main idea ("gangs are an ego boost") and suggests that Rusty "put this idea up front and arrange [his] experiences and details so they all show this idea." Although she does not go so far as to tell the student what his main idea should be, Stock presents Rusty with a series of questions designed to help him generate more material and think about the connections between various parts of the essay.

Because Rusty's paper contains more mechanical errors than most of the essays in our sampling, it is worth noting how readers deal with these problems in their responses. Although 5 of the 11 responding to this essay do mention editing problems, none of the teachers seems overly concerned with the quality of the editing at this stage in the drafting process. Those who mention editing relegate it to a future time when the draft is more nearly finished. Gere is typical of those who mentioned error. Rather than drawing Rusty's attention to mechanical flaws, she tells us she would want to help him avoid his tendency to "hide behind his usual concern with 'grammar and structure.'" She feels that his obvious interest in this subject may well help him overcome some of those mechanical problems.

As we look at their notes to us, it becomes clear that most of our readers have a rather well-developed concept of the writer behind the text. Larson sees Rusty as a "teachable" and "interesting" student, someone with whom he should have no difficulty working. Peterson also looks forward to working with Rusty, calling him an "enjoyable" and "familiar" student. She hopes that her marks on the paper will let him know that she cares about what he is saying.

Gere reveals her image of Rusty in saying that she feels this assignment can be important in helping him "to overcome his feelings of insecurity about writing and 'find' himself as a writer." Hull wants to be sure that Rusty knows that she is interested in what he has to say. Although she does not directly characterize him, she implies that she sees him as somewhat fragile: She will withhold needed instruction on sentence boundaries until he is ready to receive it.

Stewart and Anson present the most well-developed characterizations of this student. Stewart sees Rusty as an intelligent student, someone "for whom one can do a great deal." He wants to tell Rusty that he is genuinely interested in what he has to say, and he is hopeful that once Rusty recognizes his sincerity, he will be receptive to receiving help in mechanical matters. Anson creates a context in which Rusty shows up in his basic writing course after having been a participant in a federally-funded summer program for "at risk" students (taught by Anson). As a member of the summer program, Rusty appeared to be having difficulty in "making the. . . transition from his home culture to the culture of the academy," and Anson worried that he "might decide the world of college. . . [is] too rarified, too little like his own world. . . ." Anson is delighted to find that Rusty has decided to continue his studies.

The readers see Rusty as a student with whom they enjoy working. They seem to have a clear idea of who Rusty is, and the various characterizations they give (or imply) have much in common with one another. The readers have rather similar things to say to Rusty about the ways he can go about developing this essay. And, they are pretty much in agreement that although he will have to deal with mechanical matters in the future, it will be to his benefit at this point to concentrate on more global issues.

WRITING 13
MULTIPLE DRAFTS: "THE JOHN COUGAR CONCERT"
Featured Responders: Stock, Hull, Larson, Stewart

This selection presents the two rough drafts and the final draft of a concert review. **Respond to the final draft.**

BACKGROUND

This assignment is the fourth of five multiple-draft assignments based on various aims of discourse. The final draft is the third draft the student has handed in. You have read and perhaps commented on these earlier drafts.

You may assume that students have the option of rewriting one of their course papers for a change in grade.

THE ASSIGNMENT

Choose a book, movie, album, product, or anything else about which we tend to make judgments, and write an essay evaluating this subject. Base your evaluations on appropriate criteria and support them with reasons and evidence. Design the essay for publication in the school newspaper.

Writing 13
Frank C.
First Rough Draft

[The John Cougar Concert]

Stated as being one of the best rock shows on the road by
Rolling Stone Magazine, John Cougar took is fans and me, on what
I call a roller coaster ride of emotion. And what a ride it was.

Before the show even started, the most noticeable thing was the
stage. There it stood, quite bare with only a white backdrop. This
plain setting pointed to John Cougar's no-nonsense approach to rock
and roll. Although it was a plain setting, the crowd knew it was
going to be a great show.

Refering back to what I said earlier about roller coaster of
emotion, the ride was about to start. Starting with "Grandma's
Theme", and "Smalltown" from the "Scarecrow" album, John Cougar got
the emotions rolling. After those semi-fast songs, John Cougar really
got the crowd on their feet with "Authority Song", "Serious Business",
and "Crumblin Down". Once John Cougar had the audience at a emotional
high, he went into an extended version of "Play Guitar" in which he
had the whole audience singing to it. Then came kind of a reflective
mood for lovers when he sang "Jack and Diane", and "Everyone needs a
Hand to Hold on to." Then the emotions turned to a more somber mood
when John Cougar talked about the plight of the American farmer. This
is a political stance he is very well known for. He also talked
briefly about Farm Aid which was a concert that he and other rock
stars were organizing to help the American farmers. After talking
briefly about those issues, John Cougar quickly went into one of his
more popular songs that tell of many typical farmers--"Rain on the
Scarecrow." This song typifies what happens when a farmer runs out of
money and the consequences he must face.

John Cougar knew that these issues were very important to him,
but he didn't want to dwell on them for too long. That is why he got
the crowd started on a climb towards another emotional peak. He sang
"R.O.C.K. in the U.S.A." which is a salute to 1960's rock and roll.
It is a very upbeat song about how some famous rockers such as James
Brown, Frankie Lyman, and Mitch Ryder finally made it in the music
business. Right after that, Cougar went into a 60's medley with
classic songs such as "Proud Mary", "Under the Boardwalk", and "Cold
Sweat." These songs topped off an incredible variety of emotions.

John Cougar, in my opinion, did a very good job at presenting his
concert in a roller coaster form. I believe he knew that by starting
off slowly, then picking up momentum, then slowing things down with
his songs for lovers, then almost putting a mood of saddness with his
stance on the situation of American farmers, and getting the crowd on
it's feet again with a classic 60's medley, would leave a very
satisfied crowd. It was a very interesting form, but effective in
every sense of the word.

Writing 13
Frank C.
Second Rough Draft

[The John Cougar Concert]

On December 13, 1985, at the Ohio Center, John Cougar took his fans and me on what I call a roller coaster ride of emotion. And what a ride it was. Rolling Stone Magazine even stated, "Forget the Springsteen comparison, this is simply one of the best rock shows on the road."

Before the show even started, the most noticeable thing was the stage. At most concerts you would expect fancy equipment and garish decor, but Cougar's stage was practically bare with only a white backdrop. This plain setting pointed to John Cougar's no-nonsense approach to rock and roll.

It was nearing 8:00 pm (the scheduled time to begin) and the crowd was starting to get excited. People were chanting, "We want Cougar, we want Cougar!" Suddenly the lights went out and the roller coaster of emotions was about to start.

A roar of elation went through the crowd when Cougar appeared on stage. There he stood dressed only in a white t-shirt, worn out Levis, and cowboy boots. Again, pointing to his no-nonsense approach to rock and roll.

Immediately he started into one of his newest hits, "Small Town" from the "Scarecrow" album. The emotions really started rolling with that song. People were jumping up and down and standing on their chairs. After that "warm up" song, Cougar got the whole crowd on their feet with "I want all of you to get up off your seat and get into it!" With that, Cougar went into his more energetic songs such as "Authority Song", "Serious Business", and "Crumblin Down". The whole audience must have listened to Cougar's command because everyone was singing along, dancing, and having a great time. John Cougar knew he had the audience at an emotional high because he went into an extended version of "Play Guitar." The crowd was in a frenzy during that song. People were releasing so much energy by cheering and dancing.

After all his high powered songs, John Cougar slowed the emotions by singing a couple of songs for lovers. Songs such as "Jack and Diane", and "Everyone Needs a Hand to Hold on to" had a few couples embracing each other. After that, Cougar paced across the stage in a very serious manner. He started to talk about an issue that is very important to him—that of the American farmer and the problems that they are facing. It is an issue he is very well known for. He also talked briefly about Farm Aid which was a benefit concert that he and other rock stars were organizing to help American farmers. With that,

1

Cougar went into a very emotional song, "Rain on the Scarecrow" off of the "Scarecrow" album. This song typifies what happens when a farmer runs out of money and the consequences he must face. [Add lines in song.] You could actually feel the emotions of saddness and despair by the incredible way John Cougar projected this song. [Explain why people like songs. Plus quote.]

John Cougar knew that these issues were very important to him, but he didn't want to dwell on them for too long. That is why he got the crowd started on a climb towards another emotional peak. He sang "R.O.C.K. in the U.S.A." which is a salute to 1960's rock and roll. It is a very upbeat song about how some famous rockers such as James Brown, Frankie Lyman, and Mitch Ryder finally made it in the music business. You could tell Cougar was really working hard because you could see sweat drip off his face. Cougar again urged the crowd to join in. He quickly went into a 60's medly with classic songs such as "Proud Mary", "Under the Boardwalk", and "Cold Sweat." These songs topped off an incredible variety of emotions.

John Cougar, in my opinion, did a very good job at presenting his concert in a roller coaster form. I believe he knew that by starting off slow, then fast, then slow, and then fast again would leave a very satisfied crowd. I could tell it was a very satisfied crowd because instead of rushing for the exit, everyone sat back down for a few minutes to relax after the show was over. It was a very interesting form, but effective in every sense of the word.

2

STOCK

Writing 13
Frank C.
Final Draft

The John Cougar Concert

On *the* cold and blustery evening ~~of~~ December 13, 1985, at the Ohio

Center, John Cougar took his fans and me on what I call a roller

coaster ride of emotion. And what a ride it was. *In a review of the concert,* Rolling Stone

Magazine even stated, "Forget the Springsteen comparison, this is

simply one of the best rock shows on the road."

why even? Before the show [even] started, the [most noticeable thing was the *audience could not help but notice the stage.*

stage.] At most *rock* concerts, [~~you would~~ *audiences*] expect fancy equipment and flashy

decor, but Cougar's stage was practically bare with only a white

backdrop and basic instruments. This plain setting pointed to John

Cougar's no-nonsense approach to rock and roll.

Editor's Note:
Why do you move from past to present in this sentence and then back again in the next sentence?

It was nearing 8:00 P.M., [the scheduled time to begin] and the

crowd was starting to get excited. People were chanting, "We want

Cougar, we want Cougar!" My [old] high school friends and I were also *were they old?*

joining in the chanting. We, like all the others, wanted to see this

man from a small town in Indiana perform. Suddenly the lights went

out and the roller coaster of emotions [was about to start.] *started up.*

A [roar] of elation [went] through the crowd when Cougar appeared on *moved or stalked or raced*

stage. There he stood with his shoulder-length black hair and *fiercely* intent

eyes. There was no fancy costume either, just a white t-shirt, worn-

note:
Want to play with lion (Cougar) imagery here? Wild cat stuff?

out Levis, and cowboy boots. [Again, pointing to his] no-nonsense *in Cougar's* *Reinforcing the stage set's message: There is*

approach to rock and roll.

Immediately he belted into one of his newest hits, "Small Town"

1

from the Scarecrow album. The emotions really started rolling with that song. People were jumping up and down and standing on their chairs. After that ["warm up"] song, Cougar [yelled at the crowd in a very urging voice,] ~urged the crowd:~ "I want all of you to get up off your seat and get into it!" With that, Cougar roared into his more energetic songs such as "Authority Song", "Serious Business", and "Crumblin Down". The whole audience [must have listened to Cougar's command] ~responded~ because everyone was singing along, dancing, and having a great time. John Cougar knew he had the audience at an emotional [high] because he went into an extended version of "Play Guitar". People released so much energy by cheering and singing during this song. I even found myself to be out of breath.

After all his high powered songs, John Cougar [slowed] the emotions by singing a couple of songs for lovers. Songs such as "Jack and Diane" and "Everyone Needs A Hand To Hold On To" [had] ~inspired~ a few couples embracing each other. After that, Cougar paced across the stage in a very serious manner. He started to talk about an issue that is very important to him -- that of the American farmer and the problems that they are facing. It is an issue he is very well known for. He also talked briefly about Farm Aid, which was a benefit concert that he and other rock stars were organizing to help American farmers. With that, Cougar went into a very emotional song, "Rain on the Scarecrow". This song [typifies] ~demonstrates? describes? suggests?~ what happens when a farmer runs out of money and [the consequences] he must face. Lines like "Called my old friend Schepman up to auction off the land, he said, John it's just my job and I hope you understand", really makes you feel discouraged, the way you would

Ed. Note:
Want to play with hot and cold throughout? Cold night; warm then hot emotions?

Ed. note:
Actually your not only play with hot and cold but high and low and fast and slow as well. Want to work all of them?

Remind me to tell you about this rule that makes no sense what-so-ever.

Ed. Note: Can you set these lines apart like the lines of the song?

feel if you had to ask your friend to sell something very dear to you.

You could actually feel the emotions of sadness and despair by the

incredible way John Cougar projected this song.

although
[John Cougar knew that] these issues were very important to him. John Cougar
knew his audience had not come
but, he didn't want to dwell on them, for too long. That is why he [got]
again
the crowd [started] on a climb towards another emotional peak. He sang

"R.O.C.K. in the U.S.A." which is a salute to 1960's rock and roll.

It is a very upbeat song about how some famous rockers such as James

Brown, Frankie Lyman, and Mitch Ryder finally made it in the music

business. I could tell Cougar was really working hard because I could

see sweat drip off his face. Cougar again urged the crowd to join in.

He rocketed into a 60's medley with classic songs such as "Proud

Mary", "Under the Boardwalk", and "Cold Sweat". These songs topped

off an incredible variety of emotions.

John Cougar, in my opinion, did a very good job at presenting his

concert in a roller coaster of emotion. For three hours, he and his

band members, including Larry Crane, and Mike Wanchic: guitar, Kenny

Aronoff: drums, and Toby Myers: bass played non-stop with no

intermissions. Even though there was no opening band, I believe John
then accelerating his pace only to
Cougar knew that by starting slow, (then fast, then slow, and then fast slow it
he involve? captivate? engage? the audience and down
again) would leave a very satisfied crowd. Satisfying it was, because again
and
instead of rushing for the exit, everyone, including myself, had to speed it
up
sit back down to relax. For $16.00, this concert was definitely worth again

filled
with
warm
feelings
on a
cold night in
Columbus.

every penny.

3

Writing 13:   Response

Dear Frank,

"The John Cougar Concert" is good. I think you should consider publishing this essay in our class anthology. It gets better every time you revise it. Let me illustrate how I think you have made it a more effective essay in each succeeding draft by reproducing your developing descriptions of the beginning of the concert. You began with one sentence that was not itself gracefully composed: "Refering back to what I said earlier about roller coaster of emotion, the ride was about to start."(Draft 1). In your second draft, you revised and expanded that sentence; in so doing, you established some tension by telling the reader that the appointed time of the concert had arrived, and you began to recreate the mood of the crowd as his fans anxiously anticipated Cougar's performance.

> It was nearing 8:00 pm (the scheduled time to begin) and the crowd was starting to get excited. People were chanting, 'We want Cougar, we want Cougar!' Suddenly the lights went out and the roller coaster of emotions was about to start (Draft 2).

In the draft you have just submitted, you have revised again; this time you have sharpened the reader's sense of the scene by dramatizing the crowd, by placing yourself and your friends into it and its mood; furthermore, you have supplied some information about Cougar that pre-figures your discussion of his commitment to the American farmer.

> It was nearly 8:00 P.M. (the scheduled time to begin) and the crowd was starting to get excited. People were chanting, "We want Cougar, we want Cougar!" My old high school friends and I were also joining in the chanting. We, like all the others, wanted to see this man from a small town in Indiana perform. Suddenly the lights went out and the roller coaster of emotions was about to start (Draft 3).

You and this essay are on a roll (not a roller coaster).

Because I thought you might want to continue to work on "The John Cougar Concert" and to submit it for a higher grade and/or for the class anthology, I have taken the liberty of copy editing it. Please take note of my editorial suggestions to you. In each case, decide if and how you would like to make use of the suggestion. I'd like to make your decisions and the reasons why you have made them my agenda item for our next conference.

I'm looking forward to talking with you more about this essay which is developing so well.   I think I'll even have to buy a John Cougar tape.

P. L. Stock

P. S. December 13th is my birthday, and I remember the night of December 13, 1985. It was snowing and cold in Grand Rapids, too. I was there talking to a group of Michigan high school principals about the teaching of writing. Who do you think had more fun that night, you or I?

Frank - you've done a fine job with the revisions. With a little fine tuning, this piece will be ready for publication. See what you think about the sentence-level suggestions I've made below—

Writing 13
Frank C.
Final Draft

The John Cougar Concert

On a cold and blustery evening on December 13, 1985, at the Ohio
Center, John Cougar took his fans and me on what I call a roller
coaster ride of emotion. And what a ride it was. *Even* ~~Rolling Stone~~
Magazine e~~v~~en stated, "Forget the Springsteen comparison, this is
simply one of the best rock shows on the road."

How does this sound to you, the even being put at the front?

Before the show even started, the most noticeable thing was the
stage. At most concerts you would expect fancy equipment and flashy
decor, but Cougar's stage was practically bare with only a white
backdrop and basic instruments. This plain setting pointed to John
Cougar's no-nonsense approach to rock and roll.

did work on this sentence a little. It might confuse some readers, this idea that the stage is visible before the show.

It was nearing 8:00 P.M. (the scheduled time to begin) and the
crowd was starting to get excited. People were chanting, "We want
Cougar, we want Cougar!" /My old high school friends and I were also
joining in the chanting. We, like all the others, wanted to see this
man from a small town in Indiana perform/ Suddenly the lights went
out, and the roller coaster of emotions was about to start.

I like your addition here you give the flavor of both the crowd and the singer and suggest a connection between them

A roar of elation went through the crowd when Cougar appeared on
stage. There he stood with his shoulder length black hair and intent
eyes. There was no fancy costume either, just a white t-shirt, worn
out Levis, and cowboy boots. [Again, pointing to his no-nonsense
approach to rock and roll.] *I wonder if there's a way to suggest this rather than say it explicitly. Maybe omit this phrase?*

Try a dash (—) here instead of a comma.

Immediately he belted into one of his newest hits, "Small Town"

I like this word here —

1

from the <u>Scarecrow</u> album. The emotions really started rolling with
that song. People were jumping up and down and standing on their
chairs. After that "warm up" song, Cougar yelled at the crowd in a
very urging voice, "I want all of you to get up off your seat and get
into it!" With that, Cougar roared into his more energetic songs such
as "Authority Song", "Serious Business", and "Crumblin Down". The
whole audience must have listened to Cougar's command because everyone
was singing along, dancing, and having a great time. <u>John Cougar knew</u>
<u>he had the audience at an emotional high because he went into an</u>
<u>extended version of "Play Guitar".</u> People released so much energy by
cheering and singing during this song. I even found myself to be out
of breath.

Why is there an indication that he knew? Does he really do this song at such a moment?

After all his high powered songs, John Cougar slowed the emotions
by singing a couple of songs for lovers. Songs such as "Jack and
Diane" and "Everyone Needs A Hand To Hold On To" had a few couples
embracing each other. After that, Cougar paced across the stage in a
very serious manner. He started to talk about an issue that is very
important to him — that of the American farmer and the problems that
they are facing. [It is an issue he is very well known for.] He also
talked briefly about Farm Aid which was a benefit concert that he and
other rock stars were organizing to help American farmers. With that,
Cougar went into a very emotional song, "Rain on the Scarecrow". This
song typifies *the consequences for a farmer when he* ~~what happens when a farmer~~ runs out of money. ~~and the~~
~~consequences he must face.~~ Lines like "Called my old friend Schepman
up to auction off the land, he said, John it's just my job and I hope
you understand", really makes you feel discouraged, the way you would

See if you think this reads better

Maybe omit? Do you see why?

I don't know—your version may be better.

Maybe use the symbol for a line break (—) where appropriate

This doesn't sound quite right broken apart by the lyrics. Can you re-arrange?

feel if you had to ask your friend to sell something very dear to you.
You could actually feel the emotions of sadness and despair by the
incredible way John Cougar projected this song.

Although
~~John Cougar knew that~~ these issues were very important to ~~him~~, *John Cougar*

Listen to both versions, and see what the difference is.

but he didn't want to dwell on them for too long. That is why he got
the crowd started on a climb towards another emotional peak. He sang
"R.O.C.K. in the U.S.A." which is a salute to 1960's rock and roll.
It is a very upbeat song about how some famous rockers such as James
Brown, Frankie Lyman, and Mitch Ryder finally made it in the music
business. I could tell Cougar was really working hard because I could
see sweat drip off his face. Cougar again urged the crowd to join in.
He rocketed into a 60's medley with classic songs such as "Proud
Mary", "Under the Boardwalk", and "Cold Sweat". These songs topped
off an incredible variety of emotions.

John Cougar, in my opinion, did a very good job at presenting his
concert in a roller coaster of emotion. For three hours, he and his
band members, including Larry Crane, and Mike Wanchic, guitar; Kenny
Aronoff, drums; and Toby Myers, bass, played non-stop with no
intermissions. Even though there was no opening band, I believe John
Cougar knew that by starting slow, then fast, then slow, and then fast
again would leave a very satisfied crowd. Satisfying it was, because
instead of rushing for the exit, everyone, including myself, had to
sit back down to relax. For $16.00, this concert was definitely worth
every penny.

See if you understand how I've used semi-colons (;) and commas here, and why.

3

LARSON

Writing 13
Frank C.
Final Draft

The John Cougar Concert

On a cold and blustery evening on December 13, 1985, at the Ohio
Center, John Cougar took his fans and me on what I call a roller
coaster ride of emotion. And what a ride it was. Rolling Stone
Magazine even stated, "Forget the Springsteen comparison, this is
simply one of the best rock shows on the road."

Before the show even started, the most noticeable thing was the
stage. At most concerts you would expect fancy equipment and flashy
decor, but Cougar's stage was practically bare with only a white
backdrop and basic instruments. This plain setting pointed to John
Cougar's no-nonsense approach to rock and roll.

It was nearing 8:00 P.M. (the scheduled time to begin) and the
crowd was starting to get excited. People were chanting, "We want
Cougar, we want Cougar!" My old high school friends and I were also
joining in the chanting. We, like all the others, wanted to see this
man from a small town in Indiana perform. Suddenly the lights went
out and the roller coaster of emotions was about to start.

A roar of elation went through the crowd when Cougar appeared on
stage. There he stood with his shoulder length black hair and intent
eyes. There was no fancy costume either, just a white t-shirt, worn
out Levis, and cowboy boots. Again, pointing to his no-nonsense
approach to rock and roll.

Immediately he belted into one of his newest hits, "Small Town"

1

from the <u>Scarecrow</u> album. The emotions really started rolling with

that song. People were jumping up and down and standing on their

chairs. After that "warm up" song, Cougar yelled at the crowd in a

very urging voice, "I want all of you to get up off your seat and get

into it!" With that, Cougar roared into his more energetic songs such

as "Authority Song", "Serious Business", and "Crumblin Down". The

whole audience must have listened to Cougar's command because everyone

was singing along, dancing, and having a great time. John Cougar knew

he had the audience at an emotional high because he went into an

extended version of "Play Guitar". People released so much energy by

cheering and singing during this song. I even found myself to be out

of breath.

  After all his high powered songs, John Cougar slowed the emotions

by singing a couple of songs for lovers. Songs such as "Jack and

Diane" and "Everyone Needs A Hand To Hold On To" had a few couples

embracing each other. After that, Cougar paced across the stage in a

very serious manner. He started to talk about an issue that is very *"FARMERS"?*

important to him – that of the American farmer and the problems that

they are facing. It is an issue he is very well known for. He also

talked briefly about Farm Aid *PUNCTUATE?* which was a benefit concert that he and

other rock stars were organizing to help American farmers. With that,

Cougar went into a very emotional song, "Rain on the Scarecrow". This

song typifies what happens when a farmer runs out of money and the

consequences he must face. Lines like "Called my old friend Schepman

up to auction off the land, he/said, John it's just my job and I hope

you understand", really makes you feel discouraged, the way you would

WHAT EXACTLY IS THE "I HERE? HOW TO HELP THEM SOLVE THEIR PROBLEMS?

WORD FORM?

2

feel if you had to ask your friend to sell something very dear to you. You could actually feel the emotions of sadness and despair by the incredible way John Cougar projected this song.

John Cougar knew that these issues were very important to him, but he didn't want to dwell on them for too long. That is why he got the crowd started on a climb towards another emotional peak. He sang "R.O.C.K. in the U.S.A." which is a salute to 1960's rock and roll. It is a very upbeat song about how some famous rockers such as James Brown, Frankie Lyman, and Mitch Ryder finally made it in the music business. I could tell Cougar was really working hard because I could see sweat drip off his face. Cougar again urged the crowd to join in. He rocketed into a 60's medley with classic songs such as "Proud Mary", "Under the Boardwalk", and "Cold Sweat". These songs topped off an incredible variety of emotions.

John Cougar, in my opinion, did a very good job at presenting his concert in a roller coaster of emotion. For three hours, he and his band members, including Larry Crane, and Mike Wanchic: guitar, Kenny Aronoff: drums, and Toby Myers: bass played non-stop with no intermissions. Even though there was no opening band, I believe John Cougar knew that by starting slow, then fast, then slow, and then fast again would leave a very satisfied crowd. Satisfying it was, because instead of rushing for the exit, everyone, including myself, had to sit back down to relax. For $16.00, this concert was definitely worth every penny.

see over

3

This essay, which seems to me to hage changed little since
the second draft, is a vivid, engaged, and specific report
of Cougar's concert. I value your enthusiasm for the
concert and your evident pleasure in it; it's good that you
expressed those reactions.

But the paper remains essentially a report of the concert
and your personal responses. The assignment, however,
asked for an "evaluation" based upon criteria and supported
by reasons. To some extent you've given criteria (the
emotional "roller coaster") and other standards (the
audience's responses), but you do less with these
bases for judgment than the assignment meant to elicit.
To put the point differently: is any concert that
could be said to create an "emotional roller coaster"
good? Is any concert good that has the audience involved? Are these the only, or the principal, bases for
judgment? Why? Does the quality of the music played
matter? The eloquence of the words as a kind of poetry?
The sentiments expressed in the songs? I don't mean to
imply that all these matters need to be touched in an
essay such as you are writing. But I think that the
bases of judgment should be formulated a little more
explicitly than you have done here, and that the
narrative of the concert might be at least somewhat subordinated
to a discussion of features that make the concert, in
your view, praiseworthy. That discussion requires <u>some</u> detachment.

Writing such a review is, of course, a matter of balance.
One <u>wants</u> the details; one wants the experience. But, even
in a school newspaper, one probably wants a bit more:
signs of a detached reflection on whether, overall,
the concert was an artistically satisfying experience--and why.

I'd like to see you rewrite this piece with the goal of
striking the balance I've just described, somewhat more
than the present essay does.

Writing 13
Frank C.
Final Draft

The John Cougar Concert

On a cold and blustery evening on December 13, 1985, at the Ohio
Center, John Cougar took his fans and me on what I call a roller
coaster ride of emotion. And what a ride it was. Rolling Stone
Magazine even stated, "Forget the Springsteen comparison, this is
simply one of the best rock shows on the road."

Before the show even started, the most noticeable thing was the
stage. At most concerts you would expect fancy equipment and flashy
decor, but Cougar's stage was practically bare with only a white
backdrop and basic instruments. This plain setting pointed to John
Cougar's no-nonsense approach to rock and roll.

It was nearing 8:00 P.M. (the scheduled time to begin) and the
crowd was starting to get excited. People were chanting, "We want
Cougar, we want Cougar!" My old high school friends and I were also
joining in the chanting. We, like all the others, wanted to see this
man from a small town in Indiana perform. Suddenly, the lights went
out and the roller coaster of emotions was about to start.

A roar of elation went through the crowd when Cougar appeared on
stage. There he stood with his shoulder length black hair and intent
eyes. There was no fancy costume either, just a white t-shirt, worn
out Levis, and cowboy boots, ~~Again, pointing to~~ emphasizing his no-nonsense
approach to rock and roll.

Immediately he belted into one of his newest hits, "Small Town"

from the <u>Scarecrow</u> album. The emotions really started rolling with
that song. People were jumping up and down and standing on their
25 chairs. After that "warm up" song, Cougar yelled at the crowd in a
very urging voice, "I want all of you to get up off your seat and get
into it!" With that, Cougar roared into his more energetic songs such
as "Authority Song," "Serious Business," and "Crumblin Down." The
whole audience must have listened to Cougar's command because everyone
was singing along, dancing, and having a great time. John Cougar knew
he had the audience at an emotional high because he went into an
extended version of "Play Guitar." People released so much energy by
cheering and singing during this song. I even found myself to be out
of breath.

"very urging" stops the other easier. Can't you think of more dramatic terms?

Put commas and periods inside quotation marks, always.

    After all his high powered songs, John Cougar slowed the emotions
by singing a couple of songs for lovers. ~~Songs such as~~ "Jack and
Diane" and "Everyone Needs A Hand To Hold On To" had a few couples
embracing each other. After that, Cougar paced across the stage in a
very serious manner. He started to talk about an issue that is very
important to him - that of the American farmer and the problems that
they are facing. It is an issue he is very well known for. He also
talked briefly about Farm Aid which was a benefit concert that he and
other rock stars were organizing to help American farmers. With that,
Cougar went into a very emotional song, "Rain on the Scarecrow." This
song typifies what happens when a farmer runs out of money and the
consequences he must face. Lines like "Called my old friend Schepman
up to auction off the land, he said, John it's just my job and I hope
you understand" really makes you feel discouraged, the way you would

agreement

feel if you had to ask your friend to sell something very dear to you. You could actually feel the emotions of sadness and despair by the incredible way John Cougar projected this song.

John Cougar knew that these issues were very important to him, but he didn't want to dwell on them for too long. That is why he got the crowd started on a climb towards another emotional peak. He sang "R.O.C.K. in the U.S.A." which is a salute to 1960's rock and roll. It is a very upbeat song about how some famous rockers such as James Brown, Frankie Lyman, and Mitch Ryder finally made it in the music business. I could tell Cougar was really working hard because I could see sweat drip off his face. Cougar again urged the crowd to join in. He rocketed into a 60's medley with classic songs such as "Proud Mary", "Under the Boardwalk", and "Cold Sweat". These songs topped off an incredible variety of emotions.

John Cougar, in my opinion, did a very good job at presenting his concert in a roller coaster of emotion. For three hours, he and his band members, including Larry Crane, and Mike Wanchic: guitar, Kenny Aronoff: drums, and Toby Myers: bass played non-stop with no intermissions. Even though there was no opening band, I believe John Cougar knew that by starting slow, then fast, then slow, and then fast again would leave a very satisfied crowd. Satisfying it was, because instead of rushing for the exit, everyone, including myself, had to sit back down to relax. For $16.00, this concert was definitely worth every penny.

you've Used This Term several Times.

what is The subject for This verb

Frank C., "The John Cougar Concert"

Your assignment tells you to evaluate your subject, in this
case a rock concert. You are supposed to develop some
criteria for judging rock concerts and then indicate the
ways in which this particular concert met those criteria.
Now, let's see what you've done.

You tell us that John Cougar took you and his fans on a
"roller coaster ride of emotion," a phrase you use two or
three times in the paper. We also learn that Cougar
operates from a bare stage, wears plain clothes, works his
audience into several frenzies during the evening, makes a
pitch for American farmers, and plays non-stop. Where, in
all this adulation, are criteria for judging this rock
group? Does one evaluate rock stars by their ability to
work audiences into a frenzy of emotion? Is it necessary
for them to wear clothes that set them off from other rock
groups? What about their ability to sing, compose music,
and play their instruments? You don't mention any of these
things. Are they unimportant when applied to rock
musicians?

If you detect a trace of sarcasm in my remarks, I apologize
for putting it there, but I can hardly suppress it. You
see, I am the most difficult kind of reader you could
imagine for this kind of piece. I hate rock music. I do
not see your star, John Cougar, as a man dressing in a no-
nonsense fashion. I see a scuzzy performer in scuzzy
clothes and infer that he is probably half coked out of his
head during this orgy. If he is like most rock musicians I
have heard, he has minimal playing skills, yells more than
he sings (which is all right because the words to the songs
he sings are little more than primitive tribal chants), and
pounds his boots on the floor of the stage.

The contrast between Cougar and a real musician is
especially apparent to me right now because as I write this
I am listening to a recording of the Dvorak Violin Concerto
performed by Nathan Milstein, one of the greatest violinists
of the twentieth century. Unlike rock stars, Mr. Milstein
did not suddenly appear, make a year's worth of hit records,
and vanish into limbo. He has been around for decades. Let
me tell you what criteria I used, as a young person, when I
measured his playing against that of other violinists.
First, I noted how well he could play. Could he get notes
that other violinists couldn't? Boy, could he. Only
Heifetz could get more. What kind of tone did he produce?
Lush, and powerfully moving. How good were his interpretive
skills? They were wonderful. He played unaccompanied Bach,
concertos by Bruch, Mendelssohn, Glazunov, and a host of
others with tremendous feeling and style. Milstein never
used amplifiers, either, but he could play with a kind of

intensity you probably never were exposed to. I could have gone to a Milstein concert and then written a piece which would have stimulated half of Kansas City to check him out the next time he came around.

In fairness to you, I suppose your fellow high school students, who undoubtedly like Cougar a lot better than Milstein, would get the idea that he was pretty good. But you might have told them just what he does that is as good as what Springsteen does. In what ways is he better than Springsteen? I really have no idea yet how to evaluate rock music groups.

I've suggested a few changes in editing and diction. If you do not understand them, see me.

C

Discussion of Responses to "THE JOHN COUGAR CONCERT"
Featured Responders: Stock, Hull, Larson, Stewart
Featured Issues:
- **Criteria-based evaluative assignment**
- **Response to multiple drafts**
- **Readers' biases**
- **Editorial help**

The responses to this essay can be placed into three categories. Stock and Hull like the essay and feel that it is ready for a final editing. Elbow, Gere, Peterson, and Anson are satisfied with the essay; or at least, they agree that it is time for the writer to move on. Larson, McClelland, and Stewart, by contrast, are troubled by the fact that the student has failed to do a criteria-based evaluation of this concert. Larson and McClelland would have the student revise; Stewart would have him repent.

Warnock does not fit neatly into any of these categories. She seems happy enough with Frank's progress through these drafts, but feels that this piece is still "alive" enough for Frank to warrant further revision.

Most of the readers of this essay take note of the process through which it has developed—in their notes to us, their comments to Frank, or both. Larson comments that the student made several changes between the first and second drafts and fewer between the second and third. He feels hindered by the fact that he doesn't "know what he [the student] was told between drafts, or what his other writing has been like." He tells us that none of the drafts responds to the assignment, thus implying that given the opportunity he would have drawn the student's attention to this problem earlier in the process. Gere also finds it "a little difficult to give this a 'real' response because some of the problems I see here (which also appear in earlier drafts) are things I would have commented on earlier."

Peterson reacts differently. She "assumed that the changes between drafts had been made in response to my comments and that, though the assignment calls for a criteria-based evaluation, what I really want (or am willing to accept) is an evaluative narrative." She says that were this not the case, she would have prompted Frank, at the first draft stage, to state criteria explicitly and organize his evaluation by means of those criteria.

Neither Hull nor Warnock objects to the way we have set up this responding task. Hull does mention the effect seeing these drafts may have had on her response: "I wonder if I would be as complimentary if I had not seen the previous two drafts. I don't know. But having seen them, I want to reward this student's effort." Warnock notes that the drafts show her a student revising "from draft 1 to 3 to fit the purpose and situation."

Elbow wants to place his end comment in the context of the entire process; so, as he says in his note to us, he has made up a little story in which he has given advice that has, in several cases, not been taken. Elbow goes on to say that he likes "to stress in (my) feedback that my perceptions are personal and idiosyncratic (rather than general, impersonal or Godlike verdicts)." In his note to us he says that Frank has resisted his advice in places and says that he is glad to see him making up his own mind.

Two readers of this essay, Hull and Stewart, offer insight into personal predispositions that certainly affect the ways they read this essay. After saying that Frank is making improvements in these drafts, Hull tells us: "it's such a relief to read about a rock concert after prayer in schools, leukemia, and alcoholism. I may be overly enthusiastic about this paper." Clearly, Hull has no predisposition to dislike the topic.

Stewart starts his note to us by saying that in his youth he "would have (been) more sensitive and less abrasive." However, he has come to think that "students are not always served by such an approach. Why should a teacher always be objective and hence bland in responding to students' work? He or she shouldn't." Given Stewart's comments to Frank about rock musicians and "real" musicians, one wonders whether Stewart can appreciate any essay on this topic. His note to us would seem to indicate his willingness to bring his biases to his reading of this essay.

Hull and Stock provide us with one final comparison. They both like this essay and feel that it is ready for a final editing. Hull tells us that she wanted to give Frank all the help she could in making the final draft a polished piece of writing. Stock tells us that she copyedits one or two papers for each student during the course of a semester; because she sees Frank's essay as a satisfactory final draft, she makes copyediting suggestions that would allow him to produce the best draft possible. Her design is not to impose her editing strategies on the student—she will copyedit only when she feels the student is "sufficiently invested" in a paper to resist her suggestions if he does not like them—but rather to provide the content for a conversation she will have with the student before he produces the final draft. A glance at these two editings shows the baffling array of choices a writer has in any revising task. Although both readers make many useful suggestions for improvement, they seldom focus on the same items, and they never make the same suggestions for revision.

Our readers do not agree on what should be done with this essay, then, because they read the essay very differently. Hull and Stock like the essay and want to help the writer polish the paper for its final presentation. Stewart and McClelland think the paper needs much work before it will be ready for polishing. At the center of their disagreement is the issue of whether the writer must produce a criteria-based evaluation and/or just what constitutes such an evaluation.

WRITING 15
MULTIPLE PAPERS IN A SERIES OF ASSIGNMENTS
Featured Responders: Elbow, White, Larson, Hull

Presented in this selection are three papers from one student's course writings. **You may respond either to the group as a whole or only to the last paper of the course, "The Right to Pray."**

BACKGROUND

These three papers—Paper 2, "The Popularity of Disney World," an informative essay; Paper 3, "Choosing a College," an evaluative essay; and Paper 5, "The Right to Pray," a persuasive essay—have been submitted at the end of the term as the major portion of this student's final course portfolio. Through the semester, students have written (and handed in according to a common schedule) five essays in response to assignments that stipulate the aim of discourse but which give students freedom to choose their own subjects. Now, at the end of the course, they are handing in what they see as their three best efforts, to be reviewed for their final grade. Although you have already read and commented on earlier drafts of papers 2 and 3, you have not yet seen Paper 5, "The Right to Pray." It is the last paper of the course, submitted as a final draft.

In preparation for this persuasive essay, the class has been examining the basic principles of argumentative and persuasive writing, including logical appeal, emotional appeal, and appeal to the writer's character. A good deal of time has been devoted to developing and supporting assertions. Some attention has also been given to the role of audience in argumentative and persuasive writing as well as to the structure of argumentative discourse.

THE ASSIGNMENT

Reflect on your experience and choose a controversial issue that is particularly interesting to you. Write a paper in which you attempt to convince your readers to accept your views on the topic. Be sure to target your essay for readers who are in need of some convincing on this matter.

Writing 15
Donna R.
Paper 2: Final Draft

The Popularity of Walt Disney World

Have you ever wondered why Walt Disney World in Orlando, Florida
is so popular? Its attractions appeal to the old and the young. The
atmosphere there makes the young, happy and the old feel young and
happy. There is something there for every age. Walt Disney World's
activities and atmosphere appeal to the people of every generation.

Every year Disney holds a "Grad Nite" for high school seniors and
seniors from all parts of Florida. At this time musical groups such
as Klymakise, Rene and Angela, Starpoint and Miami Sound Machine that
appeal to the young generation perform. It starts at eleven o'clock
p.m. and ends a five o'clock a.m. The brilliant flourescent light of
Disney shines brightly against the sky's dark complexion. There is
the laughter and the chatter of teenagers mingles, with the blasting
music in the background. The dress code is semi-formal and the
youngsters are dressed in an array of colors. Of course there are
chaperons who rather spend their night in lounges or coffee shops
while the night lingers on. The teenagers wish the night would never
end.

Most senior citizens prefer a more quieter atmosphere and Disney
World provides one. They usually explore Disney's attrations during
the off season, which is approximately from September to March or
April. Older couples can be seen paired off holding hands and
strolling down Main Street wearing multi-colored plaid shorts and
Hawaiin shirts. Most would not dare to tackle Space Mountain or
Thunder Mountain, but there are places such as the Presidential Hall
of Fame that are more their speed. They can buy souvenirs and crafts
from different shops along Disney's streets. Mickey's big smile and
equally big ears on pendants decorate souvenir shop windows. Other
shops are dedicated to making specific crafts like leather products.
Here, leather belts, purses and vests are produced for tourists.

Senior citizens are not the only ones who take advantage of
Disney during the off season, this is the time when most schools take
field trips. Hundreds of giggling elementary school aged children
race off of yellow school buses. Frantic teachers try to herd up
these energetic kids. The kids have more time to enjoy Disney because
it is less crowded and does not take as long to get to the attactions.
They also have a greater chance of seeing and meeting some of the
Disney Characters. The kids scamper around Disney in their vivid
colored shortsets enjoying the activities.

Many kids love the field trips because it takes the place of time
spent in school but during summer vacation is when most of them would

rather visit. There are more people their own age and a larger crowd with a more exciting atmosphere at Disney at this time.

The rides are what excite the younger generation. Long lines consisting of hundreds of people can be seen waiting to ride some of the more exciting rides. Space Mountain is one of the favorites. It is a roller coaster inside of a building. The tracks for the ride are in a dark part of the building. The riders cannot see what direction the ride is going. After the ride a conveyor belt transports the riders to the outside. During the trip there is a section where they can see themselves situated along the side of the conveyor belt. Further down there is a section of technologically advanced homes. The home had computerized operated applicances and lights. It even had a monitor and a computerized baby sitter. Another favorite is Thunder Mountain. It has not been at Disney as long as Space Mountain but it is equally as popular. It has an "Old West" setting. A train takes the riders through what looks like a mine in the desert. It is also a roller coaster like ride. The train moves with speed so great that it stops the voices of the riders in their throats. Time and time again people put themselves through this. There are rides for the very young children from age 1 to six or seven. The carousel has blinking lights and jeweled horses to ride. There is even a ride with gray and pink Dumbo elephants for the kids to ride. The rides are accompanied by a cheery little tune.

Another thing at Disney that interest the young children is the Disney characters. Mickey, Donald and Goofy flash winning smiles at their small admirers and readily give handshakes and hugs. This usually brightens the day of children and it is the topic of conversations for days.

Even though there is a wide generation gap, Walt Disney World is a place that everyone can enjoy together. It can be said that Disney brings the family closer together.

Writing 15
Donna R.
Paper 3: Final Draft

Choosing a College

Should I attend college? If so, should it be a small private
college or a state university? What are the differences between the
two? How different are they in cost, dorm life, regulations, class
size and reputation?

These are just some of the areas pondered upon by teenagers as
they approach high school graduation. In their decision to choose a
certain institution, the cost, financial aid, class size, the
reputation of the school related to their major, rules, and the dorm
life, are important factors. When all of the information is gathered
it shows that a state university offers a freer environment and a
better education.

Probably the most important area to consider is cost. This
usually includes tuition, room, board and meals. At a state
university, the average paid by each student is $4,200 a year. State
universities are able to offer many scholarships and other forms of
financial aid to help students pay. This is because they receive
local and state tax funds along with endowments and gifts or
donations. Private colleges do not recieve help from the government.
They have to depend on endowments and donations as well as the student
fees to keep them operating. This causes the tuition to be higher.
The average cost is about $8,500 per student a year. These colleges
are able to supply scholarships and other financial aid, but not as
much as a state university.

Cost is considered more by the parents, but the teenager
concentrates on what he is allowed to do while in college. Most
private colleges have strict rules and regulations for which the
students are held responsible. For instance, at Christopher College,
a private college in Tamarac, Illinois, the students are given curfews
of 11:00 o'clock p.m. on weekdays and 1:00 a.m. on weekends. If these
curfews are broken, they are required to pay a $50 fine. They also
must pay a $25 fine if they are caught walking on the grass. State
universities, on the other hand, do not impose a curfew on their
students. They are given two (2) keys. One is to their room and the
other is to the dorm's lobby. This is to accomodate the time the
student chooses to come back to the dorm.

Another area that would get a lot of attention from the teenager
is dorm life. They now know that they do not have a curfew and
they've found out that there are co-educational dorms on state
university campuses. They also have dorms that are strictly male or
female. Intervisitation in all three types of dorms is allowed. Many

private colleges do not have coed dorms. The dorms are either all male or all female. They do not allow visitation between the sexes in the dorms past the lobby. This is also present at Christopher College. If a male is caught in a female's dorm room, he is either put on probation or expelled. The same goes for a female in a male's dorm room.

Even though private colleges cost more and have stricter rules concerning dorms, they do have a positive quality that a lot of students consider. This is the size of the classes. Since the enrollment of most private colleges are smaller than state universities, the student to teacher ratio is smaller. Most private colleges have an average ration of 15:1. These students recieve more personal attention from the professors. On the other hand, students at state universities usually have to hire tutors to get the same one-on-one attention. Most state universities have an average of 45:1. At Central State University in Capitol, Illinois, there are lecture classes. These classes consist of any where from 200 to 250 students. There is no way one professor could see each student separately in a short 50 minute class period.

Also in considering a college the students should check the accreditation of the school related to their major. Most of the smaller private colleges, such as St. Anthony's College in Norwich, Illinois, do not have well developed academic schools like the state universities. St. Anthony has a very poorly developed medical school. They can only accomodate 10 to 15 students at a time. St. Anthony does not have the funds to improve the different academic schools on their campus. The University of North Indiana has a very technologically advanced medical school. They have more money to develop their medical college. University of North Indiana recieves funds from the government to help them.

Millions of students have to make this big decision every year. The majority choose to further their education at a state university. After gathering and weighing the advantages and disadvantages of both a small private college and state university most choose to further their education at a state university.

Writing 15
Donna R.
Paper 5: Final Draft

                    The Right to Pray

    It is nine o'clock a.m. seven years ago in a small classroom. A
bell rings to signify the beginning of school. "Would everyone please
stand for the flag salute and a moment of silence," blares over the
intercom. Twenty-seven sixth graders noisily shift chairs and stand
to their feet. After they salute the flag, the teacher asks, "Who
would like to lead us in prayer today?" Every child raises a hand and
shouts, "Me, me, me!"

    These days have been long lost. Prayer in schools has been
abolished because it has been argued that it interfers with some of
the children's religious preferences. But what about the other kids?
They are being deprived of a religious freedom. To give both the
religious preference and freedom the constitution grants, prayer
should be present, but optional, in schools.

    We believe the reason this country is in such a bad shape is
because it has turned away from God. One example is taking prayer out
of schools. With all of the trouble and evil in the world, we want
our children to learn to ask for God's protection. Now more than ever
protection in school is essential. Schools are now corupt with drugs,
fights and murders, and they are getting worse as times passes. God
is the only one able to protect kids while they attend school.

    The people who oppose prayer in school say school is not the
place for prayer. Schools are for learning. Anywhere can be the

place for prayer. The prayer does not have to be long and extensive.
It can be a short simple prayer, like thanking God for watching me up
this mourning and giving me strength to attend school, that will not
interfer with time used for getting an education. The prayer does not
even have to be aloud. God sees the heart. Silent prayers are just
as effective. One prayer that I used to use in class went like this:

> "Dear God, I want to thank you for my life,
> health, and strength. I ask that you protect
> me through the day. Amen."

Atheist are among the people who wanted prayer out of school.
These people do not believe there is a God. Naturally, they pass it
on to their children. They do not want their children exposed to
religion in school. Some say the prayer was forced on the students.
If prayer was optional in schools, the students would be given a
choice.

I got lost here—can't follow your thoughts

Opposite of the atheist's beliefs, some parents believe in god
and want Him in every aspect of their child's life. These are the
people that suffer from the decision to take prayer out of school.
They can not practice their religious beliefs and therefore they have
no religious freedom. One of my friends told me, "I was really
shocked when they [Congress] passed the law taking prayer out of
schools. How could they do that? Religious freedom is given to us by
the constitution. I felt so deprived!" How would the opposition feel
if one of their inalienable rights, such as liberty, taken away from
them? They would be very upset. Well, this is how we feel. This is a
grave injustice to some of the Americans.

In the 1700's and 1800's, thousands of people set out for this

country. Many had suffered beatings and imprisonment in their home
country because of their religious preferences. News had gotten to
them that they would be able to practice their choice of religion in
the New World. It was known to some as a religious haven. During the
journey, which sometimes lasted for three months, many contracted
diseases and some lost their lives. Now, some of their descendents
are being deprived of that self-same freedom. No compromises were
made when the decision was finalized to remove prayer from schools.
These people have a right to practice their religious beliefs. Just
as students are given the choice of saluting the flag, they should be
given the choice to pray.

WRITING 15, MULTIPLE PAPERS: PORTFOLIO

Dear Donna,

I'm afraid you've got to move fast to get this ready to submit. I'm certain it won't pass on the grounds of mistakes in mechanics, and I feel pretty sure that it will still fail even if you clean up all mistakes.

Mechanics: lots in the first paper and quite a few in the second and third. I've marked some. But I'm afraid there's more that's needed.

Disney. If you clean it up, it <u>might</u> pass but I'm disappointed that you didn't really revise it at all. Notice how in the second and third papers you have a genuine voice and presence. The good news is that by putting these three papers together you give me a vivid sense of your increasing voice and presence on paper. With each paper there is more sense of you as a writer daring to speak out--a person <u>there</u> in the text and a caring energy.

By not revising the Disney paper you've left that timid fake voice from the beginning of the semester when you were scared to speak out on paper. Playing it safe. Notice how the second paper is in a way nothing but information, (and I don't mean that as an insult) yet there is voice and presence in that information: I hear a real person--you--finding and weighing and giving us that information. I don't trust the Disney voice: it's like one of those "pretend" voices in a travelogue movie. With your skills now, you can go back and actually <u>be</u> there a bit and give us something real about that evening.

2nd paper. Go back to my earlier comments and revise. Remember I talked about how your picture of private colleges is really not accurate as a picture of all or even most private colleges--and how that one distrust what you say. Whereas in truth, what you say would be fine if you talk about them as the small, religious-based private colleges you happen to know. (Are they perhaps the ones you considered? Is this by any chance trying to be an account of the thinking <u>you</u> went through in deciding where to go? As such it would be much more compelling--and oddly enough it would be more persuasive to others for not pretenting to fit

everyone--just being a story of your thinking and deciding.

New paper. You take more chances, you wade into deeper water. Serious prob-

lems, but again more energy and presence. You're acting like a real writer here.

About revising:

--Terrific opening. Captures. Says much of what you want to say--without

having to argue. <u>But</u> it undermines your argument. You say (lower 2) you want reli-

gious freedom, but that scene shows that it's the atheist child who is having his

freedom denied. He's being made to take part in prayers. Whereas to have no public

prayers doesn't stop anyone from praying. (Your example of your own prayer sounds

like the kind of thing you can say to yourself.)

--You suffer from not making your case clear enough. Even I (who've been read-

ing you all semester) can't quite tell whether you're saying that there should be

public prayers for all, or just times of silent prayer during which some kids can do

other things.

--Also that "we" on the first page made it seem for a moment as though you

weren't giving your own thoughts but just quoting what others say in some pamphlet.

But it didn't <u>sound</u> as though you were doing that. Can't you say "I"?

Best,

Peter

Writing 15
Donna R.
Paper 5: Final Draft

The Right to Pray

It is nine o'clock a.m. seven years ago in a small classroom. A
bell rings to signify the beginning of school. "Would everyone please
stand for the flag salute and a moment of silence," blares over the
intercom. Twenty-seven sixth graders noisily shift chairs and stand
to their feet. After they salute the flag, the teacher asks, "Who
would like to lead us in prayer today?" Every child raises a hand and
shouts, "Me, me, me!"

These days have been long lost. Prayer in schools has been
abolished because it has been argued that it interfers with some of
the children's religious preferences. But what about the other kids?
They are being deprived of a religious freedom. To give both the
religious preference and freedom the constitution grants, prayer
should be present, but optional, in schools.

Is this the real argument? Be fair!

Define what this means.

Who is this? We believe the reason this country is in such a bad shape is
because it has turned away from God. One example is taking prayer out
of schools. With all of the trouble and evil in the world, we want
our children to learn to ask for God's protection. Now more than ever
protection in school is essential. Schools are now corrupt with drugs,
fights and murders, and they are getting worse as times passes. God
is the only one able to protect kids while they attend school.

How does this occur?

The people who oppose prayer in school say school is not the
place for prayer. Schools are for learning. Anywhere can be the

1

place for prayer. The prayer does not have to be long and extensive.
It can be a short simple prayer, like thanking God for watching me up
this mourning and giving me strength to attend school, that will not
interfer with time used for getting an education. The prayer does not
even have to be aloud. God sees the heart. Silent prayers are just
as effective. One prayer that I used to use in class went like this:

> "Dear God, I want to thank you for my life,
> health, and strength. I ask that you protect
> me through the day. Amen."

Atheists are among the people who wanted prayer out of school.
These people do not believe there is a God. Naturally, they pass it
on to their children. They do not want their children exposed to
religion in school. Some say the prayer was forced on the students.
If prayer was optional in schools, the students would be given a
choice.

[Opposite of the atheist's beliefs,] But some parents believe in god
and want Him in every aspect of their child's life. These are the
people that suffer from the decision to take prayer out of school.
They can not practice their religious beliefs in school and therefore they have
no religious freedom. One of my friends told me, "I was really
shocked when they [Congress] passed the law taking prayer out of
schools. How could they do that? Religious freedom is given to us by
the constitution. I felt so deprived!" How would the opposition feel
if one of their inalienable rights, such as liberty, taken away from
them? They would be very upset. Well, this is how we feel. This is a
grave injustice to some of the Americans.

In the 1700's and 1800's, thousands of people set out for this

2

country. Many had suffered beatings and imprisonment in their home country because of their religious preferences. News had gotten to them that they would be able to practice their choice of religion in the New World. It was known to some as a religious haven. During the journey, which sometimes lasted for three months, many contracted diseases and some lost their lives. Now, some of their descendents are being deprived of that self-same freedom. No compromises were made when the decision was finalized to remove prayer from schools. These people have a right to practice their religious beliefs. Just as students are given the choice of saluting the flag, they should be given the choice to pray.

Now that you have gotten such a good start on this complex topic, you need to get more information. See the Supreme Court decision (the reference librarian will show you where it is) and notice the arguments.

You have a conflict here between two versions of "freedom," which you need to define carefully. The paper is not yet convincing, and you need to develop definitions and arguments to make it so.

3

Writing 15
Donna R.
Paper 5: Final Draft

The Right to Pray

It is nine o'clock a.m. seven years ago in a small classroom. A
bell rings to signify the beginning of school. "Would everyone please
stand for the flag salute and a moment of silence," blares over the
intercom. Twenty-seven sixth graders noisily shift chairs and stand
to their feet. After they salute the flag, the teacher asks, "Who
would like to lead us in prayer today?" Every child raises a hand and
shouts, "Me, me, me!"

These days have been long lost. Prayer in schools has been
abolished because it has been argued that it interfers with some of
the children's religious preferences. But what about the other kids?
They are being deprived of a religious freedom. To give both the
religious preference and freedom the constitution grants, prayer
should be present, but optional, in schools.

We believe the reason this country is in such a bad shape is
because it has turned away from God. One example is taking prayer out
of schools. With all of the trouble and evil in the world, we want
our children to learn to ask for God's protection. Now more than ever
protection in school is essential. Schools are now corupt with drugs,
fights and murders, and they are getting worse as times passes. God
is the only one able to protect kids while they attend school.

The people who oppose prayer in school say school is not the
place for prayer. Schools are for learning. Anywhere can be the

1

place for prayer. The prayer does not have to be long and extensive.
It can be a short simple prayer, like thanking God for watching me up
this mourning and giving me strength to attend school, that will not
interfer with time used for getting an education. The prayer does not
even have to be aloud. God sees the heart. Silent prayers are just
as effective. One prayer that I used to use in class went like this:

> "Dear God, I want to thank you for my life,
> health, and strength. I ask that you protect
> me through the day. Amen."

Atheist are among the people who wanted prayer out of school.
These people do not believe there is a God. Naturally, they pass it
on to their children. They do not want their children exposed to
religion in school. Some say the prayer was forced on the students.
If prayer was optional in schools, the students would be given a
choice.

Opposite of the atheist's beliefs, some parents believe in god
and want Him in every aspect of their child's life. These are the
people that suffer from the decision to take prayer out of school.
They can not practice their religious beliefs and therefore they have
no religious freedom. One of my friends told me, "I was really
shocked when they [Congress] passed the law taking prayer out of
schools. How could they do that? Religious freedom is given to us by
the constitution. I felt so deprived!" How would the opposition feel
if one of their inalienable rights, such as liberty, taken away from
them? They would be very upset. Well, this is how we feel. This is a
grave injustice to some of the Americans.

In the 1700's and 1800's, thousands of people set out for this

2

country. Many had suffered beatings and imprisonment in their home
country because of their religious preferences. News had gotten to
them that they would be able to practice their choice of religion in
the New World. It was known to some as a religious haven. During the
journey, which sometimes lasted for three months, many contracted
diseases and some lost their lives. Now, some of their descendents
are being deprived of that self-same freedom. No compromises were
made when the decision was finalized to remove prayer from schools.
These people have a right to practice their religious beliefs. Just
as students are given the choice of saluting the flag, they should be
given the choice to pray.

SEE PREVIOUS PAGE, AND FINAL COMMENT.

NOT ACCORDING TO YOUR FIRST #. IT LOOKED AS IF ALL HAD TO SALUTE

When one is trying to convince
another person or persons of
he soundness of one's views on
an issue on which you and
they disagree, one has to be
sure that one understands the issue
clearly. In this instance I'm
not sure you state *clearly* the issue you
are raising. Are you urging that
there be public, group silent
prayer daily in school for a
stated period of time, for all
students at the same time? Or
are you urging that students
be allowed to pray silently during
school hours at times of their choice?
If you are urging the latter, why
can't students pray silently even
now, when they wish? If you're urging
the former, you should make that clear.
And you should take more extensive account of why those who do not
agree with you take a different view. In order to consider the
views of these others, you should probably have done some reading,
or interviewed some of those who differ with you, so as to be able
to understand and state their views clearly.

I'd urge, also, that you think carefully about statements suggesting
that without the opportunity to pray in the schools, people have
lost their religious freedom. Do people not have all of the
days when they are not in school for communal prayers of their

3

(over)

choice, and many of the minutes when they are in school for
silent prayer of their choice? In these circumstances, can it
fairly be said that religious freedom has been lost?
If you think it can fairly be said that religious freedom
has been lost, then why do you think so?

If time allows, I'd encourage you to revise this essay
and resubmit it. I'll withhold a final grade in the course
for you until I receive the revision, if you elect to do
one.

This is a better focused paper than the other two in this portfolio. It is clearer in this paper (though still not
totally clear) what you want to focus on. In that sense
the paper is an improvement over the previous two. I'd
encourage you now to make this one still better.

```
Writing 15
Donna R.
Paper 5:  Final Draft
```

                        The Right to Pray

        It is nine o'clock a.m. seven years ago in a small classroom. A

bell rings to signify the beginning of school. "Would everyone please

stand for the flag salute and a moment of silence," blares over the

intercom. Twenty-seven sixth graders noisily shift chairs and stand

to their feet. After they salute the flag, the teacher asks, "Who

would like to lead us in prayer today?" Every child raises a hand and

shouts, "Me, me, me!"

This is an effective beginning for me -- dramatic and poignant.

I hear your regret already. These days have been long lost. Prayer in schools has been

what would be the effect of postponing it until later in the paper? abolished because it has been argued that it interfers with some of

the children's religious preferences. But what about the other kids?

They are being deprived of a religious freedom. To give both the

religious preference and freedom the constitution grants, prayer

should be present, but optional, in schools.

        (We) believe the reason this country is in such a bad shape is

because it has turned away from God. One example is taking prayer out

of schools. With all of the trouble and evil in the world, (we) want

our children to learn to ask for ~~God's~~ protection. Now more than ever

Are you speaking on behalf of a group, here? should you identify them or use I? protection in school is essential. Schools are now corupt with drugs,

fights and murders, and they are getting worse as times passes. God

is the only one able to protect kids while they attend school.

Your argume seems to be that the only hope for problem that face school: is divine intervention. In terms of your audience, who is likely to accept this argument?

        The people who oppose prayer in school say school is not the

place for prayer. Schools are for learning. Anywhere can be the

                                1

place for prayer. The prayer does not have to be long and extensive.

It can be a short simple prayer, like thanking God for watching me up

this mourning [*SP*] and giving me strength to attend school, that will not

interfer with time used for getting an education. The prayer does not

even have to be aloud. God sees the heart. Silent prayers are just

as effective. One prayer that I used to use in class went like this:

> "Dear God, I want to thank you for my life,
> health, and strength. I ask that you protect
> me through the day. Amen."

Atheist [*S*] are among the people who wanted prayer out of school.

These people do not believe there is a God. Naturally, they pass (it) *their... beliefs?*

on to their children. They do not want their children exposed to

religion in school. Some say the prayer was forced on the students.

If prayer was optional in schools, the students would be given a

choice.

Opposite of the atheist's beliefs, some parents believe in god

and want Him in every aspect of their child's life. These are the

people that suffer from the decision to take prayer out of school.

They can not practice their religious beliefs and therefore they have   *I like your*

no religious freedom. One of my friends told me, "I was really   *use of*

shocked when they [Congress] passed the law taking prayer out of   *quote*

schools. How could they do that? Religious freedom is given to us by   *from*

the constitution. I felt so deprived!" How would the opposition feel   *friend*

if one of their inalienable rights, such as liberty, were taken away from

them? They would be very upset. Well, this is how we feel. This is a

grave injustice to some of the Americans.

In the 1700's and 1800's, thousands of people set out for this

what right would the "opposition" say they are losing if there is prayer in schools? How would you answer them?

country. Many had suffered beatings and imprisonment in their home country because of their religious preferences. News had gotten to them that they would be able to practice their choice of religion in the New World. It was known to some as a religious haven. During the journey, which sometimes lasted for three months, many contracted diseases and some lost their lives. Now, some of their descendents are being deprived of that self-same freedom. No compromises were made when the decision was finalized to remove prayer from schools. These people have a right to practice their religious beliefs. Just as students are given the choice of saluting the flag, they should be given the choice to pray.

Historical arguments can be powerful. But how would the "opposition" answer your point?

Donna— this paper would work well for readers who already believe in the right to pray in schools, but not, I don't think, for the "opposition," the people who hold different beliefs.

Let me show you what I mean. Re-read your paper, and mark all the words and phrases you use to refer to people who believe in prayer in schools. Then go back and mark the terms used to refer to people who oppose prayer in schools. What do you notice about your choice of terminology for the two groups? What do your choices tell you about your relationship to your audience? Who is your audience? If it includes people who oppose prayer in schools, will your paper persuade them

↓

to think differently? Why or why not?

Sorry to bombard you with questions! But I know it's difficult to find a way to talk persuasively to the "opposition" about issues that you feel deeply about, and I'm hoping the questions will prompt you to think a little more about what is involved in argumentation for an academic audience.

Discussion of Responses to "THE RIGHT TO PRAY"
Featured Responders: Elbow, White, Larson, Hull
Featured Issues:
- **Arguments that readers find problematic**
- **Portfolios**

In choosing this essay, we were interested in two questions. First, how would the teachers in our study respond to a student who has written an argument that makes assumptions that will be unacceptable to the readers she is supposed to be addressing? Second, how would these teachers respond to a student's semester portfolio?

All of the readers of this essay tell the writer that, as it stands, the essay does not work. White suggests that the student add information and clarify definitions—especially what she means by "freedom." Elbow also implies that she needs to examine the meaning of freedom. He says that her opening example shows that prayer in schools actually denies freedom to the atheistic child. Hull also deals with this issue, asking Donna what right her "opposition" would be losing if prayer should be put back in school.

Larson counters Donna's argument from a slightly different perspective, asking her how eliminating the chance for group prayer prevents anyone from practicing his/her belief in silent prayer. Stewart, whose response is not presented above, also makes this point in asking the following questions:

> Does it [taking prayer out of schools] prevent you from attending the church of your choice? Does it prevent you from practicing your religion at home or in informal groups with those who belong to your church or faith? I think not.

McClelland (not presented above) notes that Donna undermines her own argument by saying that prayers can be short and silent. He also suggests that Donna deal with what the Constitution says about separation of church and state. Similarly, O'Hare (not presented above) tells Donna that she has failed "to mention a central issue in the controversy: the Constitution's separation of Church and State."

It is clear, then, that all of the readers see Donna's argument as problematic. They point to her inexact definition of key terms, such as "freedom" and "separation of church and state," and her flawed logic, that is, the assumption that taking prayer out of schools denies one freedom of worship. However, they do not give Donna much insight into how she might go about constructing a workable argument. If taking prayer out of schools does not impinge on religious freedom and, in fact, putting it in schools would, then how can Donna construct a successful argument for her point of view?

The readers devote most of their response, not to constructing a better argument, but rather to how Donna can frame her argument for her intended audience. Hull assigns Donna an exercise designed to help her discover problems in her tone. Anson, whose response is not presented above, spends nearly all of his time explaining why this essay will be ineffective with the "intended" audience. He uses a well-developed analogy in which he asks Donna to consider how she would write to a landlord, for whom she has little regard but needs something from, and compare that tone with the one she is using here. Near the end of his comment, he asks Donna to "try to imagine someone you really like and trust, who doesn't go along with your views," in order to approach the essay in a less "harsh, a less adversarial way." O'Hare also wants Donna to reconsider her tone; he asks Donna if she has discussed the issue with people who disagree with her position. McClelland tells Donna that the assignment asked her to write for readers who are in need of convincing; he goes on to show her why her essay will be ineffective with an audience of people opposed to her point of view.

Given their evaluations of the shortcomings of Donna's essay, it is somewhat surprising, perhaps, that six of the eight readers find something positive to say to Donna. However, their remarks are, for the most part, couched in guarded terms, as the following examples illustrate:

This is a better focused paper than the other two in this portfolio. It is clearer in this paper (though still not totally clear) what you want to focus on. In that sense the paper is an improvement over the previous two. (Larson)

You argue most effectively for your point in the short, fifth paragraph. (McClelland)

Your conclusion is fairly effective but the compromises you mention should have been dealt with in detail. (O'Hare)

Such faint praise as this is found mixed with some of the harshest criticism given to any of the essays used in our study. For example:

[I]n the third paragraph you launch into a negative statement that qualifies for the description "religious tirade." (McClelland)

In this paper, you virtually ignore your opponent's arguments. . . . You have dealt with an important subject superficially. (O'Hare)

After this you seem to hop from one point to another, like a rabbit hitting different patches of clover in a meadow. I don't have any sense of a sustained and developed argument or set of arguments. I have more a sense of your putting down what has come into your head, probably from outside influences, at random. . . . Overall, and I'm sorry to say it, this is not a very good paper. (Stewart)

Not all of the readers are so openly critical, but, as a group, they are certainly more critical of this essay than of any other essay in the sampling. It would appear that the readers' reactions are caused, at least in part, by the way Donna approaches this essay. She is writing from a point of view inside a group, and despite the directions in her assignment to write for readers who do not agree with her on this issue, she has invoked an audience that adheres to the basic tenets of this group, as the following passage indicates:

We believe the reason this country is in such a bad shape is because it has turned away from God. With all of the trouble and evil in the world, we want our children to learn to ask for God's protection.

Nearly all of the readers respond directly to this passage. White underlines the "we" at the beginning of the passage and asks "who is this?" Hull circles the "we," and asks: "Are you speaking on behalf of a group here? Should you identify them or use I?" Other readers respond to this passage in the endnotes they write to the student:

There's a lot of that accusatory tone still, in fact in some ways it's even stronger, especially with this 'we' pronoun that you use, because that makes it seem as if you're writing as part of some coalition. (Anson)

The third paragraph begins with "We" with no attempt to explain who is being referred to. (O'Hare)

That "we" on the first page made it seem for a moment as though you weren't giving your own thoughts but just quoting what others say in some pamphlet. But it didn't *sound* as though you were doing that. Can't you say "I"? (Elbow)

Too many of your arguments sound like those you have been given by conservative religious groups or their spokesmen. I cease hearing Donna R. telling me why prayer should be allowed and hear, instead, someone else talking through Donna R. (Stewart)

Although many of the readers seem troubled by Donna's failure to identify with (and speak to) an audience that might disagree with her, only one of the readers, Glynda Hull, expresses any doubt that Donna can write a successful essay on this topic. According to Hull, Donna is a student who "believes deeply in having prayer in schools," and is hindered by those beliefs from seeing her audience's point of view. To make any progress, Donna "must understand the relationship she's set up with the audience, the people she's supposed to persuade." Hull believes Donna is reducing matters to a "we/us" level, and she suggests that Donna go back to the essay and look at the terms she has used to name people who believe as she does and people who oppose prayer in the schools. She hopes the exercise will help Donna "imagine the opposition's point of view." On reflection, however, Hull is not very hopeful that her tactic will work, as her note to us indicates:

> As I re-read my comments, I know that one of the reasons I'm hard on this paper is that I disagree with her. . . . I think this student is drawing for her rhetoric on a membership in a discourse community that I don't belong to. In some ways, it is not going to be possible for her to persuade people like me. It would be interesting to let this paper raise this issue in class discussion.

Next we move to the question of how the readers responded to a portfolio. We presented three essays by a student and gave readers the choice of responding to all three essays, or to limit their responses to the last essay in the collection.* With the exception of Elbow, all the teachers who responded to this assignment chose to focus on the last paper.

Four of the teachers do acknowledge the portfolio in their responses or their notes to us. In her note to us, Hull says that in order to comment on the first two papers she would have to know what she had suggested on earlier drafts. Larson refers to the portfolio in telling Donna that "The Right to Pray" is the best of the three essays in the group because its focus is clearer; he makes no further mention of the portfolio, however. In his note to us, White remarks that the first two papers "show gaps in logic and inability to use sources well."

Elbow is alone in responding to the entire portfolio. In his note to us, he says that he is assuming a system such as the one he worked with at Stony Brook: Donna is handing this portfolio to him in preparation for submitting it to the outside portfolio readers at the end of the term. He will suggest any changes he thinks necessary before the portfolio is turned in. In order to show us how he functions as a "coach" in a portfolio system, Elbow creates a context that includes the comments he has made on previous drafts of each of the essays in this group. With such a backdrop, Elbow's comments to the writer of "The Right to Pray" take on the character of a conversation that has been going on throughout the semester.

*   *   *

We come now to the end of one part of our study and the beginning of its second phase. We have presented sample essays and allowed the teachers' responses to these essays to, more or less, speak for themselves. In Chapter 3, we present a rubric for analyzing teacher comments, and in Chapter 4 we use that rubric and our readers' responses to other sample essays to develop detailed analyses of their responding styles.

*We are using the term broadly here to refer to a group of essays chosen by the student to represent his work in a given course. We are aware that many writers such as Kathleen Yancey, and the writers represented in her collection, *Portfolios in Practice: Voices from the Field*, use the term in a much more narrow and exacting fashion.

3 | A Method for Analyzing Teacher Comments

Even after a brief survey it is clear that the 12 readers' responses differ markedly from traditional ways of responding to student writing and, in their broad outline, reflect many of the practices endorsed by contemporary theory. These readers respond in full and often highly elaborate statements, not in symbols, abbreviations, or the cryptic language that only teachers use when they mark student writing. They spend most of their time commenting on matters of content, organization, and purpose, often in subtle and complex ways, and give only moderate attention to the obvious and outward features of writing: mechanics, word choice, sentence structure, and style. Beyond the conventional forms of teacher commentary—criticism, commands, and corrections—they make regular use of advice, descriptions, reader responses, and all manner of questions. These are not the kind of responses that Sommers (1982) criticized as vague, contradictory, unhelpful, and mean-spirited. They are the kind she called for when she said:

> Our comments need to offer students revision tasks of a different order of complexity and sophistication . . . , by forcing students back into the chaos, back to the point where they are shaping and restructuring their meaning. (p. 156)

Given their richness and complexity, we had to find a way to describe precisely what they did in their responses and to make distinctions among their responding styles. The difficulty in such a task may be seen easily enough in the following sets of responses, presented in end comments by three of our readers on Writing 6, "The Four Seasons." The first example is an excerpt from Donald Stewart's detailed letter to the student:

> [N]ow we run into some problems. Have you described the four seasons in Syracuse, or have you described four idealized seasons? I think the latter, and I'll tell you why. In describing Spring, you mention the trees blossoming, flowers working their way out of the ground, geese flying overhead, and a long winter's nap ending for bears, squirrels, rabbits and other hibernating animals. These are all cliches about Spring. If you must use them, particularize them. Instead of telling us about blossoming trees, tell us how you look forward to the blooming of the redbud tree in your front yard, and of the flowering crab which follows right behind it. Tell us about the particular flowers which blossom in your yard in Syracuse. We'll skip the geese, but let's take a hard look at your list of hibernating animals. How many bears roam the streets of Syracuse? Or do you make frequent trips to the zoo to see them come out of hibernation? If you lived in Yellowstone Park in the winter, mention of hibernating bears would be quite natural. Here, a reader does a double take. What bears are there in Syracuse, or anywhere nearby? Even more to the point, tree squirrels do not hibernate. In winter they are busy digging in places where they buried seeds during the summer. Are you talking about ground squirrels? Do they live in Syracuse? Rabbits don't hibernate either. The fact that

you used these examples suggests to me that you were just tossing off cliched descriptions of Spring rather than giving us some honest description of Spring in Syracuse. There were, however, a couple of places where you provided some very fine detail. For example, the line, "the faint smell of pollen lingers in the air" is terrific. That's a superb detail. Even the moist ground wanting to seep into one's shoes is pretty good.

The second example comes from Patricia Stock's letter to the student:

I thought it was effective of you to contrast the fall, strolling into Tallahassee and shriveling the flowers, with fall parading (You didn't use the word, your description made me feel it.) into Syracuse, showing off its auburn, garnet, and gold leaves. I must say, I liked the fact that you chose auburn as a color because Auburn the city is so close to Syracuse. I actually stopped to think if that might be why Auburn has the name it does. Do you know? And I liked the precious gem, precious metal allusions you invoked by choosing garnet and gold as colors. The season moves you inward into enclosed, secure beds of leaves and outward into majestic displays of ornamental leaves.

If you had not told me that winter was your second favorite season, I would not have guessed it. I would have guessed it was spring because your descriptions of spring have almost as much vitality as your descriptions of fall. As I read the section of your essay you devoted to winter, I was struck by how heavily you relied on overused language to express your feelings about Syracuse's winters (my understanding is that Syracuse's winters are WINTERS). I guess you were aware of your reliance on all-too-familiar language yourself because you enclosed some of it in quotation marks: "winter wonderland," "feel Jack Frost nipping at your nose." To be sure, it is a tough problem: How to communicate one's special understandings. After all, you have not invented the language, you have inherited it. All you have in language is what you have been given. I find, however, that you can take the given and give it an original turn ("soft scrunching of that magical white carpet underneath your feet"), and as I read your essays, I hope for that from you. I'm actually anticipating your development as an even more creative, even more effective writer this semester.

The third example is Glynda Hull's endnote to David, in its entirety:

You've got an unusual paper here in that some readers will love it and some will feel just as strongly in the opposite direction. What I want you to do is to figure out what it is about your paper, and about different readers, that could produce such different reactions. For example:

1. Your seasonal portraits could have, with a few exceptions, been written by someone who grew up in Tallahassee. What will some readers like about this quality; what will others dislike?
2. You say at the end of your paper that you've told only the good things about the seasons. Why might this be pleasant to some readers but offensive to others?
3. You use a lot of phrases that are often used in conjunction with the seasons. Again, what will some readers like about this, others dislike, and why?

Given your consideration of these questions, would you now make any changes in your paper? Why or why not?

On a first reading, what stands out in these three sets of responses are their similarities. All three engage in full-fledged discussions with the writer, focus on the cliched language and content of the writing, and offer specific ways to turn the student back into the process of revision. Yet each set clearly differs from the others. Whereas Stewart and Stock go into great detail in their comments, Hull limits herself to several general statements and questions.

Although all three readers directly address the issue of cliched language, they choose somewhat different ways of talking about the problem:

Stewart: [N]ow we run into some problems. . . . In describing Spring, you mention the trees blossoming, flowers working their way out of the ground, geese flying north overhead, and a long winter's nap ending for bears, squirrels, rabbits and other hibernating animals. These are all cliches about Spring.

Stock: As I read the section of your essay you devoted to winter, I was struck by how heavily you relied on overused language to express your feelings about Syracuse's winters (my understanding is that Syracuse's winters are WINTERS). I guess you were aware of your reliance on all-too-familiar language yourself because you enclosed some of it in quotation marks: "winter wonderland," "feel Jack Frost nipping at your nose."

Hull: You use a lot of phrases that are often used in conjunction with the seasons. Again, what will some readers like about this, others dislike, and why?

Stewart comes right out and criticizes the student's use of cliches. Stock makes something of the same assessment, but mutes her criticism, and Hull seems to go out of her way to avoid making any negative comments at all. Although all three readers seem to present some kind of evaluation of the writing, it can hardly be said that their ways of presenting these evaluations to the student are the same. Further, both Stewart and Hull present a large portion of their comments in the form of questions. But even here some distinctions might be made, as the following examples show:

Stewart: What bears are there in Syracuse, or anywhere nearby? Even more to the point, tree squirrels do not hibernate. In winter they are busy digging in places where they buried seeds during the summer. Are you talking about ground squirrels? Do they live in Syracuse?

Hull: Your seasonal portraits could have, with a few exceptions, been written by someone who grew up in Tallahassee. What will some readers like about this quality? What will others dislike?

Whereas Stewart seems to have a definite agenda behind the questions he asks, some specific answer or place he wants the student to come to, Hull is content to pose an open-ended question for the student to consider on his own. Stewart and Hull also both call on the student to engage in certain revisions. Here again, though, they take different tacts:

Stewart: If you must use [these cliched expressions], particularize them. Instead of telling us about blossoming trees, tell us how you look forward to the blooming of the redbud tree in your front yard, and of the flowering crab which follows right behind it. Tell us about the particular flowers which blossom in your yard in Syracuse.

Hull: What I want you to do is to figure out what it is about your paper, and about different readers, that could produce such different reactions.

Whereas Stewart uses direct commands to prompt the student to make particular changes in the text, Hull gives the student an issue to think about as a writer. Interestingly, Stock follows her close reading with still a different type of response:

To be sure, it is a tough problem: How to communicate one's special understandings. After all, you have not invented the language, you have inherited it. All you have in language is what you have been given. I find, however, that you can take the given and give it an original turn. . . .

This commentary does not describe or evaluate the writing. It does not call on the student to make a revision. It does not offer advice. It is a kind of lesson, a strategy the teachers regularly employ in their responses.

From the start, we were interested in analyzing *what* these teachers respond to and *how* they present their comments. We wanted to know the extent to which they emphasize the content and purpose of student writing, as contemporary composition studies suggest teachers should, and we wanted to know how they deal with local matters of writing: sentence structure, wording, and correctness. We also wanted to examine how often these teachers make corrections to student texts or criticized the writing, for instance, or how often they frame their comments in the form of interpretations and questions.

Any method of classifying these readers' comments would have to provide a way to make sharp distinctions that would capture the diversity in their comments and the patterns that make up their individual styles. Because the readers make a majority of their comments on the content and purpose of writing, methods of analysis that distinguish a series of discrete categories for local matters but establish only one area for content would not be adequate for our purposes. We needed a way of capturing the different ways they respond to the writer's ideas and deal with the various factors that influence the content and structure of student writing. Similarly, methods that distinguish only a few, broad types of response—implicit or explicit, brief or extensive, positive or negative, directive or facilitative, reader-based or criteria-based—would not allow us to adequately distinguish among their ways of framing their comments.[1] All 12 of the readers regularly make comments that explicitly present their readings and their calls for revision. They all make comments that are detailed and text-specific and that guide—not dictate—revision. They also have a variety of ways of presenting both positive and negative commentary. Although some readers make greater use of reader responses than others, the distinction between reader-based and criteria-based response would also be too broad for our purposes because all of the readers base most of their comments on criteria-based concerns.

Not even more elaborate methods of classification would be adequate to capture the nuances we wanted to capture. Although fairly detailed, Lees' (1979) division of response into seven modes—correcting, emoting, describing, suggesting, questioning, reminding, and assigning—would not provide categories that were precise enough to see distinctions in the ways these teachers evaluate writing and call on the student to make revisions.[2] Searle and Dillon's (1980) system offers a fairly detailed analysis of what teachers address in their comments, identifying one broad area for content and three subcategories under form: "style," "structure," and "mechanics." But the system provides only three broad categories for how comments may be presented: as "evaluations" of the writing, as "assessments" of the student's abilities, or as "instructions" (including explanations, corrections, and encouragement) (p. 236).[3]

Influenced by the recent scholarship of Sommers and Knoblauch and Brannon, we wanted, in particular, to look at how the readers responded to student writing in terms of teacher control, one of the central issues in contemporary composition theory and practice. How much, and in what ways, can teachers most productively intervene in students' writing? Such a lens would also allow us to investigate some of the most compelling questions about teacher response:

How much should teachers decide what specifically needs to be revised in a piece of writing? How much should they allow students to make their own choices as writers?

To what extent should teachers lay out definite plans for helping students improve a piece of writing and guide them to produce polished written products? To what extent should they use their responses to turn students back into their writing and give them practice in certain writing activities?

We were particularly interested in the extent to which our teachers would make use of what Knoblauch and Brannon call *directive* and *facilitative* commentary.

In *Rhetorical Traditions and the Teaching of Writing*, in one of the most comprehensive and insightful treatments on response, Knoblauch and Brannon (1984) use these terms to distinguish between two general types of teacher commentary according to the degree to which the teacher takes control over the student's writing. In *directive* commentary, the teacher takes excessive control over the writing and prescribes what the writer should do (or should have done). The function of such commentary is "either simply to label the errors in writing or to define restrictively what a student would (or will) have to do in order to perfect it in the teacher's eyes" (p. 123). They consider the following comments part of a directive style because they assert the teacher's agenda to such an extent that they overlook the student's purposes for writing and diminish her role in deciding on revisions:

This is obvious—cut it out.
Rephrase.
Run on sentence. Break it up.
Unnecessary—this weakens what you want to say.
Unclear!
Keep yourself out of the essay. This is a formal essay. (pp. 123-125)

In *facilitative* commentary, the teacher refrains from taking control over the text. Instead of pointing to problems or telling the writer what to do, the teacher dramatizes a reader's understanding of the text, so that the writer may see where the writing is and is not yet realizing her intentions. Facilitative readers try "to preserve the writer's control of the discourse" (p. 128) and treat the text at "the level of meaning, line of reasoning, intellectual potentiality" (p. 128). Knoblauch and Brannon cite the following comments as characteristic of a facilitative style:

How important are these factors? Do you imply that they are relative or that they don't always matter? Is your essay going to be about these factors?

What criteria lead you to decide this? Size? Location? Program offerings? The kind of student body?

If some are "lower ranked" then in what sense are they all "the same."

Is this a difference between colleges? Are you saying that it really doesn't matter? Do you believe that?

This sounds interesting—have you been rejected? Would it be worth talking about? (pp. 126-127)

The purpose of such response, they note, is "to create motivation for immediate and substantive revision by describing a careful reader's uncertainties about what a writer intends to say" (p. 126). Whereas directive comments project the teacher's vision for the writing onto the student, facilitative comments guide the student to consider where the text is allowing her to achieve her intentions and how it might be made to work better. The emphasis is on helping the student make improvements, not on pointing out problems or necessary changes.

Although Knoblauch and Brannon suggest that directive comments tend to focus on correctness, organization, and style and to take the form of commands and criticism, and although they suggest that facilitative comments tend to focus on the student's overall content and purpose and to take the form of praise and questions, they claim that the difference between the two does not lie in the outward form of the comments.[4] Rather, they say, it lies in the attitudes or the stance of the teacher behind the comments:

The essential difference between the two commenting styles is the degree of control over choices that the writer or the teacher retains. In directive commentary, the teacher says or implies, "Don't do it your way; do it *this* way." In facilitative commentary, the teacher says or implies, "Here's what your choices have caused me to think you're saying—if my response differs from your intent, how can you help me to see what you mean?" The essential difference . . . lies more in attitude and outlook than in perceivable changes of technique. (p. 129)

Thus, rather than conducting a comment-by-comment analysis of teacher response, Knoblauch and Brannon look to discern the general trend of a given set of responses, whether they are *mostly* directive or *mostly* facilitative.

Knoblauch and Brannon's discussion of teacher control was a valuable starting point for our analysis. Their pioneering work encourages teachers to reflect on their styles of commenting and offers them a new language for distinguishing between comments that tell the student what is right and wrong in her writing and comments that consciously attempt to engage the student in taking up global revisions. Their talk about the teacher's "idealized text" and "students' rights to their own texts" has helped teachers become more aware of the roles they assume and the relationships they establish with students when they respond to their writing. It also has pointed to ways that teachers could put the clarion call to "teach writing as a process" into practice.

But given the rich and subtle diversity among the readers' comments, we were led to make finer and finer distinctions than Knoblauch and Brannon make, both about what teachers focus on in their responses and how they frame their comments. We designed a method of analysis that would allow us to distinguish among the different ways these teachers talk about large conceptual matters of content, context, and form, to describe the different ways in which their comments are directive and facilitative, and generally to study the different ways they exert control over student writing.

ANALYZING THE FOCUS AND MODE OF TEACHER COMMENTS

Our method of analysis provides two perspectives from which to examine a teacher's written comments. The "focus" identifies *what* a comment refers to in the writing—for instance, whether the comment mainly addresses the writer's wording, organization, or ideas. The second perspective allows us to examine *how* the comment is framed. It directs our attention to the shape of the comment, or what we call its "mode." The mode of commentary characterizes the image a teacher creates for herself and the degree of control she exerts, through that comment, over the student's writing.

We examine the focus and mode of each teacher comment—in effect, each new statement the teacher makes to the student, whether it appears in isolation or as part of a cluster of comments, whether it is placed in the margins or in a separate note. We classify each comment into one of 7 categories under "focus" and into one of 10 categories under "mode."[5] Table 3.1 outlines our rubric for analyzing teacher comments:

Table 3.1. Categories for Analyzing Comments.

FOCUS	MODE
Global	Corrections
Ideas	Evaluations
Development	Qualified Negative Evaluations
Global Structure	Imperatives
	Advice
Local	Praise
Local Structure	
Wording	Indirect Requests
Correctness	Problem-Posing Questions
	Heuristic Questions
Extra-Textual	Reflective Statements

Essentially, the various focuses of commentary may be seen in terms of three broad categories: local issues, global issues, or issues about the larger contexts of writing. **Local structure, wording,** and **correctness** deal with microscopic areas in student texts, or *local matters*:

You might try to combine these sentences.

Good, sharp naming.

You can use some type of punctuation here.

Ideas, development, and **global structure** deal with macroscopic areas in student texts, or *global matters*:

This is an insightful observation.

You might add some explanation about how these drugs are dangerous.

In what way do these two paragraphs go with your ideas on page 1?

Other comments go beyond the immediate concerns of the text and deal with the *contexts* that inform a piece of writing. These **extra-textual comments** call attention, for example, to the rhetorical context or the classroom setting:

Who do you envision as the main audience for this paper?

The assignment also asked you to express your views.

Similarly, the various modes of commentary may be seen in terms of several general functions. When responding, teachers frame their comments in essentially five ways, with different modes assuming different degrees of control. They *correct* the writing by making changes in the student's text. That is, they make **corrections**:

[The teacher changes "its" to "it is" in a student sentence.]

They *evaluate* the writing in various ways, through **negative evaluations, qualified negative evaluations,** and **praise**:

This point is underdeveloped.

I'm not sure I see your point.

An insightful observation.

They also *explicitly call on* the student to make revisions, by way of **imperative comments** or **advice**:

> Add more details.
>
> I'd consider adding another example.

These types of commentary exert appreciable control over the writing. Through the use of other types of comments, teachers may temper their control. They may *indirectly call* on the student to revise the writing by way of **questions**, whether they are open questions or closed:

> In what ways was it a "delightful" relationship?
>
> How have your views about the relationship changed?
>
> Was it your first date?
>
> Can't you say this about any couples?

And they may use **interpretive comments, explanatory comments,** and **reader responses** to *reflect on* their understanding of the text or *explain* the meaning of their other responses:

> You seem to have two main points in the paper.
>
> One way to emphasize a point is to hold the news for the end of the sentence.
>
> As I read your essay, I thought about my own memories of Boston.

Whereas some teachers base their responses on controlling modes of commentary, others make extensive use of less controlling modes. By charting a teacher's responses comment-by-comment in terms of her focus and mode and studying the patterns in the larger context of her commentary, we can identify a reader's predominant features of response and describe her responding style. In the following sections, we explain the focuses and modes of teacher comments in detail.

The Focuses of Commentary

The focus of a comment describes what a comment refers to, whether it is a formal feature in the student's text or a feature of some larger context of the writing. Most classification systems either pose only broad, highly generalized categories such as "form" and "content" or, when they establish more specific categories, give a disproportionate weight to the more distinguishable features of writing: diction, style, structure, and mechanics. We have identified six formal categories of response—three dealing with global matters (ideas, development, global structure) and three dealing with local matters (local structure, wording, correctness). We identify one additional category for comments that treat issues beyond the immediate text, for example, comments about voice, audience, the assignment, and the student's composing processes (extra-textual comments).

Ideas

Under "ideas," we place comments that deal with matters of content at or beyond the level of the sentence: the thoughts, assertions, arguments, lines of thought, and reasoning of the writing.[6] The following examples show the vast range of comments that are placed in this category:

- An insightful observation.
- I like this passage.
- This paper is filled with excellent descriptions.
- Your text is more effective in the winter scene than elsewhere.
- Do a little check on the reasoning behind your statements.

Comments about "ideas" are distinguished from comments about "development," "wording," and "global structure" by the language of the teacher's comment. If a comment about the content of the writing does not draw attention to the selection of individual words or to the need for development, we place it under "ideas." The following comments, for example, would be labeled as ideas:

- Text: "People abuse their right to use alcoholic beverages."
  Response: "All people?"

- Text: "Why allow something to be done when it is wrong?"
  Response: "Do you mean morally wrong or dangerous?"

These comments would have been placed under "wording" if they had read:

- Text: "People abuse their right to use alcoholic beverages."
  Response: "Get more precise."

- Text: "Why allow something to be done when it is wrong?"
  Response: "'Wrong' seems inexact or inappropriate."

If a comment about the main ideas in a piece of writing does not call attention to the organization or form of the essay, we place it under "ideas," not "global structure." For example:

- This seems to be one of your most important ideas.
- Are these your two main concerns in the essay?

Development

Comments about "development" ask for additional support, definition, elaboration, or explanation of the writer's ideas. They do not call for new ideas or assertions so much as they ask for the development of statements that are already present in the text. The teacher does not question or disapprove of what the writer says, but simply calls for more information. This information requires additional sentences (not just additional words or phrases) and can be added to the text without making significant changes in the existing structure. Here are some examples:

- What happened? Tell us more.
- Evidence? Examples?—Can you provide a definition?
- Characterize the "feeling" a bit more.
- What else could you say in favor of your position?

Comments that acknowledge or compliment the writer's detail, examples, definitions, or support are considered as "ideas," not as "development," because the material is already present in the writing and is not being requested:

- Good use of examples.
- This is the kind of elaboration that helps me follow what you're saying.

Global Structure

We use the term "global structure" for comments that are concerned with the organization of large units of discourse. This category includes comments about the overall arrangement of the essay, the relation of materials within different paragraphs, and the order of paragraphs. It also includes comments about the effectiveness of introductions and conclusions:

- Does this paragraph belong with your discussion of membership?
- How does this personal narrative fit in with your informative aim?
- Seems like you've tried to build yourself a good framework and foundation.
- Okay—I see you're setting up the paper as the assignment suggested.

The category includes comments about the unity, coherence, and emphasis of the essay as a whole:

- You seem to get off track here.
- Why do you include these points when you don't refer to them later?

It also includes comments about the thesis, focus, or main point(s) of the writing—but only when the wording of the comment explicitly calls attention to their function as *structural* features:

- If this is your main idea, put it up in the first paragraph.
- I'd recommend that you focus on your favorite season, fall.

Also included here are comments that deal with the omission of large units of discourse, including the omission of paragraphs:

- Do you need this paragraph?
- This material doesn't seem to add much to your point.

Local Structure

We use "local structure" to identify comments that deal with the structure within a sentence, between consecutive sentences, or within a paragraph. Typically these comments are concerned with the arrangement of sentences (or parts of sentences); the clarity, directness, coherence, and emphasis of sentences; or the connection between sentences:

- I have trouble following this sentence.
- Try to rework these sentences to avoid the repetition.
- How could you combine these sentences?

Also included here are comments that deal with the omission of words, phrases, clauses, and sentences:

- You can cut this word without any loss of meaning.
- I'd consider cutting the last phrase so you can end on a strong note.

Wording

Comments about "wording" deal with the writer's word choice within a sentence. Comments in this category address problems in wording or phrasing—for instance, problems with clarity, economy, or appropriateness:

- Pretentious language.
- Right word?
- What does this refer to?
- [Teacher changes "yelled at the crowd" to "urged the crowd."]

They also address wording within sentences—*naming*—that is sharp, precise, vivid, or insightful:[7]

- Sharp word choice.
- Another neat image.
- The roller coaster image works well.
- This word seems just right for here.

Included in this category are comments that ask the student to get *more specific* with the wording or phrasing *within a sentence*. In such comments the teacher does not disapprove of the wording but simply calls on the writer to provide sharper language or additional detail. The request for greater specification can be addressed by adding a word or phrase or by making a minor substitution in the wording of the sentence:

- Try to get more precise here.
- Which songs?
- First impressions about what? Neatness?
- When did this happen?

Corrections/Conventions

Comments in this category typically deal with errors in grammar, mechanics, punctuation, and spelling—matters that are conventionally viewed in terms of right and wrong, correct and incorrect:

- Subject-verb agreement error.
- Comma splice: should be period or semicolon.
- Commas and periods always go inside quotes.
- You shift tenses in the beginning of paragraph two.

The category also includes comments that deal with formal conventions such as paragraphing, citation and documentation, titles, and manuscript format:

- Start a new paragraph here.
- Captivating title
- Good use of quote.

Extra-Textual Comments

Comments that refer to concerns outside of the formal text—the audience, the writer's intentions or purpose, the topic, the writing assignment, the student's writing activities, and the student's experience—are placed in this category:

- Who is your audience?
- The assignment called for an expository piece.
- You've chosen a good topic for yourself.
- This paper is a real improvement on your previous draft.
- Before beginning a second draft, I suggest you do a barebones outline.
- How much do you know about the seat-belt law?
- Are you exercising your mind as you write or are you coasting?

Comments about voice—that is, the sound of the writing, tone, persona, point of view, authority, the credibility of the writing, and the writer's "own" voices—are also considered "extra-textual":

- Artificial tone.
- This sounds like a news report.
- How do you come across here?
- Your use of second person is effective.
- Your enthusiasm comes through clearly here.

In addition, we place in this category comments that address the essay as a whole and the student's general work on the writing:

- I think you have the makings of a very good paper here.
- This is a very moving and effective piece of writing.
- You've done some promising work here.

We also place here any miscellaneous comments that do not fit into one of the other categories of response, for example, comments about the student's reading of another text or comments in which the teacher tells the student *not* to be concerned about some feature of the writing:

- I read "Young Goodman Brown" somewhat differently from the way you have.
- Because this is a rough draft, you don't need to worry about fine tuning your sentences.

The Orientation of Teacher Comments

As part of our analysis of the focus of teacher commentary, we also note when any comment goes "beyond the text" and makes reference to some context outside the writing itself. Most comments explicitly address only some formal feature of writing, that is, an element that can be seen in the text, as in the following examples:

Good detail.

Combine these sentences.

How does this paragraph relate to the previous one?

Such comments are "oriented" to the formal text. Often, however, a comment addresses or makes some reference to an element of writing that, even as it addresses some formal concern, goes beyond the text, by speaking about the writing topic, the assignment, the audience, another text, the writing classroom, a discourse community or culture, the student's writing processes, or the student's experience. Such comments still focus on the text; they simply do so from a broader perspective:

This is the kind of good detail your readers will need.

Combine these sentences in the ways we practiced in class last week.

Try to do some brainstorming to see what additional ideas you can come up with.

In each of these comments, the orientation expands from the text itself to some larger context of the writing. The first example looks at an issue of wording in terms of the audience. The second looks at a matter of local structure in terms of the student's classwork. The third examines a comment about development in terms of the student's writing activities. Figure 3.1 illustrates the various contexts of writing that a teacher's comments may invoke: the formal text, the rhetorical situation, the student's writing processes, the student's personal contexts, and the larger social setting.

Whenever a comment refers explicitly to some element outside the immediate text, we label its textual focus and, in addition, identify all the contexts it refers to beyond the text.[8] Even when we identify these additional references to some outside context, we still count the comment only once, according to its focus. We simply note any additional references the comment makes to other contexts.

Are you describing these seasons for people who have experienced or just read about them? (A comment about ideas seen in terms of the rhetorical context)

The introduction seems to prepare us more for a report on the subject than for a personal exploration, as the assignment called for. (One comment about global structure seen in terms of the rhetorical context and the classroom assignment)

This is an interesting description of winter. What other details would help your readers picture the season? (Two comments: the first, a comment about an idea in the text; the second, a comment about development with a reference to the rhetorical context)

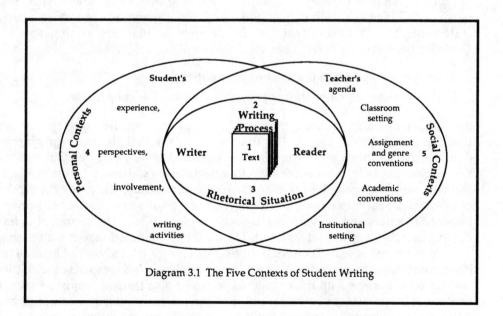

Diagram 3.1 The Five Contexts of Student Writing

Figure 3.1. The five contexts of student writing.

Whenever a comment makes no reference to a textual feature but explicitly addresses some element outside the text, we place it in the category extra-textual and note the context to which it refers. These comments refer to no particular part of the writing but instead emphasize some concern beyond the immediate text:

> Who did you have in mind as readers? (rhetorical context)
>
> The assignment asked you to illustrate your points with specific examples. (classroom context)
>
> This is a real improvement over your earlier work in the course. (student's classroom experience)
>
> You might start by jotting down a list of examples that come to mind. (student's writing activities)

The "orientation" of comments allows us to examine the extent to which the 12 readers look at student texts in terms of the full context of writing, as contemporary theorists urge us to do.[9]

The Modes of Commentary

Our "modes" of commentary analyze the different ways that teachers speak to students and set up tasks for them to do. They define the typical ways teachers give shape to their responses and the different degrees of control these types of comments imply. Our analysis is based on two complementary assumptions. First, the form of a comment strongly influences how the comment functions and what it comes to mean. Second, the form of a comment is not enough: Any analysis of how comments function must consider, not only the form of the comments, but also their content and voice. We also assume, as will become apparent when we look at the modes in full sets of responses, that the meaning and control implied by any given comment may very well be influenced by the surrounding comments.

Our analysis of modes is especially concerned with the form of teacher comments but goes beyond a simple analysis of the outward, grammatical form—that is, whether they are presented as statements, commands, or questions. As Knoblauch and Brannon rightly note, the "superficial form" of a comment is an unreliable way to distinguish among different types of teacher responses. Some statements are more controlling than other statements, some questions are more controlling than other questions, and some questions are more controlling than some statements. But we believe that the surface forms of teachers' comments are not unimportant. Consider the following two comments, for example:

> Move this paragraph to the start of your paper.
>
> You might want to move this paragraph to the start of your paper.

It might well be argued that these two sentences perform the same speech act, that is, request that the paragraph be moved. But that is not to say that the two are synonymous. There is a definite change in meaning—and in the relationship between teacher and student—when the sentence changes from an imperative to a declarative statement. Although we would grant that the two sentences may be taken to mean the same thing when they are presented in the full context of a real classroom setting, given the power relations that conventionally adhere between teachers and students, we think the different ways the comment is framed does make a difference in the way it is interpreted. The form of a comment makes a difference in meaning.

At the same time, we believe that it is not enough to analyze the form of teacher comments. If we are to capture the different ways teachers shape their responses and, through them, enact various relationships with their students, we must also take into consideration the voice and the content of their comments, because changes in the substance of a comment may make a critical difference in its meaning and in its implicit control, as in the following case:

> Add more detail.

Try to see what you can do to fill out this discussion.

Both comments are presented as commands, but one clearly invokes a strong teacher presence and implies greater control than the other. In analyzing the modes of a teacher's comments, then, we look to describe the different ways that teachers bring together the voice, content, and form of their comments and, in doing so, establish different relationships with students. Different modes implicitly create different images and roles for the teacher, establish different roles and tasks for students, and enact different degrees of teacher control over student writing.

The proposed set of modes provides 10 ways of characterizing the different images teachers create for themselves on the page and the different degrees of control these comments imply. Whereas some modes tend to exert firm control over the student's writing (corrective, evaluative, and imperative comments), other modes tend to exert moderate control (qualified evaluations, advisory comments, praise, closed questions), and others only modest control (open questions, reflective statements). The detailed classification should help us make fine discriminations about what teachers attempt to do in their comments—the relationships they establish and the tasks they set forth—and help us to describe teachers' responding styles more fully and consistently.

Corrections

The teacher makes a change in the text:

- "When I have tried my best, ~~it should make me feel~~ as if I have achieved something." [The teacher crosses out the words and adds above the crossouts: "When I have tried my best, I should feel as if. . . ."]

Negative Evaluations

The teacher makes what is presented as an objective criticism about the writing:

- Vague description.
- Poor sentence structure.
- This paragraph needs detail and clarity.
- The writing gets very abstract and general at times.

Qualified Negative Evaluations

The teacher presents a negative evaluation of the text, but qualifies it in some way or draws attention to its subjective nature. These comments refer explicitly to the teacher behind the comment through the pronouns "I" or "me," making it clear that they express one reader's views, not the detached, "objective" evaluations of a judge:

- I have trouble seeing your main point.
- I'm not sure about your interpretation of the story.
- I need to know more about specific techniques.
- This is a bit too technical for me.

Comments that assess the writing and include "I think" or the qualifier "seems" are also considered qualified evaluations:

- I think you could introduce this paper a bit more engagingly.

- This seems like a stereotype of spring.
- It seems as though you are being closed-minded.

Praise

The teacher makes a positive judgment about the writing, whether it is presented objectively or in a way that acknowledges the subjectivity of the responder:

- A vivid image.
- This is an interesting way to start the paper.
- Your text is more effective in the winter scene than elsewhere.
- I hear a strong voice in this paper.
- I think you've got a good start here.
- The example about your grandmother worked well for me.

Affective comments that suggest a positive judgment about the writing are also considered as praise:

- Yes!
- Exactly.

Imperatives

The teacher requests a change in the text or some action by the student, usually by means of a command:

- Add more details.
- Put the conclusion in a separate paragraph.
- You need to add some examples.
- You must first provide some information about the damage drug use does to people.
- Make a list of every specific instance you can think of when your parents have overguided.

This category also includes most "soft" directives, statements that call on the student to be vigilant about some issue of writing, or statements that are virtual commands:

- Be careful with your transitions.
- Watch out for cliched language.
- Check use of "enormous."

Advice

The teacher recommends or suggests a change in the text, offering advice that leaves a measure of choice to the student. Advisory comments are typically stated in the conditional mood. They also tend to be more specific about what they are calling for than either evaluative or imperative comments. Here are a number of examples:

- You might add some detail here.
- I'd try to state this more directly.

- I suggest you put this material about the gang's name at the start of the essay.
- Don't worry if you start out strongly and modify your position.
- What about starting with this point?

Comments are classified as "advisory" when they use imperatives to call on the student to *reconsider* something he has written, to *try* to do something by way of revision, or to *remember* some point or lesson:

- Think about whether you need to provide another example.
- Try stating that point in a sentence or two.
- Remember that you'll need to get mechanics up to snuff for the final draft.

Indirect Requests

The teacher uses a question that begins with "Can you" (or "Could you") to prompt the student to engage in some activity of revision. Such questions often refer explicitly to some technical language of composition ("detail," "example") or to some operation of writing ("develop," "connect"):

- Can you give an example?
- Could you develop this argument?

Problem-Posing Questions

The teacher uses a question to identify a problem in the text or some issue that needs to be considered. Problem-posing comments do not directly call on the student to make changes; instead, they present critical questions about the writing, especially about its form. They are aimed at calling attention to something that may not be working as well as it might.

Problem-posing comments take one of two forms, depending on how much room they leave the student to decide whether a change is to be made. In *closed problem-posing questions*, the teacher strongly implies that something is wrong with the text and insinuates in the wording of the comment itself the teacher's answer to the question. In doing so, the teacher limits the realm of possible responses from the student. In a way, these comments are imperatives or evaluations cast in the form of a question. They often contain a negative or an intensifier. Here are a number of examples:

- Can't this be said of fall in any northern city?
- Is this paragraph really necessary?
- Isn't one example enough?
- In Syracuse is everything ideal? predictable? perfect?

In *open problem-posing questions*, the teacher calls attention to some issue or potential problem in the writing yet leaves it to the student to figure out what, if anything, needs to be done. The teacher implies that something might need to be changed and prompts the student to consider the matter:

- Is this your main point?
- Do you see this material about your membership in the gang as your key point?
- What would you have to do with this paper to make it more than just a "pass"?
- What will some readers like about this quality, and other readers dislike?

Characteristically, closed problem-posing questions are phrased in a way that draws attention to the *teacher* and places her in the role of trouble-shooter; open problem-posing questions are phrased in a way that draws attention to the *student* and casts him in the role of critic.

Heuristic Questions

The teacher asks the student to add to or think further about the content of the writing.

There are two types of heuristic commentary, one which presents "closed" questions, the other which presents "open" questions. In *closed heuristic comments*, the teacher uses a question to guide the student to add specific information to the text. The teacher adopts the stance of an interested reader and asks the student to add information to specify, clarify, or expand on a point. The teacher does not approve or disapprove of the writing; she just asks for more information. The student is left to come up with information that is usually readily available from his experience. The key terms of the comment are usually based on words taken from the student's text. They commonly begin with interrogatives:

- What beach?
- How old were you?
- Which flower is the first to appear?
- How cold does it get?

In *open heuristic questions*, the teacher invites or challenges the student to consider his ideas further. These comments are always concerned with the content of the writing, specifically, with turning the student back into his statements and thoughts. They may focus on the ideas within the text or on the student's thinking beyond the scope of the immediate text. They are typically written out in an extended form (not in phrases or fragments), using much of the student's own language:

- How is fall in Syracuse different from fall in other northern cities?
- In what ways has your illness changed your outlook and behavior?
- What did your parents do when they "overguided," and how did you react?
- How does overguiding remove individuality and independence?

These questions are "open" in the sense that they do not request specific information but instead allow the student the freedom and responsibility to think about the subject on his own.

Reflective Statements

This category is a catch-all for descriptive, interpretive, explanatory, reader-response, and hortatorical statements—and all other statements that are not evaluative, directive, or advisory. They usually present the teacher's reflections on the writing, either as an instructor or as an individual reader.

Teacher Reflections

In *explanatory* comments, the teacher explains or elaborates on an earlier comment:

- [Good, vivid descriptions.] They get at your feelings about spring.
- [I'd consider adding an example.] It would solidify your point.

Such comments are made "explanatory" by the way they function in relation to a previous comment on the same focus. In such cases, the explanatory function typically overrides the mode that the comment would assume if it were seen in isolation. For example, the following comments, in isolation, would both be considered qualified negative evaluations:

- I wonder about your last line, "drugs are wrong, therefore, should not be legal."
- This statement seems a little circular to me.

But when they are put together in a response, the second comment serves to go back over the ground of the first one, explaining it, and is therefore considered "explanatory":

- I wonder about your last line, "drugs are wrong, therefore, should not be legal." It seems a little circular to me.

In another type of *explanatory* comment, the teacher explains some concept or informs the student about outside knowledge or material that is related to the writing:

- A comma splice occurs when two main clauses are connected with a comma.
- Writing is meant to express, not impress.
- Garrison Keillor has written a similar comparison of the seasons in last month's Atlantic.
- In academic writing, the trick is to express your opinion with authority—but to make sure your argument is more than just your opinion.
- Perhaps you and I found the argument so different because we have had different life experiences.

In *hortatorical* comments, the teacher encourages or exhorts the student to adopt some attitude or take some action:

- I bet you can come up with a lot of descriptive details about this.
- This is the kind of personal involvement you can use throughout the essay.

Reader Reflections

In *interpretive* comments, the teacher describes what the text says or interprets its meaning or significance. The teacher "plays back" the writer's words and ideas but does not offer a judgment or reaction:

- First, you say that the law is a violation of a person's freedom.
- You write that the feeling was "almost like an 'ego-trip.'"
- Here is your second argument.
- You seem especially interested in talking about fishing this one time at Lake Ivanhoe.

In *reader-response comments*, the teacher assumes the role of a reader more than a teacher and says something about her way of reading the writing. There are three types of reader-response comments: reader-experience comments, reader remarks, and reader reactions.

In *reader-experience comments*, the teacher illustrates how she processes particular passages of the student's writing, by giving a moment-by-moment reading of the words on the page:

- As you moved fall forward with a dusting of frost into "sweater-weather," I thought: This is nice. He is doing more than sketch the season here, he is shading it, subtly he is easing it into winter.

- I actually stopped to think if that might be why Auburn has the name it does.
- What I noticed first are the places where you talk about your feelings while being in the gang.
- Then I am led to believe that things are alright—but with a lingering fear and keeping my fingers crossed.

In *reader remarks,* the teacher presents her own thoughts and associations—not about the writing itself—but about the writer's subject or something the writer has said:

- I love winter too.
- I hadn't thought of people hibernating.
- This reminds me of the movie *Tin Men.*
- Since I'm from a part of the country that has four equally balanced seasons, I don't think I'd like the Sun Belt at all.

In *reader reactions,* the teacher presents her reading or interpretation of the text and, as she does so, insinuates some evaluation about the writing:

- It took me a while to figure how this sentence follows from the previous one.
- I don't disagree with your *position*, but somehow I find myself fighting you as I read.
- I was struck by how heavily you relied on overused language to express your feelings about Syracuse's winters.
- When I was reading this paper I began to think that a native of Tallahassee who had never been north could have written it.

*   *   *

These 10 modes of response attempt to characterize the various ways teachers phrase their comments to students, and in doing so suggest different degrees of control over their writing. It is important to note, however, that all comments by their very nature employ some degree of control. Every time a teacher responds to a student's text, the comment identifies some issue the teacher finds significant and wants the student to attend to in some way. In a sense, then, all comments are evaluations of the writing and directives to the student. The question of control lies in the extent to which the teacher overtly evaluates the writing and directs the changes that are to be made.[10] Each of the modes, we suggest, creates a different role for the teacher and a corresponding task for the student, as Table 3.2 indicates.

Meaning in the Modes: The Immediate Sense of Teacher Comments

In our analysis of teacher responses, our goal is not to determine how the teacher actually intended a given comment or to predict how the student would likely understand it. Such determinations, as Knoblauch and Brannon (1981) rightly point out, cannot reliably be made without access to the actual context in which the comment was made:

A single comment on a single essay is too local and contingent a phenomenon to yield general conclusions about the quality of the conversation of which it is a part. Any remark on a student essay, whatever its form, finally owes its meaning and impact to the governing dialogue that influences some student's reaction to it. Remarks taken out of context can appear more restrictive or open-ended, more facilitative or judgmental, than they really are in light of a teacher's overall communicative habits. (p. 287)

Table 3.2. Teacher Roles Implied in the Various Modes of Commentary.

MODE	*TEACHER ROLE*
Corrective	proofreader
Evaluative	critic
Qualified evaluative	subjective reader
Imperative	editor
Advisory	advisor
Praise	supportive coach
Indirect request	supervisor
Closed problem-posing	trouble-shooter
Open problem-posing	problem-poser
Closed heuristic	interested reader
Open heuristic	fellow inquirer
Reflective	teacher as reader
	or teacher as instructor

We agree with Knoblauch and Brannon that teachers may be able to make "superficially similar comments" mean "vastly different" things and that the ultimate meaning of a teacher's comments depends on the larger context of which they are part, including, of course, the individual relationship between the teacher and the student (p. 287). At the same time, we would assert that the way a teacher's comments are shaped on the page—how the comments are presented and what they say—creates its own context and plays a significant role in determining how comments come to mean. Although it is true that comments written on a student essay are shaped by the larger classroom context, it is no less true that the context itself is shaped by the teacher's comments. Arguably, during the time the student looks over the comments, they *are* the context of instruction and have an immediate impact on how the student reads and interprets those comments. To the extent that these responses stay fixed in the student's mind, they may even become the focus of his attention. In short, the precise form of a comment significantly influences the meaning of the comment, with different forms establishing different relationships between teacher and student.[11]

With Knoblauch and Brannon, we are interested in the substance of a comment and the stance of the teacher behind it, what they call "the posture beneath the surface appearance of a comment" (p. 129). But whereas they are concerned with the *actual* teacher's attitudes and virtually disregard the form of the comments, we are concerned with the attitudes that are *implied* in teacher comments and look to their form as a key clue to the teacher's underlying attitudes and roles. By looking at the form and content of a comment in its intrinsic context, we are attempting to determine the "immediate sense" of the comment—the conventional meaning that is derivable from the words the teacher puts on the page. Our analysis of modes of commentary, then, is a study of the textual meaning of a teacher's comments, a meaning that exists independent from its original, holistic context, but that is construable from the words on the page.[12] Consider, for example, the following comment written in response to Writing 6, "The Four Seasons":

Is this reference to Tallahassee necessary?

We are not interested in interpreting the teacher's actual intentions in making the comment—that is, in determining whether the comment is intended to request the student to remove the sentence about Tallahassee. We are also not interested in predicting how the student writer would actually interpret the comment—that is, whether he would take it as a genuine question or as a veiled command. In either case, our interpretation would require information about the teacher-student relationship and the actual classroom context, both of which are beyond the scope of this study. Given the clinical and formalistic nature of our project, we decided to concentrate our analysis on the immediate sense of the comment, by inferring the context from the teacher's comments and the student's text and giving a close reading to the substance and form of the comment. The comment "Is this reference to Tallahassee necessary," then, is neither a command telling the student to omit the reference to Tallahassee nor a request that is cast in the form of a question. As we see it, in its immediate sense, the comment simply poses a problem that the teacher wants the student to consider. The comment may be *intended* to suggest that the student should not have introduced this idea to the paper or even to urge him to remove it in a revision. But in its *immediate sense*, it merely asks the student to consider the problem. Different forms of the "same" response, we are suggesting, amount to different comments—as Pascal says, words differently arranged have different meanings. Thus, the following comments deal with the same issue and can be seen as having the same general goal— to lead the writer to consider deleting his comparison between autumn in Syracuse and autumn in Tallahassee—but they are all different comments:

> Stick to describing the seasons in Syracuse. (imperative)
>
> You might concentrate on just the seasons in Syracuse. (advisory)
>
> This sentence about Tallahassee does not belong here. (evaluative)
>
> I stumbled on this comparison the first time I read it. (reader reaction)
>
> Can you find a better way to get at this comparison? (indirect request)
>
> Would it be better to focus on the seasons in Syracuse? (problem-posing)

Although all six versions of the comment—in a particular context, with particular teachers, and particular students—may have the force of a request, each of the comments has a different immediate sense. Only the first example, "Stick to the seasons in Syracuse," immediately directs the student to make a change. The other versions offer advice, present evaluations of the sentence, or ask the student to consider its relevance. The case suggests how different modes of response may enact different roles for the teacher and exert different degrees of teacher control.

We are dealing, then, with the teacher's persona—the *figure* of the teacher we see in and through her written comments, the teacher as she appears in the text, construed from the words on the page. Nevertheless, we would think that a teacher's comments on the page should inscribe her actual intentions. A teacher who wants to be a facilitator would presumably emphasize comments that would offer some guidelines but leave room for students to make their own decisions about their writing. Comments that present mostly commands and criticism would be incompatible, we would think, with this teacher's responding goals. Similarly, a teacher who wants to emphasize writing as a way of thinking or as a means of personal expression would not make a majority of comments in corrective, imperative, or even advisory modes; if her comments on the page were to reflect her actual goals, she would make appreciable use of heuristic questions designed to turn students back into their thinking. A close reading of the roles teachers create through their comments is foundational to our study.

PROCEDURES FOR ANALYZING TEACHER COMMENTS

For our analysis of the 12 readers' responses to the sampling of essays, we established a system for counting comments and for labeling the focus and mode of each comment. We then trained outside raters to label the comments, and computed the totals for individual readers and for the 12 readers as a group.

Counting and Labeling Individual Comments

The term *response* is a general name for the various ways teachers offer students feedback to their writing. As Figure 3.2 indicates, there are two broad types of response, written and spoken, each of which may be further divided into specific types.

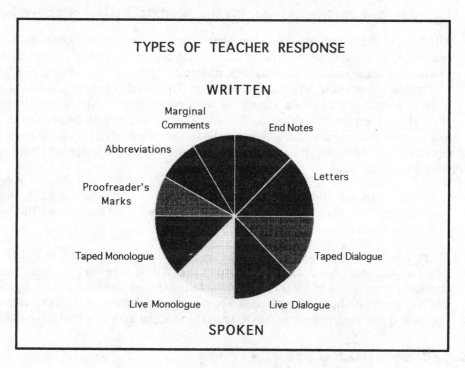

Figure 3.2. Types of teacher response.

Our analysis does not treat the entire range of teacher response, but concentrates on teachers' *written comments*. (We examined one group of comments that were not written— Chris Anson's tape-recorded comments, which he presented to us in transcripts.) As we use the term, a *comment* is any response that is written out in words (a single word, a phrase, a clause) and speaks to one area or issue of the writing—whether it occurs on the student's text near the passage it addresses, in a note at the end of the text, or in a separate note or letter.[13]

Generally, each sentence or group of words that addresses a new issue or passage in a piece of student writing constitutes a new comment. Marginal comments pose few difficulties in counting because they are usually set off distinctly from each other in the student's text. The following responses, from Glynda Hull's marginal comments on "The Four Seasons," are each counted as one comment because they are presented on the page as a unit and address one passage or one issue in the student's text:

A vivid image.

This word seems just right.

I hadn't thought of people hibernating too.

Wow—the smell of dried leaves must conjure up powerful images for you.

When two or more comments are placed in a group and act as a unit, they form what we call a *combination comment*, or a *cluster*. Rather than labeling a cluster of comments as a whole or identifying one comment within a cluster as predominant, we distinguished and labeled each comment. Whenever the focus or mode changed, we identified a new comment and labeled it accordingly. The following responses are combination comments from Hull's commentary:

I hadn't thought of people hibernating too—this is a neat comparison.

> Wow—the smell of dried leaves must conjure up powerful images for you. I bet you could write an interesting paper just about this.
>
> Another neat image—but I don't get how "strolling" is a way of "shrivelling."

All three of these combination comments are made up of two comments. The first combines a reader remark and a positive evaluation about one of the writer's ideas. The second starts with a reader remark about an idea and then makes a hortatorical comment designed to encourage the student to think about writing a new paper. The third presents a positive evaluation about one word in a sentence and then a qualified negative evaluation about another word.

The same principles are used for numbering continuous responses in endnotes and letters. In a sequence of comments, whenever the focus or mode changes, we identified a new comment. Consider the following paragraph from Donald Stewart's letter to David on his description of winter in Syracuse:

> Winter turns out to be a popular song. Why don't you tell us what Syracuse winters are really like? Are they as bad as those in Buffalo, with all that snow? How cold does it get? Any ice skating available?

There are five comments in this sequence, with each new sentence either framed in a different mode or focusing on a different concern in the writing. The first is a negative evaluation about the student's description of winter. In the next two, Stewart presents a closed problem-posing question and then an open heuristic question about winter in Syracuse. The last two comments are closed heuristic questions that are meant to help the student add specific information to the writing.[14]

Reading a Comment in Light of the Student's Writing

Sometimes a comment can be readily interpreted solely on the basis of the comment itself, without reference to the student's writing, as in the following examples:

> Great verb choice.
>
> I'm jarred by the change in tone here.
>
> Do squirrels really hibernate?

In these cases, the comments create their own adequate context. But it is often the case that the comment itself is abbreviated or vague or for some other reason does not provide enough information for raters to determine its focus and mode. Without the context of the student's text, the following comments, for example, are indeterminate:

> I like this.
>
> Detail needed.

In order to determine the focus of these comments, we need to look at them in light of the passages to which they refer. In the first case, the meaning of the comment "I like this" becomes clear once it is seen written directly above the underlined words of the following student sentence: "You can feel the moist ground wanting to <u>seep into your shoes</u>." The teacher likes the student's naming. In the second case, the comment "Detail needed," without its immediate context, can be taken to mean that the text needs a more specific word, that is, sharper wording *within* the sentence. Or it can be taken to mean that the text needs further elaboration *beyond* the sentence, that is, a matter of development. That the comment focuses on wording is suggested by its referent in the text, in which the teacher underscores a general term within the following sentence: "Wives are planting <u>new flowers</u>. . . ." The interpretation of each of these comments takes shape only when read in conjunction with the passage to which it refers. Even in such cases, however, the interpretation of a comment is determined *mainly* by what the teacher writes, not by the student's text.

Reading Parts of a Comment in Light of the Rest of the Comment

The meaning of any given comment in a cluster of comments may be influenced by the meaning of the rest of the comment. For example, in the following cluster, the meaning of the second comment depends on the meaning of the first and third comments:

> Is this the best focus for your paper? How can you come up with specific details about all four seasons? Maybe you need to focus on one of the seasons?

As an isolated comment, the meaning of the second statement, "How can you come up with specific details about all four seasons?" is ambiguous: It can be taken as an open problem-posing question in which the teacher is asking the student to figure out how he could add details to the writing, or it can be taken as a closed problem-posing question in which the teacher is indirectly challenging the student's decision to try to describe all four seasons. But in the context of the rest of the comment, it is clear that the question is not asking the student to consider adding material to the four sections of the essay. It is asking him to consider the problems he is running into by trying to develop a paper around such a broad focus as a description of all four seasons in Syracuse. It is a *closed* problem-posing question, presenting a veiled criticism within the form of a question: How can you present enough specific details in a paper devoted to describing all four seasons.

Now consider how the meaning of the second comment—and the cluster as a whole—changes in the following version of the commentary:

> This seems like a manageable focus for your paper. How can you come up with specific details about all four seasons?

The opening praise comment influences the way the second comment is to be taken, as an *open* problem-posing question, an invitation to get more details for all four seasons.

Below is another example of how the labeling of a comment may be influenced by surrounding comments:

> [W]e need to know what beaches you're talking abut. The "going-to-the beach" detail is a cliché for many parts of the country.

There are two comments in this sequence, both of them dealing with the student's wording. The first is a negative evaluation. In isolation, the second comment would also be considered a negative evaluation. But in this context, it serves the function of explaining the preceding comment and is labeled "explanatory." These sample comments demonstrate how the meaning—and, hence, the mode—of a comment may shift according to the context of that comment.

SAMPLE ANALYSES OF TEACHER COMMENTS

The following analysis of the three sets of responses presented at the start of the chapter—written by Stewart, Stock, and Hull—illustrate how our method of analysis may be used to describe comments and make fine distinctions among even apparently similar response styles. All three readers deal for the most part with the ideas and the wording of the writing—in particular, with its overgeneralized language. All three also use the student's own words to offer a close reading of the text. But they focus on different areas of writing and frame their comments differently, exerting various degrees of teacher control.

STEWART

[N]ow we run into some problems. Have you described the four seasons in Syracuse, or have you described four idealized seasons? I think the latter, and I'll tell you why. In describing Spring, you mention the trees blossoming, flowers working their way out of the ground, geese flying north overhead, and a long winter's nap ending for bears, squirrels, rabbits and other hibernating animals. These are all cliches about Spring. If you must use them, particularize them. Instead of telling us about blossoming trees, tell us how you look forward to the blooming of the redbud tree in your front yard, and of the flowering crab which follows right behind it. Tell us about the particular flowers which blossom in your yard in Syracuse. We'll skip the geese, but let's take a hard look at your list of hibernating animals. How many bears roam the streets of Syracuse? Or do you make frequent trips to the zoo to see them come out of hibernation? If you lived in Yellowstone Park in the winter, mention of hibernating bears would be quite natural. Here, a reader does a double take. What bears are there in Syracuse, or anywhere nearby?

Stewart is most concerned with the problems in the writing. His comments show how the cliched images about spring are connected to the larger problems of careless thinking. He frames almost half of his comments in highly controlling modes. Three of them are presented as criticisms—one a qualified negative evaluation, the other two straight criticisms:[15]

I think [you have described four idealized seasons], and I'll tell you why.

These are all cliches about Spring.

Here, a reader does a double take.

When he calls on the student to revise, he does so in the form of an imperative, setting forth a definite path for revision:

If you must use them, particularize them.

But, having presented this firm directive to the student to make the writing more substantive, he writes two comments that, although in isolation they take the form of imperatives, function (in the larger context of the surrounding comments) as follow-up examples and guides for revision:

Instead of telling us about blossoming trees, tell us how you look forward to the blooming of the redbud tree in your front yard, and of the flowering crab which follows right behind it. Tell us about the particular flowers which blossom in your yard in Syracuse.

These two comments, then, are explanatory: They are there to help the student follow Stewart's call to make the writing more concrete and particular. He goes on to point to other weak descriptions; however, this time he does not do so directly, through evaluative comments, but indirectly, through several closed problem-posing questions:

Have you described the four seasons in Syracuse, or have you described four idealized seasons?

How many bears roam the streets of Syracuse?

What bears are there in Syracuse, or anywhere nearby?

The comments are framed as questions and are less controlling than overt criticism or imperatives, but they are used to lead the student to see the text a certain way and to consider particular changes that the teacher sets forth. As a whole, the comments, although they are not extensively controlling, establish what Stewart sees as the problems with the writing and are firmly controlling.

STOCK

I thought it was effective of you to contrast the fall, strolling into Tallahassee and shriveling the flowers, with fall parading . . . into Syracuse, showing off its auburn, garnet, and gold leaves. I must say, I liked the fact that you chose auburn as a color because Auburn the city is so close to Syracuse. I actually stopped to think if that might be why Auburn has the name it does. Do you know? And I liked the precious gem, precious metal allusions you invoked by choosing garnet and gold as colors. The season moves you inward into enclosed, secure beds of leaves and outward into majestic displays of ornamental leaves. If you had not told me that winter was your second favorite season, I would not have guessed it. I would have guessed it was spring because your descriptions of spring have almost as much vitality as your descriptions of fall. As I read the section of your essay you devoted to winter, I was struck by how heavily you relied on overused language to express your feelings about Syracuse's winters (my understanding is that Syracuse's winters are WINTERS).

Whereas Stewart is mostly concerned with the problems in the text and directing the writer to make specific changes, Stock is mostly concerned with providing a close reading of the writing. But rather than relying on her authority as a teacher and presenting criticism, she foregrounds her role as a reader and presents her comments in the form of reader responses. She presents three positive comments that emphasize her perspective as an individual reader:

> I thought it was effective of you to contrast the fall, strolling into Tallahassee and shriveling the flowers, with fall parading . . . into Syracuse, showing off its auburn, garnet, and gold leaves.

> I must say, I liked the fact that you chose auburn as a color because Auburn the city is so close to Syracuse.

> And I liked the precious gem, precious metal allusions you invoked by choosing garnet and gold as colors.

She also offers some criticism, but submerges it in comments that, at the same time, play back her reading of the writing:

> If you had not told me that winter was your second favorite season, I would not have guessed it.

> As I read the section of your essay you devoted to winter, I was struck by how heavily you relied on overused language to express your feelings about Syracuse's winters.

These evaluations, which are written in the form of reader reactions, are woven into the fabric of her readings and interpretations. Several other comments take the form of reflective statements, but they are not evaluative: one reader remark, in which Stock expresses a personal view about the subject ("my understanding is that Syracuse's winters are WINTERS"); a reader-experience comment, in which she gives an account of her moment-to-moment thoughts as she reads ("I actually stopped to think if that might be why Auburn has the name it does"); an explanatory comment ("I would have guessed [your favorite season] was spring because your descriptions of spring have almost as much vitality as your descriptions of fall"); and an interpretation ("The season moves you inward into enclosed, secure beds of leaves and outward into majestic displays of ornamental leaves"). In choosing these modes of response, Stock seems to be content to show the student how his writing has affected her and allow him to decide which revisions, if any, he should take up. She presents no straight criticism, no imperatives, and no advice, and assumes modest control over the writing.

HULL

You've got an unusual paper here in that some readers will love it and some will feel just as strongly in the opposite direction. What I want you to do is to figure out what it is about your paper, and about different readers, that could produce such different reactions. For example:

1) Your seasonal portraits could have, with a few exceptions, been written by someone who grew up in Tallahassee. What will some readers like about this quality? What will others dislike?

2) You say at the end of your paper that you've told only the good things about the seasons. Why might this be pleasant to some readers but offensive to others?

3) You use a lot of phrases that are often used in conjunction with the seasons. Again, what will some readers like about this, others dislike, and why?

Given your consideration of these questions, would you now make any changes in your paper? Why or why not?

Hull focuses her comments less on the text or her reactions to the text and more on how the writing may be interpreted by different readers. In contrast to both Stewart and Stock, she makes no criticisms. Instead, she points to several issues and then leads the student to think about them. The heart of her response offers several interpretive comments—(1) Your seasonal portraits could have, with a few exceptions, been written by someone who grew up in Tallahassee, (2) You say at the end of your paper that you've told only the good things about the seasons, and (3) You use a lot of phrases that are often used in conjunction with the seasons—that are followed directly by open problem-posing questions that are designed to engage the student in considering his choices:

What will some readers like about this quality? What will others dislike?

Why might this be pleasant to some readers but offensive to others?

Again, what will some readers like about this, others dislike, and why?

Hull does not call for any specific changes in the text; she asks the student to think about his choices as a writer, making what amounts to an assignment. Although she matter-of-factly lays out a plan for revision and assumes a clear control over the work to be done, she throws the weight of responsibility on the student.

Table 3.3 presents an analysis of the focuses and modes used by Stewart, Stock, and Hull. It indicates how the three readers have somewhat different concerns in their commentary and clearly different ways of presenting those concerns. (For a comment-by-comment analysis of the focuses and modes of their responses to Writing 6, see Appendix B.)

Overall, the three responders assume varying degrees of teacher control in their comments. Stewart calls for particular changes in the text. By making several criticisms, presenting his major call for revision in the form of a command, and using a series of closed problem-posing questions, he exerts a firm control over the student writer and creates a fairly directive style. Stock's emphasis on providing a close reading of the text without overt criticism, which allows the student

Table 3.3. Sample Analysis of Three Teachers' Comments.

	Stewart	Stock	Hull
Focus	9 ideas 3 wording	7 ideas 3 wording	5 ideas 2 wording 4 other
Mode	2 neg evaluative 1 qual evaluative 1 imperative 3 closed prob-posing 1 closed heuristic 4 reflective	3 praise 1 heuristic 6 reflective	1 imperative 6 open prob-posing 4 reflective

to decide on which changes are to be made, makes her commentary nondirective. Hull's style falls somewhere between the two in terms of teacher control. Although she directs the student to consider the particular choices he has made as a writer, she makes no evaluative comments and leaves it up to the student to think about these issues on his own; she does not call on him to make specific changes according to her plan. By asking the student to consider the ways that different audiences might react to his writing, she calls attention to the rhetorical context of the writing and shifts her concern away from text production and squarely into the student's evolving understanding of how language works. The relatively few comments she writes also contribute to what amounts to a style that, while it offers some direction, is only moderately controlling.

A SUMMARY ANALYSIS OF THE 12 READERS' COMMENTS

In order to draw a composite both of the 12 readers' individual response styles and their patterns of response as a whole, we did a careful comment-by-comment analysis of a large sampling of these readers' comments. To do so, we reduced our sampling from the original 15 writings to 10. We eliminated the three pieces to which our readers most frequently chose not to respond (Writings 3, 14, and 15). We also eliminated two additional writings in order to get the same number of rough drafts and final drafts in the revised sampling. Writing 7 was omitted because it proved to be one of the most problematic essays in the sampling, and Writing 8 was omitted because it shared a number of attributes with Writing 9. (See Appendix F for the writings that are not displayed in the text.) Both groups of writings, the rough drafts and final drafts, included essays that were shaped for various aims and that displayed a range in overall quality.[16] The final sampling, then, was made up of the following writings:

ROUGH DRAFTS

Writing 1: [Against the Seat Belt Law]
Writing 2: "What If Drugs Were Legal?"
Writing 4: [Overguiding Teenage Children]
Writing 5: "Attention: Bass Fishermen"
Writing 12: "Street Gangs: One Point of View"

FINAL DRAFTS

Writing 6: "The Four Seasons"
Writing 9:   "A Broken Man"
Writing 10: "Leukemia"
Writing 11: "Being a Good Waitress"
Writing 13: "The John Cougar Concert"

In making these adjustments, we reduced our data from 156 sets of responses on the original 15 writings to 113 sets in the revised sampling.[17] The 2,529 comments our readers made on these 10 writings, both in the margins and in separate endnotes, became the data base for our analysis.[18] The individual comments on each set of responses were numbered and all names and identifying marks were removed from the writings. The 113 sets of responses were labeled by three raters, with each rater reading and labeling comments independently.[19] The raters labeled the 2,529 comments our 12 readers made on the 10 writings in the sampling, rating each comment once for focus and once for mode. They achieved an agreement of 84% in labeling the readers' individual comments, for a .91 interrater reliability coefficient. (See Appendix D for a description of this analysis.) After the raters individually labeled all 113 sets of responses, they negotiated disagreements and made final decisions about the labeling of each set of comments. These final decisions represent the final counts that comprise our overall analysis of the 12 readers' responses to the sampling, presented in summary in Tables 3.4 and 3.5.

Among other things, Table 3.4 shows the readers' emphasis on global concerns, i.e., global structure, development, and ideas (55% of their comments), and their comparatively moderate treatment of local concerns, i.e., local structure, wording, and correctness (21%). It also shows the extent to which the readers as a group try to temper the control they assume over students' writing choices. Only 29% of their comments are cast in authoritative modes (corrective, evaluative, qualified evaluative, imperative, advisory), including only 15% in the three modes that tend to be the most controlling: corrections, negative evaluations, and imperatives. Twelve percent are presented in the form of praise. Significantly, well over half of their comments (59%) are framed as questions and reflective statements, the least directive modes of commentary.

Table 3.4. Analysis of the 12 Readers' Focuses of Commentary.

	Number	Percentage
Ideas	736	29
Development	351	14
Global structure	313	12
Local structure	107	4
Wording	275	11
Correctness	144	6
Extra-textual comments	603	24
TOTAL	2529	100

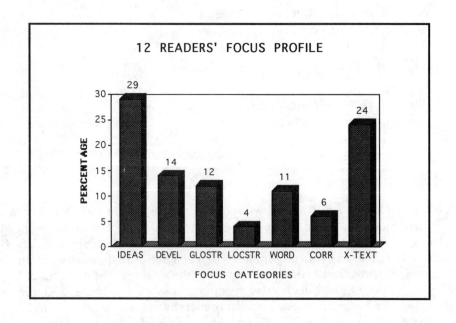

Table 3.5. Analysis of the 12 Readers' Modes of Commentary.

	Number	Percentage
Corrections	94	4
Negative evaluations	189	7
Qualified negative evaluations	101	4
Imperatives	143	5
Advice	243	9
Praise	294	12
Indirect requests	43	2
Closed problem-posing questions	175	7
Closed heuristic questions	99	4
Open problem-posing questions	171	7
Open heuristic questions	130	5
Interpretive comments	201	8
Explanatory comments	319	13
Reader response comments	200	8
Other	127	5
TOTAL	2529	100

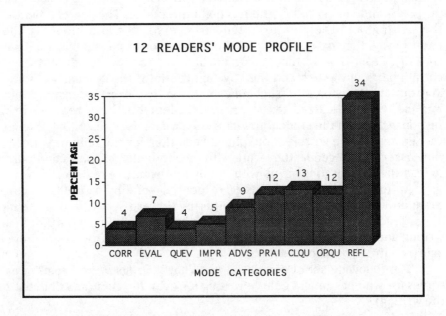

In the next chapter, we use the figures from our analysis to describe the responding styles of each of our readers. In Chapter 5, we use these figures to identify the similarities in the 12 readers' responses as a group.

4 | Control in Teacher Commentary: An Analysis of the 12 Readers' Responding Styles

How do accomplished teachers who are familiar with current scholarship respond to college student writing? How many comments do they make? What do they focus on? What modes of commentary do they employ? To what extent do they assume control over student writing? In this chapter we use our analysis of the 12 readers' comments to come up with a description of their individual responding styles.

By their example, the 12 readers seem to endorse Knoblauch and Brannon's (1984) stand against "directive" response.[1] As a group, these readers eschew commentary that is so highly critical and takes so much control over the writing that the student is led to forego her own purposes and simply follow the teacher's directions. They rarely dictate particular changes for the writing, and they do not attend to every error and infelicity they come across. Most importantly, they do not "ignore writers' intentions and meanings in favor of their own agenda" (p. 119). From time to time, some of the readers may decide how the student should revise certain parts of the text and thereby "appropriate" the student's writing.[2] However, they rarely appropriate the choices to such an extent that they exert extensive control over the writing and impose their "idealized texts" on the student.[3] If these readers bring an agenda to their responses or lead the student to follow their vision for the writing, they do not suggest that their way is *the* way the writing should have been done or the only way it can be revised. Even when they assert their agenda, they work with the student's meanings and purposes and in general try to lead the student to come up with her own substantive revisions.[4]

An examination of two sets of responses—one by a teacher whose style Knoblauch and Brannon would call "directive," the other by Edward White, one of the most controlling readers in our study—demonstrates the difference between commentary that takes control over student writing and commentary that assumes firm control and provides definite direction but does not usurp control from the student.

The following set of responses to "What If Drugs Were Legal?" was written by an English professor who has taught college writing for over 20 years (see Chapter 2 for the full context for the writing).[5]

Writing 2
Nancy S.
First Rough Draft

What If Drugs Were Legal?

What if drugs were legal? ~~Could~~ Can you imagine what it would do to
our society? ~~Well according to~~ John E. LeMoult, a lawyer with twenty[20]
years of experience on the subject, feels we should at least consider
(it) I would like to comment on his article "Legalize Drugs" in the
June 15, 1984, issue of the New York Times. I disagree with LeMoult's
idea of legalizing drugs to cut the cost of crime.

what? (margin)
Keep yourself in the background just state your position. (margin)

LeMoult's article ~~was~~ is short and sweet *cliché*. He gives the background
of the legalization of drugs. For example, the first antidrug laws of
the United States were passed in 1914. ~~The laws were put in effect~~
because of the threat of the Chinese (imagrants). In addition, he
explains how women were the first to use laudanun, an over-the-counter
drug, as a substitute for drinking because it was unacceptable for women to
drink. By explaining this he made the reader feel that society was
the cause of women's using the substitute, laudanun, for drinking.
LeMoult proceeds from there to explain how the money to buy drugs
comes from ~~us as~~ society. Since drug addicts turn to crime ~~to get~~
money, we become a corrupt society. Due to this we spend unnecessary
money protecting inocent citizens by means of law enforcment, jails,
(and ect). LeMoult says that if we legalize drugs ~~that~~ "Overnight the
cost of law enforcement, courts, judges, jails and convict
rehabilitation would be cut in half. The savings in tax would be more
than $50 billion a year."

condense (margin)
wordy (margin)
good material— needs to be tightened a bit (margin)
No!! (margin)

1

Punct.

LeMoult might be correct by saying that our cost of living in society would be cut in half if drugs were legalized, however, he is justifying a wrong to save money. ~~In my opinion~~ legalizing drugs is *?* the easy man's way out. Just because crime is high due to the fact *] awk S* that the cost of drugs is unbeleivable it doesn't make legalizing them right. We all know drugs are dangerous to the body and society *awk* without any explanation, therefore, you shouldn't legalize something that is dangerous. *NO!!*

Stay out of it — make it 3rd person

My only and most important argument to LeMoult is the physical harm it would bring by legalizing drugs. People abuse their right to use alcoholic beverages because they are legal. For example, LeMoult himself says the amount of drug addicts is small compared to alcoholics. Why?—of course it is because of the legalization of alcohol. When you make something legal it can and will be done with *diction too low* little hassel. Why allow something to be done with ease when it is wrong? LeMoult's points are good and true, but I believe he is approaching the subject in the wrong manner. Drugs are wrong, therefore, should not be legal!

Your general organization is fine, but you need to tighten up your thinking as well as your expression. You can make it much more powerful by attention to above suggestions.

Have you proved the "wrongness" of drugs just by saying that they are? Is alcohol also "wrong"?

2

It does not take a fine-tuned instrument to see how these comments are extremely controlling—or, in Knoblauch and Brannon's terms, "directive." The teacher seems to stalk the writing, looking to catch any errors or problems that spring up and rigorously marking or fixing most of them along the way. She makes 45 responses on the paper. Half of them take the form of circles, underlines, cross outs, and other graphic symbols or abbreviations—marks that are unaccompanied by any written commentary. Only half of the responses are written out as statements, and most of these are cast in cryptic one-word comments and short phrases, creating a voice that is editorial, critical, and demanding.

The responses cover a wide range of concerns, but they are mostly focused on local matters: 38 of the 45 responses address correctness, wording, local structure, and the writer's use of "I." The teacher's interest in cleaning up surface features leads her to give only cursory attention to the student's ideas and purposes. She is more concerned with seeing how it lives up to her agenda as a teacher (which emphasizes formal propriety) than she is with using her comments to help Nancy figure out what she wants to say and how she might say it better. Tellingly, 17 of her 23 comments are presented in the most controlling modes: five corrections, eight negative evaluations, and four imperatives, not to mention all the other corrections and evaluations she makes by way of proofreader's marks. Although she asks two questions about the writer's ideas, both of them are closed problem-posing questions that have the feel of evaluations as much as interrogatives: "Have you proved the 'wrongness' of drugs just by saying that they are? Is alcohol also 'wrong'?" These are the modes and strategies used by teachers who extensively "appropriate" and take control over student writing in order to fulfill their purposes: in this case, to get the student to produce clean, cosmetically correct prose. These comments clearly impose the teacher's idealized text on the writing.

Now compare those responses with the following set of responses that White makes on this rough draft:

Writing 2
Nancy S.
First Rough Draft

What If Drugs Were Legal?

What if drugs were legal? Could you imagine what it would do to
our society? Well according to John E. LeMoult, a lawyer with twenty
years of experience on the subject, feels we should at least consider
it. I would like to comment on his article "Legalize Drugs" in the
June 15, 1984, issue of the New York Times. I disagree with LeMoult's
idea of legalizing drugs to cut the cost of crime.

LeMoult's article was short and sweet. He gives the background
of the legalization of drugs. For example, the first antidrug laws of
the United States were passed in 1914. The laws were put in effect
because of the threat of the Chinese imagrants. In addition, he
explains how women were the first to use laudanun, an over the counter
drug, as a substitute for drinking; it was unacceptable for women to
drink. By explaining this he made the reader feel that society was
the cause of women using the substitute, laudanun, for drinking.
LeMoult proceeded from there to explain how the money to buy drugs
comes from us as society. Since drug addicts turn to crime to get
money we become a corrupt society. Due to this we spend unnecessary
money protecting inocent citizens by means of law enforcment, jails,
and ect. LeMoult says that if we legalize drugs that "Overnight the
cost of law enforcement, courts, judges, jails and convict
rehabilitation would be cut in half. The savings in tax would be more
than $50 billion a year."

Now that you are clear on what you have to say (see your last ¶) revise the opening to begin your argument.

Select the parts of LeMoult's article that are appropirate for your paper and omit the rest. Be sure to quote accurately.

Your first argument here: the financial reasons are not good enough for legalization. Focus this ¶ on this argument and develop your case

LeMoult might be correct by saying that our cost of living in society would be cut in half if drugs were legalized, however, he is justifying a wrong to save money. In my opinion legalizing drugs is the easy (man's) way out. Just because crime is high due to the fact that the cost of drugs is unbelievable it doesn't make legalizing them right. We all know drugs are dangerous to the body and society without any explanation, therefore, you shouldn't legalize something that is dangerous.

Not so. Look at the previous ¶

My only and most important argument to LeMoult is the physical harm it would bring by legalizing drugs. People abuse their right to use alcoholic beverages because they are legal. For example, LeMoult himself says the amount of drug addicts is small compared to alcoholics. Why?—of course it is because of the legalization of alcohol. When you make something legal it can and will be done with little hassel. Why allow something to be done with ease when it is wrong? LeMoult's points are good and true but I believe he is approaching the subject in the wrong manner. Drugs are wrong, therefore, should not be legal!

second argument. Now develop this one.

Make this into a full closing ¶.

The paper is a good discovery draft that could become a good paper. As you revise, be sure you focus each ¶ on its central idea. I enjoy the energy of your style.

2

White sets forth in no uncertain terms what this student needs to do in order to turn this draft into a "good paper." His series of imperative comments helps establish the persona of a teacher who knows just what the student should do and who does not hesitate to lay out necessary revisions:[6]

> Now that you are clear on what *you* have to say . . . , revise the opening to begin your argument.
>
> Select the parts of LeMoult's article that are appropriate for *your* paper and omit the rest. Be sure to quote accurately.
>
> Focus this prgh on this argument and develop your case.
>
> Now develop this one.
>
> Make this into a full closing prgh.
>
> As you revise, be sure you focus each prgh on its central idea.

Clearly, the responses emphasize White's authority as a teacher. They are surely controlling. But they hardly belong in the same category as the first teacher's responses.[7] Most obviously, White does not smatter the page with markings about surface features. He deals with a range of concerns, but most of his responses address the ideas and development of the writing. Although he marks several sentence-level problems, he does not dwell on them. In addition, most of his responses take the form of full statements. They have the feel of conversation and, although they may not initiate much interaction, create some kind of exchange with the writer. Although he has a certain idea of what can be done to improve the essay, he does not set forth a rigid plan according to specific features and organizational strategies he has in mind.[8] He works with the student's meanings and purposes and tries to indicate where they should be more fully brought out.

White makes six comments in modes that do not assert significant control over the writing: two praise comments, two interpretations, and two explanatory comments. These comments indicate where the essay is working well, how it is coming across to a reader, and what his other comments mean. He makes only one negative evaluation, when he disagrees that the writer's "only and most important argument to LeMoult" occurs in the last paragraph. Although White's responses assume a substantial degree of control, they do not impose an "idealized text" on the writing, and they do not "usurp" control from the student by dictating sweeping changes. The same can be said of White's responses in general and of the other two most controlling readers in the study: Donald Stewart and Richard Larson.

As a group, the 12 readers show they are aware of the problems with commentary that takes excessive control over student texts. They try to keep responsibility for the writing choices in the hands of the student. Nevertheless, it would be misleading to suggest that they believe all forms of "directive" commentary are to be avoided. In fact, most of our readers make at least occasional use of the most controlling modes of commentary. The group as a whole writes an average of 16% of their comments in these three highly controlling modes. Three of the readers—White, Stewart, and Frank O'Hare—write over 20% of their comments in the form of corrections, commands, and negative evaluations.

It would also be misleading, however, to say that all 12 of our readers adopt a "facilitative" style. Clearly, some readers are more or less "facilitative"—or more or less controlling—than others. The readers differ significantly in the modes of commentary they employ, in the range and detail of their comments, and in the extent to which they try to engage the student in a real exchange about revision. Through the various ways they respond to our sampling of writings, the 12 readers demonstrate that there are many ways for readers to be "directive" and to be "facilitative," many ways to exert control over student writing or share responsibility with the writer. Looked at closely, their comments reveal just how complex the concept of control in teacher commentary really is.

The readers' comments also reveal an underlying truth. In a sense, all teacher comments assume control over the student's writing. Amid the complexities about response styles, there are two constants: All teachers' responses are somehow evaluative, and all teachers' responses are somehow directive. When they respond, teachers indicate what's working (if only by their silence) and what's not working in the text. They also indicate, however implicitly or explicitly, what can be done to improve the writing. Given the power relations that adhere between teachers and students in the classroom, any responses will take on the sense of evaluations and directives.

Because the very act of response is an act of control, the question, then, is not *whether* the teacher—or any responder—should assume control over a text; the question is *to what extent* the teacher, given his overall style and the goals for instruction, should assume control or allow the writer to retain control over the writing. It's a question of how much and when to evaluate, how much and when to be directive: when to tell the student that something is not working effectively, when to simply play back the text or pose a question; when to direct the student to take up particular revisions, when to offer several options for her to consider; when to give explicit, detailed advice, when to stand back and let the student herself figure out what is working and what can be made to work better. Some writers may need more direction than others. Some teachers may be more inclined and more adept at using one type of response or another. Some types of writing or some stages of drafting may require more teacher guidance. And some approaches to teaching writing may demand more or less controlling styles of response. The more a teacher bases instruction on the completion of written products, the more likely he will intervene in the student's writing and the more controlling his responses will be. The more a teacher bases instruction on the student's learning principles of writing and practicing activities of composing, the more likely he will encourage the student to make her own writing choices and the less controlling he will be. Response styles, then, are distinguished by (a) the extent to which teachers evaluate texts and direct the student toward revision, and (b) the way in which they present their readings and call on the student to make revisions.

In the following section, we outline a spectrum of responding styles that is based on the different ways teachers exert control over students' writing choices.

A METHOD FOR DESCRIBING TEACHERS' RESPONDING STYLES

Our method of describing teacher responses provides a detailed system for classifying response styles in terms of teacher control. The method differs from Knoblauch and Brannon's in that we are looking at comments independently from actual classroom contexts, using information derivable only from the student texts and the teacher comments. It transforms Knoblauch and Brannon's two-type classification into six general responding styles, each one invoking a different predominant role for the teacher and reflective of a different degree and type of teacher control. These general styles provide six prototypes against which an individual teacher's style may be constructed. They fall into two broad categories, "authoritative" and "interactive," and in Figure 4.1 are presented left to right from more controlling to less controlling.

Teachers who use an "authoritative" style tend to write comments that directly identify what can or should be done by way of revision. They use their authority as teachers to set in motion the changes that are to be made. Teachers who use an "interactive" style try to engage students in actively making their own choices about revision, relying less on the teacher's authority and more on the interplay between reader and writer. These teachers do not concentrate on announcing the need for changes or even suggesting them; they write comments that offer interpretations, ask questions, and provide information to help the writer see how they are reading and reacting to the text. They identify issues for the student to consider and indicate only indirectly what might be made to work better. They attempt to engage the student in reenvisioning the text and leave her to decide what changes to make on her own. Rather than setting "authoritative" commentary in opposition to "nonauthoritative" commentary, we prefer to place responses that explicitly foreground the teacher's authority ("authoritative") at one side of a continuum that gradually gives way to responses that rely less and less on the teacher's authority and attempt in different ways to place the teacher in a dynamic exchange with the student ("interactive").[9]

There are three kinds of authoritative response: authoritarian, directive, and advisory. Each is associated with one overriding function that suggests its relative degree of control,[10] as Figure 4.2 shows.

An **authoritarian** style typically *corrects* and *criticizes* the student's writing. It is highly judgmental and dictates a variety of changes, rigidly imposing the teacher's agenda and taking substantial control over the text. Such a style is usually marked by a predominance of corrective, imperative, and evaluative comments, and by a clipped, critical voice. A **directive** style *directs* or *firmly guides* the student about what to do to improve her writing. It points to problems the student should address or (when it takes on a more positive tone) presents a number of specific directions for revision. Teachers who use a directive style are not highly judgmental, but they are nevertheless critical. They do not go so far as to demand changes; they just point to the need for

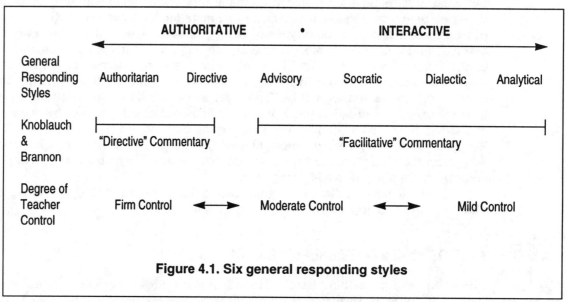

Figure 4.1. Six general responding styles

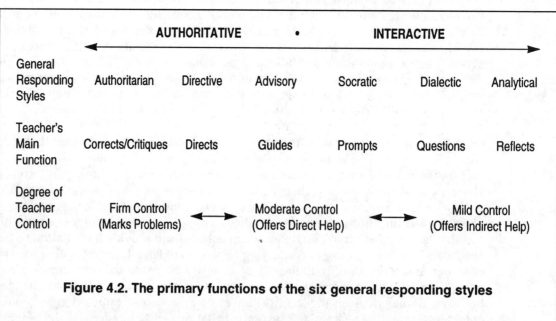

Figure 4.2. The primary functions of the six general responding styles

them. Both authoritarian and directive styles of response assert the teacher's authority and frequently "appropriate" the student's writing. But whereas authoritarian commentary usurps control from the student, demanding exacting changes across the text, directive commentary identifies the need for changes and, at least as often, engages in other, less authoritative types of commentary. The third type of authoritative response—**advisory**—primarily *makes suggestions* or *offers options* that are designed to help the writer decide what to do by way of revision. Advisory response is typically less controlling than directive commentary because it suggests changes more than it dictates or requests them. An advisory style is also more conversational and deferring than the other two types of authoritative response, allowing the student greater control over making her own writing choices.[11]

There are three kinds of interactive response—Socratic, dialectic, and analytical—again, each one progressively less controlling. A **Socratic** style *prompts* the student to make particular changes in the text. It relies heavily on the kind of closed questions Socrates is known for in Plato's dialogues: questions that seem to imply the questioner's answer (closed problem-posing questions) or that attempt to elicit specific information that the questioner assumes the respondent has readily available (closed heuristic questions). A Socratic style allows the teacher to create an interplay with the student even as it keeps the teacher in control of how the student sees the choices. A **dialectic** style makes the student more responsible for making her own writing decisions by *asking open-ended questions*, questions that lead her to consider issues and possibilities on her own. Finally, in an **analytical** style the teacher mainly reflects on how he understands the writing. He usually gives the student a close reading of the text or provides lessons about the writing but assumes little direct control over revision.[12]

The teacher's choice of modes is the most significant factor in determining his responding style. In Figure 4.3, we indicate how different modes of response, when they occur

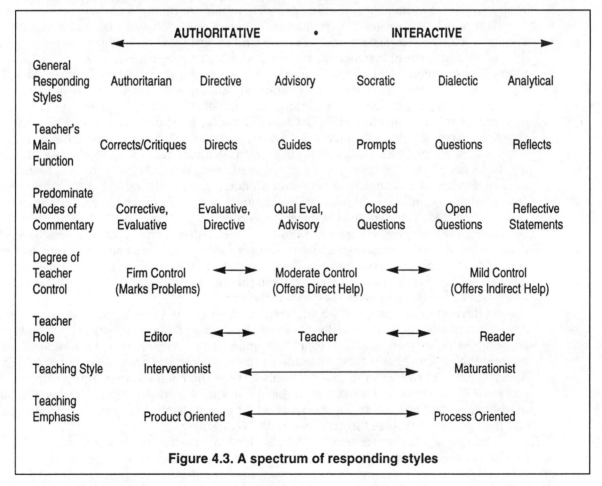

Figure 4.3. A spectrum of responding styles

extensively across a teacher's responses, may be linked with different styles. For instance, responses that make heavy use of corrective and evaluative statements are typically going to be part of—and help establish—an authoritarian style. Responses that make substantial use of open-ended questions are typically going to be part of—and help establish—a dialectical style. Other factors, as we shall see, also influence teacher control, including the number and range of comments, the length and specificity of the comments, the focus and orientation of the comments, and the extent to which the teacher reads the student text in terms of his own agenda. These various patterns of response, as they come together in a set or sets of commentary, make up a teacher's responding style.

We also indicate in Figure 4.3 how different modes of commentary and styles of response link up with different images and roles for the teacher. Instead of delineating all the images and roles that are associated with the various types of response, we indicate here the three general roles that teachers tend to invoke in their commentary. We assume that most teachers' responses place the responder in the role of a teacher, someone who (among other things) provides instruction, offers guidance, or gives advice. From this base at the center, the teacher may move out either in the direction of an editor or in the direction of a reader. The more a teacher devotes his responses to indicating changes that need to be made in the text, the more he will take on the role of an editor and the greater control he will assert over the writing. The more a teacher devotes his responses to playing back his way of interpreting the text or identifying issues it raises for him, the more he will take on the role of a reader and the less control he will exert over the writing. Teachers, of course, take on many roles in their responses, not just one or two. They may assume different roles for different students, for different assignments, or at different points in a course. They may also assume a variety of roles with the same student, even on a single piece of writing. In this analysis, we are concerned with examining the predominant roles the 12 readers assume in their responses.

Figure 4.3 also suggests a connection between styles of response and styles of teaching. Teachers who lean toward the role of editor tend to write authoritative comments and adopt an interventionist style of instruction; teachers who lean toward the role of reader tend to write interactive comments and adopt a maturationist style of instruction.[13] Of course, most teachers do not assume either the pure role of editor and simply proofread the text or the pure role of reader and simply play back their interpretations of the writing. Their style is usually some mixture of roles: a teacher-editor, a teacher-critic, a teacher-advisor, a teacher-coach, a representative reader, a sympathetic reader, or some other kind of teacher-reader. Just as editors and readers assume different roles and tasks, teachers may incorporate different roles and tasks in their central task of using comments to help students learn to write better.

As Figure 4.3 indicates, teachers who predominantly make strong authoritative comments (corrections, commands, and negative evaluations) and lean toward the role of editor tend to be product-oriented. They are usually most concerned with helping students learn to write better by leading them to produce better, more complete written texts. Teachers who predominantly make reflective comments (especially reader-response comments) and lean toward the role of reader tend to be process-oriented. They are usually most concerned with helping students learn to become better writers by giving them practice in writing activities and placing the major responsibility on them to make their own revisions.[14]

In the rest of this chapter, we analyze the styles of our 12 readers. As we noted in Chapter 3, we are not attempting to describe these readers' *actual* responding styles, but their *images* as responders as may be inferred from their comments themselves in this clinical setting. Of course, the control that a teacher assumes in comments she makes in an actual setting is a direct function of the larger classroom context. How she comes across in the comments will be influenced by how she comes across in the classroom. We are attempting to describe the types of teacher control and the styles of response that emerge from these readers' words on the page and the figures they create through their written responses.

The rest of the chapter unfolds in three sections, each one analyzing the responding style of four of our readers, each of whom, in turn, typically assumes a different degree of control.

Each section begins with a reader whose style is the most controlling in that group (and whose style is among the most controlling in the 12 readers as a whole) and concludes with a reader whose style is the least controlling in that group (and among the 12 readers as a whole). In between, we will see readers whose styles are moderately controlling. Table 4.1 outlines the 12 readers' styles according to their group and their relative degree of control.

Table 4.1. Degrees of Control in the 12 Readers' Styles.

	Most controlling ⟵⟶ Least controlling			
Group 1	White	O'Hare	Peterson	Gere
Group 2	Stewart	McClelland	Hull	Elbow
Group 3	Larson	Anson	Stock	Warnock

In each section we illustrate the teachers' response styles by displaying their comments on a common sample essay. In the first section, we describe the response styles of Edward White, Frank O'Hare, Jane Peterson, and Anne Gere, and present their responses to Writing 12, "Street Gangs: One Point of View." In the second section, we describe the response styles of Donald Stewart, Ben McClelland, Glynda Hull, and Peter Elbow, and present their responses to Writing 2, "What If Drugs Were Legal?" In the third section, we describe the response styles of Richard Larson, Chris Anson, Patricia Stock, and Tilly Warnock, and present their responses to Writing 4, "Overguiding Teenage Children." In each case, the sample essay selected for the individual reader is one that is representative of his or her comments on the sampling as a whole. In each write-up, in addition to providing a sample set of responses, we describe the reader's general responding style, present a chart that gives a quantitative analysis of their responses, analyze the modes and focus of their responses, and offer an overview of the roles they adopt and the type of control they assume as responders.[15]

GROUP 1: EDWARD WHITE, FRANK O'HARE, JANE PETERSON, ANNE GERE

EDWARD WHITE

Edward White offers students more direction in his comments—and is more controlling—than any other reader in the study. His commentary is a good starting point for this analysis of responding styles because it marks one end of the scale for our readers as a group and because it helps define the boundary that separates styles that are directive (in our sense of the term) from those that are authoritarian (or "directive" in Knoblauch and Brannon's sense).

White's commentary shows some of the characteristics of both authoritative and interactive styles of response. On the one hand, he focuses almost a third of his comments on matters of correctness, wording, and local structure. Assuming the roles of editor and judge, he frames many of his comments in the form of corrections and negative evaluations and unhesitatingly directs the student to make changes in the text. On the other hand, he focuses over half of his comments on content and organization and frames almost half of all his comments in the form of questions, reflective comments, and praise. He often takes on the roles of an expert reader and knowing guide and uses his comments to lead the student to consider issues of revision, not simply to hand down editorial changes. His comments are usually cast in complete statements and use specific language from the student's text to help her understand what he is saying.

White's mixture of authoritative and interactive methods of response come together in a style that is neither overbearing nor collaborative, but authoritative and decisive. He inserts a definite hand in student writing and tells students in no uncertain terms what works and what can be made to work better. But he does not dismiss their meanings, and he is not overly controlling in the way that Knoblauch and Brannon have in mind for "directive" response— nothing that extreme. He seems intent on identifying students' intentions and pointing to specific changes that would help them better realize those intentions, and he is more concerned with what students might do in a revision than in what they failed to do in the draft in front of him. Nevertheless, White frames almost half of his comments in the form of correctives, critical evaluations, and commands—by far the most of any reader in the study.[1] He also tries to cover a lot of ground in his responses and deals with local concerns on every paper, regardless of the stage of drafting. These comments have the feel of directions to the writer, the requests of a teacher-editor who expects certain changes to be made.

The physical shape of White's responses captures the decisive, directive nature of his commentary. His marginal responses are spread across the student's text in bold strokes that mark his presence as a teacher, addressing a wide variety of issues as they come up. His endnotes typically are short and direct (the one presented here on "Street Gangs" is longer than most). He usually begins these endnotes with a positive comment. Then he points to the central problem or need in the writing and tells the writer how to deal with it, usually framing these comments in the form of negative evaluations and imperatives. In many cases, he goes on briefly to explain his commentary or offer a short lesson, and then closes with some encouragement. White leaves little doubt about what needs to be addressed in the writing, yet his comments are clearly designed to speak to the student.

An overview of White's responses is presented in the following table.[2]

WHITE

SETS OF RESPONSES	NUMBER OF RESPONSES		
5 rough drafts 4 final drafts		Rough Drafts	Final Drafts	Total
	Marginal Comments	53	36	89
15 comments/writing	End Comments	29	18	47
3.2 issues/writing	Total	82	54	136

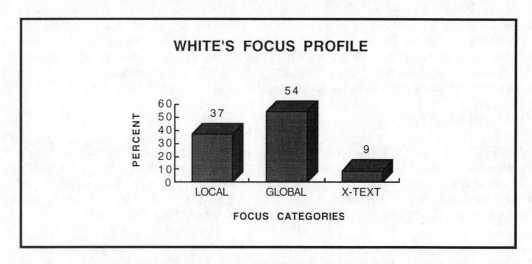

WHITE'S FOCUS PROFILE

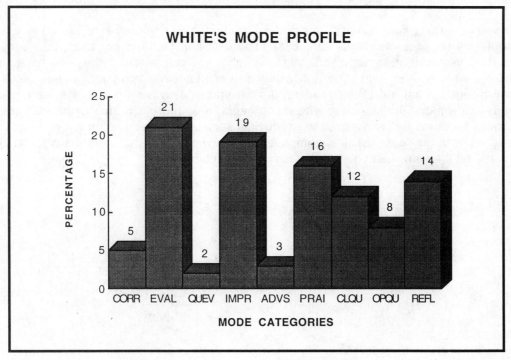

WHITE'S MODE PROFILE

WRITING 12
"STREET GANGS: ONE POINT OF VIEW"

BACKGROUND

This informative paper is the third paper of the course, the third time students have taken an assignment through several drafts with in-draft commentary. The class has been studying the principles of informative writing and paying special attention to the use of examples. Students have already completed invention activities and a first rough draft toward this paper, neither of which you have made written responses to. They will take the assignment through two more drafts.

Rusty is the kind of student who comes into writing classes apprehensive and expecting not to do well, largely because, as he wrote in his journal at the beginning of the course, his "grammar and structure are not too good." He keeps to himself in class, and he has not talked with you after class or in conference about his writing or his performance in the class, even though your written responses on his first two papers indicated that you expected more from him—in substance and correctness—in his future papers. Now he hands in this paper.

THE ASSIGNMENT

For your third paper, I'd like you to write about a hobby or activity in which you regularly engage and in which you have some level of authority or proficiency. In an informative essay of 600-900 words, inform or advise a general audience (say, the members of this class) about an aspect of this hobby or activity. As you write, try to say as best you can what precisely you mean, in a way that perhaps will spark your readers' interest in the subject.

In our work on this paper, we will pay special attention to the use, as distinct from the mere *citation*, of examples to examine and illustrate a point. As you write, keep this objective in mind.

We will take this paper through four drafts. The first is an exploratory draft, a place where you should try to get some words and ideas produced and begin to get them into some general shape. It may well be sketchy and rough. Do what you can to make it a place where you think through and discover what you want to say. You need not concern yourself with being neat and orderly—this is not a draft for readers, but for you as a writer at work. The second and third drafts are working drafts, places where you begin to do more careful shaping and crafting, and perhaps some more discovering and producing, some more experimenting. The fourth is a "final draft"—not in the sense that it is complete and forever done with, but in the sense that you can "finally" let it go now that your writing is ready for readers.

Writing 12
Rusty S.
Second Rough Draft

Street Gangs: One Point of View

I'm writing this paper on street gangs because I was once part
of one, and I feel that this gives me some authority to write a
legitimate opinion. *about them from the inside.*

I never asked or set out to join a gang, it just happened by
association. I knew some guys who were members of the Cripps and by
hanging around them I was sort of "taken in" by the gang and generally
thought to be a part of them by everyone else.

Unlike some members, I tried to maintain a low profile. I didn't
provoke fights or do destructive things on purpose, but we had a
strong bond. If one person was in trouble, no matter who or what kind
it was, everyone was there regardless, *of the cause. (?)*

This sticking together almost always occurred in a physical sense.
If one of our guys were to be beaten up, the rest of us would take a
revenge of some sort, whether it be by beating someone up or *;*
vandalizing someones property, we always got even. That was a basic
rule, nobody could "be one up on us", we always had to get even. *:*

Except for this one occasion, I can't really remember us actually *This sentence*
going out and starting trouble for no "reason". We were at the pool, *makes us expect*
and what we did was single out one person at a time. Once we had a *something else.*
target, one of us would go up to that certain someone and "sucker *Begin with "On*
punch" him and before he could retaliate the rest of the gang would *one occasion..."*
break it up.

This is the kind of detail
we need. But we need more, 1
even here.

Being a member had its ups and downs. The worst part was being
paranoid about something happening to you. It wasn't a frightening
feeling, but more like a burden. You knew something, somehow,
somewhere would eventually happen, either to you or the gang. Many
times I paid the price for being part of the Cripps with black eyes or
broken noses. I even had my windshield busted once.   *oral tone*

The good side was the family type atmosphere between us, we were
more than friends, almost like cousins or even brothers. That sense   *(?)*
of support that I got from being part of that gang was unmeasurable.   *very important to me.*
Walking down the halls of school and having everyone know that your in
this gang was great, almost like an "ego-trip". For it did make some
What did they   of the guys cocky. This overall feeling is hard to explain, it deals
do when   a lot with acceptance and friendship. I guess these two things were
"cocky"?   what kept me in the gang so long. I liked the feeling of being part
Detail.   of something that (where I come from) is almost like a status symbol.
My parents called this insecurity, this may be, but more importantly
it gave me a purpose and an identity.

During the time I spent in the gang, we were more a "party" gang.   *more than what?*
We got into trouble and fights, but not with other gangs. Gangs at
More than   the time were more friendly and were only gangs by name. I mean
when?   everyone knew each other and it was only the name of the gang and
their symbols that separated us.

Our symbols were one, a blue and red hankerchief worn around the
right ankle, a diamond stud earring in the left ear and most important
the thin white cane each member had. This was in relation with our
name: "THE CRIPPS".

2

This sign (⊥) means you are using a comma to connect sentences. Review the Handbook, chap 4, on this. We will talk about this at our next conference.

I left the gang last year because it started getting (to) violent⊥ *disliked* especially ˄the growing conflicts between gangs. Many gang fights started to break out in the streets, ˄*in* schools, and ˄*at* school related events. I just couldn't handle this,⊥ somebody could get really hurt or killed. I also felt I didn't need the ego boost anymore. I felt I could be my own person, with my own traits and characteristics. To sum it up, I grew up.

this is an interesting paper that promises to become very good. Your major idea is solid: gangs are an "ego boost" for immature kids.

Notice that you don't get around to saying this until the last paragraph. You need now to put this idea up front and to arrange your experiences and details so they all show this idea. Remember: we need lots of details and descriptions, so we can see what you mean.

Remember to edit the next draft, with a particular eye to sentence punctuation.

I want to know *more* about your subject and about your *experiences*. You have certainly "sparked my interest," as the assignment called for.[3]

Mode

What makes White's style stand out as the most controlling both in this group and among the 12 readers as a whole is his use of corrective comments and his abundant use of imperative and critical comments. Tellingly, 45% of White's responses to the sampling are cast in strong authoritative modes (corrections, negative evaluations, and imperatives), the highest in the study. The next highest uses of these modes occur in Donald Stewart's (29%) and Frank O'Hare's responses (21%).[3]

White's comments on "Street Gangs" are among his most directive responses in the sampling; they are also the most directive responses that this essay received from our readers.[4] In this second rough draft, half of White's comments are cast in strong authoritative modes. Three of these comments are editorial corrections. Another two are corrections qualified by a question mark. Across his responses to the sampling, White makes editorial changes (in the form of comments or editing marks) on every paper, with the exception of Writing 10, where he makes no marginal comments. He makes more corrective comments than all but two other readers.[5]

White also frames four of his comments to Rusty in the form of negative evaluations:

> This sentence makes us expect something else.
>
> [This is the kind of detail we need.] But we need more, even here.
>
> Oral tone.
>
> Notice that you don't get around to saying this until the last paragraph.

After corrective comments, negative evaluations are the most controlling form of response. They point out flaws in the text and implicitly dictate specific changes the student should make (or should have made). White writes 21% of all his comments in the sampling in the form of negative evaluations—easily the most in the study. (Stewart, who is second behind White, frames 16% of his comments as straight criticism; as a whole, the 12 readers write an average of 7% of their comments in this mode.) White's frequent use of negative evaluations accounts, more than any other feature of his commentary, for his highly controlling style.

In addition, White presents three imperatives in the marginal comments and two more in the endnote. The first two direct the student to engage in some activity of revision; the last two request changes in the text:

> Review the Handbook, chapter 4, on this.
>
> Remember to edit the next draft, with a particular eye to sentence punctuation.
>
> [What did they do when cocky?] *Detail.*
>
> You need now to put this idea up front and to arrange your experiences and details so they all show this idea.

All four of these comments dictate a course of revision and are clearly controlling. Still, the first two are softened somewhat by the commands "Review" and "Remember," verbs that are less forceful and less authoritative than commands White might easily have used in their place: "Correct all sentence boundary errors" and "Edit the next draft." They are also tempered by the fact that they call for the student to engage in some activity of revision, not to make a particular change in the text. The third comment, which we read as an elliptical command ("Add more detail"), has more force behind it, especially because it requests a specific change in the text and because it is underscored.[6] The last command is the most assertive that White makes on this set of responses, in part because of its form (the definitiveness of "You need now to put") and in part because it focuses on such a large issue of the writing, its controlling idea. As these commands show, White does not shy away from pointing to changes he feels should be made. Notably, however, he modulates some of his control either by framing the imperative in combination with some other comment ("What did they do when cocky?" and "We will talk about this at our next conference.") or by citing a reason for the request ("with a particular eye to sentence revision," "so they all show this idea"), not just presenting the command itself. Such additions give some reasoning behind White's comments and place some of the weight of the choice outside of himself.

Even as White scatters assertive, controlling comments across his responses, he also makes regular use of interactive commentary. On "Street Gangs," for instance, he tempers some of the control he exerts over Rusty by casting 9 of his 24 comments in the form of questions, reflective statements, and praise. His questions, especially the one open question in the middle of the writing—"What did they *do* when cocky?"—leave it up to Rusty to come up with his own additional materials. His explanatory comments, although he uses them less frequently than most of the other readers, also put him in a role other than that of editor or critic:

> This sign ( ) means you are using a comma to connect sentences. [Review the Handbook, chap 4, on this.]
>
> Remember, we need lots of details and descriptions, so we can see what you mean.

These explanatory comments help to ease the otherwise strong emphasis on White's authority as a teacher and ground the comments in some authority outside of himself, in certain conventions of writing. He uses these explanatory comments—and, elsewhere, interpretive comments—sparingly but regularly across his responses to the sampling.

White's four positive remarks also help ease some of his control over the writing:

> *This* is the kind of detail we need.
>
> This is an interesting paper that promises to become very good.
>
> Your major idea is solid: gangs are an "ego boost" for immature kids.
>
> You have certainly sparked my interest, as the assignment called for.

Although such praise controls the student's choices in ways that are similar to the control implied in negative evaluations, largely by determining what the writer attends to, it does not exert the kind or the degree of control that criticism does.[7] By using praise, the teacher turns his attention away from the changes that can be made to improve the text. He steps back from his role as editor, and, adopting the role of a coach or a motivator, acknowledges what has already been accomplished. But in doing so he also likely closes down all subsequent revision on the writing he praises.[8]

White's comments on four other essays (Writings 2, 4, 6, and 11) also make extensive use of strong authoritative comments, each essay having no fewer than 42% of the comments framed as correctives, criticism, or imperatives. Notably, however, even in these—his most controlling—sets of responses, White nearly balances strong authoritative comments with interactive ones. He frames 48 of his 100 comments as corrections, criticism, and imperatives; he frames 34 comments as questions, reflective statements, and praise.[9] He also tempers some of his control as a responder by giving many of his comments a conversational tone and offering explanations for his choices. White's full statements, frequent praise, and interactive comments—not just strong authoritative comments—help show how his responding style does not simply dictate changes to be made, but directs and guides the student toward revision.

Focus

White addresses a range of issues in most of his responses. He treats three or more areas of commentary on seven of his nine sets of responses—and treats four or more areas on four sets of responses.[10] White restricts his comments to the formal text more than anyone else in the study, framing only a handful of comments that call attention to the rhetorical situation, the classroom, or the student's relation to the writing. He also focuses on local matters more than any other reader in the study, with 37% of his responses given to local structure, wording, and correctness. (The median for the group of readers is 15%.) The more a teacher's comments focus on the formal text and especially on local concerns, the more controlling the comments because they may readily lead to specific changes in the writing with little input by the student. As Sommers (1982) notes "Th[e] appropriation of the text by the teacher happens particularly when teachers identify errors in usage, diction, and style in a first draft and ask students to correct these errors when they revise" (p. 149).

In "Street Gangs," 11 of White's 16 marginal comments (and 12 of his 24 comments overall) address local concerns. If he limited his comments to such local concerns, he would be more controlling. But that is not the case. Unlike the directive readers Brannon and Knoblauch denounce, White looks beyond matters of "prose decorum" and considers the writer's content and organization. Six of his comments to Rusty are concerned with ideas and development:

> *This* is the kind of detail we need. But we need more, even here.
> What did they do when cocky? *Detail.*
> Remember, we need lots of details and descriptions, so we can see what you mean.
> I want to know *more* about your subject and about your experiences.

Another three comments, all of which occur in the endnote, address the controlling idea and the organization of the essay:

> Your major idea is solid: gangs are an "ego boost" for immature kids. Notice that you don't get around to saying this until the last paragraph. You need now to put this idea up front and to arrange your experiences and details so they all show this idea.

Across his responses to the sampling, 54% of White's comments deal with global concerns: ideas, development, and global structure. So, although White's interest in dealing regularly with student writing at the local level helps make his commentary directive and at times leads him to appropriate student texts, his emphasis on global matters gets him into areas of writing that are less prone to immediate, specific revisions and that are more likely to place greater responsibility on the student.[11]

Overview of Teacher Control

Edward White is a close critical reader. It seems he goes to the text looking for, and in his comments is able to put his finger on, what he sees as the key problems that need to be worked out in the writing. He then instructs students about what to do by way of revision or poses questions that will lead them to make specific changes in the text. He does not shy away from telling students precisely what their writing needs or offering them specific directions for revision. And he is content, it seems, to let his comments rest on his authority as a teacher. White occasionally explains the rationale behind his comments, but only occasionally. He rarely qualifies his comments or uses qualifying modes. In fact, among the 12 readers he has the lowest percentage of qualified evaluative comments and advice—comments that temper the teacher's control when he presents evaluations of the writing and calls for revisions. He also seldom makes reference to contexts beyond the text to provide some perspective for his responses.

Throughout his comments, White also exerts a strong presence as a teacher and as an expert reader, an authority. He seems inclined to shape his comments around his sense of how the writing should proceed. To say that White takes an "idealized text" to his reading is too strong and emphasizes the negative side of directive commentary. It would be more accurate to say that he offers firm direction or guidance to the student, that he wants to give her something explicit to work on. This direction comes out most clearly in White's tendency to determine the controlling idea of the writing. He exerts such control, for example, in his final comment on "Street Gangs," when he inserts his sense of what the main thrust of the essay should be:

> This is an interesting paper that promises to become very good. Your major idea is solid: gangs are an "ego boost" for immature kids.[12]

This tendency to offer a strong reading of the writing can also be seen in White's comments on other papers:

> The basic problem to work on for your next draft has to do with supporting your assertions with evidence. (Writing 1)
>
> Now that you are clear on what *you* have to say (see your last prgh), revise the opening to begin your argument. (Writing 2)
>
> The best tone [approach] for this assignment is the one you set in your opening prgh, in which the details show what is special for you about fishing. (Writing 5)
>
> Your revision should keep the good organization and concept, but show careful attention to making the memories *yours*, by detail, rather than just anyone's. (Writing 6)

Even though these comments can be seen as White's attempt simply to help the student locate the main idea or thrust of the writing, they also show him making decisions for the student, virtually imposing his views on the focus of writing, which is perhaps the most significant choice a writer makes—and perhaps the choice that most makes one an author.

White's emphasis on the formal text, his wide range of focuses, his tendency to deal with local structure, and his heavy use of corrective, imperative, and critical modes together make his responses stand out as the most controlling in the study. The brevity of many of his comments, the lines that underscore his responses, the thick inscription of his felt-tip pen, and his inclination to give strong readings, in addition, emphasize his presence as a responder and increase his control over student writing. His commentary creates a voice that is, although not authoritarian, firmly authoritative. These are comments of the teacher in the role of a sure-handed critic and expert guide. They are not to be considered so much as they are to be addressed.

FRANK O'HARE

Frank O'Hare alternates between authoritative and interactive strategies of response, creating a mixed style that is ultimately more directive than it is facilitative. At the heart of his responses, he is a critic. When he looks at a piece of writing, it seems his impulse is to evaluate it, and when he records his reactions for the student, he does so directly and without apology. In isolation, his evaluative comments would unquestionably be considered controlling. But in the full setting of his responses, his critical side is tempered by comments that establish a context for his evaluations and that share control with the student. Throughout his responses, O'Hare shifts between negative evaluations, imperatives, and advice, on the one hand, and open questions, interpretations, and positive comments, on the other. He asks more questions than the most authoritative readers in the study, and he uses many more negative evaluations and imperatives than the most interactive readers. He is best seen as a facilitative critic.

Across the sampling O'Hare makes regular use of criticism, praise, and reflective statements, but he varies his use of advice, commands, and questions from essay to essay. He is intent above all on providing his reading of the text, playing back what he understands the writer to be saying and judging the relative strengths and weaknesses of the writing. There is also a clear difference between the way he comments on rough drafts and on final drafts.[1] On rough drafts, O'Hare regularly uses imperatives and advice and makes abundant use of questions, especially open questions. He writes fewer comments on final drafts and cuts back dramatically on his use of questions and imperatives (although he still uses a moderate amount of advice). His comments on "Street Gangs" are representative of the way he generally establishes a foundation for his commentary through reflective statements and evaluations. They also are representative of his comments on other rough drafts in his use of questions, commands, and advisory comments. But they are exceptional in at least two ways, which may well be related. O'Hare makes almost 10 more comments on this essay (26) than his average. And he makes almost as many comments on local matters and voice on this one essay (7) as he does on the other eight essays combined (8). Evidently, he thinks this writing (unlike, for example, Writing 1, Writing 2, or Writing 10) is far enough along to deal with such concerns, and he deals with them simply by adding comments, not taking away from his usual interest in the content and purpose of the writing.

O'Hare's method of response offers a middle ground between marginal comments and full-fledged letters to the student. He makes a running list of discrete comments separate from the student's text—comments that address particular passages and that could easily be presented in the margins. Other than the symbols he uses to connect his endnotes with the student's actual writing, he makes no responses on the essays themselves.[2] The method gives him a way to offer detailed responses to specific passages, and thereby communicate his ideas more fully to the student. It also allows him a device for at least physically distancing himself from the writing and offering a check on becoming overly directive, because it is more difficult for teachers to appropriate student writing or even dictate specific changes when they do not write on the text and instead present a separate set of notes to the student. As we shall see, the decision to make comments outside of the student's text also leads teachers to make more interpretive comments, whose purpose is to identify or paraphrase what the student has said so that other comments can be made. Extensive use of such comments emphasizes the teacher's role as reader and—as in O'Hare's case—has the effect of easing teacher control.

O'HARE

SETS OF RESPONSES

5 rough drafts
4 final drafts

17 comments/writing

3.3 issues/writing

NUMBER OF RESPONSES

	Rough Drafts	Final Drafts	Total
Marginal Comments	00	00	00
End Comments	94	56	150
Total	94	56	150

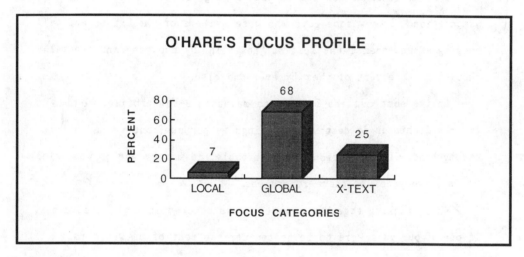

O'HARE'S FOCUS PROFILE

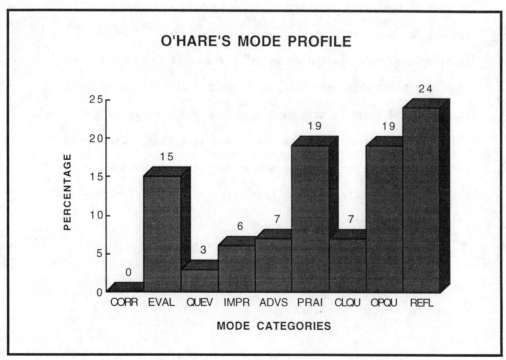

O'HARE'S MODE PROFILE

Writing 12
Rusty S.
Second Rough Draft

Street Gangs: One Point of View

I'm writing this paper on street gangs because I was once part
of one, and I feel that this gives me some authority to write a
legitimate opinion.

I never asked or set out to join a gang, it just happened by
association. I knew some guys who were members of the Cripps and by
hanging around them I was sort of "taken in" by the gang and generally
thought to be a part of them by everyone else.

Unlike some members I tried to maintain a low profile. I didn't
provoke fights or do destructive things on purpose, but we had a
strong bond. If one person was in trouble, no matter who or what kind
it was, everyone was there regardless.

This sticking together almost always occured in a physical sense.
If one of our guys were to be beaten up, the rest of us would take a
revenge of some sort, whether it be by beating someone up or
vandalizing someones property, we always got even. That was a basic
rule, nobody could "be one up on us", we always had to get even.

Except for this one occasion, I can't really remember us actually
going out and starting trouble for no "reason". We were at the pool,
and what we did was single out one person at a time. Once we had a
target, one of us would go up to that certain someone and "sucker
punch" him and before he could retaliate the rest of the gang would
break it up.

Being a member had its ups and downs. The worst part was being
paranoid about something happening to you. It wasn't a frightening
feeling, but more like a burden. You knew something, somehow,
somewhere would eventually happen, either to you or the gang. Many
times I paid the price for being part of the Cripps with black eyes or
broken noses. I even had my windshield busted once.

The good side was the family type atmosphere between us, we were
more than friends, almost like cousins or even brothers. That sense
of support that I got from being part of that gang was unmeasurable.
Walking down the halls of school and having everyone know that your in
this gang was great, almost like an "ego-trip". For it did make some
of the guys cocky. This overall feeling is hard to explain, it deals
a lot with acceptance and friendship. I guess these two things were
what kept me in the gang so long. I liked the feeling of being part
of something that (where I come from) is almost like a status symbol.
My parents called this insecurity, this may be, but more importantly
it gave me a purpose and an identity.

During the time I spent in the gang, we were more a "party" gang.
We got into trouble and fights, but not with other gangs. Gangs at
the time were more friendly and were only gangs by name. I mean
everyone knew each other and it was only the name of the gang and
their symbols that separated us.

Our symbols were one, a blue and red hankerchief worn around the
right ankle, a diamond stud earring in the left ear and most important
the thin white cane each member had. This was in relation with our
name: "THE CRIPPS".

2

I left the gang last year because it started getting to violent, especially the growing conflicts between gangs. Many gang fights started to break out in the streets, schools and school related events. I just couldn't handle this, somebody could get really hurt or killed. I also felt I didn't need the ego boost anymore. I felt I could be my own person, with my own traits and characteristics. To sum it up, I grew up.

Writing 12
Rusty S.

    Rusty, I get the feeling that you are still thinking through your experiences with the gang and that you haven't yet decided the significance of this experience.

    In the first paragraph, you seem hesitant about your right to write about this subject. Of course, your opinion about this subject is of value. Your opinion will be not only legitimate but authoritative.

    This hesitancy has, I think, caused you to neglect focusing on your purpose in this paper. It would probably be useful for you to sketch quickly an informal outline of your draft. What major points do you want to establish?

    Why did you talk about keeping a low profile?

    You seem to be combining the bonding issue with "starting trouble."

    You claim that your gang didn't look for trouble, and yet the fifth paragraph discusses the only time you did.

    Paragraph six needs specifics. What incident or incidents led you to use the terms "paranoia" and "burden"? You suffered black eyes and broken noses and yet weren't afraid. Please explain.

    Paragraph seven does a good job of establishing your sense of identity.

    Paragraph eight is confused and confusing. Are you saying that gang rivalries weren't as nasty as they appear to be? If so, the point is interesting and well worth explaining to your readers.

    Paragraph nine: what point are you establishing here?

    This subject is well worth writing about, but you must decide what your major points will be.

Two comments about code:
1. The level of your vocabulary is just a little too informal.

2. I have marked six places where you failed to recognize sentence boundaries. Please examine these examples and see if you can rewrite them correctly. Please come in for a conference and we'll discuss this problem. All six are, in reality, examples of just one problem.

Mode

Like Edward White, O'Hare does not shy away from making commands and critical evaluations. But a closer look at the extent to which the two use these comments begins to reveal the differences in their styles. Whereas White frames 45% of his comments in strong authoritative modes (correctives, negative evaluations, imperatives), O'Hare uses 21%. Further comparisons are even more revealing. White and O'Hare use evaluations more than anyone else in the study: one-third of their comments are cast in the form of evaluative modes. Yet, whereas White uses more criticism than praise, O'Hare balances positive and negative evaluations.[3] White frames his comments in the form of imperatives 19% of the time, the highest in the study; O'Hare casts his comments as imperatives only 6% of the time, an average rate for our readers. White regularly makes corrections in his comments; O'Hare makes no corrective comments on the sampling. If White and O'Hare share a propensity for making authoritative comments, they do not share it to the same degree, or use them with the same assertiveness and authority.

Still, O'Hare's style is fairly directive. On "Street Gangs," 8 of his 26 comments are either imperatives or negative evaluations:[4]

> You claim that your gang didn't look for trouble, and yet the fifth paragraph discusses the only time you did.
>
> Paragraph six needs specifics. [You suffered black eyes and broken noses and yet weren't afraid.] Please explain.
>
> Paragraph eight is confused and confusing.
>
> [This subject is well worth writing about,] but you must decide what your major points will be.
>
> The level of your vocabulary is just a little too informal.
>
> I have marked six places where you failed to recognize sentence boundaries. Please examine these examples and see if you can rewrite them correctly. Please come in for a conference and we'll discuss this problem.

For the most part, these evaluations and commands are straightforward and authoritative. However, they are softened by the interpretive comments and praise that are around them. This strategy establishes O'Hare's role as a reader and coach as well as a critic. There is a conversational tone in his comments as well, partly because they are framed in full sentences and read like letters.

Across his other sets of responses, O'Hare regularly presents frank criticisms that assert his authority as a teacher and a critic:

> Your first paragraph is a series of claims with no discussions of the reasons for your claims. (Writing 1)
>
> [I have no doubt about your sincerity in this paper . . .] but you fail to help your readers see Syracuse as you see it. (Writing 6)
>
> The third paragraph is not well organized. (Writing 11)

Frequently, though, he mutes his evaluations and blunts the sharpness of the criticism by the way he expresses his comments:

> The level of your vocabulary is just a little too informal. (Writing 12)
>
> You use only one example (the policeman and your friends) to support your opinion. (Writing 1)
>
> In the second paragraph, you tell your readers that LeMoult gives the historical background on how drugs became restricted by law, but you haven't yet explained why he does so. (Writing 2)

In the first example, he softens the criticism by specifying that the student's vocabulary is "just a little" too informal. In the second, he states his evaluation in terms of what the student already does (but does not yet do enough of), rather than simply in terms of a fault: "You don't have enough examples." In the last case, he again presents his evaluation in terms of what the student does and in terms of what he has yet to do. The comment would have been more critical, for instance, if it had been stated more directly: "Your summary is incomplete." At other times, O'Hare takes some of the bite out of his evaluations by placing them among other comments that find something to praise in the writing or that explain a negative comment, as in the samples cited earlier:

> I have no doubt about your sincerity in this paper . . . but you fail to help your readers see Syracuse as you see it. (Writing 6)
>
> The third paragraph is not well organized. It covers too many concepts superficially. (Writing 11)

O'Hare also makes his commentary less directive by presenting as many comments in the form of advice as in the form of imperatives and by making a high percentage of positive evaluations, reflective statements, and open questions (19%, 24%, and 19% respectively). In fact, he tends to use a range of modes in all of his responses, with his authoritative comments followed up by and moderated by interactive ones.

The feature that most effectively plays against O'Hare's authoritative comments and gives his style an interactive quality is his use of open questions. In "Street Gangs," for example, he writes five open questions:

> What major points do you want to establish?
>
> Why did you talk about keeping a low profile?
>
> What incident or incidents led you to use the terms "paranoia" and "burden"?
>
> Are you saying that gang rivalries weren't as nasty as they appear to be?
>
> Paragraph 9: what point are you establishing here?

O'Hare's questions often stand on their own. Frequently, however, they follow other types of response and may be read as his way of helping the student address the problems he sees in the writing. Three of the questions from "Street Gangs" fit this pattern:

> It would probably be useful for you to sketch quickly an informal outline of your draft. What major points do you want to establish?
>
> Paragraph six needs specifics. What incident or incidents led you to use the terms "paranoia" and "burden"?
>
> Paragraph eight is confused and confusing. Are you saying that gang rivalries weren't as nasty as they appear to be?

These follow-up questions direct Rusty's attention away from what he has not yet done in the draft to what he can do in revision. In the process, they temper O'Hare's control and shift more responsibility to the student.

O'Hare makes frequent use of this strategy of following authoritative comments with open questions in his response to other essays:

> You use only one example . . . to support your opinion. Can you think of others? (Writing 1)
>
> Your audience needs to be shown by examples dealt with in some detail

how beliefs that work well for parents don't work quite as well or even badly for teenagers. How would your guidelines work? (Writing 4)

The last full page of your draft "After fishing" to the end is a narrative of one day you spent fishing. You merely mention the fishing you did at the lilypads . . . and then, too briefly, hooking the monster bass. What is your overall purpose and who is your audience? (Writing 5)

He also tends to write questions after he provides interpretations of the writing, as in the following examples:

You seem interested in the different kinds of techniques demanded by different locations in that one lake. Should you focus on that lake exclusively or talk about Central Florida in general? In other words, what is your overall purpose? (Writing 5)

In the last paragraph, you say that "LeMoult's points are good and true but I believe he is approaching the subject in the wrong manner." What of LeMoult's points are "good and true"? How is he "approaching the subject"? Why is he approaching the problem in the wrong manner? Why are drugs wrong? (Writing 2)

O'Hare chooses to identify problems explicitly before (or instead of) simply raising questions to prompt revision, feeling perhaps that the student must be appraised of a problem before she can understand the full meaning of his question.[5] By following his criticism and interpretations with questions, he gives the student a chance to become actively involved in her revision, thus making his commentary interactive. As a result, O'Hare's comments, although they are directive, are far less directive than White's.

Focus

O'Hare limits the control he exerts over student writing by treating a moderate range of issues on each set of responses. He addresses more than three issues on only three sets of responses. He also limits his control by dealing only occasionally with local matters of correctness, wording, and sentence structure and by focusing most of his attention on global concerns. On Writing 12, for example, O'Hare writes 10 comments on ideas, among them the following:

Why did you talk about keeping a low profile?
You seem to be combining the bonding issue with "starting trouble."
You claim your gang didn't look for trouble, and yet the first paragraph discusses the only time you did.
Paragraph nine: what point are you establishing here?

He uses another four comments to lead Rusty to develop the assertions that are already there, including three in the following sequence:

Paragraph six needs specifics. What incident or incidents led you to use the terms "paranoia" and "burden"? [You suffered black eyes and broken noses and yet weren't afraid.] Please explain.

His responses across the sampling are dominated by comments about ideas and development. Fifty-six percent of his comments are given to these two focuses, the second highest in the study.[6]

O'Hare looks at most pieces of writing in terms of a conceptual model that highlights a standard set of concerns. This model, which he calls PACES (an acronym for purpose, audience, code, experience, self), offers a handy set of terms that helps O'Hare connect his written responses to the larger classroom conversation. It also may lead him to focus the majority of his comments on large matters of content and context because only one of the PACES categories—code—deals with local concerns. Although one might expect such a model to prompt O'Hare to address all five areas on each set of responses, he rarely does. In his responses to the sampling of essays, he tends to focus predominantly on only three areas: purpose, audience, and experience. He mentions the student's "self" on five essays and addresses matters of "code" (i.e., our categories of correctness, wording, and local structure) on five sets of responses.

O'Hare routinely sees student writing in terms of the rhetorical situation. Although he looks at Writing 12 explicitly in terms of the audience and purpose in only two comments, most of his commentaries are checkered with such references.[7] The following samples from his comments on Writings 5 and 9, displayed in Chapter 2, are representative:

> You obviously enjoy fishing and know enough to make it attractive for people who haven't experienced the Orlando bass-fishing experience. (Writing 5)
>
> What is your overall purpose and who is your audience? (Writing 5)
>
> Is your audience people who have never fished before or people who have never fished for bass, especially in the Orlando area? (Writing 5)
>
> Elizabeth, you have a keen sense of what your readers need in order to understand this difficult and complex problem facing you and your family. You assume sensitivity and intelligence in your audience and convince your readers not just by the logic of your evidence and argument, but by the effectiveness of your style. (Writing 9)

By looking at the writing in terms of its impact not only on himself but also on other potential readers, O'Hare is able to maintain his emphasis on the content and the context of writing and to temper some of the authority he exerts over the student. He is able to project his concerns as the concerns of the larger audience, deflecting some attention from his own position as a teacher and making his style less controlling. Nevertheless, although he looks to the context of the writing and makes a moderate number of references to the student's knowledge, experiences, and composing processes, he remains committed first of all to the role of the critic. He fastens his attention on the text to help the student come up with a better written product.

Overview of Teacher Control

O'Hare uses a fairly large portion of his responses to direct students' attention to specific areas of the writing that are not working well and others that need improvement. Often he presents sharp, no-nonsense evaluations of the writing that assert his authority as a teacher and a critic. Like White, when he gives his readings he takes on the role of an expert reader, a reader whose judgments are informed and authoritative.[8] Yet he often mutes the harshness of these evaluations by acknowledging the strengths of an essay and offering some guidance for revision. This guidance gives students some direction, yet allows them to decide specifically what to do. The combination of criticism, recommendations, praise, and questions makes his commentary critical yet facilitative, both authoritative and interactive.

Across his responses to the sampling, O'Hare judges the writing not against the requirements of the assignment but in terms of his sense of the writer's evolving purpose. Although he is more than willing to point to areas that need improvement, he seems ambivalent about how much control he is willing to assert over the student. He is obviously interested in providing a clear direction for revision, yet at the same time seems reluctant to determine what specific revisions the student should take up. For example, in his comments to "Street Gangs" he freely identifies places where he thinks the writing fails to work or where it needs more information. Yet unlike White, who identifies what he sees as the focus of the writing (gangs are an ego boost), O'Hare resists telling Rusty what specifically he should do. After telling the student that it seems as though he has not yet decided the focus of his writing, O'Hare asks questions that might help him order his thinking and then offers encouragement and an open-ended command: "This subject is well worth writing about, but you must decide what your major points will be." He leaves the decision—and the responsibility—up to the student. Similarly, in his comments on Writing 1, O'Hare offers general advice, but little in the way of specific direction:

> If your audience is the general public or even the members of your writing class, you will want to consider carefully what different people think about this issue and why. You might brainstorm, cluster or freewrite on their opinions and on yours.

Elsewhere, even as his commentary asserts greater control over the student's choices, it is less directive than White's and puts greater responsibility on the student. On Writing 5, for instance, O'Hare points to the conflict between the narrative and expository elements of the writing and calls on the student to emphasize the expository function in the revision. But he leaves it up to Steve to decide how to make it more "expository," offering questions that might help him think through the matter:

> You seem interested in the different kinds of techniques demanded by different locations in that one lake. Should you focus on that lake exclusively or talk about Central Florida in general? In other words, what is your overall purpose? Is your audience people who have never fished before or people who have never fished for bass, especially in the Orlando area?

In his response to Writing 6, one of his most directive sets of commentary, O'Hare strongly recommends that the writer refocus the essay on one of the seasons in Syracuse. But later in the comment (perhaps feeling uneasy about this advice) he implies that the student may well not take up the recommendation.

> I'd recommend that you focus on your favorite season, fall, and capture it for your audience. . . . If you decide to focus on the fall in Syracuse, try to make your audience want to join you there.

Again, although O'Hare at one point seems interested in directing the student to make certain revisions, at another he seems reluctant to make decisions or provide material for the writer. Responders who are more directive would be more willing to assert their agendas and lead the student to make particular changes. Responders who are less directive would be more likely to make fewer evaluations and allow the student even more room to make his own decisions. O'Hare is not unwilling to offer his sense of how the student may best revise a piece of writing; he is intent on pointing out problems and giving the student some definite ideas to work on in revision. But he is also interested in having the student make his own choices about what specifically to do in the way of revision.

Finally, O'Hare positions himself as an interactive critic in his comments, pointing unhesitantly to areas for improvement, yet leaving the content of the changes in the hands of the student.

JANE PETERSON

Jane Peterson is a facilitative responder.[1] She assumes the stance of an interested reader and then, invoking her role as a teacher, indicates how students can shape the text better for their audience.[2] Her comments suggest that she is genuinely interested in what students have to say and that she is mainly concerned with helping them say what they have to say more effectively. Unlike Edward White and Frank O'Hare, who stand back from the writing and assume the stance of editor or critic, Peterson takes on a positive, encouraging stance and places herself in only a slightly superior position to the student. She seems to look at the writing, first of all, to get a sense of what is working and then to identify, not so much what needs to be fixed, but what can be improved. Instead of laying out criticisms in her comments or playing back her reading of the text, she shows her reactions and needs as a reader and frames comments that are designed to prompt the student to work on improving the text on his own.

Peterson's style of response is less controlling than O'Hare's commentary and considerably less controlling than White's. She is careful not to rely too much on her own authority and risk upsetting the delicate balance she tries to maintain between her role as a representative reader and her role as a guiding teacher. Yet, as we shall see, she is more controlling than most of our interactive readers. She stands with O'Hare in the middle of the 12 readers in terms of teacher control. While O'Hare's commentary has more the feel of directive response, Peterson's has more the feel of interactive response.

Peterson and White are the only readers in our study who make more marginal comments than end comments (Peterson 105-44, White 89-47). On almost every essay to which she responds, she makes twice as many comments in the margins as she does in her endnotes. These marginal comments usually offer brief interpretations, evaluations, and questions that are designed to note what has been done and lead the writer to consider how he might enhance what is already there. Her imperative and advisory comments, though rare, are still fairly controlling, concentrating as they do on specific point-by-point concerns. At times the number and brevity of the marginal comments give them the staccato manner of a somewhat demanding reader. In her endnotes Peterson typically starts with a positive evaluation of the writing or some compliment to the writer, and then goes on to present in a brief, general way some recommendations for revision. Like White and O'Hare, she is interested in leading students to produce (more) complete texts at all levels, a goal that leads her to devote a significant portion of her comments to local concerns and that ultimately contributes to her directiveness as a responder.[3]

PETERSON

SETS OF RESPONSES	NUMBER OF RESPONSES		
		Rough Drafts	Final Drafts	Total

SETS OF RESPONSES		Rough Drafts	Final Drafts	Total
5 rough drafts 4 final drafts	Marginal Comments	61	44	105
17 comments/writing	End Comments	31	13	44
3.4 issues/writing	Total	92	57	149

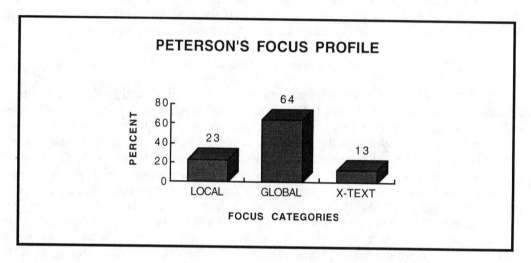

PETERSON'S FOCUS PROFILE

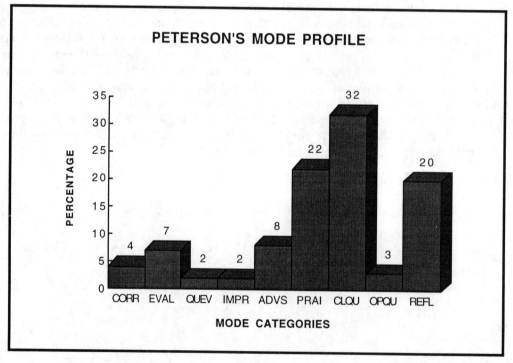

PETERSON'S MODE PROFILE

Writing 12
Rusty S.
Second Rough Draft

Street Gangs: One Point of View

I'm writing this paper on street gangs because I was once part
of one, and I feel that this gives me some authority to write a
legitimate opinion.

yes - as an
insider you
have info most
readers don't
have

I never asked or set out to join a gang, it just happened by
association. I knew some guys who were members of the Cripps and by
hanging around them I was sort of "taken in" by the gang and generally
thought to be a part of them by everyone else.

how old were
you ? Were you
in 7 th grade ?
in 10 th ?

did you consider
yourself a member ?
did they consider
you a member ?

Unlike some members I tried to maintain a low profile. I didn't
provoke fights or do destructive things on purpose, but we had a
strong bond. If one person was in trouble, no matter who or what kind
it was, everyone was there regardless.

This sticking together almost always occured in a physical sense.
If one of our guys were to be beaten up, the rest of us would take a
revenge of some sort, whether it be by beating someone up or
vandalizing someones property, we always got even. That was a basic
rule, nobody could "be one up on us", we always had to get even.

anyone or just
the person who
beat up your
gang member ?

good - you've
got the idea
of using
examples to
explain

Except for this one occasion, I can't really remember us actually
going out and starting trouble for no "reason". We were at the pool,
and what we did was single out one person at a time. Once we had a
target, one of us would go up to that certain someone and "sucker
punch" him and before he could retaliate the rest of the gang would
break it up.

1

Being a member had its ups and downs. The worst part was being

paranoid about something happening to you. It wasn't a frightening

feeling, but more like a burden. You knew something, somehow,

somewhere would eventually happen, either to you or the gang. Many

times I paid the price for being part of the Cripps with black eyes or

broken noses. I even had my windshield busted once.

good quick examples

The good side was the family type atmosphere between us, we were

how many were in your gang?

more than friends, almost like cousins or even brothers. That sense

of support that I got from being part of that gang was unmeasurable.

Walking down the halls of school and having everyone know that your in

how did others know? Did you wear the symbols + carry the cause in school

this gang was great, almost like an "ego-trip". For it did make some

of the guys cocky. This overall feeling is hard to explain, it deals

a lot with acceptance and friendship. I guess these two things were

what kept me in the gang so long. I liked the feeling of being part

of something that (where I come from) is almost like a status symbol.

My parents called this insecurity, this may be, but more importantly

it gave me a purpose and an identity.

how long was that?

examples? what kind of trouble with whom? teachers? police? your parents?

During the time I spent in the gang, we were more a "party" gang.

We got into trouble and fights, but not with other gangs. Gangs at

the time were more friendly and were only gangs by name. I mean

everyone knew each other and it was only the name of the gang and

their symbols that separated us.

Our symbols were one, a blue and red hankerchief worn around the

right ankle, a diamond stud earring in the left ear and most important

the thin white cane each member had. This was in relation with our

name: "THE CRIPPS".

2

I left the gang last year because it started getting to violent, especially the growing conflicts between gangs. Many gang fights started to break out in the streets, schools and school related events. I just couldn't handle this, somebody could get really hurt or killed. I also felt I didn't need the ego boost anymore. I felt I could be my own person, with my own traits and characteristics. To sum it up, I grew up.

Rusty, your topic is very interesting and you have something of value to give readers, but you need more detail (as my questions suggest), and you also need more focus — to select & shape info so readers can easily understand what you're saying. Let's talk for a few minutes *as the end of* class about how you might select and organize what you know. I'm really interested in learning more about what it's like to be a gang member. I'd also like you to go by the writing lab and make an appointment for next week, so you can get some extra help on editing your paper between your 3rd and final drafts.

3

Mode

Throughout her commentary, Peterson integrates the roles of teacher and reader, gently but surely guiding the student even as she presents the needs of an audience. Most of Peterson's comments, on Writing 12 and throughout the sampling, are cast in the form of closed questions. These questions are designed to elicit specific information or lead the student to recognize some problem with the writing, usually with the aim of directly improving the text. In fact, one in every three of Peterson's comments is presented as a closed question—far and away the most in the group. Closed heuristic questions, which typically call on the writer to add readily available information in specific places, make up 15% of her total comments, the highest percentage in the study. They are the distinguishing feature of her responses.

In the margins of "Street Gangs," Peterson makes 11 closed heuristic comments, some calling for specification, others for development:[4]

> How old were you? Were you in 7th grade? 10th?
>
> How many were in your gang?
>
> How long was that?
>
> Did you consider yourself a member? Did they consider you a member?
>
> How did others know? Did you wear the symbols and carry the cane in school?

Such comments offer help without wresting control from the student. They indicate where information may be needed, but they leave room for the student to come up with the information on his own. By contrast, evaluative, imperative, and even advisory comments tend to exert more control over the writing. Compare White's advisory comment and O'Hare's evaluative comment to Rusty about the need for greater clarification in paragraph 8, for example, with Peterson's questions about the same issue:

> I want to know *more* about your subject and about your experience. (White)
>
> Paragraph eight is confused and confusing. (O'Hare)
>
> Examples? What kind of trouble and with whom? Teachers? Police? Your parents? (Peterson)

With such questions, the student is left with some room to decide not only *what* to add but first of all *whether* to add anything.[5] Peterson's closed heuristic comments, because they are specific, offer guidance; because they imply that certain changes should be made, they are rather controlling. They ride the fine line that separates assistance from teacher directiveness.

Peterson also makes frequent use of closed problem-posing questions. These questions tend to exert more control over the writer than closed heuristic questions because they usually present a correction, an imperative, or an evaluation in the form of a question. In Writing 1, for example, she calls into question the student's claim that the seat belt law is "a violation of your freedom" by asking: "Don't all laws and regulations limit freedom—speed limits, state inspections for cars, life jacket requirements for small boats, etc.?" In Writing 2, she calls several of the student's assertions into question through such closed problem-posing questions. In response to the student's claim that drug addicts lead to a "corrupt society," Peterson writes in the margin: "Crime-filled?" In response to the claim, "We all know drugs are dangerous to the body and society without any explanation, therefore, you shouldn't legalize something that is dangerous," she writes five problem-posing comments that are designed to make the student reconsider her claim, if not to throw the entire statement into doubt:

> Do we? [i.e., Do we all know that drugs are dangerous?]
>
> All drugs? [i.e., Are all drugs dangerous?]

Cigarettes? Alcohol? Car racing? [i.e., Aren't cigarettes, alcohol, and car racing dangerous yet legal?]

How? Legal or illegal? [i.e., How are drugs dangerous to society? Are you talking about legal or illegal drugs?]

These comments ostensibly allow the student to consider the issue being raised instead of directing him to make certain changes. But the very form of the comment enables the teacher to insinuate her preferences into the responses even as she asks a question. There is a questioning tone in each of the comments, a hint that Peterson does not agree with the student's statement. As a result, the comments exert a certain control over the writing. By contrast, open questions do not insinuate the teacher's judgments into the comment so much as they invite the student to consider an issue of writing, as in the following questions Peterson writes across the sampling:

How important is this [argument] to you? If there had been a funding rider, would you favor the seat belt law? (Writing 1)

Do you know of other instances when seat belts were (or would have been) dangerous? (Writing 1)

What's [LeMoult] doing in the first 3 prghs? (Writing 2)

Peterson's closed questions, then, allow students room to make decisions about their writing, but they also allow her to keep a sure hand in them as well.

Positive evaluations work in a similar way. These praise comments are clearly less controlling and authoritative than criticism because they place the teacher in the role of appreciative reader or satisfied critic, rather than the role of problem finder. They nevertheless assume certain control over how the student looks at the writing and how he makes choices for revision. Even as positive comments deflect some authority from the teacher and place the locus of attention on the text, they subtly endorse the teacher's values and agenda. After all, they come from the same perspective as criticism, invoking as they do the teacher's role as critic or judge. They fit in well with Peterson's general style because they allow her to encourage the student even as they allow her to point to issues of writing with which she is concerned and nudge the student into accepting her terms and plans.

Peterson is second only to Anne Gere in offering positive evaluations, using them in 22% of her comments. She presents an average of almost four praise comments on her nine sets of responses, making at least one on every set of responses and usually three or more. She compliments Rusty's use of examples in "Street Gangs" three times in her marginal comments and makes two more positive comments in the endnote. Although she is willing to be critical, she makes two-and-a-half times as many positive evaluations as negative. She uses this praise not only to note accomplishments and encourage the student but also to provide short lessons by embedding explanations within them:

Good—you've got the idea of using examples to explain. (Writing 12)

Good addition that places you clearly in the audience as participant (not just observer) . . . . (Writing 13)

Good—you're an expert on these lakes and can write about them to bass fishers who have just moved into the Orlando area. (Writing 5)

Good detail to show the contrast. (Writing 9)

Good place to use the dash for emphasis. (Writing 10)

Good idea to return to opening metaphor to give a sense of closure. (Writing 8)

She uses a similar strategy in many of her criticisms, using them as vehicles for briefly explaining her commentary:

> To make this into a feature article for the campus newspaper, you need to start over. (Writing 5)
>
> You might have stated directly why you're including this—I assume because of the "self-esteem" issue. (Writing 11)
>
> I suggest you do a barebones outline on the article (you're missing a couple of LeMoult's points). (Writing 2)

These comments would be more authoritative and offer less direction if they were presented without the added explanations:

> You need to start over.
>
> You might have stated directly why're you're including this.
>
> I suggest you do a barebones outline on the article.

Not content to be just an editor, Peterson responds as a facilitator in these comments. As she sets out possible revisions, she takes care to offer reasons for the suggested changes. She does not simply rely on her authority as a teacher; she also explains her choices and suggests the reasons behind them.

In a similar way, she frequently follows one comment with another comment that offers more specific help:

> How old were you? Were you in 7th grade? 10th? (Writing 12)
>
> How did others know? Did you wear the symbols and carry the cane in school? (Writing 12)
>
> What kind of trouble and with whom? Teachers? Police? Your parents? (Writing 12)
>
> Don't all laws and regulations limit freedom—speed limits, state inspections for cars, life jacket requirements for small boats, etc.? (Writing 1)
>
> Was it a one-car accident or a collision? Did the car roll over? (Writing 1)

Such explanations and follow-up comments offer additional guidance and direction to the student, and they provide some balance to the terse, elliptical comments she often makes in the margins. These fuller comments are more conversational and take on the feel of the two-way exchange between teacher and student that is essential to interactive commentary.

Peterson's middle-range response style is defined as much by what is absent in her choice of modes as by what is there. It is made less controlling than it might be, in particular, by her limited use of strong authoritative comments. Across the sampling she makes only six corrective comments (none of them on rough drafts) and only three commands (all of them on Writing 5). Whereas 45% of White's comments are cast in strong authoritative modes and 21% of O'Hare's, only 13% of Peterson's are presented as correctives, commands, or critical evaluations.[6] Instead of framing her calls for revision in the form of commands, she frames them as advice.[7] At the same time, her response style is made less student-oriented and less interactive by her limited use of open-ended questions and reflective statements. Peterson poses the lowest percentage of open questions among the readers, 3% of all her comments. She writes interpretive comments infrequently and rarely makes reader-response comments. She is content to work almost exclusively with the formal text and the material the student already has on the page. Although she likes to put responsibility onto the student, she does not like to forego offering some clear direction for revision.

Focus

Peterson addresses a range, but not a wide range, of issues in her responses. She addresses three areas of commentary on six sets of responses and more than three areas on only three sets—the average number for our readers. She most frequently deals with matters of content and organization, especially with development, about which she writes more comments than anyone else in the study. Twenty-three percent of her comments are concerned with the writer's development of his ideas, 27% with ideas, and 14% with global structure. But, like White, Peterson also deals regularly with sentence-level issues. Twenty-three percent of her comments address local structure, wording, and correctness. She is especially willing to address such local matters on final drafts. On "Street Gangs," a rough draft, 6 of her 23 comments deal with local matters. This concern for dealing with local issues suggests a larger interest in the evolving written product.

Peterson tempers some of her control as a responder by casting many of her comments in terms of the needs and interests of prospective readers. Instead of asserting her authority as a teacher, she deflects attention from herself as a single reader and grounds her comments in a community of readers. In her comments on "Street Gangs," for example, she indicates the questions she has as a representative reader and engages the student in figuring out what the text needs to help readers understand:

> Your topic is very interesting and you have something of value to give readers, but you need more detail (as my questions suggest), and you also need more focus—to select and shape info so readers can easily understand what you're saying.

Her rhetorical orientation has the effect of tempering her control by looking at the written product in light of the student's purpose.[8] As the following comments suggest, Peterson regularly makes such references to prospective readers:

> Having lived in Texas, I can identify with your excitement at the prospect of "real lakes," but this section doesn't help *inform* readers about bass fishing or Orlando lakes. (Writing 5)
>
> I've put a few questions in the margin to help you see where readers might want even more detail to understand the effects better. (Writing 10)
>
> To help readers see more clearly what you mean, you need specific examples for each of your points. (Writing 4)

The last example is especially revealing, making clear the distinction between Peterson as a single reader ("I") and the larger community of potential readers. She speaks explicitly of other readers on five of her nine sets of responses. Such an orientation deflects the student's attention from the formal text itself and, because it expands the authority of the responses beyond her as an individual teacher, eases her control as a responder.

Overview of Teacher Control

Peterson's responses create the image of an interested reader—but a reader who is at once feeling hungry for more information and in need of sharper prose. On the one hand, her comments show her interest in understanding what the writer has to say, allowing him to make whatever changes he feels would be necessary to get his points across. On the other hand, her comments establish, subtly but clearly, her rather defined expectations as a reader and her own agenda as a writing teacher. Her commentary as a whole focuses on text production and on leading students to make their writing more complete. Evidently, she believes the more students work to get to finished texts, the more they will learn to produce such texts on their own and develop as writers.

Peterson assumes moderate control over student writing. Although she points to specific areas for students to revise, she usually refrains from determining the focus of their writing and never lays out a detailed course for revision. Her comments to "Street Gangs," for example, guide the student's revision and yet allow him to retain control over the changes that are made. Her marginal comments for the most part identify places for additional material, leaving a good measure of responsibility to the student. Her endnote is more directive. But it balances direction and openness, criticism and praise, and it refrains from dictating specific changes:

> Your topic is very interesting and you have something of value to give readers, but you need more detail (as my questions suggest), and you need more focus—to select and shape info so readers can easily understand what you're saying. I'm really interested in learning more about what it's like to be a gang member. I'd also like you to go by the writing lab and make an appointment for next week, so you can get some extra help on editing your paper between your 3rd and 4th drafts.

Peterson gets more controlling in her responses to Writings 1 and 5, especially in her endnotes:

> The last paragraph is what really helped me see why [the seat belt law] is important to you, and that's the point that needs much more detail. (Writing 1)

> To make this [writing] into a feature article for the campus newspaper, you need to start over. I suggest focusing on the lakes—you can give background info on the lakes (how they were formed—general characteristics, etc.) and then select 3-5 specific lakes to discuss in detail (tell the size and location of each from a bass fisher's point of view). (Writing 5)

But usually she does not exert such control. Her comments on Writing 4 and Writing 2 show her exerting her authority over what students should consider in their revision, but guiding their work more than controlling it:

> To help readers see more clearly what you mean, you need specific examples for each of your points. I've indicated some possible places for these, but they're just possibilities. (Writing 4)

> Before beginning a second draft, I suggest you do a barebones outline on the article (you're missing a couple of LeMoult's points) and then do one on your response (you seem to have at least two objections instead of one). (Writing 2)

In the degree of teacher control, then, Peterson's comments are less like White's and more like (although still less controlling than) O'Hare's.

Peterson's choice to make many marginal comments—many of them terse or elliptical, some of them even cryptic—makes her commentary more directing and controlling than it might be if she made fewer responses or made the ones she wrote more discursive and conversational. But throughout her responses, her voice is supportive and encouraging—the voice of a facilitative responder—placing her on just a slightly higher level than her students. Although she asserts her own direction for the writing more than most interactive responders, ultimately she is an interactive responder.

ANNE GERE

Anne Gere raises issues for the student to consider and provides some direction for revision, but she refrains from directing the student's choices and instead puts the impetus on the student to make his own decisions as a writer. Her style is among the least controlling and most interactive in the study.

Gere's comments are lean and simple. She identifies what she sees as major issues for revision, but she streamlines her responses by addressing only representative cases of these issues and providing only brief guidance. She seems to view her comments as starting points for the student's work, not as blueprints for revision. The student is left to decide how to enact her suggestions, to identify additional areas in which her comments may be put to use, and to come up with his own changes.

In Gere's responses we find the voice and stance of a supportive, yet expectant, mentor. Her task seems to be to select the main issues the student needs to deal with at a particular time, to point his attention to representative places where those issues come up in his writing, and to engage him in a dialogue about them. She does not hesitate to identify strengths and weaknesses in the writing, but she prefers simply to suggest what the student might work on. Instead of directing the writer to make particular revisions, as Edward White does, or instead of prompting him to make point-by-point changes on his own, as Jane Peterson does, Gere invites him to plan his own practical course for revision. Like Frank O'Hare, she makes frequent use of praise and questions. But whereas O'Hare tends to base his comments on negative evaluations, Gere tends to base hers on advice.

Still, she is always careful, it seems, not to give the student too much to handle. She usually restricts herself to commenting on one or two priorities, either assuming that by working on these larger issues the student will also address other, less important matters, or assuming that those other areas do not have to be addressed, at least not immediately. She also seems less concerned than White, O'Hare, or Peterson with leading students to come up with a finished piece of writing. She is more willing to allow the student to explore options that, although they may not lead to his producing a neater, more complete text, may lead him to develop his thinking or practice some principle of writing.

The look of the comments, the way they fall plainly and unobtrusively on the page, symbolizes her hands-off style of commentary. She makes only a few marginal comments, almost all of them in full sentences. There are no lines or other markings, and the comments never spill over into the student's text. Most of the comments here take the form of questions or praise. Her endnotes, themselves compact and typed on a separate page, are also unobstrusive. They are relatively short, ranging between 7 to 16 comments. They typically start out with a positive evaluation, identify both the strengths and the weaknesses of the writing, and then suggest a general plan for revision, often using open questions to help the student with his thinking. She is the least controlling of the four readers in this group—and among the least controlling of the 12 readers as a whole—because she does not lay out a specific plan for revision but instead leaves it to the student to come to terms with his writing on his own.

GERE

SETS OF RESPONSES	NUMBER OF RESPONSES		
5 rough drafts 5 final drafts 18 comments/writing 3.3 issues/writing		Rough Drafts	Final Drafts	Total
	Marginal Comments	36	38	74
	End Comments	59	48	107
	Total	95	86	181

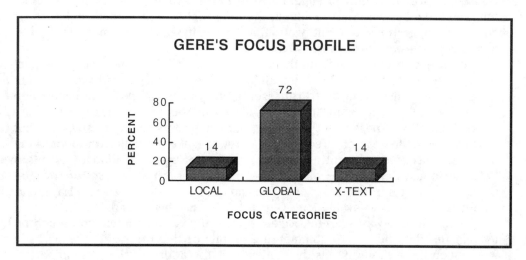

GERE'S FOCUS PROFILE

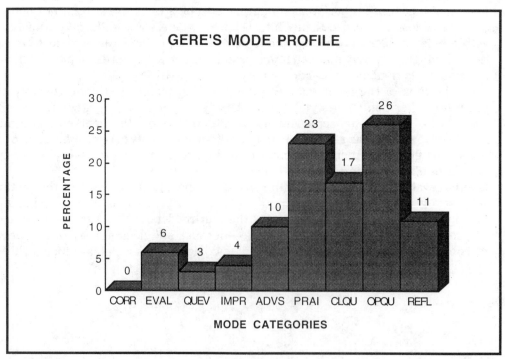

GERE'S MODE PROFILE

Writing 12
Rusty S.
Second Rough Draft

Street Gangs: One Point of View

I'm writing this paper on street gangs because I was once part *[Can you start with one specific experience drawn from your life with street gangs?]* of one, and I feel that this gives me some authority to write a legitimate opinion.

I never asked or set out to join a gang, it just happened by association. I knew some guys who were members of the Cripps and by hanging around them I was sort of "taken in" by the gang and generally thought to be a part of them by everyone else.

Unlike some members I tried to maintain a low profile. I didn't provoke fights or do destructive things on purpose, but we had a strong bond. If one person was in trouble, no matter who or what kind it was, everyone was there regardless. *[These ¶'s seem to deal with the issue of "membership." What else can you say about membership in the gang? Is there a way to make connections among these ¶'s?]*

This sticking together almost always occured in a physical sense. If one of our guys were to be beaten up, the rest of us would take a revenge of some sort, whether it be by beating someone up or vandalizing someones property, we always got even. That was a basic rule, nobody could "be one up on us", we always had to get even.

[What does this "exception" show? What do you want your readers to draw from this?] Except for this one occasion, I can't really remember us actually going out and starting trouble for no "reason". We were at the pool, and what we did was single out one person at a time. Once we had a target, one of us would go up to that certain someone and "sucker punch" him and before he could retaliate the rest of the gang would break it up.

1

Being a member had its ups and downs. The worst part was being

paranoid about something happening to you. It wasn't a frightening

feeling, but more like a burden. You knew something, somehow,

somewhere would eventually happen, either to you or the gang. Many

times I paid the price for being part of the Cripps with black eyes or

broken noses. I even had my windshield busted once.

this section sets up a nice contrast. Can you say more about advantages and disadvantages of membership?

The good side was the family type atmosphere between us, we were

more than friends, almost like cousins or even brothers. That sense

of support that I got from being part of that gang was unmeasurable.

Walking down the halls of school and having everyone know that your in

this gang was great, almost like an "ego-trip". For it did make some

of the guys cocky. This overall feeling is hard to explain, it deals

a lot with acceptance and friendship. I guess these two things were

what kept me in the gang so long. I liked the feeling of being part

of something that (where I come from) is almost like a status symbol.

Does this relate to your conclusion

My parents called this insecurity, this may be, but more importantly

it gave me a purpose and an identity.

During the time I spent in the gang, we were more a "party" gang.

Is this related to your point about not starting trouble for no reason?

We got into trouble and fights, but not with other gangs. Gangs at

the time were more friendly and were only gangs by name. I mean

everyone knew each other and it was only the name of the gang and

their symbols that separated us.

Our symbols were one, a blue and red hankerchief worn around the

Does this belong with your discussion of membership?

right ankle, a diamond stud earring in the left ear and most important

the thin white cane each member had. This was in relation with our

name: "THE CRIPPS".

2

I left the gang last year because it started getting to violent, especially the growing conflicts between gangs. Many gang fights started to break out in the streets, schools and school related events. I just couldn't handle this, somebody could get really hurt or killed. I also felt I didn't need the ego boost anymore. I felt I could be my own person, with my own traits and characteristics. To sum it up, I grew up.   *this last sentence is really interesting. What does the issue of growing up say about gangs? What, finally, is your point of view about gangs?*

Rusty--

I think you have the makings of a very good paper here. You clearly know
a great deal about gangs, and you have a rich store of illustrations and examples
to draw upon. At this stage you should give some thought to how you want to
shape your material. A good beginning is to try to summarize your "point of view"
in a sentence. What advice or information do you want to give your audience about
gangs? Then think about how you can convey this advice/information most
effectively.

As my marginal questions indicate, I wonder if you can rearrange parts of
your paper to bring related ideas together. What connections do you see among
issues of membership, identity and growing up? Does the topic of gangs raise
other issues for you?

Don't worry about sentence structure, spelling and punctuation in the next
draft. Just concentrate on what you want to tell your audience.

Mode

Gere keeps the control in her responses to a minimum by using nondirective modes, especially questions. Forty-three percent of her comments are framed as questions, 26% as open questions, the highest in the study. Twenty-three percent of her comments take the form of praise, again the highest in the study.[1] Fewer than 10% of her comments are cast in strong authoritative modes (corrections, imperatives, and negative evaluations), among the lowest for the 12 readers.

She is especially nondirective in her marginal comments. Three out of every four of her marginal comments take the form of questions. Almost all of the others are positive evaluations. Gere offers more direction—and becomes more controlling—in her end comments. In fact, she places in endnotes all 10 of her negative evaluations, all 7 of her commands, and 17 of her 18 advisory comments.[2]

In "Street Gangs" Gere raises issues about the focus, development, and organization of the writing. But she leaves it up to Rusty to decide what matters to take up and how to address them. She makes two positive evaluations and one interpretive statement in the margins. All of the others are questions. Two of the questions are indirect requests, questions that virtually advise the student to make a change:

> Can you start with one specific experience drawn from your life with street gangs?
> Can you say more about advantages and disadvantages of membership?

Eight of the questions are open. Three of them are open heuristic questions that invite the writer to think further about what he has to say:

> What else can you say about membership in the gang?
> What does the issue of growing up say about gangs?
> What, finally, is *your* point of view about gangs?

Five others are open problem-posing questions that ask Rusty to reconsider his choices for shaping his ideas into text. Although several of these comments are posed in the grammatical form of yes/no questions, the comments leave it up to Rusty to determine the appropriate response:

> What does this exception show? What do you want your readers to draw from this?
> Is there a way to make connections among these paragraphs?
> Does this relate to your conclusion?
> Is this related to your point about not starting trouble for no reason?
> Does this belong with your discussion of membership?

Both kinds of open questions implicitly ask Rusty to consider making changes, but they do not outwardly direct or even advise him to do so. They give more room to the student by not actively calling for a change to be made and implicitly calling on him to make his own decisions. Although they obviously exert some control over the student by determining what he attends to in the writing, they do not set out a course for revision. These are questions to consider, not recommendations to be taken up. They help create Gere's image as a mentor or counselor inasmuch as they offer questions for the student to grapple with on his own. Just how much responsibility they place on the writer can be seen, in contrast, by looking at similar comments that are framed in modes that are more directive:

> Tell us more about membership in the gang. (imperative)
> You're not making your point of view about gangs clear. (negative evaluation)
> Connect these paragraphs. (imperative)
> This paragraph is out of place. (negative evaluation)
> You might put this with the info about not starting trouble for no reason. (advice)
> Doesn't this belong with your discussion of membership? (closed problem-posing question)

These sample comments address the same concerns as Gere's open questions to Rusty, but they assume more authoritative forms and exert greater control over the student's choices.

Gere's endnote on "Street Gangs" offers more direction than her marginal comments. But still she does not dictate or direct changes. After opening with a series of positive remarks about the draft, she makes several forthright recommendations for revision. She presents the heart of her suggestions in imperative modes, but, notably, they are soft imperatives. She does not command the student to "Shape this material" but tells him "you should *give some thought* to how *you want* to shape your material" (emphasis added). She then follows the statement with an advisory comment and an open question:

> At this stage you should give some thought to how you want to shape your material. A good beginning is to try to summarize your "point of view" in a sentence. What advice or information do you want to give your audience about gangs?

These comments do not so much direct the student to make specific changes as they prompt him to consider matters of revision. The second imperative Gere makes in her endnote is also muted. She does not say, "Convey this advice," or less stridently, "Try to convey this advice." She says: "Then *think about how you can convey* this advice/information most effectively" (emphasis added). Her subsequent comments, which deal with the arrangement of the essay, use similar strategies for softening her suggestions:

> As my marginal questions indicate, I *wonder if you can rearrange* parts of your paper to bring related ideas together. What connections do you see among issues of membership, identity and growing up? Does the topic of gangs raise other issues for you? (emphasis added)

Her advice is designed to nudge Rusty to reexamine the organization of the essay; her questions indicate the first few steps he might take in trying to work out the matter for himself. Although her marginal comments pose questions for him to consider, her endnotes offer a general sense of direction.

Focus

As much as anyone else in the study, Gere limits the number of comments she makes and restricts the scope of her responses. In doing so, she modifies the control she exerts over student writing. Whereas White and Peterson make an average of 11 marginal comments per paper, she makes only seven. Her comments are simple and direct and only rarely elaborated in multiple comments.[3] Yet they are almost always cast in full sentences and have the feel of conversation. They are also usually focused on a limited range of issues. Seven of her 10 sets of responses address three or fewer areas of response.

In her marginal comments Gere addresses only one or two instances of her main concerns. She refrains from identifying every, or even most, of the areas in which these concerns might be raised in the writing. And she rarely addresses any other matters. In her comments on "Street Gangs," for example, she uses her marginal comments to point to some, but not all, of the areas in which Rusty might add detail, and she makes no comments on the wording, voice, or sentence structure, much less on matters of correctness. She uses her endnotes to assess the relative strengths and weaknesses of the content and purpose of the writing and to suggest one or two areas for revision.

Across the sampling of essays, she focuses primarily on three areas of response—ideas, development, and global structure. She addresses 72% of her comments to these areas, the highest in the study. On "Street Gangs," 21 of her 26 comments address global concerns: six on ideas, five on development, and 10 on global structure, among them the following:

> This last sentence is really interesting. What does the issue of growing up say about gangs? (ideas)
>
> [Y]ou have a rich store of illustrations and examples to draw upon. (ideas)
>
> What else can you say about membership in the gang? (development)
>
> Can you start with one specific experience drawn from your life with street gangs? (global structure)
>
> Does this belong with your discussion of membership? (global structure)

Gere resists calling attention to correctness, wording, and sentence structure on rough drafts, making a total of only three comments across the five in-draft writings. (In fact, she tells the writer of "Street Gangs" to hold off dealing with local matters until after his next draft.) However, she is willing to take up such matters on final drafts; she makes 23 comments at the sentence level across the sampling, at least two on each paper.

Gere also frequently makes comments that go beyond the formal text and look at the writing in relation both to the audience (on four papers) and to the writer's knowledge or experience (on five papers). Both these orientations may be found in her comments on "Street Gangs." At one point, she calls on Rusty to consider his ideas in relation to his audience:

> What advice or information do you want to give your audience about gangs?
>
> Just concentrate on what you want to tell your audience.

At another point, she asks him to see his writing in terms of his own views and experiences:

> Can you start with one specific experience drawn from your life?
>
> What, finally, is *your* point of view about gangs?

Gere makes reference to the writer's own ideas more than any of our other readers. In her other sets of responses, we can see this same tendency to speak of the writing in terms of the student writer's personal experiences:

> Your choice of topic is excellent because you clearly know a great deal about bass fishing. (Writing 5)
>
> You can certainly draw on your own experiences to illustrate points you make, but try to prevent the narrative from taking over. (Writing 5)
>
> The significance of the seasons for you remains somewhat vague. (Writing 6)
>
> Although I understand that you take pleasure in each of the four seasons, I'm still not sure if they have any other meaning for you. (Writing 6)

To the extent that such comments leave the materials and choices of writing to the student's own ideas and experiences, they regulate the teacher's control over the writing.

Overview of Teacher Control

Gere's comments never risk taking center stage. If she controls the spotlight, she is intent on throwing the light on the student, not on her role as a responder. Although she determines through her very choice of comments what the student initially may attend to,[4] she leaves it up to the student to decide how to use her suggestions and to find ways to address her concerns. She does not lay out a script to be followed or overtly guide the student about how he might take up the tasks. Once she has selected the areas of writing she thinks it best for the student to work on, she frames questions, points to things to keep in mind, acknowledges the successes, and gently urges the student to discover what he can say and how best to say it. Still, her comments, although they defer much control to the student, are nevertheless quietly demanding. By not laying out changes that should be made or even charting specific courses for revision, they challenge the student to assume responsibility for his own writing choices.

Gere clearly refrains from imposing her idealized text on the student or presenting her own sense of how the writing might best be revised. She does not attempt to identify or endorse one idea as the "main" or "central" idea of the writing. Although she tells Rusty in an imperative that he should begin thinking about his focus and offers a bit of advice on how he can do so, she keeps control of the decision making in Rusty's hands. Similarly, although she points to the need for Rusty to develop and relate his thoughts, she does not make specific recommendations or tell him what to do. Consistent with her tendency as a responder, she turns the matter into a question for him to consider and figure out on his own:

> What advice or information do you want to give your audience about gangs?
> What connections do you see among issues of membership, identity and growing up?

She even opens the issue up beyond the parameters of his original discussion—"Does the topic of gangs raise other issues for you"—inviting him to search for additional ideas on his own and open himself to another possible focus, perhaps even a different kind of essay altogether.

To a large extent, the dialogic, interactive quality of Gere's style grows out of her attention to the student's writing processes. Whereas White, O'Hare, and Peterson all seem intent on leading the student to come up with a better, more formally complete and communicatively effective piece of writing in the next draft, Gere routinely seems to suspend her concern for the written product in favor of using her comments, first of all, as a way to give the student practice in working on his writing. Using the text in front of her, she engages the student in practicing certain processes (especially the decision-making strategies) of writing. Freed from seeing the improved subsequent draft as the goal for her response, her comments can be—and typically are—less directed toward an immediate text-based goal and more open-ended.

Consider, for example, the comments that White, O'Hare, and Peterson make on "Street Gangs." Most of them have the immediate or ultimate goal of leading the student to making the next draft more complete. White makes a number of corrections and suggested corrections in the actual wording of the text as he goes through the writing. All of his marginal comments are directed toward leading the student to make specific improvements in the text, for example:

> This sentence makes us expect something else. Begin with "On one occasion. . ."
> This is the kind of detail we need. But we need more, even here.

His endnote underscores his interest in directing the student to come up with a more tightly shaped piece of writing: "You need now to put this idea up front and to arrange your experiences and details so they all show this idea." O'Hare's comments show a less immediate concern for the written product, or perhaps a less comprehensive concern, but behind them there is a sense that he has his eye on the shape of the next draft:

Paragraph six needs specifics. What incident or incidents led you to use the terms "paranoia" and "burden"? You suffered black eyes and broken noses and yet weren't afraid. Please explain.

Paragraph eight is confused and confusing. Are you saying that gang rivalries weren't as nasty as they appear to be? If so, the point is interesting and well worth explaining to your readers.

These and many other comments indicate changes that he hopes will result in an immediate improvement in the text. Peterson is less controlling than White or O'Hare in the way she frames her comments, but she is no less interested in having the student work directly on textual improvements, as the following comments indicate:

> Anyone [?] or just the person who beat up your gang member?
>
> How many were in your gang?
>
> [Y]ou need more detail (as my questions suggest), and you also need more focus—to select and shape info so readers can easily understand what you're saying.

Each of these comments has the immediate design of eliciting a particular change in the text, with the aim of achieving a demonstrable improvement in the next draft. The more a reader's comments are geared toward the written product, the more likely they will call for particular changes and the more controlling the response.

Although many of Gere's comments may be seen as offering ideas for the improvement of the next draft, many are only indirectly concerned with immediate changes in the text and more concerned with having the student consider his choices as a writer. Many of her comments on "Street Gangs," for instance, are obviously concerned with making immediate improvements in the next draft:

> Can you start with one specific experience drawn from your life with street gangs?
>
> These prghs seem to deal with the issue of "membership." What else can you say about membership in the gang? Is there a way to make connections among these prghs?
>
> This section sets up a nice contrast. Can you say more about advantages and disadvantages of membership?
>
> A good beginning is to try to summarize your "point of view" in a sentence.

Yet as Gere's comments unfold, it seems clear that she is also trying to prompt him to think about certain issues of revision, whether or not they lead to a fuller, more complete next draft. As she does so, her comments also become more open-ended and interactive.[5] The following comments, for example, may lead to particular changes in the text, but they also suggest Gere's interest in giving the student practice in making choices as a writer:

> Does this relate to your conclusion?
>
> Is this related to your point about not starting trouble for no reason?
>
> At this stage you should give some thought to how you want to shape your material. A good beginning is to try to summarize your "point of view" in a sentence. What advice or information do you want to give your audience about gangs? Then think about how you can convey this advice/information most effectively.

With these comments, Gere leads the student to *consider* these issues. She deflects some of the emphasis from the revised product and attends to the student's activities of revision. She even raises an issue at the end of her marginal comments that might well lead to an entirely new line of thought, and perhaps a new focus or even a new paper:

> This last sentence is really interesting. What does the issue of growing up say about gangs? What, finally, is your point of view about gangs?

For Gere, these open heuristic comments, in which the teacher asks the student to return to the chaos of his thinking without any necessary concern for how those ideas would fit in the existing structure of the paper, are fairly common. They reflect her qualified interest in the written product, and epitomize her interest in the student's composing processes and the development of the thought in his writing.

Of course, all writing teachers look at the text before them as the site for instruction. Most of them would also want to have the student work toward producing fuller revised drafts. But whereas some teachers look to help students develop as writers by having them revise their texts to a certain stage of completeness, others look to those texts as opportunities to raise issues for students to think about and practice as writers, whether or not they come up with better, more polished writing at the end of the process. The latter is the case for Gere. For her, the text is there to raise issues and provide a staging area for the student's practice as a writer.

With her brief marginal comments, the limited areas of writing she addresses on each paper, and her use of nondirective modes, Gere encourages and challenges the student more than she either guides or directs him. She is one of the least controlling readers in our study, an example of a teacher who takes on the role of mentor, a counselor who leaves it up to the student to practice making his own choices as a writer.

GROUP 2: DONALD STEWART, BEN MCCLELLAND, GLYNDA HULL, PETER ELBOW

DONALD STEWART

Donald Stewart is the most thorough responder among the readers in the study. He is also one of the most controlling. Across his responses to the sampling, Stewart presents sharp critiques of the writing, pointing matter of factly to the problems in the text and explaining ways to make the next version better. He seems to operate from the premise that students learn to write best through practice in producing complete, polished texts.

Driven by this goal to help the student come up with the fullest, most effective piece of writing (or at least showing her what such a finished text might require), Stewart immerses himself in the student's words, ideas, and textual strategies. Using the assignment and specific genre conventions as the basis for his judgments, he acknowleges the strengths of the writing and then, more incisively, indicates where it falls short. Once his diagnosis is complete, he presents the student with detailed directions on how the writing may be improved. Along the way, he carefully explains and illustrates his comments, making sure that the student comes to understand not only that some strategy did not work, but why it did not work and how it might be made to work better. However, his thoroughness and control do not come without a cost. Not infrequently, Stewart appropriates the student's writing by pointing out specific places where the writing should be changed. On some responses, he even takes over the student's text by making important decisions and projecting on the writer his views about specifically how the writing should be revised.

At first glance, what stands out in Stewart's responses (especially among this group of readers) is the spattering of editorial marks he puts on the pages of the student's text. If these were the only responses he made to the paper, we would say that he takes over the writing, replacing the student's purposes as a writer with his purposes as a responder. These markings do little more than attempt to tidy up the superficial features of the text and take no account of what the student has to say or how purposefully she says it. Of course, Stewart goes on to do much more, making these editings a part—and only a part—of a much larger and far richer style of response. In separate full-blown letters to students, Stewart systematically addresses a range of concerns, apparently in order of priority. He deals first with content and organization, then style, and finally editing and correctness, usually the shortest section and always saved until the end.

Stewart's responses attempt to balance contraries. Through one lens, they are sharp, critical, and demanding, directing the student's revision according to Stewart's vision for the writing. Through another lens, they present detailed assistance about how to deal with the problems of the paper; his motivation is to guide and teach the student more than simply to edit, judge, or correct the writing. Although he is unmistakably directive, Stewart limits the control he exerts over the student by offering well-developed, specific responses in a relatively casual style.

STEWART

SETS OF RESPONSES	NUMBER OF RESPONSES		

SETS OF RESPONSES

5 rough drafts
4 final drafts

35 comments/writing

5 issues/writing

NUMBER OF RESPONSES

	Rough Drafts	Final Drafts	Total
Marginal Comments	46	31	77
End Comments	131	111	242
Total	177	142	319

STEWART'S FOCUS PROFILE

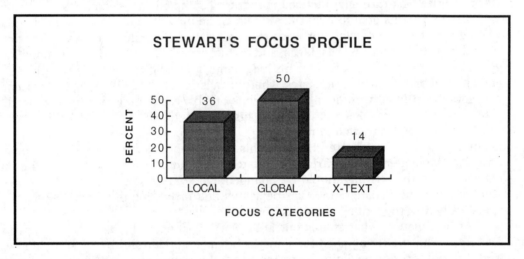

STEWART'S MODE PROFILE

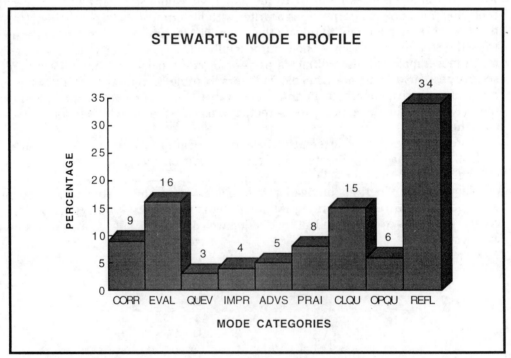

WRITING 2
"WHAT IF DRUGS WERE LEGAL?"

BACKGROUND

This is the first rough draft of an argumentative response essay. Through the first several weeks of the course, the class has focused on various kinds of expressive writing, and students have been writing essays mostly from their personal experience. Now the class is moving into transactional writing on topics which may include, but which must extend beyond, their first-hand experience. As a bridge into the second half of the course, students are to write a response essay in which they express their views on what another writer has to say about an issue. In anticipation of this assignment, students have been given practice in summarizing and paraphrasing the ideas of others. Although they have written several essays up to this point, this is the first paper that they will take through several drafts and receive another's comments on before they hand in the final draft.

This particular student, Nancy, sees herself as a "good writer." As she has told you a few times already (both verbally and in her course journal), she "has always gotten A's in English." Evidently, she is confused, or even put off, by your view of writing and, particularly, your assessment of her work thus far in the course. She has been somewhat resistant to changing her style and process of writing and has not been very responsive to your comments on the four previous course papers.

THE ASSIGNMENT

Select from a journal, magazine, or newspaper, a recent article on an issue you are interested in, one that presents a view you disagree with or that you find some problem with. In an essay intended for the same publication, write a response to the article. You may respond to the article as a whole or to parts of it. Your task is not to review the article for its own sake but to express your views on what this writer has to say. Your final draft should identify the author, title, and issue you are responding to and summarize what the author says about it, and then present your response.

We'll take this essay through two rough drafts before the final draft is due, two weeks from today. I will respond to both the first rough draft and the second rough draft.

Writing 2
Nancy S.
First Rough Draft

What If Drugs Were Legal?

What if drugs were legal? Could you imagine what it would do to

our society? [Well according to John E. LeMoult, a lawyer with twenty   *you can go*
Two ways with
years of experience on the subject, feels we should at least consider   *This sentence:*
it.] I would like to comment on his article, "Legalize Drugs" in the   *(1) ~~done~~ omit*
June 15, 1984, issue of the New York Times. I disagree with LeMoult's   *"according To:*
                                                                            feels"
arguments for
~~idea of~~ legalizing drugs to cut the cost of crime.   *(2) omit "feels"*

The way it is
Tense   LeMoult's article was short and sweet. He gives ~~the~~ background   *now, you have*
Consistency *on*   *a clumsy mix*
         ~~of~~ the legalization of drugs. For example, the first antidrug laws ~~of~~ *in   of two different*
the United States were passed in 1914. The laws were put in effect   *structures.*
because of the threat of the Chinese imagrants. In addition, he   *sp.*
explains how women were the first to use laudanun, an over-the-counter   *sp.*
drug, as a substitute for drinking; it was unacceptable for women to
                          with   example
drink. ~~By explaining~~ this, he made the reader feel that society was
                          as a
the cause of women using ~~the~~ substitute, laudanun, for drinking.   *Syntax needs work*
                                                                        here.
Tense LeMoult proceeded from there to explain how the money to buy drugs

comes from us as society. Since drug addicts turn to crime to get

money we become a corrupt society. Due to (this) we spend unnecessary   *refers to?*

sp. money protecting inocent citizens by means of law enforcment, jails,

etc. means and ect. LeMoult says that if we legalize drugs ~~that~~ "Overnight the   *lc*

"and so cost of law enforcement, courts, judges, jails and convict

forth." rehabilitation would be cut in half. The savings in tax would be more

than $50 billion a year."

1

LeMoult might be correct by saying that our cost of living in society would be cut in half if drugs were legalized, however, he is justifying a wrong to save money. In my opinion, legalizing drugs is the easy man's way out. Just because crime is high due to the fact that the cost of drugs is unbeleivable it doesn't make legalizing them right. We all know drugs are dangerous to the body and society without any explanation, therefore, you shouldn't legalize something that is dangerous.

My only and most important argument to LeMoult is the physical harm it would bring by legalizing drugs. People abuse their right to use alcoholic beverages because they are legal. For example, LeMoult himself says the amount of drug addicts is small compared to alcoholics. Why?—of course it is because of the legalization of alcohol. When you make something legal it can and will be done with little hassel. Why allow something to be done with ease when it is wrong? LeMoult's points are good and true but I believe he is approaching the subject in the wrong manner. Drugs are wrong, therefore, should not be legal!

2

Nancy S., Rough Draft of "What If Drugs Were Legal?"

Let's look first at the things you did which were right.
You chose an article whose argument you disagreed with and
gave us a full citation. Good. You've also defined the
particular issues with which you do not agree and summarized
the author's arguments. No problem of note there.

Now, we have to look at those things which must improve in
your next draft. First, you don't provide any arguments for
your position. All you offer are assertions: drug use is a
crime and should not be legalized; drugs are dangerous to an
individual's health and to society; legalization will
promote even more of this harmful activity; drugs are wrong.
If it would make you feel any better, I can tell you that I
share your antipathy for drug use. But, if we are going to
answer Mr. LeMoult, we must use more than assertions. For
example, I don't think we'll get anywhere with the circular
argument that drug use is criminal and should not be
legalized. That's the issue he wants to argue. Let's look
at the assertion that drug use is dangerous to individuals
and to society. You have something to work with there. You
must first provide some very specific information about the
damage drug use does to people. The hippies of the sixties
argued that smoking marijuana was not as harmful as smoking
cigarettes. Then some research was done on long-term
smokers of marijuana. They discovered that it left a
residue in the brain, interfering with synapses and
producing early senility (at age 28 or so). Similar
information is available, I am sure, about the effects of
cocaine use. And you must show, in more specific terms,
exactly what damage society suffers from drug users: loss of
productivity, cost of care for those disabled, costs of law
enforcement, breakdown of families, etc. You might also get
somewhere with the argument that legalization will only
promote increased use. The argument against alcohol
prohibition was that legalizing it again would reduce law
enforcement costs and not contribute significantly to
alcoholism. Trouble is that bootleg alcohol continued to be
produced, and alcoholism is a national problem not only in
our country but many others. I don't think one can muster
good arguments for prohibiting alcohol again, but the
arguments against the 19th amendment proved to be equally
fatuous. So, you do have something to work with.

You must also do a much better job of editing the paper.
There are some problems with syntax and pronoun references,
as well as common garden variety errors in punctuation and
spelling. If you don't understand the marks on your paper,
see me and I'll explain them to you.

Mode

Although there are other factors that contribute to Stewart's directive style, the most important is his substantial use of strong authoritative modes. Stewart frames more of his comments in these modes than all but one other reader. Thirty-nine percent of his comments are framed as correctives, imperatives, and negative evaluations.[1] His comments on the sample writing above demonstrate the extent to which he employs such directive modes. Fourteen of his 35 comments on "What If Drugs Were Legal?" are strong authoritative comments: four corrections, three imperatives, and seven negative evaluations. By comparison, the other three readers in this group—Ben McClelland, Glynda Hull, and Peter Elbow—*together* make a total of only eight strong authoritative comments (no corrective comments, six imperative comments, and only two negative evaluations).

Stewart does not shy away from wielding his authority and establishing specific goals for the revision. Stripped of the surrounding responses, his criticism and commands in his letter to Nancy show just how directive his comments can be:

First, you don't provide any arguments for your position. All you offer are assertions. But [you] must use more than assertions. You must first provide some very specific information about the damage drug use does to people. And you must show, in more specific terms, exactly what damage society suffers from drug users. You must also do a better job of editing the paper.

There are six comments here. The first two are negative evaluations; the next four, strong imperatives. The comments are probing and precise; Stewart's voice is teacherly and superior, at times even harsh. The comments leave little to wonder about his overall judgment of the writing.

Across the sampling Stewart uses such sharp directive commentary as the basis for his responses. It is especially prominent in Writings 1, 4, and 5, as the following excerpts from those responses show:

There are two significant problems with the content of your paper. First, you were supposed to tell readers why this subject was important to you. You don't do that. Second, the arguments you offer to support your position just will not hold up. . . . [I have seen a great deal of evidence that clearly demonstrates the fact that seat belts do save lives. You argue . . . that this is not so,] but in support of your argument you offer but one rather flimsy example. You will have to show me a lot of statistical evidence to prove that wearing seat belts is dangerous. I simply don't believe you. (Writing 1)

After that, unfortunately, things go downhill. The tone changes and becomes didactic. You almost start to lecture these parents. . . . Even more troublesome is the abstract nature of much of what you say. We must have some specific examples of parents forcing their prejudices on their children or not allowing them to work out their problems for themselves. (Writing 4)

Too much of your paper is given over to your love of fishing for bass in Orlando and an account of one days' fishing on Lake Ivenhoe. . . . After you've announced the prey, large mouth bass, you should immediately begin with your discussion of habitat. This is the place to bring in the information you have provided in your narrative about the habits of the bass, under differing conditions. After that, talk about equipment. You mention two types of lures, but you never tell us what kind of rod you use, how to cast for bass, and what motions to impart to the lure to attract bass. (Writing 5)

As these excerpts indicate, these three sets of responses are built on directive comments that assert Stewart's views about the writing. In his letters of response about these papers, 32% of Stewart's comments are cast in the form of criticism or commands. Another 10% are cast as advice or qualified negative evaluations. Such commentary sets out to tell the student what needs to be done to improve the writing and unquestionably asserts his control.

But although Stewart exerts a definite control over the student by his frequent use of directive modes (i.e., corrective, imperative, and negative evaluative comments), he tempers this directiveness somewhat through his use of interactive commentary. He regularly plays back his reading of the text, asks questions, and, in general, liberally elaborates on his comments. Across the sampling, 15% of his comments are given to interpreting the text and providing reader responses to the student, 21% are given to questions, and 12% are given to explain other comments and offer instruction.[2] Well over half of his comments are not framed in authoritative modes.[3]

It is Stewart's liberal elaborating that sets him apart from most other directive readers. Whereas Edward White, for example, tends to be concise and somewhat general in his commentary, Stewart tends to provide well-developed responses with plenty of elaboration. Such elaboration usually follows Stewart's authoritative comments and serves to temper some of his control. Just how much tempering it does depends on the control implied in the surrounding comments.

At times, Stewart elaborates on his strong directive comments in order to clarify and reinforce his position. When he does so, he offers more direction than assistance and moderates his control only slightly, if at all. In his responses to Writing 6, "The Four Seasons," for example, Stewart uses explanatory comments to follow up on his criticism of the writer's cliched language:

> Have you described the four seasons in Syracuse, or have you described four idealized seasons? I think the latter, and I'll tell you why. In describing Spring, you mention the trees blossoming, flowers working their way out of the ground, geese flying north overhead, and a long winter's nap ending for bears, squirrels, rabbits and other hibernating animals. These are all cliches about Spring. (Writing 6)

The follow-up comments elaborate on the problem he identifies in the opening comments. In the same response, he uses closed problem-posing questions in a similar way—not to raise issues for the student to consider, but to explain and reinforce his criticism:

> [T]he same kinds of problems show up in your descriptions of the other seasons. In Summer, for example, you talk about families going to the beach. In Syracuse? Isn't the nearest beach Lake Ontario . . . ? (Writing 6)
> Winter turns out to be a popular song. Why don't you tell us what Syracuse winters are really like? (Writing 6)

In his responses to Writing 13, following a summary of the student's main points, he uses a closed problem-posing question to carry the full weight of his criticism:

> You tell us that John Cougar took you and his fans on a "roller coaster ride of emotion," a phrase you use two or three times in the paper. We also learn that Cougar operates from a bare stage, wears plain clothes, works his audience into several frenzies during the evening, makes a pitch for American farmers, and plays non-stop. Where, in all this adulation, are criteria for judging this rock group? (Writing 13)

In cases such as these, Stewart's elaboration serves to clarify his other responses, but does only a little to offer assistance to the student or to moderate his control over the writing.[4]

More often than not, however, Stewart's elaboration shows the student how she might begin to address his authoritative comments, and it tempers his control. In his letter to Nancy, for example, Stewart explains how to support her claim that drug use is dangerous by illustrating how a similar argument about marijuana has been waged:

> Let's look at the assertion that drug use is dangerous to individuals and to society. You have something to work with there. **You must first provide some very specific**

information about the damage drug use does to people. The hippies of the sixties argued that smoking marijuana was not as harmful as smoking cigarettes. Then some research was done on long-term smokers of marijuana. They discovered that it left a residue in the brain, interfering with synapses and producing early senility (at age 28 or so). Similar information is available, I am sure, about the effects of cocaine use.

The response might have been cast in barebones form as a simple imperative comment (in boldface type). But Stewart couches the command between interactive comments. He starts with informal direct address to the student and offers her some encouragement. Then, after the call for additional support, he offers her an extended explanatory comment. The surrounding comments take some of the emphasis off Stewart as a critic and focus on what the student might do by way of revision. Across his comments on Writing 2, Stewart modifies his other strong authoritative comments, as well, by way of the comments that surround them. He complements his five imperative comments with three praise comments, three statements of direct address to the student, and 10 reflective comments. Half of these reflective comments are interpretive comments or reader responses comments, for example:

> You chose an article whose argument you disagreed with and gave us a full citation. (interpretive)
> You've also defined the particular issues with which you do not agree and summarized the author's arguments. (interpretive)
> If it would make you feel any better, I can tell you that I share your antipathy for drug use. (reader remark)

Half of them are explanatory comments that either explain other comments or offer brief instruction, for example:

> [I don't think we'll get anywhere with the circular argument that drug use is criminal and should not be legalized.] That's the issue he wants to argue. (explanatory)
> The argument against alcohol prohibition was that legalizing it again would reduce law enforcement costs and not contribute significantly to alcoholism. (explanatory)

These follow-up comments help temper—or at least redirect—Stewart's otherwise strong control over the writing.[5] The added commentary provides help more than it dictates the student's revision.

Stewart's elaboration is even more open-ended when it is tied to comments that are less directive, as in the following sequence from his response to Rusty on Writing 12:

> So, what other improvements might be made? You might give us a bit more detail about other gang members. What were their names and what characterized their behavior? Was there one, for example, who had to be restrained because he was likely to blow up like a firecracker at the slightest provocation? Did you have an enforcer, one guy who was bigger than and stronger than the rest? . . . Adding this kind of detail would make an interesting paper even more interesting.

Here, rather than stating his calls for revision as commands, Stewart begins by presenting an open problem-posing question and a piece of advice. These comments invoke less teacher control than commands and allow the subsequent comments to be seen as offering assistance more than directing particular changes. Similarly, in his response to Writing 10, a personal essay on the writer's battle with leukemia, he follows a qualified evaluation with a series of questions based on his own personal experience:[6]

I can think of many things you could have but did not say. For example, do you now understand, in ways you did not before, how precious yet how fragile life is? Do you find that your ability to sympathize with others who suffer has greatly increased? How about the pattern of your life? You mention the treatments and the discomfort that went with them. But the treatments that go with it have altered your lifestyle. Considering the amount of chemotherapy you have had, aren't your blood counts depressed, making you vulnerable to infections? And hasn't this caused you to avoid crowds, any kinds of social gathering in which people might be sick and infectious? Do you wash your hands excessively and generally maintain a very high level of personal hygiene? How do you feel about health professionals now? I have come to have very great regard for good doctors and trained and sympathetic nurses.

The more Stewart uses such interactive comments to elaborate on his other commentary, the more he takes on the voice, not of the teacher-critic, but of a guide. Even as they present more of the teacher's views, these comments offer the student guidance. Whether written in the service of directive comments, advice, or other interactive comments, they temper Stewart's directiveness and channel greater responsibility to the student.

Focus

Stewart's extensive responses illustrate the complex relationship that exists between the number of comments a teacher makes and the extent of his control. Although it may be true that the more comments a teacher makes, the more likely he will impose his vision of the text on the student, it is not necessarily so. It is what the teacher does with his comments, not the number of comments itself, that determines how directive or how interactive he will be. The large number of comments that Stewart makes in some ways contributes to his directiveness; in other ways it tempers his control.

Stewart's detailed commentary leads him to be more directive inasmuch as it involves him in a wide range of issues and extensive treatment of local concerns. He makes an average of 35 comments per paper. Although this total is less than Chris Anson's (37 comments per paper) and the same as Patricia Stock's (35 comments per paper), he covers a lot more ground in his responses. Stewart addresses five or more issues on seven sets of responses and six or more on four sets.[7] The range of comments shows his interest in having his hand, at any given stage of drafting, in all levels of revision—an interest that leads him to be more directive than he would be if he were to limit himself to fewer concerns. But, paradoxically, the large number of comments (as distinct from the wide range of issues he takes up) arguably makes his style less directive than it might be because the extra comments allow him to follow up his authoritative comments with questions and other nonevaluative responses. As we have seen, they allow him to explain, illustrate, and contextualize his directive comments and point the student down the right path without dictating specifically how she should go. If Stewart made fewer comments, he might well be more directive, not less.

Stewart's way of attending regularly both to local matters and global matters also helps explain why he is among the most directive of our 12 readers and, intertestingly, why he is not even more controlling. Across his responses to the sampling, Stewart deals fairly extensively with local matters. More than a third of all his responses address sentence structure, wording, and correctness. In fact, he makes more comments on correctness than any of the other 12 readers,[8] and more comments on wording than all but one other reader.[9] Generally, the more a responder deals with local matters, the more he will likely lead students to make specific changes in the writing and the more controlling his commentary will be.[10]

Alternately, Stewart's emphasis on the content of student writing leads him to be less directive than he might be. Stewart writes almost half of his overall comments about the writer's ideas and the development of those ideas. In his letters to students, the primary forum for his response, he devotes 89% of his comments to ideas, development, and other conceptual matters such as the topic, audience, and writing assignment.[11] Such responses to content, although they may be highly charged because they deal with the student's perceptions, do not tend to be as directive as comments about local concerns or about matters of form in general.[12] Thus, Stewart's commentary, although it is directive, is not as controlling as authoritarian response, which tends to deal more fully with conventional matters of organization and style.

Stewart's control is also mitigated somewhat by the way he situates many of his comments within a broader rhetorical context. Instead of focusing narrowly on the formal text, he addresses many of his comments to the audience and purpose of the writing. In Writing 2, for example, he calls attention to Nancy's rhetorical situation when he cites LeMoult as her prospective audience: "If we are going to answer Mr. LeMoult, we must use more than assertions." In other responses as well he also occasionally looks at the writing in terms of the specific target audience:

> [W]hile your personal experience can certainly be incorporated into this kind of paper, it's not what the editor of *Field and Stream* wants. (Writing 5)

> You almost start to lecture these parents. . . . You become almost patronising, explaining parents' faults to them but hoping that they will have wisdom enough to overcome them. I don't think many parents of teenagers would respond too warmly to such advice. . . . (Writing 4)

More often, he speaks generally in terms of "the reader":

> Explaining your interest in a subject means telling a reader why this particular problem concerns you. (Writing 1)

> This is developing into a most interesting paper because it provides readers a point of view they seldom are privileged to get: the perspective on gang membership from inside. (Writing 12)

> Your account of the diagnosis of your disease and the treatment is also moving. I suspect most readers will fully empathize with the physical suffering you experience and wish you a return to good health. (Writing 10)

Typically, calling attention to other readers lessens a teacher's control. It removes some of the emphasis on the reader as a teacher and implicitly puts some of the authority for his responses in the hands of a general audience. By indicating what other readers would be interested in and what they would need, Stewart removes some of the emphasis on his own individual preferences as a teacher.

Overview of Teacher Control

As a responder Stewart is direct, sure-handed, and critical. But he is also guiding and supportive. His responses, which are based on authoritative methods but make use of a number of interactive strategies, create the image of a tough but helpful critic. He is definite about what he wants students to achieve in their revisions. But he is also very much a teacher, one who offers his students abundant assistance. It is as if, through his responses, Stewart says: "I am here to give you my estimation of what you have and have not done in your writing and to present some expert advice on what you need to do. I am here to push you to do your best to produce purposeful, acceptable writing. But I'll give you a lot of help along the way."

From start to finish in his responses, Stewart casts himself in the roles of teacher and critic. Even though he commonly presents his responses from the stated point of view of "the reader," such talk often seems a thin disguise for Stewart's own goals and preferences as a teacher. In a number of his responses he speaks about "the readers" but ends up including himself as a member of the audience or talking about himself as the main reader. On Writing 1, for example, after pointing out some of his own counterpoints to the student's arguments, he says, "Convince me that wearing seat belts is unsafe and that by not wearing them you will not infringe upon my rights" and "Convince me that I am wrong," presenting himself as the target audience. Midway through his response to Writing 13, after holding little back in his criticism, he apologizes by noting how difficult it is for him to be a reader for such a concert review:

> If you detect a trace of sarcasm in my remarks, I apologize for putting it there, but I can hardly suppress it. You see, I am the most difficult kind of reader you could imagine for this kind of piece. I hate rock music.

Throughout his responses, he asserts control over the writing by invoking himself as the primary reader of the text and giving strong readings to the writing based on his own ideas about music and his own expectations as a teacher.

Stewart also exerts his control as a responder through his emphasis on the writing assignment. Six out of his nine sets of responses call on the student to revise the writing so that it fits the requirements set forth in the assignment. Most of his responses also accept or call into question the feasibility of the student's choice of topic, again in light of the assignment and its stated rhetorical constraints. Those papers that do not prompt him to talk about the assignment or the topic already conform to these expectations. By holding fast to the demands of the assignment, Stewart is less able to give students room to find their own materials and purposes and is more likely to direct them along the lines he has drawn.

Ultimately, however, Stewart's control is most clearly seen in the way he, on a few occasions, brings an idealized text to his reading and imposes on the student his way of seeing the revision as a whole. Such extensive appropriating occurs when teachers look at improved written products as the goal of their responses and direct the student to make sweeping changes according to their vision for the writing. Stewart's commentary meets both conditions. He is committed to leading students to come up with better written products, and his responses are typically tied to specific features of the written text and designed to help the student come up with a revision that is more complete and polished. For instance, he takes over Louise's text in Writing 1 when he requires her to speak about how a particular personal experience motivated her interest in the subject. He seems to have decided that any response to this assignment must include the student's personal experience, and he seems set on eliciting this experience in her revision. He is more forceful in a subsequent comment: "You will have to show me a lot of statistical evidence to prove that wearing seat belts is dangerous. I simply don't believe you." This response directs the student to come up, not with support, but with statistical data as a particular kind of support for his argument. Evidently, arguments from examples (even personal examples) or arguments from expert sources will not do. In doing so, he severely limits the student's options.

If these two comments represented a minor portion of his overall response or if he went on to make other comments that served to put more control for decision making on the student, Stewart could hardly be seen as taking over the student's text. But he goes on to make other comments that foist on the student his sense of how the writing should look. The accumulation of such comments across the response as a whole leads him to impose his idealized text—his overall sense of how the writing should look—on the student's revision.

Stewart more obviously imposes his idealized text on Writing 5. This time he projects his sense of how any paper written for this assignment should follow the conventions of expository writing and how this particular paper on bass fishing should be (or would best be) written:[13]

> After you've announced the prey, large mouth bass, you should immediately begin with your discussion of habitat. This is the place to bring in the information about the habits of the bass, under differing conditions.
>
> After that, talk about equipment.
>
> Remember: your *first* obligation is to tell the reader where the fish are, what to use, and how to catch them.

> Having established that structure for the paper, you can put in the
> necessary details and then end with your zinger: the story of the big bass
> you caught.
>
> In this paper, you give us only two sentences after hooking it. That's not
> enough. The reader wants a longer report of the battle you had landing this
> big fish.

All of these comments deal with the student's own words and ideas; they work with what the student has put before him. Nevertheless, by making these moment-by-moment decisions about how the text should unfold, Stewart takes over the writing and imposes his idealized text on the student.[14]

These responses, however, are the exceptions. Stewart does not usually take such extensive control.[15] In his other letters of response, he may have certain ideas about where the draft goes wrong or how it might be improved, but he does not foist his decisions on the student or impose a specific course of action on her revision.[16] Across his responses, his control is often moderated, as we have shown, by the way he precedes his imperative comments with close readings of the student writing and follows them with detailed explanations and examples. Moreover, even in his most directive sets of responses, he is finally more concerned with the evolving content and purpose of the writing than with the formal propriety of the text, which is much more likely to lead a teacher to co-opt the student's reasons for writing with his own.[17]

Although it is arguable just how effective such directive responses will be in helping students develop as writers, it seems clear that, even if they are followed in a rote, mechanical way, they would lead students to produce better pieces of writing. In the end, Stewart leaves us to wonder about a number of questions that are at the heart of this study. How much direct control should teachers provide over revision? How much should they leave to the student to figure out on her own? How much should teachers, especially those who privilege the written product, present detailed commentary that closely guides the student's rewriting? How much should they leave issues of revision for the student to work through on her own? Is there a point at which such detailed directing and guidance may become counterproductive? Stewart's commentary, combining as it does contrary methods in a unique style, is a fertile ground for teachers who wonder how much control—and how much help—they would do best to provide.

BEN MCCLELLAND

Ben McClelland uses many of the same strategies of response that Donald Stewart uses in his commentary. Both of them are sharp, critical readers. Both of them rely heavily on their authority as teachers. And both of them write comments that are designed to help students produce completed texts according to the demands of the assignment. They assume that leading students to make detailed revisions on a given paper will eventually help them produce other, similar papers on their own. But whereas Stewart provides only brief summaries of the student texts and detailed directions for revision, McClelland presents close, detailed readings and only general directions for revision. And whereas Stewart seems comfortable with assuming the role of the teacher and leading students step by step through their writing projects, McClelland seems both to rely on and resist his authority as a teacher. On the one hand, he asserts his agenda in his readings and lays out in no uncertain terms his advice and commands. On the other hand, he uses a number of strategies, including questions, brief lessons, and other explanations, to make his commentary less directive and more interactive.

All of McClelland's responses take the form of letters to the student. They are more crafted than Frank O'Hare's listing of comments, but they are not as long or detailed as Stewart's letters. (McClelland writes an average of 20 comments per paper, Stewart 35.) Whereas Stewart systematically addresses three broad areas of response—content and purpose, style, and correctness—McClelland deals almost entirely with content and purpose. He makes no comments in the margins and very rarely deals with local concerns.

Unlike Stewart's letters, McClelland's letters of response do not follow a certain format, but they do have a broad overall shape. He usually begins his responses by giving a reading of the text, with his interpretive comments giving way to various kinds of criticism. Along the way, he offers brief lessons and asks questions that are designed to engage the student in her own analysis of what she has written. He typically closes by charting out a general plan for revision.[1] Although these comments present only general goals and leave the actual work—the actual materials and the specific changes—to the student, they give McClelland decided control over the writing.

McClelland is a demanding reader, sure-handed about his analysis of the problems in student writing and firm about what the writer should work on in the way of revision. Ultimately, he is more authoritative than interactive, a close, critical reader more than a guide.

McCLELLAND

SETS OF RESPONSES			
5 rough drafts			
5 final drafts			
20 comments/writing			
2.8 issues/writing			

NUMBER OF RESPONSES

	Rough Drafts	Final Drafts	Total
Marginal Comments	00	00	00
End Comments	119	82	201
Total	119	82	201

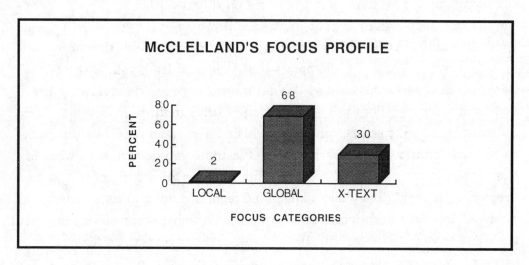

McCLELLAND'S FOCUS PROFILE

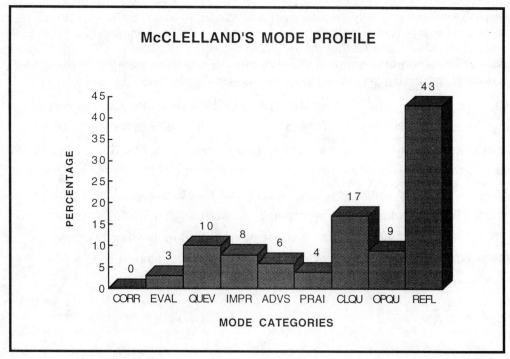

McCLELLAND'S MODE PROFILE

Nancy S.' s First Rough Draft: "What If Drugs Were Legal"

What is it that you want me most to know about your position on LeMoult's article, "Legalize Drugs," Nancy? Try stating that point in a sentence or two. In order to understand your position on LeMoult's article then, just what do I need to know about his article? That is, what specific points do you need to summarize from his article and which ones may you disregard? I ask you to work out these two matters because, as I read your draft, I need a clearer sense of both. Before reading further in my comments, please jot down a list of items on them.

First, with regard to your position, did you say that you were against legalizing drugs because they were physically harmful and, therefore morally wrong? Those are the points that I gleaned from your last two paragraphs. However, you say, "We all know drugs are dangerous to the body and society <u>without</u> <u>any</u> <u>explanation</u>..." [my emphasis]. Given the nature of LeMoult's radical proposal (which I also have read), I think some further explanation is due us readers. Of course, you do give somewhat of one in the last paragraph, don't you? But your causal linking of illegal drugs and their relatively few addicts and legal alcohol and its relatively many addicts fails to convince me. But perhaps there is something that you could use to your advantage in the behavior of other sorts of addicts: smokers, gamblers, shoppers? What else could you say in favor of your position?

Second, with regard to what you summarize from LeMoult, what main point of his do you want to focus on? In a sentence, what is his major reason for suggesting that we consider legalizing drugs? At two points (paragraph 2 & 3) you indicate that it has to do with crime and the cost of enforcement of drug laws. Why do you include the points on the first antidrug laws and on women's use of laudanum when you don't refer to them later? Do they relate to your argument with LeMoult over legalizing drugs? Moreover, when you say, "LeMoult's points are good and true," to what specific points are you referring? Sometimes it's useful to make a concession to an opponent, but it must be qualified or limited to some specific point that does not detract from your main objection to the opponent's position.

If I were pressed to say what your argument with LeMoult came down to, I would say that you stacked some general point about the harm of drugs against his proposition that legalizing drugs would cut crime and law enforcement costs dramatically. Is that what you attempted? Look again at his data and his logic. Search for ways of composing a more effective argument by 1) calling his conclusions into question and 2) making your case more detailed and convincing.

Mode

McClelland distributes his commentary over a wide range of modes, employing a relatively high number of reflective statements and making regular though not extensive use of authoritative commentary. He writes 43% of his comments in reflective modes, the fourth highest in the study, and a relatively moderate 27% of his comments in the five authoritative modes.[2] Nevertheless, he assumes appreciable control over student writing, in large part because he brings a strong teacher's agenda to his commentary—both to his authoritative comments and his interactive comments alike.

McClelland devotes most of his responses to providing close, critical readings of the student's text.[3] These readings are often framed in modes that conventionally moderate teacher control—qualified evaluations, interpretations, and explanatory comments—but that he often uses to present criticism.

This tendency to use moderate modes to present strong, authoritative comments can be seen in McClelland's use of interpretive comments, which appear in 8 of his 10 sets of responses.[4] At times, he uses interpretive comments conventionally, to simply play back his reading of the text; at other times, he uses them less conventionally to subtly inject some criticism into his readings. The following comments, for instance, are simple interpretations:

> This text shows you moving away from recreating the personal experiences of participating in an activity in and of itself (as you did in the first two assignments) and moving towards "presenting an understanding about" the activity. For you, Steve, this movement is from something like "My Bass Fishing Experience with My Grandfather" to "How to Bass Fish the Lakes of Orlando." (Writing 5)

> Your opening two questions set forth what you will talk about in this essay, Barbara. In the first half of the piece you talk about technical (or "mechanical") requirements of the work; in the second, making tips. Implied in both is pleasing the customer; in concluding you allude to feeling good about doing good work. (Writing 11)

These comments provide a gloss on the text and leave it up to the student to consider how effectively she is achieving her intentions in the paper. Often, however, McClelland's interpretations are tinged with assessments of the writing and verge on reader reactions:

> If I were pressed to say what your argument with LeMoult came down to, I would say that you stacked some general point about the harm of drugs against his proposition that legalizing drugs would cut crime and law enforcement costs dramatically. (Writing 2)

> That's what the voice in this draft sounds like, a Disembodied Authority who knows what's what about this topic. (Writing 4)

> You also say that your parents called your need to belong to the Cripps "insecurity"; however, while you do not refute their point . . . , neither do you agree with them. . . [Reading your sentence over a few times, I wonder if both you and your parents were right.] (Writing 12)

> Your personal response to "Young Goodman Brown" gives us an inside look at a family headed by such a character, even if your essay brings more light to the plight, in yours and your sister's cases, of Faith's innocent children than to the counterpart of *Good*man who now ironically sees himself and all others as bad men and women. (Writing 9)

These comments play back the reader's understanding of the text, but as they do so they go beyond interpretation and insert some criticism into the reading: "you stacked some general point" against the author's arguments; the draft sounds like it is coming from a *disembodied* authority; you say your parents saw this as insecurity, *but* you say nothing in response to their claim; "*even if* your essay brings more light to the plight . . . than to the counterpart of *Good*man." In effect, they move from invoking McClelland's role as a reader to subtly asserting his role as a critic.

He uses his evaluative commentary in a similar way. In contrast to Stewart, who uses straight evaluative comments, McClelland casts his judgments in the form of qualified negative evaluations and, less frequently, reader reactions.[5] Conventionally, these indirect evaluations are less controlling than overt evaluations because they acknowledge the reader's subjectivity and speak as much to the reader's way of processing the text as they do to the text.[6] McClelland's qualified negative evaluations often operate in this conventional way and moderate his criticism, as the following cases show:

> Given the nature of LeMoult's radical proposal . . . , I think some further explanation is due us readers. (Writing 2)
>
> As I read your paper, Louise, I am confused by your selection of a topic. (Writing 1)
>
> What's missing for me as a reader is some basis for such authoritative talk. (Writing 4)
>
> I need to know more about specific techniques: HOW to do it. (Writing 5)
>
> As I read over your paper, it sounds like the voice of someone who just began talking about the "bad old days." (Writing 12)

These comments clearly point to something that is not working in the text, but they soften the evaluation somewhat by noting the reader's way of processing the writing rather than simply calling attention to a problem in the text. But, just as often, McClelland's qualified evaluations operate unconventionally and are sharp and authoritative:

> I don't learn anything from your draft. Furthermore, I wonder why you choose to argue an issue that the American public appears to have accepted years ago rather than to inform readers about some particular interest that you have or to explain to them some knowledge that is uniquely yours. In particular, your calling the government's method of incentives to get state adoptions of seat belt laws "communistic" makes me feel that not only are you lacking any special knowledge about this particular law's legislative history, but, worse, that you are unfamiliar with the traditional American system of federal-state relations. (Writing 1)
>
> I give a low priority to the reverie about your early childhood days. (Writing 5)
>
> My pleasure was measurably diminished because your depiction lacked precise, sensory details. Thus, rather than experiencing the actual scene of your hometown, I caught only dim glimpses into an overgeneralized world. (Writing 6)
>
> [As a reader, I can vicariously experience just about everything there—] except, that is, for the main event: Cougar's music. (Writing 13)

Although they are cast in the form of qualified negative evaluations, these comments present strong criticisms of the writing, emphasizing McClelland's role as a teacher and critic over his role as a reader. They assert—not modify—his control as a responder. (Tellingly, McClelland writes only nine positive evaluations, fewer than all but one other reader in the study.)

McClelland's agenda also often shows through his explanatory comments.[7] At times, he uses short lessons to instruct the student about a principle of writing, and he does so in a way that is meant to facilitate revision:

> Sometimes it's useful to make a concession to an opponent, but it must be qualified or limited to some specific point that does not detract from your main objection to the opponent's position. (Writing 2)
>
> The intellectual challenge of writing about a matter in which you are deeply implicated emotionally is that it is difficult to analyze human relations when you lack the distance (in emotion and time) from which to view them. (Writing 9)

In a shift of this nature you must gauge how much "showing" and how much "telling" to do in the text. (Writing 5)

Mostly, though, he uses explanatory comments to remind students about the assignment or to explain the conventions of a particular type of writing:

I'd say [your membership in the gang] authorizes you to write about an aspect of first-hand experience, *using "examples to examine and illustrate a point."* I underscore this line from the assignment sheet because it's central to fulfilling this particular assignment. (Writing 12)

Recall that the assignment reminds you "not to forget that good expository writing is informed by our personal knowledge and experiences." Furthermore, the assignment calls on you to discuss parent-child relationships *because* of your "firsthand" knowledge, "to consider what you have learned through your own relationship with your parents." (Writing 4)

Although these comments are not directive, they invoke the teacher's agenda and authority. Moreover, they often lead directly into explicit evaluation of the writing, as the following responses illustrate:

As I read your paper, Louise, I am confused by your selection of a topic. The assignment calls for you to write about something "you know a great deal about." Does the seat belt law really fall into that category? . . . My expectation for this assignment is that writers will have some expertise about their subjects, that I'll learn something about the topics from reading the essays. I don't learn anything from reading your draft. Furthermore, I wonder why you choose to argue an issue that the American public appears to have accepted years ago rather than to inform readers about some particular interest that you have or to explain to them some knowledge that is uniquely yours. (Writing 1)

This essay recounting your painful recovery experience certainly qualifies you to fulfill this assignment, to write about something that "has had an impact on you, either changing you in some way or teaching you an important lesson." However, you narrate the course of the diagnosis and your recovery at length and never get to the heart of this assignment. Reread the assignment, Kevin, and you'll see that you are to focus primarily on the effect of the event, not on the event itself. (Writing 10)

These responses—and others in which he evaluates how the writing stacks up against the standards of the assignment—are some of McClelland's most directive in the study. The readings are firmly controlling even though many of his comments are not cast in authoritative modes.

McClelland's calls for revision are also firm, but they are not as assertive or as controlling as his close readings. He presents a moderate 14% of his comments as imperatives or advice. But he uses them regularly and at key points in his responses,[8] especially toward the end of his letters, when he usually explicitly lays out his plan for revision. Although he uses slightly more advisory comments than commands, many of his comments blur the line between the two forms:

If you are committed to this topic, become knowledgeable about it so that you can write an informative essay on it. Begin by reading widely on it and by interviewing local public safety experts and automobile dealers. Moreover, if it's feasible, perhaps you could also interview via telephone state and federal legislators and appropriate individuals from a couple of the major automobile manufacturers. (Writing 1)

Let me suggest that you focus on your experiences and those of friends you know well in order to have a knowledge base from which to build the sort of essay this assignment calls for. (Writing 4)

While you take a more pragmatic approach to the work, consider how you might include some information for readers with our interests within your approach. (Writing 11)

On several occasions across the sampling, he also presents advice in terms of his preferences as a reader:

> I'd like to know specifically in what ways it [the gang] was and in what ways it wasn't [like an ego trip]. (Writing 12)

> If I were to apply for a waiter's job at your establishment, I'd like to know more about the work and the money. (Writing 11)

> I'd like to hear more about Cougar's music, especially what you think about it. (Writing 13)

Many of his imperative comments, however, are geared toward particular changes in the product and are rather directive:

> Look again at his data and his logic. Search for ways of composing a more effective argument by 1) calling his conclusions into question and 2) making your case more detailed and convincing. (Writing 2)

> Of course, with such requirements for "telling" us such things you have to make some trade-offs, some reduction in the amount of "showing" us the scene. . . . So you need to examine carefully what to include and what to let drop to the editor's floor. (Writing 5)

> To shape your text into a more evocative reading you need to emulate my approach of sensory and personal details, though not necessarily my style, as embodied in the paragraph above. Using that approach as a guide, rework each of the seasonal scenes to build each into a vicarious, sensory experience for your readers. (Writing 6)

> Help me decide from your characterization of his music whether to buy an album of his. To do this you need to assess the songs' lyrics (some of which you already do). But also you need to define and rate the musicality of his work—both the composing and the performing. (Writing 13)

These commands do not tell the student specifically what to change in the writing or how to change it, but they do establish definite goals for revision and exert a firm control over the writing. Just how much control they exert depends on what McClelland does in the way of introducing and elaborating these calls for revision.

When McClelland makes a number of interpretive comments and follows his advice and commands with questions, his responses are only moderately directive. This is the case on Writings 2, 4, 11, and 12, in which he makes 23 of his 29 interpretive comments and asks 50 of his 53 questions.[9] They are easily McClelland's most interactive responses in the sampling, providing students with a keen sense of how their writing is being interpreted and guiding them to make the called-for revisions.

When he uses few or no interpretive comments and no questions, as in his comments on Writings 5, 6, 10, and 13, his criticism and commands dominate the response and make his comments particularly directive. Across his responses, in fact, McClelland's strong readings and sharp, concise calls for revision highlight his expectations as a teacher-critic more than they offer guidance for revision. Like Stewart, he sets forth in no uncertain terms his criticism of the writing and directs the writer to produce the text he envisions. In contrast to Stewart, he usually offers little elaboration on his plans for revision. He calls on the student to take up certain activities or specifies certain goals, and, although he sometimes briefly explains or illustrates these prompts, he expects the student to come up with these revisions on his own.[10]

Focus

McClelland gives less attention to local matters—and more attention to the content and context of writing—than any other reader in the study. Only 6 of his 201 comments on the 10 essays in the sampling—less than 3% of his comments—are made on correctness, wording, and local structure.[11] On Writing 2, 23 of McClelland's 25 comments are given to global matters. Sixteen comments focus on ideas, among them the following:

> With regard to your position, did you say that you were against legalizing drugs because they were harmful and, therefore, morally wrong? Those are the points that I gleaned from your last two paragraphs. However, you say, "We all know drugs are dangerous to the body and society *without any explanation*. . . ."

Four comments deal with development:

> Given the nature of LeMoult's radical proposal, . . . I think some further explanation is due us readers.
> But perhaps there is something that you could use to your advantage in the behavior of other sorts of addicts: smokers, gamblers, shoppers?
> What else can you say in favor of your position?
> Search for ways of composing a more effective argument by . . . making your case more detailed and convincing.

Three comments deal with global structure, in this case, with the focus of the essay or the relation of ideas to this focus:[12]

> Try stating [your] point in a sentence or two.
> Do [the points on the first antidrug laws and on women's use of laudanum] relate to your argument with LeMoult over legalizing drugs?
> Is this what you attempted?

The remaining two comments address conceptual matters beyond the text. One calls on Nancy to do some work with invention; the other asks her to look back at her reading of LeMoult.

In each of his commentaries, McClelland also addresses a limited number of areas. Five of his letters cover only one or two areas of response; only two letters address four or more areas.[13] In contrast to Stewart and Edward White, he does not try to lead the student to improve all levels of writing and does not mark various incidental problems as they arise. By focusing on fewer areas of response and especially by dealing minimally with local matters, he moderates the control he exerts over student writing.

McClelland also takes some of the emphasis away from the formal text by orienting many of his comments to the rhetorical context and the individual student's work in the course. He speaks of the needs of the reader—usually, as we shall see, on his particular needs as a reader—on 9 of his 10 responses. These comments, such as the following from Writing 2 and Writing 12, help place his responses in a rhetorical context:

> Given the nature of LeMoult's radical proposal . . . , I think some further explanation is due us readers. (Writing 2)
> What remains is to commit yourself to the work of developing and organizing that knowledge for us readers in your new community who are relying on you for a look inside the gang and inside your membership to it. (Writing 12)

In half of his letters, McClelland goes beyond commenting about the text and the rhetorical situation and talks in terms of the writer's composing processes, her earlier coursework, and the student behind the text. On Writing 2, for instance, McClelland suggests that Nancy "jot down a list of items" that might lead her to better understand the focus of the writing and to decide which of LeMoult's points she should summarize. He looks at six writings in terms of the student's earlier papers or earlier drafts. In his responses to five papers, he speaks about the writing in terms of the student's knowledge about the subject. On Writing 1, for instance, he calls on Louise to base her writing on "knowledge that is uniquely yours." On Writing 12, he assures Rusty that he has "the personal knowledge to do the job" laid out in the assignment. Although these comments are written with the aim of leading the student to improve the draft, they are less concerned with the immediate changes to be made in the text and moderate his control as a responder.

Overview of Teacher Control

McClelland is a sharp, critical reader and a demanding responder. He offers close analyses of student writing, pinpoints problems in the text, and in a general way directs the student to make revisions. Although he looks to place some of the responsibility for revision on the writer, he asserts a clear-cut control. In each of his responses, he seems to know exactly what the student should do with a piece of writing and confidently sets out the tasks for revision. He does not impose an idealized text on the student's writing. He does not lay out specific changes to be made in the text or dictate revisions. Nevertheless, his commentary is carefully guided by his sense of what the writing must do or what improvements would best be made. He strictly holds to the demands of the writing assignment and reads with a definite set of expectations in mind. He often makes key decisions for the writer and does not hesitate to indicate his preferences about how the writing would best be revised.

Although McClelland does not refer to the assignment in his comments on Writing 2, he does so on 8 of his 10 sets of responses. Frequently, after explaining the demands of an assignment, he goes on to evaluate the writing strictly in terms of these expectations. Of course, the more closely a responder judges the writing against the requirements of the assignment, a teacher-oriented concern, the more likely he will control decisions about the writing and the more directive his style.

McClelland's emphasis on the writing assignment goes hand in hand with his image as a reader. Although he frequently calls attention to other prospective readers in his responses, he envisions himself as the primary reader of the writing. Like Stewart, he assumes the role of a detached, expert reader—that is, as an authoritative teacher—more often than he does the role of a representative reader.[14] Even on those occasions when he speaks from the perspective of the target audience, he presents his very defined expectations. On Writing 5, for example, he speaks about how the writing works for him both as a reader and a novice fisherman:

> [Y]ou must gauge how much "showing" and how much "telling" to do in the text. As a reader, I want to experience vicariously the primary sensations of the activity, while also needing your commentary to explain how to catch that wondrous large-mouth. What I find most effective in your draft, Steve, is the technical information. . . . I need to know more about specific techniques . . . . The more scientific information . . . and the more lore . . . you present, the better for us readers.

He goes on to underscore his own preferences as a reader, preferences that are tied to his role as a teacher:

> So you need to examine carefully what to include and what to let drop on the editor's floor. As far as relevance to my needs as a reader, I give a low priority to the reverie about your early childhood days. . . . There are more than two hundred words tied up in it.

Although in his responses to Writing 12 he speaks of himself and others as "readers in your new community who are relying on you for a look inside the gang and inside your membership to it," he once again presents himself as the primary audience:

> Assuming that you'll continue along this line of describing the Cripps and explaining why you joined and quit, I'd like to know more about how the gang functioned. My brother belonged to a gang in the early sixties, so I have some knowledge of his gang's structure and functions. I wonder if your gang was similar to his "Black Hawks."

By asking the student to focus attention on this particular area of the writing, he focuses attention on himself as the main reader of the writing and asserts his control as a teacher. His large number of interpretive comments notwithstanding, McClelland does not read as a representative or a general reader; his reading is filtered through the expectations of a discriminating reader, one whose interests are unmistakably those of a teacher.

Together, McClelland's emphasis on the writing assignment and his own views toward the writing lead him to present strong critical readings and to create himself in the role of a teacher-critic. These readings, which are presented in a variety of modes, present sharp judgments or make key decisions about the writing. They emphasize his authority and allow him to determine the specific focus or content of the paper. Although his commentary is only mildly directive on several sets of responses, keeping responsibility in the hands of the student,[15] he makes or implies important decisions for the writer in almost all of his responses.

In Writing 5, for example, McClelland tells the writer that he wants greater attention placed on "the primary sensations" of fishing. He also tells him he needs to explain more fully the technical aspects of bass fishing, noting that, "The more scientific information (like that about barometric pressure change) and the more lore (your particular tricks of the trade) you present, the better for us readers who are novices to this sport." In Writing 6, he does not simply point to the lack of detail; he points to the lack of "precise, sensory details." He goes on to provide a model of his own writing that highlights the use of such detail. In Writing 13, he calls for a particular type of concert review, one that concentrates on the music itself and that is written for a rather particular rhetorical purpose—convincing the reader to purchase the singer's music:

> To be sure, you do explain some basic things . . . . But, Frank, a concert review *evaluates* the music. Suppose I've never heard about Cougar. Help me decide from your characterization of his music whether to buy an album of his.

In his response to Writing 9, he implies that the writer should have interpreted her father's turning away from his family as a typical male midlife crisis, not just as a parallel to Young Goodman Brown's rejection of his wife and faith.[16] Although these strong readings do not dictate specific revisions, they still impose McClelland's vision for the writing onto the student and make important decisions about the writing. In doing so, they take control over the writer's choices, appropriating the writing.

McClelland's strong readings, sharp evaluations, and pointed calls for revision make his style critical and, for this group of readers, fairly directive. His interpretive comments, questions, modelling, and short lessons often give his responses an interactive quality that tempers his control. But although he alternates between interactive and authoritative strategies, his strong presence as a reader and critic and his definite sense of how the writing may be improved finally make his style more critical and authoritative than guiding and interactive. Like Stewart, White, and O'Hare, he uses his authority as a teacher to point directly to the problems in the writing and to set forth a clear plan for revision. But whereas these other directive readers express their assessments briefly and frequently play back the student's writing in comments that simply interpret the text, McClelland gives detailed critical readings of the text and often filters his interpretations through his own views and judgments as an individual reader. Unlike Stewart and (to a lesser extent) O'Hare, he does not further elaborate his calls for revision; instead, like White, he sets forth general plans for revision and rarely expands on them.

McClelland, then, is a critical teacher-reader. He is less directive than White and Stewart, but he is more directive than O'Hare and Peterson. He is also far more directive, as we shall see, than the next two readers in this group, Glynda Hull and Peter Elbow.

GLYNDA HULL

After the detail of Donald Stewart's and Ben McClelland's comments, Glynda Hull's comments seem sparse. Whereas Stewart writes 35 comments per paper and McClelland 20, Hull writes an average of 12 comments per paper. She not only writes fewer comments, she also elaborates less on those she does present.[1] But the number of comments only begins to account for their differences. In number, type, and purpose, Hull's comments are radically different from Stewart's and McClelland's. The features of her responses may be seen sprinkled through the commentary of other readers. But Hull's unconventional use of a few conventional strategies—using imperatives, limiting the scope of her responses, and focusing on students' writing processes—makes her commentary unique in this study.

Whereas Stewart and McClelland look for areas for improvement and offer ways to refashion the written product, Hull uses the writing to determine the activities or issues the student would do best to work on. Stewart and McClelland use most of their comments to evaluate student texts, present lessons, and somehow direct the student to improve the text. Hull uses most of her comments to devise assignments for students to take up on their own in order to learn about writing by practice more than precept and by self-guided work rather than directed point-by-point revision. She is less concerned with the revision of drafts than with engaging students in working on those issues and activities they most need to work on for their ongoing development as writers.

More than any other reader in the study, Hull also shapes her responses to the needs of the individual student. She usually focuses on only two or three concerns, deciding what to take up (and how far to go with it) according to the image of the student she sees reflected in the text. As a result, her responses assume a variety of purposes. She writes comments that are designed to improve the text, either in part or as a whole; comments that are designed to engage the student in some writing activity; and comments that are designed to familiarize the student with the conventions of writing.

Hull usually writes few marginal comments. She tends not to make many, if any, marginal comments on early or immature drafts, and avoids making marginal comments on underdeveloped "final" drafts as well.[2] Most of the real work in her responses is reserved for the endnote. Her style is characterized by the informal voice of her comments, her penchant for zeroing in on one or two key concerns, and her frequent use of three modes of response: praise, problem-posing questions, and process-based imperatives.

For Hull, then, less is more: The less she evaluates the text, the more she can make assignments for students; the less she takes up in her responses, the more she can help students focus their work; the less she indicates what students might come up with in their next drafts, the more they will have to make their own decisions and come up with their own material.[3] She seems as comfortable laying out a course of action for students as she seems committed to putting the real responsibility for revising and learning on them. Hull is neither as directive as Stewart or McClelland nor as open-ended and nondirective as Anne Gere or (as we shall see) as Peter Elbow. Her response style, situated midway between the most directive and the least directive readers in the study, swings continuously in both directions, nodding to, but never touching on, either extreme.

HULL			
SETS OF RESPONSES	**NUMBER OF RESPONSES**		
5 rough drafts 4 final drafts 12 comments/writing 2.3 issues/writing		Rough Drafts	Final Drafts	Total
	Marginal Comments	13	30	43
	End Comments	38	31	69
	Total	51	61	112

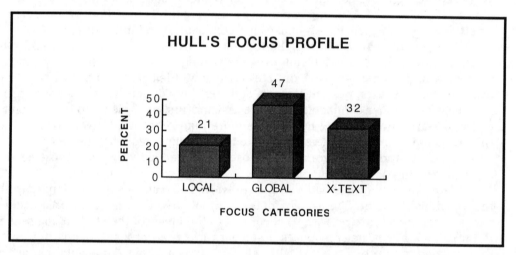

HULL'S FOCUS PROFILE

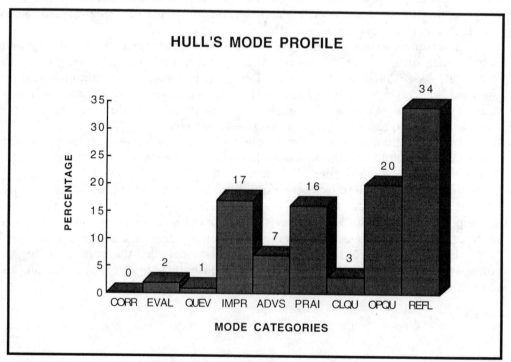

HULL'S MODE PROFILE

Writing 2
Nancy S.
First Rough Draft

What If Drugs Were Legal?

What if drugs were legal? Could you imagine what it would do to our society? Well according to John E. LeMoult, a lawyer with twenty years of experience on the subject, feels we should at least consider it. I would like to comment on his article "Legalize Drugs" in the June 15, 1984, issue of the New York Times. I disagree with LeMoult's idea of legalizing drugs to cut the cost of crime.

LeMoult's article was short and sweet. He gives the background of the legalization of drugs. For example, the first antidrug laws of the United States were passed in 1914. The laws were put in effect because of the threat of the Chinese imagrants. In addition, he explains how women were the first to use laudanun, an over the counter drug, as a substitute for drinking; it was unacceptable for women to drink. By explaining this he made the reader feel that society was the cause of women using the substitute, laudanun, for drinking. LeMoult proceeded from there to explain how the money to buy drugs comes from us as society. Since drug addicts turn to crime to get money we become a corrupt society. Due to this we spend unnecessary money protecting inocent citizens by means of law enforcment, jails, and ect. LeMoult says that if we legalize drugs that "Overnight the cost of law enforcement, courts, judges, jails and convict rehabilitation would be cut in half. The savings in tax would be more than $50 billion a year."

Okay — I see you're setting up the paper as the assignment suggested —

you're beginning to respond to LeMoult's argument. What if you saved evaluative comments until later? How would this choice affect your argument?

1

LeMoult might be correct by saying that our cost of living in society would be cut in half if drugs were legalized, however, he is justifying a wrong to save money. In my opinion legalizing drugs is the easy man's way out. Just because crime is high due to the fact that the cost of drugs is unbeleivable it doesn't make legalizing them right. We all know drugs are dangerous to the body and society without any explanation, therefore, you shouldn't legalize something that is dangerous.

My only and most important argument to LeMoult is the physical harm it would bring by legalizing drugs. People abuse their right to use alcoholic beverages because they are legal. For example, LeMoult himself says the amount of drug addicts is small compared to alcoholics. Why?—of course it is because of the legalization of alcohol. When you make something legal it can and will be done with little hassel. Why allow something to be done with ease when it is wrong? LeMoult's points are good and true but I believe he is approaching the subject in the wrong manner. Drugs are wrong, therefore, should not be legal!

Controversial issues -- drugs, abortion, the death penalty -- are hard to discuss in an even-tempered way because we all have such strong opinions and feelings about them. As LeMoult said, we all tend to express our "moral opposition" in such cases. In academic writing, the trick is to express your opinion with authority -- but, to make sure your argument is more than just your opinion.

In your next draft, I think you should work on 2 things:

① In your response, offer some persuasive evidence against legalizing drugs -- evidence that goes beyond saying "we all know that drugs are harmful." How about, for example, the connection between drug abuse and other serious human problems, like AIDS?

② After you've offered this evidence, go back and imagine how LeMonet would respond to it. Would he have an answer for the AIDS argument? Can you strengthen your argument accordingly?

It will be interesting for us to talk in class about the extent to which it is possible to persuade when the issue involves moral opposition. If it's not possible, then who becomes the audience for such papers?

Mode

The outstanding feature of Hull's responses is her use of imperative comments. Only Edward White uses more imperatives than Hull (19% to her 17%). They are at the heart of eight of her nine sets of responses. Of course, teachers who make regular use of commands typically assume significant control over the student's writing. Although commands may assume a range of forms—from bald directives to helpful prompts—they usually take on an authoritative tone and call on the student to make specific changes in the text. Consider, for example, the following imperative comments that Stewart and McClelland present in their responses to Nancy:

> You must first provide some very specific information about the damage drug use does to people. . . . And you must show, in more specific terms, exactly what damage society suffers from drug users: loss of productivity, cost of care for those disabled, costs of law enforcement, breakdown of families, etc. . . . You must also do a better job of editing the paper. (Stewart)

> Look again at his data and his logic. Search for ways of composing a more effective argument by 1) calling his conclusions into question and 2) making your case more detailed and convincing. (McClelland)

These imperatives are text-based and highly authoritative. Stewart makes no bones about what he expects Nancy to do. His voice is straightforward, if not strident. McClelland's calls for action are less defined, but they still direct Nancy to make specific revisions in the text, his voice urging and demanding.

But even though most teachers use commands to direct the student to make specific changes in the text (e.g., Add some detail, Combine these sentences), Hull characteristically uses them to engage the student in processes that are not necessarily or immediately tied to producing a better subsequent draft. Typically, her imperative comments are assignments, invitations for the student to consider some issue of writing or to practice some composing activity. They prompt the student—even as they encourage him—to learn on his own, by hands-on practice.[4] These process-based imperatives are the kind of assignment-making comments that Lees (19) advocates. Hull's comments on "What If Drugs Were Legal?" are a case in point. She writes two imperatives to Nancy:

> 1) In your response, offer some persuasive evidence against legalizing drugs—evidence that goes beyond saying "we all know that drugs are harmful."
>
> 2) After you've offered this evidence, go back and imagine how LeMoult would respond to it.

Like Stewart's and McClelland's imperatives, Hull's first imperative is targeted toward the text, calling on the student to add some evidence on her revised draft. But such text-based imperatives are, for Hull, the exception and not the rule. Only 6 of her 19 imperatives in the sampling are geared toward specific changes in the text.[5] The second comment is far more characteristic of Hull's commands. For the moment, it delays trying to effect any immediate change in her next draft. It simply prompts Nancy to think about her arguments. The comment would be much different—more geared toward the written product and more controlling—if Hull had said: "Go back and insert arguments that will refute LeMoult's claims."

In her responses throughout the sampling, Hull's impulse is to lead students to practice writing activities on their own rather than direct them to make specific changes in their texts, as the following examples indicate:

> Take a look at the sentence in your draft that I've bracketed: it is good advice! How could you follow this advice in your paper? (Writing 1)
>
> Try your hand at another draft of this assignment, this time on a different

> topic. . . . What we'll want to do is compare their voices. (Writing 1)
>
> What I want you to do is figure out what it is about your paper . . . that could produce such different reactions. (Writing 6)

Perhaps the clearest example of Hull's willingness to make assignments that engage the student in the process of revision occurs in her endnote to Writing 5:

> In your next draft, keep those wonderful details, but pay attention as well to how you can make this more an expository essay than a personal experience piece. If I had to pick a title for this draft, it would be something like: "The Day I Caught My Monster Bass." What would you need to do to your paper to make the following title fit it: "Fishing in the Lakes of Central Orlando"?

Here she uses imperative comments to call on the student to consider some advice, experiment with different voices, and consider various conventions of writing. On other occasions, as we shall see, she uses them to engage students in other writing activities: coming up with lists, brainstorming ideas and evidence, and cutting and pasting sections of a paper. Although such imperatives, of course, clearly exert control over the student writer, they are less controlling than conventional imperative comments because they guide the student to create and work with his own material—not simply follow directions on how to change a text.

Hull's commands, however, are different from Stewart's and McClelland's in other ways as well. Whereas Stewart and McClelland state their directives assertively, Hull expresses hers diplomatically. She does not say "Add evidence" or "You must find stronger arguments"; she says "offer us some persuasive evidence." She does not say "Anticipate LeMoult's reactions to your arguments"; she says "go back and imagine how LeMoult would respond." Her directives are cast in language that is more informal and hortatorical—and less authoritative—than conventional imperatives. She seems to go out of the way to soften the harshness of her directives. Notice, for example, how she introduces and follows up on her imperatives to Nancy:

> In your next draft, I think you should work on two things:
>
> 1) In your response, offer some persuasive evidence against legalizing drugs— evidence that goes beyond saying "we all know that drugs are harmful." How about, for example, the connection between drug abuse and other serious human problems, like AIDS?
>
> 2) After you've offered this evidence, go back and imagine how LeMoult would respond to it. Would he have an answer for the AIDS argument? Can you strengthen your argument accordingly?

She eases her way into the comments by noting that these are matters she *thinks* Nancy should work on. Then, after presenting the assignments, she offers open-ended questions for the student to consider. Together, the surrounding comments emphasize that these responses present issues to consider, not orders to follow.[6]

Hull's directives, then, are different from conventional directives in three ways. First, they are usually directed toward the writing process, not the written product. Second, they mute the authority that goes along with most directive comments, invoking instead a posture that is guiding and interactive, her voice more informal and hortatorical, her calls to action more open-ended. Third, they are typically framed by comments that are interactive. The calls to action are usually preceded by interpretive comments, positive evaluations, or (as in the case above) metadiscourse designed to prepare the student for the imperative to come. They are often followed by problem-posing questions, which serve to turn the matter back into a question for the student to consider. By casting her imperatives in these ways, Hull moderates the control she exerts over the writing and puts the burden of revision on the student. Consider, for example, her responses to "Street Gangs":

> You have the makings of a very interesting paper here. Here are two suggestions for your next draft:
>
> 1) **I want you to add some extended examples—not just one sentence or two, but whole paragraphs**. On the first page, for example, you might tell specifically about a time when someone got in trouble and everyone was there. **Give details: what time, when, what situation, where**. These long examples should be used to illustrate and provide evidence for points you're making.
>
> 2) After you've added the examples, **get some scissors and tape, and cut your paper up— one paragraph per strip of paper. Experiment with putting these paragraphs in different orders**. Which ones seem like beginning material? Which ones come next? And so on?

Imperatives (in bold) are at the heart of these two groups of comments.[7] The imperatives in the first item are geared to the text and consequently are more conventional and more controlling than the second. Still, the opening command mutes Hull's authority: "I want you to add," she says, not "Add examples" or "You must add examples." The next command, following on an example and followed by several guiding questions, functions less as a new request than it does as a helpful prompt or suggestion. The second series of commands—which comprise one comment—are process-based imperatives, or assignments. The comment perfectly illustrates how Hull's imperatives are, paradoxically, interactive. In a style that is straightforward but not commanding, they prompt the student to engage in an activity, yet at the same time leave the decision about what specifically to do up to him. At the end of the sequence, the imperatives segue into a series of open problem-posing questions, which serve to offer some direction, yet leave the answers for Rusty to work out on his own.

This strategy of combining directives and open problem-posing comments is a common characteristic of Hull's responding style. Some combination of these modes occurs on six of her nine sets of responses. In fact, Hull casts more comments as open problem-posing questions (15%) than all but one other reader.[8] Examples are easy to find:

> Go back and imagine how LeMoult would respond to it. Would he have an answer for the AIDS argument? Can you strengthen your argument accordingly? (Writing 2)[9]
>
> Take a look at the sentence in your draft that I've bracketed. How could you follow this advice? (Writing 1)
>
> What I want you to do is figure out what it is about your paper, and about different readers, that could produce such different reactions. For example, your seasonal portraits could have, with a few exceptions, been written by someone who grew up in Tallahassee. What will some readers like about this quality; what will others dislike? (Writing 6).

Hull also combines process imperatives and open problem-posing questions in her comments on Writing 11, "The Most Effective Ways of Being a Good Waitress." After opening her endnote by affirming that this midterm essay "is certainly a 'pass,'" Hull continues:

> But now, let's consider how to make [this paper] more than a pass. . . . Here are some things to get you started thinking before we meet to talk about a "good money" paper:
>
> 1) Underline the parts of your paper you think a reader would like best. What is likable about those parts?
>
> 2) Put an asterisk at places where you might do more to interest a reader or where you're not satisfied with your paper. What's the problem with those places?
>
> 3) Think back to your experiences as a waitress and make a list of the most memorable ones . . . .

After establishing a light tone in her opening statements, Hull presents three imperative comments that call on Barbara to engage in a process activity. The tone of all three imperatives, if matter-of-fact, is also light and inviting. Moreover, two of the three imperatives are framed by interactive comments—at the start by direct talk to the student about the comments to come and after by open-ended questions.

Throughout her responses, Hull turns her commands into facilitative comments by surrounding them with open-ended questions and helpful explanations. Consider the following pared-down version of Hull's responses to Writing 4, an argumentative essay in which the student writes in rather abstract terms against parents who "overguide" their teenage children:

1) Make a list of every specific instance you can think of when your parents (or the parents of your friends) have overguided.

2) Look over the list and see if you notice any interesting patterns.

3) Pick one specific instance from your first list . . . and describe that instance in detail in a few paragraphs.

Even stated without the surrounding comments, these three "process" imperatives are informal. They have the feel of help more than requests or commands. But they take on a highly interactive quality when they are seen in their original context, framed by direct speech to the student and modified by examples and questions:

I have some ideas about how you can shape your next draft on this topic that I want to talk to you about. In preparation for that conference, would you do these things:

1) Make a list of every specific instance you can think of when your parents (or the parents of your friends) have overguided. (For example, "the time I wanted to go to Tijuana during spring break, the time. . . .")

2) Look over the list and see if you notice any interesting patterns. In what situations do parents tend to overguide? What form does the overguidance take? How do teenagers typically react?

3) Pick one specific instance from your first list—one that seems "representative" of guidance behavior, and describe that instance in detail in a few paragraphs.

We'll work with what you've done in our next class meeting.

The response, with all its devices to help as well as direct the student, demonstrates the extent to which Hull presents imperatives—not to control what the student writes—but to guide him in process tasks. In their full context, these process imperatives and open problem-posing questions help make her style both directive and interactive. Combined with her encouraging tone and her liberal use of praise, they create the persona of a supportive teacher who shares responsibility with students even as she demands it of them. They allow her to decide what is best to work on and leave the students to work out their revisions on their own. In this way, Hull directs, guides, and helps students learn by going where they have to go.

Focus

Hull individualizes her responses—and achieves her diversity as a responder—through the focus of her comments. Although she takes up very different concerns from paper to paper, she addresses a very limited number of concerns on most sets of responses. She tends to address only two or three areas of writing—and to pursue only one of them—in most of her commentaries. In fact, she deals with fewer issues in her responses than anyone else in the study, just above two per paper.[10] By limiting the areas she addresses, she is able to adapt her responses to the needs of the individual student, give him more room to decide what to revise, and assume less control over his writing.

The issues she takes up from paper to paper follow no explicit pattern. Instead, they seem to be selected according to the needs of the individual student, based especially on what she sees in the writing. On Writing 1, for example, Hull delays work on the next draft in order to have Louise work on her voice as a writer. On Writing 10, she puts aside all concern about sentence-level problems and concentrates on having Kevin simply add some analysis of his experiences. On Writing 13, she offers sample editorial comments that will help the writer polish the writing for publication.

On Writings 4 and 12, two rough drafts that share the problem of inadequate development, Hull takes very different strategies. On "Overguiding Teenage Children," she suspends work on the draft as a whole and focuses Anne's attention on coming up with examples and drafting one of the examples in a separate writing. On "Street Gangs," perhaps because it is further along in its use of specific details and experiences, Hull tries to help Rusty come up with a full next draft. After praising his ideas in her marginal comments, she directs Rusty (through text-specific comments) to develop his ideas and then calls on him to experiment with the organization of the writing. The very different ways of approaching these rough drafts indicates just how far she is willing to go to shape her comments to the individual student.

Hull spreads her responses across the various focus categories. More than anything else, though, she is concerned with helping students improve the content of their writing and develop their practical understanding of how texts must be shaped according to certain conventions of writing and the expectations of readers. On all but two of her responses, she looks at the writing and her plans for revision in terms of conventions and readers:

> I hear a strong voice in this paper. The question is, what kind of voice will readers hear and be persuaded by? (Writing 1)
>
> In academic writing, the trick is to express your opinion with authority—but to make sure your argument is more than just your opinion. (Writing 2)
>
> This notion of overguidance for teenagers is an interesting one because it argues for just the opposite of what many people would expect in a paper on parents and kids. (Writing 4)
>
> You've got an unusual paper here in that some readers will love it and some will feel just as strongly in the opposite direction. What I want you to do is figure out what it is about your paper, and about different readers, that could produce such different reactions. (Writing 6)

She is also inclined to shape her comments as process tasks. Instead of simply identifying changes that can be made in the next draft and directing students' attention mainly to the written product, Hull gives students hands-on activities that will help them discover the need for changes and come up with materials on their own. She not only presents students with a task but also gives them a way to take up the task.

This way of looking at student revision in terms of the writer's composing processes, not in terms of its outcome in a final text, is part of a larger strategy that goes far toward characterizing Hull's responding style: her emphasis on the processes and principles of writing more than on the written product. Hull always seems ready to suspend work on completing a paper so she can concentrate on having the student work on an activity or principle that she thinks the student needs to practice. The papers they write in the course seem less the *target* for instruction and more *occasions* for instruction. They are places where teaching and learning can most productively be taken up. In Writing 1, for example, Hull suspends work on the draft about the use of seat belts and calls on Louise, first, to consider how she might have presented both sides of the issue (in anticipation of a conference on the subject) and, second, to draft another essay on a topic about which she is more knowledgeable. She asks her to do this not to help her produce a better essay but to help her work on her voice as a writer. In a similar way, she foregoes having Anne work on coming up with a revised draft of Writing 4, "Overguiding Teenage Children," in order to have her concentrate on discovering personal examples and developing *one* of them in a separate piece of writing. In her responses to Writing 6, "The Four Seasons," she does not call on David to revise his cliched language; she asks him to consider why some readers might like such language while others might react against it. In Writing 11 she does not call on Barbara to revise her in-class essay; she asks her to analyze the writing to see what might be useful to keep if she were to try to write something more than just a "passable" essay. Such hands-on work may eventuate in a better draft, perhaps even in a draft ready to be called final, but it is not taken up with the primary aim of producing a better paper. It is taken up for the experience of practicing revision, for the occasion for practical learning it will provide.

Even when Hull looks to help the student produce a better text, she is more interested in working on one major area of writing than in guiding the student to come up with a finished product. On both Writings 5 and 10 she limits her response to one issue and gives the students free rein (and almost all of the responsibility) to decide on their own changes:

> I like the feel of this draft. You've captured something of the pleasure and skill involved in bass fishing. . . . In your next draft, keep those wonderful details, but pay attention as well to how you can make this more an expository essay than a personal experience piece. If I had to pick a title for this draft, it would be something like: "The Day I Caught My Monster Bass." What would you need to do to your paper to make the following title fit it: "Fishing in the Lakes of Central Orlando"? (Writing 5)

> I'd like you to take one more pass at this paper. Specifically, I'd like you to think about whether your illness has in some sense made you a different person, to add some paragraphs on how having leukemia has changed or affected you. (Writing 10)

Although these revisions may lead to fuller drafts, they are meant first of all to give the students practice in writing—in Writing 5, practice in producing expository prose, in Writing 10, practice in generalizing about, and gaining insight into, one's experiences.

The same emphasis can be seen even in Hull's most elaborate and text-oriented commentaries. On Writing 2, Hull guides Nancy to produce a revised draft even as she calls her attention to issues that transcend the individual piece of writing. She points to two changes that will help Nancy develop her arguments in the next draft, but she also invites her to consider the special problems that occur when a writer tries to persuade someone else about a highly controversial and emotional topic. She extends her discussion beyond a concern for the next draft and into a lesson on the conventions of academic writing. On Writing 12, "Street Gangs," she looks to help Rusty come up with a fuller next draft, yet she limits the areas she addresses in her detailed marginal comments and endnotes to development and global structure. On Writing 13, her fullest response in the study, Hull calls a halt to further global revision and helps Frank edit the paper for possible publication. She deals briefly with the content of one sentence, makes two comments about correctness, and then, in detailed marginal comments, offers specific help with one major area of response, local structure.

Hull, then, focuses her commentaries on one major issue, according to the needs of the individual student. She talks about revision in terms of specific writing activities and in terms of the conventions and contexts of writing, and she uses her comments to engage students in practical lessons as much as to produce more complete drafts. These ways of focusing on student writing put more emphasis on the student's learning and less emphasis on the way a piece of writing turns out. They also moderate the control Hull exerts over the student and help make her style highly interactive.

Overview of Teacher Control

Unlike a number of other readers in the study, Hull leans neither toward being an editor nor being a representative or facilitative reader. Her comments are those of a teacher, a diagnostician. When she picks up a student text, it seems that she looks through the text to the student behind the writing and, on the basis of what he has written, determines what he needs most to work on at this time. She decides on a course of action for the student and then turns the matter over to him, to work through on his own. Whereas Stewart is inclined to identify specific areas for improvement and even offer detailed suggestions about how those areas may be improved, Hull simply identifies the issue, clarifies it briefly, and then sets the writer out to address the matter. Whereas McClelland casts himself as a demanding expert reader who embodies the expectations of the community and challenges the student to write for him, Hull identifies herself as an insider who will help the student learn the ropes, a sort of personal sponsor whose job it is to help the student gain entry to the club, as the following passages illustrate:

> In academic writing, the trick is to express your opinion with authority—but to make sure your argument is more than just your opinion. (Writing 2)

> I want you to add some extended examples—not just one sentence or two, but whole paragraphs. I've marked several places you could make some additions with an asterisk (*). On the first page, for example, you might tell specifically about a time when someone got in trouble and everyone was there. Give details: what time, when, what situation, where. These long examples should be used to illustrate and provide evidence for points you're making. (Writing 12)

> You said in your paper that a waitress can decide to make "good money." Well, in a way, a writer can, too. That is, a writer can decide to go beyond what is required, or maybe go out on a limb by trying something different to please a reader. If you wanted to make "good money" in terms of this paper—if you wanted to go beyond what the assignment requires, what would your paper be like? (Writing 11)

Yet, although Hull adopts the stance of a teacher, using the authority of the role to decide what the student should work on, she does not take on the teacher's authoritative voice. Instead, she is informal and easygoing. Her voice is direct yet encouraging, not businesslike; it is decisive yet supportive, not demanding. She comes across as if to say: "OK, I've thought about this writing. Now, based on what you've done so far, what should we work on?" Throughout her responses she builds a sense of camaraderie between herself and her students, a shared responsibility. Hull is in charge of deciding what to work on, the student in charge of doing the work itself. It seems fitting, then, that in a number of her responses Hull speaks of the work to be done on a paper as a joint effort that she and the student will do together, as in the following instances:

> What we'll do is compare their voices. (Writing 1)
>
> We'll work with what you've done in our next class meeting. (Writing 4)
>
> We'll use [these tasks] to think about how to write a "good money" paper. (Writing 11)

At other times, she achieves this sense of camaraderie through frequent praise. She seems to have little trouble balancing her attempts both to set the agenda for the student and to act as an ally for him. In fact, she may draw much of her authority from her obvious interest in helping the writer:

> I like the feel of this draft. You've captured something of the pleasure and skill involved in bass fishing. Details like using top-water buzz bait in patches of lillypads will make your readers want to buy some waders and head on out to Ivenho. In your next draft, keep those wonderful details, but pay attention as well to how you can make this more an expository essay than a personal experience piece.

Hull exerts control over the student's writing and learning by deciding what he would do best to work on and laying those tasks out in process directives. She relinquishes control, however, by leaving the student to come up with his own revisions. Ultimately, Hull's response style is far less controlling than it is guiding. She is a supportive teacher who integrates authoritative and interactive methods of response in a light, advisory style.

PETER ELBOW

More than anyone else in the study, Peter Elbow offers a reader's response to student papers. His comments reflect how he experiences and reacts to the writing as he reads. Most responders emphasize their roles as critics, teachers, or guides, and, maintaining a certain critical distance from the student and from their immediate experience as readers, read with an eye toward identifying problems and laying out revisions. Elbow, however, is first of all a reader and only second a critic or a teacher. He strips away some of the layers and distance that typify most teachers' readings and shows the writer how the words on the page act on him, personally and subjectively, as a reader. He reads most of all for *what* the writer has to say, for the content of the writing. He plays back his understanding of the text, reacts freely to what the writer says, and openly expresses his views about the subject. He nods at ideas and passages he likes, and he voices his concerns about what he has trouble agreeing with or does not like.

Yet his readings do not simply play back and react to what the writer says. They also deal with *how* she says it: how she shapes her meaning and allows a reader to reconstruct what she means. They deal with the text as a piece of student writing, addressing how it is written as well as what it has to say. He notes when the writing is working for him, when it gets difficult to follow, when he sees the writer reaching to try something new, or when he sees her straining. His purposes as a reader and as a teacher become enmeshed and indistinguishable, and he ends up analyzing and evaluating the writing as much as he takes in and responds to the ideas in the text.

Elbow's responses always take the form of quick, informal letters to the student. Whereas Donald Stewart and Ben McClelland average 540 and 478 words per response, respectively, Elbow averages 369. Whereas theirs are deliberate and crafted, his are spontaneous and irregular, following the contours of his thinking. They have the feel of someone talking to himself, trying literally to come to terms with the words on the page. The letters are punctuated with "I" comments, underscoring the fact that these are statements that reflect his particular views as a reader. Many of the sentences take the form of fragments, and his comments often shift suddenly into entirely new lines of thought. Elbow makes few marginal comments—only 6 on the 10 essays in this sampling. Although he is willing to mark on the text itself, his marks are restricted to lightly penciled lines: straight lines indicating places where he likes the writing and squiggly underlines indicating areas where he has some difficulty. In most of his letters, Elbow plays back the text, evaluates where the writing works and does not work as well for him, raises a question or two about the writer's choices, and indicates what the writer might think about in the way of revision. But he does not take up these or other concerns in any set order, and he never lays out an explicit agenda for revision, choosing to leave such decisions up to the student.

ELBOW

SETS OF RESPONSES	NUMBER OF RESPONSES		
		Rough Drafts	Final Drafts	Total
5 rough drafts 4 final drafts	Marginal Comments	01	05	06
25 comments/writing	End Comments	118	101	219
3.6 issues/writing	Total	119	106	225

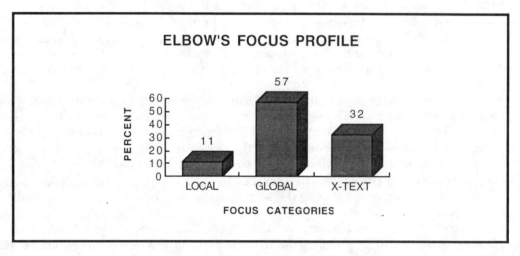

ELBOW'S FOCUS PROFILE

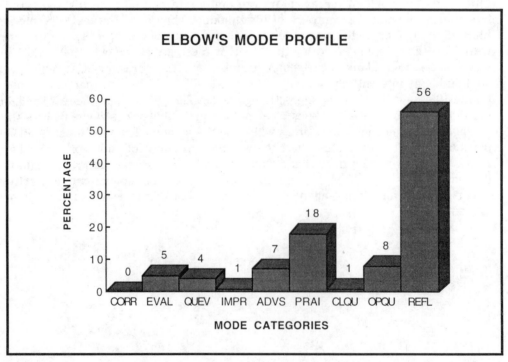

ELBOW'S MODE PROFILE

WRITING 2, "WHAT IF DRUGS WERE LEGAL?"

Dear Nancy,

It's fine not to worry about mechanics or correctness or nice sentences on a rough draft (I don't either); a way to put all attention on your train of thought; but remember that you'll need to get mechanics up to snuff for the final draft.

Seems like you've tried to build yourself a good framework and foundation--to build on for future drafts. You do an ok job of introducing the article. You don't give a full summary, but weren't asked to. And it strikes me that you move fairly quickly to one of your best arguments: alcohol. The widespread abuse is so undeniable.

My reactions. I don't disagree with your <u>position</u>, but somehow I find myself fighting you as I read. I'm trying to figure out why. I don't want to legalize drugs, but somehow I want to <u>listen</u> more to that writer. After all, he has a delicate thesis: not that we should do it but think about doing it. There's nothing wrong with you picking on part of his argument (legalizing) and ignoring the other part ("let's just think about it")--but the effect is somehow to make it seem as though you are having a closed mind and saying "Let's not even think about it." I guess I feel that the drug situation is so terrible that we have to let ourselves think about more things; I'm feeling stuck. So I think (self-centeredly) that the question for your next draft is this: what can you do to get a reader like me not to fight you so much? Try thinking about that; see what you can come up with.

I'd be happy to talk more about this in a conference.

Best,

Peter

Mode

Elbow's emphasis on his role as a reader may be seen clearly in his choice of modes. He makes no corrective comments and presents virtually no imperatives, only moderate advice, and just a few questions.[1] He writes only 17% of his comments in authoritative modes, fewer than anyone else in the study.[2] Instead, he devotes most of his responses to presenting his reading of the text in evaluative comments and reflective statements. Two out of every three of his comments are given to interpretations, reader responses, and positive and negative evaluations.[3]

All nine sets of Elbow's responses are dominated by his readings of the students' texts and are remarkably consistent in texture and style. All of them make use of some form of criticism. All of them make use of praise. And all of them use a variety of reader responses. Elbow's readings weave in and out of interpretive comments, reader-responses, and evaluations, moving freely from comments that play back the reader's views to comments that evaluate the writing. But it is his reader-response comments, in particular, comments that he employs more than anyone else in the study, that account for his moderate control as a responder and make his commentary distinctive.

At times in each of his responses, Elbow simply plays back the text by offering interpretations. In these readings, he identifies what he understands the text to say without making judgments about the writing, as in the following comment from Writing 2: "You don't give a full summary, but weren't asked to." Elbow simply tries to mirror what the text is doing. He plays back how he understands the text, without evaluation or additional comment, on all but one set of his responses:[4]

> [T]hen you go on to make your main argument—in effect to lay off a bit. (Writing 4)
>
> In the voice there you communicate a kind of "no-nonsense, we can't afford to fool around" tone that seems like it's part of the job. (Writing 11)
>
> At the bottom of 1 you give the example of picking on people at the pool. You tell it in a kind of deadpan way. . . . (Writing 12)
>
> Where it was mostly, "what he did," it's become a bit more, "what it was like for me going to the concert." (Writing 13)

These comments describe or interpret what the writing says, but they do not present any reaction or state or imply any real judgment about it. They call far more attention to the text than to the reader.

More frequently, Elbow creates readings that foreground his subjectivity as a reader. His main strategy is to verbalize his moment-by-moment experiences, understandings, associations, and reactions on reading the words on the page—to create what Elbow in his own scholarship calls "movies of the reader's mind."[5] These reader responses account for 30% of his comments and take three forms: *reader-experience comments, reader remarks*, and *reader reactions*.

Elbow's *reader-experience* comments are similar to interpretations in that they play back his way of understanding the text without making or implying any evaluations about it. But while interpretive comments minimize the reader's role in the act of interpretation, reader-experience comments highlight it. Even as they play back the text, they reveal something about the reader's experience or process of reading the writing. Consider, for instance, the following interpretive comments, which might be found in a response to Writing 10, a personal essay about the student writer's battle with leukemia:

> At first, you downplay the extent of your illness. Gradually, though, it becomes clear that you were seriously ill.

Now compare these interpretive comments with the following reader-experience comments that Elbow writes in response to the same essay:

> It took me a while to realize that you were seriously ill. At first I thought it was just
> mono or some such thing. . . . And then I get to feel as though I'm going to end up
> reading the story of a tragedy. And then finally I am led to believe that things are
> alright—but with a lingering fear and keeping my fingers crossed.

Although the interpretive comments provide an impersonal gloss of the writing, Elbow's
reader-experience comments render his personal moment-to-moment reading of the text. The
comments do not evaluate the writing. They simply show what happened to him as he read
the text, verbalizing his way of taking in its meaning. The following comments from Elbow's
other responses show how reader-experience comments (what amount to reader-based
interpretations) sidestep evaluation as they present an interpretation that is filtered explicitly
through the reader's subjectivity:

> What I noticed first are the places where you talk about your feelings while being in
> the gang: the oddly, interestingly, low-key "burden" as you put it. . . . Also the feeling
> of support and family. (Writing 12)

> I wasn't sure you were meaning to be that cynical or pragmatic. Gradually it seemed
> to me that you didn't mean that. (Writing 11)

Both passages show Elbow's particular way of making sense of the text, highlighting his own
experiences as a reader: "What I noticed first," "I wasn't sure," "Gradually it seemed to me."
Yet both stop short of evaluating the writing. Although he does not use such
reader-experience comments extensively, they appear in five sets of his responses.

Elbow also makes occasional use of *reader remarks,* comments that provide a reading of
the text without evaluating the writing. These comments note a reader's own thoughts and
associations—not about the writing itself or about his experiences while reading the text—but
about the subject under discussion. In his response to "Street Gangs," for example, Elbow
notes that if he were confronted by the circumstances that Rusty calls a burden, he "would
feel flat out fear." He also notes how Rusty's description of the sucker-punching incident is
"kind of horrifying for me. I think *I* was the kind of person who was picked on—or always
about to be." Such personal responses to the ideas may be found on four different sets of
Elbow's commentaries, among them:

> I can understand how it is that you got completely involved as if it were
> "just telling a story": what a story! (Writing 10)

> [A stray thought: by calling the banker "Schepman," do you think he was
> trying to imply he was Jewish?] It bothered me. (Writing 13)

These comments do not address the writing so much as they express the reader's response to
something in the writing.

If reader-experience comments and reader remarks were the only or the principal types of
reader-response comments Elbow made, his style would be only slightly evaluative. As it turns
out, however, 10% of his comments occur in these modes. Twice as many comments take the
form of *reader reactions,* comments that have the double function of presenting the reader's way
of processing the text *and* making evaluations about it. In these reader reactions, Elbow
indirectly identifies problems or strengths he sees even as he presents his way of understanding
the writing. The comments point to places where he is struck favorably by the writing, where he
has difficulty following a sentence or a line of thought, or, in general, where he is led to react
positively or negatively to the writer's choices. In Writing 2, for example, Elbow writes five
comments in the form of reader reactions. The first reaction is positive, the next four negative:

> [I]t strikes me that you move fairly quickly to one of your best arguments:
> alcohol.

[S]omehow I find myself fighting you as I read.

[S]omehow I want to listen more to that writer.

[T]he effect is somehow to make it seem as though you are having a closed mind and saying "Let's not even think about it."

I guess I feel that the drug situation is so terrible that we have to let ourselves think about more things; I'm feeling stuck.

Any of these comments, of course, might easily be framed as straight evaluations:

You do well to move quickly to one of your best arguments: alcohol.

Your arguments are not convincing.

You don't take enough care to present what LeMoult says.

Your ideas are narrow-minded.

The paper seems to be against even thinking about new solutions.

But Elbow chooses to mute the evaluations by embedding them within his readings of the text. Such reader reactions appear in every one of his letters, frequently at key points in his commentary. On Writing 9, for example, as he shares his reading of the end of the essay, he evaluates the student's mixture of literary analysis and personal narrative, writing two negative reader reactions:

At the end of your piece I feel things as strained ("I will be a good girl and talk about the story the teacher wants me to talk about"). In the 2nd and 3rd parags you sort of manage but I begin to feel a slight strain.

In a similar way, Elbow inserts judgments into his reader responses at key points in Writing 11 and Writing 12. On Writing 11, 9 of his 35 comments are framed as negative reader reactions. Four of them occur in the following sequence:

I actually wasn't quite clear, even at the end, what you meant by saying the tips are our decisions. [At the end I decided you were saying that if we do x, y, and z, we'll make the money,] but somehow I felt a little unclear on this. I somehow didn't like the third paragraph as much; found myself resisting you. . . . I felt you kind of preaching at me, and I didn't really get so much of a feeling of what it's like to be a waitress.

In each of these statements (except for the reader-experience comment enclosed in brackets), Elbow couches an evaluation in his reading. He does not just identify a problem in the text; he shows how a problem arose for him as he read and processed the writing. On Writing 12, when Elbow gives his reading of the sucker-punching episode and responds to the voice of the writing, he moves from two interpretive comments and two reader remarks (in the first three sentences) to a positive reader reaction and a negative reader reaction (in the two main clauses of the last sentence):

At the bottom of 1 you give the example of picking on people at the pool. You tell it in a kind of deadpan way, but it's kind of horrifying for me. I think I was the kind of person who was picked on—or always felt I was about to be. There's something intriguing or even moving about your low key tone here, but I'm also curious to know more how you actually felt—and feel.

To say that he found the writer's low-key approach "intriguing or even moving" is, of course, to suggest something positive about the writing. To say that he is "curious to know more" is to suggest that the writing has not yet provided enough detail. Both statements present his way of processing the text and contain an implicit evaluation. Overall, Elbow frames more comments as reader reactions than any other single mode: 20%.[6] They are the defining feature of his style.

Elbow makes use of the more conventional, explicit forms of evaluation as well. Straight negative evaluations or qualified evaluations make up 9% of his comments and appear on seven of his nine sets of responses, among them the following examples:

> You're not talking to me, you're speechifying, orating. (Writing 1)
> [I]t's a little bit of a soggy opening as you have it. (Writing 12)
> I still think there's a confusion there for readers. (Writing 11)

On first reading, then, Elbow appears to provide mostly nonevaluative readings of student texts. But actually his letters are filled with evaluative commentary. Forty-seven percent of his comments take some form of evaluation—whether direct or indirect, positive or negative—by far, the most in the study.[7] Moreover, he writes more criticism across his responses than all but one other reader in the study. Twenty-three percent of his comments present some form of negative evaluation, whether it is framed in the form of straight evaluations, qualified evaluations, or reader reactions.[8] Although the small number of explicit evaluative comments employed by Elbow suggests he is only moderately evaluative, his frequent use of reader reactions shows how deeply his responses are rooted in evaluation—albeit, most of them are presented as a reader's muted evaluations.

Nevertheless, Elbow's style remains nondirective and only moderately controlling—mainly for three reasons. First, he presents many of the judgments he makes about the writing in indirect modes. Second, he makes only modest use of comments that call on the student, directly or indirectly, to make particular revisions: imperatives, advice, and questions. Third, he creates a voice that is informal and nonauthoritative, the voice of a supportive reader.

Elbow's indirect evaluations allow him to give students some direction through his comments but not direct or tightly control their revision. His reader reactions in particular allow him to identify potential strengths and problems even as he dramatizes how the writing is working on him as an individual reader. Students are *shown how* the text is working and not working for a reader rather than being *told what* is not effective by a teacher in the role of critic. Such comments assume a subtle, moderate control over what students attend to and still leave a lion's share of the responsibility on them. They are less authoritative and controlling than standard imperative comments. At the same time, they are more controlling and offer more direction than interpretive comments, which simply play back the text without evaluation.[9]

Elbow's control is also moderated by his infrequent use of imperative comments and his selective use of advice. In fact, he writes fewer prompts than any other reader in the study. Typically, he leaves decisions about rewriting in the hands of the student—perhaps because he is more interested in having the student practice making her own decisions as a writer than he is in helping her improve the draft at hand. He seems committed simply to offering his readings of the text so that the student can see how her words are working for him and to discern on her own what she might do by way of revision.

In addition, Elbow asks the lowest percentage of questions in the group of readers: only 9% of his comments. By comparison, the group as a whole asks an average of 26%. Almost all of Elbow's questions are open-ended problem-posing questions that occur in response to rough drafts. They typically ask the writer to consider or reconsider the reasoning behind the choices she has made in her writing, and they leave a lot of room for the student to decide on her own materials:

> What can you do to get a reader like me not to fight you so much? (Writing 2)
> What is it that made you able to solve this tricky problem in the first parag? (Writing 9)

> [You're not talking to me, you're speechifying, orating. It makes me defensive and resistant and distrustful.] Do you know what I mean? Do you know why you do this? Is it that previous teachers wanted you always to take a position and hammer hammer hammer reasons? Would you be persuaded if I hammered you with reasons like that? (Writing 1)

Tellingly, through his nine sets of responses, Elbow writes only one heuristic question. He rarely tries to prompt students to supply more information or to push their thinking further on the subject. He is usually content to give a reading of what is already on the page and leave it up to the student to decide what to do in a revision.

Elbow's informal voice also helps develop his role as a sympathetic reader and modifies the control he exerts over student writing. From start to finish, when he is giving his reading of the text, evaluating the writing, or directing revision, Elbow presents his commentary in a searching, tentative, yet quietly persuasive voice:

> When I read your exam the first time I stumbled as I read your first 2 sentences: seemed as though you were saying that being a good waitress is the same as making a lot of money; but I wasn't sure you were meaning to be that cynical or pragmatic. Gradually it seemed to me that you didn't mean that. (Writing 11)

> You've made your final draft much stronger and tighter. In almost every case it seems to me as though what you add is more detail, more specifics. (Even down to naming the names of the co-musicians—and I like that. I like hearing people's names even when they don't mean anything to me. Makes it all sound more real.) These details help sharpen the piece; help us see or hear. (Writing 13)

In these passages and throughout his commentary, Elbow creates the voice of someone telling a story about his reading, talking out his understanding as he tries to figure out how the text is working on him. His comments have the informality of talk: There are frequent interruptions, quick changes of thought, and many statements that go over the same ground as earlier ideas. His explanatory comments briefly elaborate on his readings and add to his ethos as a helpful reader.[10]

Across his responses to the sampling, Elbow brings these various strategies of response together—subjective readings, indirect criticism, praise, and only some questions and advice—to create a style that is nonauthoritative, moderately controlling, and mildly interactive. They all can be seen clearly in his comments on "What If Drugs Were Legal?" Elbow starts out the letter, not altogether characteristically, with a lesson and a piece of advice about correctness. However, he establishes a voice and style that are representative of all of Elbow's responses. The fragments and colloquial language create a reader who is easygoing and supportive. The second paragraph shows his tendencies to look for something positive to say, offer a general overview of the writing, and establish a cooperative and encouraging atmosphere about his exchange with the writer:

> Seems like you've tried to build yourself a good framework and foundation—to build on for future drafts. You do an ok job of introducing the article. You don't give a full summary, but weren't asked to. And it strikes me that you move fairly quickly to one of your best arguments: alcohol. The widespread abuse is so undeniable.

The five comments in the passage deal with the content and structure of the writing: one positive qualified evaluation, one positive evaluation, an interpretation, a positive reader reaction, and a reader remark. Here, as in all of the other sets of his responses, Elbow looks for the positive in student writing. Although one of every four comments is given to some type of negative commentary, one of every four is also given to some type of positive evaluation. Another feature of Elbow's style that stands out here is his frequent use of qualifiers. Phrases such as "Seems like you've tried to build" and "it strikes me that" underscore the tenuousness and subjectivity of his responses, reminding students that these readings are not objectified criticisms of an evaluator but the moment-by-moment readings of a single reader—necessarily indefinite and consequently tentative. These qualities are present to an even greater extent in the second half of the letter.

At the heart of his response, Elbow gets more critical, although he continues to present comments as a reader intent mostly on showing how he reads the writing. He moves in and out of playing back the text and evaluating it. Seven of the 11 comments in paragraph 3 are in the form of reader responses. He starts off with a reader remark that presents his own position on the subject and then shifts into a reader reaction: "I don't disagree with your *position*, but somehow I find myself fighting you as I read." He next presents two comments about his experience as a reader and his views on the subject ("I'm trying to figure out why. I don't want to legalize drugs"). Then he offers another reader reaction, again a negative one: "but somehow I want to *listen* more to that writer." As in the opening sentence of the paragraph, Elbow casts his evaluations within the language of a reader's experience, not in the language of an evaluator. The evaluation is presented indirectly, in the context of a reader trying to come to terms with the writing.

Notably, Elbow does not rely on his own authority to make such an evaluation, regardless of how muted it is. He goes on to explain something of the reasoning behind his reaction, in the form of two explanatory comments:

> After all, he has a delicate thesis: not that we should do it but think about doing it. There's nothing wrong with you picking on part of his argument (legalizing) and ignoring the other part ("let's just think about it"). . . .

In order not to allow these explanations to take too much away from his point, he then comes back with two more reader reactions:

> [B]ut the effect is somehow to make it seem as though you are having a closed mind and saying 'Let's not even think about it.' I guess I feel that the drug situation is so terrible that we have to let ourselves think about more things; I'm feeling stuck.

He frames these indirect evaluations within the context of a reader's (highly qualified, tentative) thoughts as he reads: "the effect is somehow to make it seem" and "I guess I feel." The final statement rivets attention on the reader's experiences, not on the failures of the text: "I'm feeling stuck."

Elbow goes on to offer some questions or advice for the subsequent drafts—after he presents his readings and reactions. But only some. Even then he is still clearly self-conscious about the role:

> So I think (self-centeredly) that the question for your next draft is this: what can you do to get a reader like me not to fight you so much? Try thinking about that; see what you can come up with.

In all, Elbow writes 19 comments in his response. Seven comments somehow point to strengths and weaknesses in the writing, five comments present explanations, and only three explicitly call on the student to make revisions. He writes no negative evaluations or imperative comments. From start to finish he presents comments from his perspective as an individual reader, nestling his instruction and brief advice among his reader responses. In this way, Elbow uses modes that blend criticism, nonevaluative response, and praise, establish his role as a reader, and moderate his control.

Focus

Only 25 of Elbow's 227 comments deal with local structure, wording, and correctness. The rest of his comments, for the most part, deal with four areas of response. In ascending order they are voice (10%), the contexts of writing (11%), global structure (16%), and ideas (35%), the third highest among the 12 readers. Elbow's comments on Writing 2 clearly reflect these patterns of focus. Seventeen of his 20 comments deal with global concerns. Two comments deal with the organization of the essay:

> Seems like you've tried to build yourself a good framework and foundation— to build on for future drafts.

> And it strikes me that you move fairly quickly to one of your best arguments: alcohol.

Eleven comments address ideas, among them the following from the heart of the response:

> I don't disagree with your *position*, but somehow I find myself fighting you as I read. I'm trying to figure out why. I don't want to legalize drugs, but somehow I want to *listen* more to that writer.

Four comments deal with some aspect of the writing context—the writer's composing process (the first and last comments below), her ethos, and the audience:

> [It's fine not to worry about mechanics or correctness or nice sentences on a rough draft . . .]; a way to put all attention on your train of thought.
> [B]ut the effect is somehow to make it seem as though you are having a closed mind and saying "Let's not even think about it."
> [W]hat can you do to get a reader like me not to fight you so much?
> Try thinking about that; see what you can come up with.

It is interesting to note—and entirely consistent with Elbow's inclination to focus on giving his reading of what the student has already said—that only 6% of his comments are given to development, the lowest among the 12 readers. His reluctance to call on the student to develop her ideas makes his commentary less controlling, less directive. But it also leads him to offer less immediate help to the writer and leaves greater responsibility on the student.

Elbow regularly goes beyond the immediate text and invokes various contexts that inform student writing: the reader, the writer, the classroom, the writer's processes. (In fact, his practice of dealing with these extra-textual matters may lead him to address slightly more areas of response than the average for this group of readers.)[11] In all his letters, he speaks of the way the writing affects him as a reader:

> If this weren't a time for exploring I might praise you for packing a lot of reasons into a small space, but I'd still have the impulse to jump up and say, "Stop. Wait a minute. Talk to me." (Writing 1)
> [I]t strikes me that you move fairly quickly to one of your best arguments: alcohol. (Writing 2)
> The main thing I feel in reading is a struggle to see your argument clearly in what I feel as somewhat foggy language. (Writing 4)

In half of his letters he also talks (though less frequently) in terms of the general audience:

> Do you really want to restrict your audience? (Writing 5)
> I'm not sure I can really feel that you are talking to parents. (Writing 4)
> I still think there's a confusion there for readers. (Writing 11)

One-third of his comments place what he has to say in such rhetorical contexts.

In addition, Elbow often orients his comments to the student's experiences as a writer. On seven different sets of responses, he addresses such things as the writer's involvement in, or personal connection to, the writing, including the following:

> I like the way you are engaged in this task. (Writing 4)

> I wish you'd put more into your writing. I don't see any reason why you couldn't write much better pieces than you do. Would you please come up after class and let me make an appointment so we can chat—to see if there's something getting in your way? (Writing 11)

In contrast to readers like McClelland and Glynda Hull, he makes few statements that are meant to lead the student to take up particular writing activities such as brainstorming and cutting and pasting. This fact is probably related to his general reluctance to direct students toward specific revisions. Finally, he is less interested in calling attention to particular changes in the text and more interested in helping the student develop an understanding of how his writing affects readers.

Overview of Teacher Control

In his responses, Elbow combines the ethos of a subjective reader and a supportive teacher. His comments dramatize how the words on the page act on him as a single reader—what they make him see, how they make him feel, where they give him trouble. They also invoke him as a discerning and sympathetic reader who teaches. Even as he is careful to note when the writing is and is not yet working well for him, he is committed to giving close, analytical readings that will help the student re-see her writing. Whereas responders like Stewart and McClelland give strong readings and assertively direct students toward revision, Elbow relies on his readings to prompt students to turn themselves back into their writing and initiate their own self-directed revisions. Whereas Stewart and McClelland often make key decisions for the writer, Elbow resists taking such control. In their comments on Writing 2, for instance, Stewart tells Nancy that she "must first provide some very specific information about the damage drug use does to people" and that she "must show, in more specific terms, exactly what damage society suffers from drug users." McClelland calls on the student to question LeMoult's conclusions and make her case more detailed and convincing. By contrast, Elbow simply tells Nancy he is "feeling stuck" about her coming across as unwilling even to consider other perspectives, and then he calls on her to see "what can you do to get a reader like me not to fight you so much" and find "what you can come up with."

In addition, whereas Stewart and McClelland look at the writing in terms of the criteria of the writing assignment and direct the student about how to come closer to meeting those criteria in a written product, Elbow seems content to deal with the writing on its own merits and allow the student to make her own choices about revision. Although half of his letters make reference to the writing assignment, they often only do so to call attention to the assignment as an issue for the writer to consider, not as a set of requirements to follow:

> I felt something interesting going on here. Seemed as though you had the assignment in mind (don't just tell a story of your experiences but explain a subject)—for a while—but then gradually forgot about it as you got sucked into telling about your particular day of fishing. . . . The trouble is I like your stories/moments. My preference would be not to drop them . . . but to search around for some way to save it/them—but make it/them part of a piece that does what the assignment calls for. Not sure how to do it. (Writing 5)

> I'm curious if you were aware of doing something different from what the assignment called for—to tell the story and then go on to explain "how you have been changed or affected." (Writing 10)

For the most part, he lets the student decide how she will deal both with the assignment and with her revision.

Like Hull, Elbow does not gear his responses to the written product and does not take significant control over the student's writing. Like Hull, too, he leaves it to the student to come up with her own ideas and materials for revision. But Elbow is less teacherly and assumes less control. Whereas Hull seems comfortable determining the course that a student's work should take, laying out specific assignments for the student to take up, Elbow prefers to provide his reading of the text and let the student decide on her own course for revision. He is ultimately concerned more with having students practice making writing decisions than with guiding their work on their writing or having them produce polished written products.

Elbow's letters have the voice of someone trying to make sense out loud of a piece of writing, a self-avowedly subjective reader searching to articulate his experiences and reactions to the words on the page. He seems self-consciously neither a critic nor an advisor. In fact, he seems to go out of his way to downplay his authority as a teacher. Instead, he comes across as a reader who is apt to be tentative, to meet some confusion, and perhaps even read the writing too strictly in terms of his own experiences and biases.[12] Although he presents a lot of evaluative commentary, the majority of it comes indirectly, in the form of reader reactions. And although this evaluation gives him a measure of control over the writing (and provides the writer with some direction), he avoids directing or guiding the student—or even advising her—about what she might take up in the way of revision or future work. He is one of the least directive, least authoritative readers in the study.

GROUP 3: RICHARD LARSON, CHRIS ANSON, PATRICIA STOCK, TILLY WARNOCK

RICHARD LARSON

Richard Larson's responses are incisive, thorough, and demanding—the responses of a teacher-editor who is intent on having students learn to write better by following his lead and producing better written products. Larson comes to a piece of writing with a keen sense of what he is looking for and evaluates the writing rigorously in terms of that agenda. He examines the writing according to the criteria of an assignment and, although he does not make any changes himself, firmly and explicitly leads the writer to produce a text that meets those criteria. His comments cover both the overall content and purpose of the writing and the word-by-word, sentence-to-sentence expression of the writer's ideas. Through his responses he hopes to show students how to fashion carefully reasoned, carefully designed writing for an audience.

Larson is sure-handed and authoritative about his commentary. He is a kind of Socratic figure who wants to involve students in an exchange about their writing but who guides the discussion along a definite path toward a goal that he determines. Like Edward White and Donald Stewart, he responds to a wide range of issues, including local matters, and frames a relatively high percentage of his comments as criticism. Like White and Stewart, he spends much of his time directing the student toward revision, with the aim of helping her come up with a better written product. But whereas White and Stewart present a majority of their comments in straight imperatives and negative evaluations, Larson prefers to cast his comments in the more moderate forms of qualified evaluations, advice, and closed problem-posing questions. These modes of response allow Larson to leave some control in the hands of the student even as they enable him to assert—sometimes forcefully through his tone and the content of the comment—his own agenda for revision. If at times he appropriates student choices by pushing his views for revision, he does not impose an ideal text on students by insisting on certain changes or providing specific materials for the text. It is his regular use of closed problem-posing questions and strong advisory comments that distinguishes Larson's responding style and, with his criticism, makes him among the most directive readers in the study.

Larson usually writes extensive marginal comments and a detailed endnote. His marginal comments, penned in a bold all-caps script and usually running down the length of the margins, tend to be spread across the categories of form and content. They are framed in a variety of modes—advisory, imperative, negative evaluative, qualified negative evaluative, and (more than any other mode) closed problem-posing questions. Like White and Stewart, he inserts additional comments and markings between the lines of the student's text. His endnotes deal mostly with large global matters of ideas and content, usually assessing the writing in terms of the assignment. They usually start out with some overall evaluation or interpretation of the writing, point out the major problems in the text, and then present (usually in some detail) his advice for revision. Most of them close with a managerial note to the student, such as advice about the next stage of drafting or a suggestion that they meet in a conference.

LARSON

SETS OF RESPONSES	NUMBER OF RESPONSES		
		Rough Drafts	Final Drafts	Total

5 rough drafts
5 final drafts

23 comments/writing

4.1 issues/writing

	Rough Drafts	Final Drafts	Total
Marginal Comments	42	68	†10
End Comments	72	51	123
Total	114	119	233

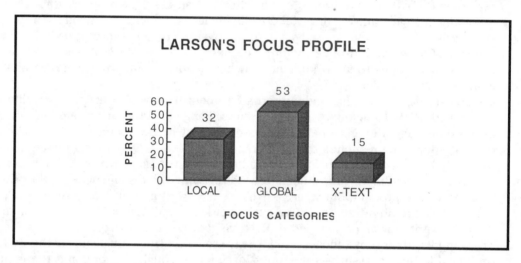

LARSON'S FOCUS PROFILE

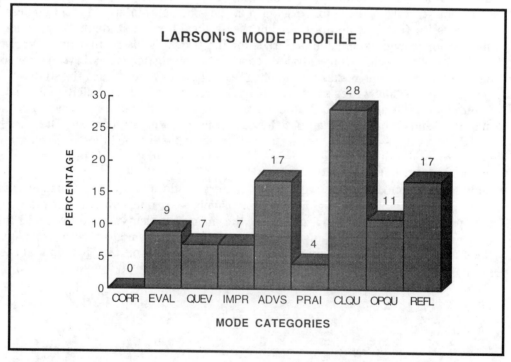

LARSON'S MODE PROFILE

WRITING 4
[ON OVERGUIDING TEENAGE CHILDREN]

BACKGROUND

This rough draft is written in response to an assignment calling for expository writing, the fourth of six required papers in the course. The first three papers focused on expressive writing and writing to learn; the next three papers are to focus on expository writing and writing to show learning. In anticipation of this change in emphasis, the class has been considering the differences between these two kinds of writing. This draft is the first piece of writing handed in for this assignment.

This student writer, Anne, has been actively working to address the issues of the course; she has been open to suggestions about how she might improve her writing.

THE ASSIGNMENT

Even though we are moving toward more expository types of writing now, we must not forget that good expository writing is informed by our personal knowledge and experiences. There is likely no topic that you know more about, firsthand, at this stage of your life than parent/child relationships. For this essay, consider what you have learned about this subject through your own relationship with your parents and share something that you have learned about such relationships. Please identify a prospective audience for this paper and shape your writing for this audience.

[She notes on her paper that she is writing to "parents of teenage children."]

Writing 4
Anne B.
Rough Draft

[On Overguiding Teenage Children]

Parenting is an enormous task and a full time job. Along with providing food, clothing, and shelter, there is something else which is very crucial to raising a child. Guidance. Whether an infant or a teenager, they need guidance from their parents. When there is no parental guidance, children sometimes end up criminals or addicts of drugs or alcohol. Child neglect is a serious problem and the issue has received much publicity. The question I have often pondered, however, deals with parents who overguide their children, more specifically young teenagers. Is this a serious problem too?

Yes, I strongly believe that it is. Parents are not only responsible for providing necessities as mentioned above, but they also have an obligation to laying down a foundation for morals. This is the guidance I spoke of earlier, and it is here that I believe the problem begins. First of all, what is a moral? A moral is a consideration or principle of right or wrong, or of good or bad character. So why here? Because morals are taught by parents. People who have already developed their own ideas, formed opinions, and activated prejudices; they have lived by these views for quite sometime. Since these beliefs they have formed work well for them, they assume they will work for their kids as well. With this assumption they set out to teach them about good and bad character and right or wrong. Are these young teens truly given only guidlines for

1

[Handwritten annotations in margins:]

COULD YOU HAVE GOT TEN TO THIS, YOUR CENTRAL QUERY, MORE QUICKLY?

THIS SENTENCE NEEDS REPUNCTUATION.

↱ REFERS TO WHAT.

WHY NOT RESTATE THE 'PROBLEM' CLEARLY AS A FOCUS FOR DISCUSSION?

CAN YOU SAY MORE DIRECTLY HERE WHAT FEATURES OF PARENTS' BEHAVIOR ARE A SOURCE OF CONCERN TO YOU?

developing good character and for forming their own ideas? Or are

they <u>told</u> what good character should consist of and receive pre-

planned ideas to believe in? It is unfortunate but the latter is

"GIVEN" TO COORDINATE WITH "TOLD"?

often true. Guidelines are replaced by rules and the understanding of

morals is lost only to prejudices. I feel that the development of

morals is a personal judgement. I am not against some guidance and

NEEDS REPUNC- TUATION

influence, it not only earns parent's respect for helping their

confused teens out, but it also gives them a feeling of being needed.

But when a stubborn force is criticizing another view, which could be

a prospect for a young mind to support, I think parents are disguising

WHAT "FORCE" AND WHAT "PROSPECT"? I DON'T FOLLOW YOUR IDEAS CLEARLY HERE.

their prejudices as morals and that is wrong.

Parents would like to see their kids be the very best they can,

yet those who overguide do not give them any opportunities. Parents,

the people who ~~are supposed~~ are most influencial, the most respected,

and have the most wisdom are pushing their beliefs on their young and

OTHER BELIEFS?

will not allow them to adhere to others. A narrow mind is something I

do not respect or consider wise. I think it is often forgotten that

young people have minds of their own. What a shame—two people bring

another precious life into this world, yet deprive it of the one thing

NOT SURE YOU HAVE THE ADJECTIVE FORM YOU WANT.

that makes [it] so unique, individual[istic] and intelligent.

WHAT?

Kids who are victimized by overguidance are only half developed.

A major ingredient of the individual is missing—self understanding.

UNDERSTANDING OF ONESELF? OR ONE'S OWN UNDERSTANDING OF ISSUES?

To find self understanding a young mind must be able to form ideas and

OMIT LETTERS IN [ ]?

make it/s own decisions. Advice does help, but it should not be so

strong as to make the final decision. It should only shine a spot

light on the feelings deep inside you that have more influence thany

ON WHAT DATA ARE YOU BASING YOUR GENERAL STATEMENTS HERE?

2

any other outside force and leave the individual to bring them to the

surface. It is freedom of the mind to explore the inner soul and find

IN ORDER?   *OR DO YOU MEAN THE "FIRE INSIDE" THAT*

the fire inside that you want to believe in something. It is also

WILL DRIVE YOU TO BELIEVE IN SOMETHING

that self understanding that allows individuals to realize they are

often confused about occurances in their life and environment. This

A WISH?

confusion is only a call for input--meaning to hear and consider other

views. These will once again throw light on those emotions that

mumble, "This is what I need." These outside views will help in the

ARE YOU DISCUSSING A SEARCH FOR FEELINGS or A SEARCH FOR GUIDING VALUES. I'M NOT SURE.

search of finding true ~~emotions~~ feelings. Then, the outcome will be

full understanding and maybe a changed belief or a stronger unchanged

one. Deprivation of this breeds ignorance--not only of the individual

COULD YOU EXPLAIN A BIT MORE CLEARLY HOW YOU THINK THIS PROCESS WORKS

but also of the environment. I feel the ignorance is the mother of

prejudices.

STEALS?

Over guidance is a terrible problem. It not only steels from the

young but it also never relieves parents of their ignorance. Parents

EVIDENCE? EXAMPLES?

feed prejudices more support by their ignorance and fear. They do not

understand, nor do they want to, the views of others only because they

are different. They have fear because they may gain interests in

different beliefs. So as a defense they fore their beliefs and

criticize others. Perhaps parents could over come their fears and

prejudices through the fresh young minds of their kids. To set the

DO YOU MEAN, "IF THEY SET..."

mind free of forced preplanned beliefs, parents will receive more

respect and love than they could ever imagine.

You've got a useful idea here--one on which you evidently
feel strongly and want very much to share with parents.
What you might work toward, in your next draft, I think:
are two things: some examples of situations in which you
think parents "overguided" children (tried to get their
children to see things entirely the parents' way?), and
some examples along with a clearer explanation of how you
think parents might guide more gently, more appropriately,
more wisely. Maybe you've had the experience of being "overguided." If so, tell what happeneed; what did your parents do,
and how did you react. If you've not had the experience of
being "overguided," you probably know some young people who have
(over)   -3-

had it; why not write about their experiences? Try to
help the reader understand where the line falls between
appropriate guidance and "overguidance," and then
say what you think parents might in fact try to do toward
their children. (The top of page three needs some
clarification.)

one

You don't need, of course, to follow / particular plan in
writing; find your own plan. But I think that if you're
addressing parents of teenagers, they'll want to know
the answers to the questions I've raised--at least, they'll
want to know <u>your</u> answers.

See the queries I've raised on particular sentences. If
there are questions you don't understand, come in and
let's talk about them.

Mode

Larson's choice of modes helps create a style that, although it is not authoritarian, is clearly authoritative. His strong teacher agenda and his heavy use of authoritative modes help make him one of the most controlling readers in the study. Forty percent of his comments are presented as imperatives, negative evaluations, advice, and qualified negative evaluations—more than any other reader except White. Nevertheless, although he does a lot of evaluating and directing, Larson, like White and Stewart, makes a number of moves that are designed to allow students to retain some control over their writing even as he leads them toward particular goals for revision. Through the entire sampling, he makes just one corrective comment. He frames his criticism in qualified evaluations almost as much as he does in straight evaluations,[1] and he frames his calls for revision in the form of advice twice as often as commands. Moreover, he presents a majority of his comments in nonauthoritative modes, including 39% in the form of questions and another 17% in the form of reflective statements. Across his responses, then, Larson's commentary shows the signs of two competing impulses: one impulse to lay out necessary improvements, the other to refrain from exerting too much control over the student's choices.

Larson's interest in tempering his control may readily be seen in all 10 sets of his responses—especially in his endnotes. It is most discernible in the way he consistently qualifies many of his comments. On Writing 4, he writes two qualified negative evaluations, and, further, couches them in mild terms:

> Not sure you have the adjective form you want.
> I don't follow your ideas clearly here.

He does the same on Writing 5, "Attention: Bass Fishermen." Instead of stating abruptly, "I can't figure out what your focus is, and I don't know what you're saying about bass fishing," Larson writes:

> I can't tell whether these procedures are part of what it always takes to fish for bass, or are simply steps you took on this one occasion. So as a reader I don't know what I'm to understand about bass fishing as a process or activity. (Writing 5)

And instead of saying, "I don't understand your technical talk about bass fishing" and "I think you spend too much time on your own experiences," he writes:

> I don't find that I understand the distinctive appeal and the special processes of bass fishing. I might add that I think you spend more time on the frustrations of the experience you tell about than on the specific steps you took to insure success and your feelings on landing the fish. (Writing 5)

In all four comments, Larson qualifies the criticism by acknowledging that it is his own subjective view (through the use of 'I') and further moderates it by adding other qualifiers ("I can't tell," "I don't know," "I don't find," and "I might add"). By anchoring his comments in the language of the student's text, he also gives the comments the feel of interpretations and constructive criticism.

Larson also softens most of his straight negative evaluations. On Writing 4, for instance, he writes three negative evaluations, but all of them are moderated in the way they are expressed. The three comments simply identify what the writing "needs," not what is wrong:

> This sentence needs repunctuation.
> Needs repunctuation.
> The top of page three needs some clarification.

His evaluative comments across his responses are similarly moderate:

> This, by the way, isn't a sentence. (Writing 13)
>
> Given the details before and after, this idea doesn't sound quite credible. (Writing 6)
>
> Not clear how one man becomes a "race." (Writing 9)
>
> It would also have been helpful for you to show how observing your father helps illuminate the story for you. (Writing 9)
>
> [Y]ou do less with these bases for judgment than the assignment meant to elicit. (Writing 13)

By smoothing the edge off his criticisms in the way he expresses them, Larson makes them less authoritative than they might be.

Similarly, most of Larson's imperatives are not as controlling as imperative comments usually are. They are cast in soft commands that give the comments the feel of advice—"reconsider," "check," "decide," and "find," rather than verbs like "repunctuate," "correct," "revise." They are also geared to the writing process as well as to the written product. Half of his imperatives call on the student to make specific changes in the text:

> Reconsider punctuation. (Writing 9)
>
> Reconsider form of word. (Writing 9)
>
> Check spelling. (Writing 10)
>
> Say more about the incidents that led you to get out. (Writing 12)
>
> [S]how us that you know your subject reasonably well. (Writing 1)

Half of the comments call on the student to engage in some activity of writing and are generally less controlling:

> Check to see *why* [LeMoult] puts forward his proposal. Check to see whether he does say some of the things you attribute to him on page 1 here. Then reconsider the notion of "harm." Sure, drugs harm people, but so does crime, and so does the spending of lots of family money on drugs rather than, say, on feeding children. (Writing 2)
>
> Write down what you decide you want the reader to know, and write down the details you want to give the reader to help him/her understand securely what you intend. Then try to find for yourself a way to arrange these details so that they will be clear to the reader. (Writing 5)

These process imperatives work in a way that is similar to Hull's process-based assignments, although Larson's imperatives are designed to help the student work on specifically recommended text-based revisions.

Probably the most significant way in which Larson tempers his authority as a responder and keeps from taking control over student writing is through the use of advisory comments. Across his responses, he frames more than twice as many of his calls for revision in advisory comments (17%) as in commands (7%). The advice allows students some control about whether to take up the revisions, as in the following examples:

> What I'd like to suggest for your next draft is that you think carefully about what you want the reader to know about bass fishing. (Writing 5)
>
> Might be useful to say more on these experiences. (Writing 12)
>
> You might explain a bit more carefully what this program is. (Writing 2)
>
> "Active" verb might be preferable here. (Writing 11)
>
> Let us know why the subject is important to you . . . . (Writing 1)

He also frames a number of his suggestions in the form of informal "why not" questions and reader-based advice—a cross between a reader-response comment and an advisory comment:

> If you've not had the experience of being "overguided," you probably know some young people who have had it; why not write about their experiences? (Writing 4)
>
> [W]hy not revise it again, with the goal in mind of shortening the narrative account and commenting, as specifically and vividly as possible, on what you've learned (or are learning) and how, if at all, your behavior has changed? (Writing 10)
>
> Why not do a sketch for a paper, following those suggestions, and let me see it. I can then see whether I can offer some help with your planning of your essay, before you actually do the next draft. (Writing 5)
>
> [I'd guess that the experience of being treated for leukemia has changed you and/or has taught you important things.] I'd like to know about them. (Writing 10)
>
> I'd be interested in knowing how your understanding of those concepts [of good and evil] has been enlarged by the story, by your father's changes in personality, and by your writing of this paper. (Writing 9)

By casting much of his advice and commands in these moderate forms, Larson sets out a clear path for revision yet tempers some of his directiveness as a responder.

Still, Larson's commentary remains firmly authoritative for a number of reasons. He makes extensive use of authoritative modes. He frequently makes editorial comments across the students' texts. He writes one-fourth of his comments in closed problem-posing questions. And, perhaps most important of all, he brings a strong agenda to his commentary.

The sheer number of Larson's authoritative comments reflects something of his directiveness as a responder. He places criticism and prompts for revision at the heart of every set of his responses. Larson writes 16% of his comments in negative evaluations and qualified negative evaluations; he offers little by way of praise.[2] Only White (23%), Stewart (19%), and Frank O'Hare (18%) use more criticism, and no other reader provides less praise. He writes 24% of his comments as commands or advice—more than all but one other reader.[3] Nine of his 10 sets of responses have six or more comments framed in these authoritative modes. Most of these comments appear in endnotes and call on the student to consider making specific changes in the written product, usually on matters of content and purpose.

Like Stewart, Larson smatters editorial comments across the margins of the student's text—almost half of them in the form of closed problem-posing questions.[4] Overall, 23% percent of his responses are cast as closed problem-posing comments—twice as many as anyone else in the study.[5] Only one set of his responses has no such comments (Writing 5), and five sets have more than six of them. Closed problem-posing questions allow the sharpness of an evaluation or an imperative and the modified control of a question. They allow the teacher to present evaluations and calls for changes even as they provide some room for the student to decide whether to take up the revision. They are the perfect form for Larson, who so often seems intent on doing two things at once: identifying areas for improvement, yet allowing the student at least some choice in the changes to be made. Used moderately, such closed questions assert less control over students than negative evaluations and imperatives. As they are used more freely or in the company of strong authoritative comments, however, they are likely to lose some of their conventional interactiveness as questions. The latter case is true for Larson.[6]

Most of Larson's closed problem-posing questions (50 of 54) appear in marginal comments and address local matters, especially wording. Even though they exert less control simply because they are framed as questions, most of them can be seen as a type of authoritative comment—a negative evaluation, an imperative, or a correction—presented with a question mark at the end. In response to Writing 4, for example, Larson writes 12 closed problem-posing questions. Some of these comments make *corrections* (or suggested corrections) that are followed by a question mark. The punctuation has the effect of turning the correction into a matter for the student to consider:

Other beliefs?

Understanding *of* oneself? Or one's own understanding of issues?

In order? Or do you mean the "fire inside" that will drive you to believe in something?

A wish?

Steals?

Do you mean, "if they set . . ."

Another comment presents an *imperative* in the form of a question, allowing the student some matter of choice and giving the comment the feel of a suggestion: "Omit letters in [brackets]?" The other comments identify issues for the writer to consider; they are *evaluations* that are framed as questions:

Refers to what?

"Given to" coordinate with "told"?

What "force" and what "prospect"?

What?

Could you have gotten to this, your central query, more quickly?

Whereas White and Stewart write evaluative, corrective, and imperative comments in response to such local concerns, Larson casts his comments in closed problem-posing questions. Although the question format arguably makes his style less directive than it would be if these comments were presented without the question marks, in straight authoritative modes, the sheer number of comments he makes in problem-posing modes still contributes to his directiveness as a responder.

Larson also uses closed problem-posing comments to call into question the student's ideas. Such questions are often marked with intensifiers and other modifiers (in boldface, our emphasis) that give them a sharp tone:

> Do you, **honestly**, think that wearing seat belts can be dangerous? (Writing 1)
>
> But does the author himself **directly** suggest that society was responsible for their doing so? (Writing 2)
>
> Does he *blame* "society"? Does he say that "society" is corrupt? (Writing 2)
>
> Is this, do you think, **really** the reason why people are outside in summer? (Writing 6)

Larson's use of these questions reflect his authority over the writing like a badge. His closed problem-posing comments about expression point out specific problems in the text and virtually lead the student to make changes according to his prompting; the closed problem-posing comments about the student's ideas often call her thinking into question. Together, the comments allow Larson to hover around the student's writing, never quite demanding that anything be changed, yet always pointing to problems that must be addressed.

Larson's end comments look less controlling than his marginal comments—and in many ways they are. But these comments are also firmly authoritative, in part because his key responses are framed as criticism and advice, but mostly because they are often tied to his strong sense of what the writing should do. Almost every set of Larson's responses asserts his agenda as a responder, through his comments about the assignment, his evaluations of the writing, or his calls for revision. The majority of his endnotes are meant to lead the student to make particular changes in the text. Few are geared toward helping students review their options or envision how they might take up the recommended revisions.

On Writing 4, for instance, although the calls for revision that dominate the endnote are cast in the form of advice, in an inviting tone, Larson's agenda shows through in the comments:

> What you might work toward, in your next draft, I think, are two things: some examples of situations in which you think parents "overguided" children . . . , and some examples along with a clearer explanation of how you think parents might guide more gently, more appropriately, more wisely. Maybe you've had the experience of being "overguided." If so, tell what happened . . . . If you've not had the experience of being "overguided," you probably know some young people who have had it; why not write about their experiences? Try to help the reader understand where the line falls between appropriate guidance and "overguidance," and then say what you think parents might in fact try to do toward their children.

Larson's agenda comes through only faintly in the opening comment, especially because he clearly introduces the comment as advice: "What you *might* work toward . . ." (our emphasis). Nevertheless, there is a clear sense that he expects something definite in the way of revision. He wants the student to provide not only examples of overguiding (a concern for all teachers who responded to the essay) but also examples, *along with a clearer explanation*, of how parents might guide without overguiding. The next two pieces of advice offer ways for Anne to think about how to come up with these revisions and, because they are process-oriented, they are more open-ended. But his agenda comes through clearly in the next piece of advice: "Try to help the reader understand where the line falls between appropriate guidance and 'overguidance,' and then say what you think parents might in fact try to do toward their children." Although the request is softened by its use of "Try" and does not depart from the student's apparent purposes in the writing, the comment lays out Larson's own rather individual sense of how the writing should be shaped.

Larson's agenda for revision similarly shows through his advice on Writing 12. After praising the essay for its honesty and detail, Larson notes that the draft, as it stands, does not fulfill the assignment. He goes on to offer Rusty several pieces of advice about how he could focus the paper on an explanation of street gangs rather than a narration of his experiences in the gang:

> [Y]our focus, for this paper, might be on letting readers know how street gangs operate, what they do, why they do it, rather than on the chronology of your experiences as a gang member. Your goal here is to enlarge the reader's knowledge of a subject that the reader might find important and might genuinely want to know more about. I think you've got such a subject. . . . But I'd like to know a bit more about gangs in general than you tell me. Maybe you could use your experiences to *illustrate* more general observations (observations that might cover many gangs, of different sorts). In using your experiences so, you might give a few more details about some of the experiences.

At first, it seems as though Larson is simply offering open-ended advice: "[Y]our focus, for this paper, might be on letting readers know how street gangs operate, what they do, why they do it . . ." He does not indicate what Rusty should add about gangs, and he does not tell him which experiences he should keep or throw away. When he starts looking at the writing in terms of the assignment, however, his commentary seems to get less suggestive and more focused, more determined. Even though his next pieces of advice have a more inviting tone, they both follow from his interest in seeing the writing conform to the demands of the assignment. By calling for the revision to focus on a detached description of "gangs in general," the comments present his expectations for the next draft more than options that the student may or may not take up.

The control Larson assumes over the student may be seen more clearly in comparison to the way Peter Elbow presents Rusty with a similar piece of advice:

> At the bottom of 1 you give the example of picking on people at the pool. You tell it in a

kind of deadpan way, but it's kind of horrifying for me. I think *I* was the kind of person who was picked on—or always felt I was about to be. There's something intriguing or even moving about your low key tone here, but I'm also curious to know a bit more how you actually felt—and feel. Something mysterious here: perhaps it's more interesting this way, despite my unsatisfied curiosity. But I do know I'd like you to flesh it out more as an example: it's a specific scene or incident, but you don't let us see *any* particulars.

Whereas the criticism that precedes Larson's advice gives his suggestions the feel of firm recommendations, Elbow's use of interpretive comments and reader responses make his subsequent advice more open-ended and inviting. Glynda Hull's advice to Rusty is direct like Larson's, but the tone is more encouraging than expectant:

I want you to add some extended examples—not just one sentence or two, but whole paragraphs. I've marked several places you could make some additions with an asterisk (*). On the first page, for example, you might tell specifically about a time when someone got in trouble and everyone was there. Give details: what time, when, what situation, where. These long examples should be used to illustrate and provide evidence for points you're making.

Whereas Larson seems to steer the student toward his sense of how the writing should go, Hull, although she is no less certain about what the writing needs in general, seems mainly intent on helping Rusty add examples to the writing. She does not direct him to make specific alterations in his focus or his purpose—perhaps because she is willing to let go of the demands of the assignment.

In a similar way Larson assumes firm control over the writer in his comments on Writing 13. After praising the writer's involvement and specificity in the draft, he again evaluates the writing against the assignment:

But the paper remains essentially a report of the concert and your personal responses. The assignment, however, asked for an "evaluation" based upon criteria and supported by reasons. To some extent you've given criteria (the emotional "roller coaster") and other standards (the audience's responses), but you do less with these bases for judgment than the assignment meant to elicit.

To put the point differently: is any concert that could be said to create an "emotional roller coaster" good? Is any concert good that has the audience involved? Are these the only, or the principal, bases for judgment? Why? Does the quality of the music played matter? The eloquence of the words as a kind of poetry? The sentiments expressed in the songs? I don't mean to imply that all these matters need to be touched in an essay such as you are writing.

With this context established, Larson goes on to suggest what might be done in a revision, but his suggestions carry the weight of the evaluative comments that precede them and, as a result, take on the force of commands:

But I think that the bases of judgment should be formulated a little more explicitly than you have done here, and that the narrative of the concert might be at least somewhat subordinated to a discussion of features that make the concert, in your view, praiseworthy. That discussion *requires* some detachment.

Writing such a review is, of course, a matter of balance. One *wants* the details; one wants the experience. But, even in a school newspaper, one probably wants a bit more: signs of a detached reflection on whether, overall, the concert was an artistically satisfying experience—and why.

I'd like to see you rewrite this piece with the goal of striking the balance I've just described, somewhat more than the present essay does. (Writing 13)

The comments that follow Larson's criticism and his initial advice emphasize his views about how the writing could best proceed. The series of questions in the second paragraph are closed problem-posing questions that are designed as much to point to considerations the writer overlooked as to suggest possible avenues for exploration on the next draft. The explanatory comments in the third paragraph reinforce his advice. Like Ben McClelland's explanatory comments, they do not serve to explain the reasoning behind his recommendations so much as they provide support for his claims.[7] The final comment reemphasizes this advice and, as it invokes his authority as a teacher, exerts greater control over the writing than most advisory comments typically exert. When all is said and done, the comments, although they are cast in the form of advice, do not offer suggestions or help so much as they set forth a recommended path for the student to follow, or a task that she would do well to take up.

More often than not across his endnotes, Larson's advisory comments are made more emphatic and more authoritative by the comments that surround them—usually comments that explain the demands of the assignment or criticize the writing. Ultimately, then, his commentary allows him to pursue his agenda and underscore his authority as a responder. Although his use of advice and process imperatives moderates his authority as a teacher and tempers his control, he still exerts substantial control over student writing.

Focus

Perhaps because he is interested in helping students learn to write better by guiding them to come up with more complete final drafts, Larson addresses a number of areas in his responses and calls on students to take up particular revisions. He addresses four or more areas on 7 of his 10 sets of responses. On all but two sets of responses (Writings 1 and 2, the two early rough drafts), he gives careful attention to matters of wording, local structure, and correctness. Thirty-two percent of his responses focus on these local concerns—the third highest in the study, just behind White and Stewart. Larson makes more comments about wording (19%) and more comments about correctness (10%) than all but one other reader.[8] He also makes a large number of comments that call on the student to develop her ideas.

There is a clear pattern in Larson's marginal and end comments. His marginal comments tend to be formalistic. Many of them are short one-word comments and phrases, and the majority of them deal with wording, local structure, and correctness, as in the following cases:

> Needs repunctuation. (Writing 4)
>
> Reconsider form of word. (Writing 9)
>
> Needs more exact referent. (Writing 10)
>
> Word needed? (Writing 12)
>
> Punctuate? Maybe omit "which"? (Writing 13)

He writes 70 of his 110 marginal comments on these local concerns. The rest are fuller statements that typically challenge students to develop or reconsider their ideas:

> But does the author himself directly suggest that society was responsible for their doing so? (Writing 2)
>
> On what data are you basing your general statements here? (Writing 4)
>
> Is this, do you think, the reason why people are outside in summer? (Writing 6)
>
> *How* did it do so? I'd like to know much more of how the story helped you. (Writing 9)
>
> You might explain a bit more carefully what this program is. (Writing 10)
>
> Might be useful to say more on these experiences. (Writing 12)

Larson's endnotes deal with the larger, rhetorical issues about content, purpose, and audience. Eighty-four of the 123 comments Larson makes in his endnotes address ideas, development, and global structure; only six address local concerns.

Larson's comments on Writing 4 show his typical concerns. He addresses five different issues in the response, one more than his average across the sampling. Seventeen out of his 24 marginal comments deal with local matters, including 12 comments that question the student's word choice, among them:

> Refers to what? "Given" to coordinate with "told"?
> What "force" and what "prospect"? I don't follow your ideas clearly here.
> Omit letters in [ ]?
> Understanding *of* oneself? Or one's own understanding of issues?

Such attention to local matters is not characteristic of Larson's other responses to rough drafts, but it is characteristic of his responses on papers in which the content is more fully realized.[9] His end comments follow the general pattern in his responses, dealing almost exclusively with global matters of content and purpose. Eight of Larson's 12 end comments advise Anne to develop her distinction between guidance and over-guidance with examples from her personal experience. Two others address the ideas she already has down on the page: one praising her main concept, the other asking her to clarify her ideas. As usual, these comments are precise, text-specific, and detailed.[10]

He also frequently calls attention to contexts beyond the text by referring directly to audience and purpose. In Writing 4, for instance, he calls on Anne to "help the reader understand where the line falls between appropriate guidance and 'overguidance,' and then say what you think parents might in fact try to do toward their children." In Writing 5, he ties most of his comments back to the needs of the audience:

> What I'd like to sugggest for your next draft is that you think carefully about what you want the reader to know about bass fishing (if that indeed is your subject) . . . . Write down what you decide you want the reader to know, and write down the details you want to give the reader to help him/her understand securely what you intend. Then try to find for yourself a way to arrange these details so that they will be clear to the reader.

Other than such references to the rhetorical context and to the writing assignment, however, he makes few comments that go beyond the formal concerns of the text. In this regard, he is similar to White and Stewart, who also give precise, thoughtful instructions for improving the text and take firm control over student writing.

Overview of Teacher Control

Larson's close, strong readings, his expectant voice, and the authority he invokes as a teacher lead him to be more controlling than we might expect from a reader who frames his comments so often in modes that ostensibly are designed to temper the teacher's control. Larson presents himself as a sure-handed, incisive critic, advisor, and problem poser. He knows what needs to be done to improve a piece of writing and is not reluctant about presenting this to the student. Although there is a hint throughout his responses that he wants to leave important decisions up to the writer, there is also always a clear sense that there is not much else to do than faithfully respond to his questions and follow his advice. There is a restraint shown in the comments, to be sure, but it is a visible restraint. It seems as if Larson wants the student to take the lead in remedying the writing and feels obliged to restrain himself from fixing the text. Yet it is clear that he is intent on using the problems he sees in a draft as opportunities for direct instruction.

Like White, Stewart, and McClelland, Larson also judges the writing firmly in terms of the specifications of the assignment. In six of his nine sets of endnotes, he bases both his evaluation and his calls for revision squarely on the terms of the assignment, among them the following:

[A]s this piece stands it is essentially an account of a period in your life: how you got into a gang, what you did, why you stopped. The assignment asked, on the other hand, to discuss an activity in which you "regularly engage" and on which you can speak from some authority. Clearly you can speak with authority on street gangs, but your focus, for this paper, might be on letting readers know how street gangs operate, what they do, why they do it, rather than on the chronology of your experiences as a gang member. Your goal here is to enlarge the reader's knowledge of a subject that the reader might find important and might genuinely want to know more about. (Writing 12)

[I]t seems to me that you've not shown much of how the story illuminates your father's behavior . . . . And, since the assignment raises the topic of "good and evil," I'd be interested in knowing how your understanding of those concepts has been enlarged by the story, by your father's changes in personality, and by your writing of this paper. (Writing 9)

[T]he paper remains essentially a report of the concert and your personal responses. The assignment, however, asked for an "evaluation" based upon criteria and supported by reasons. To some extent you've given criteria . . . and other standards . . . , but you do less with these bases for judgment than the assignment meant to elicit. (Writing 13)

By consistently holding the student to the criteria of the assignment (rather than, say, allowing her to pursue her own evolving purposes apart from it), Larson removes some power of choice from the student and adds to his control. In fact, much of his control seems to grow out of his conviction that he can be most effective as a responder by requiring close textual revision and guiding students to turn drafts into finished products, based on the conventions of writing and the expectations of readers, as they are laid out in the writing assignment. Unlike Hull or Elbow, whose comments have the feel of try-it-again invitations, teachers like Larson, White, Stewart, and McClelland encourage students to follow their lead in order to produce a more clear and coherent next draft. Their focus of instruction is not so much the student as it is the student's developing text.

Also like White, Stewart, and McClelland, Larson invokes his teacherly persona as the principal reader of the writing. He does not take on the reader's role that he is implicitly asked to assume by the writer; he reads and evaluates the writing from his perspective as a teacher and a critic, one who stands apart from the rhetorical context and whose task is to assess the overall effectiveness of the writing for the stated rhetorical situation. Whereas other teachers (like Hull and Peterson) temper their authority by making reference to the rhetorical context, Larson uses such references to establish the basis of his authority and demonstrate the need for revision. In contrast to Elbow, who creates himself as an individual reader and positions himself on a level with the writing, Larson casts himself as a representative authority and stands above the writer and the writing.

Larson, McClelland, White, and Stewart all come right out and identify changes that need to be made in student writing and call, in no uncertain terms, for specific revisions. But whereas White and Stewart seem willing to take on the role of master to apprentice and present unqualified directions for students, Larson and McClelland seem intent on smoothing the edge of their directions. Even though they are as clear as White and Stewart about what they expect from a revision, they are not as willing to lay out specific problems or ways the text should be revised. Finally, however, Larson, like McClelland, is far more authoritative than interactive. His incisive criticisms, the range of his responses, his explicit and detailed calls for revision, and his frequent use of closed questions, all lead to a style that—his nods toward placing the impetus on the student notwithstanding—is finally one of the most controlling in the study.

```
CHRIS ANSON
```

Chris Anson's comments offer a good example of responses that provide abundant help to the student without ever coming across as taking over her choices as a writer. Like Richard Larson, Anson concentrates on giving the student specific advice for revision. But whereas Larson makes firm recommendations that invoke his authority as a teacher, Anson creates himself as a supportive teacher-reader who offers suggestions and options. His comments do not direct the student so much as they provide direction. If Larson takes on the role of an editorial consultant, Anson takes on the role of a writing counselor—a sort of close advisor to student writers. He is at ease and personable in his commentary, characteristics that might be achieved through any method of response but that are encouraged by Anson's particular method: spoken, tape-recorded messages to the student.[1] He takes full advantage of this informal, interactive forum for response by using these tapes not only to address the student's own expressed concerns about the writing (as they are presented in a short tape-recorded message the student hands in with her paper) but also to voice the concerns of students from the writer's conference group.

Transcribed, Anson's commentaries run from one to three single-spaced pages. Typically, Anson starts out with some metadiscourse to the student to break the ice or bring up something the student said in her tape-recorded remarks. He briefly reviews the assignment and considers the paper in terms of the type of writing it calls for. Then he immerses himself in the main issues of the response. He defines these issues, evaluates the strengths and weaknesses in the student's handling of them, and provides detailed advice about how the writer can address specific problems in the text. Along the way, he points to sample trouble spots, offers elaborate explanations, and informs the student about the conventions that govern this type of writing. He closes almost every set of responses with a summary of his major concerns and some note of encouragement.

ANSON

SETS OF RESPONSES	NUMBER OF RESPONSES		
		Rough Drafts	Final Drafts	Total
5 rough drafts				
5 final drafts	Marginal Comments	00	00	00
37 comments/writing	End Comments	198	170	368
4.2 issues/writing	Total	198	170	368

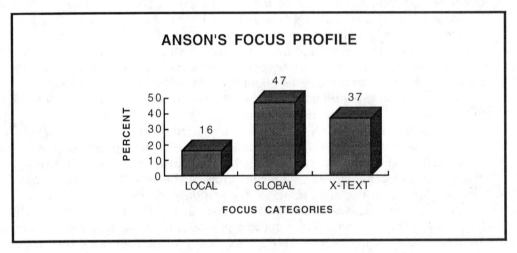

ANSON'S FOCUS PROFILE

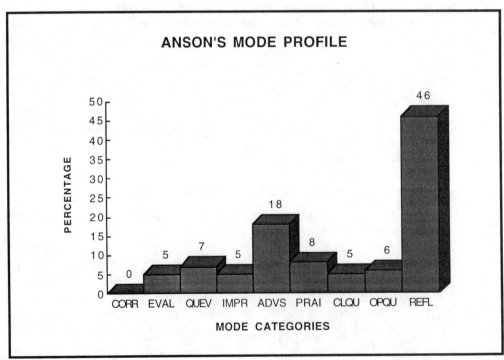

ANSON'S MODE PROFILE

Additional Context

Anne B. is the only "returning" student in the class of twenty 18-19year-old freshmen. She is in her mid-40's, a housewife with two high-school aged children; she has lived in the area for most of her life. She has worked remarkably well in the class in spite of the age difference. The students respect her experience and, for her part, she has taken an attitude of openness to improvement and respect for the students' closeness to the educational experience (at first, she was apprehensive about taking the course because, since graduating from high school in 1963, she hasn't taken anything more academic than non-credit mini-courses at local community centers on topics such as planning a vegetable garden or managing stress).

In Anne's taped commentaries, she has mentioned more than once that the course's focus on expressive writing, the frequent discussions of the writing process and of past writing experiences, and the work with strategies for inventing and exploring ideas--that all of these have come to her as a "revelation." Her high school courses in the early 1960's were traditional, and although she praises her teachers for helping her to gain command of good English, she recognizes now that they hadn't spent much time on the nature of writing, or some of its complexities. The essays she wrote were typical schoolroom "themes," with little or no freedom to define a context or audience beyond the classroom.

Anne's expressive writing has been voluminous. Her journal entries are long and often very associative, winding from one topic to the next through connections that, she reports, often "get her mind way ahead of her pen." At this point, I have been spending more time helping some students who can't seem to generate much prose, and haven't worried too much about Anne's tendency to be prolix. But now, as we shift toward more polished and carefully structured prose, I recognize a need to help her arrange and order her thoughts, and to become sensitive to the difference between the style and lexis of expressive or exploratory writing and writing which reaches out to an audience of sometimes demanding readers. In one sense, then, the predominance of expressive writing in the course, designed to help the younger freshmen generate and explore ideas, now threatens to push Anne away from economy, careful design, and the logical progression of ideas. Encouraged by the loose, comfortable feel of her journal writing, Anne slips instantly into an expressive, associative mode as soon as she begins writing anything.

In this context, her first draft of the parent/child relationship paper seems at least halfway structured and logically organized. My goal in the response is not to squelch the appeal of expressive writing but to show how it can be used as a **starting point** for something conceptually much tighter. Anne is also a very competent giver and receiver of commentary, so I'm not nearly as worried about being direct with her as with other students who have a less a less balanced sense of self.

Anne's tape to me with her draft asks me to focus on the usual questions of whether her points make sense, what she can do about her style, and so on, and she again requests specific comments on her grammar and usage, which I will provide after giving my general impressions. But at one point she says this: "Oh, another thing. Your assignment asks us to write about our relationship with our parents. I know this will be what most students will do, but I've learned a lot more from my relationship with my own kids. Can I write about that instead?"

Glancing through her essay, I realize that Anne has written at an abstract level about the topic--something she usually doesn't do. This, together with her comment, suggest to me that she has avoided being concrete, or using examples from her own experience, for fear of not "doing the assignment the right way." I decide to address this problem in my comments.

Transcription of my Taped Comments on Anne's Draft

Hi, Anne, how's it going? Um, well I've read your, the rough draft of your paper for this third assignment and I've also listened to your tape. First of all, let me say something about your question at the **end** of your tape about the assignment (I guess I feel like working backwards today!) [laughs] I think it's perfectly appropriate, and I hope I've been encouring this strongly enough in the class, to define the assignments, to set the direction for the assignment in any way you choose, as long as you have a good rationale for it, so I think that, um, it's perfectly appropriate to write about your experiences with your own kids. Because, and I've been going through this myself for the first time, I think you really learn a great deal in retrospect about the relationship you have with your own parents when you begin having children of your own. So the fact you can do that in the paper is great.

Now, one thing I noticed is that this draft is, um, well I think it's kind of abstract; it sounds rather philosophical? I don't know if you get that impression too, because it wasn't something you pointed out in your tape to me. But I raise that as a question because it seems like a lot of your writing in here hasn't taken on that abstract quality; it's been pretty concrete and you usually have lots of examles for things and so on. Um, so that's something to think about. And I also wondered if that was your choice, or if you worried--I mean, if you look at this, it could be about your parents or about being a parent, because it's so general, so if you're uncomfortable about being specific **because** you were worried about whether you were taking the right focus in the assignment, just don't! [laughs] So I think it's, this is the kind of paper where, uh, you really have a choice about whether you want to illustrate some of your points with, you know, with something a little more specific, some kind of examples or--for **example** [laughs], if you wanted to talk about, um, an incident when you felt you were making too many decisions for one of your kids and overguiding them, and--or for that matter you could include experiences both from your relationship with your parents and with your kids, since you've had both. If you wanted to focus on specific experiences as examples to illustrate some of the general points you make, you're in a good position to do that from both perspectives.

One reason why I bring up this question is that, as a reader, I guess I got a little lost in this piece at times. And I don't know how the others will react but I felt especially when I got to page two, in that longish paragraph there before the first full paragraph on that page, I felt vague, I guess; I don't know if that's a good way of putting it, but I think that part of it--you asked about style and structure in your tape--comes from a tendency to focus on everything all at once. And what you could do is look for--this is a more structured kind of writing--and you could look a little more for some overarching ideas within the general focus of overguidance. So, for example [flipping through text] . . . on the bottom of page two, it seems like you're starting another related focus on overguidance which is something about development, but some of the points you make in that section relate to points you make in other sections, and this takes away the sense of structure. I think what you've got here is a really good beginning and you've got to wade through it and find some overarching perspectives or angles on the main topic--problems with overguiding kids. Then try to restructure in some way. What you might try is a loose tree diagram or topic diagram that can show you what you're doing in each part of the paper, and then you can see any relationships between or among those. Let me be more specific here [laughs]. If you had to say what the focus of the paragraph on the bottom of page two is, what would you say? Because there are some really interesting points about development, self-understanding, advice, freedom of mind, and so on. But do you see what I mean? What would happen if you chose the idea of development: how does an overguiding parent inhibit a child's development? Start with that, and then brainstorm just on the specific ways this happens. Then take another idea: the tendency, um, on page two at the top, the tendency for parents to disguise their prejudices as morals and guidance. How does that happen? What examples can you think of? Or take, take your point about freedom for kids to be individuals. So for the purposes of focusing and structuring, you're going to want to look at different aspects of the topic. And that might mean that you'll collapse lots of your paper into one perspective (**problems** resulting from overguidance) and add others (how does one achieve a balance between **guidance** and **freedom**). In a sense, this sort of beginning is ideal for coming up with ideas, because it's like a freewrite, but at the same time what you gain in exploration you lose a little in structure. At this point, you've got a tough task of working through a lot of interrelated ideas and look for patterns for developing the essay into something with distinct parts. So the reader. . . and this is the point of that structuring . . . so the reader knows where she is at each stage. An analogy I like to use is the tour guide--you're introducing each new piece, each sight, or perspective on the topic, so the reader knows what she's looking at each time you move on to something new.

I think that you're writing in a style that's a little reflective, not quite, but like a philosophical journal entry, so you might ask yourself how much "I" you want in this piece. Um, for examle, "I strongly believe," "I have often pondered," "I think," "I feel," "I am." You might experiment with taking those out. See what happens when you take those out, what affect they have on the paper. Obviously these are choices--you can make a very heavily opinionated piece, where you're central to it and insisting on your feelings--and sometimes you don't even need the "I's" because simply making the assertions means that you're expressing them as feelings. And it might take on a less oral quality, a little more polished a feel.

Some things that really worked for me--I think you get going on page two and over to page three: "The major ingredient . . . dash . . . self-under-standing," the spotlight metaphor, "it is freedom of the soul" [reads lines]. That's nice. Oh, while we're on style, something that I think leads to an abstract feeling are all these anaphoric . . . well, that's a fancy term for the way that certain words refer to other ideas or sentences. So on page three, if you use lots of words like "these" and "those" and "this," those words [laughs] connect with something else, they refer to some assertion of a noun in the previous sentence. If you use them too often, it gives the writing a rather abstract or unspecific feel, so you might try varying the sentences there--don't just keep repeating all the nouns they refer to, but try rearranging the sentences to see what happens to the style if you get rid of some of those "theses" and these "thoses" [laughs].

There are a couple of sentences--when you get to the point of doing a more final draft, read the whole thing aloud and you might pick up on any cases when a sentence "derails." Um, take a look [flipping through pages] at, um, here it is, let me read this to you on page three: "Parents feed preju-dices more support by their ignorance and fear." You know, I think I had to read that about six times before I saw, um, what you were saying. Because I started reading it this way: "Parents feed prejudices more **ad-verb**," like *quickly*, and then I got to the "support" and the "by" and I was lost. And it's because the "feed" and the "more" are misleading, I guess, and what you mean is that parents feed more support to, that is, their ig-norance and fear simply feed their prejudices.

So to sum up, this is a good start, and I'd experiment with the abstract and concrete issue and make some decisions there, try throwing in something specific. The point here is to try out some possiblities. One thing I don't want you to feel is that expressive writing is the only place where you can write about your own experiences; it's appropriate in a lot of what we might call "expository" writing.   So see if it works here to concretize and make specific some of the more general assertions in here. Oh, you asked also about grammar and usage, and I would worry about that only when you've worked out the larger questions. But a good procedure is to circle anything you **think** is spelled incorrectly or is ungrammatical and then try to do what you can to figure it out. Some problems you might not recognize, such as the fact *judgement* with an -e is a British spelling, and those will be pointed out to you, I'm sure [laughs]. But words like "occurences" are hard for everyone, and you can probably guess when they might be misspelled. We'll talk more about these little things later on down the line. So I'd focus on the larger matters of organization, level of specificity, where you want to be in the piece, and what purpose you imagine for it, or, for that matter, what sort of audience.

Ok, Anne--I've really rambled on here, so see you in the conference group.

A Note on Tape-recorded Comments

Tape-recorded comments, of course, lead a double life. On the one hand, because they are spoken, they take on the attributes of conversation. They are typically informal in tone and have the feel of dialogue. On the other hand, because they are recorded without the interlocutor present (i.e., because technically they are monological), they have the attributes of one-way discourse. They are not as susceptible to the shifts and lulls of conversation and are generally more discursive than comments that occur in a conversation. Tape-recorded comments, then, are usually more pointed and less interactive than spoken comments. But they are usually more loosely shaped and less directive than written comments—or at least less directive than similar comments presented in a written format.[2]

Anson's tape-recorded comments, because they are highly conversational and take special advantage of the intimacy of speech, are more interactive than they would likely be in written form.[3] His comments have an abundance of metadiscourse, quick shifts, false starts, pauses, interruptions, alternatives, repetition, and emotion. Many of these qualities of speech are evident right from the start of his responses to Writing 4:

> Hi, Anne, how's it going? Um, well I've read your, the rough draft of your paper for this third assignment and I've also listened to your tape. First of all, let me say something about your question at the *end* of your tape about the assignment (I guess I feel like working backwards today!) [laughs]. I think it's perfectly appropriate, and I hope I've been encouraging this strongly enough in the class, to define the assignments, to set the direction for the assignment in any way you choose, as long as you have a good rationale for it, so I think that, um, it's perfectly appropriate to write about your experiences with your own kids.

The opening sentences—the direct talk to Anne, the humorous aside, the intensifiers, the laughing, the meandering quality of the talk—immediately establish a casual atmosphere. They create the persona of an open, approachable, and supportive teacher. These and other qualities of speech are evident throughout the response, for example, in the section that soon follows the opening remarks:

> One reason I bring up this question is that, as a reader, I guess I got a little lost in this piece at times. And I don't know how the others will react but I felt especially when I got to page two, in that longish paragraph there before the first full paragraph on that page, I felt vague, I guess; I don't know if that's a good way of putting it, but I think part of it— you asked about style and structure in your tape—comes from a tendency to focus on everything at once. And what you could do is look for—this is a more structured kind of writing—and you could look a little more for some overarching ideas within the general focus of overguidance.

There is a kind of tentativeness in these sentences, as well as an impulse to clarify or explain: "I guess I got a little lost." There is also a sense of discovery throughout the passage: "I felt vague, I guess; I don't know if that's a good way of putting it, but I think part of it . . . comes from a tendency to focus on everything at once." The halting, start-and-stop quality of speech offers a glimpse of a teacher coming to terms with the text, evaluating the writing, and working out his responses as he goes. There is an openness to the comments, a willingness to look into the possibilities for this piece of writing: "what you could do is . . . look a little more for some overarching ideas . . . ." The spoken forum offers Anson a greater opportunity to use language to gradually focus on what he has to say, to go back over the ground to define or sharpen his comments, or even to reverse or qualify his line of thought. The shifting focus, the pausing, the continual monitoring of what he says—these mannerisms of speech reveal Anson's process of interpretation and give the comments an intrinsic authority. These are not criticisms that are handed down to the student, sharp and complete. They are comments that are offered up with all the messiness of meaning making.

Anson's taped responses are made even more dialogic and more interactive when his discussions are instigated by something the students bring up themselves (in the fictional situations he creates for us) in the tape-recorded messages they hand in with their writing.[4] These messages allow Anson to take his key from the students and base his comments on their concerns. The practice provides a built-in check on the control he exerts over the writing by giving him an opportunity to shape the agenda of his response according to the students' own sense of what they need to work on. Anson focuses his comments on issues that the student raises on Writing 4 (about the appropriateness of using personal experience for the assignment) and on Writings 2 and 5. In several sets of responses, he also addresses concerns that are identified (again, in the fictional contexts he creates for us) by members of the writer's conference group.

Perhaps because the taped responses allow Anson to make more comments over a shorter period, he easily presents more words per commentary than any other responder. He produces an average of 1,100 words on each set of responses, over 300 words more than Patricia Stock, who makes more written responses than anyone else in the study. But, interestingly, perhaps because many of his words are taken up in false starts, metadiscourse, and repetition, he does not make many more comments, on the whole, than Stock or Donald Stewart. Anson makes an average of 37 comments per paper, Stock and Stewart an average of 35. Ultimately, Anson uses this commenting style not to take up more issues in his responses but to address more fully the issues he does take up.

Although the fact that the comments are spoken makes Anson's style more casual and open-ended—and perhaps fuller—than it would likely be if they were written, the format accounts only in part for his easygoing, moderately directive, yet fairly interactive style.[5] His style is actually determined by the larger choices he makes as a responder: his choice of modes, his voice, his range and focus of response, and the extent to which he tempers his authority as a teacher. If he were to make spoken comments that were packed with criticisms, corrections, and imperatives, his style would likely be only slightly less authoritarian than if he were to write them.[6]

Mode

Anson's moderate style is largely the result of his extensive use of advisory comments and detailed explanations. Anson uses more advisory comments than anyone else in the study: 18%.[7] His advice, however, rarely stands alone. It is accentuated—its authority tempered into helpfulness—by his tendency to augment his advisory comments with examples, explanations, and lessons. He writes 31% of his comments in explanatory modes: almost twice as many explanatory comments as advisory comments and over twice as many explanatory comments as any other reader in the study. If Anson's ardent use of advice characterizes his comments, his elaborate explanations make them distinctive. Like Larson and Glynda Hull, Anson frames one-quarter of his comments in the form of advice and imperatives. But his prompts are neither as directing as Larson's firm recommendations nor as open-ended as Hull's assignments. They fall somewhere in-between, offering detailed advice, but in an open, inviting way.

A good deal of the inviting, interactive quality of Anson's advice is achieved simply through the easy, conversational voice of the comments themselves. Notice how the voice of the following comments from Writing 4 moderates the directiveness of Anson's advice:

> [S]o if you're uncomfortable about being specific *because* you were worried about whether you were taking the right focus in the assignment, just don't! [laughs]

> I'd experiment with the abstract and concrete issue and make some decisions there, try throwing in something specific. The point here is to try out some possibilities.

Most of his advice is also cast in moderate, open forms, in which Anson does not assert his advice so much as offer it up for the student's consideration. All of the advice in Writing 4 fits this description:

> And what you could do is look for—this is a more structured kind of writing—and you could look a little more for some overarching ideas within the general focus of overguidance.

> [S]o you might ask yourself how much "I" you want in this piece. For example, "I strongly believe," "I have often pondered," "I think," "I feel," "I am." You might experiment with taking those out. See what happens when you take those out, what effect they have on the paper.

> [S]o you might try varying the sentences there—don't just keep repeating all the nouns they refer to, but try rearranging the sentences to see what happens to the style if you get rid of some of those "theses" and these "thoses" [laughs].

Ultimately, though, Anson's advice is made interactive—not directive—by the way he contextualizes and elaborates his advice. Whereas most readers present a comment and briefly follow it up with an example or explanation (if they add anything), Anson persistently follows up his advice with examples, lessons, and explanations, as well as with more specific advice and questions. Without these additions, without the specific help they provide, his commentary would be far more authoritative. His advice would present calls to action without offering much guidance. Consider, for example, the following version of Anson's comments to Writing 4, stripped of all but the essential points Anson makes in the actual commentary, in his own words and altered in only minor ways for readability. (The asterisks denote places where material from the original response has been removed.)

> I think it's perfectly appropriate to set the direction for the assignment and write about your experiences with your own kids. But it's kind of abstract.* If you're uncomfortable about being specific because you were worried about whether you were taking the right focus in the assignment, just don't.*

> One reason why I bring up this question is that, as a reader, I guess I got a little lost in this piece at times.* Some of the points you make relate to points you make in other sections, and this takes away the sense of structure.* What you could do is look for some overarching ideas within the general focus of overguidance. I think what you've got here is a really good beginning, but you've got to wade through it and find some overarching perspectives or angles on the main topic—problems with overguiding kids. Then try to restructure it in some way.* You also might ask yourself how much "I" you want in this piece.*

> Some things that really worked for me—I think you get going on page two and over on page three.* There are also a couple of sentences you might pick up on any cases when a sentence "derails."*

> So to sum up, this is a good start, and I'd experiment with the abstract and concrete issue and make some decisions there, try throwing in something specific.* Oh, you asked also about grammar and usage, and I would worry about that only when you've worked out the larger questions.*

This skeleton response is not directive: Anson's casual voice and casual advice—along with the four comments that praise Anne's work—ensure that it does not take control over the writing. Yet, stripped of the surrounding comments, it is far more controlling than Anson's actual response. Ten of the 14 comments in this pared-down version take the form of authoritative comments: three criticisms, one imperative, and six pieces of advice.[8] These comments offer advice about what the student *might* do rather than presenting imperatives about what she *should* do. The voice of the comments is, for the most part, moderate and conversational.

But these comments do not have the give-and-take quality, the interactiveness, of Anson's original comments. The difference lies in the extent to which Anson, in his original, full response, establishes the groundwork for, and elaborates on, his principal comments. The pared-down version has no comments that help the student understand the basic points of the commentary or that promote real interaction between teacher and student. By contrast, the original version contains 54 comments, 40 more than our pared-down version. Eleven of the additional comments that appear in Anson's original commentary present his reading of the text (in interpretations, reader responses, and positive evaluations) and provide a context for the response that follows, among them:

> I think that you're writing in a style that's a little reflective, not quite, but like a philosophical journal entry . . . .

> You know, I think I had to read that about six times before I saw what you were saying. Because I started reading it this way: "Parents feed prejudices more *adverb*," like *quickly*, and then I got to the "support" and the "by" and I was lost.

Nine of the comments suggest how Anne might go about making the called-for improvements through more specific advice, for example:

> What you might try is a loose tree diagram or topic diagram that can show you what you're doing in each part of the paper . . . .

> So for the purposes of focusing and structuring, you're going to want to look at different aspects of the topic. And that might mean that you'll collapse lots of your paper into one perspective (problems resulting from overguidance) and add others (how does one achieve a balance between guidance and freedom).

> You might experiment with taking those [references to yourself] out.

Four of them ask questions:

> If you had to say what the focus of the paragraph on the bottom of page two is, what would you say?

> But do you see what I mean?

> How does that [the tendency for parents to disguise their prejudices as morals and guidance] happen? What examples can you think of?

But most of the additional commentary, the bulk of Anson's elaboration, is presented in explanatory comments. Sixteen of the 40 comments—or 30% of Anson's full response—are cast in the form of explanatory comments. Some of these comments explain other points:

> But I raise that as a question because it seems like a lot of your writing in here hasn't taken on that abstract quality; it's been pretty concrete and you usually have lots of examples for things and so on.

Other explanatory comments cite examples:

> So on page three, if you use lots of words like "these" and "those" and "this," those words connect with something else, they refer to some assertion of a noun in the previous sentence. If you use them too often, it gives the writing a rather abstract or unspecific feel.

Still others offer brief lessons or explain some concept:

> So the reader . . . and this is the point of that structuring . . . so the reader knows where she is at each stage. An analogy I like to use is the tour guide—you're introducing each new piece, each sight, or perspective on the topic, so the reader knows what she's looking at each time you move on to something new.

Oh, while we're on style, something that I think leads to an abstract feeling are all these anaphoric . . . well, that's a fancy term for the way that certain words refer to other ideas or sentences.

These explanatory comments help to flesh out Anson's commentary, to clarify and develop the main points of his response.[9] By adding such explanations and giving some reasoning for his comments, Anson takes on less of the role of an advisor and more the role of an instructor, and thereby tempers his control as a responder. Without this explanation and all the other elaboration, Anson's advice, and his commentary as a whole, would be moderately authoritative. But with the elaboration it becomes specific, open-ended, and clearly interactive.

Anson uses such explanation and elaboration throughout his response to "Overguiding Teenage Children." As he typically does on all his responses, he identifies a concern and offers some ideas about how to make improvements. Then he explains his advice, points to sample cases in the text, and generally opens up his suggestions. A good example occurs in the second paragraph of his response to Writing 4. The opening sentences present the issue (in this case, the vagueness of the writing), offer his reading of the problem, and explain his reasons for raising it:

Now, one thing I noticed is that this draft is, um, well I think it's kind of abstract, it sounds rather philosophical? I don't know if you get that impression too, because it wasn't something you pointed out in your tape to me. But I raise that as a question because it seems like a lot of your writing in here hasn't taken on that abstract quality; it's been pretty concrete and you usually have lots of examples for things and so on. Um, so that's something to think about. And I also wondered if that was your choice, or if you worried—I mean, if you look at this, it could be about your parents or about being a parent, because it's so general.

Having defined the issue at stake—notably, in evaluations that are muted[10]—Anson goes on to offer some advice, which itself is presented in an open, easygoing manner:

So if you're uncomfortable about being specific *because* you were worried about whether you were taking the right focus in the assignment, just don't! [laughs]

Everything that follows explains and elaborates this advice:

So I think it's, this is the kind of paper where you really have a choice about whether you want to illustrate some of your points with, you know, with something a little more specific, some kind of examples or—for example [laughs], if you wanted to talk about an incident when you felt you were making too many decisions for one of your kids and overguiding them, and—or for that matter you could include experiences both from your relationship with your parents and with your kids, since you've had both. If you wanted to focus on specific experiences as examples to illustrate some of the general points you make, you're in a good position to do that from both perspectives.

Without indicating which options he sees as preferable, he lays out several ways that Anne can give substance to her claims. They are options to consider, not requests to be automatically taken up. Such open-ended elaboration is a distinguishing feature of his commentary, the marks of which may easily be found on any other of Anson's responses.[11]

Anson typically uses explanatory comments to elaborate on his calls for revision. But he also uses other types of comments to elaborate and make his style of response more interactive. First, he makes abundant use of advisory comments that are designed not to elicit particular changes in the text but to engage the student in some process of writing. Whereas Larson's advice is geared primarily to the written product, one out of every three of Anson's advisory comments is designed to help the student envision ways to make use of his other advice.[12] In the sequence from Anson's response to Writing 4, there are several of these "process suggestions."

Although each of these guides is connected to an earlier call to make some change in the text, they temper Anson's control by offering ways of going about the task of revision:

> What you might try is a loose tree diagram or topic diagram that can show you what you're doing in each part of the paper, and then you can see any relationships between or among those.

> What would happen if you chose the idea of development? Start with that, and then brainstorm just on the specific ways this happens.

> At this point, you've got a tough task of working through a lot of interrelated ideas and look for patterns for developing the essay into something with distinct parts.

These process-oriented advisory comments, because they guide the student's process of revision yet permit her to come up with her own materials, attentuate the teacher's control over the writing and make Anson's style more interactive than it would be if the comments were aimed soley at making changes in the text.[13] Second, Anson makes his advice more specific and provides additional guidance through the use of open questions. Half of his questions, in fact, are presented after some piece of advice, as part of his attempt to elaborate and offer more specific guidance for the student's revision. Over half of these questions, in turn, are followed by some sort of explanation or advice: They are rarely left to stand on their own without further development.[14] He also elaborates his advice and, in doing so, makes his responses more interactive by offering alternatives from which the student may choose. Rather than getting more restrictive as he provides more and more details, he opens up more options for the student to consider and allows her to take up these suggestions as she sees fit. As Anson notes in his comments to Anne, "The point here is to try out some possibilities."

Ultimately, these strategies for elaboration make Anson's commentary less authoritative and more interactive. It is interactive not in spite of all his advice, but because of it; and not in spite of the breadth and detail of his responses, but because of them. The additions do not direct the student so much as they offer her direction and, even as they quietly urge her to make changes, allow her to decide which options to choose. The more comments he makes, the more deeply he goes into his concerns and the more options he provides for the student to consider. The elaboration helps make his commentary guiding, not directive or controlling.[15]

Focus

Anson covers more ground in his responses than all but one other reader in the study.[16] He speaks to four or more issues on six sets of responses and to five or more issues on four sets of responses. In many ways, the scope of his commentary indicates that he is interested in helping students produce completed texts. Anson usually shuttles from large global concerns of focus and structure to matters of development to matters of wording and (at times) correctness. He seems willing to talk about whatever issues come up as he looks over a paper and composes his responses on tape. The detailed advice he presents on these issues gives further evidence of his interest in textual revision. At the same time, he is also interested in teaching students principles and strategies for completing such revision on their own.

Most readers in the study deal extensively with global concerns, sparingly with local matters, and moderately with concerns beyond the formal text. But Anson spreads his attention more fully across the range of focuses. He addresses 47% of his comments to global matters of content and structure, 16% to local structure, and 37% to extra-textual matters.[17] In fact, he devotes more comments than any other reader to contexts beyond the formal text.

In Writing 4, for example, Anson presents 37 comments on formal concerns—21 on global matters, 12 on local matters, and 4 on matters of correctness. Essentially, he calls on the student to get more specific in her talk about overguidance, to identify her key assertions, and to structure the essay around one or two key ideas. He presents another 16 comments that go beyond the formal text.[18] These comments do not focus on any specific formal concerns but address some larger context. In paragraph 2, for example, after reacting to the abstract language of the writing, Anson immediately looks beyond the text and talks about this issue in terms of Anne's own view about the writing and her earlier work in the course:

> Now, one thing I noticed is that this draft is, well, I think it's kind of abstract, it sounds rather philosophical? I don't know if you get that impression too, because it wasn't something you pointed out in your tape to me. But I raise that as a question because it seems like a lot of your writing in here hasn't taken on that abstract quality; it's been pretty concrete and you usually have lots of examples for things and so on. So that's something to think about.

He then tries to discern the reasons for the abstract language by looking into Anne's feelings toward the assignment:

> [I]f you look at this, it could be about your parents or about being a parent, because it's so general, so if you're uncomfortable about being specific *because* you were worried about whether you were taking the right focus in the assignment, just don't! [laughs]

Through the rest of the paragraph, he talks about her choices for revision in terms of the constraints that govern the personal essay:

> So I think it's, this is the kind of paper where you really have a choice about whether you want to illustrate some of your points with, you know, with something a little more specific, some kind of examples or—for example [laughs], if you wanted to talk about, um, an incident when you felt you were making too many decisions for one of your kids and overguiding them, and—or for that matter you could include experiences both from your relationship with your parents and with your kids, since you've had both. If you wanted to focus on specific experiences as examples to illustrate some of the general points you make, you're in a good position to do that from both perspectives.

Anson addresses the formal text in reference to some larger context of writing in 10 additional comments.[19] Whereas the formal comments help the student see what can be done to improve the writing in the next draft, the extra-textual comments help her to understand how she might make such changes or why they might be important to consider.

Anson uses extra-textual comments to explain and extend his text-based comments across his responses to the sampling.[20] On all but one set of responses, for example, he looks at the student's text according to the conventions and expectations that govern the type of writing called for by the assignment. He often speaks at length about the options that students have for structuring their essays, calling attention to the choices and constraints that different types of writing conventionally allow, as the following examples from three sets of responses show:

> First of all, let me say something about your question at the end of your tape about the assignment. . . . I think it's perfectly appropriate, and I hope I've been encouraging this strongly in the class, to define the assignments, to set the direction for the assignment in any way you choose, as long as you have a good rationale for it, so I think that it's perfectly appropriate to write about your experiences with your own kids. . . . I think that you're writing in a style that's a little reflective, not quite, but like a philosophical journal entry, so you might ask yourself how much "I" you want in this piece. (Writing 4)

> So I think this is an OK start, and I'm not so much worried about whether it fits the assignment perfectly (which was to write about something that you've got some special knowledge of) as how *you* can define and shape it. This seems to be pretty opinion-based, and so you might turn it into a sort of editorial essay, something you might read in an opinion section of the newspaper. If that feels right, go with it. (Writing 1)

> So I would encourage you to think about how much you want of yourself and your experiences, and . . . how much straight information you want to provide. . . . [T]here's

this narrative within an informational piece here, "I went fishing on this lake in Orlando and here's my story about this monster bass." And it may be that that's something you could use pieces of here, talk in brief about pulling a seven-and-a-half pound bass from the lake as a way of illustrating what a great fishing lake it is, but I think this piece has to decide which direction it goes in. And if you want to redefine it as a full-blown narrative, that's fine, and come up with another context for it. (Writing 5)

Instead of directing the student to follow certain conventions and produce a particular kind of text, he uses the draft in front of him to teach the student about various genre constraints and, ultimately, to help her produce a better next draft.

Anson also frequently looks at the text in terms of the rhetorical context of the writing and its effects on prospective readers. Although Anson often invokes himself as the main reader of the text, in his role as a teacher, he also commonly speaks of the general readers who are the target audience for the writing. In doing so, he reduces some of his control and places it in the hands of other readers. In Writing 4, for instance, he takes the opportunity to talk about Anne's revision in terms of what "the reader" would need to make it meaningful:

At this point, you've got a tough task of working through a lot of interrelated ideas and look for patterns for developing the essay into something with distinct parts. So the reader . . . and this is the point of that structuring . . . so the reader knows where she is at each stage. An analogy I like to use is the tour guide—you're introducing each new piece, each sight, or perspective on the topic, so the reader knows what she's looking at each time you move on to something new.

In other sets of responses he uses a similar strategy when he speaks, as on Writing 5, in terms of what bass fishermen or a general audience of newspaper readers would need or, as in Writing 11, when he talks about what college teachers would expect from an in-class essay exam.

Anson relies on student conference groups to provide additional perspectives on student writing. He makes oblique references to Anne's writing group in his comments on Writing 4.[21] But more explicit ones occur on other writings. On Writing 5, for example, Anson qualifies his views by suggesting that other readers in the group might have different reactions to Steve's mix of personal experience and technical information in his essay on bass fishing:

Now, my impression right now, and we'll see how the others react, is that you're probably a little bit over toward the extreme of personal memory as opposed to the informational.

In Writing 1, after mentioning his reservations about Louise's reasoning on the danger of seat belts, he suggests how some of the readers in her conference group will likely have the same reactions:

I imagine that one or more members of the conference group may feel differently—Sam, for one, anyway—and this will be good because they'll present a different argument, and you should really try to jot those down as we talk about the draft, or bring along a tape recorder, because you can then deal with them in the paper.

By citing the diverse views of peer readers in this way, Anson deflects attention from himself, tempers his authority as a responder, and makes the student more responsible for her own writing decisions.

Another way in which Anson looks beyond the formal text is through talk about writing processes. These comments usually accompany Anson's advice about some textual change and offer suggestions about how students might go about making changes. On Writing 4, for instance, after directing the student to think further about the structure of the essay, Anson suggests some ways Anne might go about identifying her main lines of thought:

[Y]ou've got to wade through it and find some overarching perspectives or angles on the main topic—problems with overguiding kids. Then try to restructure in some way. What you might try is a loose tree diagram or topic diagram that can show you what you're doing in each part of the paper, and then you can see any relationships between or among those.

In subsequent comments, he suggests some invention activities she might try to help develop her ideas. Similarly, in his comments on "What If Drugs Were Legal?" he suggests some ways for Nancy to anticipate counter-arguments and to find stronger arguments for her position:

What if you tried listing as many things you can think of that are legal that are also dangerous, like cigarettes, firearms, in a sense, certain kinds of recreational—all-terrain vehicles, over-the-counter drugs, and so on. Now what makes these sorts of things different from illegal drugs? You see, then when you find reasons why they're different, your points will seem more carefully thought out and developed. So the all-terrain business, for example, these can be safe with the right training and helmets and so on, while it's hard to imagine any doses of crack that could be considered perfectly ok on the human body and people's behavior.

He is not so concerned with identifying what needs to be presented in the writing as he is with helping her see what she can do—what processes she can take up—in order to make improvements in the next draft. In Writing 10, Anson calls on Kevin to proof and edit his paper and then offers the following process-based advice:

It's hard work, sometimes boring, certainly often frustrating when we're trying to focus on meaning, but it's also absolutely necessary. The strategy I've suggested, I don't see you doing this in your drafts. But whenever you think there's *any* reason to doubt a spelling, or comma, or whatever, just circle it. Do a once-through, very slowly, at the end of your writing, and just circle *anything* that you think might be incorrect. Don't look them up until the end. You really know how to spell some of these words, and they're not easy, since you've acquired a kind of specialized language having gone through this ordeal. But don't get complacent; I wouldn't just guess on everything. For example, on the top of page two, *immunity*; if you have any doubts that it's spelled wrong, and it is, just circle it, and look it up before you prepare the final draft. Are you sure "pleasant" is spelled right here? Or is there only one 'l' in "uncontrolled"? The more often you look these up, the less often you'll have to later on.

Nine sentences later, he completes the lesson. By not only pointing out specific changes that can be made in the text but also by suggesting ways of coming up with those changes, Anson offers additional help to the writer and, without taking control over the writing, makes his commentary more interactive.

Anson also frequently goes beyond the text and talks about the writing in relation to the student behind the text. In Writing 4, he takes into consideration Anne's apprehension about using her personal experience in the essay. In Writings 6, 10, and 11, seeing some complacency in the students' efforts, he calls on the students to push themselves more in their work. In Writings 1, 2, and 5 (and again in Writing 4), he shapes his commentary around the students' own expressed concerns about the writing, as they are gleaned from their (hypothetical) taped statements to him. He also looks at the piece of writing before him in relation to earlier drafts, to past writings, and to future coursework. In doing so, Anson validates the students' experiences and authority, engages them in the give-and-take relating of interactive response, and eases his control.

Anson's commentary seems to integrate Larson's emphasis on text production and Hull's emphasis on using the text to promote students' hands-on work with writing and revision. He looks to help students come up with as complete a draft as they can, yet he consistently offers explanations for his ideas about revision and frequently encourages them to practice composing strategies, to look for possibilities, and to try things out. The issues he treats and the way he deals with them in terms of the larger contexts of writing go hand in hand with the moderately authoritative, noticeably interactive style he forges through the voice and modes of his responses.

Overview of Teacher Control

Anson exhibits the strategies and emphases of a reader who is intent both on using his authority to guide students through their writing and on having students practice their own decision making as writers. While he roams about student texts, freely making suggestions about what revisions might be made and offering detailed lessons, he moves back and forth along the line that separates authoritative and interactive response—at times, for example, presenting advice but then offering a number of ways to go about taking it up, or explaining a principle but then showing how it can be used to produce a better final draft. Whether he is finally a rigorous guide or an open-ended facilitator is moot. Time and again he alternates or merges the two roles.

Anson's voice, like Hull's, is teacherly even as it is casual:

> Now, I think you've got a good start here, Nancy, but it's clear that it's just a start, and there are some really good opportunities here to think through the issue and develop this into a strong paper. (Writing 2)

> Part of the problem, for me anyway, stems from two things—a tendency to exaggerate without providing specific, realistic details, and a tendency to interpret the phenomenon you're describing very subjectively, so that *your* impression, *your* sensations and feelings are at the center of the piece. (Writing 6)

> Now this is a narrative, so it's got a fairly chronological structure, you know, first you discover you're sick, then there's the diagnosis, then the different parts of the treatment. But I really did notice how much you improved on that from the rough draft (and also from your first two papers). This is *much* . . . your paragraphs are *much* more carefully developed here. (Writing 10)

Even as his comments set forth his ideas about the writing, they try to establish a dialogue with the student, an inquiry into the possibilities for revision. Although in some ways they direct and guide, in others they simply offer options for the student to consider.

Anson also straddles the line between directing revision and offering direction when he speaks about the student's work in terms of the writing assignment. He frequently looks at the student's text according to the conventions that govern the type of writing called for by the assignment. He does not use these genre features to judge the quality of the writing. Instead he usually tries to clarify the assignment and encourage the student to decide how to use it as a springboard for devising her own purposes as a writer. Whereas some readers enforce the implicit demands of the assignment and thereby assert their authority as teachers, and whereas others put aside these requirements in favor of allowing the student to decide the direction of the writing, Anson, like Hull, characteristically uses the conventions of the assignment to teach the student about writing. Yet even as he indicates what the student might take up by way of revision, he finally leaves the choices up to the student.

Anson's penchant for ranging across student texts looking for the many ways they can be improved, the rich detail of his commentary and his abundant advice, his insistence on turning students back into the chaos of revision, and the sheer breadth of his responses—all make his style more controlling and less interactive. His colloquial language, the halting rhythms of his spoken comments, his casual voice, his many ways of deflecting authority from himself as a teacher, critic, and advisor, his way of encouraging students to try out possibilities rather than following a pre-set path, and his way of looking at student texts in terms of the larger rhetorical and pedagogical contexts—all these features make his style less controlling, more guiding, and more interactive.

Anson's commentary is less controlling than Larson's and even McClelland's and

O'Hare's. He makes far fewer criticisms than these readers, and his advice is less firm and authoritative than any of theirs. He is much more given to explanation than proclamation. Yet he is more controlling and offers more direct help than Elbow and Hull. Like these teachers, he creates himself as an ally to the student. But Elbow prefers to stay in the role of reader and does not take up the roles of advisor or instructor. And Hull prefers to direct the student to take up new writing tasks but elaborates on her comments very little, choosing instead to leave much of the work to the student. In a sense, Anson combines the elaboration of Stewart's responses (without the control he exerts in his evaluations and commands) and the student-oriented advice and options of Hull's responses (without the openness she maintains in her brief, learn-by-doing style).

Ultimately, what may best define Anson's style of response is the way in which he offers help to the student even as he allows her the freedom and the burden of considering her options and coming up with materials on her own. His style falls in the middle of this group of 12 readers: He is a facilitative teacher-advisor.

PATRICIA STOCK

For Patricia Stock, the student's essay is an occasion for getting together to talk about writing. Her responses, which take the form of highly elaborate, highly individualized letters to the student, are one-to-one tutorials. They have the feel of comments made by someone who has established a strong rapport with the student, has an intimate knowledge of his work, and is comfortable grounding her instruction in her own personal experience. Her letters of response are carefully crafted texts in their own right, written as much to involve the student in a lesson as to comment on the paper. More than seeking the improvement of a particular text, she tries to cultivate the student's practical understanding of writing.

Stock's response style is best seen as falling somewhere between Peter Elbow's and Chris Anson's. All three readers rely on lengthy commentary to the writer.[1] All three readers make their comments into informal conversations with students. And all three frame a majority of their responses in the form of reflective comments—more than any of the other nine readers. But Stock's letters are more elaborate than Elbow's and more focused and concentrated than Anson's. Whereas Elbow moves steadily from point to point and Anson gets involved in a variety of issues, Stock usually concentrates on only one or two concerns per paper, going into great detail on each one she takes up.[2] Whereas Elbow uses his letters to present his interpretations and reactions as a reader and Anson uses his talk to offer advice and instruction, Stock regularly attends to both tasks. She moves easily from giving close readings to presenting sophisticated lessons and explanations to offering detailed advice and questions. If Elbow creates himself as a reader and Anson creates himself as a close advisor, Stock creates herself as a reflective, nurturing teacher.

Stock's responses vary widely—in content, scope, and purpose—from student to student. She presents her major comments about every piece of writing in a full letter to the writer. But in four sets of her responses, in which she evidently feels the writing is far enough along to merit sentence-by-sentence revision, she also presents detailed comments in the margins, including suggested editorial changes.[3] In some cases, Stock offers close readings of the text and focuses on some issue of writing. In other cases, she foregoes making detailed comments about the text in favor of giving the student practice in some strategy of writing, whether or not he takes up a formal rewrite. In still other cases, she offers abundant advice for across-the-board revision. Although she usually limits her responses to one or two concerns, at times she addresses as many as seven.[4]

Although Stock's letters are highly individualized, they all share a common framework. Early in her response she shows that she has come to identify with what the student is saying, offers some praise for the work, and establishes a personal connection with the writing, using her experience to create a footing for the comments to come.[5] At the heart of her responses, Stock either gives a close reading of the paper and segues into advice and questions or, more often, presents a lesson and then guides the student toward revision. She usually concludes her letters with some kind of direct address to the student, a comment that tries to inspire him, challenge him, or invite him to try his hand at revision.[6] From start to finish, she roots her comments in the concrete detail of the student's writing and her own personal experience, creating a rich context that allows her to illustrate—not just present—her ideas to the writer. She exerts only modest control over the writer's choices, using reflective comments, encouraging advice, interactive questions, and plenty of examples and explanations.

STOCK

SETS OF RESPONSES	NUMBER OF RESPONSES		
		Rough Drafts	**Final Drafts**	**Total**

5 rough drafts
5 final drafts

35 comments/writing

3.7 issues/writing

	Rough Drafts	Final Drafts	Total
Marginal Comments	26	64	90
End Comments	140	116	256
Total	166	180	346

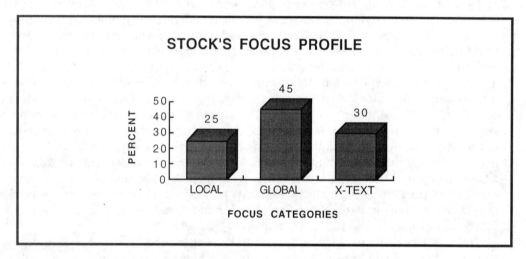

STOCK'S FOCUS PROFILE

STOCK'S MODE PROFILE

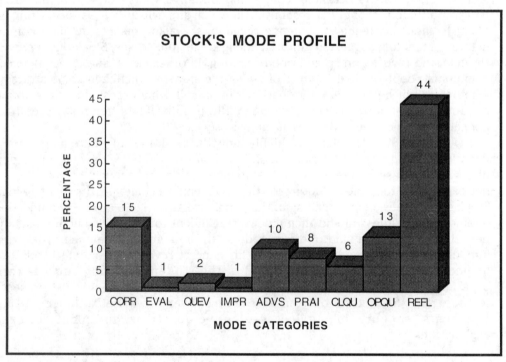

Writing 4: Response

Dear Anne,

Your essay spoke to me. I think of myself as a parent who has tried to do what you are recommending--to provide guidelines and at the same time not to make those lines so tight that my children could not find a way to move with them. It is tricky, however. I have tried to allow my children to chart their own courses even when I knew they were making mistakes and would pay the consequences of those mistakes. My reasoning went this way: They need to make mistakes now and learn that they will have to live with the consequences of their decisions and their actions. It is better they learn that now with smallish aches and pains than later with big ones. The trick for a parent, of course, is to know when to stay out and when to step in. It isn't always easy to decide.

Recently I lived through a situation with my son in which I was trying to provide guidelines and to leave a little slack in them. Andrew, who is nineteen--not among the young teens, the group you are focusing on--wanted to apply for a year-long, student exchange program in the Soviet Union. If accepted, he might not have known which city he would study in until he arrived in the Soviet Union. In two other programs, he might have chosen, he would have known. In one program, he would study in Moscow; in the other, Leningrad. Furthermore, in each of the second two programs would have been the Soviet Union for a semester, not a year. I was uncomfortable with the fact that he could have been anywhere in the Soviet Union. I kept dreaming about Siberia and salt mines. (Perhaps I've seen too many anti-Soviet films and read to much Solzhenitzen.) I thought that for a first stay to the Soviet Union, it might better for him to live in a European city like Moscow or Leningrad. I was also concerned about his living away from the United States, in a rather different culture, for an entire year. I thought a semester might be a better period of time. I expressed these concerns to Andrew. He countered with his thoughts. The first program was a superior one in his opinion. He knew some students around the country who were going to participate in it. He is self-reliant. He would manage. In fact, he would thrive. Well, I thought: He has to live it; he has to decide. If it is the wrong decision, he'll learn from that choice. He applied. He was accepted. And--thus far--this story has a happy ending from my pespective. Because he is a history major, he has been assigned to the Institute for History in Moscow which opens its archival papers this year. It is likely to be a busy place next year with lots of exciting activity and with many scholars coming and going from it. His decision seems to have been a good one for him...and for me. I realize that you wish to focus on how parents' overguide young teenagers' moral decisions. Andrew is not a young teen, and his decision was not a moral one, I know. But the decision he made and in which I had to choose a role to play was one in which I might have overguided. I tried to guide, but not overguide.

I am really interested in learning more about what you mean by the moral decisions you write about. You suggest what you might mean when you allude to prejudice. I read into your essay your worry that parents' prejudices may be passed on to their children in the guise of moral guidance. I am uncertain if I would always correlate the instilling of prejudice with overguiding. I don't think you want to do that either. I think you are saying that overguiding can be a vehicle for the passing on of prejudice. But, I am really not certain. I think I need to know more concretely what you see as the dangers to young people of overguiding parents. Maybe some specific examples, like the one I offered you concerning Andrew and me, might help me understand better just what you mean.

I hope to learn from your essay as it develops. As a parent, I need all the help I can get. I need to learn as much as I can about how to guide responsibly, about how not to "victimize" them with overguidance, as you put it. I look forward to reading your next draft of this essay. In preparation for writing it, I wonder if you might profit from thinking and talking with friends about the categories and concepts you have introduced in the essay, some of which you suggest are polar opposites in your essay. Although you do not do this, I'll set the up here as polarities: neglect vs. guidance; guidance vs. overguidance; guidelines vs. rules; wisdom vs. prejudice; nurture vs. victimize; education of the child vs. education of the parent. I am wondering how these concepts are related to one another in your thinking? I am wondering how you want them to work in your essay: to complement one another? to play off one another? to contrast with one another? in some other way?

One other thing that strikes me as I read your essay: You mix your use of the notions of *thinking* and *feeling* almost indiscriminately (e.g., page three, first paragraph: "freedom of the mind to explore the inner soul...," "These outside views will help in the search of finding true feelings," "Deprivation of this breds ignorance....") Do you understand these notions as carrying synonymous meanings? I am also uncertain of the meanings you invest in some other of the abstract terms you use, among them: beliefs, thoughts, feelings, ignorance, prejudice, fear. Can you illustrate what you mean by them in your essay? And clarify how you see them relating to one another?

Can't wait for the next draft.

P. L. Stock

Mode

Like Elbow, Stock almost never explicitly criticizes a piece of writing or directs the student to make changes in the text. Out of her 346 comments on the 10 essays in the sampling, she writes only four negative evaluations and three commands. Although on occasion she edits papers, she always makes it clear to the student that these are models and suggestions, not corrections to be automatically accepted. Whereas the most directive responders in the study use from 23% to 42% of their comments to evaluate student writing and direct revision, Stock writes only 4% of her comments in these modes—by far the fewest among our readers.[7] Most of the criticism that does occur in her commentary is presented indirectly, couched sometimes in qualified evaluations and more often in reader reactions. Still, across her responses she writes only six qualified negative evaluations and 11 negative reader reactions—just 5% of her comments.

Instead, Stock devotes herself to three primary tasks in her responses: she gives close, reader-based readings of the writing, presents detailed lessons, and offers advice and questions for the writer to consider in the way of revision. Although she usually emphasizes one or two strategies on a given commentary, she uses all three regularly across her responses. She spends more time sharing lessons and guiding the student's revision than Elbow, and she spends more time giving her readings of the text than Anson. Her letters of response are always richly textured. She frequently gives detailed interpretations of the writing and typically elaborates her lessons and calls for revision; her goal apparently is to initiate a collaboration between reader and writer, teacher and student. Almost three out of every four of her comments are cast in nonauthoritative modes—as reflections, praise, and questions. Forty-four percent of her comments take the form of reader responses and teacher reflections, among the highest in the study.[8] She also makes use of a range of other modes, especially advice, open questions, and (on special occasions) corrective comments.[9] Almost all of these strategies, as we shall see, are employed in her responses to Writing 4.

Stock establishes the stance of a highly personal, sympathetic reader through her reader responses. She makes such responses on all but one set of comments, and on six sets she makes five or more of them.[10] Most of these responses are reader remarks and reader-experience comments, in which Stock either relates the writing to her own life or describes her way of processing the text. In her responses to Writing 4, for example, she offers a glimpse into her own thoughts and experiences as a parent who has struggled with the issue of how much guidance to provide her children:

> Your essay spoke to me. I think of myself as a parent who has tried to do what you are recommending—to provide guidelines and at the same time not to make those lines so tight that my children could not find a way to move with them. It is tricky, however. I have tried to allow my children to chart their own courses even when I knew they were making mistakes and would pay the consequences of those mistakes.

With these reader remarks she establishes herself as one of the implied readers Anne seems to have in mind for her audience and creates a common ground for their discussion. She starts her commentary on Writing 5 in a similar way, this time with one reader remark (three sentences long) and several reader-experience comments:

> Where is my pole? Where is the bait? I want to go fishing. As I read your essay, Steve, I felt as if I were there with you, motoring along I-75, imagining Lake Ivenho in increasing detail as first one and then another fishing hole floated past my car window. I navigated the dense lilypads, felt the cool of the conditioned air that had worked its way down from the tops of the giant oaks to the shaded shoreline of the lake. As I joined you in the night fishing you described, I could hear the after-dark socializers, the insects and the frogs and the snakes, spreading the word that we were around. And, I felt my sleepy muscles strain into play when the wide-mouthed bass challenged them to a game of tug-of-war.

A number of her reader responses, however, edge into evaluation and take the form of reader reactions, among them the following comments from Writing 5:[11]

> You hooked my interest immediately not only with your call for the attention
> of bass fishermen but also with the dramatic details in your first paragraph.

> I was stopped by lines 7-11 on page 1 and lines 3-6 on page 2.

These reader responses help form a base for her other strategies as a responder. Whereas readers like Richard Larson and Donald Stewart establish themselves as critics through their use of evaluative comments and Ben McClelland and Frank O'Hare establish themselves, in part, as expert readers through their use of interpretive comments and criticism, Stock establishes herself as a sympathetic reader by framing her readings mostly in reader responses. With this foundation established she usually goes on to engage in her primary work: to offer lessons in writing and suggestions for revision.

Stock's favorite strategy as a responder is to devise individualized lessons based on the student's writing. In them, Stock dramatizes some problem she sees or some area of language use she thinks the student would do well to work on as a developing writer. The lessons often emerge from, or lead into, Stock's readings of the text and give the student a way of looking at his text in terms of some general principle of writing. They take the form of explanatory comments and are typically quite detailed.

In her comments to Writing 4, for instance, Stock presents a complex lesson through a lengthy example about her own experience as a parent. Although the example starts off with a number of reader remarks, it gradually becomes more pointed, more directed toward the issues of the writing and more explanatory. An implicit lesson begins to take shape at the end of paragraph one, when she moves beyond simply offering her views and experience as a parent and begins to explain the reasoning behind her decisions about how to guide her children. It takes clearer shape as a lesson midway through the second paragraph, as Stock, assuming the role of a teacher, describes in detail how she tried to guide—but not overly guide—her son's decision about a college exchange program:

> I was uncomfortable with the fact that he could have been anywhere in the Soviet Union. . . .
> I thought that for a first stay to the Soviet Union, it might be better for him to live in a
> European city like Moscow or Leningrad. I was also concerned about his living away from
> the United States, in a rather different culture, for an entire year. . . . I expressed these
> concerns to Andrew. He countered with his thoughts. . . . Well, I thought: He has to live it;
> he has to decide. If it is the wrong decision, he'll learn from that choice . . . . I realize that
> you wish to focus on how parents overguide young teenagers' moral decisions. Andrew is
> not a young teen, and his decision was not a moral one, I know. But the decision he made
> and in which I had to choose a role to play was one in which I might have overguided.

Although on the surface the example is meant to suggest something about the complex choices parents often must weigh when they try to offer their children guidance, underneath it is an extended lesson on a writer's use of personal experience to examine a subject. The sample case is designed to lead Anne back into her thinking about overguidance and perhaps to complicate her views on the subject. It also serves as a model for the work she must do in developing her thoughts on the next draft, as becomes clear at the end of paragraph three: "Maybe some specific examples, like the one I offered you concerning Andrew and me, might help me understand better just what you mean." Characteristically, the lesson is illustrated through her own personal experience.

In a similar way, in her comments to Writing 1, Stock offers a lesson about spotty arguments, starting with a reaction to Louise's rough draft and then easing, by using a lengthy personal example, into the instruction:

I smiled as I read your essay arguing against the law that requires us to wear seat belts. One of your arguments sounded like one my mother used to offer me. My mother didn't like to wear a seat belt when she was in the car so she always found putting one on as an occasion to mention that some people were actually killed in car accidents because they were wearing seat belts. And she could always remember a story that Ethel had told her or Mildred had told her about some individuals who had died because they were wearing seat belts. She often had a few terrible details of those accidents to share with me. I would usually answer my mother's complaints by expressing my horror at the details she mentioned and my sympathy for the injured individuals whom someone she knew knew about. Following her account of a terrible accident, I would customarily ask my mother how Ethel or Mildred learned about the accident, where it had taken place, and so on. Probably it wasn't very nice of me to put my mother on the spot that way. I knew the stories she was sharing with me were her way of resisting the seat belt. Somehow I thought that resistance was more characteristic of older people, who formed their car-riding habits before seat belts were commonplace to cars, than of younger people. That is why I was surprised at your stand on seat belts. And I was really surprised that you offered as support for the position you are taking about seat belts, the same kind of heard or over-heard story my mother used to tell. Nameless people, an authority whose qualifications are questionable, insufficient details. I would not have reached the same conclusion you seem to have accepted because someone told you that a person you do not know, whose judgment you cannot evaluate, had reached such a conclusion.

Using an everyday experience, Stock explains how listeners tend to balk at arguments that come from second-hand sources and are left unsupported. The example is meant to mirror and indirectly criticize a similar tact in Louise's writing, as becomes clear when, at the end of the passage, Stock calls into question her mother's line of reasoning and then presents three reader reactions to Louise's arguments. Stock's story about her mother turns into an elaborate explanation of a principle of writing that is made understandable by its expression in a common language about day-to-day events.[12]

Across her responses, Stock routinely moves from her reading of a text to these sophisticated lessons, using such examples drawn from her experience on seven of her 10 sets of responses.[13] The examples offer analogies to the students' work, giving her a way to identify with the writer, indirectly evaluate the text, illustrate strategies of writing, and give students a different lens for looking at their work. Her object seems to be to help them conceptualize issues of writing in terms of everyday experience and language use, not simply present evaluations and revisions in isolation.

Lessons dominate Stock's commentary on five sets of her responses.[14] In a number of other responses, however, she provides elaborate readings and, instead of extended lessons, presents advice and questions for revision. These readings often are short, but sometimes become detailed, as they accumulate across her response. They are usually cast—like Elbow's—in reader responses, not in explicit evaluative comments or interpretations. When they make positive evaluations, they usually go on to explain what was good about the writing. When they present or imply negative evaluations, they are typically followed by short lessons, advice, or questions that are designed to guide the student's revision. Because her readings and lessons frequently accompany each other, her role as a sympathetic reader merges with her role as a supportive teacher, establishing her dominant image as a helpful tutor.

In her responses on Writing 4, Stock gives a short reading of Anne's rough draft and then presents two pieces of advice, with all of the comments, notably, grounded in Stock's needs as an interested reader:

I am really interested in learning more about what you mean by the moral decisions you write about. You suggest what you might mean when you allude to prejudice. I read into your essay your worry that parents' prejudices may be passed on to their children in the guise of moral guidance. I am uncertain if I would always correlate the instilling of prejudice with overguiding. I don't think you want to do that either. I think I need to know more concretely what you see as the dangers to young people of overguiding parents. Maybe some specific examples, like the one I offered you concerning Andrew and me, might help me understand better just what you mean.

The comments indicate why she would like more information and, in doing so, resist taking authority over the writing: Both her evaluations and her advice are muted by her references to her own interests as a reader. The comments not only keep control in the hands of the student, they also engage her in looking at the revision in terms of her audience.

Stock gives her most detailed readings—and some of her most elaborate suggestions for revision—in her responses to Writing 5 and Writing 6. She begins her reading of "The Four Seasons" by praising the strengths in David's seasonal portraits, characteristically, in highly subjective reader responses:

I like the way you get into the essay, immediately contrasting the four seasons that exist in Syracuse your "other home" with the pleasant heat and sunshine of Tallahassee (a climate you know that all of us in the class have experienced). I especially liked your discussion of fall in Syracuse. The particular details and events you chose to write about to create fall in your essay were effective ones for me. As I read them, I said, "Yes, that's it." I know "the crazed feeling" that sends even playful adults into a humungus . . . mountain of multi-colored leaves. I like the fact that you had those leaves fall, that you raked them together into a comfort zone, and that you crawled into them to find security.

These are not the detached assessments of a critic or a teacher; they are the highly individualized and personal judgments of a reader. There are three praise comments in the excerpt. Another three comments are used to explain and elaborate on this praise. Two paragraphs later, Stock indirectly criticizes other parts of the writing, again using reader-based comments that are no less elaborate:

If you had not told me that winter was your second favorite season, I would not have guessed it. I would have guessed it was spring because your descriptions of spring have almost as much vitality as your descriptions of fall. As I read the section of your essay devoted to winter, I was struck by how heavily you relied on overused language to express your feelings about Syracuse's winters (my understanding is the Syracuse's winters are WINTERS). I guess you were aware of your reliance on all-too-familiar language yourself because you enclosed some of it in quotation marks: "winter wonderland," "feel Jack Frost nipping at your nose."

Three of these comments are negative reader reactions; the others develop her reactions.

She follows the reading with a short lesson about worn language and an attempt to encourage the student to put the lesson into practice:

To be sure, it is a tough problem: How to communicate one's special understandings. After all, you haven't invented the language, you have inherited it. All you have in language is what you have been given. I find, however, that you can take the given and give it an original turn ("soft scrunching of that magical white carpet underneath your feet"), and as I read your essays, I hope for that from you. I'm actually anticipating your development as an even more creative, even more effective writer this semester.

Having identified an area for improvement, Stock goes on to offer the student detailed advice and questions to help him with revision:

Let me suggest how you might dig into some of what I am proposing in a revision of "The

Four Seasons," should you choose to revise this paper for a higher grade later. In the essay as it is, you under-represent Syracuse's summer. Did you mean to? Did you do it because you felt those of us in the class would know summer because we have so much of it in Tallahassee? Is Syracuse's summer like Tallahassee's? Can (Should) the summer in Syracuse and the summer in Tallahassee go by the same name? What would happen if you demonstrated the changes in summer and winter in Syracuse the way you demonstrated them in spring and fall? Or are summer and winter seasons that are characterized by a sameness while spring and fall are not? Maybe these are not questions that interest you, maybe others are. Maybe a set that distinguish the dramatic changes of seasons in the northeast with the subtle changes in the southeast would be more interesting ones for you to tease out and develop in a revision of this essay should you choose to write one.

Rather than presenting only a call for revision, or rather than following her advice with only a broad question, as Glynda Hull often does, Stock offers a litany of specific questions. As the opening and closing sentences of the excerpt indicate, they are intended to open up possibilities for revision, not direct it. Ten of her 50 comments across the letter are questions.[15] Thirty-one are cast in reflective modes, half of them interpretations and reader responses, half of them explanatory and hortatorical comments. These interactive comments are typical of Stock's practices.

Stock presents detailed readings, advice, and explanations in a similar way on Writing 5, "Attention: Bass Fishermen." After praising Steve's descriptions in her opening paragraphs, she spends the rest of the letter giving brief reader-based evaluations of the writing and then immediately offering advice about how to make it more effective:

> Throughout, you allowed me to live the events with you because you offered me specific places to be, sights to see, and sensations to feel. . . . Because I like the detail you provide about the Orlando lakes and the strategies for fishing for wide-mouthed bass, I suggest that you offer your reader more of them. For example, on page 1 you might provide a phrase defining and/or describing sink holes for those of us who don't know what they are. . . . Similarly, on page 2, you might define/describe "waders," "the problem," "top-water buzz bait," "plastic worm." On page 3, you might explain why the night fishermen use a "big, black worm". . . .

The advice, like the readings, is text-specific and detailed, with Stock often explaining one comment in a follow-up comment. She does not simply offer advice; she goes over the advice in some detail, pointing to sample passages and explaining how it may be used. She also explains the reasoning behind her calls for revision and often even offers models for revision. Halfway through the response, for example, Stock advises the student to reorder several sentences at the start of his second paragraph, explains the reasoning behind her suggestion, and then offers her own way of revising the sentences:

> I'd re-write the two sentences into one myself, making the second the first and showing the relationship of the idea in it to the paragraph before and the material that will follow it. This is how I would do it:

>> Because I grew up on them and know most of their hidden underwater structures, like the fallen trees and the sand-bars that extend out into the lakes, I have an advantage over most people in fishing these lakes. There is a certain lake in Orlando that is my favorite place to fish: Lake Ivenho is actually a chain of four lakes connected by links of water. One of the things I love the most about this lake is that almost . . .

She then adds seven comments to explain the suggested revision:

Written as it is here, the first sentence of this paragraph does a lot of work for you: it makes the link between your growing up in Orlando and your claim to be an expert fisherman on Orlando's lakes and what you are about to explain to your readers; it demonstrates what you know about Orlando's lakes, and it illustrates your knowledge. (Don't forget, I'd like more of this kind of stuff.) This sets you up to remark that you like one of those lakes particularly. If you change the end mark after "place to fish" to a colon (a punctuation mark that says elaborating or amplifying material follows) that move will ask the reader to hold the first part of the sentence-like construction in mind while you add another thought. This allows you to clarify that Lake Ivenho is four lakes while still keeping the reader focused on the fact that Lake Ivenho is your favorite place to fish. You can see that with my suggested revision I am trying to make your sentences each do more than one job for you. If you elaborate and amplify your text by embedding more material in it, you can get your language to do several jobs at once for you. Look back for a minute to my first paragraph in this letter to you. I am trying to build purposeful allusions into those sentences with words like "motoring," with expressions like "conditioned air," and with carefully chosen, carefully placed words like "sleepy muscles strain into play when the wide-mouthed bass challenged them to a game of tug-of-war."

Including the advice at the start of the passage, there are nine comments in this sequence: two pieces of advice, a sample revision, and six comments that explain other comments.[16] What another responder would present as corrections or suggested changes, pronouncements based mainly on the teacher's authority, Stock turns into a highly detailed, highly interactive discussion with the student. Like Anson, she elaborates freely on her calls for revision, yet keeps her commentary open-ended. Such a practice goes hand-in-hand with Stock's general principle of using comments to explain and teach, not simply to help the student produce a better draft.

Every one of Stock's letters provides close readings of the text, lessons, and detailed explanations. Five of them present some form of modeling.[17] Seven sets of her responses include advice that is followed up with questions, and six of her letters present hortatorical comments or a note of encouragement at the end. This same ebb and flow, the movement from close readings to lessons, or from indirect criticism to advice and questions, may be seen in all but one of Stock's other letters.[18] It is the signature mark of her response style.

Focus

Across her various responses, Stock addresses a wide range of concerns. She addresses three or fewer areas of response on five of her letters, and four or more areas on her other five. Twenty-five percent of her comments are devoted to local structure, wording, and correctness, the fourth highest percentage of local comments among the 12 readers.[19] Only 45% of her comments address ideas, development, and global structure, the lowest in the study. But these numbers are misleading, as becomes apparent when we consider that Stock makes most of her comments about local matters on just two essays. Of the 87 comments she writes about local structure, wording, and correctness, 65 occur in the marginal comments to Writing 10 and Writing 13, final drafts on which Stock presents detailed editorial suggestions. Half of her responses include no comments on local matters at all.[20]

The different areas Stock takes up from response to response reflect her concern for matching her comments to the needs of the individual student. Like Hull, she attends to quite different concerns at different times—depending on her sense of how far along the student's drafting is, how well the student evidently understands the principles involved in the type of writing he is doing, and where he stands in the course.[21] She often defers work on the completion of a writing assignment in order to pick up on a principle, technique, or activity that she thinks the student would do well to stop and work on.

On five sets of responses Stock sees the student's text not as the target of revision but as a point of departure for the student's ongoing work with writing. These responses focus on two or three issues and occur on writings that are either in the very early stages of drafting or at a point at which Stock is willing to suspend further textual revision. On Writing 4, for instance, Stock focuses on helping Anne make sharper distinctions among her key terms. On Writing 1, she concentrates her entire response to Louise on her reasoning about the danger of seat belts. On Writing 2, she suspends work on the draft and calls on Nancy to reconsider her way of reading LeMoult's article. On Writing 11, she decides not to engage Donna in any further revision, but instead takes the opportunity to offer a lesson on investment in writing. In time, these responses may lead to better written products, but they are immediately concerned with having the student work on some particular principle or activity of writing. On Writing 9, a final draft handed in at the end of the term, Stock decides simply to compliment the writer on her work in the course and does not engage in any additional commentary.

In her five other sets of responses, in which Stock is more interested in leading the student to produce another draft, she addresses a wider range of concerns. Although she still limits these letters to only three or four issues, on four of them she offers, in addition, detailed editorial suggestions in the margins, usually on matters of wording, local structure, and correctness. She addresses four issues on "The Four Seasons"—half with the intention of helping David revise the paper again, half with the larger aim of encouraging him to get more involved in his work in the class. She addresses four issues on "The John Cougar Concert," although she really has only one concern in her letter (acknowledging the improvements in Frank's successive drafts) and only one concern in her marginal comments (helping him with local revision). She deals with five areas of response on "Street Gangs," presenting comments in the margins and in her letter on global structure, wording, and formal conventions, as well as on ideas and development. She covers the most issues and deals extensively with specific sentence-by-sentence revisions on two papers, Writing 5 and Writing 10. She sample edits both essays, noting that she would like the writers to rework their papers and submit them for publication in a class anthology.

Stock regularly goes beyond the formal text and looks at student writing in terms of the larger rhetorical context. Only one set of her responses—her commentary on Writing 1—does not make some explicit reference to the reader. She also routinely looks at the writing in terms of the student behind the text, commenting on the student's attitudes toward his work or suggesting various composing activities he might try in order to improve his writing. She frequently links her comments to work students have done in class and speaks of their daily lives outside of the classroom.

Overview of Teacher Control

Stock exerts only modest control over students because she frames few of her comments in evaluative and imperative modes, spends a lot of time talking about a limited number of issues, and makes plenty of reflective comments. She devotes most of her responses to describing her other comments, creating individualized lessons, and supportively offering ideas for revision. But she exerts even less control than she might because of the way she creates herself as an interested reader.

In playing back her reading of student texts, Stock takes on the role of a sympathetic reader. Like Elbow, she offers a sounding board for how the words on the page strike her as an individual reader. Perhaps even more than Elbow, she tries to understand what the student has to say and makes personal connections with the writing. She writes many remarks about what the writing makes her think and feel and infuses her interpretations with her own subjective views. Whatever evaluating she does grows out of her experiences, needs, and interests as a reader.

Although both Elbow and Stock present their views as highly involved, individual readers, they go about the task somewhat differently. Elbow brings the writing to where he stands as an individual and from this subjective vantage point presents his views and reactions toward it. Stock brings herself to the writing and fashions herself as the student's ideal reader for that text. She adopts the role she is asked to adopt by the writing and then personalizes it, searching her personal experience to find a role that matches the one the writer expects of her and responding from that perspective. In Writing 4, Stock steps into her role as a parent and shares how she tried to guide her son in making a decision about an overseas study program. In Writing 1, she describes how she reacted when her mother told her stories about the danger of seat belts. In Writing 6, she plays herself again. Noting that she is about to move to Syracuse, she expresses how much she welcomes information about the seasons in the area. In Writing 10, a personal essay about the writer's bout with leukemia, she establishes herself as a sympathetic, knowledgeable, and interested reader by telling Kevin about experiences she has had with friends who have gone through similar ordeals. Stock brings herself to the text, shaping herself in the image of the student's ideal audience yet presenting herself as an individual member of that group.

Furthermore, whereas Elbow creates himself as a sympathetic reader and devotes most of his responses to giving his readings of the text, Stock creates herself both as a sympathetic reader and as a supportive teacher. She gives almost equal time to playing back her readings of the text, presenting instruction, and making suggestions for revision. Yet even when she moves from her readings to her lessons and advice—a move that conventionally invokes one's role as a teacher—she maintains something of her stance as a reader and moderates her control over the writing. Her lessons and advice grow naturally out of her reader responses and are presented in a reader's language, as her comments on Writing 4 aptly show. The lessons and advice also tend to be accompanied by open-ended examples, questions, and explanations, all of which offer the student more direction without becoming more directive. She consistently keeps a good deal of responsibility on the student to come up with his own materials and revisions.

Stock also moderates her control by not making many comments about how well the writing responds to the dictates of the writing assignment. Instead, like Elbow and Gere, she works with what the student puts before her, trying to find areas of writing the student would do best to work on, regardless of the stated requirements of the assignment. In contrast to White, Stewart, McClelland, Larson and (to a lesser degree) Anson, she seems intent on cutting through the technical conventions that distinguish various types of discourse. She speaks about the student's writing in practical everyday terms, using her common experience as a reader and her personal experience outside the classroom to explain principles of writing. By deflecting attention from the assignment and looking at the writing in terms of the student's apparent objectives, Stock puts aside some of the authority that is typically assumed by teachers. Because she is driven less by her own expectations as a teacher, she can have more room to work with the student's ideas and purposes and make her commentary more interactive.

Moreover, she is one of the few readers in the study who gears her responses directly to the student behind the text. Like Elbow and Hull, she uses the student's writing as a starting point for her response, not the target, and focuses her comments on attitudes, processes, and principles more than particular changes in the text. Elbow looks to help students work on their attitudes toward writing and their processes of composing. Hull sets up assignments to help students come to a practical understanding of certain conventions of discourse. Stock identifies principles of writing students would do well to work on and engages them in immediate hands-on practice with these principles. Text production and revision are seen in terms of what they may contribute to the student's larger, ongoing development as a writer. This emphasis allows Stock to bridge the distance between her and the student and exert less control over the student's text and writing choices.

By shaping her comments more to the individual student's development than to the completion of the written text, limiting the range of concerns she takes up in a given essay, making extensive use of personal experience, eschewing directive modes of response in favor of reflective ones, offering detailed readings and elaborate explanations, and generally treating her written comments almost as one-to-one tutorials, Stock creates herself as one of the least directive and most interactive readers in the study.

TILLY WARNOCK

Tilly Warnock is easily the least controlling responder in the study. In fact, she frequently removes her hand so much from evaluating the text and directing changes that she does little by way of controlling student writing and initiating revision. In some cases, Warnock's responses are rather sharp, text-specific, and detailed. These responses encourage the student to look closely at his writing and offer him a sense of direction without making particular decisions for him. They reflect Warnock's engagement with the words of the student's text, and they are fairly interactive. In other cases, her responses are so brief and general that they offer little direction and verge on being detached. In still other cases, her responses mix general, detached comments and precise, text-specific comments.

Warnock makes the fewest comments of the 12 readers. She writes an average of 12 comments per paper—10 fewer than the average made by the group as a whole. Many of them are brief, and a number of them are brief and general. It is clear from her responses themselves that of the 12 readers who participated in the study Warnock was the least comfortable responding to the sampling.[1]

If Edward White, by framing a significant number of comments in strong directive modes, treads the line that separates authoritative and authoritarian response, Warnock, by framing a significant number of comments in detached and general terms, treads the line that separates interactive and detached response. Authoritative responses become problematic when they assume too great a control over the student's choices and turn authoritarian; nonauthoritative responses become problematic when they do not direct or guide the student enough and become detached, noninterventional. In her responses, Warnock vacillates between interactive response and detached response. She assumes the posture of an informal, hands-off coach, one who is content to raise general issues for students to consider and work out on their own.

WARNOCK

SETS OF RESPONSES	NUMBER OF RESPONSES		
4 rough drafts 5 final drafts 12 comments/writing 3.1 issues/writing		Rough Drafts	Final Drafts	Total
	Marginal Comments	20	31	51
	End Comments	23	35	58
	Total	43	66	109

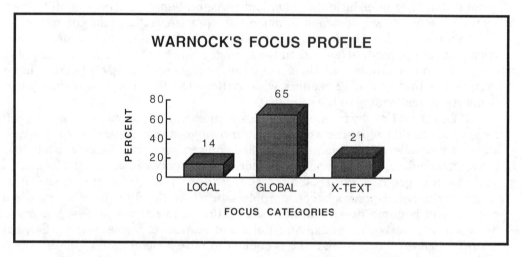

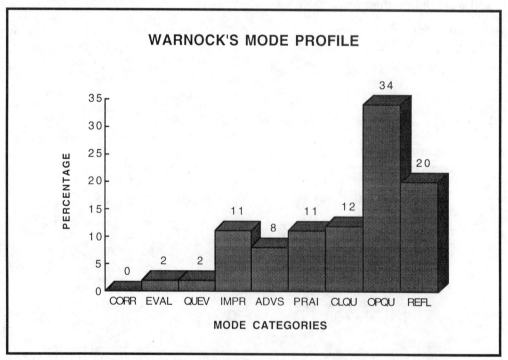

Writing 4
Anne B.
Rough Draft

[On Overguiding Teenage Children]

Parenting is an enormous task and a full time job. Along with
providing food, clothing, and shelter, there is something else which
is very crucial to raising a child. Guidance. Whether an infant or a
teenager, they need guidance from their parents. When there is no
parental guidance, children sometimes end up criminals or addicts of
drugs or alcohol. Child neglect is a serious problem and the issue
has received much publicity. The question I have often pondered,
however, deals with parents who overguide their children, more
specifically young teenagers. Is this a serious problem too?

Yes, I strongly believe that it is. Parents are not only
responsible for providing necessities as mentioned above, but they
also have an obligation to laying down a foundation for morals. This
is the guidance I spoke of earlier, and it is here that I believe the
problem begins. First of all, what is a moral? A moral is a
consideration or principle of right or wrong, or of good or bad
character. So why here? Because morals are taught by parents.
People who have already developed their own ideas, formed opinions,
and activated prejudices; they have lived by these views for quite
sometime. Since these beliefs they have formed work well for them,
they assume they will work for their kids as well. With this
assumption they set out to teach them about good and bad character and
right or wrong. Are these young teens truly given only guidlines for

Will you form a moral guidance?

1

developing good character and for forming their own ideas? Or are
they _told_ what good character should consist of and receive preplanned ideas to believe in? It is unfortunate but the latter is
often true. Guidelines are replaced by rules and the understanding of
morals is lost only to prejudices. I feel that the development of
morals is a personal judgement. I am not against some guidance and
influence, it not only earns parent's respect for helping their
confused teens out, but it also gives them a feeling of being needed.
But when a stubborn force is criticizing another view, which could be
a prospect for a young mind to support. I think parents are disguising
their prejudices as morals and that is wrong.

You might address those questions in your next draft.

   Parents would like to see their kids be the very best they can,
yet those who overguide do not give them any opportunities. Parents,
the people who ~~are supposed~~ are most influencial, the most respected,
and have the most wisdom are pushing their beliefs on their young and
will not allow them to adhere to others. A narrow mind is something I
do not respect or consider wise. I think it is often forgotten that
young people have minds of their own. What a shame—two people bring
another precious life into this world, yet deprive it of the one thing
that makes it so unique, individualistic and intelligent.

   Kids who are victimized by overguidance are only half developed.
A major ingredient of the individual is missing—self understanding.
To find self understanding a young mind must be able to form ideas and
make it's own decisions. Advice does help, but it should not be so
strong as to make the final decision. It should only shine a spot
light on the feelings deep inside you that have more influence thany

2

any other outside force and leave the individual to bring them to the surface. It is freedom of the mind to explore the inner soul and find the fire inside that you want to believe in something. It is also that self understanding that allows individuals to realize they are often confused about occurances in their life and environment. This confusion is only a call for input—meaning to hear and consider other views. These will once again throw light on those emotions that mumble, "This is what I need." These outside views will help in the search of finding true ~~emotions~~ feelings. Then, the outcome will be full understanding and maybe a changed belief or a stronger unchanged one. Deprivation of this breeds ignorance—not only of the individual but also of the environment. I feel the ignorance is the mother of prejudices.

Over guidance is a terrible problem. It not only steels from the young but it also never relieves parents of their ignorance. Parents feed prejudices more support by their ignorance and fear. They do not understand, nor do they want to, the views of others only because they are different. They have fear because they may gain interests in different beliefs. So as a defense they fore their beliefs and criticize others. Perhaps parents could over come their fears and prejudices through the fresh young minds of their kids. To set the mind free of forced preplanned beliefs, parents will receive more respect and love than they could ever imagine.

Anne - You seem to have written & discovered in your final paragraph the specific points you want to address. You might flip-flop the draft and begin with your conclusion to see if you can further define your purpose & audience. Can you explain the points made at the end and develop them with specifics? How can you use earlier information to support ideas given here?

An Inquiry into Detached Commentary

Warnock's comments on "Overguiding Teenage Children" are brief and unelaborated. She makes two succinct comments in the margins, the first an open question that occurs in the middle of page 1: "Will you focus on moral guidance"; the second a piece of advice that is presented at the top of page 2: "You might address these questions in your next draft." Although the comments are text-specific, referring to the words from the student's text, they offer only modest direction. Her endnote (presented here as Warnock typed it up in a note to us) is short and general:

> You seem to have written and discovered in your final paragraph the specific points you want to address. You might flip-flop the draft and begin with your conclusion to see if you can further define your purpose and audience. Can you explain the points you make at the end and develop them with examples? How can you use earlier information to support the ideas given in the conclusion?

In the immediate company of the responses presented by Richard Larson, Chris Anson, and Patricia Stock, Warnock's comments to "Overguiding Teenage Children" seem lean and restrained. Looked at one way, the comments cut right to the issues at stake, offer some direction, and resist directing the student's choices about revision. They allow Anne to determine for herself how well the writing is working and what she might take up in the way of revision. Looked at another way, the comments are general and not text-specific. They indicate what the student might look to do in her revision, but only briefly and generally. In effect, they say: You might begin with the conclusion, define your purpose and audience, explain your main points, and develop them with examples. They do not speak of the issues they raise specifically in terms of this particular paper, but leave it up to the student to make sense of them on her own. From this perspective, the comments offer little in the way of direction and place a great deal of responsibility in the hands of the student.

Warnock's comments on this rough draft appear all the more general when her endnote is placed next to Larson's and Stock's end comments. All three responders speak to Anne's need to define and develop her ideas more fully. But notice how Larson and Stock specify their comments and elaborate on them:

> What you might work toward, in your next draft, I think, are two things: some examples of situations in which you think parents "overguided" children (tried to get their children to see things entirely the parents' way?), and some examples along with a clearer explanation of how you think parents might guide more gently, more appropriately, more wisely. Maybe you've had the experience of being "overguided." If so, tell what happened; what did your parents do, and how did you react? If you've not had the experience of being "overguided," you probably know some young people who have had it; why not write about their experiences? Try to help the reader understand where the line falls between appropriate guidance and "overguidance," and then say what you think parents might in fact try to do toward their children. (Larson)

> I am really interested in learning more about what you mean by the moral decisions you write about. You suggest what you might mean when you allude to prejudice. I read into your essay your worry that parents' prejudices may be passed on to their children in the guise of moral guidance. I am uncertain if I would always correlate the instilling of prejudice with overguiding. I don't think you want to do that either. I think you are saying that overguiding can be a vehicle for the passing on of prejudice. But, I am really not certain. I think I need to know more concretely what you see as the dangers to young people of overguiding parents. Maybe some specific examples, like the one I offered you concerning Andrew and me, might help me understand better just what you mean. (Stock)

Whereas Larson and Stock make their responses to Anne detailed and text-specific, Warnock chooses to leave her comments brief and general.[2]

Warnock's responses to Writing 4 are the most sparse and general comments she makes across the sampling. But they are representative of a number of her responses. Her comments on Writings 5 and 6 (and, to a lesser extent, Writing 10) get somewhat more specific, yet they too do not elaborate or define her points. On Writing 5, Warnock addresses five issues in seven comments:

> This is such a rich draft that it's difficult to take in one swallow. You hook me with your opening, but what's your specific focus? Is it fishing at Lake Ivenho or is it one day of fishing there? Can you break this up into paragraphs to give your readers time to digest what all you say? As you do, consider what points exactly you're trying to convey. Do these points fall into paragraphs?

Her initial comment about the disjointed focus of the essay is briefly followed with a specific comment ("Is it fishing at Lake Ivenho or is it one day of fishing there?"), and the issue of paragraphing is augmented by one of her four marginal comments ("Check the newspaper for paragraph lengths and how information is divided up for readers"). Nevertheless, the commentary remains general and unelaborated.

Other readers, by comparison, get more specific and detailed in their responses. Anne Gere and Jane Peterson, for instance, make a comparable number of comments on this rough draft, but they deal more explicitly with the student's text than Warnock. After telling Steve that the accounts of his own fishing experiences "raise some problems," Gere goes on to explain the problems in precise terms that refer to specific statements he has made :

> When you begin to recount specific experiences they tend to take over. Instead of explaining fishing you move into a narrative of one event. This is particularly true beginning in the middle of page 2 with the section that begins "After fishing the lilly pads that morning . . ." This account leads into the narrative that closes the paper. By concentrating on this event you abandon your role as expert explaining bass fishing.

Then she offers specific advice for revision:

> As you revise this draft try to concentrate on explaining bass fishing rather than telling the story of one fishing trip. You can certainly draw on your experiences to illustrate points you make, but try to prevent the narrative from taking over.

Peterson points out the problem with the lack of focus and presents direct advice and specific examples about how the writing might be revised:

> [Your essay] tells more about you than about bass fishing or Orlando lakes. To make this into a feature article for the campus newspaper, you need to start over. I suggest focusing on the lakes—you can give background info on the lakes (how they were formed, general characteristics, etc.) and then select 3-5 specific lakes to discuss in detail (tell the size and location of each and the good and bad points of each from a bass fisher's point of view).

By getting more specific and presenting their judgments about the writing, Gere's and Peterson's comments assume greater control over the writing and offer the student more direction than Warnock's. In part, the direction they provide and the control they assume come from their use of authoritative modes. Gere frames four of her comments as negative evaluations and advice. Peterson presents one negative evaluation, one command, and three pieces of advice. But the direction comes, in addition, from the specificity of their comments. Both responders set out a possible path for revision and explain in specific terms what might be done. Although Warnock identifies the issues at stake for revision, she leaves it up to Steve to figure out what exactly his main idea is and what points he wants to convey.[3] Her responses to Writing 6 also defer to the student's own decisions about the writing:

> You're giving yourself good advice to follow in the last paragraph. The descriptions are brief and limited to only the good aspects of the seasons. What exactly about the seasons makes you want to return to Syracuse? Your last sentence suggests that you're not yet satisfied with what you've done because you haven't let your reader experience the seasons. Follow your advice and let your reader be there.

By not getting more specific in these responses, Warnock refrains from assuming much control over the students' texts and yields to their authority as writers. At the same time, she must settle for responses that offer them only a general direction for their continuing work with the essay.

If the brief, general responses she makes on Writings 4, 5, and 6 were representative of her responses, Warnock's responding style could justifiably be called detached. But they are the most sparse and general responses she makes in the study. Three other sets of responses—on Writings 1, 10, and 13—are fairly evenly mixed with general and specific comments. And three other sets of comments—on Writings 2, 9 and 11—have the kind of specificity that is characteristic of interactive response.

Warnock's response to Writing 1 is relatively short and offers little in the way of specific direction, yet her comments (all of which appear in the endnote) clearly and specifically point to areas for further investigation:

> You have selected a topic that clearly matters to you. What more do you want to know about the use of seat belts? What more do you know about your friends' accident? Have you talked to them recently or to the police? What other information do you have for and against the use of seat belts? Who exactly are your readers? Can they change the law? What arguments might convince them?

It is one of her most focused and precisely worded responses. It is also fairly text-specific. But even here Warnock does not go into great detail. She brings up the idea of adding information about the seat belt law and asks Louise to examine her friends' experience more closely. But she goes no farther than that. She does not, for example, suggest what kind of information Louise might look for on seat belts or why she might consider her friends' accident, and she offers no suggestions about who the audience might be or what arguments a given group of readers may or may not find convincing. The comments are somewhat specific, but they offer little in the way of direction.

Her responses to Writing 2 are more specific, informative, and helpful, alternating general comments and sharp, text-specific comments. (See Chapter 2 for the full set of responses.) Some of the direction she provides here is created by the sheer number of comments—19 altogether. But most of it is achieved through the specificity of many of the comments, all but one of which are presented in the margins, where they may more readily assume some specificity:

> What specific points does LeMoult make that you can argue for or against?
>
> What's your main point here? If it's that you disagree, put that idea up front and explain.
>
> How do these ideas relate to your purpose as stated in the last sentence of prgh 1?
>
> You summarize the article here, but how does what you say relate to your view stated in the last sentence of paragraph 11?
>
> Is this your only and most important argument?
>
> You've given us a summary of the article. Why?
>
> Here you're giving your views.

Each of these comments is tied directly to the student's own words and clearly identifies an issue for the student to consider. Warnock frames most of these comments as open questions and so does not assert significant control over the writer. Nevertheless, the comments offer

Steve some direction and assume a modest degree of control.

Warnock's most elaborate and specific responses—and, not coincidentally, the responses in which she offers the most direction—occur on Writings 9 and 11. Like the interactive responses of Gere, and in many respects like all interactive commentary, Warnock's responses to these essays begin to establish a mutual give-and-take relationship between teacher and student—the teacher pointing to issues and laying out possible options, the student left to assume responsibility over revision. Most of her comments in her endnote to Writing 9 are sharp open questions:

> You have been direct in presenting your understanding of your father and how Goodman Brown helps you see him. Would you prefer writing this paper about your father without bringing in the Brown connection, or would you prefer writing about good and evil in the story only? Here you give details about your father's change and suggest that his mother's death and his guilt and sins were the causes, but you say that you still cannot understand. Do you undertand that change? How exactly does reading the story help you understand how your father came to his realization. Is that your overall purpose here or is it to explore the similarities between your father and Brown? Is your father's story also an initiation story? Try reading your paper aloud to figure out what you want to do next.

Although they obviously refrain from telling or even advising the student about what to do next, these questions are rooted in the words of the student's text and identify particular issues for revision. They also provide greater detail that might help the student initiate her revision.

Warnock's comments on Writing 11, an essay about what it takes to be a successful waitress, are more specific and refer more consistently to the student's text than any of her other responses. Both her marginal comments and endnote offer clear direction but with the openness that is characteristic of interactive response:

1. Who is your audience? Experienced waitresses and waiters?

2. How can this happen? Do restaurants allow practice time?

3. I've never thought about how aggressive and in control the waitress has to be.

4. The first sentence in this paragraph (#3) confuses me, although I get your point later.

5. Does "good money" also depend on the restaurant, the time of day, and other matters?

6. Do neatness, first impressions, and practice only matter as ways to get good tips?

7. You might try flip-flopping this prgh and begin here.

Donna—

> I never realized before how much waitresses can control the situation and determine the amount of tips. Is the overall purpose here to explain how to be a good waitress or to help other waitresses or would-be waitresses learn how to get more money from customers? Your last paragraph suggests that you want to focus directly on ways to control the situation so that your readers—waitresses—get more money. Try another draft with your purpose and audience in mind throughout.

Even as these comments indicate what the student might work on, thereby exerting some control over the text, they also engage the student in looking back on the text and guide her revision. They provide the kind of detail and direction that initiate interactive response, in which the teacher opens a path for possible revision and then allows the student to make the journey on her own.

Modes

If Warnock's way of expressing her comments in general terms makes her style noncontrolling, at times to the point of almost being detached, they are made all the less controlling by her choice of modes.[4] Almost half of all her comments—the most in the study—are cast in the form of questions that typically allow students a good deal of room to decide whether and how they address the issue at stake.[5] Only one out of four of her comments is cast in authoritative modes—imperatives, advice, or criticism. (She makes no corrective comments.) In fact, only four of her 109 comments across the sampling are cast in the form of critical evaluations (straight or qualified) and all four address sentence readability. She never criticizes a student writer's ideas, focus, or organization.

Warnock makes regular use of imperatives and advice (21% of her comments), but they do not exert the kind of control that these comments conventionally exert over student writing. Although most of her commands occur on final drafts, presumably after the student has had an opportunity to work on his own, when she feels more willing to provide direction, her advice is spread evenly across rough drafts and final drafts. Instead of calling for specific changes in the text, these prompts usually make broad calls for revision.[6] They are usually cast in general terms, and consequently do not place the demands on students that such comments often do. In fact, her advice and commands are the most consistently general of all her responses, perhaps because she feels uncomfortable controlling students' choices. Seven of these prompts are generic calls for the student to reread his text and make appropriate revisions, one of Warnock's favorite strategies:

> Read aloud. (Writing 9)
>
> Read aloud and try several versions. (Writing 13)
>
> Try reading your paper aloud to figure out what you want to do next. (Writing 9)[7]

Eleven others are only slightly more defined, among them:

> Consider what points you are trying to convey. (Writing 5)
>
> Try another draft with your purpose and audience in mind throughout. (Writing 11)
>
> You might flip-flop the draft and begin with your conclusion to see if you can further define your purpose and audience. (Writing 4)
>
> [Why do you disagree?] If it's that you disagree, put that idea up front and explain. (Writing 2)
>
> [You've given us a summary of the article. Why?] You can give us your view. (Writing 2)

It makes little difference whether these comments are cast in the form of a command or in the form of advice because they are so general that they offer only broad directions to—and assume only a vague control over—the student writer. By comparison, consider the prompts that Larson, a directive responder, and Anson, a moderately directive responder, write on the same essay:

> [T]ake another look at LeMoult, and at the idea of "harm." Check to see *why* he puts forward his proposal. Check to see whether he does say some of the things you attribute to him on page 1 here. (See my queries.) Then reconsider the notion of harm. . . . Then decide how to answer LeMoult's arguments, and supporting arguments. Then try your next draft. [Larson]
>
> Another thing I'd do here is to take each of your counterarguments and see if there's any

exception to them, and try to take them and apply them to similar situations. Let me be specific here. If, on page two, one of your main points is this issue of danger to one's health. What if you tried listing as many things you can think of that are legal that are also dangerous, like cigarettes, firearms, in a sense, certain kinds of recreational—all-terrain vehicles, over-the-counter drugs, and so on. [Anson]

Only three of Warnock's prompts even begin to approach such specificity:

> Check the newspaper for paragraph lengths and how information is divided up for readers. (Writing 5)
> You might try flip-flopping this paragraph and begin here. (Writing 11)
> You can put this in the opening paragraph to let your reader know. (Writing 11)

But here, and in other responses across the sampling, she never infuses or follows her advice or imperatives with more specific commentary.

Warnock makes her most specific comments when she frames them in the form of questions. Open heuristic questions and open problem-posing questions are the staple of her commentary, accounting for 34% of her responses, easily the highest in the study. Many of these open questions are cast in general terms and are presented without elaboration:

> Who exactly are your readers? What arguments might convince them? (Writing 1)
> What's your main point here? (Writing 2)
> How can you explain and support views so they will be more convincing to readers of the publication? (Writing 2)
> What's your specific focus? (Writing 5)

The majority of her open questions, however, are specific:

> What more do you know about your friends' accident? Have you talked to them recently or to the police? (Writing 1)
> What specific points does LeMoult make that you can argue for or against? (Writing 2)
> Does Hawthorne explain the causes of Goodman Brown's change? Do you understand that change? How exactly does reading the story help you understand how your father came to his realization? (Writing 9)
> Is the overall purpose here to explain how to be a good waitress or to help other waitresses or would-be waitresses learn how to get more money from customers? (Writing 11)
> Does "good money" also depend on the restaurant, the time of day, and other matters? (Writing 11)

Notably, most of these questions appear on, and contribute to, her most interactive responses—to Writings 1, 2, 9, and 11. The questions offer the kind of help and moderate direction that is characteristic of interactive response. Paradoxically, the more specific and elaborate a response, the more likely it will be seen in terms of the help it offers the student and the less it will be seen in terms of the control it exerts over the writer's choices.

When Warnock concentrates on giving readings of the text or offering advice and imperatives, her responses tend to get general, provide little direction and help, and sometimes verge on being detached. But when she concentrates on asking questions, as she does in her responses to Writing 11 and Writing 9, they tend to get sharper and more text-specific. In fact, her most specific sets of responses—her responses to Writings 1, 2, 9, and 11—have at least seven questions apiece, many or most of which are precise and text-specific. It is specific open questions like these that, more than any other responses, make several sets of Warnock's comments mildly interactive.

Focus

In keeping with her nondirective style, Warnock makes relatively few comments. None of her endnotes has more than 10 comments; four have fewer than five. In most sets of her responses, Warnock also takes up only a few issues. Only three sets of her comments deal with four or more concerns. She rarely deals with matters of wording or correctness, issues of writing that of course invite greater teacher control, although she does make a number of comments about local structure on final drafts. In fact, almost all of the comments she does make on local concerns occur on final drafts.[8]

Across her responses to the sampling, Warnock deals mostly with ideas, development, and global structure. Together, these global concerns make up 65% of her responses. She devotes an uncommonly high percentage of her comments to global structure—23%, the highest among the group of readers:

> You summarize the article here, but how does what you say relate to your view stated in the last sentence of paragraph 1? (Writing 2)
>
> How does LeMoult set up reader expectations in the essay and how can you establish your reader's expectations? (Writing 2)
>
> Will you focus on moral guidance? (Writing 4)
>
> You might flip-flop the draft and begin with your conclusion to see if you can further define your purpose and audience. (Writing 4)
>
> You hook me with your opening, but what's your specific focus? (Writing 9)
>
> I notice on page 3 that you seem to shift from telling us a chronological account of events to explaining the three phases of treatment. (Writing 10)
>
> Your last paragraph suggests that you want to focus directly on ways to control the situation so that your readers—waitresses—get more money. (Writing 11)

As these comments on global structure suggest, Warnock also routinely casts many of her responses within the larger context of audience and purpose. She makes at least one comment about audience and purpose on every paper to which she responds, and often more. All but one set of her responses make explicit reference to the reader; four sets of responses have four or more comments that refer explicitly to readers. She does not use these comments to foist on students her view of how the writing should proceed; she uses them simply to raise the rhetorical purpose of the writing as a central concern that the writers might attend to in their revisions. She presents few of her comments, however, in the context of the student's writing processes, the topic choice, or the assignment—other signs of her hands-off style.

Overview of Teacher Control

Warnock's style is the least controlling among the 12 readers—in part because she does not make many comments and in part because she frames so many of the comments she does write only in general terms. Her mildly interactive, moderately detached style of response shows an unwillingness to influence the student writer's choices. Warnock does not assert her own agenda on students. Instead, she prefers to encourage them to come up with their own assessments of their work and their own revisions. For example, in her endnote on Writing 5, Warnock asks, "What's your specific focus. Is it fishing at Lake Ivenho or is it one day of fishing there?" She then leaves it up to the student to decide. By contrast, most of the other readers, with an eye to the assignment, guide or direct Steve to emphasize his advice about how to fish the Orlando lakes. In Writing 9, she puts her concern about the paper's focus squarely on the shoulders of the student:

> How exactly does reading the story help you understand how your father came to his realization? Is that your overall purpose here or is it to explore the similarities between your father and Brown? Is your father's story also an initiation story? Try reading your paper aloud to figure out what you want to do next.

Her response to Writing 11 similarly resists offering much in the way of direction. Instead it places the responsibility fully on the student:

> Is the overall purpose here to explain how to be a good waitress or to help other waitresses or would-be waitresses learn how to get more money from customers? . . . Try another draft with your purpose and audience in mind throughout.

Even when Warnock offers some sense of direction in her responses, she offers little in the way of actual suggestions for revising. In her response to Writing 4, she says, "You seem to have written and discovered in your final paragraph the specific points you want to address." But, having said this, she does little to direct the writer to reorganize and develop the writing around these specific points, which also go unidentified, leaving the student to find her own way. On Writing 10, after praising the student for the detailed account of his treatment for leukemia, she asks him to explain how the disease has affected him, apparently so that the paper might better fit the assignment. Nevertheless, by the end of her response she characteristically opens it up again: "If you could write about leukemia in any way, how would you and who would your intended readers be?" In a similar way, she offers some subtle direction in her comments to Writings 1 and 6, only to return to an open-ended style that defers the real decision making to the student.

Warnock's inclination to provide little direction to students sets her apart from other nondirective responders and makes her responses at times seem detached. Gere, Stock, and Elbow routinely resist taking control over student writing, yet they provide enough specificity and direction to actively engage the student in revision. Gere tempers her control by asking open questions and presenting only a limited number of follow-up responses. By providing specific suggestions yet leaving the particular tasks of revision to the student, Gere, like all interactive responders, achieves a productive tension between providing direction and assuming control. Stock moderates her control by eschewing criticism and teaching the student how to reenvision his writing on his own. But she provides the direction that is needed to turn this openness into interactive response by giving the student a lot of information to consider before he revises. She offers reader responses, brief lessons, detailed models, and a variety of possible options for the student to use in revision, but she does not push any particular way of revising. In a similar way, Elbow modifies his control by concentrating on reader responses and offering little in the way of explicit advice and direction. Yet he offers the kind of direction that initiates interactive response by inserting a good measure of evaluation into his reader responses and encouraging (and subtly directing) the writer to find a way to address his concerns as a reader.

By comparison, Warnock does not provide much in the way of specific readings or detailed calls for revision. She avoids taking control over student writing not only by writing very few comments in authoritative modes and by casting half of her comments in the form of questions, but also by expressing many of her comments in rather general terms and leaving most of her key responses unelaborated. Although several sets of her responses are sufficiently detailed to offer the student some direction, several others may remain so general that they do not engage the writing sufficiently to coax the student toward revision. Ultimately, her response style wavers between mildly interactive and somewhat detached.

* * *

All responses, in some ways, to some degree, evaluate the writing and direct the student toward revision. The question, as we have often noted, is the extent to which different readers choose to do each and how they do so. As a group, authoritative responders explicitly make judgments about student writing and point to particular ways of improving that writing. Interactive responders typically make judgments about the writing indirectly, and they do not so much *direct* student revision as they *suggest* or *encourage* it, usually subtly and moderately. If White's response style suggests the strengths of authoritative response and the limits of authoritarian response, Warnock's style suggests the strengths of interactive response and the limits of detached response. Their responding styles mark the extremes for this group of readers, from the most controlling to the least controlling.

5 | In Search of Consensus: Seven Principles for Responding

We focused in Chapter 4 on the many differences in the responding styles of the 12 readers in our study. We now turn our attention to the similarities in their responses. Depending on one's perspective, it would no doubt be possible to find many similarities in these readers' responding styles. Our discussion below identifies seven similarities. Three of them characterize how the readers present individual comments:

1. These readers write well-developed and text-specific comments.
2. They focus their comments on global, not local, concerns.
3. They frame most of their comments in nonauthoritative modes of commentary.

Four characterize their responses as a whole:

4. Their responses are carefully thought out and purposeful.
5. They are designed to help students approach writing as a process.
6. They are mindful of the rhetorical situation for the writing.
7. They are adapted to the student writer behind the text.

CHARACTERISTICS OF INDIVIDUAL COMMENTS

Length and Specificity

A glance at the responses we presented in Chapter 2 should make it obvious that the readers in this study make lengthy comments on student essays. In our overall sampling, they average 22 comments and over 400 words per essay, including marginal and end comments.[1] As we observed in Chapter 2, six of our teachers (Chris Anson, Peter Elbow, Ben McClelland, Frank O'Hare, Donald Stewart, and Patricia Stock) use no, or very few, marginal comments. In limiting themselves to end comments, these readers enact a conversational model in which the student writes full statements to them and they write full statements back to the student. The readers who make marginal comments on the student papers are careful to fashion them in sentences or long phrases and clauses that create a context in which the student can interpret their responses and get the sense of someone talking to them. In fact, a sizable number (one-fourth of the marginal comments that these teachers make) consist of more than one statement, with one comment setting up or following through on another. Three sequences of comments written to Nancy on "What If Drugs Were Legal?" illustrate what we mean:

Not sure how you are interpreting LeMoult here. Does he blame "society"? Does he say that "society" is corrupt? (Larson)

You're beginning to respond to LeMoult's argument. What if you saved evaluative comments until later? How would this choice affect your argument? (Hull)

This is in his 4th paragraph. What's he doing in the first 3 paragraphs? (Peterson)

Richard Larson begins his comment by pointing out something that is wrong with the essay, but he does not end the conversation there; he goes on to guide Nancy—with a shift to the problem-posing mode—to specific questions with which he wants her to wrestle. Glynda Hull begins with a description of what Nancy is doing at this particular point. She moves from this description to advise Nancy to consider putting off her negative reactions to LeMoult for a while, and then continues the conversation in another vein by asking her to consider (in an open problem-posing comment) how such a strategy would affect her argument. Jane Peterson also begins with a description and then moves to a question that asks Nancy to consider information she has left out of her discussion.

In addition to being lengthy and full, the comments written by these teachers tend to be text-specific. Sommers (1982) labels as "rubber-stamped" a class of comments that give students very little insight into how to revise their texts. Such comments as "awkward," "elaborate," "be specific," "not clear," and "thesis sentence needed" could be placed on a rubber stamp and used on hundreds or thousands of student essays. The teachers in this study resist the temptation to deal in such generic comments, choosing instead to fashion responses that refer to specific language in the student's text. The marginal responses Hull makes on the second page of "Street Gangs: One Point of View" illustrate what we mean by "precisely crafted text-specific" comments.

Being a member had its ups and downs. The worst part was being
paranoid about something happening to you. <u>It wasn't a frightening
feeling, but more like a burden.</u> You knew something, somehow,
somewhere would eventually happen, either to you or the gang. Many
times I paid the price for being part of the Cripps with black eyes or
broken noses. I even had my windshield busted once. ✳

This is a great way to describe the paranoid feeling.

The good side was the family type atmosphere between us, we were
more than friends, almost like cousins or even brothers. That sense
of support that I got from being part of that gang was unmeasurable.
Walking down the halls of school and having everyone know that your in
this gang was great, almost like an "ego-trip". For it did make some
of the guys cocky. This overall feeling is hard to explain, it deals
a lot with acceptance and friendship. I guess these two things were
what kept me in the gang so long. I liked the feeling of being part
of something that (where I come from) is almost like a status symbol.
<u>My parents called this insecurity, this may be, but more importantly
it gave me a purpose and an identity.</u>

ⓐ This is interesting too. ⓑ I don't think most people recognize the family-like attraction of being in a gang

I admire the way you're able to acknowledge your parents view but go on to give your own.

During the time I spent in the gang, we were more a "party" gang.
We got into trouble and fights, but not with other gangs. Gangs at
the time were more friendly and were only gangs by name. I mean
everyone knew each other and it was only the name of the gang and
their symbols that separated us.

Our symbols were one, a blue and red hankerchief worn around the
right ankle, a diamond stud earring in the left ear and most important
the thin white cane each member had. This was in relation with our
name: "THE CRIPPS". *ⓐ This is interesting — ⓑ is it common for gangs to choose names and symbols that could be associated with disability or weakness?*

Hull's comments are crafted to show that she is engaged with Rusty's essay. They pick up the concerns in, and use the language of, Rusty's text. For example, instead of simply saying "Good description," Hull says, "This is a great way to describe the paranoid feeling." To illustrate more clearly what we mean in calling these comments text-specific, we offer the same page from Rusty's essay with comments from a traditional responder outside of this study:[2]

[handwritten annotations: "of a gang", "cliché.", "avoid "you"", "ask S", "comma splices", "than what?", "awk", and various corrections]

Being a member, had its ups and downs. The worst part was being paranoid about something happening to you. It wasn't a frightening feeling, but more like a burden. You knew something, somehow, somewhere would eventually happen, either to you or the gang. Many times I paid the price for being part of the Cripps with black eyes or broken noses. I even had my windshield busted once.

The good side was the family-type atmosphere between us, we were more than friends, almost like cousins or even brothers. That sense of support that I got from being part of that gang was unmeasurable. Walking down the halls of school and having everyone know that your in this gang was great, almost like an "ego-trip". For it did make some of the guys cocky. This overall feeling is hard to explain, it deals a lot with acceptance and friendship. I guess these two things were what kept me in the gang so long. I liked the feeling of being part of something that (where I come from) is almost like a status symbol. My parents called this insecurity, this may be, but more importantly it gave me a purpose and an identity.

During the time I spent in the gang, we were more a "party" gang. We got into trouble and fights, but not with other gangs. Gangs at the time were more friendly and were only gangs by name. I mean everyone knew each other and it was only the names of the gangs and their symbols that separated us.

Our symbols were one a blue and red hankerchief worn around the right ankle, a diamond stud earring in the left ear, and most important, the thin white cane each member had. This was in relation with our name: "THE CRIPPS".

This responder offers several comments that Sommers would label as generic, or rubber-stamped: "cliche," "avoid 'you,'" "awk S," "comma splices," "awk." Although the teachers in our study do occasionally write generic comments, the vast majority of their comments are text-specific. Three out of four of their marginal comments use the language of the student's text to key the student in to what the comment is saying.

Focuses

The 12 readers clearly emphasize global, conceptual matters of writing over sentence-level concerns, as Table 5.1 shows. They also devote a consistently high percentage of their comments to matters that go beyond the immediate text, that is, to the audience and purpose of the writing, the assignment, the writer's composing processes, and the student behind the text. The following examples of these different types of comments are taken from responses the 12 readers made on Essay 10, "Leukemia," in which the student, Kevin, writes about his ongoing fight against the disease.[3] (The text of this essay appears on pp. 358-361.)

Global Focuses

You have done a very good job of explaining your experience of being a leukemia patient. (ideas)

You will need to compress this paper into a paragraph or two, so you can attend to the job of the assignment. (global structure)

You might explain a bit more fully what this program is. (development)

Local Focuses

Needs more exact referent. (wording)

Consider reconstructing sentence. Can you see how? (local structure)

Check spelling. (correctness)

Extra-textual Focuses

I suspect most readers will fully empathize with the physical suffering you experience and wish you a return to good health. (audience)

Now that you have written an account of your experience, try to address the other part of the assignment by thinking about how this experience has changed you. (assignment)

Excellent work, Kevin. You really have been through an ordeal. (whole essay; student's experience)

Table 5.1. The 12 Readers' Focuses of Commentary.

	Global Matters (%)	Local Matters (%)	Extra-Textual (%)
Anson	47	16	37
Elbow	57	11	32
Gere	72	14	14
Hull	47	21	32
Larson	53	32	15
McClelland	68	2	30
O'Hare	68	7	25
Peterson	64	23	13
Stewart	50	36	14
Stock	45	25	30
Warnock	65	14	21
White	54	37	9
AVERAGE	55	21	24

Given the prevailing trends in contemporary composition studies, we expected marking and commenting on errors to be a low priority for these teachers—and that is exactly what we found. Table 5.2 shows the percentage of errors these teachers marked in each of the 10 essays used as the data base for Chapter 4.[4] As we have already noted, Stewart marks nearly all grammatical and mechanical errors on students' texts. Even with Stewart's data included, errors were marked less than 10% of the time on rough drafts and less than 14% of the time on final drafts. Table 5.2 reveals another important trend: The teachers are less concerned with error at the early stages of writing than they are at the final stages.

Table 5.2. Analysis of Errors Marked by the 12 Readers.

	Percentage of Errors Marked	Percentage of Errors Marked (Without Stewart)	Number of Readers Marking Errors
ROUGH DRAFTS			
Essay 1	11	2	2 of 10*
Essay 2	10	3	3 of 10
Essay 4	9	5	4 of 11
Essay 5	3	1	2 of 9
Essay 12	15	8	3 of 9
FINAL DRAFTS			
Essay 6	6	1	2 of 8
Essay 9	13	13	7 of 9
Essay 10	22	17	6 of 9
Essay 11	16	11	3 of 9
Essay 13	16	11	6 of 7
AVERAGE	13	11	6 of 7

*Each of these numbers is reduced by one when Stewart's data are removed.

This last observation warrants further discussion. These teachers are not unconcerned about matters of correctness, particularly when students are in the last stages of producing an essay. Their responses to Essay 10, "Leukemia," provide us with rather striking evidence of that concern. Even though most of our teachers are impressed by much of what the writer, Kevin, has to say, and even though he is writing about an extremely sensitive subject, the teachers do not back away from the issue of error. Nine of the 12 teachers mention editing problems to Kevin. In his notes to us, Anson comments on the choice he has to make concerning the editing problems in the essay:

> Since I've been pushing the students much harder lately to do some careful editing and proofreading, my response is all the more problematic because I feel a responsibility to remind Kevin that he has to work on the surface details of his writing—and that responsibility conflicts with my need to respond to Kevin as a human being trying to battle a serious illness.

In the end, Anson decides he must resist the temptation to act as if one can fully separate "what" one is saying from "how" it is said. Thus he broaches the issue of editing in his comment to Kevin:

A second way to improve on what you're doing here when you're in the final stages is to remember the value of proofing and careful editing. It's hard work, sometimes boring, certainly often frustrating when you're trying to focus on meaning, but it's also absolutely necessary. . . . And again, that's part of that agreement we've talked about; you want your reader to have the most . . . I can't say pleasurable here, because this is an essay that makes you knit your brow, you know, it's a concerning or disconcerting essay that makes you feel a lot of sympathy; but whatever effect you *do* want, you don't want it distorted by lots of little problems.

Anson speaks for the readers as a group, who, though they are very selective in addressing matters of error, nevertheless do not overlook the issue.

Modes

Although the readers in our study certainly differ in the amount of control they exercise over student texts, as a group they use significantly more nonauthoritative comments than authoritative modes of response. In authoritative commentary, the responder somehow directs the student about how the writing may (or even should) be improved, using corrective, negative evaluative, qualified negative evaluative, imperative, or advisory comments. The following comments illustrate the range of authoritative commentary:

"I disagree with LeMoult's ~~idea of~~ legalizing drugs to cut the cost of crime." [The teacher changes "idea of" to "arguments for"] (corrective)

Paragraph eight is confused and confusing. (evaluative)

I'm not sure I see your opinion in the paper. (qualified negative evaluation)

Focus this paragraph on this argument and develop your case. (imperative)

Maybe you can take four or five pieces of paper and just list each episode you tell about here and then write as much as you can about it in more detail. (advisory)

Such comments tend to invoke the teacher's control over the writing. In nonauthoritative commentary, the responder either praises the writing or uses interactive comments to engage the student in a give-and-take exchange about revision. The following comments offer several examples of nonauthoritative commentary:

This word seems just right. (praise)

How old were you? Were you in the 7th grade? 10th? (closed heuristic questions)

Do you really need this? (closed problem-posing question)

How do you distinguish between morals and prejudices? (open heuristic question)

How do you think readers will respond to this choice? (open problem-posing question)

First, you say that the law is a violation of a person's freedom. (interpretive)

The point of the essay is essentially to give the reader an experience through words. (explanatory)

What strikes me is that you seem to plunge immediately into a set speech. (reader reaction)

As I read your essay, Steve, I felt as if I were there with you, motoring along I-75, imagining Lake Ivenhoe in increasing detail as first one and then another fishing hole floated past my car window. (reader experience)

Although these comments enact different degrees of teacher control, they all leave a good deal of responsibility to the student writer to decide what, if any, changes should be made. Table 5.3 shows that almost all the readers (though to varying degrees) favor interactive comments over authoritative comments and make regular use of praise. The readers shape less than one third of

Table 5.3. The 12 Readers' Modes of Commentary.

	Authoritative (%)	Interactive (%)	Praise (%)
Elbow	17	65	18
Gere	23	54	23
Peterson	23	55	22
Warnock	23	66	11
Hull	27	57	16
McClelland	27	69	4
Stock	29	63	8
O'Hare	31	50	19
Anson	35	57	8
Stewart	37	55	8
Larson	40	56	4
White	50	34	16
AVERAGE	29	59	12

responsibility to the student writer to decide what, if any, changes should be made. Table 5.3 shows that almost all the readers (though to varying degrees) favor interactive comments over authoritative comments and make regular use of praise. The readers shape less than one third of their comments in authoritative modes. And even when they do use these modes, they frequently temper the control they exert by framing their comments in the moderate forms of authoritative response. In place of straight negative evaluations, they sometimes use qualified negative evaluations; in place of straight imperatives, they resort to softer advisory comments.

The 12 readers frame 71% of their comments as questions, praise, and nonevaluative statements. Twenty-five percent of their comments take the form of questions, half of them open, half of them closed. They are used for a range of purposes and assume varying degrees of control. Problem-posing questions, which present issues for the student to wrestle with, are used slightly more than heuristic questions, which generally guide the student to add information and push her ideas.

The group as a whole makes it a point to identify strengths in student writing. Ten of the readers write at least 8% of their comments in the form of praise; six of them make more than 16%. However, the readers do not settle the debate about the use of praise or blame. There is no evidence to suggest that these readers, as a group, would urge teachers to balance praise and criticism in their responses, or to use one more than the other.[5]

In one of the most interesting findings in the study, we were taken by the frequency with which these readers as a group write statements that are not evaluative. In fact, less than one-fourth of their responses are framed in some form of positive or negative evaluation. The readers present 34% of their responses in what we are calling "reflective statements." In these comments, the responder approaches the student text, not as an editor or a judge, but as a teacher, a reader, a coach, or a co-communicator. He writes comments that play back the student's text, offer explanations, present reader responses, or offer encouragement to the writer. Like questions, these comments are designed to engage the writer in a discussion about the writing, but leave most of the choices about revision in the hands of the student, as the following comments on "Leukemia" illustrate:

> The first paragraph is a clear report on your illness, diagnosis, and entry into the hospital. (interpretive)
>
> I especially liked [the statement] 'Will I die?' I don't remember what I thought—I was just stunned. (positive reader reaction, reader experience)
>
> A few years ago a good friend of mine got leukemia. He underwent what

[O]ne of the goals of this assignment is to think of ways to create a kind of nonfiction, personal piece of writing . . . that other readers find interesting, entertaining, moving, whatever. (explanatory)

[I am surprised that it is not more intense in places.] This is truly a life and death subject. (explanatory)

These reflective comments help make response a two-way street between reader and writer, teacher and student. They dramatize the responder's way of reading the text and point to issues for the writer to consider, thereby allowing her to make decisions about how to revise the writing so that it more fully realizes her intentions. They are by far the most abundant form of commentary used by the 12 readers.

CHARACTERISTICS OF WHOLE SETS OF RESPONSES

The characteristics we examine next might seem, on the surface, to be simple common sense. One might assume that most writing teachers' responses would exhibit these traits. We believe, however, that these strategies of response help make these teachers' responses distinctive.

Selective Commentary

The teachers in our study are clearly selective in the comments they place on student essays. From the scores of remarks they could make, they choose those that fit within the teaching purposes they bring to a given piece of writing. Their notes to us about "Leukemia" reflect this purposefulness:

I have purposely avoided any detailed analysis of the organizational and stylistic flaws— because one can overpower a student like this with too much correction. Let him deal with the problem of responding fully to the assignment first. (Stewart)

The "I can imagine" note at the bottom of the first page is there to help the student see that I am thinking about the content, not just surface problems. . . . [H]e had so many errors in that first paragraph that I felt I needed something on that page to reassure him that I was listening. (Peterson)

The essay is well-developed, and I want to make sure that Kevin is aware of how effectively he has organized it. I also plan to tell Kevin that because it is so well-written, I have acted as if he had submitted "Leukemia" to me for publication in the class anthology. (Stock)

The paper is, of course, filled with errors of all sorts. But there is no point in marking them, because the paper should *not* be edited; the writer missed the assignment almost entirely, and must rewrite an essay that fulfills the task. (White)

There is an obvious problem in neglecting the assignment, but I tend to think of the final draft as a time for celebration more than for saying what's wrong: too late to fix things. If at all possible at this point, I want the student to feel positively about what he has done. (Elbow)

My response will be necessarily conflicted because I want to tell Kevin how moved I was by the circumstances he describes in the paper and how interested I am in knowing more, but I also need to comment on the paper as an artifact in the course. Since I've been pushing the students much harder lately to do some careful editing and proofreading, my response is all the more problematic because I feel a responsibility to remind Kevin that he has to work on the surface details of his writing. . . . (Anson)

But I'd still wear kid gloves in making suggestions about revision and analysis. I'd have to find some way to let him know I understand what a tough experience he's going through.

remind Kevin that he has to work on the surface details of his writing. . . . (Anson)

But I'd still wear kid gloves in making suggestions about revision and analysis. I'd have to find some way to let him know I understand what a tough experience he's going through. And then I'd need to turn the focus back to writing. . . . This paper cries out for revision in stages. After I'd gotten him to add some analysis, I'd get him to shape the narrative. (Hull)

It may seem to be stacking the deck to examine the readers' treatment of "Leukemia." One would expect teachers to weigh their words carefully in responding to writing on such a sensitive topic. But a review of their notes about the other essays reveals in each case the same kind of purposeful approach to their responses. The readers target the areas in each paper that they want students to focus on. Rather than marking each issue as they come to it, the teachers select a limited number of concerns to draw to the attention of the writers.[6] The responses of Hull and Anne Gere to "Leukemia" are excellent examples of this type of purposeful responding (see pages 358 and 363).

Gere begins her response by asking Kevin if he can eliminate some of the preliminary detail, a matter of global structure. This becomes an *issue* when Gere treats it in the endnote after having already dealt with it in a marginal comment: "As you find more to say about what you have changed, try to find places where you can tighten your description of the experience itself." In her second marginal comment, Gere suggests that he specify the point at which the family realized he was really ill, but she does not go on to identify other areas that could benefit from such sharper specification. The remaining five marginal comments all ask Kevin for more details; thus, they concern a single issue—development. Gere returns to this issue with four different comments in her endnote, making development a strong theme in her response. She raises two other issues in the endnote: correctness and ideas. In three comments, she praises Kevin for careful spelling of medical terminology and asks for more care in this area; she also makes three comments praising the overall effectiveness of his ideas. Thus, Gere raises four issues: global structure (3 comments), development (9 comments), correctness (3 comments) and ideas (3 comments). Of the 22 comments in her response (marginal and final comments), 18 deal with these four targeted issues.

In the first section of her response, Hull deals with the essay as a whole, not focusing on any specific matter of content or form.[7] Rather, she tells Kevin about the experiences of a friend of hers who has leukemia. This shared information makes up the first issue of her response. She follows these comments with a call for Kevin to revise: "I'd like you to take one more pass at this paper." Her next comment moves to a specific area that he is to consider—the details that he may add to his description. In her remaining comments, Hull continues to ask for, and suggests ways of providing, greater detail. Thus, there are but two main issues in this response—the information about Hull's friend and the call for more detail. (In a sense, there is but one issue inasmuch as the information on Hull's friend is designed to help Kevin see how he might be able to add material.)

The limited number of issues that Hull and Gere address in responding to "Leukemia" is typical of their practices overall and, in general, of the practices of the 12 readers in our study. The readers average just over three issues for each response to an essay. Given the number of comments they make (on average over 22 per essay), this is a rather small number, and it is diminished even more when one takes into account that very often these issues dovetail; for example, the teacher may point to problems with spurious arguments (an issue regarding the writer's ideas) and then go on to suggest ways for the student to develop more substantial support for these claims (an issue of development).[8]

Writing 10
Kevin H.
Final Draft

LEUKEMIA

   In April of 1986 I was very sick. I always had a fever and some
sort of a infection. I was very lathargic and I was tired all the
time which led to having no energy most of the time. I was not very
active and I did not like to do things like I did before I was sick.
Later that month I had a very severe pain in my upper arm. The pain
was unbearable. I also could not move my neck if I did it would
hurt. My parents and I did not know what was causing this not even
the doctor. My parents finally took me to another doctor that one of
our friends suggested. He gave me a blood test and found out that my
liver was enlarged. He admitted me into the hospital and he had
another doctor look at me. The day after I was admitted the second
doctor diagnosed me as having Accute Lymphatic Leukemia. He explained
it to my parents and I very throughly. He also said that this type of
leukemia is the curable type of leukemia.

   The whole family was shocked and they did not what to do or say.
It finally came to them that I was really sick about a month later.
They did not say much to me when they found out. At first when the
doctor told me that I had leukemia I did not think much about it then.
I did not know what leukemia was or what it did to people. I thought
to myself, "Will I die?" I do not remember what I thought — I was
just stunned. Later I found out that leukemia is a disease of the
blood. The leukemia cells kills the white blood cells which weakens

1

> the immunitty system in the body. This is caused by the uncontroled increase in leukocytes. This is what causes the decreasing of white blood cells. The same day when the doctor diagnosed me as having leukemia he sent me to The Ohio State University Hospital, where I was to be admitted. When I first arrived there it seemed so big. The doctor at the hospital seemed really nice and friendly to me. There must have been at least three residents and interns that gave me a physical. It was not very pleasent to go through three physicals in one day.

How did your life change as a result of being in the hospital?

> A couple of days after I was admitted in the hospital my doctor wanted my family to have a blood test to see if their blood is the
> same type as my blood. Unfortonely they did not have the same type of blood. The reason why she (the doctor) wanted them to do this is because she wanted to check to see if I could have a bone marrow
> transplant. Because of my parents blood types and mine were not
> capable, I had to take chemotherapy treatments. I did not know what to expect from the treatments. All I knew was that people get very sick when they take it.

Before I could take any chemotherapy I had to sign a contract saying that I understood what I had read in the contract. I felt that I was making a big decision whether or not I wanted to take chemotherapy. My parents and a witness also had to sign the contract. The contract listed all of the types of chemo, the use of the chemo, and all of the side effects. When I read over the contract some of the treatments that they were going to do on me made me think twice before signing. The contract was for a protocal program which is

Did signing the contract change you in any way?

2

connected with the nation for statistics.

There were three phases of treatment that I had to go through in it. The first was called the induction therapy treatments. It consisted of various types of chemotherapy. I had to take Prednisone during the whole thirty six days of induction therapy. I was all swollen and puffy which was caused by taking prednisone. At night I had severe cramps in my legs, feet, arms and hands. I really hated these cramps. There was nothing the doctor could do about them. All I could do was to relax where ever the cramps were and wish that the cramp would go away. I thought that there ought to be someway to releive me from the cramps, but they say they don't. I had to take different types of chemo such as Vincristine, and Adriamyacin.

The second therapy treatment was called the consolidation therapy period. This period was really long and I had to take some more types of chemotherapy. It lasted for about one hundred and fifty days. I had to take some new types of chemo called Ara-9 and many more types. The other phase of treatment is called the maintence therapy treatment. This is the longest of the three other phases of treatment, but it is the last one I will have to go through. This therapy period lasts for three years. Now I am in the Maintence therapy treatment phase, but I have two and a half years to go. Most of the chemotherapy that I have taken was given by IV and some of the chemo was taken by mouth which were pills.

Because my veins are hard to find to get blood tests and chemo, the doctor suggested that I get a Hickman Catheter placed in my chest. The catheter runs into the main artery that is in my chest. All the

3

GERE

catheter is is a tube that was inserted in my shoulder and runs down ~~out~~ through my chest ~~which is just dangling out~~. When ever I needed to get a blood test, receive blood products or get chemotherapy they would just inject it through the tube instead of poking at my arms trying to find a vein. I was very glad that they had something like this because I do not know what I would do if I had to go through four years of needles poking in my arms all of the time.

Has the catheter had any effects beside making the treatment easier?

Now I am in the maintenance therapy phase. I do not have to stay in the hospital any more to receive treatments, but I do have to go to the clinic every week for a check up and to get new chemo. I am glad that I am out of the hospital. I have not yet gotten sick from the chemo in the maintence program yet, and I do not plan on it. I have to keep taking chemo for the next two years. I have a long road ahead of me.

What have you learned from this whole experience?

Kevin--

You have done a very good job of explaining your experience of being a
leukemia patient. The chronological organization and the details about your
treatment help me understand what you have gone through. Even though this is a
final draft, I think this is a paper worth revising because you clearly have
something important to say.

Now that you have a written account of your experience, try to address the
other part of the assignment by thinking about how this experience has changed
you. Has the leukemia experience changed your thinking in any way? Do you have
a different view of yourself or of others? How has the illness changed your
behavior? What do you do differently now? You have clearly learned a good deal

about medicines and treatment procedures. What else have you learned as a result
of your experience? As you find more to say about what you have changed, try to
find places where you can tighten your description of the experience itself.

Because I would like you to rewrite this paper, I have not indicated all
usage problems. Your careful spelling of medical terminology tells me that you
have an eye for words, so I have indicated other words you may wish to spell
correctly. The occasional omitted/wrong words suggest that you would do well to
read your next version aloud before you turn it in.

Kevin— a few years ago a good friend of mine got leukemia. He underwent what sounds like a similar treatment program to yours. I remember how difficult the chemotherapy was for him. I also remember that he emerged from the illness a somewhat different person. He told me, for example, that he gained a troublesome hyperawareness of time; if he had to do something that seemed like a waste of time, he got really irritated.

4

↓

I'd like you to take one more pass at this paper. Specifically, <u>I'd like you to think</u> about whether your illness has in some senses made you a different person, <u>to</u> <u>add</u> some paragraphs on how having leukemia has changed or affected you. Do you, like my friend Tim, feel differently about how you spend your time? Do you think you've learned something you didn't know before? In other words, I'm asking you now to <u>analyze</u> your experience as well as to describe it.

Process

Recently, several researchers have suggested that many so-called process teachers do little to engage students in their writing processes.[9] Such is not the case with this group of readers. They do much more than pay lip service to helping students return to their writing and actively engage in revision.

We have noted earlier that the teachers in this study mark a larger percentage of errors on final drafts than they mark on earlier drafts (See Table 5.2). This difference is indicative of an overall sensitivity to the stage of drafting that the readers in this study bring to their responding. The responses of Anson and McClelland to Essay 1 (an extremely brief and underdeveloped rough draft) and Essay 6 (a reasonably well-organized and well-developed final draft) are representative of how the readers as a group address rough drafts somewhat differently than final drafts.

> Maybe one thing you can do is to sit down and write out each of your points, the main points, for example, this point in the middle paragraph about the government, and then go back to some of the strategies we've used and try working your way more deeply into each point, try expanding on them a little. (Anson, Essay 1)

> What can you do to resolve my reader's dilemma? Two options come to mind: 1) If you are committed to this topic, become more knowledgeable about it so that you can write an informative essay on it. Begin by reading widely on it and by interviewing local public safety experts and automobile dealers. Moreover, if it's feasible, perhaps you could also interview via telephone state and federal legislators and appropriate individuals from a couple of the major automobile manufacturers. Finally, if you want to include your friends' accident as a case in point, examine the accident report and interview your friends and the reporting police officer so that you can supply precise information. (McClelland, Essay 1)

> The exaggeration problem is pretty quickly remedied. Bruce talked about how he was bothered by the image of bears and squirrels and rabbits all carrying on a kind of woodland conversation, and I think I agree, but you really didn't rethink that much. Along those lines, some specific expressions we questioned in the conference group were things like "enormous amounts of families" (by the way, if you're going to say that, it should be "numbers," and we've talked already about that mass vs. count noun business), and "humongous pile," and "stimulating your olfactories," and the cliché about Jack Frost. (Anson, Essay 6)

> [McClelland gives student a model descriptive passage that he has written, then says:] I compose this version of a neighborhood scene in early spring not for you to copy, but to give you an example of the "sense of place" that this assignment calls on a writer to depict for readers. To shape your text into a more evocative reading you need to emulate my approach of sensory and personal details, though not necessarily my style. (McClelland, Essay 6)

Both Anson and McClelland offer the writer of Essay 1 detailed and specific advice on how she can develop her topic, indicating not only the kind of changes that can be made in the text but also supplying the student with suggested activities or procedures by which to make her own improvements. Anson suggests that she write down some of the main points she wants to focus on and then use the strategies they have discussed in class to develop them. (His other responses would indicate that he is talking about such strategies as making lists, brainstorming, and freewriting.) McClelland charts a specific plan for Louise to gather information on her subject: She can begin reading on the topic and call automobile makers for information. Neither of these readers suggests that Louise concern herself with any sentence-level structuring matters or with any grammatical or mechanical corrections.

Their responses to the writer of Essay 6 indicate more satisfaction with the material in the essay. Anson and McClelland offer no plan for developing additional information; rather, they call on David to give attention to the language he is using to capture these seasons in Syracuse and Tallahassee. Anson refers to specific words in David's text that seem clichéd or inexact. McClelland composes a sample description for David and advises him to follow his (McClelland's) model in revising the language of the text.

As we noted above, Anson and McClelland's responses are broadly typical of the responses of the readers in our study. Table 5.4 quantifies differences in the readers' responses to three immature rough drafts (Essays 1, 2, and 4) and three fairly mature final drafts (Essays 6, 9, 13). The table suggests that these readers take the drafting stage into consideration when commenting on student writing.[10] Most striking to us are the percentages of comments devoted to local matters as one moves from rough drafts (13%) to final drafts (27%). Even though the rough drafts could be improved at the local level—and are very much in need of editing—the teachers devote very little attention to these matters. Instead they concentrate on global concerns. Sixty-three percent of their comments address ideas, development, and global structure. They give twice as much attention to these local matters on the final drafts. Not surprisingly, they also make noticeably more comments calling for development on the rough drafts (19%) than on the final drafts (4%).

Table 5.4. Analysis of Comments on Rough Drafts vs. Final Drafts.

	ROUGH DRAFTS (Essays 1, 2, 4) Number %	FINAL DRAFTS (Essays 6, 9, 13) Number %	DIFFERENTIAL %
FOCUS			
Global	63	45	-18
Local	13	27	+14
Extra-textual	24	28	+ 4
MODE			
Authoritative	32	25	- 7
Closed questions	14	12	- 2
Open questions	15	11	- 4
Reflective	31	34	+ 3
Praise	8	18	+10

The readers also use more authoritative comments on the rough drafts than on the final drafts—on average, two more on each set of responses. In particular, they use three times as many imperative and advisory comments on the rough drafts (152) as the final drafts (48). Alternately, they use twice as many praise comments on the final drafts (116 vs. 59). It seems, then, that the readers make a special effort on rough drafts to guide students back into their writing, back into their ideas and purposes and drafting, with the aim of leading them, in Sommers's (1982) words, "back into the chaos, back to the point where they are shaping and restructuring their meaning."

Rhetorical Situation

Two primary elements of any rhetorical situation are audience and occasion. The teachers in this study consistently call students' attention to their readers and to the assignments given them, which, in a sense, outline the primary occasions for their writing.

Audience

Responses to student writing in the past have often assumed a new critical framework in which the focus was on the text. Working within this model, teachers avoided appeals to authors' intentions (intentional fallacy) and effects on readers (affective fallacy). Acting as new critics, they presumed that they held the key to what texts meant. Any communication between teacher and student would center on the ways the student could make the text say more clearly what it "should" say. Obviously, such a framework was not conducive to a conversation because there was no real interaction between teacher and student.

With poststructural criticism came concern for the role that readers play in making the meaning of texts. Composition teachers who were influenced by this criticism began to make student writers sensitive to the readers' responses to their writing and, along with these affective responses, asked writers to compare the effects achieved with their intentions. This new paradigm, then, allows for meaningful conversation between teachers and student writers. Rather than assuming that they know exactly what writers intend and that all readers will read texts as they read them, these teachers set the goal of helping writers explore the effects of their writing on the concept of audience. It is not surprising, then, to find that, to varying degrees, the teachers in our study invoke readers in their responses to student writing. Below are examples of direct reference to readers in their comments to the writer of Essay 10:

> If you could write about leukemia in any way, how would you and who would your intended readers be? (Warnock)

> You have done what it is so hard to do: you have taught your readers about the disease leukemia by giving them a description of the symptoms of the disease that you experienced. (Stock)

> I've put a few questions in the margins to help you see where readers might want even more detail to understand the effects better. (Peterson)

> And so as a personal experience paper written for, you know, in a context where you know your readers (in this case, the class) and your readers know you, I think in that kind of a setting it works pretty well. At some point you have to think of this as a narrative which is sharing a personal experience in a way that readers who may not know you are interested, moved, informed, affected in some way from the process of reading this. (Anson)

> I suspect most readers will fully empathize with the physical suffering you experience and wish you a return to good health. (Stewart)

In many cases such as those just illustrated, the reader is mentioned directly by use of the word "reader" or "audience." In other cases, the teacher implies the existence of these readers by placing himself in a "community" of readers. In the comments below, for example, Edward White does not mention readers directly, but the "we's" and "us's" here show that he wants the writers to envision a broader audience than the teacher:

> You give *us* only the first step, then quit. Give *us* all the steps. (Essay 11)

> This sentence makes *us* expect something else. . . . (Essay 12)

> This is the kind of detail *we* need. But *we* need more, even here. (Essay 12)

An examination of the 10 essays in our data base indicates that our teachers invoke the reader in a large majority of cases. In the 113 responses to those 10 essays, a reader is mentioned, or implied, in 92 cases. All of the teachers except Peterson and White refer to readers regularly in at least 7 of the 10 essays in the sampling. Peterson refers to readers in responding to six of the essays; White refers to readers in two essays. Given our analysis of White's responding style in Chapter 4, in many ways the most directive in our study, it is no surprise that he refers to readers less often than other teachers. Yet White tells us in his Questions on Responding that the first drafts of students' papers often receive a response from their peers. It would seem, then, that he is attempting to help students move beyond a simple model of composing in which the teacher is the only audience for one's writing. It is certainly clear that the other teachers in our study do so.

Writing assignments

Their responses and notes to us make it clear that, with the possible exception of Tilly Warnock, these readers encourage students to fulfill the writing assignments they have been given. Larson, White, McClelland, and Stewart are the most insistent that writers attend to assignments. Larson, for example, is very direct in telling the writer of Essay 5, Steve, that he has not yet met the requirements of the assignment:

> The assignment asks you to help your reader to share your understanding of an idea, process, or activity. I take it that you want to talk about bass fishing (I infer that from your title). But what you've done here is primarily to recreate a particular experience you had.

In his notes to us about Essay 10, White shows his concern for writing assignments: "The writer missed the assignment almost entirely, and must rewrite an essay that fulfills the task." McClelland also feels that Kevin has failed to fulfill the requirements of this assignment, as is obvious from his comments: "Re-read the assignment, Kevin, and you'll see that you are to focus primarily on the effect of the event, not on the event itself." In his statement of philosophy, Stewart makes it clear that following the dictates of assignments is important: "The teacher's first job, therefore, is to help students recognize and respond to the demands of a particular context." For Stewart, the assignment is very much a part of that context, as the following comments he makes to student writers indicate:

> Now, we have to talk about what you didn't do. The assignment said you should report the experience and then "examine various ways in which the event affected you." (Essay 10)

> Now, what must you do to make succeeding drafts of this paper better? First, you're going to have to focus on the assignment. (Essay 5)

> Your assignment tells you to evaluate your subject, in this case a rock concert. You are supposed to develop some criteria for judging rock concerts and then indicate the ways in which this particular concert met those criteria. (Essay 13)

Peterson also encourages students to give attention to the requirements of their assignments. In some cases, she is quite direct, as when she tells the writer of Essay 5 that his draft "talks more about [him] than about bass fishing" and that he should "start over" and write an essay that fulfills the assignment. She is a bit less direct in talking to Kevin, the author of Essay 10: "I've put a few questions in the margin to help you see where readers might want even more detail to understand the effects [of leukemia] better." Nevertheless, her comments to Kevin make it clear that he has not followed the directions of the assignment.

As we indicated above, most of the readers in this study take writing assignments seriously. However, several of them had difficulty asking students to fulfill the particular assignments they were given in this study. The most vocal critic of these assignments is Larson.[11] His chief disagreement would seem to center on the lack of continuity from assignment to assignment. In his statement of philosophy, Larson speaks to this issue:

> In building a course, I try to make assignments build directly on earlier assignments, and even if an assignment does not build directly on earlier writings, I try to make later assignments fall within the same general area—maybe it's within the same "semantic field"—as earlier assignments, so that students will be aware that their work is enriched by prior work. I try hard to avoid assignments that are totally disconnected from each other.

In addition to building continuity in assignments, Larson argues that assignments in writing courses should challenge students to "think" and "learn" in the process of writing. In a note to us about our assignments, Larson comments that: "'The papers in this project seem to me not very good at these activities (i.e., reflecting the students' "thinking" and "learning"), but the reasons may be the assignments students were answering and the kinds of instructions they received about them."

Larson is by no means the only reader critical of the assignments in this study. In her statement of philosophy, Hull suggests that she too had some objections to these assignments:

I am often perplexed, for example, by the kinds of writing assignments we still ask our students to carry out—assignments that are only once removed (by the writing process generation) from directions to write about what you did on your summer vacation. I am disturbed that so much of school writing and writing in composition classes is still an ersatz activity, an artificial substitute for genuine projects that have a chance of engaging students' intellects and inspiring their commitment. To my mind, an "authentic" writing task has got to be at the center of composition instruction, one which invites students to take part in writing and reading activities that are socially meaningful in the context built and shared by a particular classroom community.

In her notes to us, she points to specific problems with several assignments in the sampling. For example, she is not sure how to read the assignment for Essay 2:

I don't know what the subtext is for this assignment. I assume the teacher wants the student first to summarize the source text without interjecting any of her opinions. . . . I'm really torn in what to do with this paper, because I wouldn't handle an assignment just this way. . .

Hull explains that she does not believe it possible to summarize a text without including one's opinion; thus this assignment is "an ersatz activity" that is not likely to produce good writing.

Anson notes problems with several of the assignments in the sampling. For example, he sees the assignment for Essay 1 as "very poorly designed—too generalized, [with] little contextual information." Gere also has difficulty with the assignment for Essay 1: "The assignment seems to ask for two things—emotion and information—and I think it sends mixed signals to students." O'Hare sees problems in the assignment for Essay 4:

I have serious reservations about this assignment. It demands that the writer, Anne, focus on her parents and her relationship with them. If Anne is unwilling to share very personal experiences with an audience of "parents of teenage children," then she should not be writing this paper in the first place. The assignment also seems to exclude evidence from Anne's experiences with friends, acquaintances and schoolmates, and their parents.

He also feels that part of David's failure in writing to the assignment for Essay 6 may be due to the assignment: "It may be that this assignment attracts failure because it almost encourages the picture-postcard, clichéd response."

Despite their criticisms of these assignments, these readers—Larson, Hull, Anson, Gere, and O'Hare—tend to expect students to write essays that, in some sense, fulfill the assignments they have been given. Of course, there are very real differences in the ways they approach assignments. We noted earlier how direct Larson is in telling the writer of Essay 5 that he has failed to meet the requirements of the assignment and must revise. Although Hull is also aware that the writer has not fulfilled the requirements of the assignment, she indicates, in her note to us, that she will deal with the issue indirectly:

So the question is how to get him to pay more attention to the actual assignment. I could always direct him to the appropriate lines of the assignment again, the ones which distinguish this paper from a single personal experience. . . . But I'm not sure the problem is conceptual. . . . I think I would praise the paper first, acknowledge that it's a good story. Then I would do something to suggest a problem with the paper, something besides saying "you haven't followed the assignment," something that would appeal to Steve's craft as a writer.

Clearly the approaches are different, but both Larson and Hull want to focus Steve's attention on the fact that he has not fulfilled this assignment.

To varying degrees, the readers we have discussed earlier assume that students should be expected to respond to the writing assignments they have been given. None of them seems to have difficulty in pointing to an assignment and suggesting that a student must write an essay that fulfills its requirements. The remaining three readers are somewhat less willing to direct students to follow the assignment. Elbow is not unconcerned about assignments, but he is troubled by a rigid approach that evaluates writing on the basis of expectations set up by the assignments. He begins to chart a course for dealing with the assignments in his notes to us about Essay 1:

There is something peculiar and interesting going on here. The assignment just says to discuss something so as to show readers why it's important to you. But Lunsford and Straub called the exercise "argumentative writing" and have given a title that the student didn't give. . . . This puts me in a bind, but it's a productive and interesting bind. Indeed this whole exercise of writing these hypothetical comments gives me a good new view of writing classes (like the view that tutors in a writing center get): I'm helping the student satisfy an assignment that's not mine.

Elbow decides to focus his comment on the call for exploration and ignore the apparent nudge we had given toward argumentation:

In so far as this is just exploratory writing, I want to say, "Stop, reflect, wonder, explore." . . . For the next step, please push harder for exploring and for discussing— and talking about why it's important to you; don't worry about arguments.

Elbow is also troubled by the assignment given to the author of Essay 9. He lets her know that the assignment is problematic, but then suggests that she try to find ways to solve the problems it presents:

"Bouncing off the story" is in a way the main rhetorical problem here—and it's inherent in the assignment itself: how to talk about your own experience using literature as "a point of departure." Tricky. I think you pull it off well in the first paragraph. At the end of your piece I feel things as strained ("I will be a good girl and talk about the story the teacher wants me to talk about"). In the 2nd and 3rd parags you sort of manage but I begin to feel a light strain. What is it that made you able to solve this tricky problem in that first parag? Whatever it is, remember: it's an important skill.

In his responses, then, we begin to see a pattern. Elbow thinks assignments have a certain value, but a large part of that value is in giving students something to work against, to resist. His response to the writer of Essay 5 shows his concern for assignments *and* his refusal to direct students to follow them:

I felt something interesting going on here. Seemed as though you had the assignment in mind (don't talk just tell a story of your experiences but explain a subject—for a while—but then gradually forgot about it as you got sucked into telling about your particular day of fishing. (You'll see my wiggly lines of slight battlement as this story begins to creep in.) The trouble is I like your stories/moments. My preference would be not to drop them ("Shame on you—telling stories for an expository essay") but to search around for some way to save it/them—but make it/them part of a piece that does what the assignment calls for. Not sure how to do it.

> Stock shares some of Elbow's ambivalence toward writing assignments. Although not unmindful of assignments in her responses, she cannot bring herself to insist that students fulfill them. At least, she does not do so explicitly. In talking to us about Rusty, the author of Essay 12, she says:

> I like what he [Rusty] has done, and although it is not exactly what I think the assignment was asking him to do, I'm going to go with his piece of writing and the direction in which he has taken it.

In those cases in which she does seem to want to hold students to the assignment, she couches her comments, not in terms of fulfilling an assignment, but rather in terms of making the paper more effective for a particular audience, as we see in her response to the author of Essay 5:

> On pages 2 and 3, you shift your perspective without indicating a purposeful reason for that shift to your reader. You go from what promises to be an essay explaining fishing the wide-mouthed bass in Orlando to an essay narrating a time when you fished for bass all day on Lake Ivenho.

> Like several of the other readers in the study, Warnock finds problems with several of the assignments in the sampling. She is particularly critical of the assignment given to the author of Essay 9. In her notes to us, she says:

> I would again encourage students to question why they are being asked to respond personally to literature and who their audience is. I would want them to question how a paper such as this helps them read. While the teacher is clearly the reader, why should they write personally to the teacher?

In her note to us about Essay 6, she makes the following comment:

> The assignment asks students to help their readers see not the place but the significance of the place and then it asks them to give the reader a sense of place. These two aims require discussion. I would hope that students would ask why they are supposed to write this and to whom.

Warnock does attempt on occasion to call the student's attention to the assignments, but when she does she approaches the subject indirectly with something like the strategy used by Stock. That is, rather than suggesting that a writer adhere to the requirements of an assignment, she responds in terms of how the writer might make a particular piece of writing more effective. Her comment to the author of Essay 5 illustrates this point: "You hook me with your opening but what's your specific focus? Is it fishing at Lake Ivenho or is it one day of fishing there?" More than any other reader in our group, Warnock seems willing to dispense with assigned topics, as her note about our context sheet for Essay 7 suggests:

> How can there be no specific assignments? The next sentence gives the course assignments. I worry when not giving topics means not making assignments. I think workshop classes do give assignments, deadlines, instructions on group work, and daily reading and writing. I'm reminded of a colleague who responds to my teaching by saying that some students need more structure. I think he locates structure only in himself, while I locate it in my purposes, students' expectations, subjects, language, and the situation.

Although Warnock goes along, as best she can with the assignments given in the sampling, she does not work well in a situation in which students are given "topics" on which to write. Warnock is here objecting to treating "assignment" and "topic" as if they were synonymous. Although the remaining teachers spend a good bit of time adjusting and otherwise reacting to these topics, it would seem that, for the most part, they are comfortable in situations in which students are given topics and they address their comments to these assigned contexts.

The Student Writer

In a letter written to us after she had responded to the essays in this study, Peterson speaks eloquently about the role her concept of the student behind the text played in her responding.

> When I sat down to begin reading and responding to the papers, my plan was to do four at a time, assuming that would take about an hour and a half including the time to comment on my responses. I read the background for the first paper in my set, "Merry Merchandizing," thought "no problem," and read through the paper once. Then panic struck. I had nothing to say—that is, nothing to write on the paper to the student. I could have talked to teachers about my evaluation of the piece (e.g. major strengths are voice and angle on topic; areas for improvement are clarity of terms and organization), but I had no impulse to write anything on the paper. To ease my panic, I decided to read the next one (after all I could omit three—why not the first one?).
>
> I hoped that my sudden (and atypical) "speechlessness" would disappear—that in reading the second or third one, I would be moved to comment. That didn't happen. I read quickly through the whole set (in the order I had received the pieces) and had only one impulse to comment on one sentence in one paper (the sentence in "Tribute" about not being able to cry when she first knew her father was dead). I was back to "Merry Merchandizing" and still speechless. As I read it again, I realized that my perception of and relationship to a student affects my responding far more than I had imagined. It affects: how much I comment, what I choose to comment on (e.g. which effective specific example I choose to praise), how I comment (the tone and form of my remarks), where I comment (mostly margin or at the end or 50-50). . . . I did not realize the extent to which the individual student affects my commenting until I tried responding to (not evaluating) the work of a nonentity. For me, commenting on papers means talking to students and to simulate that, I will have to envision a student I have had for each piece. When I tried reading "Merry Merchandizing" as the work of Allan, a former 101 student, I had much to say.

The 12 readers' responses to our sample essays indicate that most of them shared Peterson's dilemma. In order to make the process "work at all," they had to rely on their experiences to help them create student writers for the essays we had given them. In anticipation of the need to envision a student, we provided brief profiles of the writers of six of these essays: Nancy (Essay 2); Anne (Essay 4); David (Essay 6); Jennifer (Essay 8); Gail (Essay 11);[12] and Rusty (Essay 12). In addition, we invited teachers to supply any other contextual information they wished us to know as we read their responses.

Many of the readers used the information we provided as a foundation on which to construct their concepts of the students to whom they were writing. For example, we described the author of Essay 2, Nancy, as someone who sees herself as a good writer, who says she has always gotten "A's" in English, and who is resistant to help in improving her writing. Peterson's response is obviously influenced by the image she has constructed of Nancy on the basis this information. She tells us that she often encounters students who show some degree of defensiveness, confusion, and even hostility at the beginning of the semester. She says she uses a "range of techniques (humor, praise, self-revelation)" to deal with such students; she goes on to say that when a student remains at midterm where Nancy is, she shifts ground. Her response to Essay 2 is a case in point. In this situation, Peterson decides to focus on structure, assuming that Nancy understands and values that.

Elbow's response to Nancy is also very much affected by his concept of who Nancy is. He tells us that he is "put off" by her writing and would like to be honest with her about his response. However, because he and Nancy have drifted into an adversarial relationship, he will write a comment that is "a kind of holding action, cop-out" and wait for a conference with her. Elbow says that an important principle he has come to understand is that "whenever there is a contest as to whether or not the course will 'reach' someone, the student can *always* win—always has the trump card."

In his note to us on his response to Nancy, Anson shares his developing sense of the student writer. He first thought that Nancy was "very sure of herself, perhaps even stand-offish and overconfident." He found himself trying to challenge her and being overly critical of her work. Now, he has come to "recognize that her criticisms of the early work in the course, her argument that she had always done well in high school, and an air of superiority she carried into the conference groups . . . were really a mask for a fundamental *lack of confidence*, perhaps even a feeling of fear that she wouldn't be able to do well." Given this view of Nancy, Anson has decided to support her as much as possible, "using her *expressed* (if not actually felt) confidence in her favor."

Most of the teachers in our study imagined the individual student behind this text and tailored their response to the needs of this individual. The two exceptions to this rule were Larson and O'Hare. Feeling the constraints of this artificial setting, they evidently preferred to deal with the persona they could infer from the text. In his notes to us about this essay (and writer) Larson says,

> In my comment, I *try* to engage the student in a dialogue, and I also ask her, since her discussion invites doing so, to think about a bit of language, the notion of "harm" and what brings it about. I make no assumptions about the student (I don't know what she's written about before, or what her writing has been like), but assume that by taking her seriously and helping her to think about the issues she raises I can assist in helping her increase her ability to see, and write about, a problem. I don't know what has "put her off," but I'll try to make my queries reasonable enough to be visibly worth considering. And I hope she's to learn from considering them.

We take Larson's statement that he makes "no assumptions about the student" as announcing his intention to deal with the persona created in this text; his response is consistent with this intention. O'Hare would also seem to be dealing, more or less, with the persona he can infer from the essay. He sees Nancy as one of those *types* of writers who would be unfair to opponents in writing letters to the editor.

In those cases in which we offered the teachers a chance to build on our student profiles, over half the time the teachers indicated (either in their notes to us or in their comments to the students, or both) that the concepts they had formed of the students were important in their responses to the students.[13] Most of the time, our information came from the teachers' notes to us, but in a few cases—such as the following end comment McClelland makes to the writer of "The Four Seasons"—the text makes it clear that the teacher's concept of the student's identity is an important factor in the response: "You and I know from some of your past writing (and from flashes of promise in this text) that you are capable of composing very effective essays." We had described the writer, David, as a "confident, perhaps even cocky, student who comes across as someone who thinks he is a better writer than (in your view) he is." McClelland wants to encourage David to work up to his potential. Stock would also like to address the issues of David's effort and his cockiness head-on, as the following comments to him make clear:

> Are you exercising your mind as you write or are you coasting. . . . In class you are astute, critical. You look for the shades of meaning. Sometimes I worry that your disdain for the obvious, your impatience with others who need time to see the layers of meaning in something we are reading or discussing, will intimidate members of our class, will make it harder for them to learn, will make it harder for them to ask questions because

they are afraid they will appear foolish. I share this worry with you because I don't think you are aware of how your attitude affects others in our class.

In her notes to us, Stock says that her response to David is intended to "ask him to stretch himself as a writer and as a person." Thus, her comment moves beyond the text and the rhetorical context in which it is set to address the student as an individual. Stock wants David to develop as a writer, but, as her note makes clear, she is concerned that he develop in other ways also.

RESPONSE AS A CONVERSATION

To summarize the discussion we have undertaken in this chapter, we offer the similarities we find among these readers' responses as principles for commenting on student texts. By their example, these 12 readers suggest that teachers' responses should be guided by the following principles:

Principle 1:	Teacher comments should be well-developed and text specific.
Principle 2:	They should be focused on global, not local, concerns.
Principle 3:	They should emphasize nonauthoritative modes of commentary.
Principle 4:	They should be carefully thought out and purposeful, with an eye to the needs and potential of the particular piece of writing.
Principle 5:	They should be suited to the relative maturity of the draft being read.
Principle 6:	They should be mindful of the rhetorical situation for the writing.
Principle 7:	They should be adapted to the student writer behind the text.

Each of the seven traits we have examined in this chapter contributes to a conversational style, in ways that we have alluded to in our earlier discussion. For example, in writing well-developed comments (Principle 1), a teacher takes the time to do more than tell the student what is wrong, or right, or what to do to improve the essay—time to describe how she reads the text, to respond as a reader, to explain why certain parts of the text seem to work in the way they do—and so forth. In using many nonauthoritative comments (Principle 3), a teacher moves away from the role of an authority telling a student how to "fix" his paper and toward a role that allows her to "discuss" a paper with the writer.

A conversation implies an active role for teacher and student. The teacher may offer direction, but the student must "talk back" to the teacher and take charge of his own writing choices. If students are to become writers, they must be encouraged to accept the uncertainty that comes when one takes responsibility to find what one wants to say in a given situation. The teacher cannot—must not—simply tell the student what is wrong with his paper. More to the point, the teacher may well not know what is "wrong" with the paper because the teacher may not know fully what purpose the writer wants to achieve and what readers he wishes to address.

In any conversation, it is necessary for each party to enunciate his or her position clearly for the other person. But when one party takes the time and care to write out his or her thoughts in complete sentences and coherent paragraphs and the other party responds simply by marking on those sentences with abbreviations and shorthand symbols, there is no real exchange and no real conversation. Our readers' comments, however, make it clear that they see their responses to student writing as part of a conversation. Even a relatively directive reader such as White uses few shorthand symbols and makes few marks in the "student's space." This is not to suggest that our readers do not make corrective responses or that they never write over the student's words. But as a rule they avoid both. On average, only 4% of their comments are in the corrective mode, and the essays presented in Chapter 2 make it clear that it is the exception to the rule when one of these readers invades the student's space. Even those who are liberal with their marginal comments—such as White, Larson, and Peterson—tend to avoid writing on the student's writing.

As we noted in Chapter 2, one of our real surprises in doing this study was to find that six of the readers (Anson, Elbow, McClelland, O'Hare, Stock, and Stewart) seldom use marginal comments. In answering our Questions on Responding, McClelland explains why he responds in a final comment only:

> My comments are always in the form of brief essays composed at the computer. For two reasons I never write on the students' texts: First, I want the writers to maintain authorship of their texts and so I refrain from writing on their papers; of course, this could be a false, symbolic act if I wrote prescriptive, controlling comments elsewhere. Secondly, I see my responding as one side of a conversation with students; it's a reader to writer dialogue about the meaning of the text, so I want to compose my reader responses in full discourse units.

We believe McClelland is right in saying that not writing on student texts is a "false, symbolic act" if teachers write extremely controlling comments at the end of student texts—and that could happen. But the opposite is not likely to occur: A teacher who continually writes over the student's words will not be leaving the student in control of her essay.

As we said in the Introduction, we undertook this study to answer a rather straightforward question of how a group of well-known teachers would respond to a common set of essays. Our initial impulse was toward simplicity; we would send the papers out, have the 12 readers respond to them, and look at their responses. To the degree possible, we followed that impulse in Chapter 2, presenting 36 sample sets of responses and keeping our commentary to a minimum. Things did not stay so simple. In order to get at the important differences in the responding styles of our readers, we introduced various types of commentary and did quite a bit of analysis in Chapters 3 and 4. When we came to Chapter 5, our impulse was once again to simplify, to step back and get a broader look at what these teachers are doing. As we come to a close, we find a rather simple way to symbolize what we have found—that is, that these teachers favor a noncontrolling style of responding that attempts to establish a conversation between teacher and student. In order to *see* what we mean, literally, one has only to place some of these responses next to the papers found lying around the offices of America's writing teachers.

Epilogue
Writing Assignments: How Might They Encourage Learning?

Richard L. Larson

UNDERSTANDING THE CONTEXT OF STUDENTS' WRITINGS

When responding to the students' writings gathered for discussion in this book, I viewed them as writings addressed specifically to the assignments given to the students by their instructors. All of the invited readers had received some information about the course in which the student wrote, the student writer, the assignment that the student was (supposedly) addressing, and the approximate point at which the assignment appeared in the course that produced it. I tried to take that information into account, just as, if I were working with each writing as a live text produced by a current student of mine, I would surely respond to that student's writing not as a free-standing text outside of any context, but as an effort to complete the responsibility I had given her, against the background of the previous instruction she had received in my class.

But in this project there were limits to how well I could respond to a student's writing as the completion of an assigned task. As an invited outside reader, I did not know fully what the task was. I did not know most features of the instructional context that contributed to making the assignment what the student construed it to be. Part of that context is what might be called the overall "ecology" of instruction: the details of what the student wrote on earlier assignments, the discussion in class (if any) that preceded the writing, the comments that the student had received on earlier writings, the discussions that had taken place at the consultations between teacher and student, perceptions that the student might have reached from revising earlier writings, the instructor's normal procedures in dealing with student writings (Did the instructor expect that student to enact directly what was assigned? How explicitly did the student have to meet that assignment?), the facial expressions, gestures, and tones of voice used in giving the assignment, the examples (if any) used to illustrate it, the readings (if any) assigned just before the current assignment (and possibly discussed in conjunction with it), and the interpersonal relationships that had already developed among the students. Also, I did not know whether the printed words given to me as representing the assignment were words the instructor actually wrote, or someone's paraphrase of an assignment given orally, or someone's paraphrase of a set of written instructions for the assignment. I could not fully infer in these assignments what actually had been, in the larger sense just discussed, "assigned."

I had, then, only the printed words on the page a representation of each assignment and a guide in responding. As a result, I had to examine very closely the relationship between the written representation of the assignment and the student's writing. I had to assume that what the student wrote was due, in part, to her understanding of what these written words told her to do.

Now I take it that most writing assignments (apart, perhaps, from journals, about which more later) present the student with a rhetorical "problem" to be solved. That problem may be "well" defined, in the sense of telling the student pretty explicitly what she has to do, and for whom she should do it, so that she will know pretty clearly when she has done it. Or it may be relatively "ill" defined, in the sense of giving the student a wide range of choices or allowing the student to invent a wide range of choices for solving the problem. The student, of course, can also reconstruct the problem presented—can elect to pursue the problem in a different direction, or from a different perspective, than that suggested by the assignment. Often such reconstructions produce especially interesting papers. But as an invited "outside" reader, I could not identify with confidence such reconstructions. Not knowing the details of the context in which the student wrote, I looked at the student's text as an effort to address the rhetorical problem, well- or ill-defined, posed by the instructor in the assignment, without knowing how the student might have understood the problem.

QUESTIONS ABOUT THE ADEQUACY OF WRITING ASSIGNMENTS

Examining the texts of the assignments and the sketchy accounts of the contexts in which they were written, however, led me to some questions about the problems posed. As a teacher of writing myself, I could not help asking: How likely is it that the directions given could elicit from the student a piece of writing that I would be inclined to consider effective? How successfully did the directions give to the student an occasion and a purpose to which the student would be moved to respond? How successfully did the instructions give the student a reason for coming before his or her reader? How well did the instructions give the student a reader before whom she would want to appear? How well did they give the student guidance toward finding fresh, interesting information and ideas to "construct" for those readers? In short, how well did the directions for writing help to guide, support, and perhaps gently shape the student's effort at writing? If the student is responsible for carrying out an assignment, the reader—this outside reader, anyway—cannot help thinking about how the directions for the writing might have influenced that writing: motivated it, supported it, made it seem worth doing, or how they might have failed to do so.

CONCEPTS OF "AUDIENCE" AND "PURPOSE" IN ASSIGNMENTS

Kenneth Burke reminded his readers that rhetoric is "addressed" (to listeners, to readers). Most of the writing prepared in first-year composition (except for specifically "private" writing, such as journals that instructor and students agree are not to be given to others) should be, in my view, *addressed* writing. (I recognize that some teachers do not share that view.) If that need was ever entirely forgotten, the attention to "audience" in research and theory on composition over the last 20-odd years testifies to its rediscovery: Many of us take pride in teaching our students to take account of their audience as they write (although Peter Elbow [1987] argues that writers might well find it useful not to write for a specifically envisaged reader, and Peter Vandenberg [1992] explores the complexity of identifying and addressing particular "audiences"). Along with giving attention to audience, we (as teachers influenced by rhetorical concepts) also assert the importance of "purpose" in writing, as both Wayne Booth (1963) and Lloyd Bitzer (1968) do. (Why, many of us ask students, are you coming before your reader at this time on this subject in the way you do?) When I look at the students' writings in this project, I ask myself how well the assignments gave students a *credible* audience and a purpose (a reason, a goal to be reached) for addressing that reader.

The notion of "purpose" in writing is complex and could invite a complete essay by itself (as could the notion of "audience"). One has to distinguish, to begin with, the "purpose" for engaging in the act of writing itself, and the "purpose" for bringing forth and setting before a reader the finished piece of writing. I have recently found it helpful, in conducting research on writing assignments, to adapt the term "speech act" (as introduced most notably by the philosopher J.L. Austin [1962] and developed by such scholars as John Searle [1971], Richard Ohmann & H. Martin [1958], and Marilyn Cooper [1984]). I use the term "discourse act" (it is not original with me, but has the advantage of embracing both speaking and writing), and I think of discourse acts as behavior engaged in with words in order to accomplish tasks with readers and to evoke specific kinds of responses from them (the number of possible responses is large). Every writing assignment, as I see it, invites one or more discourse acts (the same writing can perform many acts). A way of phrasing the question that I confront in thinking about a writing assignment is this: Does the assignment invite a discourse act that the student can perform, and will want to perform, well? I speculate that a student will want to perform a discourse act well if the student finds value (beyond just getting a grade) in doing it. I further speculate that a student will find value in carrying out an assignment if in the process of doing so the student learns and can tell that he or she is learning. The "learning" may lie in the enlargement (perceived by the student) of her ability at writing, or in the broadening of a student's understanding of a specific subject or of the student's world. A piece of writing submitted on an assignment, that is, should carry out effectively the requested act of discourse and reward the student, with learning, for making the effort to do so. In this short discussion I try to apply this framework to writing assignments as a group and specifically to the assignments carried out by the students whose writing we studied in this project.

KINDS OF WRITING ASSIGNMENTS

I begin by looking at journals, which these days many students are asked to keep as a kind of continuing assignment. (Many students are expected to write daily, or at least weekly, in their journals.) For the writer, writing in a journal can be a way of recording thoughts, reflecting on observations, verbalizing feeling, linking what has been read to what has been observed, trying out judgments, and so on. It is a discourse act engaged in chiefly for the writer's benefit; the writer is her own audience, and the very act of verbalizing on paper, for later reflection, different observations or data or insights can be instructive. The benefits for the student are often not realized unless the instructor gives the student some specific guidance in writing in her journal, but with such guidance a writer can gain enlarged knowledge of self (and maybe ideas for writing papers addressed to readers outside herself).

Journals may, on the other hand, not be strictly private. What might be the purpose of showing a journal to a reader? To let the reader "overhear" the writer? To let the reader share in the act of reflecting, quite informally, with no sense that the reflection is finished thought? Some teachers require the student to place the journal in their hands not only for these reasons but so that they can engage in a written conversation with students about its contents. (Other teachers, less defensibly, simply check the journal for the number of pages or the number of entries.) The journal, then, can illustrate two kinds of credible "purposes" for the act of writing.

But journals, as most (though not all) teachers invite them, are primarily private writings: writings done by the student for his or her own purposes, sometimes not even read by the teacher, like the informal notes and sketches that James Britton and other scholars designate as "expressive" writing; they are not designed primarily to affect readers other than the writer. But most student (and other) writings are addressed to a person or persons beyond the writer. I turn here, therefore, to the value of some discourse acts performed in these other kinds of writings— writings typically asked of students in courses such as those from which came the students' work presented in *Twelve Readers Reading*.

Before doing so, however, I need to reflect briefly on another of what for many teachers is, like the journal, a kind of continuing assignment: asking students to engage deliberately in various composing "processes." (The phrase is often used in the singular, "composing process," but probably most observers would recognize that writers working on different pieces under different circumstances will compose differently, and that individual writers differ in the processes they employ.) This sort of continuing assignment, unlike the keeping of a journal, does not by itself connect to or result in the production of just one particular kind of writing, but instead affords a kind of "scaffolding" on which many different kinds of writing, containing many different discourse acts, can be constructed. Teachers regularly ask, indeed assign, students to traverse these processes, but the outcome of their doing so is seen each time in the specific piece of writing— the specific discourse act, if you will—that they are working on.

The teacher who asks students to go deliberately through a "composing process" (essentially a sequence of procedures, which can be repeated at any time during the act of writing) is usually one who has become convinced that these procedures are what the student needs to learn, primarily, about writing. Typically these procedures include some form of activity to "generate" thoughts (e. g., "brainstorming," "mapping," "cubing," or the like), some form of "planning" and "drafting," some form of "revising," and finally "editing." Many of those who deliberately teach the conscious application of composing processes in the creation of different kinds of discourse emphasize the "recursiveness" of these processes; they call attention to ways in which writers at virtually any point in any of the component processes can move out to, or return to, other processes. Even a writer engaged in "invention," scholars of composing processes point out, can draft phrases and organize what has been invented.

Attention to the procedures followed by writers in writing, of course, is neither new nor idle: the earliest teachers of rhetoric taught invention and ways of classifying subjects and issues; their attention to planning and the perfecting of style suggests the same belief in the importance of revision that teachers today try to instill into their students. Indeed, most of us, in one way or another, follow the recommended procedures, and most of us employ, and teach, the procedure that is often thought to represent most clearly the attention to a composing process: revising drafts of our work. Some of us revise more than others, and some of us revise in our heads before writing or while writing (we "shape at the point of utterance," in Britton's [1970] phrase), but most of us do revise. The procedures students are taught to follow are thus by no means unimportant. But the teacher and the student both need to remember, of course, that using the scaffolding of composing processes to facilitate writing does not produce, or assure the success of, any kind of writing. The success of any writing is determined by the quality of the information included, the clarity of the organizational plan and its development, the lucidity of style, the "ethos" of the writer, the appropriateness of the writing for its reader(s), and the suitability of the writing to its occasion and purpose. Engaging adroitly in composing processes does not relieve the writer of the responsibility for producing "effective" discourse, although on occasion (I have perceived) some teachers seem to suggest that the skillful traversal of processes—skillful execution of this "continuing assignment"—is all one needs for successful writing.

If engaging deliberately in the processes of composing is for some teachers (though by no means all) a kind of "continuing," or if you will "underlying," assignment, what are the kinds of writings or assignments that students are often asked to build on that foundation? The first, in the classification I offer here, is simply *to display: to demonstrate ability, often essentially outside of the context of a genuine occasion, a purpose (outside of meeting an assignment), and an audience other than a teacher (and maybe fellow students)*. I have elsewhere designated this sort of writing as "semi-rhetorical": not, in fact, designed to influence belief or action in regard to the subject of writing, but mainly to win a favorable judgment of the writer. The abilities students are to display—besides the ability to control English syntax, punctuate reasonably, use appropriate words, and handle English idiom tolerably well—will vary from assignment to assignment. I suggest that these kinds of assignments typically ask students to demonstrate essentially one or both of two kinds of abilities: the ability to lay out information for the reader or the ability to perform a cognitive operation. Among assignments inviting mainly the display (as is often required in a test, for example) of ability to lay out information, one might identify those requiring writers to tell the steps in a process; to tell the contents of a piece of writing through summary or paraphrase; to report data retrieved from a library; to lay out the causes and/or effects of an event previously studied; to array the similarities and differences between familiar items/events or between items/events previously studied; or to summarize the known effects of a cause or the causes of an effect. Because in these kinds of assignments the writer is doing little more than presenting information or ideas she has heard about or arrived at *before* writing, the writer has little chance to reach genuine discoveries.

Among assignments requiring display of ability to carry out a cognitive operation might be those asking students to construct an argument according to, say, a model derived from Stephen Toulmin (1964); to infer cause-effect relationships between items/events not previously discussed; to conduct comparisons between items not previously compared; to comment on written texts or works of art; to make and defend decisions about problems; and so on. (Examples: Discuss the differences between

Shakespeare's Lady Macbeth and Gertrude. Compare what Samuel Johnson and Jonathan Swift say about poverty. Write a "research paper" on what happened at the Battle of Little Big Horn. answer the question, was Mary Shelley or George Eliot the more committed feminist?)

Alhough the student may need to display these abilities and perform the assigned operations in order to produce successful writing in various contexts and forms, in class or outside it, and although these various cognitive activities can indeed lead to the discovery of insights and perceptions that the student may value, the *assignment* that focuses on these abilities and operations often asks simply that the student execute the maneuvers; it often does not visibly invite the student to reach new learning or to achieve a worthwhile purpose by executing them.

Sometimes such "display" assignments ask the writer to do more than just display the ability to perform an operation; some assignments ask the students to address an audience (one present in the classroom or "invoked"—Ede and Lunsford's [1984] term—imaginatively). The student is not only to perform an operation but also to present the fruits of that operation forcefully to the present or invoked audience: to engage in a "rhetorical" act of discourse. But such an invitation in many assignments is often not backed with any serious instruction in marshaling ideas and reaching readers and reading from the point of view of another person; the discourse act requested is "pseudo-rhetorical," and everyone in the class knows that it is such. The student may learn little about the subject of the writing or about reaching living readers. The student is often given no hint about—and no encouragement to discover—why the physically present reader or the invoked reader might want or be willing to read with interest the student's work. The student is often invited, as these kinds of assignments are worded by the instructor, to demonstrate exultantly: See! I can do the job! I know how to analyze! I can put what I've analyzed before readers! I can complete this "dummy run" (Britton's [1970] term) of "communication" here in school when I have to.

Of these assignments one might well ask: Does the request to perform (one hopes, skillfully) before one's audience—the instructor, maybe one's classmates—give the student adequate encouragement to produce serious, committed writing? Often the answer is no, and an instructor or reader, therefore, cannot expect to see great accomplishments. The instructor's initial response to assignments of this sort—or, at least, my response—usually is to see whether the required abilities are displayed and the designated operations performed. If the student does more—reveals unexpected ideas about the subject, sees previously unrecognized relationships among data, or turns the writing into a forceful address to a reader on a subject of concern, for example—the instructor can applaud. But, absent an understanding between instructor and students that the students should, whenever possible, reach beyond the literal assignment, an instructor or invited reader cannot require this more complex kind of performance or make adverse judgments about the writing if such complexity is missing.

In a second typical kind of writing assignment, the student *is invited to report, reflect about, and consider the value or significance of an event or events in her personal history*—particularly events that the student (as she writes) believes affected her emotionally or intellectually. In the late 1960s and early 1970s, such assignments were especially valued (they are still valued today) because they were thought to contribute to the student's "personal growth," the advancement of which was then viewed as one of the major goals of instruction in English. Today the goal of such assignments is still, for many instructors, promoting self-knowledge within students, not to mention getting students to craft an artistically attractive, engaging text—a text that readers will take pleasure in reading. (Such writing lends itself especially well to the kind of workshop discussions within student groups that are often a central practice in courses built around the continuing practice of "composing processes.")

Such assignments are thought to be particularly useful in a writing course because, if the student knows (or can find out) nothing else, she presumably knows, and perhaps can evaluate, significant events in her personal history. And recounting personal history gives practice in narrating and describing and making interpretive judgments, which also contribute to a good deal of writing that is not concerned only or mainly with personal history. What's more, narrating personal history can offer the student an opportunity and incentive for working toward vivid and exact language and for trying out metaphor, irony, and synecdoche, that is, for the *re-creation* of dramatic, emotionally moving events.

Assignments in the reporting and especially in the evaluating of personal history, of course, can indeed have all these values, not to mention building a foundation on which the writer can later move (I use James Moffett's [1965] phrase) toward higher "abstractive altitude" in her essays. From such assignments, if carefully explained in such a way that the student knows the goals and how to reach them, the student can learn about herself and about the act of interpreting personal history. In revising them, she can sharpen her perception of the experience and of self. In reading and reacting to such writings, the teacher, classmates, and the student herself can reach insights into human predicaments and feelings that will enlarge their understanding of what it means to be human. That is, this sort of writing, unlike "display" writing or writing designed for a simulated audience, can bring students to discovery.

But such learning does not happen by itself. An assignment intended to promote such learning, and the environment in which teacher and fellow students will respond to the writing (sympathetically, with genuine interest, and with understanding of what is being done and said by the writer), has to be planned. The student is much less likely to learn what she can, and the audience is less likely to be genuinely (and informedly) pleased or moved, if the teacher's assignment, the supporting instruction, and the ambiance of the classroom have not given the writer and readers the necessary guidance in composing such writing. Such writing is both craft and art; it is not just, on the one hand, disengaged retrospection, or, on the other hand (with apologies to Wordsworth), the "spontaneous overflow of powerful feelings." Students need to be helped to understand how their writings on such an assignment can embody both acts, and much more.

ASSIGNMENTS THAT PROMOTE LEARNING AND DISCOVERY THROUGH WRITING

The last kind of assignment that I discuss here I derive not from textbooks or from theoretical scholarship, but from reading syllabi gathered during a research project on college curricula in writing, and from talking to experienced, interesting teachers about approaches to teaching and to students' learning. Such assignments give the student *a genuine opportunity to learn, to extend her store of knowledge, insight, and wisdom in the process of preparing for and doing the writing, and to alter the beliefs or perspectives of real readers by giving them the fruits of hard-won discoveries.* This is the kind of assignment that I think should predominate in our composition courses, although I recognize the value of carefully drawn assignments of retrospection on personal history and the occasional appropriateness of assignments to report data, to summarize a text, or to paraphrase a text. (These latter activities can, of course, *contribute* to assignments or sequences of assignments that facilitate learning.) Assignments in this last genre need not be complicated; for instance, one might ask the student to observe closely the language used by those around her and then to describe the patterns of language she sees. That observation will almost always result in students' learning, not just about writing a report of observation, but about language, too. Such assignments ask students to discover new knowledge and write about it. In my experience, students will listen eagerly to those kinds of reports and often discuss them energetically.

This genre of assignment traces its identity, obviously, to the classic phrase first used, I think, by Janet Emig (1977): "'Writing' [is] a mode of learning." This is the concept, whether we recognize it as such or not, on which we base many of our efforts to assure that writing plays an important role in courses in academic fields. Proponents of these kinds of assignments apply to them the term "epistemic," quite justifiably insisting that they activate and enlarge students' ways of knowing. They contribute especially well to what Ann Berthoff (1981) calls "the making of meaning" (journal keeping and autobiographic retrospection can accomplish this goal also); in the act of writing, the writer constructs, and invites readers to join her in constructing, a fresh reading of some text, some experience, some body of data, some culture, some part of the world.

The essence of this kind of assignment is that it invites the student to undertake a genuine, not a canned or spurious, act of inquiry. Frequently it asks the student to discover or recognize something *problematic* in her world and to deal with that problem, though by no means in a mechanistic or algorithmic way. It asks, in the words of theorists of learning, for a *reconstruction* of knowledge, not simply a setting forth of data essentially in the order in which it was received or has previously been sorted. An example: is "reverse discrimination" ever justifiable? Examine these [named or assigned] readings along with a Supreme Court decision of your choice and a relevant news report and, carefully citing appropriate parts of these materials, give and explain your answer to the question. Another example: at the end of this class (in an academic subject outside of English), write down one significant question about our subject that remains genuinely unanswered for you, and then try to answer it as well as you can, or at least say how you might go about finding the answer to it. (I take this example from the literature on "classroom research" and on writing in the disciplines.) Such questions invite the student to compose in such a way that, after composing, the student has a larger, fuller understanding of her subject than before she went to work. To put the point differently, the goal is to assist the student in bringing new perspectives to bear on a subject, in problem *finding*, and in reconstructing knowledge through active inquiry and reflection. Such assignments often require writing about reading that is genuinely problematic or provocative, as well as writing about conversations, dialogues, and observations—writing that reflects on and synthesizes, after reflection, ideas from diverse sources. Assignments that *fail* to engage students in such discovery of data, ideas, and meanings run the risk of eliciting from them empty exercises in the communication of unexamined thoughts. But when writing is assigned as the outcome of an inquiry whose results give the writer a serious purpose in coming before civilized readers (she has something to tell them—something she has *learned*), we can have, in my view, an instructive, worthwhile writing assignment.

THE WRITING ASSIGNMENTS GIVEN TO THE STUDENTS IN *TWELVE READERS READING*

Where, then, do the writing assignments from the teachers who contributed students' texts to *Twelve Readers Reading* fit into these categories (categories admittedly invented for this discussion)? What incentives to learning and to serious communication of the results of inquiry do these assignments offer? I select six of these assignments that I find demonstrably problematic for discussion here. But I could offer similar analyses of most of the others, too.

The assignment for Writing 6 asks the student to "depict [a] scene, mood, or setting in a way that will allow your reader—someone who does not know about it—to see the significance it has for you." The student is told that she "will do well to use specific details." The assignment asks the student for a display of abilities—this time the ability to describe a scene, using sensory details, to reveal the "significance" it has for the writer. There is no suggestion that the scene/setting chosen should have any urgent or distinctive meaning for the student, or that reexamining the scene or setting should enlarge the writer's perception or understanding of self. There is no suggestion that the writer needs to think carefully about what she proposes to describe. Although a nominal audience is specified, no context is provided that suggests a reason for the readers' being interested in what the writer describes. The background statement allows us to infer that the curriculum has asked the student to display ability to write some standard types of essays ("description," "narration," "comparison", and so on), but these activities appear to have been taught as self-contained forms that do not invite cumulative learning. (The standard forms do not connect to each other; there is no hint that writing one form builds on what the student has learned from displaying an ability to write the previously assigned form.) The assignment suggests that students are engaged in some composing processes, but there is no hint that traversing the processes helps students understand how to learn about their subjects: the processes are not linked, in the language of the assignment, to observation and reflection. The assignment promises to leave the student with no larger understanding of her subject than she had before writing: the place presumably has already had, and continues to have, whatever significance the writer will ascribe to it. I am not sure that this assignment could very easily be made an occasion for learning, but in order to try to make it so, the teacher would have had to help the student develop the ability to explain *how and why* the place or setting acquired significance for her, when it first took on that significance, whether that significance has changed over time, what importance the student attaches to the change, and so on. Informal note making and guided discussion with classmates might have helped the student carry on this reflection. The resulting paper would focus as much on the student's understanding of her perceptions of the place as on sensory details; the details would help mainly to make clear how or why the student's perceptions became clear and changed (if they did). Such a paper could interest thoughtful classmates, who could find themselves learning important elements in the growth of one of their friends.

Similar comments might be offered about Writing 11: although the topic for discussion is a "subject" or "activity," the instructions are essentially the same as for Writing 6 ("tell . . . the members of the class about this subject or activity . . . in such a way that [they] can begin to see it as you do"); in short, tell us about your subject so that we can see your thoughts or feelings. The designated audience is not shown to have much serious interest in what the student might write, and the student is given no guidance on how the writing might be shaped as inquiry and how it might enlarge knowledge. As an in-class essay (to be composed in the unrealistically restrictive time period that casts doubt on the validity of essay tests), the assignment asks for little more than a display of previously developed ideas and abilities. The reference in the directions to an "expository" essay signals that the curriculum may be constructed around essay types; such a curriculum seemingly implies that writers, when they write, sit down to produce specimens of one or another "type." They do not, of course, and therefore asking the student in effect to produce a specimen of a type quite simply misteaches. A teacher does not *need* to write into an assignment any reference at all to a "type" of essay. He can designate the discourse act invited (see my earlier discussion of the concept), or simply ask the writer to take up a subject and address her audience in whatever genre the student finds appropriate.

Writing 1 is like 6 and 11. The student is asked to discuss a topic "in a way that will help readers see why it is important" to the writer. Presumably it is already important; the writer learns nothing new by writing. The readers are not shown to be interested. No inquiry is asked, only a recitation of previously formed opinion. What will the writer learn by writing this piece? From the student paper given to us, it would seem that she did not learn, or think, much about the subject.

Writing 15 offers the invited reader a portfolio, made up of papers in which the student is evidently to demonstrate that he or she can write essays of different "types." The final paper in the portfolio is labeled "persuasive." We are told that the student has practiced using different appeals and has engaged in some discussion of "audience." But the student is given no advice to do more than recycle her previous ideas about the subject. Although a broadly stated "purpose" is offered (a purpose that might be said to drive many, many student writings), there is no language in the assignment to suggest that the writer even consider changing her mind on her subject (she is to try to convince the reader to "accept her views" on the subject, probably views already formed and long held). Nor is there a suggestion that the student feel any urgency about coming before the reader with a forceful discussion. The student has received, so far as we know, no guidance in analyzing issues, confronting substantial questions, or reasoning to conclusions by writing. No inquiry is encouraged; the student experiences no serious need to reflect on what she will say. The only way for such an assignment to invite learning, I would guess, would be for the instructor to "problematize" in some way, or require the student to problematize, the topic. One way to force the student to see the problems possibly involved in the topic might be to ask the student to locate, in newspapers or other media, pieces supporting and opposing the student's position, to summarize both kinds of pieces, and then to reflect in her own writing a recognition of the views opposed to hers. A redrafted assignment might also drop the designation of "aims" of writing. There is almost never a single aim in any writing, and the designation of an "aim," anyway, hints at the belief that a writer sits down to write in order to produce an example of an "aim," instead of sitting down to write a piece that will induce a reader to believe what she is saying.

Writing 4 moves us from displays of pre-formed, unexamined views to accounts of personal history and its significance. It does so, unfortunately, by connecting personal history with "more expository types of writing," and thus suggesting that the course is simply leading students to try to display competence in arbitrarily designated, unconnected forms of writing. The term "expository" tells the student nothing, but as an arbitrary label it suggests that writing is an act of producing examples to fit categories. The audience is left to the student to specify; the assignment blandly urges that the writing be shaped to "this audience." There is a suggestion that the student should *have learned* from thinking about her relationships with her parents, but the assignment suggests that the learning has ended and that the student will set forth only information already shaped and ordered in the student's mind. ("Consider what you *have learned* about this subject . . . and share something that you *have learned* . . . ") The assignment does not invite the kind of thoughtful retrospective attention to personal history that might lead to fresh insights, and there is no guidance in possible ways of reaching such insights. The assignment might have promoted learning through writing if it had asked the student to reflect further on her relationships with her parents, to recall and report, perhaps, central incidents in that relationship, and possibly to say whether she now sees those incidents and relationships as she did earlier. If she sees them differently, she might say how and why. Her audience of classmates, as we have discussed before, might find value in learning more about a friend and get some guidance about how they themselves might learn from changed perceptions of their parents' treatment of them.

Writing 9 asks the student to say "what she has learned about good and evil" from her own and others' experiences. In some undefined way, poems and stories read in class are to serve as "points of departure." The student is given no guidance in reflecting about her experiences or in connecting them to the literary texts. No suggestion is offered to the student about how connecting personal history to literary texts gives the student fresh insight into herself or into the texts. The student, it seems, has already learned about good and evil from her experiences and is somehow to compare those lessons from experience with lessons taught by the poems and stories—read as if they "contained" moral teachings. No audience or reason for writing is suggested. Yet the subject is perhaps potentially more useful than many in the collection because it invites the student to problematize her readings and experiences and also to draw on other readings, discussions, and experiences. If the poems and stories read are in the slightest degree ambiguous (or ambivalent), for instance, the student can be asked how she knows what is "evil" and what is "good" in those texts, or, if she has doubts, whence those doubts arise. Then she can be invited to consider whether similar doubts arise in judging her experiences as "good" or "evil," and why those doubts arise. And she can be asked how these reflections about literature and about life help her to understand the difficulty, if she experiences such, of making moral judgments of good and evil. If she has no difficulty, she can be asked to explain the reasons or the authority that makes her so sure. Such reflections, shared with classmates, might well evoke stimulating and instructive discussions of how one can make moral judgments.

And one more. Writing 12 asks the student to talk about a "hobby or activity" in an "informative" essay, advising a "general audience" about an "aspect" of this hobby or activity. (One wonders, what essay on any subject is not potentially "informative"? The instructor is again asking students to deliberately try to produce a specimen of a fossilized category from a taxonomy of writings that gives us, in fact, *dis*information about what writers do when they write.) No reason is given for the student to come before the reader on this subject, and no guidance is offered (beyond the general admonition to "*use*," as distinguished from merely "*cit[ing]*," information) about how the student might explore the subject or gain fresh insight about the subject from writing about it. The assignment directs the student to follow what many teachers would call a "process" of composing, although what is being asked for, as previously pointed out, is a procedure—a set of neatly arranged steps. The procedure is not in any way directly related to possible ways of exploring the subject or to possible kinds of learning. The procedure essentially stands by itself, as if the teacher who wrote the assignment thought that the procedure was generally a useful succession of steps for students to traverse, irrespective of the subject or the student's possible reasons for wanting to discuss the subject. Writing this paper might give the student drill in a frozen procedure; would the student learn about the subject on which she was writing, or find a reason for writing about it? It is hard to say: Rusty wrote an essay that added to my store of knowledge, though probably not to his own. I would be disinclined to use an assignment worded so loosely, although I can imagine an instructor asking a student what he learns about himself, or his associates, from considering the fact that he practices a particular hobby or engages in a particular activity. But that instructor would need to help the student understand how to learn from such reflection.

CONCLUSION: WRITING TO LEARN INSTEAD OF SIMPLY TO DISPLAY

What is missing in these assignments—and, in spite of differences in "topic," they are remarkably similar in what is asked of the student, and how it is asked—is any suggestion that writing is a way of knowing, or knowing better, or learning. There is no hint that that which one comes to know (or know better) *through* writing can be worth presenting to a reader because that reader may want to participate in the knowing, or may want to share the ideas discovered, or may find the ideas genuinely illuminating. The assignments do not suggest that the constructing of ideas can be made genuinely vivid to readers. Writing, the assignments strongly suggest, is numbingly routine and unexciting.

If the writing to which the invited readers on this project were asked to respond, therefore, is banal, unoriginal, lacking in vividness, or not resonant with the voice of an author to whom the ideas matter, some of the explanation probably lies in the directions given to the student and in the views of writing implied by those directions. If the assignment suggests that writing is a routine packaging of predigested ideas, a display of the ability to produce a specimen of a self-standing form or "mode" of writing, is it any wonder that the resulting essay has all the vigor of a routine practice session, not intended for serious viewers? In some of these writings (the piece on street gangs, for instance, which could be genuinely illuminating for many readers) the student accomplished more than the teacher might reasonably have expected, given her or his directions. But most of the writings are not pieces we would pick up with enthusiasm or read attentively unless we interest ourselves in a subject simply because our students write about it.

These assignments were no doubt selected because they are substantially representative of those that many teachers of writing use in their classes. Conceding that point, I find it discouraging because it supports the view held (I fear) by many students that required instruction in writing is not an activity from which they will learn much (except perhaps the importance of editing for correctness) or about which they care. These attitudes are among the forces that make it essential for colleges and universities to see that attention to writing is extended throughout a student's college career, into courses where the student can indeed learn by writing because the instructor can show how writing *brings* learning. The representativeness of these assignments is discouraging, too, because assignments for writing do not need to be as they are in this book. If teachers reflect and exercise some imagination, assignments can be created that will leave students knowing much more after completing them than they did before.

The only *book* about writing assignments I know that illustrates how writing can become a genuine exploration of problematic concepts is William Coles's *The Plural I* (1978); some of Coles's articles about the curricula in his own writing courses demonstrate the same approach. But I have seen assignments and sequences of assignments from experienced and intellectually engaged teachers at Bryn Mawr College and Syracuse University in which the student is invited to reflect, seek and evaluate information, explore ideas, refine thought, and reach discoveries through writing. These assignments (unfortunately not thus far published) avoid hinting to students that a piece of writing is a specimen to be hung somewhere in a taxonomy; they demonstrate that writing is inquiry. But *any* teacher of writing can simply (though I realize that reorienting one's teaching is not "simple") resolve that the writing assignments in her class, or at least a majority of those assignments, are going to give students the opportunity to learn, through observation and reading and reflection and writing, about matters that the student did not previously understand as fully as she could. The teacher, that is, can resolve to assign writings in which the act of writing is genuinely the act of discovering meaning. Learning is, as scholars of cognition point out, the *reconstruction* of knowledge; the student takes what she thought she knew, reexamines it, and produces a new structure of thought worth preserving and sharing. There may, of course, be a place in the writing curriculum for the kinds of functional and narrowly transactional writing advocated by teachers such as Maxine Hairston (1986). But in my view the work of a writing course, if it is to claim a place in a liberal arts curriculum, is to help students learn and communicate what they learn—perhaps even learn in the act of communicating. If writing includes discovery, then perhaps students can be led to want to come before readers to share those discoveries. Some of that writing may be about what a well-known teacher of rhetoric, Donald Bryant (1965), once referred to as the "undecidable questions"—problems that do not admit of ready or final solutions. Not all assignments in the writing course need concern undecidable matters; some can invite students to present observations, perceptions, recollections, and reflections that the student is fairly sure about. Some writings can display the student's abilities at discovering and reconstructing knowledge. (Summarizing another's writing, reporting another's findings, evaluating a text or a body of data, and so on, can be a part of learning and do figure prominently in civilized discourse.) Whatever the assigned *subject* for writing, the specific writing, if the teacher is willing to "problematize" assigned subjects or present them as a matter for serious reflection rather than for packaging in a display case, *can* become a stimulus to learning.

Our goal in making assignments for writing, in my view, should finally be to help students ask questions, inquire, discover, and thus learn through writing in such a way that they will *want* to come before readers and invite those readers to share, participate in, and be moved by, their learning. That spirit, if developed, can help students become eager to write about whatever topics and issues confront them, in all academic and professional fields, throughout college and throughout their lives. That spirit can help lead students to recognize writing as one of the supremely important acts of a human being.

WORKS CITED

Austin, J.L. (1962). *How to do things with words*. Cambridge, MA: Harvard University Press.

Berthoff, A. (1981). *The making of meaning: Metaphors, models, and maxims for writing teachers*. Portsmouth, NH Boynton/Cook.

Bitzer, L. (1968). The rhetorical situation. *Philosophy and Rhetoric, 1*, 1-15.

Booth, W. (1963). The rhetorical stance. *College Composition and Communication, 14,* 139-145.

Britton, J. (1970). *Language and learning*. Allen Lane, UK: The Penguin Press.

Bryant, D. (1965). Rhetoric: Its functions and its scope. In J. Schwartz & J. Rycenga (Eds.), *The province of rhetoric* (pp. 3-36). New York: The Ronald Press.

Coles, W. (1978). *The plural I.* New York: Holt, Rinehart, and Winston.

Cooper, M. (1984). The pragmatics of form: How do writers discover what to do when? In R. Beach & L. Bridwell (Eds.), *New directions in composition research* (pp. 109-126). New York: Guilford.

Ede, L., & Lunsford, A. (1984). Audience addressed/audience invoked: The role of audience in composition theory and pedagogy. *College Composition and Communication, 35,* 155-171.

Elbow, P. (1987). Closing my eyes as I speak: An argument for ignoring audience. *College English, 49,* 50-69.

Emig, J. (1977). Writing as a mode of learning. *College Composition and Communication, 28,* 122-128.

Hairston, M. (1986). Different products, different processes: A theory about writing. *College Composition and Communication, 37,* 442-452.

Moffett, J. (1965). I, you, and it. *College Composition and Communication, 16,* 243-248.

Ohmann, R., & Martin, H. (1958). *The logic and rhetoric of exposition*. New York: Holt, Rinehart, and Winston.

Searle, J.R. (1971). What is a speech act?" In J.R. Searle (Ed.), *The philosophy of language* (pp. 39-53). London: Oxford University Press.

Toulmin, S. (1964). The layout of arguments. In *The uses of argument* (pp. 94-145). Cambridge: Cambridge University Press.

Vandenberg, P. (1992). Pick up this cross and follow: (ir)responsibility and the teaching of "writing for audience." *Composition Studies, 20,* 84-97.

Appendices

APPENDIX A: DIRECTIONS TO THE 12 READERS

Here are the directions we provided the 12 readers and the questionnaire on response to which we asked them to reply.

DIRECTIONS

A. Your Statement of Philosophy

In a brief essay of 1000 words, please enunciate the basic philosophy which underlies your writing instruction. Obviously, you will be greatly constricted in your discussion by the 1000 word limit; you will not be able to do more than outline the basic principles you teach by.

We intend to present this statement *as is* in our introduction to the study so that our readers can place comments teachers must make on essays in the context of the contributors' basic philosophies. We will also use these statements as information for our own discussion in the introduction.

B. Questions on Your Responding Practices

Obviously you could spend much time answering these questions in great detail. We do not intend you to do so. Rather, we are asking that you treat them as interview-styled questions which you answer to the best of your ability in the language that comes to mind immediately.

We will not be presenting these answers per se in the text. Rather, we will use them as data in our analyses of your responses to student texts. You may handwrite or type your answers in the spaces provided or on an attached sheet.

C. Your Responses to the Sample Essays

We need to mention several matters to you before you begin the task of responding to these essays. First, you will note that there are 15 items here, rather than the 12 we originally projected. It has come to our attention that various factors could cause one to two essays to be discounted in the sampling, for example, should we fail to get permission to use an essay. Thus, it seems good to include two additional essays. Also, several of you noted the fact that you would be interested to know how readers might, or might not, respond to prewriting materials. Thus, we have added a slot in which you may choose to respond to one of three different pieces of planning for essays. In order to keep your workload at the level we originally projected, we are asking that you choose 12 of the 15 samples here to respond to. You may simply write "Omit" on the context sheets for the remaining three. Of course, if you wish to respond to those three, you may certainly do so.

We should say a word about the time this task will require. When we first planned this task, we assumed that teachers would respond to these essays in the exact fashion that they respond to their own student essays; we projected that the 12 essays (our number at that time) would take no more than three hours or so. As we have worked with our concept, we have grown to think our earlier expectations a bit unrealistic. Such a study as we are undertaking is inherently artificial and cannot purport to represent your "day-to-day" responding practices. Rather than seeing your responses to this sampling as representative of what you would always do in responding to your students, we suggest that you see it as representative of the best efforts of good teachers who espouse your composition philosophy. Your responses could serve as a clinic for inexperienced teachers who would like to learn something about teaching methods.

Now, a few comments about the essays. The names given are not the students' real names. The essays have been retyped exactly as they were submitted to writing teachers. Except in cases where the introductions to papers tell you differently, you should assume that papers were written in first semester composition courses.

Please mark the essay in the fashion you would if you were the teacher who received them. If you customarily write comments on the papers, draw lines, circle words, or whatever, make these marks on these papers. If you type out comments on a typewriter or computer, please do so for us. We should make one qualification here. If you use pencil, you will need to go back over your comments in black ink after you have finished. Pencil marks will not copy satisfactorily, and we intend to present many of the essays as marked in our text. This last comment raises another point. It would be a good idea to copy the papers before you begin marking them so that you would be able to throw out a paper and begin again should you decide at a certain point that the comments you have made are not satisfactory.

As we said above, you should feel free to use any marks, symbols, phrases, or abbreviations you would use in your actual classroom responses. If such marks need explanation, you may provide it in your commentary on the first essay in which they are used.

Since our responses to student writing always occur within a certain pedagogical context, however tacit it may be, each of the pieces of writing in the sampling is accompanied by a hypothetical context (usually based on the actual classroom circumstances). Of course, we would prefer to present all 15 essays with all of the students' earlier writings. And, ideally, we would provide a more elaborate set of information detailing the outward circumstances that influence teachers' individual responses when they sit down to read a set of papers. But no amount of detail would capture the complex, individualized nature of responding to student writing in actual situations. We have had to be content to give each paper a brief hypothetical context which identifies the assignment, the drafting stage, and some of the circumstances under which the paper was presumably written. Nevertheless, in three instances, because we wanted to capture something of the highly dynamic, highly contextualized nature of responding, we have chosen to present the piece of writing you are to respond to with earlier drafts of that paper or papers written by that student earlier in the semester. In such instances, respond only to the last draft given, which will be double-spaced for your convenience in marking.

Please read the context statements carefully and be sure you are reading papers in light of the specified stages of drafting, *if* such considerations are important to your ways of responding.

Since the contexts we give you are necessarily incomplete, you should feel free to make additions to the contexts given; for example, you may base a general comment to a paper on information which you would have given to your students in class at the time when this particular type of paper was being written. (Be sure to let us know about such additions in your commentaries following the essays.) However, other than making additions such as these, we would like to ask that you please accept the contexts and assignments for essays, even if they run contrary to your classroom practices. In such a situation, you might pretend you have taken over a class for a sick (no pun intended) colleague. Of course, you should feel free to give your opinions on contexts and assignments in the commentaries at the end of essays.

D. Commentaries

After you have responded to an essay, please write a brief commentary on your responding process. (You might simply handwrite or type these in the section provided on the context sheet for each essay, using the front and back, as needed.) You might want to keep a notepad beside the essay and record your thoughts as you mark the paper. Then, you can simply summarize or record those thoughts in the commentary. Commentaries may include thoughts that come to you about your responding practices as you read and mark these essays, dilemmas these essays presented you with, disagreements you had with the contexts given for essays, and so forth.

E. Your Reactions to the Sampling

After you have completed the responding process, would you please answer the three informational questions on the Reaction Sheet.

QUESTIONNAIRE ON YOUR RESPONDING PRACTICES

1. Assume that you are teaching a freshman writing course. How many, and what kind of assignments do you typically ask students to write? What materials do you typically ask students to turn in for a given assignment?

2. At what point(s) in students' composing processes do you typically make comments? To what extent do you make comments on planning, rough drafts and final drafts? What form(s) do these comments usually take? Handwritten? Typewritten? Spoken? At what point(s), if any, do you comment on errors. And how?

3. What kinds of comments do you typically make on papers? (What issues do your comments address?) What specific forms—statements, questions, symbols, abbreviations, diagrams, and so forth—do your comments normally take? Do your comments change over the course of a term?

4. Define the relation between responding and evaluation. At what point, if any, do you put grades on student essays? Do you ever use split grades?

5. How does your theory of responding to student texts fit in with your overall philosophy of teaching writing; that is, how do you see the purpose and value of responding to student texts in respect to other modes or aspects of writing instruction, such as assignment making, peer responding, pre-teaching, and discussing model essays?

APPENDIX B

Here is a comment-by-comment analysis of the focuses and modes from each of the three sample responses from Chapter 3. They are written by Donald Stewart, Patricia Stock, and Glynda Hull on Writing 6, "The Four Seasons."

STEWART

[N]ow we run into some problems. — Metadiscourse

1. Have you described the four seasons in Syracuse, or have you described four idealized seasons? — Ideas — Cl Prob Posing
2. I think the latter, and I'll tell you why. — Ideas — Qual Neg Eval
3. In describing Spring, you mention the trees blossoming, flowers working their way out of the ground, geese flying north overhead, and a long winter's nap ending for bears, squirrels, rabbits and other hibernating animals. — Ideas — Interpretive
4. These are all cliches about Spring. — Ideas — Neg Eval
5. If you must use them, particularize them. — Word — Imperative
6. Instead of telling us about blossoming trees, tell us how you look forward to the blooming of the redbud tree in your front yard, and of the flowering crab which follows right behind it. — Word — Explanatory
7. Tell us about the particular flowers which blossom in your yard in Syracuse. — Word — Explanatory

We'll skip the geese, but let's take a hard look at your list of hibernating animals. — Metadiscourse

8. How many bears roam the streets of Syracuse? — Ideas — Cl Prob Posing
9. Or do you make frequent trips to the zoo to see them come out of hibernation? — Ideas — Cl Heuristic
10. If you lived in Yellowstone Park in the winter, mention of hibernating bears would be quite natural. — Ideas — Explanatory
11. Here, a reader does a double take. — Ideas — Neg Eval
12. What bears are there in Syracuse, or anywhere nearby? — Ideas — Cl Prob Posing

STOCK

1. I thought it was effective of you to contrast the fall, strolling into Tallahassee and shriveling the flowers, with fall parading . . . into Syracuse, showing off its auburn, garnet, and gold leaves. — Ideas — Praise
2. I must say, I liked the fact that you chose auburn as a color because Auburn the city is so close to Syracuse. — Word — Praise
3. I actually stopped to think if that might be why Auburn has the name it does. — Ideas — Rdr Exper
4. Do you know? — Ideas — Cl Heuristic
5. And I liked the precious gem, precious metal allusions you invoked by choosing garnet and gold as colors. — Word — Praise

6.	The season moves you inward into enclosed, secure beds of leaves and outward into majestic displays of ornamental leaves.	Ideas	Interpretive
7.	If you had not told me that winter was your second favorite season, I would not have guessed it.	Ideas	Neg Rdr React
8.	I would have guessed it was spring because your descriptions of spring have almost as much vitality as your descriptions of fall.	Ideas	Explanatory
9.	As I read the section of your essay you devoted to winter, I was struck by how heavily you relied on overused language to express your feelings about Syracuse's winters	Word	Neg Rdr React
10.	(my understanding is that Syracuse's winters are WINTERS).	Ideas	Rdr Remark

HULL

1.	You've got an unusual paper here in that some readers will love it and some will feel just as strongly in the opposite direction.	Whole	Interpretive
2.	What I want you to do is to figure out what it is about your paper, and about different readers, that could produce such different reactions. For example:	Whole	Imperative
3.	Your seasonal portraits could have, with a few exceptions, been written by someone who grew up in Tallahassee.	Ideas	Interpretive
4.	What will some readers like about this quality?	Ideas	Open Prob Pos
5.	What will others dislike?	Ideas	Open Prob Pos
6.	You say at the end of your paper that you've told only the good things about the seasons.	Ideas	Interpretive
7.	Why might this be pleasant to some readers but offensive to others?	Ideas	Open Prob Pos
8.	You use a lot of phrases that are often used in conjunction with the seasons.	Word	Interpretive
9.	Again, what will some readers like about this, others dislike, and why?	Word	Open Prob Pos
10.	Given your consideration of these questions, would you now make any changes in your paper?	Whole	Open Prob Pos
11.	Why or why not?	Whole	Open Prob Pos

APPENDIX C

Below is a copy of the original rubric we used to chart the 12 readers' responses to the modified sampling of 10 essays and, following it, our revised rubric.

Twelve Readers Reading

Responder #   Rater   Essay

FOCUS

Global Structure							
Local Structure							
Expression.							
Correction/Conv							

Voice							

Naming							
Development							
Ideas							

Whole Essay/Other							

MODE

Corrective							
Directive							
Advisory							
Evaluative							
Qualified Evaluative							
Other							

Requests							
Heuristic							
Problem-Posing							

RUBRIC FOR ANALYZING COMMENTS

Responder: _____   Writing: _____

FOCUS

Comment :

Ideas																	
Development																	
Global Structure																	
Local Structure																	
Wording																	
Correctness																	
Extra-Textual																	

MODE

Corrective																	
Evaluative																	
Qualified Eval																	
Praise																	
Imperative																	
Advisory																	
Indirect Request																	
Closed Prob-Pos																	
Closed Heuristic																	
Open Prob-Pos																	
Open Heuristic																	
Interpretive																	
Explanatory																	
Reader-Response																	
Other																	

APPENDIX D

The job of labeling the 113 sets of responses proved to be complicated and time-consuming. Originally, our rubric consisted of nine focuses and nine modes:

FOCUS	MODE
Global Structure	Corrective
Local Structure	Evaluative
Expression	Qualified Evaluative
Correctness	Imperative
Advisory	
Voice	
Naming	Indirect Request
Development	Problem-Posing
Ideas	Heuristic
Other	Other

In addition, four of the mode categories called for further division. Evaluative and qualified evaluative comments were divided into positive and negative, and problem-posing and heuristic questions were further divided into open and closed.

Using these original categories, the raters' agreement was around 70%—to a great extent, we suspected, because of the large number of categories we were working with. In order to give credit for near matches in categories that were closely related and proved the most difficult to distinguish consistently, we sought to identify agreement in *degree* as well as agreement in *kind*. That is, in addition to giving full credit when two of our raters labeled a given comment in the *same* category, we gave partial credit when two of them labeled a comment in contiguous categories, categories which we designated as so closely related as to merit partial agreement. We stipulated six such contiguous categories, three in focus, three in mode:

Ideas—Development
Ideas—Other (Extra-Textual)
Expression (Wording)—Correctness
Imperative—Advisory
Open Problem-Posing—Open Heuristic
Evaluative—Other (Reflective)

We gave full credit (a value of 1) for full agreement, i.e., for the same rating by two raters. We gave half credit (a value of .5) for near agreement, i.e., for a contiguous rating by two raters. Thus, when all three raters agreed on the same category, they achieved three out of a possible three agreements (Rater A agreed with Rater B, for one agreement; Rater B agreed with Rater C, for a second agreement; and Rater C agreed with rater A, for a third agreement: a total of three agreements, for a value of "3"). When two raters agreed on a given comment and the third labeled the comment in a noncontiguous category, the group made one agreement, or a value of "1." However, when two raters agreed on the *same* category and the third rater labeled the comment in a *contiguous* category, the group made one full agreement and two partial agreements, for a total value of "2" (Raters A and B made one agreement; Rater C and Rater A made a partial agreement, for a value of ".5;" and Rater C and Rater B made a partial agreement, for a value of ".5"). When two raters reached partial agreement and the third made no match, the group achieved a .5 value on the classification of the comment.

For example, consider how we would tabulate agreement on the raters' classifications of the following comment:

Is there anything about Syracuse winters that people do *not* enjoy?

If all three raters labeled this comment "ideas," they would achieve three out of a possible three agreements, for a total of three full agreements, or a value of "3":

Rater A agrees with Rater B = one agreement, a value of "1"
Rater B agrees with Rater C = one agreement, a value of "1"
Rater C agrees with Rater A = one agreement, a value of "1".

If two raters placed this comment under "ideas" and the third called it "development," a category that is contiguous with ideas, the raters would achieve one full agreement and two "half" agreements, for a total of two agreements, or a value of "2":

Rater A agrees with Rater B = one agreement, a value of "1"
Rater B agrees partially with Rater C = half agreement, a value of ".5"
Rater C agrees partially with Rater A = half agreement, a value of ".5".

As a final illustration, if two raters labeled the focus of this comment "development" and the third rater labeled it "global structure," the raters would achieve only one agreement, for a value of "1":

Rater A agrees with Rater B = one agreement, a value of "1"
Rater B does not agree with Rater C = no agreement
Rater C does not agree with Rater A = no agreement.

There would be no partial agreement between the third rater and the other two raters since the category "global structure" is not contiguous with "development."

We obtained our rate of agreement for each of the 2529 comments in the sampling by using a coefficient of determination, comparing three things three at a time (in this case, identifying how frequently the three raters agreed with one another on individual comments). In labeling the *focuses* of the comments, the raters made 6287 out a possible 7587 agreements, for an 83% agreement. The number of possible agreements (7587) was arrived at by multiplying the total number of comments on the sampling (2529) times three (i.e., three possible agreements per comment). In labeling the *modes* of the comments, they made 6395 out of a possible 7587 agreements, for an 84% agreement. The resulting .91 interrater reliability (the square root of 83.5%) gives us a firm foundation to make claims about our readers' responses on the basis of these categories and counts.

Later, in the name of simplicity, we collapsed several categories. We joined expression and naming into the broad category "wording." We included "voice" within the category "other," which we renamed "extra-textual comments." And we separated negative evaluations and qualified evaluations from praise. We were left with the final version of the rubric presented at the start of Chapter 3.

APPENDIX E

Here are the 12 readers' statements of philosophy–that is, their theoretical statements about the teaching of writing.

Chris Anson
Teaching Composition, Circa 1989

Early in my career in composition, my engagement in some research on response to writing (and my reading of various theorists) convinced me that our primary responsibility as educators is to create a context which gives students the initiative and confidence to take control of their own learning, especially through writing and reading. I began to listen carefully to the ways students talked about their writing. Those who made the most progress seemed, during the various processes of drafting and revising, very uncertain. They weighed alternatives. They wrestled with rhetorical choices. They shaped, embellished, and rejected directions for their texts. Yet at the same time they seemed to embrace this uncertainty, to relish it. Those who had the most trouble, by contrast, were afraid of admitting uncertainty, as if to guess that good writers (like good teachers) always know exactly what they are doing. The more I examined these two attitudes toward uncertainty, the more convinced I became in their connections to learning. Students who accepted uncertainty were more deeply engaged in the relationship between their thinking and their emerging texts. I started to hypothesize that by reflecting tentativeness and possibility in my response to their work, I would encourage a relativistic and learning-rich view of writing.

Experimenting with this notion, I soon discovered that when I expressed certainties (as formulas or absolute principles of good writing), I made my students revert to pleas for "what I wanted," so that my agendas would take over their writing and turn them into scribes of my own beliefs. Yet I held my conviction loosely, aware that at a higher level I could fall prey to a contradiction—being certain of my belief. Peter Elbow's marvelous book, *Embracing Contraries*, helped to reify my thinking by giving assurance that, like the process of writing, instructional uncertainty is not only natural but healthy. And so, to a great extent, expressing my "basic philosophy" of writing instruction must remain a reflection of what I have settled on for the moment—after the questioning that comes from trying to put it down in a thousand words—in the summer of 1989.

1. **Purpose is the key to writing.** Although it's been said countless times by everyone from Applebee to Zinsser, when we strip writing of its purpose and use it primarily for the assessment of discourse-specific skills such as the control of surface mechanics, we make it lifeless. Without rhetorical and personal reasons for writing, students simply go through the motions of making meaning without being, as Vygostky has put it in an analogy to practicing piano scales, "involved in the essence of the music itself." Such a principle seems so commonplace that it is hardly worth saying; yet again and again we find evidence of writing being used in intellectually and personally meaningless ways in classroom settings. Even when our instruction focuses on the processes and social construction of texts, we are often so much at the center of our own agendas that there is not room for students to develop their own purposes for writing, or find ways of making our purposes theirs. The implication of such a view for the classroom is, I think, obvious, and it means at times we must learn to facilitate instead of dominate, to guide the **creation** of knowledge instead of simply giving it, even when our own heads may be teeming with brilliant things to say.

2. **"Writing ability," like the spoken language, best develops naturally, through constant engagement in socially and intellectually purposeful textual activities.** Our public view of writing still sees it as a technology which can be learned or mastered like typing—through short required courses. This view is especially pervasive in higher education, where faculty in many disciplines look upon the teaching of composition as a necessary accumulation of "skills" to be used in the service of "clean English prose." Unfortunately, such views militate against a more vital and self-fulfilling conception in which writing best develops naturally, in parallel with the spoken language, through constant use. In reducing writing to skills that must be learned in a few short weeks, we make it socially and pragmatically meaningless, or meaningful only in debilitating and sterile ways, leaving behind what James Britton calls "dummy runs"—writing used primarily for the purpose of measuring how well students have learned the technology.

I want, as a teacher of writing, to expose such misconceptions for what they are, and in the process help students to acquire more productive models of writing which will make their improvement self-fulfilling. If they can want to write, for a variety of reasons, then they will; and in so doing, there is no question that they will become more effective writers, with or without instruction.

3. **Writing competence is strategic, not purely informational.** We cannot hope to give students a "how-to" formula for every kind of writing they will find in any possible context. What they need is a strategic way of thinking in which they can use their existing knowledge of discourse to solve new problems they encounter as writers. Each new experience, especially if it is challenging, enhances this strategic knowledge, making them successively better able to cope with ever more complex or unfamiliar tasks.

4. **Writing inscribes the self.** This much seems certain. But what is not often explored is the way that the self is changed in that inscription. In teaching writing—any kind at any level—we are also teaching people how to explore who they are and, in the process, change what and how they think. This happens, I believe, at two levels simultaneously. The first is personally reflexive, as the process of making words compels writers to examine their expressed truths or the thinking from which they have emerged. The second is socially reflexive, as someone in a specific context reads those words and responds to them interpersonally. I can think of no better manifestation of these principles than a pedagogy of self-assessment and socially dynamic response, primarily in the form of opportunities to think about one's writing, to experiment with alternatives, and to have others respond to it, ideally in small groups in the classroom and in the public response afforded by sending or submitting material to readers beyond the classroom.

At a time when it is becoming increasingly popular for teachers to confess their ideological dispositions from the start of a class as a way of openly justifying their selection of readings, course structure, or writing assignments, I still find myself clinging to pedagogical relativism. My aim is not so much to turn students "into" something—feminists or secular humanists or corporate executives—as to help them to see alternatives, to position themselves relative to other positions. In the process, there is much **repositioning**, and this inevitably leads to a sort of intellectual tentativeness that strikes me as fundamental to good learning. I would much rather incite than expound, problematize than proselytize, question than provide truth. For young students, especially, this is hard to accomplish with abstractions. I like to energize the class with some contextualized problem—a rhetorically deep case or a simulation—that they can immediately connect to their own thoughts, experiences, or beliefs.

Writing instruction, when it works well in a classroom setting, makes use of all language activities, particularly rich, open discussion. At those moments when students are discussing their writing or the issues surrounding and infusing it, I like to lose myself among them. I delight in listening. The students, for their part, learn to expect and understand my frequent abrogations of authority, my interested silences. Writing works only in a community, and we have an obligation to establish one in our classrooms as a way to demonstrate its relationship to the texts we create there. There is a danger, of course, of over-challenging students with chaos.

Surrounding the challenge of relativism must be a safe, meticulous structure of procedures, policies, and social maxims for participation.

5. **Writing inscribes the community.** The classroom experience, especially when it is energetic and enjoyable, involves what I believe to be the most valuable part of the writing process: being read and responded to by interested and trusted people. I don't believe such readers always need to be "experts"; a friend's honest engagement in a writer's text may be more telling and valuable than a professor's scholarly pronouncements about the techniques of discourse—as Russ Hunt has pointed out in his marvelous little article, "Could You Put In a Lot of Holes? Modes of Response to Writing," [Language Arts, Vol. 64 (1986), 229-232]. The balance, especially, of "reader-based" feedback by peers and the more exacting critiques which we as teachers often provide can be illuminating.

The assumption that discourse varies across different communities is now fairly commonplace and supported by a good deal of research. Its translation into practice, however, is weak. "Writing across the curriculum" has, at least in some composition programs, become a process of reading essays about different multi-disciplinary topics, without regard to the fundamental differences in the ways that those disciplines see, study, and talk about the world. Teaching writing should accept the diversity of communities which students are in or wish to enter, while simultaneously respecting an over-arching goal of the academic "conversation," the discourse of which is inclusive and intellectually fulfilling.

Peter Elbow
Principles That Underlie My Teaching

Given the subject of this book, I need to start by emphasizing my belief that teacher responses to student writing are *not* the most important thing in a writing course—not the major source of student learning. I take to heart the extensive research that shows how often students ignore or misunderstand what we write. That might be heart-breaking if what we wrote were always brilliant, but because of the conditions under which we read and comment on student writing, what we write is often highly problematic. Writing was not meant to be read in stacks of 25 or 50 pieces—writing comments while feeling tired, rushed, and grumpy. Thus my summary of principles central to my teaching tends to point to *other* features of a writing course that I tend to see as more important than my comments on student writing:

• Students, like the rest of us, learn more by doing than by hearing or reading precepts—more from the experiences I set up than by the diagnosis and advice I give. Thus the most important part of my course is the collection of writing activities I devise—both as in-class workshop writing activities and at-home assignments. Through these activities I am trying to teach *experientially* what are perhaps my main principles about writing:

— That writing requires two opposed cognitive abilities, namely the ability to generate copiously and the ability to criticize cuttingly; that trying to generate and criticize at the same time makes writing hard; but if we consciously clear arenas in our writing process for each opposing cognitive ability to flower unobstructed by the other, we tend to write much better and with less frustration.

— That we all have unlimited supplies of words and ideas inside our heads and can reasonably expect writing sometimes to lead us to thoughts that surprise us (this being probably the most rewarding experience for writers).

— That it makes sense to get students to think of themselves as writers—people who already have lots of verbal skill and things to say. I expect that even the most unskilled of them can produce writing worth reading.

• About revising: it's important—but not *that* important. That is, I need to help them learn genuine revising—reseeing, reshaping—not just editing. I build in revising by having them turn in midprocess drafts and final drafts on separate weeks—often working on other assignments in intervening weeks; and by making sure they get feedback on early and midprocess drafts (sometimes from me and always from peers). Yet I build in *non*revising too. We all need chances to write lots of things, try them out, see what pleasure and learning we can get from them, put them aside or throw them away and go on. We learn from making lots of starts. The idea that we should revise everything we write is one of those school myths that is totally out of whack with the practice of real writers—and a formula for making students hate writing. One of the marks of a good writer is knowing when *not* to revise: either because it's good as it is—or good *enough*— or not worth the effort. Thus I try consciously to make sure they do plenty of unrevised writing such as freewriting, sketches, foolings around, and quick tries.

• The climate of the course. I don't think people learn well or take the risks necessary for learning unless they feel safe and supported. That is, even though I try to expect a lot of them, I work at being their ally more than their adversary. I think people learn more from praise and positive reinforcement than from judgment and criticism. I also try for a climate of community and supportive collaboration. That is, even though writing has a private dimension (and usefully so), I try to design procedures that emphasize the social and cooperative dimension to writing.

• Liking writing. It obviously helps when students like to write. But I'm getting more and more interested these days in the proposition that students improve their writing faster when they like *what* they write. Let me explain. It might seem as though improvement happens this way:

> We write something. We see that it has terrible faults. Therefore we hate it
> and we improve it.

But I wonder about that model. I suspect it works more like this:

> We write something. We see it has terrible faults. But we *like* it. And *that's*
> what drives us to work on improving it. When we hate what we write we tend
> to put the piece aside and say, "I've really got to work on this piece some day."

It's beginning to dawn on me that many of the things I've tended to do instinctively (which I'm now learning to do more deliberately and with less guilt) are really designed to help students learn to like what they write. Yes, I also want them to see the faults, but it doesn't bother me if students go for a while with "too high" an opinion of their writing. They'll find faults soon enough if they care about what they write, and it's their caring that will in fact lead to more improvement in writing in the long run than my pointing out of faults. I think I've noticed over the years that good writing teachers are better than most of us at liking their students and what they write. I've always figured this was kind of an accident: who could hang in there very long with any energy and good spirits without this gift (or this blindness) of liking the kids and their writing? But now I'm sensing that the liking is central. I've begun to realize that there's usually a crucial turning point somewhere in the first weeks of my course: am I going to *like* this class or not? When I do, everything seems to go better; when I don't, my teaching goes badly and they seem to make less progress. Thus I have begun to ask myself more consciously now, What can I do to increase the chances that I'll like these students and their writing—and they'll like their writing.

• About "proper" vs. "improper" discourse. This issue plays at different levels: correctness vs. mistakes in mechanics; standard vs. nonstandard English; academic discourse vs. other discourses (such as standard English, expressive/personal discourse, or other dialects or idiolects). My position at all three levels is what I like to call productively schizophrenic:

- Correctness. I try to teach students to turn off awareness of mechanics at early points in the writing process (and many of them have difficulty learning this—particularly the weak students). But I also stress the importance of (and I require) surface correctness on important final drafts.

- Standard English. I try to teach them to allow themselves to write in nonstandard English (even about "serious" topics on "formal assignments") if that's more linguistically comfortable or cognitively productive. But I also try to teach them to achieve standard English on certain drafts.

- Academic discourse. I try to teach them to write expressive, personal discourse and engage in imaginative writing. But I also try to teach them to use academic discourse on certain occasions (and sometimes require two final drafts of the same paper, one in academic discourse and one not.)

• About audience. My understanding of audience gives me a conceptual framework within which to see teacher responses to student writing. My main principle here is that students (like all of us) need a balance of audiences, of audience orientations, and of kinds of feedback. For example students have tended to write for only one audience: teachers (and for a grade). As a result they tend to be unrealistically deferential or even craven about trying to please us, yet underneath scorning our criteria and the kind of writing we want. They need to write to other audiences, such as to each other and to persons outside the class. In addition they need a balance among three *audience orientations*.

- Private writing. We all need a place for writing where we suit only ourselves and don't worry about other readers. (Of course we have various audiences swimming around in our heads which shape our private writing, but that doesn't diminish the safety that comes from not having to show to actual readers.) I sometimes even minimize the self as audience—trying to teach students to give themselves permission to put down words that do *not* satisfy that sometimes-demanding audience of self.

- Shared writing—writing that one gives to an audience but doesn't get feedback on. This may sound artificial in a school setting (sometimes we teachers can't think of anything to do to a text but give feedback). But actually, "mere sharing" is a natural activity in the world: it's what usually happens when writers give readings or publish articles or stories. I get students just to read what they've written to a partner or to a small group or even to the whole class; I have students give copies to each other of what they've written; and I publish a class anthology three times a semester (funded by a Writing Program lab fee).

- Writing that one gives to an audience for feedback or response.

Each of these audience orientations promotes its own kind of learning. Private writing gives students the most safety and practice and takes none of my time to read. Students probably learn most from just writing a great deal—without instruction or feedback. (They're not writing enough unless they're writing more than I can possibly read.) To share writing without getting feedback increases audience awareness and teaches us how our writing feels in our mouth and sounds in our ear—all this with no instruction. Most writers agree that the ear and the voice are the main organs for improving writing. As for the third audience orientation—writing for the response—the benefits to learning are obvious. Yet this third orientation must also be divided, for writers need three kinds of response or reader:

- Reader as everyday human who focuses on the message—who reads to see what the writer has to say and then replies with his views on the topic.

- Reader as trusted ally: someone who gives support no matter how poor the writing or debatable the message. A writer can confide things in this kind of ally that she wouldn't confide with others; she can take chances or write things she can't control or understand yet.

- Reader as diagnostician, coach, giver of advice.

Most students have almost never written except for teachers and in the third audience orientation (for feedback) and almost never gotten any kind of feedback except for the third sort (diagnosis and advice). The damage is considerable. Therefore in my teaching I try hard to create a balance of audiences, audience orientations and kinds of response.

But I have omitted to list a *fourth* kind of reader—reader as evaluator or judge: someone who can grade the piece or evaluate how good it is in relation to some standard. For it's important to realize that a diagnostician or coach is not the same as a judge. We can diagnose problems in a paper and give useful advice without grading it. I have almost never given conventional grades to individual papers, but have sometimes appended to my comments a kind of grid or analytic framework—giving a '+', 'ok', or '-' on three to five criteria (e.g., Effectiveness of Reasons, Organization, Clarity of Syntax and Diction, Voice/stance, Mechanics). This was an attempt to ally student anxiety in hopes they'd pay more attention to my comments—comments which usually don't answer the question, "But, *how good* was my writing?"

I have finally given myself permission to act on my sense that evaluation is not very important for learning to write better—indeed that the emphasis on evaluation and grading in schools is usually a hindrance to learning. I am therefore currently experimenting with a system where course grades are based entirely on tasks and activities and responsibilities students must fulfill—not on my evaluation of their writing. For grades above a B, I specify an extra set of tasks (somewhat daunting for most students). As I continue to experiment with this principle, these are my goals: that I not grade their writing (though sometimes permitting myself an evaluative dimension in my comments); that the requirements for an A or A/B are sufficiently daunting that not everyone will try for them; that those students who get a B or higher will have worked very hard on their writing and will probably write creditably.

Anne Gere
Statement of Philosophy

As a parent I aim to work myself out of a job. I love my children, of course, and delight in remaining intimately connected with them as long as we all live, but I want them to become independent adults who make their own decisions and take responsibility for their own lives. Each of their steps toward autonomy—cooking for themselves, learning to drive, developing the skills that will enable them to earn their own incomes—provides me a measure of success. When they ask for advice I am happy to offer it, but I am even more pleased when they tackle hard choices on their own. As a teacher of writing I am likewise interested in working myself out of a job.

As is true in parenting, working myself out of a job as a writing instructor does not mean separating myself from my students or refusing to help them. It does mean encouraging them to write for themselves, to make their own choices, instead of concentrating their energies on pleasing me. The philosophy that guides my teaching can be summarized by five statements:

- WRITERS NEED A WIDE REPERTOIRE OF APPROACHES TO COMPOSING.
- STUDENTS SHOULD HAVE AUTHORITY OVER THEIR OWN TEXTS.
- WRITING IS A SOCIAL ACT.
- COMPOSING CONTRIBUTES TO INTERTEXTUAL CONVERSATION.
- GRADES BELONG LATE IN THE COMPOSING PROCESS.

Implementation of this philosophy, like implementing my philosophy of parenting, varies with circumstance and with my continued learning, but these statements suggest the general direction.

WRITERS NEED A WIDE REPERTOIRE OF APPROACHES TO COMPOSING

Composing is not like riding a bicycle. One does not learn a single set of skills and apply them everywhere and always the same. Writers need to learn contextually because there is no one right way to compose. Different tasks, circumstances and constraints require different strategies. Writers who rely on one strategy for composing find themselves immobilized when faced with an unusual or difficult writing task.

Whether the issue is ways of generating ideas for writing or effective strategies for proofreading, I encourage multiple approaches to composing. One student will find a set of heuristic questions useful for beginning writing while another will insist that free writing works best. We talk about the relative merits of reading aloud versus reading backwards to catch errors. By regularly assigning and sharing "process papers" in which students detail their own ways of writing, by reading accounts of published writers, and by talking about my own writing, I demonstrate that composing takes many forms, that different strategies work well for different writers, and that when one approach isn't working good writers turn to another.

Many students come to class initially with the assumption that there is a "right" way to write, and they seek a set of rules by which to practice this orthodoxy. Although I will acknowledge that there are some "wrong" ways to go about writing—such as concentrating exclusively on forming the perfect first sentence or spending hours on workbook grammar exercises—I concentrate on helping students see that there are many right ways to compose.

STUDENTS SHOULD HAVE AUTHORITY OVER THEIR OWN TEXTS

Authority over one's texts takes on problematic dimension in school-sponsored writing. After all, students are frequently composing in a required class writing in response to an instructor's assignment. This context can militate against students feeling that they have any stake in the writing, much less have authority over it. Yet, students must "own" writing for it to be effective. The instructor faces the challenge of giving students authority over texts they are required to write.

Although they ask it in various ways, one of students' most frequent questions is: "What do you want?" They aim to please the teacher and want to make their writing conform to whatever the teacher wants. I try to turn that question back to students so their writing becomes increasingly what they want. This isn't easy in the face of competition, grades, and years of schooling, but I am most successful when I remember to pay attention to what students feel as well as what they know. When I can help students recognize that most writers experience feelings of insecurity, of apprehension, of being not good enough, I can usually help them move toward feelings of confidence, comfort, and even pleasure in writing. With these positive feelings about writing comes a clear sense of what they want in writing. From this point forward my job becomes one of asking the kinds of questions any interested reader would ask about a text. Rather than insisting that students conform to my vision of what their papers should be, I probe and question to help them define their own purposes more clearly. My own purpose is for students to retain authority over their own writing, to write what they want rather than what they think I want.

WRITING IS A SOCIAL ACT

Our culture perpetuates the myth of writing as a private and isolated activity. From real estate ads for "isolated cottage suitable for writer" to publishing conventions that group collaborators in an "acknowledgements" section while reserving the title page for a single name, our society emphasizes singularity in writing. While I recognize the existence of individual aspects in writing, I see writing as social.

Many students accept unquestioningly the cultural mythology that describes writing as a solo performance rather than a social act. They assume that writers, who are born not made, always work in isolated garrets completely removed from other human beings. They often eschew any form of sharing in writing because it seems to them a form of cheating.

One strategy for helping students see writing in social terms is to invite them to respond to one another's drafts. Once students know and begin to trust one another, I ask them to participate in writing groups where they discuss ideas for writing, share drafts, and work on problems of editing. As they participate in writing groups, students begin to recognize the social dimensions in writing, to see that receiving suggestions for revision is not a form of cheating. At the same time that they see writing in social terms, students begin to envision themselves as writers rather than as conscripts fulfilling an assignment.

COMPOSING CONTRIBUTES TO INTERTEXTUAL CONVERSATION

Making meaning with texts, whether in reading or writing, involves intertextual transactions. As we read we catch allusions, draw upon our experiences with other texts, and devise meanings based as much on what we bring to the text as what it contains. Similarly, when we write we draw, both consciously and unconsciously, upon other texts. We make meanings in response to and with the aid of texts already in existence.

Accordingly, I encourage students to think of composing as reading as well as writing, to see that they compose meanings in their minds when they look at texts much as they compose meanings when they put pen to paper. Seeing reading and writing as two halves of the same whole leads students to a more flexible view of texts in general.

In addition to recognizing that they need not be bound to their own first drafts, they begin to see others' texts as invitations rather than as implacable surfaces of perfection. They start to see texts as posing questions and raising issues to which they can respond rather than merely as models to be admired. They begin to talk back to texts.

GRADES BELONG LATE IN THE COMPOSING PROCESS

All writing instructors face the inherent tension of the dual role often characterized as coach and referee. The coach encourages writers, urges them on when they falter, and makes constructive suggestions to help them improve their writing. The referee, charged with evaluating students' performances, ranks them in relation to one another through grades.

One way to reduce this tension is to postpone the referee role as long as possible. I do not grade papers as they are produced during the term although I read them carefully and make extensive comments. At the end of the term I ask students to select a certain number for grading, and I base my final grade on what appears in their folders.

One of my recurring nightmares involves being pursued by hordes of former students who want me to continue to serve as their teacher. But by teacher they really mean proof-reader, editor, or muse. These nightmare students want me to give them ideas for writing, to suggest revisions, to fix all the commas. In my waking hours I know that my former students may occasionally stop by to talk about what they are doing, but they will not chase after me flapping their papers because I teach them to become writers who form their own discourse communities and make their own choices.

Glynda Hull
Seeing with a Different Lens:
Thoughts on the Teaching of Writing

> Class and culture erect boundaries that hinder our vision—blind us to the logic of error and the ever-present stirring of language—and encourage the designation of otherness, difference, deficiency. . . . To truly educate in America, to reach the full sweep of our citizenry, we need to question received perception, shift continually from the standard lens.
>
> —Mike Rose, *Lives on the Boundary* (1989)

What I've most wanted to do as a teacher is to see with a different lens. In any composition class, but particularly in those labeled "basic" or "remedial," there will on occasion be puzzling student performances: essays that don't come close to addressing the assignment, at least the one that we imagined; sentences that rock you with awkwardness or error; answers and comments in a tutorial or a class that collide with our expectations about how such discussions will likely proceed. In those situations, unless we're careful, unless we can "shift continually from the standard lens," we are apt to label a student as different and therefore deficient. This happens, not because we are uncaring teachers or don't have good intentions, but because we are all most at home in our own discourse communities, so at home, in fact, that we take our own language and literacy practices as natural and right and look askance at different ways of using words. What I've wanted to do as a teacher is to find ways to understand the logic and history that stand behind any learning performance, and to use that understanding to inform whatever instruction I provide—whether it occurs through comments on a student's paper or a conversation in a conference or a discussion in the classroom. I've wanted to make it my normal business to assume coherence and sense, to take for granted that, given a better angle of vision, we can see a student's text and discourse anew.

If you believe in the coherence of learning performances, you will also be sympathetic to the ways in which students' sentences and essays and patterns of conversation, though sometimes departing from the conventions valued in schooling and the academy, do nonetheless adhere to rules and models—just a different set. One way to understand acts of reading and writing, then, is to uncover the rules and strategies and points of view that underlie students' constructions and interpretations of texts. Similarly, I'd argue that if students are to learn to produce and take part in academic discourse, their education will include a deconstruction of the notion of conventions. Instead of acting as if the standard forms and practices that we adhere to in order to produce what will be recognized as academic writing— that is, our ways of marshalling evidence and seeming like authorities and handling source texts and developing an argument—instead of acting as if these ways of using language were right and obvious and second nature to anyone who has his wits about him, we'll need to find ways to treat conventions as conventions, to expose them as culturally-bound and socially-defined.

There's a not-so-subtle agenda behind what I'm saying. Writing courses have traditionally been our institutions' gatekeepers, and thus many teachers have had to work to find ways to let more students inside and to help them remain. Like others, I have wanted to acknowledge the logic and history of reading and writing performances, but I've also wanted to remember the sanctity of academic forms and traditions. This is not to say that I do not revere the classic or would discard western analytic thought and logic. Actually, I've been interested for a long time in finding out through research how we can help underprepared writers acquire a very "basic" knowledge about sentence correctness and, more recently, essayist conventions at the level of discourse. I do often think, however, that the future will see us expanding our notions of what constitutes a literacy practice that can be valued in the classroom and by the academy, and rightly so. As more and more students come to us from cultural backgrounds that vary from the white middle class norm on which so much of schooling practice is based, we need to keep our eyes open for ways to honor that diversity, to put its richness to work in our classrooms. We might, for example, examine what have been called "unofficial literacies"—the uses of reading and writing which flourish apart from schooling—to see what such practice can teach us about the acquisition of reading and writing skills and the forms and functions of texts outside the essayist tradition. We might celebrate the tension between academic and non-academic writing, pushing towards an appreciation of varieties of language use and coaxing the growth of a meta-awareness of how language functions.

All of this—acknowledging the logic and history of reading and writing performances, representing academic discourse as socially agreed upon convention, broadening our notions of literacy by asking what our students and their communities and the workplace can teach us—all of this suggests for me particular practices and routines and structures for the composition class, while disallowing others. I am often perplexed, for example, by the kinds of writing assignments we still ask our students to carry out—assignments that are only once removed (by the writing process generation) from directions to write about what you did on your summer vacation. I am disturbed that so much of school writing and writing in composition classes is still an ersatz activity, an artificial substitute for genuine projects that have a chance of engaging students' intellects and inspiring their commitment. To my mind, an "authentic" writing task has got to be at the center of composition instruction, one which invites students to take part in writing and reading activities that are socially meaningful in the context built and shared by a particular classroom community. In such a setting, students can work collaboratively to carry out joint projects too taxing or complex for individual effort, or alternately, they can proceed more independently but with a joint sense of enterprise and purpose. To be sure, there will be room for activities valued in current practice—occasions for multiple revisions, talk about process, pre-writing aids—but these activities will have only a reflected glory, a secondary importance dependent upon their variant relevance and usefulness in accomplishing the authentic task at hand.

Our students are going to learn to write and to value writing, not merely to master the construction of themes or essays that fit the genres of college composition—not just to produce an expository paper or an argument or a book review (which is not to say that these forms and the literacy practices surrounding them do not have a place). Our students are going to learn to write and to value writing as a means of human interaction and knowledge building to which we all have a right, and in order to understand and experience the varieties, power, and constraints of language use. If we can allow this kind of larger purpose to inform our programs—beginning composition as well as advanced, "remedial" writing alongside honors English—then we can also begin to envision an education for all our students that has potential to embolden and empower.

> **Richard Larson**
> **A Statement of 'Philosophy' About the Teaching of Writing**

In my writing courses, regardless of their level, I work to help students understand what it means to have, and to express, an idea. To "have and express" an idea includes, for me, finding that idea, evaluating it (deciding whether it is worth placing before a reader), putting it into words, explaining it, illustrating it (if it admits of illustration), supporting it, defending it against differing views—in short, earning the reader's respect for that idea, as developed. I take it that literate citizens, many of whom will enter professions and callings in which they must explore ideas, need to know what it means to have and express an idea.

I also want students to develop the ability to assess the ideas of others: to identify the ideas as these people (students and professionals) express them, see why these writers come before readers with their ideas, see how these writers try to win the assent of readers (how they illustrate, how they support, how they show the significance of those ideas). I want students to recognize how other writers ask them as readers to respond to their ideas. I would like students to learn to judge the credibility, the value, the significance of other writers' ideas—and then to make judgments about their own ideas. I find that students have had next to no encouragement toward such evaluation of others' writing.

My courses focus, so far as I can make them do so, not on students' personal histories (unless those histories are related to the ideas they are discussing), but on significant, current social and cultural issues, such as the wisdom of "reverse discrimination," the value of "scientific" research, the limits of individual autonomy in a free society. I encourage students to read carefully, think seriously, and write informedly about the issues they are confronting.

In my courses, most assignments are focused on readings. I ask students to read specific pieces (ordinarily *not* from textbooks, but from current books, articles and reports), and to find for themselves readings that extend their thinking about the readings assigned. As I've said elsewhere in print, I don't think there is any such genre in writing as the "research paper" (no serious writer other than a burdened college student ever sat down specifically to write a "research paper"); I think all writing should, as appropriate, reflect the fruits of reading and investigation into topics and issues before the student. I want students to find information and ideas, evaluate what they find, and compose inquiries based upon what they have read, what they have located, and what they have discovered for themselves through reflections. So far as possible, I ask students to discuss *issues*, not people, places, or memories, unless the people, places, and memories are related to issues they are confronting.

So my class periods are devoted, primarily, to discussion of others' writings—students' writings, professional writing—to help students understand issues and to help them understand how to go about developing *their* ideas about those issues. (Occasionally I discuss questions of style and problems of expression, as well as ways of *reading* texts. I never discuss grammar or mechanics or paragraphs or thesis sentences, unless these topics will clearly help students discuss issues they are facing.) Class meetings center on readings that incorporate ideas.

I do not focus much on so-called "composing processes." (I think that research on writing has pretty well established there is no such thing as "the composing process.") I take it that every writer who ever wrote goes through a process of some sort, and also that what *finally* counts to a reader is not how the writer got to his/her final text, but how effective that final text is in accomplishing the action sought by the writer (or in accomplishing some action that the writer might value—writers don't always know what acts they intend). But I do put a good deal of emphasis on how one searches for, invents, and develops ideas: invention is the central act by a writer—as it has been since classical times. I also encourage students to revise their draft writings in response to their colleagues' comments and in response to my readings of those drafts. But I freely admit that my readings may be wrong; if a student disputes my reading, I try to help him/her to eliminate the possibility of misunderstanding in doing *what* the student wants to do. I concur with the suggestion that students can help themselves learn by collaborating with other students. In dealing with students' drafts, I try to hold regular conferences with students; when I cannot confer with a student, I try to write the student a specific, typed commentary exploring how well he/she addressed an issue.

In making assignments, I try to encourage students to address difficult problems. In building a course, I try to make assignments build directly on earlier assignments, and even if an assignment does not build directly on earlier writings, I try to make later assignments fall within the same general area—maybe it's within the same "semantic field"—as earlier assignments, so that students will be aware that their work is enriched by prior work. I try hard to avoid assignments that are totally disconnected from each other, such as assignments that take the students mechanically through someone's taxonomy of "modes" or "aims" of discourse (writers don't write to exemplify "modes" and "aims" of discourse). I try to help students see the connections between current and earlier work in the course.

Perhaps most drastically (in the sense of violating students' expectations), I assign no grades, ever, to individual papers. Every paper, at every point, can be revised to improve it; I tell students that every writing is a work in progress, and one doesn't grade a work in progress. Further, they themselves are "in progress" as learners during the entire course, and one doesn't try to sum up, by means of a "grade," human beings who are in the process of growth. (I also believe, seriously, that no grade can ever capture the complexity of a piece of writing. Grades can never do more than hint crudely at what they purport to suggest, and they often mislead seriously.)

I ask students, at the end of my courses, to compile a portfolio of writings they have done during the course, revised to make them the best works of which the student is capable. I stipulate that the portfolio must contain writings on particular assignments (one or two), then give them a choice of two or three other writings to include. Hereafter I will probably ask students to include analyses of themselves as writers, saying where they started, where they have come, and where they have still to go at the end of the course, and why they included the papers they did in response to my request that they choose. I tell the students, frankly, that I'll assign a grade, for the Registrar's use, on the basis of the portfolio, but that any grade I assign is simply my best guess about where they are, and what they've accomplished, at the end of the semester.

In looking at the papers on the current project, I have approached them from the perspective of one for whom the central goal of teaching college courses in writing is, as noted earlier, to help students engage in discussion of ideas, and win their readers' respect for their ideas. The papers in this project seem to me not very good at these activities, but the reasons may be the assignments students were answering and the kinds of instructions they received about them. None, for me, is a successful example of what I'd like students to learn to do.

Ben McClelland
Philosophy of Learning and Teaching Composition

Read your students' minds through their texts. Then search—neither for a way of setting them straight, nor of showing them the right answer—but search for a question or a counterstatement that will challenge them to build more powerful texts.

My educational philosophy follows from a Bakhtinian theory of language that sees language development in any community as an ongoing conversation that individual speakers and listeners join and leave. New speakers, joining in the conversation, use words that others have used before, infusing words with new meanings and intentions as they employ them in new contexts. In a writing class this means that communication is not a one-way street, from writer to reader through a text. Rather, communication proceeds complexly and not just back and forth between writer and reader, but also back and forth between writer and text and between reader and text. According to this notion of language, the text is a dynamic participant in the communication process, filled as it is with context-laden and richly-implicated words. This interactivity, or dialogism, in the very nature of language gives it unique epistemic properties: As language users integrate the meanings and histories of words into their own consciousnesses, they learn by connecting the concepts in new words with ones existing already in their minds.

Accordingly, I see Freshman English as an introduction to academic discourse, a basic course in reading, writing, and thinking in the special language of the academy. As newcomers, freshmen must learn the community's special languages and writing conventions in order to join the conversations of the academy: to read the textbooks, to perform laboratory experiments and write reports on them, to respond to teachers' examination questions, and to write essays based on their own research. Before they leave the university with a degree they will have to become initiated community members, perusing the social historian's reading of the world, checking the calculus expert's proofs, challenging the philosopher's abstract reasoning. In short, they will be judging many discourses that they hear on facts and figures and values—and they will be thinking for themselves. For many of our students, to perform this act of advanced literacy requires basic intellectual and social changes over four years of study; they must both deepen their understanding of language and assert themselves as community participants. To begin such fundamental changes is our goal in Freshman English. How to do it?

My attempt is a course conducted according to reading and writing workshop principles, proceeding through writing journal entries, reading published texts, collaborating with peers in small-group discussion, scoring sample essays holistically, drafting essays, reading and responding to each other's drafts, and revising and editing their texts; it concludes with an evaluation of writing portfolios. Just listing these activities oversimplifies the curriculum's overall effect because it overlooks its empowering matrix: the classroom as context for student interaction to build reading comprehension and writing development socially, the classroom as a special locus for learning—an educational environment enriched by the integration of the coursework elements, the interactivity of the participants, and the connections made between the content of the coursework and students' personal lives. Thus, the course's workshop method (conversing about texts we are reading and writing) and content (connecting personal ideology with public issues) authorizes individual effort and collaborative learning, aiming to develop articulate, literate democrats. To situate my teaching in contemporary pedagogy, I would say that it is based on "social-epistemic rhetoric: as characterized by James Berlin in an issue of *College English* (1988).

Throughout the course a major goal is to guide students through an incremental series of reading-writing-discussing activities that lead them to teach themselves. In the space of this essay I cannot discuss all the course activities in detail. However, I do want to explain that a central activity is peer reader response to drafts which precedes my teacher response to revisions. The response I work to nurture is that of an interested reader who responds with comments and questions which flow directly out of the reading experience with the text. For example, I ask students to paraphrase the draft's main point, to state what is effective or engaging in the draft, and to focus questions and comments on content that occur to a reader who is trying to follow a writer's development of ideas. For the most part, the reader's role I ask students to adopt here parallels that of the reader of published texts. The two ways in which this reading-writing activity differs from the one with a published text are that the writers are present and the drafts are works-in-progress; therefore, readers may speak directly to the writer about their feelings, expectations, and interpretations. Over the semester as they continually write and read in this activity, students carry on dialogues with each other in and through writing about their writing and reading. I believe that—in addition to providing feedback to writers—this activity helps students build a vocabulary and metadiscourse, a way of talking about academic discourse. As John Trimbur (1985) observes, "By emphasizing the social activity of writing, collaborative learning can play a significant role in helping students make the transition from one community to another. Collaborative learning can help students generate a transitional language to bridge the cultural gap and acquire fluency in academic conversation" (101). Reader response activities, then, are a central, but not sole, means of helping students gain membership in the academic community.

I contend that my philosophy of teaching writing gives a wholeness to the various activities of the course, a wholeness deriving from the interactivity of learners, the integration of multiple activities of reading and writing, and the connection of course content to the lives of the learners. The student's introduction to the language and conventions of the academic community occurs incrementally in activity after activity, but because of this holistic philosophy, I believe, the student's total learning experience equals more than the sum of the course's parts.

I believe that by being immersed in the discourse of Freshman English, students begin to develop individual voices for speaking out in the academic community. Moreover, through the particular method and content of our reading, writing, and discussing activities, students begin to construct and articulate their ideologies in friendly, conflictual discourse. They transform themselves and their peers from merely passive consumers of information into active makers of meaning. It is just such empowered people as these who, understanding the social implications of academic literacy, can revitalize our democratic society (Clifford, 1988, 18).

Works Cited

Berlin, James. (1988, September). "Rhetoric and Ideology in the Writing Class." *College English*, 50, 477-494.

Clifford, John. (1988, September 17). "Literacy and Teacher Training: Alternative Strategies." Paper read at MLA's Right to Literacy Conference, Columbus, Ohio.

Trimbur, John. (1985). "Collaborative Learning and Teaching Writing." *Perspectives on Research and Scholarship in Composition*. Ben W. McClelland and Timothy R. Donovan (eds.). New York: MLA.

Frank O'Hare
Statement of Philosophy

Whenever I am asked to serve as a consultant to help design a series of writing courses at the elementary, secondary or college level, I usually suggest that everyone sketch briefly an informal philosophy of composition to establish a common framework for our curriculum planning. The following brief, unelaborated list is typical of those I have shared in these meetings.

Principles and Assumptions

1. Writing is a highly complex skill, difficult to begin and difficult to see through to a conclusion. Robert Crichton, author of *The Secret of Santa Vittoria*, said, "There is nothing in writing harder than to start." John Steinbeck, near the end of a distinguished career, confessed, "I suffer as always from the fear of

putting down the first line. It is amazing the terrors, the magics, the prayers, the straightening shyness that assails one." Ernest Hemingway put it more succinctly, "I write with my blood."

2. One can grow and learn through writing. Many writers have addressed this idea—Henry Miller: "Writing is a voyage of discovery"; E. M. Forster: "How do I know what I think until I see what I said"; W. H. Auden: "Language is the mother, not the handmaiden, of thought; words will tell you things you never thought or felt before"; C. Day Lewis: "We do not write in order to be understood; we write in order to understand"; Adrienne Rich: "Poems are like dreams; you put into them what you don't know you know."

3. Writing should be viewed as process rather than product. Because it involves a complex, seemingly endless series of choices, rejections, and additional choices, writing is of necessity a messy undertaking. It is no surprise then that most writers throw away a substantial portion of what they write.

4. Writing should be responded to in constructive ways *while* the writer is still working on it. Giving a writer advice after the work is finished is very like trying to cure a patient after he or she has expired. Surgery should be performed while the patient is still alive.

5. Writers should not only accept but welcome error as one of the most important means of improving their writing skills. Lewis Thomas, in a *Saturday Evening Post* article, October 1976 said: "Mistakes are at the very base of human thought, embedded there, feeding the structure like root nodules. If we were not provided with the knack of being wrong, we could never get anything useful done. We think our way along by choosing between right and wrong alternatives, and the wrong choices have to be made as frequently as the right ones. We get along in life this way. We are built to make mistakes, coded for error." Error then is a necessary, not an accidental step on the way to writing improvement.

The principles and assumptions discussed here demand a different kind of writing curriculum from that of the current-traditional paradigm, a curriculum that focuses on multiple drafting, with invention and revision at its center. Listed below are Writing Curriculum Guidelines based on these principles and assumptions. Many school systems and colleges have found them useful when they were designing their writing programs.

Writing Curriculum Guidelines

1. *Multiple Drafts.* Most major writing assignments should require an exploratory draft, a working draft(s), and a final draft. Proofreading becomes extremely important only at the final-draft stage.

2. *The Writing Class as Art Class.* The writing classroom should resemble an art class or a creative writing workshop—i.e., the course should be activity-centered, and students' writing should be the central focus. Using sets of criteria questions, students will respond to their peers' drafts. Writing instructors should be facilitators not purveyors of knowledge; lectures should be brief and rare. Writing instructors don't teach composition so much as design environments where the acquisition of writing skills can take place.

3. *Student as Authority.* Whenever possible, students should be given a variety of writing assignments on subjects which are significant to them and about which they are knowledgeable. The students have a right to their own

texts. Teacher comments should help students to achieve their purposes. Teachers should try not to appropriate their students' texts. To help them generate and analyze material for their papers, students should be given abundant practice with many of the following invention techniques: brainstorming; clustering; mapping; writing itself; Burke's pentad; the journalistic questions; cubing; looping; free writing; journals; the tagmemic heuristic—particle (static), wave (dynamic), field (relative), contrast, range of variation, and distribution; analogy; the writing of others. Students should engage in invention and planning activities throughout the writing process.

4. *Purposes(s) and Audience(s)*. A writer usually has a variety of purposes and more than one audience in any writing task.

5. *Reading*. Grammaticality, style, coherence, cohesion, mechanics, usage, organization, strategies of thinking and development, the modes—all are more often acquired by extensive reading than learned by being taught.

6. *Sentence Sense*. Students develop sentence sense by writing, by extensive reading, and by revising their own work. Practice with sentence combining helps students deal with many of the most common errors in student writing, for example the sentence boundary. It also improves their style and sharpens their revision skills.

7. *Mechanics and Usage*. We need effective and, if possible, jargon-free explanations/lessons, preferably in a writer's dictionary to which students could refer. Most handbooks are written for teachers. Their explanations are seldom helpful to students.

8. *Correctness*. Although conformity to the conventions of written English should not be stressed initially, correctness is of importance at the final-draft stage. The rules for writing are mere conventions. Error is not a moral issue.

9. *The Portfolio Method of Grading*. Students should not be given a letter grade on every assignment. Instead of averaging by including every paper a student has written, allow students to select a reasonable number of their best pieces for evaluation.

Jane Peterson
In Search of Congruity—Or Trying to Practice, Not Preach

I grew up in a fundamentalist no smoking, no drinking, no dancing, no movies, no card playing Baptist home. We congratulated ourselves on being reasonable—stopping short of no sleeveless blouses, no slacks, no make-up, no jewelry, no doctors. We were the elect—saved and baptized—bearers of the "good news," God's own stewards of truth, right, goodness, et cetera, et cetera, and so forth.

Preaching love and forgiveness, this community practiced public humiliation and rejection. No one was exempt. One Sunday evening, the preacher announced his teenaged daughter was pregnant and that, after talking with her and the father (a high-ranking deacon's son), he fully supported her decision to have and keep the baby though the couple did not wish to marry. The congregation fired him. Why? Because he had not immediately sent his daughter away. When, a few weeks later, she had a miscarriage, the congregation asked him to stay since his daughter would not, after all, be embarrassing the church. He refused.

Those years of painful incongruities between what was said and done, belief and action, matter and method, have probably shaped my philosophy of teaching as much as anything. Congruity is my touchstone, consonance between theory and practice my goal. As I read, write, learn, and teach, what I know and believe about reading, writing, and learning changes, sometimes quickly and dramatically but more often slowly and subtly as I bring new ideas, information, and self-awareness to the time I invest in consciously reflecting on what I do, what I ask students to do, what happens, and why.

Assumptions

Several assumptions underlie my current philosophy of teaching composition. If I were to draw these assumptions, I would represent them as equal and interactive, together creating a foundation for teaching composition.

- Students can learn to become not just competent writers but good writers;
- Good writing is writing that works—writing that communicates something of value (information, ideas, feelings) to the intended audience;
- Students are people to be respected—they enter classrooms with knowledge and expertise in many areas, with personal goals and other commitments, and with assumptions about writing and themselves as writers, readers, and learners;
- Teaching composition is important and interesting work—valuable for both students and teachers, challenging, fun; and
- Learning (i.e., developing and internalizing concepts) does not proceed linearly or uniformly—it's active, recursive, interactive, unpredictable.

Goals

The community college students I teach enter the first semester freshman course (expository writing) with different experiences and needs as writers, readers, and learners. Many still view writing and reading as mechanical acts of encoding and decoding, not as acts of making meaning. My primary concern is to create contexts for learning that help students move from "where they are" toward understanding writing and reading as active processes of meaning-making. More specific goals—what I hope students leave the course with—fall into four areas: performance, metacognition, affect, and knowledge.

Performance: that every student experience the satisfaction of producing at least one good piece of writing;

Metacognition and Affect: that students leave with a greater awareness of and confidence in their own developing abilities as writers, readers, and learners;

Knowledge: that students have written enough, read enough, talked enough, listened enough, observed enough, and reflected enough on their experiences to begin internalizing these concepts:

- writing has value (not just writing for others, but writing for themselves—thinking, remembering, expressing feelings);
- writing for others is a complex activity that takes time, involves both thinking and feeling, and proceeds according to no set pattern (strategies and processes vary not only from person to person, but task to task);
- readers' expectations and needs vary, so audience and purpose should guide decisions about form, content, order and tone.

Because learning is recursive and genuine understanding (not mere "information about") deepens through experience, I have the same goals for our second semester research and argumentation course, with two concepts added about the value and complexity of research.

To begin (or continue) the process of internalizing these concepts, students need to experience writing and reading as acts of making meaning. They also need to reflect on their experiences, to discover and articulate these developing concepts for themselves. Such learning does not proceed quickly or predictably, and few students, if any, leave either course with all concepts fully internalized. They do, however, usually leave having experienced "moments of ownership" that empower.

Principles and Practices

The theories of reading, composing, and learning embedded in my assumptions and goals suggest an active, interactive classroom where students work alone, with partners, in small groups, and occasionally as a class. They read, write, speak, listen to one another, observe, and reflect on their experiences. To increase the odds of becoming invested in their writing, they choose their own topics, specific audiences, and forms within broadly assigned purposes, e.g., to inform or evaluate. In my current first-semester course, papers may be essays, brochures, letters, whatever would work for the audience and purpose. Students have three to five weeks to work on each out-of-class paper, which means some time to play with topics, envision audiences, and perhaps discover new ideas or beliefs. In the second semester, students each choose a topic to work with all semester, engaging in various forms of research and writing three papers: an informative paper for classmates that provides an overview of the topic and the student's research processes and two argumentative pieces for audiences of the writer's choosing.

As a teacher, the real challenge lies not in making those basic decisions about course design congruent with what I believe, but in living the theories I espouse. If I ask students to consider their audiences and purposes, reflect on their experiences, and trust the process of learning by doing, I must try to do the same.

To consider my audience, I need to focus on students—the real people I see and talk with regularly, not some abstract notion of students. I need to find out, for instance, what their questions or concerns are, not bury them in my questions or suggestions. I need to ask what they want to accomplish in their writings and how much more time or energy they're willing to invest in revising, not push them onto a track built on my assumptions about what they should do. To focus on purpose, I need to connect their activities and mine to goals. What do I want the comments on this draft or journal entry to accomplish? What does John or Sarah or Brian or Kim need now to work productively? And if I expect students to invest in their work, I need to be invested in mine, reflecting on my experiences—the successes and failures of this inductive, rhetorical approach to teaching—observing, questioning, revising, learning.

All of this "needing to"—this search for congruity at several levels—may sound tiresome, but it doesn't feel tiresome. Instead it generates the ideas and questions that make teaching composition fun as it places me in the position of listener and learner, a position that grows richer each year as students from more diverse backgrounds become my teachers.

Donald Stewart
Statement of Philosophy

The practice of composition, when it is well taught, arouses in the pupil feelings of health, power, sanity and hope—the invariable attendants of mental growth. Badly taught it arrests development, and the result is a feeling of abnormality, a feeling of exhaustion, a feeling of powerlessness and failure.

What is the reward of the teacher of composition? It is the knowledge that from his teaching men and women have gained power—power to strike hard blows for truth, good government and right living.

Fred Newton Scott and Joseph V. Denny

I hesitate to call my approach to the teaching of writing a "philosophy." That seems too profound a term for the collection of attitudes which govern the things that I do. I do not, of course, wish to suggest that I do not take this work very seriously. Quite the contrary. In fact, over the past thirty-six years I have spent more time thinking and re-thinking my approach to the teaching of writing than anything else I have done professionally.

The things I do now are grounded in a few simple but comprehensive axioms:

(1) *Writing, like speaking, occurs in a staggering variety of contexts.* The variables include the subject, the writer, the audience, the purpose, and the constraints operating on any of the above in a particular situation. *Good writing, therefore, is writing which is superbly adapted to its context.*

(2) *The teacher's first job, therefore, is to help students recognize and respond to the demands of a particular context.*

(3) *Good classroom writing occurs when each student is given as much freedom or as much direction as he or she requires and desires.*

(4) *The priorities in any piece of writing are, in order, substance, organization, style, and editing.* Each is evaluated as contributing to or detracting from the success of a particular piece in a specific context.

Now let me explain, in a little more detail, the consequences of acting on each of these axioms. Winston Weathers put the first succinctly when he said: "Context is everything!" Precisely. In letter-writing alone, one runs through a considerable gamut of contexts. Yesterday I wrote my sister a birthday letter. She likes to kid about being perpetually 39, but I won't let her do that. Since I am her brother, I am allowed considerable teasing latitude. I also tell her family news and wish her a happy birthday. Organization barely exists in this letter, and the style is very informal, the voice of the brother she grew up with, still unreformed and a bit on the edge between uncouth and civilized. An hour later I am writing to a New York publisher, trying to get him to take a look at one of my manuscripts. It's brief, formal but not stuffy, and very tightly organized. He wants to know, quickly, what the book's about, why readers would be interested in it, and what my qualifications for writing it are. Still later, I'm writing a letter to the newspaper, telling readers that the city council's decision to re-zone an area near my property is stupid and short-sighted. I'm angry. I'm not writing to persuade anyone; the damage is done. I'm writing to needle those on the city council who voted foolishly and to remind them that I'll do my best to see that they don't get re-elected. Finally, I write a brief note of condolence to an old friend whose wife has just died. This has to be sympathetic but not sentimental. He's an extremely intelligent scientist, not given to fake displays of emotion and not likely to be moved by anything which suggests a hint of insincerity. It's a difficult note to write.

Students write a similar range of papers: newsy letters to family and friends; reports, formal essays, and term papers; letters to their college and university newspapers; and, unfortunately, those terrible letters expressing condolence to the parents, brothers, and sisters of close friends who have died or been killed. Context is everything! It causes subtle adjustments in the information presented, the order in which it is presented, the tone in which it is conveyed, and even in the editing skills.

A student conditioned to churn out five-paragraph essays in *words for teacher,* as Robert Zoellner once called them, is bewildered, at first, by the idea of adapting organization and style to the world of the context. He or she has never had to worry about it. The teacher is the audience, and his or her attitudes, prejudices, and reputation define everything the student does. This teacher assigns the topics, prescribes the organizational pattern, and, frequently, creates an artificial context. Some students become, in high school, very comfortable working in this hothouse environment. They are not at all pleased by the approach I take. Since life is a constant adjustment to contexts, however, I insist that they get used to it.

Giving students as much freedom as they want or as much direction as they require has certain hazards. The danger of plagiarism is the most obvious one, but I have had much less trouble with it under this system than the old. A student who chooses her own subject will, I have found, pick a subject in which she is interested or about which she is irritated. Thus, one will tell me funny stories about guiding horseback parties in Yellowstone in the summer, and another will give American students the devil for showing so little interest in foreign language study. Those who draw a blank get some intensive work in inventional techniques.

The priorities are easy to establish and apply. Reading each paper, I try to discern the context for which it was written and to determine whether or not the content of the paper is appropriate and effective for that context. Content here could include information presented, arguments mustered, jokes told to entertain, etc. After judging the content I turn to the arrangement of the piece. My students learn very early in the course that I have no particular love of the five-paragraph essay, the thesis statement and supporting reasons laid out in block form, etc. I'm open to any organizational pattern that works. Sometimes a thesis statement and proofs will be right. Other times a meditation or an analogy would be better.

Among all the aspects of style which I consider, voice is the most important. If I don't hear an authentic voice, I'm turned off. I do not subscribe to the detached cerebral style of the cognitive psychologists or the socially constructed person of the collaborative learners who are making waves these days. Mark Twain had a voice which permeated all his writing. So did D. H. Lawrence, Virginia Woolf, William Shakespeare. Nothing is less interesting to read than the dry, lifeless prose of technical report writers who have been taught that the total submersion of any personality the writer has is a consummation devoutly to be wished in that kind of writing. I don't agree. All it guarantees is writing which is difficult to read, become interested in, or follow.

Editing is a given. If students can't spell, punctuate, or observe the usage conventions required by differing contexts, they must get a handbook and do some reading. I don't spend much time on these matters, unless a particular problem is giving an entire class trouble. Then we have a brief editing session and then go on to important matters.

That, in brief, is the way I conduct composition classes. It is a successful method because my students write a variety of papers on a variety of subjects, and most do so with the enthusiasm generated by the freedom they have to do what they want to do and what they can do best. And we spend class time doing what needs to be done: helping those who are short on ideas learn how to generate more; encouraging those afraid to experiment organizationally to take courage; sensitizing those who do not realize what their style is telling a reader about them; and giving an occasional kick in the pants to someone who edits sloppily. It's not a tidy method; it's not a chaotic one either. But it does generate a lot of good student writing.

Patricia Stock

Philosophy of Teaching Composition
A Personal Statement

Recent conceptions of literacy—studies emerging from anthropology, history, literary theory, philosophy, psychology, and sociology—emphasize its character as situated action, as a complex of processes shaped by and shaping social relationships. Studies emerging from the fields of rhetoric and composition and education, undertaken by researchers into literacy teaching and learning, further emphasize that:

1. Language learning is a self-generated, creative process.
2. Language learning is holistic. The different components of language—function, form, and meaning—are learned simultaneously.
3. Language learning is social and collaborative.
4. Language learning is functional and integrative.
5. Language learning is variable. Because language is inherently variable, the meanings, the forms, and the functions of [individuals'] language will depend on their personal, social, and cultural experiences (Angela A. Jagger, "Observing the Language Learner," in Angela Jagger and M. Trika Smith-Burke (Eds.) *Observing the Language Learner.* Urbana, IL: NCTE, 1985, p. 4).

Persuaded by the research to which I refer, I believe that language development is a process in which students must study not only the forms of language but their functions as well in order to learn, think, and communicate in various contexts, and that this process is one in which context influences both language functions and language use, and that talk and writing are in fact seamless uses of language. Because I believe that language learning is **self-generated, creative, holistic**—not a matter of learning forms as items but rather a matter of learning forms and their functions and their meanings and all three together in contextualized acts of making meaning, I invite students in composition courses to talk and write as well as to listen and read their way to understanding; furthermore, I allow students a measure of choice in the subjects about which they read and write. Because I believe that language learning is **social and collaborative**, I join with my students in a community of language users not only to model effective language use for them but also to demonstrate that it is only in community that the functions of language use find their meanings and values. Because I believe that language learning is **functional and integrative** only in a community bonded by common language and by the systems of values reflected in that language, I ask students to speak and listen, write and read for one another to dramatize and thus come to understand how common language is constructed—how common worlds and their values are made, how "local knowledge" is constituted.

Conceived as an enactment of these beliefs and practices in particular settings, the composition courses I teach are not designed as a body of content but rather as the discourse students can and do produce. For this reason I ask students to bring their own subjects to these courses, and I provide students opportunities to talk and write about those subjects, both for each other and for me. I also provide students a model composer—the teacher—someone who struggles to make meaning just as they do.

With the syllabus I give to students the first day we meet together, I open the conversation of each course this way: We shall write the text for this course—you and I together. Teaching one another from the range of experience and knowledge we each bring to it, we shall all be inquirers in our course of study. It will be our responsibility, yours as well as mine, to teach each other what we need to know to build our common text. If we are to become authors who are also authorities, then we must write "the textbook" for this course—individually and together.

By asking students to write for one another and for me, and by writing for and with my students, I intend for composition classes I teach to dramatize the tension between personal and community language that is both inevitable and essential for all who would be readers and writers in any new social community. By definition, any community of which individuals can be a part must include them as active participants, thinking their own thoughts, speaking those thoughts in their own languages. I know full well that students must come to be familiar with the academic community's various languages—their peculiar forms and vocabularies, their different ways of introducing discussions, shaping questions, framing problems, posing solutions, expressing concepts; but I also believe that composition courses can provide the setting for students to speak and write their various ways toward such familiarity, not merely listen and read their ways toward it. By encouraging students in composition classes to read and write for one another about subjects of their own choosing, I intend that they will demonstrate for one another that writers and readers behave in much the same way as speakers and listeners do; that individuals who speak and hear, write and read for and with one another over a period of time in a given context come to constitute what Stanley Fish has called an "interpretive community," a community of individuals with shared expectations and values.

For an interpretive community to take shape, it is essential that its members enact publically and communally the constitutive hermeneutics of the forming community. Not only should composition courses provide students and their teachers occasions to enact the requisite hermeneutics—the patterned negotiations over meanings and values—that will characterize the interactive uses of language in the particular discourse community they are forming; but composition courses should also provide students an analogic drama they may imagine when they inquire into the meanings and values that have already been invested in the requisite hermeneutics of the other discourse communities in which they will participate in the university.

When students in my composition classes and I come together to compose from a variety of social perspectives in a new academic community, we do so of necessity in a language that has already been partly shaped and created in the social setting in which we find ourselves; but as we encounter that language and seek to use it for our own purposes, we renew and change it. The social worlds of conversation and letters are ones that continually make and remake discourse and shape and reshape knowledge; the perspectives and expressions that students bring from the worlds of their prior experience have place and purpose in them.

Tilly Warnock
An ABC's of Writing

Instead of a philosophy of composition, I have developed an ABC's of writing: Aristotle's definition of rhetoric as discovering the possible means of persuasion in a given context; Kenneth Burke's theories of language as symbolic action and as performance, by people, for specific purposes, in particular situations, using language; and Composition research on context, collaboration, and critical judgment. Here I want to focus directly on Aristotle's definition and only indirectly on Burke and composition research, although I obviously read backwards from current research to Burke to Aristotle.

Aristotle makes a cut between rhetoric and poetics. Rhetoric is the act of discovering what will work in a particular situation. Poetics is the naming of parts, kinds, and species. Rhetoric is concerned with thing-making, while poetics is concerned with thing-made. Rhetoric examines the function of figures and tropes, and poetics classifies figures and tropes. Rhetoric deals with probabilities; poetics with certainties. Rhetoric is not figures and tropes nor is it a body of knowledge about how to persuade. Rhetoric, that which persuades, changes according to the situation. Although the two approaches of rhetoric and poetics often treat the same material, for example, the metaphor, they do so for different purposes and with different consequences.

Rhetoric and poetics are ways of doing; they are performances: they are not referentially true. I try to remember that Aristotle made this and other cuts for his own rhetorical reasons and that I have my own motives for using his definition of rhetoric.

For me, the definition has practical consequences in teaching. I think first of myself as a teacher, a person concerned with thing-makers; therefore I tend towards theories involving people, motives, consequences, and contexts, as well as texts, rather than towards those which emphasize texts primarily.

I also think of myself as a rhetorician, more interested in what changes than in what stays the same. I understand both discovering and naming as actions, but I believe that the motive for rhetoric is change and the motive for poetics is stasis. The need to discover means of persuasion arises in times of doubt and indeterminacy and when change is possible. I'm not so sure that I and students can effect change, especially the revisions we want, but, because I perceive the world as changing, I want to help students gain what Burke called "strategies for coping" and "equipment for living" and what I call critical judgment.

My bias towards probability, and the strengths and limitations of my "terministic screen," became clear to me many years ago when I read an article by Dan I. Slobin, "The More It Changes: On Understanding Language By Watching It Move Through Time." Awareness of my "occupational psychosis" as a rhetorician was heightened more recently when I read Sarah Warshauer Freedman's *Response to Student Writing*.

Slobin's point is that "language maintains a universal character across all of these continuing changes, so that the more it changes, the more sure we can be of what it is." I don't argue with the referential accuracy of his study, but I do know that I am as interested in changes as in constancies and in specifics as in universals.

For example, Slobin explains that the third charge to language is that it be quick and easy because of communicative needs and short-term memory constraints. I certainly though tentatively accept these now familiar cooperative and cognitive principles, but I am drawn to cases where these principles are modified or broken in order to do things with words in particular contexts.

Therefore, I teach principles, rules, and strategies, but I also try to teach students how to modify these for specific situations. I define writing as an action by people, for specific purposes, in particular contexts. I assert metaphorically not referentially that writing is a matter of probabilities.

More recently I confronted my bias as I wrote "good problem" in the margin of page one of *Response to Student Writing* where Freedman discusses the confusion caused in students by teachers' varied and often conflicting responses to their writing. I put "Use" beside the following:

> In the bleakest scenario, students develop a folk theory about response in which they believe that the nature of the response is dictated solely by the responder's taste. They become frustrated when they perceive inconsistency in 'tastes' and receive mixed messages about their writing. They give up trying to learn to write, and often, in frustration, adopt a strategy of learning to please a particular teacher at a given time and then consciously, upon encountering the next teacher, try to forget everything they 'learned' so that they can start anew to satisfy the next teacher's taste. Teachers express similar complaints: a feeling of having to "start over" with each new class, a feeling of discontinuity in writing instruction.

I find this scenario exhilarating, not bleak. Students know that certainties are few and far between and that *kairotic* moments, those moments of harmony, wholeness, and seeing anew, are rare in this otherwise chaotic world. Most messages are mixed, if not downright infelicitous. Students realize that there is no one right way to write nor one way of writing that will work in all situations. They know that the first requirement of writing is to figure out what the situation calls for and to decide how to accomplish one's own purposes in that context. If students give up, I believe it's because what they know through years of speaking, writing, reading, and listening is contradicted by what they are taught. I'm not sure whether they give up on English teachers who teach what's right not what's rhetoric, or whether they buy our view of writing as something that must be done a certain way and therefore give up on something which doesn't make sense in the world as they understand it.

I fear that our desire as teachers to find the standard, the right response, is a desire to establish and maintain our own authority. If we don't know what works, how can we teach others? We know that every writing performance is different because the people, purposes, and places change, but we don't teach to the differences. Sometimes we say it's because students can't handle everything at once and so we reduce writing to a series of steps or rules. We often work part to whole, never getting to the wholeness and messiness of meaning, and we wonder why students aren't motivated. But as Cole and Scribner say, people learn that which is valued in their community and that which they have time to practice.

I prefer to admit that we as English teachers don't know and that our students are right in their suspicions: We don't know what will hold true across time and space. What I think we and our students *do* know is that writers have to scramble and figure out what might work, by reading situations critically and deciding how to act and by reading drafts critically and judging how to revise. Writers must know their options and how to choose among them. We know that what we do in writing might not work and that our choices are context-bound, but we can improve our chances through practice, experimentation, help from others, reading, and a language-rich environment. I encourage students always to have an eye open for what's standard and certain, but meanwhile to proceed.

Freedman ends her book discussing the same problem she began with, and I think she's right on target: the major problem with writing is that it can't be fixed. Naming the parts, kinds, and species isn't enough, if our goal is to *use* language—to find the possible means of persuasion in a given context. We can redefine this problem as the challenge of writing and teaching writing. Not knowing, not being able to solve the problem once and for all, is what keeps us at it.

Beside the following passage, I drew four stars and wrote "imp." At the top of the page, I wrote "All":

> The teachers in the survey and in the observational study have a clear sense of what they teach and why. However, there is little evidence that they feel that they can depend on their students' coming into their classes with previously learned skills in writing, beyond the most mechanical; there is little evidence that they can count on their students' building on what they learn in this class in their future classes, in any specific ways. . . . The students seem to feel that they have to adjust to each teacher individually. . . . We need large-scale studies of the effects of students' greater education experiences on what they take away from individual classrooms. We need to experiment with ways of providing students with more coherent education experiences across time.

I believe that many students are learning what is most valuable—that writing changes—despite what we are teaching—that writing is stable. I want to acknowledge what they know intuitively and help them make the most of the situation at hand, because this is the most practical approach to teaching I have found. And what I hope will carry over from one class to another, from one writing task to another, is the understanding that because people, purposes, and places change, we must develop not only skills and strategies but also our critical judgment, our ability to read situations and decide what probably will work. There are standards for "good writing," which we can teach and help students figure out, but we can also help students discover the probable means of persuasion in specific situations—the "writing good for" particular people, purposes, and places.

Once students understand writing is a judgment call, that there are no answers which some (particularly teachers) have and others (themselves for instance) don't have, then they're usually willing to act.

Edward M. White
Philosophical Statement

The place of writing at the center of the liberal arts undergraduate curriculum derives from its double role as a socializing discipline (enforcing and confirming student membership in an educated community) and as an individualizing discipline (demanding critical thinking and an active relation of the self to material under study). While both of these functions are important, the second one is more significant for the undergraduate curriculum. That is, writing instruction becomes a *liberating* activity, and hence properly an essential part of the liberal arts, when it demands and rewards thinking for oneself. When we look closely at the undergraduate program most American students pursue, with its fragmented view of knowledge and its emphasis on the accumulation of information, writing emerges as a unifying and integrating force. Writing, as an active form of critical thinking, demands that students make sense of what they think they know. But such writing never comes easily to students and is much harder to teach than the conventions of discourse.

But, much of education is not really concerned with stimulating individual thought. Nor are most of our students particularly interested in such matters. While writing teachers may and usually do welcome original ideas, we are rather less hospitable to original spelling and punctuation—mainly because, as part of the political and social structure, we owe it to our students to help them acquire the "right" language, the language of the rich and powerful. If we neglect that task, even in the name of equality, our students will rebel, for they are seeking the linguistic tools that will help them fit into and advance within, not challenge, the social structure. We can—and should—also help them examine and question the social structure, but no teacher working within a writing program can be separate from the socializing institution. Thus, even the most politically and socially aware writing teachers are always forced to socialize their students, even as they urge them to become more fully themselves through their writing.

There is no professional consensus on the curriculum of writing courses, at any level. There is also no shortage of advice from researchers and practitioners; whatever approach to instruction an individual instructor might elect or inherit seems to have its prominent exemplars and promoters, and the profusion of textbooks is legendary. How can we arrange a sensible and useful syllabus in the face of so many theories, texts, research findings, pedagogical truisms, content suggestions, and methodologies? The overabundance of advice and materials sometimes seems overwhelming even to the specialists and is often beyond comprehension to the novices who are commonly entrusted with writing classes in universities.

Until more agreement emerges, if it ever does, writing teachers need to follow just a few common sense guidelines that follow from conceiving the writing class as a critical thinking course fundamental to the liberal arts curriculum: focus on *writing* in the class, maintain an appropriate intellectual content, plan for discovery and revision, use evaluation as part of teaching, organize a series of writing tasks that relate to each other and call for a broad range of writing and reading skills.

Whatever curriculum design emerges from consideration of the students and goals of the particular course, instruction should focus on writing tasks that *matter*, that engage our students' natural desire to make connections between their lives and their courses, to make sense of what they are learning.

This kind of intellectual vitality and creativity leads to good writing. Such writing, at all levels, is never neutral, voiceless, wholly detached; sometimes it even verges on personal expression and personal experience, a form of writing that is out of favor in high schools and almost extinct at the college level beyond the early weeks of freshman composition courses. James Britton and his research team (1975) found very little of such important writing in the London secondary schools; many college faculty feel that it is somehow undignified to ask students to write about themselves in relation to events or ideas. But the very essence of learning is the putting of oneself in relation to the material under study. I am not advocating the intellectual aridity of unsupported personal opinion or unreflective narratives about one's own past. Too much writing in college remedial (even freshman) courses stays only with narrative, concrete descriptions, the day's news. Such a limitation essentially restricts student possibilities for learning and for an expanded context for thought. But a course that draws on and helps to integrate the general education program, a course that asks students to evaluate what they read and say, leads to the critical thinking that can generate writing worth writing and reading.

A college-level writing course, then, treads a narrow curricular line, whatever the material it uses or the approach it makes. It needs to help students place themselves in contact with their topics, using some kind of appropriate voice, even as it asks them as writers to discover and develop ideas found in reading and discussion beyond themselves. The class needs to attend to the machinery of writing, from punctuation and spelling to audience awareness, but only in passing and as appropriate to the real focus of the course: inventing, reading, critical thinking, drafting, and revising. Further, the reading and the writing assignments need to relate to each other and to move in some discernible way from the beginning of the term to the end.

Finally, more than any other course at the university, the writing course depends upon the simple humanity of the teacher. The teacher must care deeply about thinking, reading, and writing, as a way of caring deeply about what students say and how they say it. The teacher must also be uncommonly open about interests and feelings, as a way of allowing students to know the final evaluator of their work. Since evaluation is central to learning anything, evaluation criteria should be open and public, not private, as well as clear and reasonable. Students must internalize some kind of evaluation scheme if they are to learn how to revise their work, and the teacher must help them see that more than simple subjectivity is involved. At the same time, the human communication that is at the heart of the course calls for a human response as well as an evaluation. So at the same time that the teacher is being superhuman (with too many students, too much to read and respond to, too much to know about, too little time, and probably too little pay), the teacher must also be intensely human and personal. But it is finally up to the teacher to determine if the writing course will be just one more set of exercises to complete for a grade, or will turn out to be one of the most intellectually exciting, inventive, useful, and transforming experiences in the university.*

* This statement is adapted by the author from Chapter Four of Edward M. White, *Developing Successful College Writing Programs*, San Francisco: Jossey-Bass, 1989.

APPENDIX F

Here are the three writings from the original sampling that we were not able to include in the text: Writing 3, a series of invention activities; Writing 7, "Merry Merchandising"; and Writing 14, a pair of essays written at different points in the course to a sequence of assignments on a common topic. These three writings were the ones that the 12 readers most frequently passed up when they chose 12 of the 15 writings from the sampling.

WRITING 3
Invention Activities

Respond to one of the following invention activities, preferably the one most similar to the kind you use in freshman writing courses. If you do not typically respond to invention work, you may choose not to comment on any of these samples.

Writing 3-A
[On Water Skiing]
Invention: Clustering and Freewriting

This invention work consists of a clustering activity and a pair of freewriting exercises done in preparation for a personal experience essay. Although the class has practiced these invention techniques in the first week of class, this is the first time students will be preparing a rough draft of their papers after this invention activity is returned.

Writing 3-B
[On Abolishing the SAT Exam]
Invention: Planning and Informal Writing

This invention work is made up of a thesis statement, an informal outline, and some informal writings toward an argumentative essay. These strategies are among a number of invention strategies students have been introduced to through the first half of the course. They have also tried freewriting, brainstorming, and the systematic questioning of classical invention. Students will be preparing a rough draft of their paper after this invention activity is returned.

Writing 3-C
[On Freedom]
Invention: Formal Questioning

As a way into an expository essay on an open topic, students have been asked to respond to the questions that comprise this formal heuristic based on Kenneth Burke's pentad. The class has also been introduced to clustering and freewriting. Students will be preparing a rough draft after this invention activity is returned.

Writing 3-A
Susan J.
Invention

Clustering: [On Water Skiing]

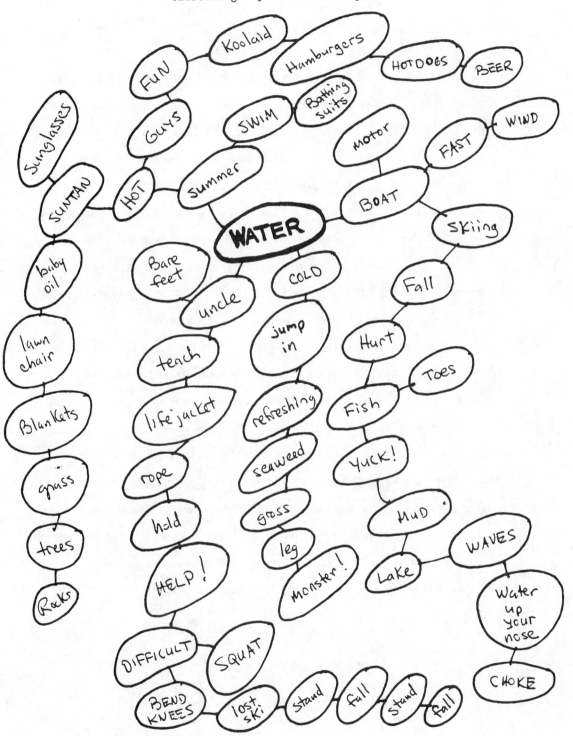

Writing 3-A
Susan J.
Invention

Freewriting 1: [On Water Skiing]

The first time I got up on water skiis. It hurts sometimes when
you fall. In fact it hurts very much. It's hard to get up the first
couple times. You're in an akward position. "Bend your knees up to
your chest and let the boat pull you up. It'll be a piece of cake.
Before you know it you'll be sliding across the water." Nothing
nothing nothing. "Easier said than done" I said. "Are you ready
yet?" he said. "As ready as I'll ever be I guess." The motor of the
boat gradually started getting louder. He was pulling me. The
pressure of the H20 felt funny against my skiis. I can't keep my legs
together. Oh--I'm falling! Shit. I let go. My body jerked as I let
go of the rope. That's pretty hard to do. "A piece of cake" he says.
Nothing nothing nothing nothing. I'm practically drowning with all
the waves the other boats are making. Bobbing up and down. That life
preserver is a pain. It doesn't even fit me right. It keep floating
and the back of it is iching my neck. ~~I can't wait~~ I'm freezing now
and my lips and fingers are blue. I can't wait to get back into the
boat where its dry and warm. Nothing nothing nothing. "Try again" my
uncle persists. Come on, one more time." By now my teeth are
chattering and I have a cramp in my leg. After 5 mill times of
struggling to get up I figure what's <u>one</u> more try. ~~He put the~~
"I'm ready." "Here goes." He put the boat in gear.

Writing 3-A
Susan J.
Invention

Freewriting 2: [On Water Skiing]

I like to water ski even though it's kind of hard. My uncle
taught me how. He's <u>really</u> good at it, but he's a <u>terrible</u> teacher—
Nothing nothing. First you need a boat and some skiis. The boat
really goes fast. At least it seems like it does when you're trying
to ski behind it. The hardest part of skiing is to jump in the water
because it's always freezing at first. I hate fish. I always imagine
they're going to swim up and bite my feet when I'm in the water. They
haven't yet but I guess I'm just paranoyed about it. I hate life
jackets too. The're a pain and so uncomfortable but since I like
living, I wear one when I'm in the water. Seaweed is gross. The
first time I tried to water ski we were in kind of shallow water and
it rapped around my legs. I thought it was jaws coming to get me so I
climbed back into the boat and promised never to get back in that
water again. But after I calmed down I jumped right back in again.

I love summer time and I love to be outside in summer especially
by the water. That's why I like water skiing so much. But I don't
like to fall even though I usually do. Why can't I be like normal
people and have the choice to let go of the rope and gracefully sink
into the water. <u>No</u>, I always end up falling on my face inhaling a
gallon of water ~~and half choke and then end the day by~~ and choking for
a half hour. It <u>hurts</u> when you fall too.

```
Writing 3-B
Lesley D.
Invention
```

Planning: [On Abolishing the SAT Exam]

Because the SAT is unfair to ~~girls~~ it should
    1) be abolished
    2) not be used as an admissions criteria.

THESIS--
The Scholastic Aptitude Test should be abolished because it does not
give accurate indication of ability. (AGAINST GIRLS)

AUDIENCE-- Test Makers? Students? College admissions officers?

          GIRLS TAKE THINGS MORE SERIOUSLY

                        discourages students
I   CREATES ANXIETY

        time pressure
        nervousness
        places pressure on student

          Takes time to prepare for
          --could be doing something else - school work

          lowers self-esteem and feeling of abilities

II   RESTRICTS COLLEGE ADMISSION

          REJECTION, DIFFICULTY GETTING IN -- Smart ~~girls~~
          with excellent ability to do work may not get into college

          SCHOLARSHIPS, GRANTS -- too heavily weighted on admission
          Schools miss out on talented students who happen to not test well

                    ~~WHOSE CUTOFF?~~

III ~~GIRLS~~ PERFORM BETTER IN HIGH SCHOOL & DURING THEIR 1st YEAR

      Lose out on scholarships grants
      Rely heavily on test results to decide recipients of scholarships

IV   DISCRIMINATORY

      Peoples, especially males, will strongly disagree with the idea
      that girls educations are being restricted because of SATs.

```
Writing 3-B
Lesley D.
Invention
```

Informal Writing: [On Abolishing the SAT Exam]

Students around the world eventually fear some form of
standarized test. For students in the U.S. the Scholastic Aptitude
Test, or SAT is the case.

INTRO-- 1. college admission
        2. loss of scholarship
        3. damaging to self esteem

Do you remember waking up early that Saturday morning when you
had to take your first Scholastic Aptitude Test, ~~to many~~ the dreaded
SAT. Your stomache was tied in knots and you just knew that if you
ate that well-balanced breakfast your mom made you would absolutely
get sick.

Well, even though you may refuse to believe it, you were not the
only one feeling the stress and anxiety that accompanies the SAT.

(Why ~~should~~ did we have to go through that awful experience?)

Every student that plans to attend college is required to take the SAT.

To most people, the SAT is . . .

The single most anxiety-provoking event of a high schooler's
academic life. Fear of the Test can develop as early as the ninth
grade. For many ~~people, especially girls,~~ the SAT creates a feeling
of nervousness and places pressure on doing well. In some cases, the
failure to do well on the SAT ~~causes~~ lowers self-esteem and ~~ability to
achieve~~ degrades a students ability.   Students are discouraged and
don't even attempt to pursue the area of the SAT that they ~~bombed~~ did
not do well on.

During the time that is spent ~~labouring over~~ preparing for the
SAT, students could be working on ~~their school grades~~ other areas of
study more pertinent to their education.

Colleges base at least part of their decision on whether to admit
a student on his or her SAT score, a score that is supposed to predict
how well a student will do during the first year of college. HOWEVER,
BY USING THE SAT AS A CUTOFF FOR ADMISSION, COLLEGES ARE MISSING OUT
on students who have the talent to succeed and happen to not test well.

Writing 3-C
Ellen G.
Invention

Formal Questioning: [On Freedom] *

What goes with freedom?
Liberty, justice, self-control, pride riots, loss of control, democracy

What is freedom?
Freedom is the state of being able to do as one chooses, think as one chooses to think, and worship as one chooses. It includes the ability to come and go as one pleases and it can also be a state of mind, a release from bonds and restrictions.

What physical entities do you associate with freedom?
Open spaces, sunshine, the making of money, the Constitution, Bill of Rights, newspapers (radical), American flag

What has been written or said in favor of freedom?
The Declaration of Independence, the Constitution, Civil Rights speeches, "I have a dream" (MLK), ERA speeches, women's rights, during the French Revolution, during the Reformation, in most Presidential speeches, the Magna Carta, in treaties of war, "La Marseillaise," existentialist writings

In what context is freedom set?
Freedom is usually used when a point regarding humanity is being made. People also bring feedom into the picture when they feel strongly about <u>any</u> particular point.

How is freedom like other things?
It is an ideal of humanity. One is never sure, like justice, if it is ever achieved. It is a tool, like money, in that by promising it a leader can sway people to his side. Freedom is like wine in that man thirsts for it but if given too much it can lead him to self-destruction.

In what class do you place freedom?
Ideals, dreams, goals

What opposes freedom?
Tyranny, close-mindedness, man (often), "the system," the church (sometimes)

What physical entities oppose freedom?
Jails (prisons), chains, fences, homes, guns, weapons

What has been written or said against freedom?
Poll tax, voting restrictions, all the restrictions on blacks, certain church doctrines/rules before the Reformation and during counter-Reformations.

1

What theoretical or philosophical opposition is there to freedom?
Governments, zen?, communism, slavery, draft

How does freedom stand out against its context?
Freedom is sometimes thought to have lost its meaning in societies of
today. It has been used so variantly that it is difficult to find a
pure meaning and therefore use of the word can cause confusion.

How is freedom unlike other similar things?

[No response]

What about freedom is odd, incongruous or unusual?
Freedom is one's right or ability to choose without being restricted,
but having no restrictions would seem to lead to chaos and disorder
and restriction, thereby cancelling freedom.

What follows or follows from freedom?
Often a democracy follows freedom. However massive chaos can follow
unlimited freedom. This qualifies "freedom" making too much bad and
too little good and causing confusion. Sometimes imprisonment follows
freedom.

How did freedom come to be?
Once man began to think intelligently of himself as an individual,
freedom was naturally one of his thoughts.

What are the causes of freedom?
Revolt, cooperation, new beginnings

What results from freedom?
Peace, happiness, chaos, crime, death, government

What problems does freedom pose? Solutions?
Too much freedom is often bad, so restrictions are placed on it. People
care only about themselves and their needs so a government is formed.

What opportunities does freedom offer?
It offers the chance to live as you choose, worship as you choose and
say what you please. It allows you to make as much money as you can
and do with it what you want. It also allows you to sometimes govern
yourself.

What are the implications of freedom?
It places the highest responsibility on the individual because it is
up to the individual to make sure that he doesn't abuse the privilege.

Is freedom good? Bad? Desirable? Necessary?
Usually. Sometimes. Yes (absolute, no). Yes.

[*This heuristic appears in Charles W. Bridges and Ronald F. Lunsford's
Writing: Discovering Form and Meaning (Belmont, CA: Wadsworth, 1984).]

2

WRITING 7
"Merry Merchandising"

BACKGROUND

This final draft is one of the pieces of writing this student has submitted in his final portfolio and designated as among his best work of the semester. There have been no specific assignments in this course. Instead, the class has followed a workshop model which asks students to write 6 to 10 papers (a total of 30 typewritten pages) on their own subjects, discovering for themselves the most appropriate form for each writing and receiving peer commentaries on their drafts throughout the term. As a way of encouraging students to consider fresh subjects for their papers, the class has been reading a variety of articles and essays from popular magazines, including the article referred to in this student's essay, on the commercialism of Christmas. Now, in the last week of class, students are handing in their portfolios for your formal review and a final course grade.

This paper is one of three pieces of writing that you will respond to independently before composing your final review of the student's performance in the class as a whole.

Writing 7
Michael K.
Final Draft

Merry Merchandising

I would like to begin by presenting us with a picture. It is
Christmas eve. The sky is clear and the reflections of small stars
shine their twinkling light back to the white covered Earth. Large,
individual snowflakes (like the ones in cartoons) slowly find their
way to the ground in a glorious pattern of swirling and dancing. To
save us trouble and time, it is a general, somewhat corny Christmas
image. We all know what it looks like. We've seen enough Hallmark
cards to get the idea. What we don't know is why I've brought you all
here today into this quaint land of enchantment. The answer is a
simple one. Christmas is drawing near and a dreadful fear is slowly
rising in the heart of mankind. Advertising, commercialism, and the
over use of the Santa Claus image have not made their appearance yet.
We have griped for years about the abuse of the holiday season by the
media. It is now these gripes which have caused a panic this year as
we realize too late that we were wrong. It is now time for us to give
a helping hand to rampant commercialism. After all, it has always
been there for us. If the jolly season of 1986 is going to be a time
which family and friends will remember merrily, you are going to have
to pay dearly for it. Please let me explain.

Our first common misconception is the idea that Christmas should
be a quiet, peaceful time devoid of the gongs and crashes of Madison
Avenue. The wildness of the season is considered pagan and

1

antagonistic to the true, peaceful image of the birth of Jesus. The church tells us often that "Advent is a quiet season of spiritual preparation for the 'silent night, holy night'" (Sheerin 164). But do any of us honestly believe that Mary and Joseph spent the weeks before Jesus' birth in quiet preparation? Mary was a young, pregnant girl. She was away from home and forced out of all local housing. She had been told that she would give birth to the son of God who would lead the world to salvation. Would this cause any of us to experience quiet preparation?

The Christmas season has traditionally been a time for chaos. Chaos is what has given us that feeling of anxiety since we were children. It is the feeling we see animals experience as they get jittery just before a storm. The charming winter scene which I have brought us to does not provide us with this feeling. It is the countless commercials and displays telling us that "time is running out" which have helped us. It is the arrray of contradicting images given to us by the media which support the craziness. The "true meaning of Christmas" would not exist without maniacal mothers clubbing people to get Cabbage Patch dolls.

This brings us to another, equally sensible gripe by those of us who cringe at the sight of Duracell-run reindeer and little Santas sliding down hills in Norelco shavers. This is the so-called "abuse" of the Christmas image. "Goods are not sold on their merits nor at bargain prices but through an appeal to mood or sentiment. As to advertising, a record player screeching out a Christmas carol in a department store is the quintessence of bogus" (Sheerin 163).

However, we are all instinctively lazy. Even when it comes to the excitement of the winter holiday we would rather place ourselves in that cozy wonderland once again then spend time ransacking the local department store. Our natural instinct is to hibernate. Yet even those of us who see the abuse of the holiday image as gross would be upset if we slept through the glory of Christmas morning. It is these "bogus" Christmas carols which shocked us out of bed in the middle of November. Would we heroicly have sprung to action if MacDonald's had not set up their "Dancing nuggets" campaign before summer had even begun? (If you answered yes, you can stop reading here. You're probably right.)

Now let us jump quickly to another problem. Those of us who would support traditional gift giving and holiday cheer constantly thwart (thwart?) the fads and "must haves" (must haves?) of modern manufacture. "Once the promoters find a fad they can gear to the unsatisfied psychological need of juveniles, they can start a fad comparable to that of Davy Crockett in size and popularity" (Sheerin 163). We fail to see that it is these fads created by business promotion which led to many of the traditions we know today. Who made the first Christmas fruitcake or put lights on the tree for the first time? It was the fads our parents and ancestors grew up with that gave us the countless traditions which we have come to know today.

We come to a final understanding that we all are instinctively guilty also. It seems that we all need a reason or justification for doing almost anything. We party during the weekend because we have worked hard all week. We chow down that extra slice of pizza because we exercised today. Media and commercial insanity is our excuse to spend a quiet Christmas at home. We are worn out, but we can relax in our beds on Christmas Eve and safely know that all the wildness has ended and the storm is over. The "all night Zayre sell-out" has given us our peaceful holiday.

The "true image of Christmas" may truly be alive in our hearts. This is where it belongs. The peace within a stable over two-thousand years ago is something that we hide from the perils of our "modern society." The dreams, anxieties, and traditions are things which we share only with ourselves and our friends. However, we do need help to round out the season and balance the magic. So please, go out and spend yourself "into the red." It's a Christmas color anyhow.

And remember: there are only 15 shopping days left.

WRITING 14
"I Want To Be Excellent"
Multiple Papers in a Sequence of Assignments

Presented in this selection are two expressive essays written by the same student at different points in a sequence of assignments. Respond to the second essay presented, paper 7.

BACKGROUND

These two papers are the second and seventh papers written in response to a sequence of nine assignments on the common general subject, Competence and Excellence. In some way or another, all of the assignments ask students to come to terms with their own ideas and experience on some aspect of this subject, with each successive paper building on the previous writings in the course. The course structure does not provide for students to receive responses to their rough drafts; each of the nine assignments, then, is handed in as a "final" draft. Students may choose to rewrite any papers they wish, although they are not required to rewrite any of them.

Paper 2 was written in response to an assignment that asked students to describe a time when they achieved what they consider a degree of "excellence" at something and, on the basis of that experience, to talk about what it means to be "excellent" in that activity. Assignments 3-6 have asked students to examine other experiences in which they or someone they know demonstrated either competence or excellence. Here is the assignment for paper 7:

ASSIGNMENT

Looking back over the writings you have done so far in the course and considering where you have come in your thinking about "competence" and "excellence," select an idea that you would like to examine more closely, more fully, or in a different light. Write an essay in which you share your thinking on this subject with the members of this class.

Writing 14
Becky C.
Paper 2: Final Draft

EXPERIENCE OF EXCELLENCE

I took a deep breath and tried to calm the trembling that quivered through me. We all hovered in anticipation as we awaited our signal to begin. Bang! The gun sounded and instantly we shot into motion.

Panic seized me. Would I remember the whole routine? I held my spine stiff and straight, allowing for no mistakes. The judges swerved by with hawk-like eyes, just waiting to tick their sheets.

I silently counted as the adrenilin flowed. Determination overpowered my fears. The flag whirled in my hands. Like a robot, I started ahead with my chin held high.

Straight from the start of the show, I knew I had everything together. Snap, twirl, flip, a sneaky smile threatened to break loose. Perfect! I had caught the arial just right.

Now for the ending. With thirty or more bands watching, I ran up the 50 yard line. While holding my breath and my flag pole high in the air, I stretched upward to then curl into a somersault and flip over the two flag poles held waist-high by my fellow corp members. I landed perfectly. With a final salute, the last note from the band rang through the air.

As I practically panted for air, the applause thundered down around us. With pride and exhileration, I knew I had done my best.

Excellence only appears after long hours of grueling practice and performances. It comes from a feeling within. The feeling which makes you dig just a little deeper for that last ounce of strength, even when you know your gage reads empty.

Perfection leaves you with an inner-glow, an indescribable feeling. Sometimes you may not have appeared "excellent" to those watching, but if you feel you did your best and it was good enough, then that is all that matters.

For me, excellence came with that extra poise, snap, and the determination to be the best.

Writing 14
Becky C.
Paper 7: Final Draft

I Want To Be Excellent

I hate competence! To me, being competent is doing something
with little effort. I don't want to be just competent. I want to be
excellent at almost everything I attempt and do. I despise not being
the best I can be and not trying and doing as well as I could. I
haven't reached self expectations. A feeling of unease and slight
bitterness towards myself engulfs me. The feelings of unease and
bitterness are a result of self-dissatisfaction. I feel uneasy about
what others may be thinking of me and what I have done. For example,
when I have finished my work at the college cafeteria and I haven't
completed it to my satisfaction, I sit and stew about what the manager
thought about my work and what the other employees thought as they
glanced over my work. I also feel bitter with regret at myself and at
those few who may have done a better job than I did.

I am ashamed of myself for not being excellent at most things I
try and wish to do well in, even though it is not expected of me from
others. Most people do what they have to do and leave their finished
product. Again, an example is my job here on campus. After we have
finished serving the students, one task is to scrub out the steam
table. I have watched other girls "attempt" an effort towards this
task. Almost everyone of them did the minimum amount of work required
of them. They would dip out the water, give a few quick swipes with a
grubby rag and they were finished, leaving behind them a trail of

1

water spots and streaks of spaghetti noodles with dried sauce. When I
have completed the same task, I can look back upon sparkling chrome
and a dry, spot-free surface. Why don't I just get by, too? Why not
finish my work and get on home? I did this once as I mentioned
before. I did what was required of me and left. Boy, did I feel
guilty! It grated on my conscious to know I weaseled out of polishing
my work. I feel as if in leaving behind a task, I have left behind
some of my character. I have demonstrated what I am and my attitude
toward things. I'm not a slap-happy person by nature, and it shows in
my work.

When I have tried my best, it should make me feel as if I have
achieved something. Instead, I get very mad at myself. Sometimes I
boil underneath when I see others achieving higher goals or my goals.
Why don't I excel in all I want to do and be? Then sometimes I think
I have been ridiculous in expecting too much of myself. I wonder, is
it possible that I'm just not meant to be excellent in some things I
attempt, or maybe even in most things? Is it too much to ask of
myself and God to help me achieve all these things? I really can't
answer my own questions, because I don't know. Maybe it's the way I
approach the matter. I might have a negative outlook on something I
am doing, and this could hamper my results. Many times I jump into
something without first thinking it through. This results in the
wrong formation of an event and eventually, mere competence.

To me, excellence is not just knowing I did my best, but knowing
I did the best possible job. I don't feel that the best possible is
perfection. Only God and Jesus are or can be perfect. But I believe

2

the best is the highest quality anyone can achieve given his/her circumstances and abilities.

I also believe that people who are merely competent are deceiving themselves. They will be "nobodies." They won't stand out as having accomplished a thing. For me, it takes energy, strength, will and determination.

I feel as if I haven't performed anything completely excellent. I have to keep trying and maybe someday I will reach my goals of excellence. I'm really not sure why I don't feel as if I have performed a task excellently. Others say I have, and sometimes for a short while, I will believe that I have, too. But then I stop and really think the situation over, and there is always another aspect within my capabilities which I could have completed to better satisfaction. For instance, I have written many poems. I enjoy creating poetry and formulating ideas. As editor of our high school literary magazine, I planned the layout for the many poems and stories. The students bragged on how the book was different from the previous annual issues. They said I had done an excellent job on the magazine. They also thought the many poems I had submitted were excellent. Instead of feeling enthralled by their praise, I could only think of the factors which I should have worked harder on, such as more illustrations, a different format, or even better ideas and rhyming words in my own poems.

Sometimes I feel very jealous of others who excel. I can see that they are giving it their all and really moving ahead. I hate the feeling that I am standing still. This also makes me a litle bitter

3

towards others who are much better than I am. I also want to experience those moments of excellence and glory when I am basking in the knowledge of my excellence. Self achievement is very important to me. I like the feeling of knowing I am excellent and having others know it, too. This feeling is not conceit. I don't want people being jealous of me or always praising me, although sometimes this is nice. I am still going to give it me all.

In applying my feelings to the present, I am struggling in schoolwork. I feel as if I study all the time and accomplish nearly nothing. Seeing others doing better in their schoolwork makes me try that much harder. Being a registered nurse is my future goal. Hopefully I'll excel in my "niche" in this world, nursing. This is what I want for my parents, myself, and God--for me, Becky C_____ , to reach an excellence I can be proud of.

4

Notes

NOTES TO THE INTRODUCTION

1. We were not assuming that people who contribute to the scholarship of the field and who are visible at national conferences are the best teachers of writing—or that they are necessarily better teachers than those who do not conduct formal research or write regularly for publication. The same study could have been done just as productively, perhaps in some ways even more productively, with responders who were recognized as master teachers, whether or not they produced scholarly publications.

2. We realize that many of the readers of this book, especially teachers with large course loads and overcrowded classes, who already have more than they can handle, might find it difficult to see some of the readers' responses as feasible for them. In fact, they may find that they are simply irrelevant to their circumstances. The depth of many of these sets of responses is daunting, the time it would take to practice such responses for three or four classes untenable. We are aware of the dire circumstances that prevent writing teachers from devoting more time than they already do to response and that keep them from commenting in ways that these teachers seem to be espousing. Nevertheless, we believe that the responses collected here will be of value even to teachers who can give no more time than they already do in responding to their students' writing. Even if the response styles displayed here were to do nothing more than suggest to teachers how they might make better use of the 15 or 20 minutes they can give to their responses on an essay, or how they might more effectively focus the handful of comments they do make, we would hope the study will prove valuable for them.

3. At least, the sampling is as representative as 15 essays could be, considering the huge range of writing that is taken up in first-year composition courses.

4. We reduced the number of responses we display in Chapter 2 to 36 (four sets of responses to nine essays). We used the teachers' responses to 10 essays—a total of 113 sets of responses—for our analysis of their responding styles in Chapter 4.

5. Originally, we asked the readers to respond as they usually do, as if they came across these writings from one of their own students, in a real classroom situation. Only later, when we realized more fully the difficulty they might have in responding to writing in our hypothetical contexts, did we ask them to look at their responses as models of their best ways of responding. It would take a good deal of effort just to recreate a context from the material we provided, so it was not feasible to expect them to respond in the time they typically spend responding to their own students' writing.

6. Throughout the book we will alternate between using "he" and "she" as our generic singular pronoun. Usually, we will use one as the generic pronoun in one section of a chapter and then switch to the other pronoun in the next. At times within certain

sections, when we speak of a teacher as "she" (or "he"), we speak of the student as "he" (or "she"). Our aim throughout has been to balance the use of both pronouns even as we try to meet the demands of clarity and style.

7.   Louise Rosenblatt distinguishes between the "text," the words on the page, and a "poem," a reader's construction of those words into meaning.

8.   Three of the readers in particular regularly augmented our contexts in their responses: Patricia Stock, Peter Elbow, and Chris Anson. The other readers worked with the contexts as they were presented, although some more fully and more comfortably than others. Two readers repeatedly expressed the trouble they had in dealing with the hypothetical contexts: Tilly Warnock and Richard Larson. For a critique of the assignments presented in the background sheets and a proposal for classifying different types of student writing, see Larson's essay at the end of the book.

9.   Of course, we are setting aside the issue of whether they would receive or accept such writing in the first place.

10.   Arguably, all readings, whether they are readings of actual texts or texts in hypothetical contexts, are shaped not merely by an "established" context but by the reader's *sense* of context, by the way he chooses or happens to create the text and by the interpretive conventions that inform his reading. See, for instance, Fish's (1980) argument in "Is There a Text in This Class?" and "How To Recognize a Poem When You See One," in his collection of essays.

11.   Even in keeping within the realm of clinical research, we might have shaped the study in different ways. We might, for instance, have had 12 (or 6 or 24) teachers respond to a number of different samplings of student writing, among them:

1.   12 pieces of writing selected by each of the 12 readers;
2.   12 pieces of writing from several students in the same class; or
3.   12 pieces of writing from one student across a semester.

Although such materials might have been closer to these teachers' actual experiences and perhaps more realistic, they would not have allowed us to make the kind of comparisons about readers, essays, and stages of drafting that we thought would be most useful at this time, given the lack of clarity about many of the issues regarding response to student writing. (For a review of the current scholarship, see Brannon & Knoblauch, 1981.)

NOTES TO CHAPTER 1

1.   See Diederich (1963), "In praise of praise"; Gee (1972), "Students' responses to teacher comments." The research of Diederich (1963) and Gee (1972) seemed to suggest it is important to balance praise and criticism in responding. However, Stevens (1973), in "The effects of positive and negative evaluation on the written comments of low performing high school students," found that high school students improved equally well regardless of whether they received a steady diet of praise or criticism.

2.   Sommers also called attention to a problem in the way teachers phrased their responses to students texts. She found that they often used vague and general language that told students little about what could be done to improve those texts or that, in many cases, failed to identify what the teacher liked or disliked. Such comments as "think more about your audience," "avoid colloquial language," "avoid the passive," "avoid prepositions at the end of sentences," "be clear," "be specific," and so forth, Sommers labeled "rubber-stamped" because they could be placed on a stamp and used on hundreds or thousands of student texts (p. 152). In place of such comments, Sommers called for text-specific responses that would communicate teachers' intentions to student writers.

3.   Two additional articles dealing with the roles teachers play are Cowan (1977) and Purves (1984).

4. The discussion here brings up the important connection between response theory (and composition theory) and modern literary critical theories. For a good review of articles dealing with composition and literary theories, see Clifford and Schilb (1985). Two particulary insightful treatments of this subject are in White (1984) and Emig and Parker (1976).

5. See Chapter 4 for a detailed discussion of directive and facilitative responding.

6. Anson's findings are consistent with those of Burhans (1983). Working with college catalogs as his data base, Burhans found that no more than 5% of them "reflect any influence whatever from contemporary knowledge about writing and the teaching of writing" (p. 646).

7. We should note here that Fulkerson's real thrust in this article is not to declare the rhetoricians the winners, but to say that a full statement of writing theory must contain more than a definition of what makes writing good. In addition, it must include a definition of the writing process, a statement about one's pedagogy in teaching writing, and a declaration of one's epistemology, that is, of what one counts as knowledge.

8. Knoblauch and Brannon (1984) speak to this issue:

> We would argue . . . that once student writers have pursued worthwhile meanings through successive drafts, assisted by readers' personal reactions to the coherence, value, and communicative effectiveness of their developing discourses, their efforts have been successful by definition because they serve the long-range goal of intellectual growth and the maturation of composing ability. (pp. 132, 133)

North (1987) echoes Brannon and Knoblauch:

> Our job [in tutoring] is to produce better writers, not better writing. Any given project—a class assignment, a law school application letter, an encyclopedia entry, a dissertation proposal—is for the writer the prime, often the exclusive concern. . . . [But] we look beyond or through that particular project, that particular text, and see it as an occasion for addressing our primary concern, the process by which it is produced. (p. 438)

NOTES TO CHAPTER 3

1. These classifications are presented, in order, by Nina Ziv, George Hillocks, Paul Diederich, Thomas Gee, C.H. Knoblauch and Lil Brannon, Peter Elbow and Pat Belanoff.

2. For instance, Lees' system would not allow us to distinguish between comments that *request* the student to make a change and those that *advise* him to make a change, a distinction that we sensed was important in determining levels of teacher control. Further, Lees' method provides no way of distinguishing the different ways that teachers evaluate student writing—some more overtly, some more subtly—than others. It also does not establish distinctions among different types of questions.

3. In looking at the 12 readers' responses, we saw that they evaluated student writing in several different ways, some of which were more direct than others. We also saw that their "instructions" took several different forms: instructions about what to do by way of revision, explanations about how to read their other comments, and explanations that informed students about their subject or that reminded them about some lesson in writing. These categories were too broad for our purposes. In addition, we felt that teachers engage in very different acts when they correct student writing and when they make explanations, two types of commentary that Searle and Dillon put in the same group.

4. As Knoblauch and Brannon note, although directive commentary tends to deal with matters of form, it can deal with content; although facilitative commentary tends to address writing at the level of meaning, at times it can address "formal problems" (p. 129).

5. Of course, these categories do not define sharp divisions that actually exist among these qualities of writing; rather, they posit ways of looking at concepts that are far more complex and interdependent than any system of classification can fully represent. Although we recognize that these categories and definitions are in many ways arbitrary, we would argue they serve as useful terministic screens (to use Kenneth Burke's term) for directing our attention to certain aspects of discourse while necessarily deflecting our attention from others (Burke, 1966, p. 45).

6. Of course, in many ways, the categories of wording, development, and ideas are often difficult to separate. Nevertheless, we maintain that comments about content at the sentence level can be distinguished from content at the word or phrase level. Teachers commonly make such a distinction when they speak of the "sharp imagery" in a sentence and then go on to talk about the same sentence as an "interesting idea." We are always concerned most with the teacher's words on the page—with whether, for example, they direct the student's attention mostly to the wording of a sentence or mostly to the ideas in the sentence.

7. In the original version of the rubric, we had two distinct categories for wording: *expression*, to indicate problems in the student's word choice, and *naming*, to indicate strengths in the student's word choice. We felt that when teachers dealt with problems in diction, they were looking predominantly at wording as a matter of form and that when they dealt with successful word choice they were seeing the writing predominantly in terms of *content*. We abandoned the distinction when it raised questions about the placement of comments about sentence-level matters that did not easily fall into these two categories, especially comments that called for greater specificity. Should the comment "What kind of flowers?" be considered a comment about expression or naming? The comment implies a problem with the word choice, and consequently would belong in expression, yet we were hard pressed to see such comments that called for greater specificity as more a matter of form than a matter of content. In order to make our labeling less complicated and more dependable, we collapsed these areas of writing into one broad category, *wording*.

8. We also counted comments as having an extra-textual orientation when they invoked the individual teacher as part of the audience, by use of the personal pronouns "I," "me," "we," or "us":

> I came away from this paper with a clear sense of place.

> How can you be sure we all know "without any explanation"?

> You chose an article whose argument you disagreed with and gave us a full citation.

Comments that used a personal pronoun but did not invoke the teacher as a reader were not included in this category:

> If I were pressed to say what your argument with LeMoult came down to, I would say that you stacked some general point about the harm of drugs against his proposition that legalizing drugs would cut crime and law enforcement costs dramatically.

In this comment, the teacher places himself as an evaluator, not as a member of the writer's audience.

9. The clinical nature of this study—specifically, the fact that these writings are presented with hypothetical contexts that might have led the readers to respond to matters beyond the text less than they might typically do in a real classroom setting—prevents us from drawing any firm conclusions about these teachers' inclinations to look at student writing in terms of these larger contexts.

10. Comments in the same mode do not necessarily enact the same degree of teacher

control. For example, consider how the following comments, all of them imperatives, enact increasingly greater control over the student:

> Check the need for this reference to Tallahassee.
> Place this reference to Tallahassee elsewhere.
> You must find a better way of organizing this material.

Control is a function of the substance and voice as well as the form of the comment.

11. Surely a teacher's actual intentions may influence the precise form of his comments. But we are not concerned with—nor, given the clinical nature of our study, are we able to make—such connections to the actual teacher's attitudes and intentions. Through our study, we hope to help teachers become more conscious about how they may frame their comments in ways that will allow them to match what they say on the page with their intentions.

12. The meaning we have in mind here is not like the autonomous meaning that the New Critics claimed to discover in literary texts, that is, meaning divorced from authorial intention and unaffected by reader bias. It is like the textual meaning that the Chicago Critics look to derive from written texts. For critics such as Richard McKeon, Wayne Booth, and James Phelan, the text embodies the intended meaning of the author. However, it does not reside there "autonomously" but is brought to life by readers who are intent on co-creating the writer's probable intentions as best they can from the words on the page. These readers assume the unity and coherence of a piece of writing and try, through a close reading of the text and its implicit cues, to understand the writer's probable meaning. For more on this approach, see Booth (1983).

13. We do not take into account responses that appear in the form of symbols or abbreviations. For example, if a teacher bracketed a sentence fragment and simply wrote "SF" in the margin, we did not count it as a comment. If a teacher circled some parts of a sentence and indicated with arrows how they might be rearranged but did not talk about these markings, we again did not count it. But if he made such markings and added any words about them (for instance, "Faulty sentence structure" or "What do you think about this change?"), we counted it as a comment. Similarly, if a teacher simply added a phrase or sentence to the student's text, we considered it a comment. Omitting responses that are presented in symbols or abbreviations does not affect our counts in any appreciable way because our 12 readers make very few of these responses.

14. The next sequence, also from Stewart's letter, is more difficult to number:

> In Summer, for example, you talk about families going to the beach. In Syracuse? Isn't the nearest beach Lake Ontario, and is it fit to swim in? Perhaps it is. I know Erie was a mess and still may be. At any rate, we need to know what beaches you're talking about. The "going to the beach" detail is a Summer cliche for many parts of the country.

There are six comments in the seven sentences of this sequence. The first sentence is an interpretive comment, the second a closed problem-posing question. Although the third sentence contains two independent clauses that might be counted as two comments, the two clauses work together as a single, closed problem-posing comment because they both address the same concern, in the same mode. The fourth and fifth sentences also count as a single comment because they address the same concern and both take the form of reader remarks: When there is no change in the topic and no change in focus or mode, there is no new comment. The sixth and seventh sentences deal with the same topic—the writer's talking in general terms about going to the beach—but they are counted as two distinct comments because the latter follows up on and explains the evaluation presented in the previous sentence, in effect, establishing a change in mode. Sentence 6, then, contains a negative evaluation about specificity, and sentence 7 is an explanatory comment.

15. We use the term *criticism* to refer to any kind of negative evaluation.

16. The following chart shows the balance between rough drafts and final drafts in the sampling. The writings are identified in parentheses:

5 ROUGH DRAFTS	5 FINAL DRAFTS
2 argumentative (Writings 1, 2)	1 evaluative (Writing 13)
2 expository (Writings 4, 5)	3 expository (Writings 6, 9, 11)
1 expressive (Writing 12)	1 expressive (Writing 10)
2 immature rough drafts (Writings 1, 2)	3 mediocre final drafts (Writings 6, 10, 11)
3 mature rough drafts (Writings 4, 5, 12)	2 above average final drafts (Writings 9, 13)

17. That is, the readers wrote 113 sets of responses out of the possible 120 sets. (Remember that each reader had the option of deleting 3 essays.) Seven readers responded to 9 of the 10 essays in the sampling. The other five responded to all 10.

18. To repeat a point we made earlier in the chapter, we are not analyzing all forms of response in this study, only responses that are written out as "comments." We do not analyze abbreviations, graphic symbols, or editings that are not written out in words. As a glance at the sample responses in Chapter 2 reveals, our readers made very few responses that were not written out in the form of comments, that is, in words, phrases, or sentences.

19. Two graduate students working in rhetoric and composition at Florida State University, Kim Haimes and Tom Thompson, were trained to use the rubric to label written comments. Over the course of 15 two-hour training sessions, they studied the definitions of the rubric, learned the principles for analyzing comments, and practiced using the categories on over 50 sets of responses. These two students were joined by one of the authors to make a team of three raters. Using the "Rubric for Analyzing Teacher Comments" (presented in Appendix C), the raters moved fully through one responder's comments before moving on to the next. They first labeled the comments made by the six readers who made marginal comments and brief endnotes; then they tackled the more difficult task of labeling the comments written in separate letters to the student. After completing their analyses on two readers' responses to the sampling, the group came together, discussed whatever difficulties they had in labeling the comments, and clarified their sense of the categories in an effort to improve agreement on subsequent sets of responses.

NOTES TO THE INTRODUCTION TO CHAPTER 4

1. See Chapter 3 for a summary of Knoblauch and Brannon's argument against "directive" comments and in favor of "facilitative" commentary. (For their full statement on the distinction, see Knoblauch & Brannon, 1984.)

2. When Sommers (1982) and Brannon and Knoblauch (1982) criticize teachers who "appropriate" student texts, we think they are really talking about teachers who *extensively* appropriate student writing—teachers who use the majority of their comments to make important decisions for students *and* impose their idealized text on the writing. As we see it, teachers "appropriate" student writing whenever they make choices that they expect the student to adopt, not just consider. We distinguish between "appropriating" selected parts of a text and "imposing an idealized text" on the writing as a whole. For us, the terms are not interchangeable. When teachers impose an idealized text they *extensively* appropriate student writing. They may appropriate it only in part and not wrest control from the writer.

3. Teachers "impose their idealized text" on student writing when they foist on the student a certain way of seeing the overall writing. Teachers can point to problems or

indicate ways to revise without taking over the text. In fact, they routinely read texts with their own agendas and terministic screens; they invariably project their views on student writing. But when they foist decisions on the writer, they "appropriate" the student's text. And when they force a large number of decisions on the student and push one way of looking at the text as a whole, they impose their rigid, detailed vision (what Knoblauch and Brannon call an idealized text) on the writing. Teachers are especially prone to take over a text when they read with an eye toward getting the student to produce a (more) complete written product that meets the teacher's purposes in a way that does not acknowledge or work with the student's meanings or choices. The student is left to follow the teacher's path for revision rather than find one for herself, according to her intentions for the writing.

Brannon and Knoblauch see this issue of control in terms of the students' rights to their own texts. They claim that teachers who impose their idealized text deny students the rights that writers normally enjoy: rights to determine their own purposes and materials. Rather than agree or disagree with them, we would like to pose the issue as a question: In what ways do the 12 readers in this study, by the evidence of their responses, assume that students should be responsible for determining their own choices? As we have noted at the start of the chapter, our readers seem to agree in principle with Knoblauch and Brannon on the general point that teachers should not usurp control from their students. At the same time, as a group they are not unwilling to make judgments about the quality or the appropriateness of the students' choices.

4. Like all teachers, the 12 readers do bring their individual agendas to these writings, but they use those agendas as guides for their reading, not necessarily as templates against which the student's writing is rigidly judged. In fact, it might be argued that no effective response is likely to result unless a teacher has a good grasp of his agenda and makes it known to students. The problem occurs when the teacher uses the agenda in a way that pushes his concerns for writing to such an extent that he takes away from the student's efforts and particular intentions in a piece of writing. Teachers may use their agendas productively to make comments, without "appropriating" the writing or "imposing an ideal text" on the student.

5. The comments are taken from another study we have initiated, in which we compare the responses of these 12 well-known teachers with the responses of 12 English teachers who represent a range of teachers who typically teach college writing: graduate students, instructors, and literature faculty. The responses reproduced here were written by a professor of literature at a small midwestern college. This teacher was given the same context as the 12 readers in this study. She was asked to make the kinds of comments she typically makes on student writing and to represent her best responding practices, as if she were to present her responses as models for less experienced colleagues.

6. Here and throughout the chapter, by *revision* we mean more than just the prospect or act of actual rewriting; we mean the general act of reenvisioning—or looking again upon—a piece of writing. A responder has a hand in revision whether or not the student goes back and makes actual changes to the text.

7. In our view, teachers may make frequent use of corrective, imperative, and negative evaluations, and still not take control out of the student's hands. They may "direct" the student writer, but do so in a moderate way, one that is directing or guiding, not appropriating or dictatorial.

8. The exceptions might be in the first and last marginal comments, in which White may be said to impose on the student his sense of what makes an adequate opening and closing paragraph.

9. We choose not to oppose "authoritative" styles of response with "nonauthoritative" styles because all teacher comments assume—though some less explicitly than others—the teacher's authority. Even the least controlling responses, for instance, ones that simply offer the teacher's paragraph-by-paragraph description of the writing, may—and, we hope, *would*—proceed from the teacher's authority and expertise.

10. All of these categories are based on the predominant strategies a teacher employs in his responses. Although a teacher who has an advisory style may, of course, use modes that are more controlling (e.g., corrective or evaluative) or less controlling (e.g., interpretive comments or heuristic questions), he bases his commentary on providing options and recommendations to the student.

11. It is difficult to find a place for what we call "advisory" response in Knoblauch and Brannon's categories. In some ways it seems "directive," in others, "facilitative."

12. Our division of teacher commentary into two broad categories—"authoritative" and "interactive"—roughly parallels Knoblauch and Brannon's "directive" and "facilitative" response. But our category of "authoritative" response identifies two kinds of highly controlling commentary. In a sense, it divides Knoblauch and Brannon's "directive" commentary into two distinct types: "authoritarian" and "directive." Our authoritarian style is closely associated with the type of commentary that they call directive, in which the teacher takes significant control over the student's writing and prescribes definite changes. We prefer the term authoritarian because it more accurately captures the extent of control the teacher exerts in this kind of response. For us, directive response invokes the teacher's authority but is less prescriptive, less harsh and critical, and less controlling than authoritarian commentary. It has the feel of constructive criticism. Our category of interactive response identifies three distinct types of response that attempt to preserve the student's control over the writing—Socratic, dialectic, and analytical—whereas Knoblauch and Brannon establish only one broadly defined type, facilitative. However, the two categories we present here—authoritative and interactive—do not represent the two extremes of teacher response. The opposite of authoritarian response is not interactive response, but "detached" response, in which the teacher gets only minimally involved in directing or helping students conceive of changes in their writing. Anson (1989) posits analogous categories. His concept of "dualistic" response is consistent with authoritarian response, his category "relativistic" with detached response, and his category "reflective" broadly consistent with our interactive response. (See Chapter 2 for a brief definition of these categories.)

13. Kroll (1980) identifies two opposing types of teachers. For interventionists, education involves the transmission of knowledge and skills. The emphasis is on the content of instruction. For maturationists, education involves the creation of climates in which the individual may work out her potential for growth. The emphasis is on the person and her processes of writing and learning. Kroll proposes the usefulness of a third type of teacher, interactionists, who try to integrate elements from the other two types. Although some of the 12 readers in our study lean toward an interventionist perspective and others toward a maturationist perspective, they usually employ some elements from the opposing perspective.

14. Of course, neither group does one without getting involved in the other. We are talking about what each group of teachers emphasizes: either the production of completed texts or the practice of writing activities. Many or even most teachers probably fall somewhere in between these two extremes.

15. Our descriptions of the 12 readers' responding styles gets increasingly complex as we move through the three groups of readers, mainly for two reasons. First, we want to get our readers accustomed to our method of analysis before moving on, in the second and third sections, to more complicated issues of response and fuller analyses. Second, the individual readers' responses become more complicated from Group 1 to Group 3. Three of the four readers in the first group—Edward White, Jane Peterson, and Anne Gere—use the relatively standard form of brief marginal comments and short endnotes; the fourth reader, Frank O'Hare, lists on a separate page what amounts to a series of marginal comments. Three of the four readers in the second group of readers—Donald Stewart, Ben McClelland, and Peter Elbow—offer lengthy letters to the student, sometimes in addition to marginal responses, sometimes without any marginal responses at all. The fourth reader in the group—Glynda Hull—greatly varies the format of her responses from essay to essay. The third group of readers brings together three of the four readers who make the most comments to the sampling of

essays: Richard Larson, Patricia Stock, and Chris Anson. Furthermore, whereas Stock attempts to simulate the full array of spoken and written comments that typify her classroom responses, Anson provides transcripts of tape-recorded comments to these hypothetical students. The fourth reader in the group—Tilly Warnock—makes standard marginal comments and short endnotes, yet presents a style that is distinctive among this group of readers because it often offers only brief, often general remarks about the writing.

Notes to White's Section

1. Throughout this chapter, we speak of a reader making "more" or "fewer" responses than others even when we are referring to the percentage of his overall responses. We also make minor changes in the capitalization and punctuation of the readers' sample comments without noting them.

2. Each of our descriptions of the 12 readers' responding styles includes such a chart summarizing our quantitative analysis of their comments. Below is a key for the labels in the charts:

   FOCUS
   LOCAL   Local matters: correctness, wording, local structure
   GLOBAL   Global matters: ideas, development, global structure
   X-TEXT   Extra-textual matters: e.g., audience, purpose, assignment, process

   MODE
   CORR   corrective
   EVAL   negative evaluation
   QUEV   qualified negative evaluation
   IMPR   imperative
   ADVS   advisory
   PRAI   praise: positive evaluations and qualified positive evaluations
   CLQU   closed questions: indirect requests, closed problem-posing questions, closed heuristic questions
   OPQU   open questions: open problem-posing questions and open heuristic questions
   REFL   reflective: interpretive, explanatory, reader response, other

3. By contrast, Peter Elbow makes the lowest percentage of comments in strong authoritative modes: 6%. The average for the 12 readers is 16%.

4. "Street Gangs" elicited probably the most directive responses from the readers as a group. Evidently, they found it a draft that was far enough along and that had enough potential to lead them to want to make constructive criticism. They apparently thought Rusty was the type of student who could use more structured guidance.

5. White presents 5% of his comments in the form of corrections. Patricia Stock makes extensive corrections on primarily two sets of responses, a total of 15% of her responses. Donald Stewart regularly makes corrective comments, a total of 9% of his responses.

6. This distinction will become clearer as we describe more responding styles that make use of imperative modes, and elucidate the difference between imperative comments that address changes in the text and imperatives that address activities or processes of revision.

7. Again, throughout this chapter, we use the term *criticism* to refer to negative evaluations and qualified negative evaluations.

8. We had a difficult time seeing praise either as a part of authoritative commentary or as a part of interactive commentary. Positive comments seem to have almost equal doses of authoritative and interactive qualities. Praise comments are difficult

to place under authoritative commentary because they do not call for any change to the text, as all other forms of authoritative commentary state or imply. They are difficult to place under interactive commentary because they do not actively encourage students to consider how they may revise the writing. They close down discussion or interaction by stating the teacher's views about what works and (presumably) does not need further attention. Consequently, we do not treat praise as part of our count of either authoritative or interactive commentary.

9. In Writing 12, 12 of 24 comments are framed in strong authoritative modes (i.e., correctives, negative evaluations, or imperatives), and 7 of 24 comments are framed in interactive modes (i.e., questions or reflective statements) or praise. In Writing 2, 9 of 15 comments are authoritative. In Writing 4, 8 of 19 are authoritative. In Writing 6, 10 of 24 are authoritative. In Writing 11, 9 of 18 are authoritative.

10. We count as an "area of response," or "issue," only those categories of response that receive at least *two* comments in the margins or *one* comment in the endnotes. That is, any matter that receives treatment in an endnote is automatically an "issue." If it receives no mention in an endnote, it requires two mentions in marginal comments to be an "issue." As a group, the 12 readers address for each paper an average of 3.3 areas of response out of the 7 areas defined by our rubric: ideas, development, global structure, local structure, wording, correctness, extra-textual comments.

11. In other words, emphasizing the content and purpose of writing runs counter to traditional authoritarian commentary, which routinely appropriates control of student writing by emphasizing the changes that could be made to surface features at the local level.

12. Indeed, other readers envision different potential focuses for the paper, for example, the way gangs provide an ego boost, the special bond among members of a gang, the differences between a party gang and a disruptive gang, and the different activities of this gang or of gangs in general. Whereas White does not shy away from indicating his preference to the student, other teachers choose not even to list the possible alternatives.

Notes to O'Hare's Section

1. The differences among O'Hare's various sets of responses made it difficult to select one set as representative of his style. Of the three essays we decided to display in the chapter, his responses to "Street Gangs" were most consistent with his usual patterns of response. His level of control and his overall style are best epitomized in his responses to "Bass Fishermen." At different times on this rough draft, he plays open-ended questions off of evaluative and imperative statements and makes frequent use of praise, all the while keeping his attention on global concerns and the rhetorical context. His other responses displayed in Chapter 2 (to Writings 8 and 9) focus, as they typically do, on global concerns. But they are less representative in terms of his use of modes. There are no critical evaluations and no questions on these papers, only interpretive comments, explanatory comments, and praise—not all that surprising when one considers how strong O'Hare finds these two pieces of writing. His responses to Writing 11, meanwhile, are far and away his most directive. Here he writes eight comments: one imperative, four negative evaluations, and three comments that explain his earlier criticisms.

2. He makes use of lines and symbols in the text to indicate places where he finds something positive in the writing.

3. O'Hare frames 19% of his comments in the form of praise (i.e., positive evaluations and positive qualified evaluations) and 18% in the form of criticism (i.e., negative evaluations and negative qualified evaluations).

4. By comparison, 9 of White's 14 comments on "Street Gangs" are commands.

5. Compare O'Hare's strategy here with the strategies used by Jane Peterson and Anne Gere in later sections. Both Peterson and Gere tend to use questions without making a prior criticism of the writing.

6. Ben McClelland writes the fewest comments on local matters (2%) and the most comments about ideas and development (58%).

7. The exception is Writing 2 in which O'Hare makes no reference to the reader.

8. By comparison, see Peterson's style, which creates a role for her of a representative or an interested reader, not an expert reader or an authority.

Notes to Peterson's Section

1. We are using the term *facilitative* here in a more narrow sense than Knoblauch and Brannon. Their concept of facilitative commentary refers to any style of response that is not highly directive or authoritarian. For them, any teacher who tries to engage students in a real exchange about their writing is facilitative, whether she does so primarily by providing reader responses, advice, open questions, or closed questions. For us, the concept refers specifically to teachers who take on the role of an interested, representative reader or a helpful teacher and use their interests and needs as readers to guide the student toward revision. Among the 12 readers, the other prime example of such a facilitative responder is Chris Anson, who also reads the writing as an interested reader and uses his comments to guide the student's revision.

2. Peterson adopts the role of an interested reader especially in her marginal comments; in her endnotes, she tends to take on the role of a supportive teacher.

3. Notably, though, both Peterson and White are more interested in making the text complete by saying what could be added, rather than by simply noting what is not working. The latter method is a mark, of course, of authoritarian response.

4. An additional comment (comment 5) is framed as a closed problem-posing question: "Anyone or just the person who beat up your gang member?"

5. Evaluative comments also allow the student to decide what changes will be made. But they leave little room for the student to decide not to make a change in the writing.

6. In their comments to "Street Gangs," White and O'Hare write 12 and 9 strong authoritative comments, respectively; Peterson writes only two, both of them negative evaluations: "you need more detail . . ., and you also need more focus."

7. With one exception, Peterson makes her 12 advisory comments in her endnotes.

8. As we will see, it is not always the case that teachers become less controlling when they refer to the rhetorical context of the writing, that is, to the audience and purpose of the writing. Teachers may use comments about the rhetorical situation to direct the student to satisfy their vision—not necessarily the student's intentions or a prospective audience's expectations—for a piece of writing.

Notes to Gere's Section

1. Gere writes much of her praise in end comments and on final drafts. She frames only 9% of her responses in negative evaluations or negative qualified evaluations, just below the average for readers in the study.

2. The more complete the draft, the more Gere makes use of evaluative comments and the less she presents advice.

3. Gere's use of combination comments, which in "Street Gangs" is extensive, is unusual for her. Across her other nine sets of responses, she makes only five multiple comments.

4. Of course, there is no telling what the student will actually attend to when he receives a set of comments back from his teacher. Clearly, different students will attend to different matters, with varying degrees of involvement. Also, a given form of commentary will likely have different effects on different individual students. We are not attempting to ignore the abundant research that shows rather powerfully the extent to which the meaning of a text—whether it be a piece of writing or a set

of teacher comments to that writing—depends on the expectations one brings to the text and that grows out of the transaction between the reader and the words on the page. We are assuming, nevertheless, that there are certain—not standard—but more or less typical ways that certain strategies of style will be taken by more readers than not. We do not intend (nor do we pretend it would be possible) to establish how some "ideal" student would respond to different kinds of comments. But we do suggest that certain forms of commentary will usually be taken one way and not another.

5. Of course, it is a chicken-or-egg matter: It may also be said that as they are more open-ended and less authoritative they become less directed toward having the student make particular changes in the written product.

Notes to Stewart's Section

1. White writes 45% of his comments in imperative modes, the most in the study. Stewart makes the second-highest number of corrective comments (9%) and negative evaluations (16%).

2. Stewart casts 11% of his responses as closed problem-posing comments, the third-highest use of these comments among the readers. As we will see, these closed questions seem well-suited to his critical style. Stewart also writes the third-highest percentage of explanatory responses in the study.

3. The high number of nonauthoritative comments is due, in part, to the fact that Stewart writes full letters to the student. This form of response is often characterized by a high number of reflective comments.

4. Stewart's elaboration contributes to his directiveness in other sets of responses as well. In his comments on Writing 4, a rough draft that tries to urge parents not to overguide their teenage children, even as he gets more specific, Stewart follows negative evaluations with other types of evaluations, or he follows strong imperative comments with other, more specific imperatives. For example, he follows his criticism about the writer's voice with examples and then additional criticism:

> After that, unfortunately, things go downhill. The tone changes and becomes didactic. You almost start to lecture these parrents. See, for example, lines three and four on page 2 and the second line of the last paragraph in the essay. You become almost patronising, explaining parents' faults to them but hoping that they will have wisdom enough to overcome them. I don't think many parents of teenagers would respond too warmly to such advice, especially coming from an eighteen-year-old whom they would see as hardly worldly wise.

In Writing 5, he often follows directive comments with other directive comments that are more specific:

> In this paper, you give us only two sentences after hooking [the big bass]. That's not enough. The reader wants a longer report of the battle you had landing this big fish.

These comments provide more direction as well as more assistance to the student.

5. In other sets of responses, Stewart follows some kind of directive comment (in the following cases, negative evaluations) with an explanatory comment:

> You also move, without transitions, from a semi-abstract discussion of bass fishing to references to a particular day's fishing. A reader can get confused by that kind of maneuver. (Writing 5)

> I am surprised that [the paper] is not more intense in places. This is truly a life and death subject! (Writing 10)

Such explanations suggest there is a reason for making changes in the writing beyond the teacher's merely saying so. They invoke an authority beyond the teacher and ease his control.

6. Stewart begins this response by telling the student of his own experience battling cancer:

    > I don't think anyone would question your choice of subject. The discovery that one has leukemia certainly has an impact. People die from this disease. As a matter of fact, I can relate to your experience better than most. I have been treating a blood cancer the past two years and have taken some of the medicines you mention: Vincristine and Adriamycin. Chemotherapy, which was an abstraction to me before this experience, is now a reality. So, we are on common ground here.

    He uses his personal experience distinctively in several other sets of responses as well: Writings 1, 6, and 13 (see Chapter 2 for his full responses).

7. He makes 35 comments on "What If Drugs Were Legal?"—more than anyone in this group of responders and, in fact, more than any one of our 12 readers. His comments on Writing 2 cover six areas: correctness, wording, local structure, development, ideas, and the assignment. None of the three other readers from this group treats more than four categories.

8. Stewart writes 13% of his comments on matters of correctness; Larson, who has the next highest percentage, writes 10%.

9. Both Stewart and Larson devote 19% of their comments to wording; White devotes 18% of his comments to the area.

10. Even when they are not framed in corrective modes, comments about correctness, wording, and sentence structure do not allow as much room for the student's choice, as the following comments illustrate:

    > [Re: "My only and most important argument to LeMoult is the physical harm it would bring by legalizing drugs."] Refers to? (Writing 2)
    > You can go two ways with this sentence: (1) omit "according to;" (2) omit "feels."
    > [Re: "olfactories"] Pretentious language. (Writing 6)
    > [Re: "rustic"] Sure this is the right word? (Writing 6)
    > [Re: "roller coaster"] You've used this term several times. (Writing 13)

    These local matters are less open to debate than matters of content and effect, and students are less likely to be invested in them. They would readily defer to the authority of such comments and make the called for change. Consequently, the more a teacher deals with such issues, the more he asserts control over the writing. Further, the more he is interested in local matters, the more likely he is interested in having students produce a finished written product, and the more he is likely to push his own vision for the writing.

11. Stewart writes only 36 of his 113 comments about correctness, wording, and local structure in his letters to the student, and 14 of those occur on one paper in which his talk about wording is closely related to the content of the essay (Writing 6). He writes the other 77 comments directly on student texts. The fact that Stewart puts almost all of his editorial comments on students' texts and separates them from the conceptual comments in his letters suggests that his emphasis is on the content and purpose of the writing, not on correctness. His comments on Writing 2 provide a good example. Although 16 of his 35 total comments are given to local matters, 14 of them occur in his interlinear comments on the student's text. His endnote is devoted to larger conceptual matters. He focuses 16 of his 20 comments in the letter on ideas and development, and two more on how the writing fulfills the demands of the writing assignment.

12. We make this assertion on the basis of two observations. First, the form of the writing, tied as it is to the text, is more overt and more readily lends itself to immediate revision. Second, the ideas, because they are usually dependent on the writer's knowledge and experience, often are simply not accessible to the teacher. What the student specifically has to say or believes is beyond the teacher's control.

It is difficult for the teacher to anticipate or presume what Nancy knows or could write confidently about in regard, say, to the damage that society suffers from drug abuse; thus it is difficult to tell her in specific ways what to do with her content.

13.   That is, an idealized text may take two forms. First, it may (super)impose on student writing the teacher's general expectations for a particular assignment or a particular type of writing. A teacher who brings this kind of idealized text to his reading looks at all the papers written to a common assignment in terms of this template of expectations. Second, it may (super)impose on student writing the teacher's idealized text for each paper he reads in a stack of papers. Instead of using a common template for looking at all the writings, he creates an individual template for the piece of writing he is reading. He assumes that he knows best what the student should do, or at least that his sense of how the text should look is what he needs to present to the student.

14.   Less perjoratively, Stewart can be seen as offering the student detailed guidance—or even specific, well-thought-out help—on how to improve the paper. We are choosing to highlight the metaphor of control in teacher commentary. We realize the judgmental connotation in the words "taking control" and "imposing his idealized text," but we do not mean to suggest whether or not the degree of control Stewart exerts over this writing is appropriate or effective.

15.   Stewart appropriates the writing in places in his responses to Writings 4 and 13, but he does not, in our view, impose an idealized text on those papers.

16.   In his response to Writing 2, the following comments come the closest to indicating his preferences for the revision:

> Let's look at the assertion that drug use is dangerous to individuals and to society. You have something to work with there. You must first provide some very specific information about the damage drug use does to people.

Stewart indicates in no uncertain terms that Nancy should add material here. But he does not indicate what kind of information or suggest that some type of information will be more useful (or expected by him) than another. Even as he calls for the additional support, he gives the student leeway to come up with her own material for revision. Because he makes perhaps only one other comment that may overpower the student's decisions (when he says earlier "I don't think we'll get anywhere with the circular argument that drug use is criminal and therefore should not be legalized"), he does not really impose his vision for the paper on the student.

17.   The concept of the idealized text, especially as put forth by Brannon and Knoblauch in their work, has been used mostly to talk about teachers' taking over student writing by attending so much to the formal propriety of the text—its correctness, style, and organization—that they deal in only a cursory fashion, if at all, with the student's ideas and purposes. Stewart's commentary, in part because it deals extensively with the writer's content and purpose, is less controlling than the kind of authoritarian commentary we presented as an example at the start of the chapter. Although several sets of Stewart's responses may cross the line of "directive" response into "authoritarian" response, we see Stewart's style of commentary as directive, not authoritarian.

Notes to McClelland's Section

1.   Eight of his 10 responses follow this pattern, six of them closely.

2.   By comparison, White writes 51%, Stewart 37%, and O'Hare 31% in authoritative modes.

3.   Here and throughout the chapter, when we talk about a "reading of the text," we do not simply mean playing back one's understanding of what the writer said. It may also include evaluation of the student's writing.

4.   McClelland makes a number of interpretive comments on Writings 5, 11, 9, 13, and a large number on Writings 2 and 12. He makes no interpretive comments on only two sets of responses, on Writing 6, in which he calls for a major revision, and on Writing

10, in which he calls on the writer to try the assignment again.

5. Across the sampling, he writes 10 reader reactions (e.g., "So, when I read sentences like 'I think it is often forgotten that young people have minds of their own,' I wonder if you are talking about your parents or a friend's parents"). He writes only seven straight negative evaluations, usually in reference to the paper as a whole.

6. This is the kind of subjective reading that Robert Schwegler (1991) advocates.

7. Unlike Stewart, who explains many of his comments by citing examples and showing the reasons behind the comments, in effect, basing his claims on arguments outside of himself, McClelland uses only six comments to explain a previous comment. He relies on his authority as a teacher and even asserts this authority.

8. McClelland ends six of his letters with imperative and/or advisory statements. He writes at least two prompts—two commands or advisory comments—on 9 of his 10 sets of responses. The exception, Writing 9, is a final draft handed in at the end of the term.

9. The number of questions is slightly misleading because they are not evenly distributed across these four sets of responses. Twenty occur on Writing 11, in which McClelland writes a series of short heuristic questions that ask the writer to consider how she might develop her writing, should she choose to do a revision. He is more likely to use questions on rough drafts and evaluative comments on final drafts.

10. In his responses to two essays, he provides models for imitation. On Writing 6, "The Four Seasons," he presents the student with a paragraph of his own description to illustrate how the writer may use details to achieve a sense of place. On Writing 13, "The John Cougar Concert," he provides two pieces of published writing to show the writer some stylistic conventions for music reviews. Such modeling works well with the dual purpose of his response, allowing him both to indicate how the writing may be improved and to put the responsibility for the actual revising on the student.

11. Actually, all five of McClelland's comments about local concerns are made on wording; he makes no comments on local structure or correctness. Sixty-eight percent of his comments are given to global structure, ideas, and development— the second highest (with O'Hare) in the study. Gere makes the most comments about global matters (72%).

12. The comments McClelland makes about global structure are often concerned with the main idea of the essay, not with introductions, conclusions, or the arrangement of the essay.

13. McClelland averages just under three issues per commentary—the second lowest in the study.

14. See Jane Peterson's responses for an example of the comments made by what we are calling a representative reader.

15. His commentary on Writings 2, 1, 4, and 12 keeps a good deal of control in the hands of the writer. His presence, for example, is moderate in his response to Writing 2, in which his questions serve to place the major decisions on the student. He comes closest to imposing his own vision for the writing when at the end of his response, he directs Nancy to call LeMoult's conclusions into question, rather than leaving it for her to decide how to respond against his views.

16. The clearest example of McClelland's strong presence as a reader, though, occurs in his response to Writing 8. Here, following a strong reading of Jennifer's relationship with her alcoholic father, he calls into question her rendering of her father's alcoholism and goes on to present his own alternate interpretation:

> In your 5th paragraph, when you introduce the subject of alcoholism, unwittingly you misstate the facts: "But alcoholism is a disease that captures and imprisons its victim and *offers no escape*" (my emphasis). While alcohol is addictive and the disease is virulent, Jennifer, people can and do recover from it. Moreover,

alcoholism is a disease; it is not literally a jailer or some sort of merciless terrorist or superhuman kidnaper. . . . To characterize alcoholism not as a disease but as a powerful, evil person elevates your father's struggle with it to some imagined heroic level.

Notes to Hull's Section

1. Hull and McClelland attend to the same number of concerns and make a similar number of main comments (about seven per paper). But McClelland elaborates on his comments more than Hull does. Stewart, of course, elaborates much more than either of them.

2. Interestingly, in cases in which Hull uses marginal comments and an endnote, she more often than not uses her marginal comments and her end comments for different purposes. For example, on Writing 12, she uses her marginal comments to boost Rusty's confidence about what he has already accomplished in the writing, whereas in her endnote she focuses on helping him to develop and shape his ideas. Similarly, her marginal comments on Writing 6 point to specific passages she likes, and then her end comment calls on David to figure out for himself how his essay might be received by readers in different settings. On Writing 2, her marginal comments deal with Nancy's summary of LeMoult; her end comments deal with developing stronger evidence and arguments.

3. Before long, the metaphor exhausts its usefulness. Of course, because doing less and less as a responder could soon lead to students' also doing less, at some point we might more accurately say that for Hull moderate is more: The more she takes moderate responsibility for deciding what students should work on, the more she can guide them without directing them and the more they may be led to work purposefully on their own.

4. Lees outlines seven different modes of commentary and claims the most effective of them is assignment making because it involves students most in making their own revisions.

5. The text-based imperatives appear in Writing 5: "In your next draft, keep those wonderful details, but pay attention as well to how you can make this more an expository essay than a personal experience piece"; Writing 10: "Add some paragraphs on how having leukemia has changed or affected you"; and Writing 12: "I want you to add some extended examples—not just one sentence or two, but whole paragraphs"; "Give details."

6. Note how Hull does not spell out any specific connection between drug use and AIDS that she may have in mind nor does she provide already formed content for the student, as she would if she had said: "How about getting into how drug use could also lead to the increased occurrence of AIDS"?

7. Although Hull refers to these comments as "suggestions," they are clearly stronger than advisory comments.

8. Tilly Warnock makes the highest percentage of open problem-posing questions, 22%. Many of hers, however, are general questions that she uses from paper to paper.

9. It is also interesting to compare Hull's problem-posing questions with McClelland's more incisive and demanding questions. McClelland asks, "In a sentence, what is [LeMoult's] major reason for suggesting we consider legalizing drugs?" and "Why do you include the points on the first antidrug laws and on women's use of laudanum when you don't refer to them later? Do they relate to your argument with LeMoult over legalizing drugs?" Hull asks, "Would [LeMoult] have an answer for the AIDS argument?"

10. Hull addresses three or fewer areas on seven of her nine sets of responses. On her other two sets of responses, she addresses four issues.

Notes to Elbow's Section

1. Elbow writes only three imperatives and 16 advisory comments across the nine essays to which he responded in this sampling. In fact, he makes fewer imperative and advisory comments than anyone else in the study. Together they account for only 8% of his comments. He also asks fewer questions than anyone else in the study (9%).

2. By comparison, Peterson, Gere, and Warnock write 23% of their comments in authoritative modes. Next to Elbow, they write the fewest authoritative comments in the study. White makes the most use of authoritative modes: 50%.

3. Nine percent of Elbow's comments are cast in the form of negative evaluations and qualified negative evaluations, 18% in the form of praise, and 39% in the form of interpretive comments and various types of reader response. In all, 56% of his responses are cast in reflective modes—easily the highest in the study. Anson and Stock have the next highest percentage of comments in reflective modes (interpretive, explanatory, reader-response, and other): Anson 46%, Stock 44%.

4. The exception is Writing 9, a final draft handed in at the end of the term.

5. Elbow (Elbow & Belanoff, 1989) speaks of such responses in terms of readers telling "what happens inside their heads" as they read the words on the page, that is, what they see in the text or what happened to them as they read it. We speak of them in terms of the reader's subjective understandings, experiences, responses, and reactions. Whereas Elbow groups these different forms of reader-response commentary together, we differentiate them. Mainly, we are interested in separating responses that evaluate the writing from those that do not.

6. Six percent of Elbow's reader reactions are positive; 14% are negative.

7. O'Hare has the next highest percentage of evaluations—explicit or embedded. He writes 39% of his comments in evaluations of some kind.

8. White also makes 23% of his comments in some form of evaluative commentary. But all of his occur in negative evaluations and negative qualified evaluations. Across his responses to the sampling, Elbow also writes more criticism than comments that simply play back the text without evaluation. Nineteen percent of his comments play back the writing in interpretive comments, reader-experience comments, and reader remarks.

9. Interpretive comments that simply play back the text in interpretive comments assume minimal control over the writing. But because they do not make judgments about the writing or indicate how it may be improved, they offer little in the way of direction for revision. They also create little give and take between teacher and student and, consequently, are only moderately interactive. The student is left on his own to decide what needs to be changed and how it can be changed.

10. Elbow writes 13% of his responses in explanatory comments, mostly on final drafts. On rough drafts, he tends to use more problem-posing questions, perhaps as a way to induce the writer to initiate her own revisions.

11. Elbow addresses three areas of commentary on four sets of his responses and four areas on five sets, for an average of 3.6 areas per response. The group averages 3.3 issues per paper.

12. Again, this is the type of reader that Schwegler (1991) endorses.

Notes to Larson's Section

1. Larson uses more advisory comments and qualified negative evaluations than any other reader (24%). His use of advisory comments (17%) and qualified negative evaluations (7%) is the second highest among the 12 readers.

2. Larson uses qualified evaluations on all but one set of responses and straight criticism on all but two sets. Only 4% of his comments praise the student's work. By contrast, Gere, who stands at the other end of the spectrum, writes 23% of her comments in the form of praise.

3. Advisory or imperative comments appear in every set of Larson's responses. Seven out of his 10 sets of responses have four or more comments framed as advice or imperatives. Hull, who writes the most imperatives and advice in the study, writes 24% of her comments as prompts, although most of hers are assignments geared toward students' writing processes. Anson writes 23% of his comments as commands or advice, but his prompts, as we will see, are also often geared toward students' writing processes and are more open than Larson's.

4. Fifty of his 110 marginal comments are closed problem-posing questions. Another 33 are presented as advice and commands. In other words, three out of four marginal comments somehow present Larson's views about specific needs for revision.

5. Peterson, who writes the second highest number of closed problem-posing questions, frames 12% of her comments in this mode.

6. A quick analysis of Larson's questions supports this claim. Although he frames 39% of his comments as questions, the third highest among the 12 readers, 28% are in the form of closed questions: indirect requests, closed heuristic questions, or closed problem-posing questions. Because these questions leave less room than open questions for the student to make her own choices, his style is more directive than the number of overall questions makes it appear.

7. From time to time, Larson does moderate his control by elaborating on his calls for revision and thereby offering students something more to go on than just his call for a change. On Writing 5, for example, after advising the writer to think about the kind of information his audience would need, Larson lists several things to consider and gives him several strategies to use to come up with the material:

> What I'd like to suggest for your next draft is that you think carefully about what you want the reader to know about bass fishing (if that indeed is your subject): where to do it, how to do it, why it's especially pleasurable, or some other knowledge. Write down what you decide you want the reader to know, and write down the details you want to give the reader to help him/her understand securely what you intend. Then try to find for yourself a way to arrange these details so that they will be clear to the reader.

On Writing 11, after calling on the student to say more about how she sees the job of waitressing, he offers a series of questions that are meant to guide invention:

> How do the parts of your discussion connect? Why are you a waitress? Why does it matter to you that you be a "good" waitress? What, fundamentally, do you want your readers to learn about being a waitress that, maybe, they had not known or thought of? What's distinctive, interesting, about your work?

Such elaboration offers students possible ways of seeing their revision.

8. Larson and Stewart make the same percentage of comments about wording (19%). Only Stewart makes more comments on correctness (13%).

9. Larson's comments on local matters also account for the high number of comments he writes on this draft: 36, compared with an average of 23 comments per paper.

10. Larson's responses also clearly shift focus according to the stage of drafting. He deals more with local structure and wording on later drafts and saves almost all of his comments about correctness (20 out of 24 comments) for the final draft. He also uses more evaluative comments and fewer commands on final drafts than on rough drafts.

Notes to Anson's Section

1. Although we did not enter into the project with the aim of soliciting spoken or tape-recorded comments, we were delighted to have the opportunity to consider how such spoken comments compare with the written comments made by others in the study. It has turned out to be a fortunate turn.

2. Of course, tape-recorded comments are not necessarily less authoritative than written

comments. The spoken comments simply allow greater room for the teacher to become interactive. The same claim, we think, can be made about one-to-one tutorial responses: Although the two-way conversation allows for the greatest degree of teacher-student interaction, it does not necessarily eventuate in more interactive commentary. Tutors may be just as directive in their exchanges with students as they may be in one-directional tape-recorded comments or written comments. In fact, a recent study by one of us suggests that tutorial talk, in which the student is present and may make greater demands on the teacher to express, clarify, and specify his responses, may lend themselves to be more directive than one-way responses, in which the teacher may feel less obliged to provide specific material or help to the student.

3. Nevertheless, it would not be difficult to revise Anson's comments to a more "writerly" form: cutting out the excessive repetition, the false starts, the interruptors (and of course letting go of the voice inflections and laughter and such). In all probability, such changes would make Anson's style somewhat less informal, somewhat less tentative, less spontaneous, and somewhat less interactive. But they would also make his comments more incisive.

4. As part of the hypothetical context for his responses, Anson assumes that the students submit a short tape in which they talk about their processes of composing the paper and sometimes direct him to look at specific concerns they have about the writing.

5. It would be difficult to estimate how much of Anson's wording, style, and voice would be altered if they were originally written, not transcribed from spoken comments. Clearly, not all spoken comments would have the same effects as they do in Anson's style. Different sets of spoken comments, framed in different ways, lead to different styles—although generally it is safe to suppose that most spoken comments will be less formal than most written comments. Of course, written comments may achieve some of the same effects, as we can see from Elbow's and Hull's comments. Still, Anson's comments raise several questions about teacher control in different forms of response: In what ways do spoken comments encourage interaction or teacher control? Do they encourage greater interaction than written comments? To what extent do written comments allow a responder to capture the nuances of speech? What advantages do written comments, in which the responder is given a greater opportunity to pause and consider what he is going to say and to shape his comments for the student, have over spoken comments? These would be interesting questions to take up in future research.

6. Arguably, they might be even more directive because their impulse seems to be to critique the writing and lead the student to produce a better text according to Anson's view of the writing. It might well be the case that spoken comments make manifest and even crystallize the favored style of a responder: Readers who are inclined to be directive will more readily display that tendency in their spoken comments.

7. Following Anson, Larson writes 17% of his comments in advisory modes; Stock and Gere write 10%. Only nine of Anson's advisory comments take the form of firm advice, for example:

> What I also suggest . . . is that you push harder during the earlier stages [of writing]. (Writing 1)

> Another thing I'd do here is to take each of your counter arguments and see if there's *any* exception to them, and try to take them and apply them to similar situations. (Writing 2)

> I mean, instead of telling us that his temperament changed, how about showing that? (Writing 9)

Even in instances in which Anson states his advice somewhat more assertively, he often opens it back up later, frequently as part of the same comment:

So for the purposes of focusing and structuring, you're going to want to look at different aspects of the topic. And that might mean that you'll collapse lots of your paper into one perspective (*problems* resulting from overguidance) and add others (how does one achieve a balance between *guidance* and *freedom*).

I'd experiment with the abstract and concrete issue and make some decisions there, try throwing in something specific. The point here is to try out some possibilities.

8. Here is the specific analysis of the comments: one negative evaluation; one negative qualified evaluation; one negative reader reaction; one imperative; one positive evaluation; three positive qualified evaluations; six advisory comments.

9. Across the 10 essays in the sampling, Anson makes the following use of the three types of explanatory comments:

    23 comments that explain another comment (6%)
    23 comments that offer an example (6%)
    69 comments that explain a concept or present a brief lesson (19%)

10. Anson does not say, "Your writing is abstract and sounds like a philosophical treatise." He qualifies his assertion: "one thing I noticed," "I think it's kind of abstract," "it sounds rather philosophical." He goes on to grant that the writer may not share this assessment and even to explain the reasoning behind it.

11. See, for example, paragraphs 3 and 4 from Anson's responses to Writing 12, presented in Chapter 2. Here, Anson identifies a concern, explains it in some detail, offers an example of where the concern comes up in the writing, and offers a number of questions to help the writer think through the issue.

12. Anson writes 21 advisory comments that are meant to help the student find ways to go about the task of revision. He writes 45 advisory comments that deal directly with changes to the text.

13. Anson's process-oriented advice is similar to Hull's use of prompts to make assignments, but Anson's advice is more motivated by a concern for the written product than Hull's. In addition, he does not use such "process prompts" nearly as frequently as she does.

14. In comparison to the rest of the readers, Anson does not present many questions. Whereas Elbow writes the fewest questions among the readers in the study (9%), Anson writes the second fewest (11%). His regular but moderate use of questions is revealing. Anson seems to prefer the added direction and control that is offered by advice rather than the indirect guidance and lesser control that is offered by questions.

15. Of course, most authoritative commentary also leaves the work to the student, but it "leaves" this work to the student in a quite different sense by pointing to changes that should be (or could be) made. Although authoritative commentary can, like interactive commentary, be quite specific in the changes that it calls for, it usually gets more directive as it gets more detailed. What makes response interactive is a *combination* of teacher direction and student control, that is, a teacher providing precise commentary or offering some specific explanation, questions, or help, yet leaving the choices and changes to the student.

16. Stewart addresses an average of 5.1 issues per commentary; Anson addresses 4.2, the second highest average in the study.

17. Anson deals with local matters on 8 of his 10 sets of responses. Writing 4 is one of four sets of responses in which he makes a substantial number of comments on local structure, wording, and correctness.

18. He makes, in addition, two comments on the essay as a whole for a total of 55 comments. The four comments he makes about correctness actually tell the student not to concern herself with it at this time in her drafting.

19. For example, in paragraph 3 of his response, Anson focuses on the global structure of the writing and looks at the issue of structure in terms of some larger context:

One reason why I bring up this question is that, as a reader, I guess I got a little lost in this piece at times. And I don't know how the others will react but I felt especially when I got to page two, in that longish paragraph there before the first full paragraph on that page, I felt vague, I guess; I don't know if that's a good way of putting it, but I think that part of it—you asked about style and structure on your tape—comes from a tendency to focus on everything all at once.

The first comment makes reference to Anson as a reader (and thus the rhetorical context); the second comment makes reference to the classroom and, specifically, the student's conference group; the third comment refers to the student's own experiences as a writer, specifically, the concerns she raised about her writing on her tape-recorded message to Anson.

20. Anson orients his commentary to contexts beyond the immediate text in 9 of his 10 sets of responses. If his extra-textual comments were removed from his responses, he would average three issues per commentary—below the average for the study.

21. In paragraph 3, Anson refers to the conference group when he notes that he does not know "how the others will react."

Notes to Stock's Section

1. Anson makes an average of 37 comments per response, Elbow 24, Stock 35. Stock's letters average nearly 800 words—second only to Anson's spoken-and-transcribed responses. The average length of her responses increases to 852 words per response when her four sets of marginal comments are considered.

2. In a letter to us, Stock notes how the elaborateness of her letters grew out of her attempts to capture the rich exchange that typifies her classroom and her overall responses to student writing: "[T]he 'responses' I wrote to the student writers whose work defined your project—of necessity—had to be full ones in order for me to suggest the responses that I normally offer students in the things I say to them in conferences, in our chat as we leave the classroom together, within class discussions, and so on, as well as in the 'notes' I customarily write to students in response to their papers." The responses, she said, "were meant to capture responses that I normally shape in both talk and writing."

3. She writes marginal comments on Writings 5 and 12, both mature rough drafts, and Writings 10 and 13, essays designated as final drafts but which many of the readers thought would benefit from further revision.

4. In Writing 1, for instance, Stock guides Louise, by using a personal anecdote, to reconsider her own arguments against wearing seat belts, and then goes on to question whether she really wants to write about the seat-belt law itself or more generally about laws that interfere with individual rights. In Writing 2, she preempts revision on "What If Drugs Were Legal?" and instead asks Nancy to work on a more careful reading of the article she is arguing against. In Writing 11, she sidesteps any specific talk about the writing and uses Barbara's ideas about waitressing to devise a lesson that will help her reenvision her concept of writing. In Writing 5, she writes almost 60 comments in a point-by-point analysis of how Steve might improve the detail, organization, and style of his article on bass fishing. In Writing 13, she praises Frank for his revisions of the concert review, discussing the successive changes he made to an idea that ran through all three versions of the article, and then sets up a conference to talk about her suggestions for further revision.

5. The following passages are typical of the way Stock opens her letters:

I smiled as I read your essay arguing against the law that requires us to wear seat belts. One of your arguments sounded like one my mother used to offer me. (Writing 1)

Where is my pole? Where is the bait? I want to go fishing. As I read your essay, Steve, I felt as if I were there with you, motoring along I-75, imagining Lake Ivenho in increasing detail as first one and then another fishing hole floated past my car window. (Writing 5)

I really enjoyed reading your mid-term essay, "The Most Effective Ways of Being a Good Waitress." I feel as if I got to know you a bit more than I have in class. I was impressed with your conception of waitressing, with your sense that the job only begins after you can already do what most people think of as waitressing, what you call the mechanics of the job. Your conception of waitressing is so gracious, so people-oriented. I hope that the waitresses who serve me when I am in restaurants think of waitressing as you do. I know I'll enjoy my meals a lot more if they do. (Writing 11)

6.   The following comments illustrate the different ways she closes her letters:

I am really looking forward to reading your next draft, Steve. This is a fine piece of work so far. Thanks for teaching me about fishing in Orlando. I'm looking forward to learning more. (Writing 5)

Let's talk in a conference this week as you are working on your second draft of this essay; let's talk about seat belts and the law requiring that we wear them. . . . I warn you, though, I'm off to the motor vehicle bureau and the library to get such facts as I can about seat belt use so that I can give you a tough time when you come in. (Writing 1)

In your future writings, I will look forward to seeing your good, critical mind fully at work. (Writing 6)

7.   The following chart shows the relative emphasis (in percentages) that the most and least directive readers in the study give to these three authoritative modes: imperatives, negative evaluations, and qualified negative evaluations.

	IMP	EVAL	QE	TOTAL
White	19	21	2	42
Stewart	4	16	3	23
Larson	7	9	7	23
Peterson	2	7	2	11
Elbow	1	5	4	10
Stock	1	1	2	4

Without her marginal comments on Writings 10 and 13, the percentage of comments Stock casts in the authoritative modes—correctives, negative evaluations, qualified negative evaluations, imperatives, and advice—would drop from 19% to 7%, by far the lowest among the 12 readers. Her percentage of comments cast in the various reflective modes would climb from 44% to 53%—just shy of Elbow's total.

8.   Stock makes the third-highest percentage of reflective comments among the twelve readers, behind Elbow (56%) and Anson (46%). Sixty percent of the comments in her letters of response are given to reflective modes. One out of every five of Stock's comments is cast as a reader response or an interpretation; one out of four presents a teacher response: lessons, explanations, examples, models, or encouragement.

9.   Although Stock makes more corrections than anyone else in the study, the count is somewhat misleading. In contrast to Stewart, who makes corrections routinely in all of his responses, or White, who when he edits student texts does so without qualification, most of Stock's corrective comments (43 out of 51) occur on responses to two papers (Writings 10 and 13) that she chooses to sample edit. (The other eight occur on Writing 5, her most thorough response.) Furthermore, when Stock uses editorial comments, she presents them as the suggestions of a teacher who is intent on modeling ways of crafting sentences and proofreading texts. Each time she uses corrective comments she makes it a point to note that they are models or "editorial

suggestions" and reminds the student that he is free to take what he can and put the rest aside.

10. Stock writes 13% of her comments in reader responses; she writes another 6% of her comments in interpretations.

11. Stock does as much criticizing from her perspective as a reader, in reader reactions, as she does in straight evaluations and qualified evaluations.

12. Stock also uses her personal experience to illustrate a lesson on Writing 11, employing her views on writing as a rhetorical act in order to expand the student's conception of writing and raise her expectations as a writer. She then makes an extended comparison between learning to wait tables effectively and learning to write effectively. Twelve of the 20 comments in the overall response are given to the lesson. On Writing 13, Stock gives a close analysis of draft revisions, not to play back her reading of the text or evaluate the writing, but to underscore a lesson about revision. She extracts the same passage from three consecutive drafts and shows the improvements that come with each of the changes. (See Stock's full response to Writing 13 in Chapter 2.) She goes on in detailed marginal comments to lay out further local revisions. On Writing 2, Stock offers a lesson in reading by modeling her way of interpreting LeMoult's article. Overall, she presents lessons in all but one of her letters of response. Sixteen percent of her comments are explanatory ones, the main vehicle for lessons and explanations.

13. In addition to Writings 1 and 4, personal lessons dominate Stock's comments on Writing 2, Writing 11, and Writing 13 (see note 12).

14. Stock does not use such lessons based on her personal experience in her responses to Writings 5, 9, and 13. The one letter in which Stock does not present any kind of lesson is on Writing 9, a final draft handed in at the end of the semester.

15. Stock uses questions regularly across the sampling to guide revision. She writes 10 or more on four sets of responses. Although she casts only 19% of her comments in the form of questions, among the lowest in the group, the low percentage may be due to the fact that she makes so many explanatory and reader-response comments.

16. Of the 57 comments she writes in her letter to Steve, 30 are cast in the form of reflective statements—10 that offer some reading of the text, 20 that present explanations or instruction. Another 12 comments are cast in the form of advice.

17. See, for example, Writing 13, in which Stock uses the student's own writing to illustrate—in effect, to model—the development of one's thought over several revisions. Stock also uses models on Writing 12, in which she provides Rusty with a student paper that more fully develops a similar topic; on Writing 2, where she illustrates her own close reading of a section of LeMoult's article; and on Writing 10, in which she models how she would outline an article in order to review it for publication. In a way, she also sets up as models her sample editing of student texts and her talk about guiding her son's decision making in her responses on Writing 4. Her models can be seen as lessons, offering the student a way to conceptualize the tasks he needs to perform in revision.

18. Stock's response to Writing 9, a strong final draft handed in at the end of the term, is the exception. Here she is content to praise the writing and the student's work in the course.

19. Stock's percentage of local comments is just behind those of the most directive readers in the study—White, Stewart, and Larson.

20. Excluding the 65 comments Stock writes as editorial suggestions in the margins of "Leukemia" and "The John Cougar Concert," the percentage of comments Stock gives to local matters drops to 10%, among the lowest in the study, and the percentage of comments she devotes to global concerns jumps to 56%, the average for the 12 readers as a group.

21. Interestingly, readers in the study who do the most to individualize their responses (Hull, Elbow, and Stock) make the lowest percentages of comments about global structure, ideas, and development. They address matters as they come up, depending on their sense of what the student would most benefit from at a given

time, regardless of whether the paper is a rough draft or a near-final draft. They also are inclined to devote more comments to concerns that go beyond the formal text.

Notes to Warnock's Section

1. Warnock says as much herself. In her notes to us on Writing 4, she says that she finds "reading this and the other papers out of a classroom context very difficult. I guess I need to be in the situation myself, participating and observing." She expresses the same difficulty in dealing with the artificial contexts on other writings. As she says in her notes to us on Writing 11: "I don't know how to take or use the background information about Gail in responding to her writing. Such information certainly affects how I read a student's paper, but out of context this information reads more like gossip. I certainly read students' papers in the context of such information which I learn in class." In effect, as Warnock explains here and elsewhere, her responses in the study do not accurately reflect what she does in actual settings for two reasons: (a) she is uncomfortable working with the limited and artificial information we provide in our created contexts, and (b) in actual classroom situations she relies heavily on spoken comments, especially on early rough drafts. Warnock herself acknowledges the artificiality of her responses in a note she makes to us on Writing 10: "I wouldn't respond as I do below except that I'm trying my best to fulfill the assignment given me."

   In our analysis of Warnock's comments, as with those of earlier readers, we examine the style of Warnock's implied teacher, the one that emerges from the words on the page, putting aside any additional information that is not directly tied to the words of her actual comments. But as we do so we should once again keep in mind the peculiarity of responding to student writing out of context and allow Warnock's actual views and practices to provide a backdrop for our description. For instance, in her notes to us about her responses on Writing 4, she says that in an actual setting she usually would not make written comments on rough drafts. Instead, she would have students respond to one another's drafts orally in groups:

   > I would probably ask Anne to read this aloud, explain it to other students in a small group, or read portions to the class in order to help her clarify her purpose and audience. I think she would hear the repetition and wandering, and I believe that she would realize that her ideas begin to come together near the end. I would usually not respond to a draft by writing comments and would do so only in response to the writer's questions about the draft.

   Her statement may shed some light on the limited number of responses she writes on the essay.

2. Although this specificity may lead to increased teacher control, it also provides clearer direction to the student. Stock's commentary shows how comments can be precise, specific, and even detailed, yet leave ample room for the student to make her own revisions. It is a paradox of response: The very specificity that may lead to teacher control may also lead to the richest interaction between teacher and student.

3. Warnock's nondirective response is also a function of her choice of modes. Three of her seven comments are open questions and another is an indirect request. In contrast to Gere and Peterson, she provides no comments that indicate specifically where the disjunction in the essay occurs or that might suggest ways to unify the writing.

4. As we shall see, any description of Warnock's modes requires an accompanying analysis of the relative degree of specificity of the comments in those modes.

5. Gere and Larson make the next highest percentage of comments in the form of questions, 43% and 39%, respectively.

6. Twelve of Warnock's prompts call for changes in the product, as in the following cases:

Play with the title to figure out what exactly you're trying to write about and use a title to set up clear reader expectations. (Writing 6).

[Y]ou can put this point in the opening prgh to let your reader know. (Writing 11)

You might address these questions in your next draft. (Writing 4)

You might try flip-flopping this prgh and begin here. (Writing 11)

Nine of her prompts call on the student to engage in some composing process:

Read these 2 aloud. (Writing 13)

Read aloud. [I'm not sure what you're saying.] (Writing 9)

Try reading it aloud to others to hear if you follow through on ideas and if your listeners can follow. (Writing 13)

By comparison, Larson gears the majority of his advisory and imperative comments to the written product and Hull the majority of hers to the writing process.

7.   In a note to us, Warnock explains her strategy of using "Read aloud" comments in this way: "I always encourage students to read drafts aloud so that they can become critical readers and get help from other listeners."

8.   Thirteen of the 15 comments she makes on correctness, wording, and local structure occur on final drafts. All nine comments on local structure occur on final drafts.

NOTES TO CHAPTER 5

1.   We should note that two of the readers—Stock and Hull—felt they wrote longer responses in a situation that allowed them no face-to-face contact with these students. Hull makes this point in answering our Questions on Responding:

I ought to point out that, for this study, I've probably made more comments on the papers than I would in actual practice. I couldn't shake off the notion that the comments I was offering on each piece of writing were to be seen as crucial to that writer's development. In actual practice, I know that you can't accomplish everything with comments on a paper.

In personal correspondence with us, Stock alluded to the fact that she was writing more than she would usually write in an attempt to capture, in these written comments, some of the give-and-take that happens in student-teacher conferences.

2.   The comments are taken from another study we have initiated, in which we compare the responses of these 12 well-known teachers with the responses of 12 English teachers who represent a range of writing instructors. Of course, the decision as to whether a comment is text-specific is not always an easy one to make. Nevertheless, it is possible to look at a teacher's comments as a whole and determine whether they tend to be generic or text-specific.

3.   This is an essay we have not displayed earlier. We offered readers an opportunity to respond to this essay for a number of reasons. First, it was written by a person labeled as a "basic writer," and, even though it was submitted as a final draft, it contained a good many usage errors. Second, it provided an opportunity to deal with writing that was very personal to the student and that treated a sensitive topic, his struggle to overcome leukemia. Because we have not dealt with this essay in previous chapters, much of our discussion in Chapter 5 refers to the

readers' responses to it. We'd like to thank our colleague Pat Naulty for providing us with the essay.

4. Even though we realize the concept of what constitutes an "error" is an extremely complicated one, it serves our purposes here to define error as something we feel a majority of writing teachers would agree to calling "wrong." We then multiplied the number of errors possible in the sampling by the number of responses to the essays in the sampling, thereby arriving at the number of possible responses the readers could make to "errors." Next we counted the number of errors marked (both in marginal and end comments) on all the responses in the sampling and determined what percentage of possible errors that number represented.

5. Although the readers, as a group, write as many positive evaluations (12%) as criticism (11%), most of them *as individuals* write significantly more praise than criticism or more criticism than praise. (These figures on the use of criticism and praise do not include the small percentage of comments the readers as a group framed as negative and positive reader reactions, which are categorized under reflective commentary.)

6. The areas a teacher addresses become what we are calling an "issue" when the teacher makes two or more marginal comments or one end comment on one of the seven focus categories: ideas, development, global structure, local structure, wording, correctness, and extra-textual comments. The readers as a group averaged 3.3 issues per set of responses. They addressed the most issues on Essay 12, "Street Gangs" (4.4 issues per response); they addressed the fewest issues on Essay 1, on the seat-belt law (2.8 issues per response).

7. Because Hull makes but one mark on this essay—underlining the sentence that begins at the bottom of page 2 and goes onto page 3—we presented her endnote only.

8. We should note here a possible contradiction in what we are saying and the method of defining "issue." Given our definition of "issue," a teacher could treat many different matters in marginal comments (with one comment devoted to each matter) and still treat a limited number of issues. What we find, however, is that Gere's essay presented in this chapter is typical of our teacher's commenting style, in that 18 of the 22 comments on the essay appeared in focuses that were among the four "issues" she treated.

9. See, for example, Sommers (1982), Anson (1989), and Burhans (1983).

10. It is difficult in this study, given its clinical design—specifically, the fact that the readers are responding to writings that were not done in their classes, by their students—to come to any definitive conclusions about how these responders (would) respond to rough drafts differently from final drafts. Often, the readers treat what we designate as a "final" draft as still requiring substantial revision, and they make comments that are intended to lead students to continue work on the writing. Also, they could not respond to one draft and then, after the student had a chance to revise the paper, respond to it again in light of their earlier comments and the student's revisions. Still, we are compelled to make several observations about how they responded to these three rough drafts and these three final drafts, according to the information we provided to them about the writing.

11. Larson's criticism of these assignments led to our asking him to write the epilogue on writing assignments.

12. Oops. In error we called this student Gail on the context sheet and Barbara on the essay. Thus, we have to deal with the confusion of these two names in readers' responses to and commentaries about this essay.

13. The following chart lists the cases, identified by Xs, in which the teacher's concept of who the individual student is seems to move beyond the persona of the text to deal with extrinsic information about the student.

	Essay 2	Essay 4	Essay 6	Essay 8	Essay 11	Essay 13	Total
Anson	X	X	X	X	X	X	6
Elbow	X				X		2
Gere	X			X		X	3
Hull	X	X	X	X	X	X	6
Larson			X				1
McClelland			X				1
O'Hare		X					1
Peterson	X			X		X	3
Stewart	X	X	X			X	4
Stock	X	X	X	X	X		5
Warnock							0
White			X			X	2
TOTAL	7	5	7	5	4	6	

The chart shows that certain readers are much more clearly affected by their sense of student identities than others, and we would argue that there is some correlation between this tendency and the responding styles that we have described in Chapter 4. That is, more controlling teachers, such as Larson and White, might be expected to take the student's identity into consideration less often than interactive responders, such as Hull and Anson. However, as we point out in Chapter 4, no one factor can account for a controlling or interactive style. We see White's style as more controlling than O'Hare's, yet O'Hare has fewer references to a writer beyond the text than does White. And what about Warnock? In a sense, our chart completely misrepresents Warnock's views about the importance of knowing about the writer of a text. Her commentary on Writing 6 indicates some of the frustration she feels in dealing with student writing outside the context of her classroom:

> Again the background information doesn't provide a context for me to respond to the paper. . . . David has written to discover, but he stopped before revising for others. I don't think a draft like this one would be turned in as a final paper if it had been read aloud and responded to by a group of students or by the teacher in a conference.

Warnock apparently depends on workshops to do much of the work in her writing classes and, in that context, students and teacher get to know much about one another and use what they know to inform their responses. Warnock is not able to simulate those interactions here and, thus, often feels that her responses do not reflect her style of teaching.

References

Anson, C. (Ed.). (1989). *Writing and response: Theory, practice, and research*. Urbana: National Council of Teachers of English.

Anson, C. (1989). Response styles and ways of knowing. In C. Anson (Ed.), *Writing and response: Theory, practice, and research* (pp. 332-366). Urbana: National Council of Teachers of English.

Arnold, L.V. (1963). Effects of frequency of writing and intensity of teacher evaluation upon performance in written composition of tenth-grade students. Unpublished doctoral dissertation, Florida State University, Tallahassee, FL.

Austin, J.L. (1962). *How to do things with words*. Cambridge, MA: Harvard University Press.

Bata, E.J. (1972). A study of the relative effectiveness of marking techniques on junior college freshmen English composition. Unpublished doctoral dissertation, University of Maryland.

Berkenkotter, C. (1991). Paradigm debates, turf wars, and the conduct of sociocognitive inquiry in composition. *College Composition and Communication, 42*, 151-169.

Berlin, J. (1982). Contemporary composition: The major pedagogical theories. *College English, 44*, 765-777.

Berthoff, A. (1981). *The making of meaning*. Montclair, NJ: Boynton/Cook Publishing.

Booth, W. (1983). *The rhetoric of fiction* (2nd ed.). Chicago: University of Chicago Press.

Brannon, L., & Knoblauch, C.H. (1982). On students' rights to their own texts: A model of teacher response. *College Composition and Communication, 33*, 157-166.

Britton, J. (1970). *Language and learning*. Allen Lane the Penguin Press.

Britton, J., Burgess, T., Martin, N., McLeod, A., & Rosen, H. (1975). *The development of writing abilities, 11-18*. London: Macmillan Education.

Burhans, C. (1983). The teaching of writing and the knowledge gap." *College English, 45*, 639-656.

Burke, K. (1966). *Language as symbolic action*. Berkeley: University of California Press.

Clark, W.G. (1968). *An evaluation of two techniques of teaching freshman composition*. (ERIC ED 039 241).

Clifford, J., & Schilb, J. (1985). Composition theory and literary theory. In B. McClelland & T. Donovan (Eds.), *Perspectives on research and scholarship in composition* (pp. 45-67). New York: MLA.

Coles, W. (1984). *The plural I*. New York: Holt, Rinehart, and Winston.

Cowan, G. (1977). The rhetorician's personae. *College Composition and Communication, 28*, 259-262.

Diederich, P. (1963). In praise of praise. *NEA Journal, 52*, 58-59.

Diederich, P. (1974). *Measuring growth in English*. Urbana: National Council of Teachers of English.

Elbow, P. (1973). *Writing without teachers*. Oxford: Oxford University Press.

Elbow, P. (1981). *Writing with power*. Oxford: Oxford University Press.

Elbow, P. (1987). Closing my eyes as I speak: An argument for ignoring audience. *College English, 49*, 50-69.

Elbow, P., & Belanoff, P. (1989). *Sharing and responding.* New York: Random House.

Emig, J. (1977). Writing as a mode of learning. *College Composition and Communication, 28*, 122-128.

Emig, J., & Parker, R., Jr. (1976). *Responding to student writing: Building a theory of the evaluating process.* (ERIC ED 136257).

Faigley, L. (1986). Competing theories of process: A critique and a proposal. *College English, 48*, 527-542.

Fish, S. (1980). *Is there a text in this class?* Cambridge, MA: Harvard University Press.

Freedman, S.W. (1984). The registers of student and professional expository writing: Influences on teachers' responses. In R. Beach & L.S. Bridwell (Eds.), *New directions in composition research* (pp. 334-347). New York: Guilford.

Fulkerson, R. (1979). Four philosophies of composition. *College Composition and Communication, 30*, 343-348.

Garrison, R. (1974). One-to-one tutorial instruction in freshman composition. *New Directions for Community Colleges, 2*, 55-84.

Gee, T. (1972). Students' responses to teacher comments. *Research in the Teaching of English, 6*, 212-221.

Griffin, C.W. (1982). Theory of responding to student writing: The state of the art. *College Composition and Communication, 33*, 296-342.

Hillocks, G. (1982). The interaction of instruction, teacher comment, and revision in teaching the composing process. *Research in the Teaching of English, 16*, 261-278.

Horvath, B. (1984). The components of written response: A practical synthesis of current views. *Rhetoric Review, 2*, 136-156.

Knoblauch, C.H., & Brannon, L. (1981). Teacher commentary on student writing: The state of the art. *Freshman English News, 10*, 1-4.

Knoblauch, C.H., & Brannon, L. (1984). *Rhetorical traditions and the teaching of writing.* Upper Montclair, NJ: Boynton/Cook.

Kroll, B. (1980). Developmental perspectives and the teaching of writing. *College English, 41*, 741-752.

Lawson, B., Sterr Ryan, S., & Winterowd, W.R. (1989). *Encountering student texts.* Urbana: National Council of Teachers of English.

Lees, E. (1979). Evaluating student writing. *College Composition and Communication, 30*, 370-374.

Lynn, S. (1987). Reading the writing process: Toward a theory of current pedagogies. *College English, 49*, 902-910.

Moffett, J. (1965). I, you, and it. *College Composition and Communication, 16*, 243-248.

Moffett, J. (1983). *Teaching the universe of discourse.* Portsmouth, NH: Heinemann. (originally published in 1968)

Murray, D. (1982). What can you say besides awk? In *Learning by teaching.* Montclair, NJ: Boynton/Cook.

Murray, D. (1982). *Learning by teaching: Selected articles on writing and teaching.* Montclair, NJ: Boynton/Cook.

North, S. (1987). *The making of knowledge in composition.* Upper Montclair, NJ: Boynton/Cook.

Perry, W.G. (1970). *Forms of intellectual and ethical development in the college years.* New York: Holt Rinehart and Winston.

Purves, A. (1984). The teacher as reader: An anatomy. *College English, 46*, 259-265.

Rose, M. (1989). *Lives on the boundary: The struggles and achievements of America's underprepared.* New York: Free Press.

Rosenblatt, L. (1978). *The reader, the text, the poem: The transactional theory of the literary work.* Carbondale: Southern Illinois University Press.

Schwegler, R. (1991). In R. Bullock & C. Schuster (Eds.), *The politics of reading student papers* (pp. 203-225). Portsmouth, NH: Boynton/Cook.

Searle, D., & Dillon, D. (1980). The message of marking: Teacher written responses to student writing at intermediate grade levels. *Research in the Teaching of English, 14*, 233-242.

Sommers, N. (1982). Responding to student writing. *College Composition and Communication, 33*, 148-156.

Stevens, A.F. (1973). The effects of positive and negative evaluation on the written composition of low performing high school students. *DAI, 34*, 1778-A

Stiff, R. (1967). The effect upon composition of particular correction techniques. *Research in the Teaching of English, 1*, 54-75.

White, E. (1984). Post-structural literary criticism and the response to student writing. *College Composition and Communication, 35*, 186-195.

Williams, J. (1981). The phenomenology of error. *College Composition and Communication, 32*, 152-168.

Woods, W. (1981). Composition textbooks and pedagogical theory, 1960-80. *College English, 43*, 393-409.

Ziv, N. (1984). The effect of teacher comments on the writing of four college freshmen. In R. Beach & L.S. Bridwell (Eds.), *New directions in composition research* (pp. 362-380). New York: Guilford.

Author Index

Subject Index